*Empire Films and the Crisis of Colonialism,
1946–1959*

Empire Films and the Crisis of Colonialism,
1946–1959

JON COWANS

Johns Hopkins University Press
Baltimore

© 2015 Johns Hopkins University Press
All rights reserved. Published 2015
Printed in the United States of America on acid-free paper
2 4 6 8 9 7 5 3 1

Johns Hopkins University Press
2715 North Charles Street
Baltimore, Maryland 21218-4363
www.press.jhu.edu

Library of Congress Cataloging-in-Publication Data
Cowans, Jon.
Empire films and the crisis of colonialism, 1946–1959 / Jon Cowans.
pages cm
Includes bibliographical references and index.
ISBN 978-1-4214-1641-0 (hardcover : alk. paper) — ISBN 978-1-4214-1642-7 (electronic) — ISBN 1-4214-1641-7 (hardcover : alk. paper) — ISBN 1-4214-1642-5 (electronic) 1. Imperialism in motion pictures. 2. Motion pictures—Great Britain—History—20th century. 3. Motion pictures—France—History—20th century. 4. Motion pictures—United States—History—20th century. 5. Motion pictures—Political aspects. I. Title.
PN1995.9.I42C69 2015
791.43'6581—dc23   2014024720

A catalog record for this book is available from the British Library.

Special discounts are available for bulk purchases of this book. For more information, please contact Special Sales at 410-516-6936 or specialsales@press.jhu.edu.

Johns Hopkins University Press uses environmentally friendly book materials, including recycled text paper that is composed of at least 30 percent post-consumer waste, whenever possible.

CONTENTS

Acknowledgments vii

Introduction 1

PART I THE PERSISTENCE OF EMPIRE: COLONIALIST FILMS IN THE DECOLONIZATION ERA 21

1 The White Woman's Burden 31

2 Heroes of Empire 56

3 Westerns 93

PART II COMING TO TERMS: CONFRONTING INSURGENCY AND DECOLONIZATION 137

4 The British Empire and Decolonization 139

5 The French Empire and Decolonization 182

6 Americans in Postwar Asia 208

PART III DANGEROUS LIAISONS: INTERRACIAL COUPLES IN FILMS 243

7 Miscegenation in Westerns 253

8 Romance across the Pacific 271

9 Black-White Couples and Internal Decolonization 289

Conclusion 335

Appendix A: Attitudes toward Indians and U.S. Conquest in Westerns *347*
Appendix B: Outcomes of Interracial Romance in Miscegenation Films *349*
Notes *355*
Index *421*

ACKNOWLEDGMENTS

The author would like to thank everyone at the following research facilities: Les Archives Françaises du Film du Centre National du Cinéma et de l'Image Animée, Bois d'Arcy; La Bibliothèque Nationale de France; La Bibliothèque Publique d'Information, Centre Pompidou; the British Film Institute; the British Library, Colindale; La Cinémathèque Française; the Los Angeles Public Library; the Margaret Herrick Library, Academy of Motion Picture Arts and Sciences; the Milwaukee Public Library; the New York Historical Society; the New York Public Library's Schwartzman branch and Library for the Performing Arts; New York University's Bobst Library; Rutgers University Libraries and Research Council; the San Diego Public Library; Stanford University Libraries and Special Collections; University of California, Los Angeles Library, Performing Arts Special Collections and Film and Television Archive; University of Southern California's Cinematic Arts Library; University of Southern California's Warner Bros. Archives; University of Texas at Austin's Briscoe Center for American History. Special thanks are due to Jonathon Auxier, Emily Baughan, Cosimo Chiarelli, Ned Comstock, Sandra Garcia-Myers, Brett Service, Christina Strasburger, and Whitney Strub.

Thanks also to Beth Gianfagna for her expert work in copyediting the manuscript, to Bob Brugger of Johns Hopkins University Press for his wise advice and his interest in the project, to Courtney Bond for production editing, and to everyone else at JHUP.

Finally, thanks to my parents for their years of love and support; to Reyther for love, patience, and many interesting conversations about film; and to Alejandra and Marcelo, who think I should be playing instead of working.

*Empire Films and the Crisis of Colonialism,
1946–1959*

INTRODUCTION

The twentieth century saw a stunning array of profound changes in world affairs, with none more significant than the dismantling of the West's colonial empires and the reordering of relations between colonizer and colonized. In 1900, Western powers ruled over much of the world, but after World War II many colonial rulers began going home, and colonized peoples began to take increasing control over their own lives. Although inequalities of wealth and power certainly persisted at century's end, the disparities that had allowed Western countries to conquer, occupy, and rule colonies with relative ease had lessened, and the very notion of colonialism had become discredited. The terms *colonialism* and *imperialism* became epithets, raising the political costs of one country's efforts to rule over another. Because so many colonial relationships involved predominantly white nations ruling over people of color, race relations were also changing in this process. Speaking in 1900, African American political activist W.E.B. Du Bois proclaimed to the First Pan-African Congress—meeting, revealingly, in London—that "the problem of the twentieth century is the problem of the colour line—the relation of the darker to the lighter races of men in Asia and Africa, in America and the islands of the sea."[1] In a century filled with fundamental changes, events bore out Du Bois's sense of the centrality of what came to be known as North-South relations and the racial questions inherent in them.

Since roughly the 1970s, scholars have shown growing interest in these questions, but if they have examined the process of decolonization in detail, few have spoken with any precision about how and when colonialism became discredited in the West.[2] This vagueness in works by first-rate scholars exists because the study of attitudes—particularly Western attitudes—about colonialism remains in its infancy despite a half century of scholarship on colonialism and decolonization. So although it seems clear that, at some point in the twentieth century, something fundamental changed in Western thinking about colonialism and relations with non-Western peoples, difficulties in specifying the timing of those changes indicate broader gaps in our knowledge. Without assuming that changes in Western thinking *caused* decolonization—the changes may be consequences more than causes—the subject merits a closer look.

The opinion polls often used to study public opinion in the second half of the twentieth century are only as good as the questions researchers thought to ask, and on this issue there are few useful polls. This book examines public opinion about colonialism in three main colonizing powers—Britain, France, and the United States—by focusing on a single arena: fiction films on colonial topics. Although important changes in Western thinking on these issues occurred before and after the peak period of decolonization, this book concentrates on the years from the end of World War II to the end of the 1950s. In 1945, the Western empires were at their peak, but by 1960, British Prime Minister Harold Macmillan's "wind of change" speech acknowledged the seeming inevitability of decolonization, even if diehard colonial regimes clung to power for a few more years.[3]

There are several reasons that the study of cinema can illuminate Western thoughts and feelings about colonialism. Despite a decline in attendance at movie theaters during these years, film remained immensely popular in all three countries, as film stars were among their most famous individuals and countless films were familiar to millions. Moreover, filmmakers in all three countries turned repeatedly—almost obsessively—to colonial topics, and the appearance of new films every year on these subjects allows for rather fine-grained historical analysis. For years, historians showed little interest in films on historical topics, simply dismissing them as wildly inaccurate. More recently, historians and other scholars have come to realize what films can tell us—not about the events they depict but about the myths, fantasies, ideologies, assumptions, and values of the societies that produce and consume them.[4] Commercial films' quest for popularity, in short, creates an overlap between the outlooks of films' producers and consumers.

A second reason for examining collective attitudes through film concerns cinema's ability to shape as well as reflect popular outlooks. Although some films are known as "message pictures," messages are embedded in virtually all films, and though proving media influence is notoriously difficult, it is hard to deny at least some potential for mass media to form, reinforce, and even alter attitudes.[5] Students of propaganda have noted how much harder it is to influence people already familiar with a subject, but given how little most Western people knew about their countries' colonies and their history, it stands to reason that films about colonialism were operating in a field conducive to influence.

A third reason for using film to examine views of colonialism is that movies on colonial themes provoked extensive published discussion in the form of film reviews. So far, scholars have done almost nothing with this rich body of sources, but this book analyzes the discussions of colonial topics that appear in American, British, and French film reviews. Interpreted carefully, reviews and other evidence of films' reception can illuminate certain patterns of opinion on colonial and racial questions.

Definitions

The term *public opinion* has meant many different things since it came into use in the eighteenth century. Since the advent of opinion polling in the 1930s, a kind of electoral definition has come to prevail, and while this notion of public opinion as a composite of the equally weighted opinions of all the individuals (or voters) in a society has its uses for polls on voting intentions or issues at stake in elections, it can be misleading to apply it to all issues. Particularly when many people have no knowledge, interest, or opinion on a given question, polls may create illusions.[6] Foreign affairs rarely interest many people, and the occasional polls on colonial questions in countries such as Britain and France often showed surprising ignorance and apathy. While noting the findings of a few polls, this study will mostly use a different concept of public opinion, one that favors active over passive opinion and privileges public actions and expressions such as buying movie tickets or writing reviews or letters to newspapers or censors. The inventors of polling critiqued the equating of public opinion with the opinions of journalists and other elites, arguing correctly that there were often differences between them, and over time they proved polling's superiority for forecasting elections.[7] But for many other issues, an opinion-poll model may misread the way the politics of opinion actually worked.

Using films and their reception to examine public opinion about colonialism requires appreciating the complexity of reception. Filmmakers must anticipate the reactions of audiences, critics, censors, pressure groups, and film-industry professionals, and for each film a different constellation of reception appears. This study focuses on the interested public for each film, made up of those who bought tickets and the critics and letter-writers who left behind evidence historians can examine. Of course not everyone's opinion counted equally—critics at the *New York Times*, the *London Times*, or *Le Monde* were far more influential than those who merely bought tickets and spoke with friends about films they had seen. Not everyone even went to the movies, and people in rural areas, for example, attended fewer films than city dwellers.[8] These issues call for treating public opinion as the array of expressions of unequally influential individuals who made up the interested public for each film, but enough people saw and wrote about films that these ad hoc publics bear some relationship to the societies in which they formed. Public opinion is a complex construct, deserving scrutiny from many angles and approaches, and this study does not pretend to offer the final word on Western views of colonialism.

Also requiring definition is *colonialism*, which, simply put, involves one country or nation ruling over another. For a fuller definition, this study proposes that colonialism has four essential components: occupation, exploitation, discrimination, and acculturation. Occupation means the physical presence of the colonizer, if only in limited numbers, including troops, administrators, business people, missionaries, teachers, and others. It entails the seizure of land and other resources and the usurping of political functions, and it implies the use of violence and coercion to keep order. Despite Western colonizers' claims that they had occupied *terra nullius* (empty land) or been invited to rule, the history of the modern Western empires is filled with wars of conquest and acts of violence, and though rulers often used one group of colonial subjects to inflict violence on another, Western commanders and overseers were rarely far away.[9] Defenders of colonialism may be correct that violence was rare for long periods in certain colonies, but the continuing threat and memory of violence helped account for that tranquility.[10] Given cost concerns, perpetual, large-scale violence was impractical, and even occasional use of violence could erode its power to intimidate.[11] Forms of occupation varied widely: only some colonies had large settler populations; some relied on direct administration by whites, while others featured indirect rule through chiefs; some saw large-scale extermination and/or removal of indigenous peoples, while others subjected them to apartheid or segregation, and still others saw large-scale mixing (*mestizaje*, *métissage*, etc.) between colonizer and colonized. Even where a few Westerners controlled vast populations, however, their physical presence remained crucial. That presence, a reminder of conquest and continuing subjugation, also brought countless daily irritations and humiliations to the colonized.

Exploitation can have different meanings, from simply making good use of something to taking unfair advantage of someone.[12] Colonizers believed they brought development for mutual benefit, while critics of colonialism saw it as a matter of pillage. Colonialism's economic harm or benefit to colonizer and colonized is too vast an issue to address here, but in ethical terms the coercion and lack of consent make it a moot point. Economic exploitation in the sense of taking unfair advantage involved violating the principles of free-market capitalism, through trade monopolies and barriers, price setting, currency-exchange restrictions, the commandeering of export earnings, slavery, and forced labor. Although many associate modern Western colonialism with capitalism, it was closer to mercantilism, and Adam Smith himself was an early critic of colonialism.[13] Exploitation was not solely economic, and many colonies lost money but served strategic goals. Colonizers routinely conscripted locals for military service inside and outside the colony, and they also exploited the colonized sexually.

Ensuring that the benefits of exploitation went to the colonizers required discrimination, a third defining trait of colonialism. This took many forms, from reserving property rights or positions of authority to whites, to rules barring the colonized from social clubs and institutions, and formal and informal rules against miscegenation. The system, in short, highlighted and stigmatized difference between colonizer and colonized, and it is not surprising that colonizers lost their grip first on colonies filled with white subjects.[14] If many colonies maintained impermeable boundaries between ruling and subject ethnic groups, others preferred the flexibility of semipermeable barriers, which used forms of cooptation and tokenism to preempt resistance, recruit collaborators, and create illusions of fairness and equality. Regimes of discrimination thus varied considerably, and colonizers often debated the relative virtues of what might be called liberal and conservative colonialism.

The importance of notions of race in these regimes of discrimination suggests that racism was another defining trait of colonialism, and there are good reasons to consider this. Although many now contest the whole notion of race—the invention of eighteenth- and nineteenth-century European pseudoscientists—perceptions of it were so ubiquitous that one needs the concept to analyze colonial discrimination, and one cannot trace the origins of racial thought without close attention to Westerners' colonial experiences.[15] England's colonization of Ireland showed that colonial discrimination could operate without differences of skin color or the racial category schemes of the pseudoscientists, but in such cases ethnic differentiation and the stigmatizing of difference still operated.[16] And although in Latin America *mestizaje* complicated things, informal ranking systems recognized fine degrees of ethnic difference and facilitated discrimination.

Not all Western colonizers believed in the biological inferiority of other races. Nineteenth-century advocates for the American Indians who insisted that they could educate and civilize them in effect rejected biological racism, no matter how ethnocentric and condescending they were. Although they stigmatized difference in the sense that they wished to eradicate Indian culture, their wish to remake Indians in their own image required them to downplay innate differences.[17] As a rule, the civilizing mission conflicted with biological racism, for it would be pointless to try to make genetically inferior beings resemble their superiors.[18] This was another issue that separated liberal and conservative colonizers.

The term *culturism* offers an alternative to racism, implying a belief in the superiority of one's own culture and the possibility of imparting it to the colonized, who are not biologically inferior but simply "behind" in historical development.[19] In making the colonized resemble themselves, colonizers eroded difference, thus undermining the basis of discrimination—and indeed threatening colonialism itself. This process, however, could take years, if it ever succeeded at all, and in the meantime, discrimination could work without biological racism. If racism is not exactly a defining trait of colonialism, then, it was nonetheless vital to its operation in most cases, and whether using biological concepts or not, colonialism required establishing and stigmatizing differences between colonizer and colonized.[20]

A fourth defining trait of colonialism is acculturation, the often forcible replacement of indigenous culture with that of the colonizer. Although cultural influence flowed in both directions, it was highly asymmetrical, operating in a framework of inequality and coercion that allowed the banning of indigenous religions, languages, and other culturally determined practices. Acculturation met stiff resistance, but children proved malleable, especially when removed from the home, as with the Australian aborigines' "stolen generation" and American Indians sent to boarding schools. Coerced acculturation was not always official policy, and colonizers debated the wisdom of tampering with indigenous cultures. The opposition sprang less from cultural relativism or respect for others' ways than from fears of provoking costly disorder or revolt. Ironically, the policy of *not* tampering interfered as well, for colonizers ended up blocking change that would otherwise have occurred.[21] Levels of effective acculturation varied greatly by time and place, in part because many colonized regions saw few Europeans—a point that underlines the importance of the occupier's physical presence.[22] However few in number the colonizers were, and however briefly they ruled, they left at least some cultural legacies everywhere.

A crucial aspect of acculturation involved the tendency of the colonized to internalize the colonizers' values and ways of thinking, and thus to accept their own inferiority. Albert Memmi's experiences as a Tunisian Jew who moved to France when Tunisia gained its independence led him to wonder how the colonized can "hate the colonizers and yet admire them so passionately," and he observed that the colonial subject, in copying the colonizer's "habits, clothing, food, and architecture," also "adopts his own condemnation."[23] This explains how "a handful of often arrogant colonizers can live in the midst of a multitude of colonized."[24] But if some colonial subjects certainly admired aspects of Western civilization, the role that Westernized elites played in anticolonial liberation movements suggests that acculturation did not always produce obedient subjects.[25] Their situation highlights the complexities of colonial acculturation and both the difficulties and possibilities of overcoming "mental colonization."

If consensus on the meaning of colonialism remains elusive, the problem is even worse for the term *imperialism*. Edward Said called it "a word and an idea today so controversial, so fraught with all sorts of questions, doubts, polemics, and ideological premises as nearly to resist use altogether."[26] Some use it as a synonym for colonialism, but Said drew a useful distinction in specifying that colonialism involves "the implanting of settlements on distant territory."[27] In this sense, colonialism is a variant of imperialism, in which the colonizer is physically present.[28] Control without occupation could occur through pressure via international institutions, boycotts and sanctions, the effects and memory of previous occupation, and stated or implied threats of military force. Formal and informal empire have been portrayed as two aspects of a single phenomenon—two ends of a continuum—with cost-conscious rulers preferring the cheaper informal variant whenever possible.[29] At the informal end, empire may shade imperceptibly into mere inequality in international relations, but the notion of a continuum involving imperialism and colonialism, distinguished by degrees of occupation, remains useful.[30]

Decolonization seems easy enough to define, as it involves the dismantling of colonial rule and the departure of the occupiers. Yet Frantz Fanon's insistence that decolonization is necessarily violent—given that colonialism is as well—suggests a stricter definition, for Fanon knew that some countries gained their independence peacefully.[31] To Fanon, decolonization implied a revolution and a rejection of Western values, so negotiated transfers of power brought only ersatz decolonization. This surely set an unrealistic standard, for if only a total rejection of Western values and ways qualifies as decolonization, then none has ever occurred. Perhaps it is useful to view decolonization as a long-term process rather than an event, and the histories of countless former colonies involve revolutions or other changes occurring years after independence, as new regimes reduced their former colonizer's influence. Decolonization thus began well before independence and continued long after it.

These issues bring up the related concept of neocolonialism, which Ghana's first leader, Kwame Nkrumah, examined in a 1965 essay.[32] Under neocolonialism, wrote Nkrumah, a state "is, in theory, independent" but "in reality its economic system and thus its political policy is directed from outside." The neocolonial power, which is not necessarily the former colonizer, controls affairs through the stationing of troops, periodic military incursions, and pressure exercised through financial institutions, usually in collaboration with corrupt indigenous elites. The result "is that foreign capital is used for the exploitation rather than for the development" of the country. The system is actually worse than colonialism, under which "the imperial power had at least to explain and justify" its actions.[33] If neocolonialism involves control without occupation, then in this view the transition from colonialism to neocolonialism is a shift from colonialism to imperialism.

One problem with the neocolonialism thesis concerns the time it took for new regimes to free themselves from lingering ties.[34] In 1965, it was simply too soon to see the outcome of decolonization. Nkrumah's complaint that "a state in the grip of neo-colonialism is not master of its own destiny" also sets an unreasonable standard, given that no state enjoys total independence from foreign pressures and influences.[35] And although the thesis rightly identifies the means by which powerful states may pressure and control new countries, to treat the colonizer's physical presence as irrelevant ignores the daily humiliations of living under foreign occupation and also overlooks the greater difficulties of controlling a country without that presence.[36] As for collaborating elites, it bears asking whether these are puppets or simply leaders who choose freely to ally with Western states and enact capitalist policies, and also whether they would fall without Western support. Certain regimes have met those tests, but it takes considerable Eurocentrism to assume that Western states control everything in the world, and many a Western client has fallen from power. The same historical forces that discredited colonialism also raised the political costs of neocolonialism and imperialism, emboldening resistance to dictators and leading Western powers to abandon them.

The neocolonialism thesis has endured despite the rising power and wealth of countries such as China, South Korea, Brazil, Chile, and India, and today the notion that nothing has changed, for example, in China's relations with the West since the days when gunboats cruised the Yangtze is hardly convincing.[37] This is not to deny that inequalities remain in international relations, or that Western powers still seek to influence third-world nations, but to dismiss the significance of decolonization is to suggest that all the anticolonial resistance of the past century accomplished nothing, a false claim and a demoralizing one for those engaged in resistance.[38]

Although a full explanation of why decolonization occurred is beyond this book's scope, one key question is what role growing Western disillusionment with colonialism played. Western anticolonialism, which dates back to the 1500s, grew after each world war, and fascist imperialism did much to discredit the concept. Ethical misgivings about colonialism may help explain why colonial powers rarely devoted all of their efforts and resources to resisting decolonization, but other explanations include the rising will and capacity of the colonized to oppose colonial rule; European financial and military weakness after 1945; hostility toward colonialism from the new superpowers and other countries; the material aid the Soviets and others gave resistance movements; and a "snowball effect" that made decolonization look unstoppable.[39] Nonetheless, changing Western views likely played some role, and the precise relationship between Western public opinion and decolonization needs further scrutiny.

Approaches to Decolonization

Decolonization merits a transnational and comparative approach, for the same basic process was unfolding more or less simultaneously in many places. The cinematic treatment of empire has been as transnational as empire itself: films in each country have influenced each other, as in the often-noted overlap between American westerns and empire films set in India.[40] While national studies of decolonization may identify unique causes and processes, they may also overlook global forces and trends.[41] Comparing national experiences thus offers valuable perspective, and indeed, when facing differences between two countries' experiences, it takes a third case to identify the aberration. National and transnational studies both have their value, but far more national studies have been done so far.

This book includes Britain and France mainly because they were Europe's two most important colonizers in the modern era. The inclusion of the United States as a third case will puzzle only those who still believe American self-images that the United States, as a former colony itself, has always rejected colonialism. It is true that Americans have long disdained lengthy tasks of occupation and administration, unlike those Europeans who denied they would ever leave their colonies. Yet even looking only at formal colonialism, indisputable American cases include the Philippines, Cuba, Puerto Rico, Guam, Hawaii, and Panama. And unless one accepts the "saltwater fallacy"—that only overseas territories count as colonies—the entire United States itself was formed as part of western colonial expansion.[42] The notion of American colonialism is plain enough to historians, and if one also considers America's informal empire in places such as East Asia and Central America, the cases become even more numerous.[43] In the Cold War, proprietary attitudes could be seen, for example, in Republicans' accusations that President Truman had "lost" China in 1949. And despite American misgivings about European colonialism, concerns about communism after 1945 led Washington into complicity with European colonialism in various places.[44] Finally, including the United States in a study of films on this topic makes sense because most of those films came from Hollywood.

The concept of decolonization applies more easily to areas such as the Philippines, where the United States granted independence and ended the occupation, than it does within the U.S. borders. For colonial relationships with American Indians, Hawaiians, Alaskans, African Americans, Chicanos, and others inside the United States, conceptualizing decolonization is more complicated. One normally gauges it by the degree of real independence eventually achieved, but when colonialism involves permanent annexation of territory and the absorption of its people, one must assess decolonization in terms of changes in components of colonialism other than occupation. Internal decolonization might be measured in terms of the cessation of discrimination and exploitation and the degree of integration and real equality subject peoples achieved.[45] The colonizer's continuing presence and the extensive acculturation produced make internal decolonization quite imperfect, but then decolonization is never total, as former colonies always reflect some measure of their colonizers' influences. So if things such as segregation, discrimination, and exploitation were ended or greatly reduced, one might speak of decolonization in a country such as the United States.

The leaders of the African American freedom struggle in the 1950s and 1960s certainly saw their efforts as part of a global process of decolonization.[46] That struggle actually mapped out two paths to decolonization: one seeking integration, assimilation, and equality, and another seeking separation and the preservation of cultural distinctions (as in black nationalism and today's multiculturalism). American Indians have also taken both paths, as some have fought for the right to live on reservations and preserve traditional ways while others have left the reservation and sought full integration and equality. Ideally, decolonization would mean the freedom to choose either path with some prospect of success. This book will consider how films and reviews grappled with the meanings and implications of internal decolonization, and whether people saw similarities between internal and external colonialism.

While Americans were expanding their overseas presence, Europeans were pondering a retreat from empire. For the British, the loss of empire raised fundamental questions of identity.[47] Some historians have depicted most modern Britons as surprisingly unaware of and indifferent to their empire, while revisionists have challenged that view, but this lively debate has focused primarily on the late nineteenth and early twentieth centuries, and the evidence for the 1940s and 1950s remains frustratingly thin (see chapter 4). This book uses films and reviews to fill in the picture, and it also considers British feelings about immigration from the colonies, a by-product of decolonization.

Although British decolonization was not always placid, many have noted France's more violent and traumatic path to decolonization. France fought and lost major wars in Indochina and Algeria, and the latter fueled bitter internal political conflicts—notably the Algiers revolt of 1958, which toppled the Fourth Republic and provoked right-wing terrorism in France.[48] While many historians maintain that the French long avoided discussing the traumas of colonialism, this book will question that picture, arguing that by the 1950s, many wanted public discussion of the recent and current crises. As in Britain, losing an empire raised questions of national identity, provoked anxieties about France's international standing, and spurred immigration from former colonies.

The Films

This book focuses on fiction films, emphasizing those that examined relations between colonizer and colonized more than those that merely used colonial settings as backdrops for tales about relations among whites. Although it privileges high-profile films, given that they were more influential and provoked more discussion, it also considers films that did poorly at the box office, for people watched both kinds of films.

Placing films in national categories became harder in this period. While some European filmmakers rejected the Hollywood style, American films nonetheless influenced European cinema, which in turn influenced American filmmakers.[49] Hollywood was also filled with European immigrants, while the British and French film industries hosted immigrants from various countries—including Americans fleeing Hollywood's blacklist.[50] Postwar European governments' attempts to protect domestic film industries caused trade disputes with the Americans, the outcome of which involved Hollywood's shooting in Europe and employing European actors and crews rather than repatriating profits. This "runaway" production, which also grew because of lower production costs in Europe, yielded a large body of Anglo-American and other bi-national films.[51] Finally, Hollywood's search for foreign markets led it to alter films to suit foreign tastes and avoid giving offense.[52] The two largest European colonial powers were also Hollywood's two largest foreign markets, so despite many Americans' distaste for European colonialism, Hollywood restrained its criticism of the British and French empires.[53]

Interwar empire films had developed certain conventions that endured after 1945. Many older films had depicted whites as courageous, intelligent, and virtuous, though some had white characters overcome their selfishness, cynicism, and immaturity and embrace their imperial duties.[54] Whites were typically outnumbered by hordes of natives, highlighting their superior resourcefulness and sangfroid as well as their knowledge and technology (guns, compasses, motor vehicles). Although individual whites might be cruel and greedy, the overall enterprise typically had noble motives, and civilization normally triumphed in the end. Also highlighting whites' courage were the dangers of the local environment, usually a jungle or desert. As these were mostly adventure films, dangerous environments and exotic images boosted their entertainment value and underlined their protagonists' heroism and courage. While real settlers generally sought an easy life with native servants and laborers doing most of the work, empire films generally showed explorers and conquerors in the dangerous early stages of colonization rather than settlers and the mature phase of colonial rule.[55] Films nonetheless hinted at an easier life to follow by showing compliant servants treating whites like royalty.

The dangers of exotic environments were moral as well as physical, especially in the South Seas films.[56] Empire films often featured scenes of sexual temptation, offering audiences the pleasures of fantasy and images of attractive, seductive, scantily clad natives (often played by whites), before they upheld Western morality in the final reel. Whether depicting natives as dangerous in moral or physical terms, films usually presented them as undifferentiated masses, often silent figures who supplied "local color," and few movies gave native characters much intelligible or intelligent dialogue. Animals often got more screen time, particularly in films set in Africa.[57] Native life was cheap in empire films, which often featured the slaughter of faceless warriors who fought stupidly.[58] Natives were typically primitive, dangerous, violent, and cruel, but there were usually a few "good natives"—loyal servants and protectors of whites, or childlike characters needing protection.[59] In contrasting civilization and barbarism, the films depicted natives who were irrational, superstitious, and ignorant. Native women varied from attractive seductresses, to ugly objects of ridicule, to selfless and noble protectors of imperiled white men.[60]

One of the purposes empire films served in their heyday in the interwar years was to bolster public support for colonialism.[61] Even when filmmakers did not benefit from official assistance, many shared colonialist mentalities or catered to Western audiences' presumed outlooks. Apart from a handful of noble-savage films critical of Western intrusion—usually set in the South Seas—interwar empire films generally looked like colonialist propaganda. Yet the continuing production of empire films *after* independence suggests that bolstering empire was not their sole purpose, and filmmakers seeking to entertain and make money kept using old, successful formulas. Particularly in the postwar era, when studios and producers were looking for visually striking wide-screen material, the temptation to shoot in exotic locales led to the production of films with no real point to make about colonialism. They conveyed messages all the same, if only inadvertently, and their content and reception deserve scrutiny.

Adhering to genre conventions led postwar films to perpetuate images and stereotypes created in very different times, but this book argues that cinematic myths and genres also evolved significantly after 1945.[62] Postwar films on colonial themes turned increasingly ambivalent, even anticolonialist, creating new functions for the genre. These included the articulation of new political perspectives as well as the defense of old ones; the addressing of current issues, directly or indirectly; the recognition and validation of the historical experiences of both colonizers and colonized; and the expression of contrition for Western crimes.

Empire films, in short, became more politically complex after World War II. This book asks of each film: Who are the "good guys" and "bad guys" (regrettably simplistic concepts that nonetheless fit most films), and what is good or bad about them? With whom do films urge audiences to sympathize? Whose stories do they tell? Do films include perspectives of the colonized, developing individual characters? Do the colonized get to speak at all? If so, do they speak in their own language, or do they struggle to express themselves in the colonizer's tongue? Do films use close-ups of colonized individuals, and if so, to demonize or to empathize?[63] Do films explain the motives for natives' violence? Do the films air their grievances and recount their past? Do they depict only men or also women and children? Do the films favor acculturation and assimilation, or do they see differences as immutable? Do they depict the culture of the colonized, and do they seek to explain and translate rituals and practices, or do they present them merely as exotic and primitive? Do films seek cultural authenticity? Do they engage in ethnic miscasting? How do films present the actions and motives of westerners? How do they depict relations between colonizer and colonized, including sexual or romantic relationships? Do these relationships end well, and if not, why not?

The Historical Analysis of Film: Disciplines and Methodologies

Historians are relative newcomers to the study of film.[64] Scholars in other disciplines have done far more work on film, including specialists in literature, cinema studies, cultural and postcolonial studies, gender studies, and area studies. While for years historians did little more than list films' inaccuracies, a growing number now set aside such issues and view films as historical artifacts and myths.⁶⁵ Instead of viewing films as faulty secondary sources, they treat them as primary sources, studying them not for information about the history they depict, but for what they reveal about the societies that produced and consumed them.⁶⁶

Despite borrowing from other disciplines, historians nonetheless approach film in their own ways. In place of many film scholars' often exclusive interest in textual analysis and the (often Freudian) reading of symbolisms, historians are more inclined to combine textual analysis with attention to historical context and research into production and reception, inquiring what historical conditions helped produce a film and what impact it had on society.⁶⁷ Less inclined toward the jargon of literary analysis, they are also more leery of overanalysis and the making of unfalsifiable or unsubstantiated claims about the meaning of cinematic images.⁶⁸ Of course it is perfectly valid to suggest *possible* meanings of film images, but to empirically minded historians, the lack of evidence presented to support them raises potential objections.

Historians may also object to generalizations about popular cinema that ignore its historical evolution and, in the case of empire films, that treat Hollywood as an eternal and unchanging supporter of colonialism and racism.⁶⁹ Of course some film scholars do see historical change, but one of historians' analytical tools—the concept of historical empathy—is crucial to the study of film. Judging the films of the past, in short, requires considering them in historical context, taking into account prevailing mentalities, constraints, and conditions. Although a given film may now seem dated, historians seek not to debate the people of the past, but to make their world understandable, and instead of judging a film's politics by today's standards, they strive to assess where it stood in relation to the prevailing ideas of its time—a task textual analysis cannot accomplish.

Just as important to the film historian is what one might call cinematic empathy. Here, fact-checking historians have been the worst offenders—criticizing historical films for taking liberties and romanticizing the past without appreciating why filmmakers do so. In a letter to Clyde Dollar, historical consultant on *A Man Called Horse* (1970), director Elliot Silverstein expressed his frustrations at Dollar's constant complaints. "Your devotion is to the mind of your reader or pupil," he explained, "and mine is directed primarily toward the heart and the emotions" and "the general sweep of building emotional and artistic effect." It is the historian's task, he added, "to try to reveal things as they once were," while "it is mine to try to entertain and enlighten" and "perhaps lend some insight into the past."⁷⁰ Films, in short, should be judged as films, not as history books. Judging commercial films also requires a clear sense of the realities of film production and the intense, conflicting pressures filmmakers faced from studios, financiers, critics, censors, audiences, and pressure groups.

The historian's usual methods—the analysis of the production, content, and reception of historical documents and artifacts—certainly work well for films.[71] But films have specific qualities, so content analysis requires attention to matters specific to the medium, including directing style, narrative structure, genre, cinematography and visual composition, acting style, casting, lighting, costumes, makeup, set design, sound design, music, editing, and location choices. In these tasks, historians have much to learn from the other disciplines.

Studying film production also borrows from literary analysis the concept of authorial intent, but identifying a film's "author" can be difficult. Despite a tradition dating back to the Renaissance of glorifying individual artistic genius, the analysis of film generally bears out historians' skepticism toward "great man" theories. As critics of the *auteur* theory have argued, not all films have a director whose artistic vision dominated the production, and even famous directors have complained about the endless compromises forced upon them.[72] While ideally one would identify the various contributions of the individuals (directors, producers, screenwriters, novelists) and institutions (studios, culture ministries, censorship organizations) who helped shape a film, archives often contain only fragments of what took place. And interviews with filmmakers can be disappointing, confirming historians' warnings that historical actors can rarely explain their own actions.

Aware of commercial pressures and the collective nature of filmmaking, students of American films often attribute authorship to Hollywood rather than to their directors. There are good reasons to do so, but this convenient term for America's commercial film industry requires some prefatory remarks. And although Hollywood has no counterpart in Europe, some of these comments pertain to Britain and France as well.

One school of thought treats Hollywood as a more or less coherent entity with its own political ideology, agenda, and aesthetic style. Exercising cultural hegemony over America and the world, it promotes and reproduces dominant ideologies and ideas about politics, society, economics, gender, and ethnic relations. In this view, Hollywood may be autonomous from governments, but it tends to share the interests and ideologies of ruling classes and elites. Pioneering this outlook were Marxists of the Frankfurt school, principally Theodor Adorno and Max Horkheimer, and their approach has proved popular.[73] In recent years, conservatives have accused Hollywood of promoting a liberal agenda and ignoring demand for films about faith, family, and traditional values—even if it means foregoing potential profits.[74]

A rival school of thought sees Hollywood as essentially devoted to making profits and thus largely indifferent to content. Whether Sam Goldwyn actually said, "If you want to send a message, use Western Union," the idea that studios "give 'em what they want" is quite common. Evidence for this outlook includes past efforts to investigate audience desires. Adolph Zukor reportedly sat in his Manhattan penny arcade to watch people watching movies; in 1912, William Fox sent out ten thousand cards asking patrons about their entertainment preferences; by the 1940s, studios held sneak previews, hired pollsters to research audience preferences, and then altered their films to suit them.[75] Viewing these efforts, scholars emphasize Hollywood's ability to sense and cater to prevailing mentalities, not its power to impose its own ideas on reluctant consumers.[76]

Both of these approaches to relations between film producers and consumers have great value. Some film-industry figures have shown more interest in learning audience preferences than others, so neither approach suffices to describe the complex and changing entity known as Hollywood.[77] The temptation to use film to advance one's own ideas is strong indeed. Orson Welles admitted that he went into film so that "people will listen to what I have to say politically," and screenwriter Philip Dunne called the prospect of influencing audiences "a headier wine than either money or fame."[78] Yet at all levels of the industry there is little job security, limiting how far one can ignore audiences' expectations, mentalities, and changing values. Drawing on both of these theories of film production, this book considers the extent to which the filmmakers and film industries of the United States, Britain, and France were leading or following the evolution of attitudes on colonialism.

Researching the reception of films is notoriously difficult, and many scholars do not attempt it at all. But the potential rewards justify the effort, and historians are accustomed to working with frustratingly incomplete documentary records. A good starting point for assessing reception is to recognize the multiple and competing means by which societies legitimize films, including measures of audience popularity (primarily theatrical ticket sales in this era); critical reaction; awards from film-industry professionals; and the eventual judgment of scholars. Societies have no definitive way to resolve conflicts among these subjective means of legitimation, and though in time a consensus may form, the entire process can be contentious.[79]

Researching audience reactions presents a great challenge, as viewers rarely leave a record of their reactions. In recent decades, media historians have emphasized "plural sense-making," the notion that different people perceive, understand, and recall different things in media images based on their own sociological traits, mentalities, knowledge, politics, and tastes.⁸⁰ Unfortunately, aside from the occasional letter to a newspaper or censor, historians have only quantitative evidence such as ticket sales. Even here, assumptions can be hazardous; poor ticket sales may reflect supply-side issues such as poor distribution and advertising. Films' life-cycles also differ, as some remain or become popular long after their initial release, often eluding annual box-office statistics. Box-office data themselves merit reservations, as they are mostly self-reported and may be overstated or understated; nonetheless, if the figures' precision deserves skepticism, the film industry's lists of the top films each year generally correspond to other, more impressionistic means of assessment.⁸¹

For the United States in this period, the best available information appears in *Variety*, which published annual rankings of earnings as well as all-time box-office charts that adjusted previous figures.⁸² Historians of postwar French film have the benefit of Simon Simsi's painstaking compilation of data from the Centre National de Cinématographie.⁸³ For Britain no such compilation exists, leaving only meager references to ticket sales of a few leading films in trade publications. Box-office charts, of course, cannot account for one person watching a film multiple times, and they lack regional or demographic breakdowns. They also fail to reveal people's reactions or motives for seeing a film. (In this period, some filmgoers attended regularly, perhaps knowing little of a film in advance.)⁸⁴ In general, however, the more popular a film was, the more likely it was that people were making informed choices.

For qualitative analysis of reception, the richest source available consists of film reviews. While many scholars have ignored reviews altogether, others have leapt to unwarranted conclusions based on woefully small and poorly constructed samples, often consisting of two or three reviews from film journals and elite newspapers and magazines. And it is practically useless to state, as many do, that a film received "mixed reviews," if that phrase means that some critics liked it while others did not. Not only is that true of nearly every film ever made, but it provides no guidance at all about quantitative patterns. The term "mixed review," however, is useful to describe a review that was neither clearly positive nor clearly negative. This study uses it that way and tallies reviews in three rather than two categories.

This book uses reviews from a wide range of American, British, and French publications, including newspapers, magazines, and trade papers. For each country, it consults periodicals from cities of various sizes, including both mass-circulation periodicals and those with narrower readerships, while also seeking out voices across a wide political spectrum. (Not all reviews fit a paper's political stance, as critics enjoyed considerable political autonomy.) It includes little reaction from small towns and rural areas, largely because small-town papers published few reviews of their own—many had no critic at all and simply reprinted reviews from urban papers. The consequent urban bias may be unfortunate, but big-city newspapers were read in suburban and rural areas.[85] Moreover, in these countries in this era, movie-going itself was more urban than rural, and the urban bias in film criticism probably mirrors similar biases in public opinion on the political issues in question here.[86]

The examination of reviews here also focuses more on the critics' political opinions on colonial issues than on their judgments of films' artistic or entertainment value. It nonetheless reports breakdowns among positive, negative, and mixed judgments of the films, because inept filmmaking distracted critics from the issues raised. Connections between the affective and cognitive dimensions of film reception are noteworthy, as research has shown that people are more likely to understand a film's message if they enjoyed the picture.[87] Specific questions include: How many people commented on the political issues raised, and what interested them most? What views did they state about colonialism and race relations? What did they understand or misunderstand about the issues? Was sensitivity to colonial issues growing? Did critics see the events depicted as part of global trends?

A reminder that public opinion does not necessarily consist of the equally weighted opinions of all individuals should preempt many objections about using film reviews to study public opinion. Scholars have often denied that critics represent audiences, and this dismissive attitude may help explain why so few have studied reviews.[88] To be sure, people who write for a living are wealthier and better educated than the general populace, and in the United States in this era, critics as a group were whiter as well. (The striking gender imbalance in Hollywood in these years was far less prevalent among film critics, many of whom were women.) Critics also differ from most audience members in that they spend far more time watching and thinking about films. A common distinction between reviewers and critics treats the latter as experts on cinema and reviewers as unskilled hacks; by that definition, many of the reviews used here come from reviewers, who presumably did not differ so greatly from their readers. Given the difficulty of drawing precise lines between these categories, however, this study discards that distinction and uses the terms as synonyms, and it contends that people who review films appear along a continuum of cinematic expertise. And because this study is specifically interested in *political* rather than *artistic* judgments, the supposed gulf between critics and audiences is even less significant, for there is little reason to believe that critics had any special expertise, training, or experience in the political analysis of colonialism. The point here is not to deny that audience reaction and critical opinion were separate means of legitimation, but rather to suggest that on specific political questions critics and ordinary viewers were not so far apart, having grown up in the same basic historical and social milieu. And although critical opinion deserves attention for its power to shape as well as reflect others' opinions, the main reason why this study takes reviews seriously is that they constitute a vital component of public opinion and a fascinating, almost totally unexplored repository of opinions about colonialism in the era of decolonization.

PART ONE

THE PERSISTENCE OF EMPIRE
Colonialist Films in the Decolonization Era

Like other major turning points in history, the end of World War II saw a complex intersection of memories and expectations. Traumatic memories of the war jostled with equally painful recollections of the Great Depression and World War I, from which many hoped humankind would at least learn useful lessons. For Western leaders, envisioning a new global order demanded grappling with the colonial question, for in the colonies the traumatic events had challenged the seeming inevitability of Western domination. Some colonies were closer to independence than others—in India it was by now simply a question of when and how Britain would hand over power, while in much of Africa independence seemed a distant prospect—but nearly everywhere colonial rulers faced unprecedented pressure to make concessions. The reasons for this new situation included the principles for which the victors claimed to have fought, the promises colonial rulers had made to secure the wartime cooperation of the colonized, the war's profound effects on the mentalities of the colonized, and the rise to superpower status of two avowedly anticolonial countries. Though colonial rulers resisted demands for independence, a stunning global wave of decolonization soon began.

While Western leaders grappled with these issues, ordinary citizens in those countries must have watched with bewilderment the unfolding events and the confusing and disturbing news from unfamiliar places. To those who knew little about the colonies or the people under their rule, movies had been a rare source of images and information, however flawed, and soon after World War II films resumed their engagement with the colonial world. While some films addressed decolonization directly, others ignored it, telling tales set in the past and justifying and glorifying the work of Western colonizers as empire films had long done. With decolonization gaining momentum, the continued production of colonialist films set in the past raises crucial questions, but before turning to those films, a few comments about the historical context of the time are in order.

The American Background

As American leaders began planning for a new postwar future, their historical distaste for European colonialism was now strengthened by their belief that a division of the world into closed trading blocs, including Europe's colonial empires, had contributed to the Depression and the ensuing war. Envisioning a free, democratic, and capitalist world marked by free movement of capital and goods, they saw little place for colonial empires. With polls and other evidence showing Americans, despite their war-weariness and isolationist traditions, now more supportive of involvement in global affairs, Washington set out to build a new international order.[1] The potential paradox of a country dedicated to freedom and self-determination exercising power over vast regions of the globe—a kind of anti-imperialist imperialism—probably did not bother many Americans, given their tendency to see themselves as benevolent and uninterested in governing distant lands. But if few Americans saw their country as imperialist, others certainly did, as the United States attained a level of global power unprecedented in world history.

The onset of the Cold War soon complicated American anticolonialism. On the one hand, concerns that liberation movements might turn to the Soviets for help gave the United States reason to support them and to pressure the Europeans to decolonize, and it set an example by granting independence to the Philippines in 1946. On the other hand, American leaders feared that pressuring the Europeans could fuel anti-Americanism, and they also believed, as Senator Henry Cabot Lodge, Jr., put it, that "we need . . . these countries to be strong, and they cannot be strong without their colonies."[2] What resulted was a contradictory policy toward European colonialism. Secretary of State John Foster Dulles spoke in 1954 of "walking a tightrope" between supporting the European allies and backing the aspirations of the colonized, and Washington ended up angering both; in Indochina, for example, the U.S. refusal to fight alongside the French angered Paris, while the economic and military aid it gave the French angered the Vietminh.[3]

Washington's postwar foreign policy also rested on new versions of the manifest-destiny concept. The old belief that God had chosen Americans to bring Christianity and civilization to the entire continent now applied to a superpower with global aspirations, and a Protestant sense of mission once again fueled American expansion. Secretary Dulles's grandfather had been a missionary and his father a minister, and he himself was a leader in the Federal Council of Churches; President Truman, a devout Baptist, declared that God intended America to lead the world; President Eisenhower also saw the Cold War through a spiritual lens.[4] This approach to international affairs coincided with a rise in the 1950s in church membership, Bible sales, and other evidence of religiousness. Expressing this outlook in global affairs, Republican Senator Edward Martin of Pennsylvania said in 1950 that "America must move forward with the atomic bomb in one hand and the cross in the other."[5] Although not all Americans saw things in quite those terms, there was a broad consensus on many aspects of foreign policy and the Cold War.

Broad consensus on many domestic issues did not extend to race relations. The war years had seen race riots and the internment of Japanese Americans, but with Nazi policies having helped to discredit racism, many Americans—including in Hollywood—now sought to distinguish themselves from the enemy by favoring racial tolerance. Members of all racial minorities had contributed to the war effort, generating expectations of reaping just rewards, and the ensuing years saw major victories for the civil rights movement. Unfortunately, bitter struggles over desegregation in the South underlined continuing divisions, and the use of federal troops to resolve stalemates in places such as Little Rock, Arkansas, in 1957 showed that progress toward racial equality required coercion as well as persuasion and negotiation. Coercion also helped produce the political consensus that many observers consider a hallmark of 1950s America, for the anticommunist witch hunts of the early Cold War crushed the far left, intimidated liberals, and forged an artificial unanimity. Nowhere was this more evident than in Hollywood.

Postwar Hollywood

Amid postwar labor strife in Hollywood, a new committee of Hollywood conservatives known as the Motion Picture Alliance for the Preservation of American Ideals (MPA) urged the House Committee on Un-American Activities (HUAC) to come to Hollywood to look for leftists.[6] Certain that films influenced viewers, HUAC began hearings in 1947, resulting in the jailing of "the Hollywood Ten" for contempt of Congress. The rattled studio moguls, mostly Jewish immigrants fearful of congressmen who were both anti-Semitic and anticommunist, then blacklisted hundreds of screenwriters and directors.[7] It thus became dangerous for films to articulate anything that might sound like a critique of "the American way."[8] The Central Intelligence Agency (CIA) even monitored and advised Hollywood on specific films in these years, and although the notion that the CIA needed to encourage the ultrapatriotic moguls to make pro-American films may seem ridiculous, concerns about impressionable foreign audiences made officials skittish about highlighting problems in America.[9] Yet even as boycott threats from conservative pressure groups such as the American Legion and the Catholic-led Legion of Decency added to the repressive environment in Hollywood, liberal and leftist filmmakers managed to keep working and to challenge the manufactured consensus through subtle critiques.[10]

Adding to Hollywood's problems was a sharp decline in ticket sales that began soon after World War II and continued for more than two decades, reducing the number of theaters and films produced.[11] The culprit usually cited is television, but equally important were migration to the suburbs, which drew people to other forms of diversion, and the baby boom, which kept potential moviegoers at home.[12] Hollywood courted audiences with wider screens and 3D, and it also sought out visually striking and exotic big-screen material, opening the way for more films in tropical and colonial settings.

Compounding Hollywood's problems, the Supreme Court's 1948 *Paramount* decision resolved a long-standing Justice Department antitrust suit by banning certain coercive trade practices and ordering the studios to sell off the theaters that had virtually guaranteed them sales of their films.[13] At the same time, talent agents such as Lew Wasserman at MCA increasingly took advantage of Hollywood's desperation for bankable stars, wresting decision-making power away from the studios.[14] As the studios began to outsource production and sell off assets, often limiting their role to financing and distributing independent producers' films, it might seem that filmmakers gained more freedom, but the retention of financing and distribution sufficed to keep independent producers under some control, and for independents unable to cover losses with hits as the studios had done, the new system afforded less creative freedom than one might expect.[15] Filmmakers did gain freedom from the weakening of both the Production Code Administration (PCA) and state and local censors. The PCA, a self-policing mechanism the studios had created in the early 1930s to preempt boycotts and censorship, functioned in the framework of the studio system, but as that system weakened, so did the PCA.[16] Filmmakers desperate for audiences grew bolder in the 1950s, increasingly defying the PCA, and the code itself was revised in 1956, reflecting changing mores.[17] Also fueling these trends was the Supreme Court's ruling in the 1952 *Miracle* case, which reversed a 1915 ruling and granted First Amendment rights to films.[18] State and local censors now retreated, and by the mid-1950s, pressure groups such as the Legion of Decency were losing power. Hollywood still had to cope with its audiences' conservatism, but the changing political and cultural landscape created space for cautious exploration of controversial themes. So despite popular images of the 1950s as a repressive, conservative era, American filmmaking in some ways now enjoyed growing freedom.

The British Background

Like the Americans, the British entered the postwar era filled with both painful memories and expectations of better times. The British, of course, had suffered much more from the two world wars, and unlike the United States, Britain emerged from the war with its standing in the world much diminished. The war had left Britain in need of physical reconstruction, and its dire financial situation made it even more dependent on the United States.[19] Now a debtor to its colonies, Britain faced a shortage of hard currency, while voters felt entitled to a better life after years of sacrifice and hardship. Their choice of Labour's Clement Attlee in 1945 mainly reflected impatience with continuing austerity and desires for a generous welfare state, but in ousting Churchill's Conservatives, they had also brought to power a party that was, if not exactly anticolonialist, at least less willing to resist decolonization. With welfare-state measures competing for revenues, the empire's future looked uncertain, even if no leader called for dismantling it.[20]

In the Depression, the empire had been an outlet for exports and a destination for the unemployed, and those benefits offset many troubles the empire brought in the interwar years, including bitter resistance in Ireland, India, Egypt, Iraq, and Palestine. World War II brought the loss of Hong Kong, Singapore, Malaya, and Burma to the Japanese, as well as new discontent in India, but again Britain derived crucial resources from its empire. Wartime unrest in India and elsewhere led London to promise future freedom, and in 1940 Parliament passed a Colonial Development and Welfare Bill that pledged new spending to better the lives of the colonized.[21] Whatever misgivings Labour's leaders had about colonialism, they resisted American pressure for decolonization, for as Foreign Minister Ernest Bevin put it, "if the British Empire fell . . . it would mean that the standard of life of our constituents would fall considerably."[22] Amid a dollar shortage, colonial exports alleviated a balance-of-payments crisis.[23] Within this context, granting independence to India and Pakistan in August 1947 must have seemed a serious blow, even if British leaders knew they lacked the resources to keep the Raj by force. Making the best of the inevitable, British leaders and newspapers cast the handover of power as the culmination of long-standing plans for India, though a few dissenters saw only British abdication.[24] Trying to adjust to growing anti-imperialism, British leaders, argues Wendy Webster, promoted the concept of a "people's empire," which "mobilized ideas of welfare, development, and egalitarianism," and King George VI's radio speeches contrasted Britain's "temperate" approach to empire with the aggressiveness of the country's Nazi foes.[25] A stoic acceptance of Indian independence and the crafting of a new image for Britain's relations with its colonies set the tone for later policies toward decolonization.

The British Film Industry

The damage Britain suffered in World War II also naturally affected the country's film industry. Facing personnel shortages and lacking capital for repairs and investment, British studios reduced output from prewar levels of more than two hundred films per year to forty full-length films in 1945.[26] Yet despite production problems, Britain's film market remained robust, reaching an all-time high of more than 1.6 billion admissions in 1946.[27] This imbalance of supply and demand in Britain created a golden opportunity for Hollywood, which earned more than half its European revenue in Britain.[28] Already sensitive to being, in effect, occupied and colonized by the United States during and after the war, Britons in both the film industry and government now resented the flood of American films, which often played in theaters Hollywood owned in Britain. Accusations of a symbiotic relationship between Hollywood and Washington (with Hollywood getting the State Department to help force open European markets) in addition to concerns about badly needed funds flowing to Hollywood, led to protectionism.[29] Alongside obvious financial and economic concerns stood cultural ones, for the cinematic invasion hampered the projection of British imagery and the shaping of British identity at a critical moment.[30] If moviegoers shared these concerns, that did not stop them from watching American films, with their lavish production values and keen sense of popular entertainment.

British protectionism went through a series of experiments, one of which foundered when Hollywood retaliated against a 75 percent duty on foreign films by imposing an embargo on exports to Britain.[31] Quotas reserving screen time for British films revealed a shortage of production and provoked stiff resistance from exhibitors.[32] As noted in the introduction, a series of agreements beginning in 1948 led Hollywood to reinvest its British earnings in filmmaking in Britain, and in the 1950s Hollywood coproduced about 170 films with the British.[33] In 1948, the government created the National Film Finance Company, whose director hoped state funding would help "in the projection of England and the English way of life to the Dominions and foreign countries."[34] The Treasury, however, proved stingy, and what money it allotted often ended up financing coproductions with Hollywood.[35]

The French Background

If Britain's recent experiences had been more painful than America's, France's were even worse. France had been a major battlefield in both world wars and had lost a higher percentage of its population, and in the second war France also suffered defeat and occupation. The French in 1945 also carried the additional burden of having collaborated with the Nazis, for most citizens had initially supported or acquiesced to Marshal Philippe Pétain's collaborationist regime. The Resistance, a broad coalition dominated by the Left but led by the moderate General Charles de Gaulle, became the nucleus of a new postwar regime, but bitter divisions between committed *Pétainistes* and *résistants* persisted, making political debates potentially explosive for many years.[36] Vichy's collaboration with the Nazis and its own role in deporting Jews to German concentration camps helped to discredit racism in France, which would prove significant as the country grappled with colonial questions.[37]

Proud memories of France's great-power status also shaped visions of the future, and de Gaulle, head of the provisional government until January 1946, looked for ways to maximize France's "rank" in the postwar world.[38] These hopes had major implications for colonial policy; a 1946 conference of colonialists warned that without its empire, France "would be a pauper condemned to servitude."[39] As in Britain, the world wars had proven the empire's value in the form of troops, workers, raw materials, and capital. After years of lingering doubts, empire now enjoyed wide support in France, for while Vichy had sounded imperial themes, the Resistance had also valued the empire as a base of operations.[40] In his radio speech launching the Resistance in June 1940, de Gaulle had sought to boost France's morale by recalling that "behind her is a vast empire," and if such statements overstated the empire's value, they nevertheless offered a useful myth that bolstered both French morale and support for colonialism.[41] In 1944 at Brazzaville, the Resistance convened a conference of colonial administrators, who dismissed any notion of granting independence but promised humanitarian development and greater administrative roles for indigenous people.[42]

When the war ended, however, a series of crises spread throughout the empire—results of the war's disruptions and raised expectations among the colonized. In Indochina, where the Japanese had taken over and had puppet Emperor Bao Dai proclaim independence in March 1945, the French responded with promises of change to placate local nationalists. In Syria, held under a League of Nations mandate, violent uprisings tested French strength until British pressure forced the French to abandon the territory altogether in 1946. In Algeria, the French faced a major uprising in Sétif on May 8, 1945, leading to a death toll in the tens of thousands, and a massacre of similar proportions followed in Madagascar in 1947.[43]

Coping with these events and with international pressure to decolonize, postwar leaders outlined new colonial policies. The Constituent Assembly of 1946 included sixty-three deputies elected in overseas territories, but it followed the Brazzaville approach on imperial questions, offering reforms such as citizenship for all French subjects and an end to forced labor but no hint of independence.[44] The finished constitution proclaimed that "France intends to lead the peoples for which it has responsibility to the freedom to administer themselves and to direct their own affairs democratically, avoiding any system of colonization founded on arbitrariness."[45] The new "French Union" fell short of these lofty sentiments: a federalist system in appearance, it remained firmly under Paris's control, with only 78 seats reserved for the colonies in an assembly of 622.[46] Like the British, the French increased appropriations for colonial development and welfare, hoping to preempt further colonial unrest.[47] The most serious crisis arose in September 1945 after Japanese power collapsed in Indochina, when the Vietminh under Ho Chi Minh seized control in Hanoi and then declared independence. War began there in November 1946, so unlike Britain and the United States, France entered the postwar period engaged in a full-scale war to keep one of its colonies.

The French Film Industry

Given the shape France was in, it is a wonder that it produced films at all.[48] Despite severe shortages of raw materials and capital, the country managed to make eighty-three films in 1946 (rising again in subsequent years), and although many people lacked sufficient food, shelter, and fuel, French theaters sold more than 369 million tickets in 1946—a telling comment on cinema's place in French society.[49] Although evidence suggests that French viewers generally preferred French films, American films were popular as well, much to the chagrin of the Communists and others.[50] Amid French calls for protectionism, the 1946 Blum-Byrnes accords, a two-year agreement between American and French trade negotiators, reserved at least four weeks per quarter for French films, set quotas for American films in France, and capped the repatriation of American earnings. Communist deputies and journalists denounced the accords; one charged that "the State Department decided to make cinema the instrument of its will for imperialist domination" and a "fifth column . . . [for] the crushing or the colonization of national cinemas," while film-industry personnel marching in the streets in January 1948 chanted slogans such as "Blum sold us out, Truman wants us dead."[51] Historian Jacques Portes speaks of a "conscious disinformation campaign" that generated a "black legend" about a deal he considers "a success for France."[52] While it is true that Hollywood now exported a backlog of wartime films, historians have vastly overstated Hollywood's domination of the French market.[53] In fact, France produced eighty-eight films in 1947 and ninety-two in 1948; French films accounted for twelve of the top twenty films in 1947 and fourteen of the top twenty in 1948, and French and American films had roughly equal market shares in those years.[54] So although alarmists warned that the Blum-Byrnes accords "call into question the very survival of the dramatic art" in France, rumors of the death of France's film industry were greatly exaggerated.[55]

Further negotiations yielded new accords in 1948, with the Americans agreeing to show even fewer films in France. Also in 1948, France's parliament began taxing tickets to subsidize film production and theater renovations, and French protectionism reached levels few other countries equaled, probably exceeding what was even necessary.[56] As for Hollywood's earnings in France, very little went to the sort of coproductions that the British and the Americans made, largely because of linguistic barriers, but Hollywood did invest in distribution and exhibition.

Despite the impressive output and performance of French films, the country did not produce films on colonial topics in the first decade after the war, in part because of government censorship. The paucity of French fiction films about the colonies makes French reviews of foreign films all the more valuable for gauging outlooks, but unfortunately shortages of paper and newsprint restricted space for film reviews in the first years after the war. French critics also tended to ignore American films in favor of French ones, but by the 1950s, more and more reviews of American films were appearing, and the following chapters examine them.

CHAPTER ONE

The White Woman's Burden

Empire films, a staple of the interwar years in America, Britain, and France, largely disappeared during World War II, and with the advent of decolonization after the war, there was reason to wonder if the genre would return.[1] But while the French mostly abandoned filmmaking in the tradition of *Princesse Tam-Tam* (1932), *La Bandera* (1935), and *Pepé le Moko* (1937), the Americans and the British revived the genre, updating it by casting colonialism in humanitarian terms, much as colonial policymakers were doing in hopes of saving their empires. These new empire films often sentimentalized their material, featured women in prominent roles, and reduced complicated issues of international relations to personal relationships. In part, this was simply how popular cinema had always worked, but these films also matched broader patterns of postwar colonial policy and ideology. Americans, for example, tended to see their actions overseas as benevolent, and they hoped for gratitude and friendship in return for American liberation and protection. Students of America's Cold War culture have observed a penchant for sentimental narratives aimed at building ties with other peoples, a cultural tradition that certainly marks many postwar films, and one that later produced the concept of winning "hearts and minds" in Vietnam.[2]

The British also moved tentatively in this direction after 1945. The concept of a people's empire helped the recasting of colonialism as an egalitarian, multiracial partnership—now increasingly referred to as a Commonwealth.[3] Indeed the phrase "hearts and minds" was coined by an Englishman, Sir Gerald Templer, high commissioner in Malaya during the counterinsurgency in 1952.[4] Also prone to sentimentalizing relations with the colonized were the French, who liked to contrast the cold calculations of British and other imperialists with their own genuine concerns and feelings for their colonial subjects.[5] Although colonial theorist Jules Harmand had warned his compatriots in 1910 that "it would be folly for the conquerors to think that they might be loved," others ignored the advice.[6] In 1923, for example, Colonial Minister Albert Sarraut explained "the profound calm that prevails in our colonies" by explaining that unlike other European colonizers, "we are affectionate" toward the native, and "we know how to hold the humble face of the black or yellow brother against our breasts, where he hears our hearts beating in unison with his."[7] Given all this sentimentalism in postwar colonial discourse, it is not surprising that empire films of the era used it so extensively.

The Anna Leonowens Films

A common figure in postwar empire films was the intrepid woman who ventured into dangerous lands and strove selflessly to civilize the natives. The first such postwar film was Twentieth Century-Fox's 1946 release, *Anna and the King of Siam*. This black-and-white film starred Irene Dunne as Anna Owens, a British widow who in 1862 relocated from India to Siam (as Thailand was known then) to support herself and her son by teaching the children of the King of Siam. Based on Margaret Landon's 1943 novelization of the autobiographical tale by the real Anna Leonowens, this Darryl F. Zanuck production was the first of several dramatizations, including the Richard Rodgers and Oscar Hammerstein musical of 1951, the 1956 film *The King and I* (discussed below), and a 1999 film, *Anna and the King*, with Jodie Foster. Shot on the Fox lot by veteran Hollywood director John Cromwell, it opens with Bernard Herrmann's haunting music and Arthur C. Miller's shadowy nighttime photography establishing an exotic, dangerous atmosphere as Anna and her young son Louis arrive by boat in Bangkok. Greeted by the King's chief minister, the Kralahome (Lee J. Cobb), Anna immediately clashes with him over what she considers rude personal questions, learning later that to the Siamese, asking such questions is polite. She also learns that they are to live in the royal palace rather than the house that King Mongkut (Rex Harrison) promised her. She objects, but the King is too busy to meet her and hear her demands, and a test of wills soon ensues.

This struggle between Anna and the King intertwines themes of gender and cultural difference. Following in a tradition of claiming cultural superiority—and justifying imperialism—by indicting non-Western cultures' mistreatment of women, the film emphasizes Asian sexual inequality. The British captain who delivers Anna to Bangkok warns her that "women do not exist in Siam," and at the royal court, Mongkut has fathered sixty-seven children with wives from his harem of three thousand women. To the Siamese, an intelligent and articulate woman is so unknown that they call Anna "sir," and her ability to stand up to a

Siamese man—even the King—expresses the film's assumptions of Western superiority. Yet this apparently feminist tale of an independent woman who defies a tyrannical male chauvinist has misgivings about the headstrong Anna, and it alternately criticizes and sympathizes with both its main characters.

The film takes Anna's point of view throughout, but she seems rude as she gloats at having annoyed the King into granting her a house, and she is also ignorant and gives unintentional offense. In effect, the film pleads for westerners to learn more about the people over whom they rule, a common theme in postwar fiction set in Asia. Although images of Siam range from mildly condescending to thoroughly horrifying, the story sympathizes with a king torn between loyalty to cultural traditions and his will to modernize Siam. From the opening scene, when Louis notices that people are barefoot and the Kralahome is naked from the waist up, Anna and Louis see Siam as uncivilized, and when they first enter the palace complex, a melodramatic orchestral chord conveys the fear they feel in this exotic land. Before long, the list of Siamese barbarities grows: everyone around the King grovels humiliatingly; the King is above the law and orders his slaves beaten if they anger him; worst of all, the King puts his imprisoned wife Tuptim (Linda Darnell) on trial in a miserable dungeon after she tries to escape to meet her true love. Her lover is brought in with his back scarred from a vicious flogging, and the King has the two burned at the stake right outside Anna's room—a location he chose to punish her for meddling on Tuptim's behalf.

Yet there was more to the film than this litany of Orientalist stereotypes of despotism and barbarity. Midway through the story, the Kralahome informs the King that they have lost part of their territory to French imperialist machinations. He warns that "the ships of Europe will crowd thick around our seas, greedy for conquest" and "they have the power and the cunning" to seize the entire kingdom. While the horrors of Siamese culture may have tempted some viewers to welcome the Europeans' arrival, the film urges a different reaction by having Anna side with the Siamese; when told of the threat, she reacts with alarm, declaring, "That's outrageous." At this point, the film makes clear why the King invited Anna to Siam; he informs her that British businessmen also have designs on his kingdom and tells her: "The greedy men of Europe are at our door. They say Siam is barbaric land and so must be ruled by them. So King *must* learn all modern things now." Although he finds Western ways baffling and unattractive, he urges his heir, Prince Chulalongkorn, and his entire family to embrace them. Anna, of course, ends up spending as much time educating and civilizing the King as she does his family, and he comes to value her political advice as well.

In presenting the European takeover of Southeast Asia from this perspective, this American film invites emotional revulsion toward European imperialism, greed, and conquest. But if it thus offsets its criticism of Siam, it nonetheless depicts an asymmetrical relationship between the two principals, for while Mongkut learns much from Anna, she learns virtually nothing from anyone in Siam. Unlike the 1999 film, in which the King teaches Anna aspects of Buddhist wisdom, here Anna has no reason to learn from a king who, while charming, is often faintly ridiculous, as he mangles English comically, wants to send two male elephants to President Lincoln in hopes that they will reproduce, and acts boorishly at a banquet held to impress Europeans. Late in the film, Anna even notices that the Prince has outgrown his garments and says, "Somebody really ought to look after you"—suggesting that the Siamese need lessons in mothering as well as Western civilization. The film, in sum, outlines a lopsided relationship in which the East has much to learn from the modern, civilized West and nothing to teach in return, so it nests anticolonialist messages in a film with fundamentally colonialist assumptions. This practice of combining political anticolonialism with cultural condescension reflects an American outlook seen in many postwar films, as Americans were quick to condemn European colonialism but overlooked the colonialist overtones of their own policies.

To say that Anna learns nothing from her hosts is not to say she earns only money for her work. As in so many cinematic battles of the sexes, the two principals gradually come to like each other, and though the film stops short of presenting a love affair, a hint of real affection appears in a touching moment when the grateful King invites her not only to share his meal but even to eat from his bowl. The film departs from the historical record in inventing a riding accident that takes Louis's life, clearing the way for her to stay in Siam; now having lost both her husband and her child, Anna finds her purpose in life as a surrogate mother for Mongkut's children, who shower her with love. If the film thus abandons its apparent feminism—Anna finds fulfillment not in professional accomplishments but in maternal love—it certainly fits broader patterns of Cold War culture, as a benevolent westerner ventures East, helps spread democracy and Western civilization, and bridges the cultural chasm through bonds of mutual affection.

Like many historical films, *Anna and the King of Siam* presents a curious blend of fact and fiction, even if few Western viewers could tell where one ended and the other began. Historians often cite Siam/Thailand as one of the few countries that escaped Western colonization, but Mongkut only granted concessions to Western nations under duress, and those concessions included the sorts of unequal treaty rights seen in China (extraterritoriality for westerners, the right to reside in the capital, and so forth).[8] The film conveys this historical point, but by ending its story with the King's death and Chulalongkorn's accession, it ignores the continuing Western encroachment that Siam failed to stop. The film rightly points out that French expansion cost the kingdom part of its territory—though those Cambodian lands themselves reflected Thai imperialism—but it lets the British off fairly lightly. Despite criticizing the covetousness of British entrepreneurs in Southeast Asia, it suggests that Her Majesty's officials intervened with more honorable arrangements. It makes no mention of how, in the year Anna arrived, British warships shelled territory Siam claimed in the south, and it does not match its denunciation of French designs in Indochina with criticism of British ambitions in Malaya and Burma.[9] And the Americans, who figure in the film only through Anna's praise of Abraham Lincoln and the King's exchange of letters with him, were also parties to the unequal treaties, even before Mongkut's reign.[10] Historians credit Siam's monarchs with skillful resistance to Western colonization, but they did this more by playing the rival powers off against each other than by hosting banquets to impress Western diplomats with how civilized they were.[11] Each new Western version of the tale has angered many Thais, both for portraying the King as something of a boob and for drastically overstating Anna's role in the country's modernization and resistance to colonialism.[12] Leonowens seems to have fabricated the tale of Tuptim's torture and burning at the stake, but the film is accurate in depicting polygamy and in showing Mongkut's heir introducing reforms and abolishing prostration.[13]

In advertisements for the film, Fox emphasized its exotic appeal, with drawings of Anna in a white gown next to the King, surrounded by provocatively posed and attired harem slaves, and an inset of a screaming woman being burned at the stake. A caption read, "Into His Strange Exotic Kingdom Came Anna . . . Bringing the Wonder of Her Western Beauty . . . The Flame of Her Courage . . . The Weapon of her Wit!"[14] The film did well at the American box office, ranking twenty-fourth on *Variety*'s annual charts with $3.5 million in film rentals (a figure roughly half of domestic ticket sales).[15] It also received five Oscar nominations, winning for art direction and cinematography, and did very well with American critics, getting twenty-six positive (84 percent), two negative, and three mixed or neutral reviews in a sample of thirty-one.[16] The cultural contrasts struck most reviewers, who used terms such as "savage," "barbaric," and "feudal" to describe Siam and its king, and most critics mentioned either the burning at the stake, the groveling, the polygamy, or the mistreatment of women, while also noting the King's modernization plans. Anna's civilizing mission impressed many critics, including nine who used the term "democracy" to describe what she was teaching.[17] The *Chicago Tribune* wrote that Anna "manages to inculcate some of the ideals of the dignity of man and the principles of democracy" while the *Los Angeles Examiner* claimed that she "brought the light of civilization and freedom of thought into the tiny kingdom." The *Dallas Morning News* emphasized the difficulty of her task—the "modernization of a barbaric Oriental monarchy" and the education of a "slant-eyed Student Prince"—while the Catholic weekly *America* wrote that the film's "slow pace is in keeping with the maturing of the democratic idea in Oriental minds." Also implying the film's relevance to current American efforts to spread democracy in Asia, the *Philadelphia Inquirer* called it "a lesson in how re-education along democratic lines may be accomplished through gentleness and patience," and the New York cultural weekly *Cue* felt Anna's efforts were "generally for the people's good."

Only two reviews even mentioned the subplot about European imperialism: the *Houston Post*, which called the King's modernization program "the best means of protecting the island [sic] from European aggression," and *Esquire*, which said the film was set in "a time when the rising tides of imperialism were threatening to inundate all Asia." *Esquire*'s Jack Moffitt added that Mongkut sought "to avoid the western enslavement, which always used a charge of 'barbarism and savagery' as its extenuating pretext," but he undermined his point by saying of the Siamese and their king: "Yet they *were* savages. And he was a savage." The only other dissent about Anna's civilizing work came from the *New Yorker*'s John McCarten, who wrote, "Eventually, [Mongkut] succumbs to her ideas, and the Siamese become part of the modern world, God help them." Like several others, McCarten objected to the ethnic miscasting, writing that Rex Harrison was "unmistakably Anglo-Saxon" and that his dialogue "sounds more like the chatter of Piccadilly" than Bangkok. But many critics who complained about one Western actor's miscasting went on to praise another; the *San Francisco Chronicle*, for example, felt that some of the Siamese were "rather obviously Occidentals in slant-eyed makeup," but it wrote that "Mr. Harrison makes a convincing enough Oriental, and so does Linda Darnell." Rather than objecting to the entire idea of westerners playing Asians, many critics believed it was a question of choosing the right Western actors for the job.[18]

British critics were less impressed. Of twenty-three reviews examined, ten were positive (43 percent), four negative, and nine mixed.[19] Like the Americans, the British often called the Siamese and their king barbaric and noted the burning at the stake, though only one mentioned polygamy—the *Daily Mirror*, which wrote that Mongkut "has more wives than a hedgehog has quills"—and none acknowledged the mistreatment of women. The *Daily Herald, Kinematograph Weekly,* and *Tribune* mentioned the advent of democracy, and several praised Anna's work. As for the subplot about European encroachment, the *Daily Telegraph* said the story was set "nearly a century ago, when acquisitive European traders and Governments were making King Mongkut uneasily conscious of the outside world," but no other paper surveyed here—not even the Communist *Daily Worker*—even mentioned European imperialism. What did bother many British reviewers was the ethnic miscasting, though more complained about the casting of an American to play Anna (and her teaching of "American" to the children) than about whites playing Asians.

In an essay on this and other iterations of this tale, Caren Kaplan speaks of "the apparently seamless acceptance in the West of literary and cinematic representations of enslaved Siamese women and childishly capricious Asian dictators."[20] Kaplan's point is well taken in terms of the films, but some critics doubted the tale's veracity. The *St. Louis Post-Dispatch* sneered at the film, calling it "schmaltz," and the *San Francisco Chronicle* liked the film but felt it "gives Anna too much credit for reorganizing Siam" and "once in a while departs radically from historical fact." London's *Daily Herald* also liked the film but warned that "this is certainly bunk historically," and the *Daily Mirror* called the King "a character as fascinating as [he] is unreal." So although Western critics enjoyed the film and endorsed Anna's civilizing efforts, their doubts about the yarn invite caution about assuming its seamless acceptance.

The film had a brief run in France: it does not appear in Simsi's box-office figures, and many critics ignored the film altogether. Of five reviews located, one was positive, three negative, and one mixed.[21] Three reviews mentioned the barbarism of Siam and its king, and *Le Figaro* praised Anna, who "strives to attract toward ideas of progress a sovereign who is sensitive but still enslaved to old atavisms." In the anticolonialist *Franc-Tireur*, Pierre Laroche wrote sarcastically that the film "shows us in all seriousness how Mme. Irene Dunne, a British schoolteacher, brings civilization to Mongkut's kingdom—and I am not making this up." He added that "it would undoubtedly be in very poor taste to remind our good friends across the Atlantic and in Hollywood that they rather violently expelled from their country these same English whose civilizing work they are praising here." Also skeptical, *Combat* noted that Anna "retains, in the far East, her prejudices and her petticoats," but it praised Harrison's performance "in spite of the obstacle of the change of race." Anglo-Saxon efforts to civilize Asia, it seems, did not impress the French.

***

The 1956 film remake, Twentieth Century-Fox's *The King and I*, starring Yul Brynner and Deborah Kerr, looked and sounded quite different. Based on the 1951 stage musical, the Walter Lang film (again overseen by Zanuck) was shot in lavish, colorful CinemaScope and was a major hit in the United States, reaching number two on *Variety*'s annual box-office charts.[22] Academy Awards went to Brynner for Best Actor and to its music, sound, costumes, and art direction. The story remained fundamentally the same, and despite a line in the song, "Getting to Know You," that said, "But if you become a teacher, by your pupils you'll be taught," the film failed to develop that idea, and Anna again learned nothing from the Siamese. The friendship between Anna and the King went further, as a dancing scene late in the film conveyed romantic tensions, but it led nowhere, and the film mainly emphasized the sentimental bonds Anna developed with the King and his family. The film also added a lengthy sequence in which Tuptim (Rita Moreno) stages a play for the King's European guests. Her production, "The Small House of Uncle Thomas," based on *Uncle Tom's Cabin*, is a thinly veiled attempt to embarrass the King for enslaving her and keeping her from her lover. Scholars have rightly objected that there were major differences between American slavery and Siamese concubinage, but the scene pleads for both gender equality and liberty.[23] Anna, it turns out, is behind Tuptim's act of rebellion, having given her Stowe's novel. (The real Leonowens supported abolitionism and introduced Mongkut's wives to *Uncle Tom's Cabin*.)[24] So just as Anna resists the King's domination by teaching her pupils songs about home in hopes of annoying Mongkut into granting her a house, Tuptim cleverly stages her resistance through a play. The other theme in both Tuptim's play and the film itself concerns liberty, an important concept in American Cold War culture. The language of slavery permeated American Cold War references to communism, so although this film again defended Siam's liberty from European colonialism, women's liberty from male domination, and the Siamese people's liberty from humiliating and stifling royal absolutism, the Cold War gave these themes new resonance in 1956.[25]

The song "Getting to Know You" has led some to see the film serving Western aims of surveillance and control over Thailand, but the film's fantasy version of Siam conveyed less useful information than one would have learned from five minutes of perusing the popular *World Book Encyclopedia*.[26] Nor was the film likely to have improved cultural relations between the United States and Thailand, where it was banned for insulting King Mongkut. It may have bolstered Western enthusiasm for bringing modernity and civilization to Southeast Asia, but suggestions that contemporaries interpreted the film through the lens of current foreign affairs find little confirmation in reviews.[27] The film was indeed popular with American critics—this sample found twenty-three positive reviews (88 percent), none negative, and three mixed—and among the many rave reviews, the *Chicago Tribune* called it "one of the finest motion pictures to reach the screen."[28] Again critics used terms like "barbaric" and "savage" to describe Siam, and the European imperialism theme registered even less often than it had in 1946—despite ten years' worth of news about decolonization and a song in which the King questions imperialism, asking, "Might they not protect me out of all I own?" The *Dallas Morning News* noted that the King staged a banquet to impress the Europeans, but it ignored his motives. Only the *Hollywood Reporter* raised the subject at all, quoting the lyric just mentioned and stating that the film was set "when the nations of Europe were absorbing in colonial expansion every small country that seemed to need 'protection.'" No American review alluded to America's current efforts in Southeast Asia.

In Britain, where the film's September 1956 opening coincided with the deepening clash with Colonel Nasser over Suez, most critics also liked the film, with fourteen of nineteen (74 percent) praising it and only the *Monthly Film Bulletin* panning it.[29] These critics hardly took the film seriously in political terms, with several calling it Hollywood fantasy and turning sarcastic about the English governess.[30] Milton Shulman of the *Sunday Express*, for example, wrote, "On this evidence, we ought to send a few governesses to Colonel Nasser. Perhaps a few smacks on the bottom could end the Suez Crisis." Fred Majdalany of the center-right *Daily Mail* wrote that "a legion of militant governesses sited strategically at all danger points between Cyprus and Tehran inclusive, and regularly boxing all ears with delusions of grandeur might do more for oil and life-lines than present arrangements. (That's *quite* enough of that, Master Nasser!)" Dilys Powell of the *Sunday Times* confessed that "the whole story, with its air of Western patronage strikes me as a bit of cheek," while the *Daily Herald* remarked sarcastically that "she teaches them all sorts of moral things like 'Rule Britannia.'" And although terms such as "barbaric," "medieval," and "savage" appeared in most reviews, the use of quotation marks in the *Monthly Film Bulletin*'s reference to the King's "attempts to 'civilise' himself" suggested a cultural relativism missing from the American reviews. Patrick Gibbs of the *Daily Telegraph* complained that "the mockery of Oriental ways was for my taste overdone" and the King "is made excessively absurd," though he admitted that his was "a minority opinion." So although a few British critics found the film patronizing, the only references to British imperialism were the wisecracks about governesses. As for France, the film did well, selling more than two million tickets, but it seems to have been the sort of film that drove a wedge between French audiences and critics, very few of whom bothered to review it.[31]

Missionaries in Postwar Empire Films

Films about female civilizers in these years often focused on missionaries, highlighting an important theme in the history of Western colonialism and calling attention to one of women's main contributions to colonization. Missionaries were often among the first Europeans to visit and report on many areas, providing what became intelligence information for conquerors, and the protection of missionaries in uncharted territories furnished a pretext for sending troops; their work also helped legitimize colonization in Western eyes.[32] Missionaries remained important after the conquest, teaching European languages, facilitating commerce, and building personal bonds with the colonized.[33] As Chinua Achebe's novel *Things Fall Apart* illustrated, their proselytizing began to undermine the beliefs and self-confidence of host societies, launching the process of mental colonization.[34] The entire missionary enterprise required a certain cultural arrogance, and missionaries went beyond proselytizing, promoting many forms of acculturation.[35] Yet missionaries also became advocates for the colonized, clashing with resentful settlers and administrators.[36]

Western missionaries' experiences in India reflect many of these points. Portuguese missionaries who offered food along with the gospels won converts among the poorest Indians—a group cynically nicknamed "rice Christians"—but when the British East India Company took over in the eighteenth century, it discouraged proselytizing. That attitude changed in the 1810s, coinciding with a trend toward greater British intervention against cultural practices such as *sati* and *thuggee*. Some Britons opposed this trend as a dangerous distraction from Britain's real business in India—business—and in 1857 the massive uprising known as the Mutiny, fueled by anger at perceived attacks on Indian religion and culture, seemed to vindicate them. After the uprising, Benjamin Disraeli reminded his compatriots of their previous "solemn engagement not to tamper with their religion," and Queen Victoria's proclamation of 1 November 1858 declared, "We disclaim alike the right and desire to impose our convictions on any of our subjects" or to interfere with their "religious faith or observances."[37] Although missionaries still won a few converts, Christians always remained a tiny minority.[38]

The 1947 British film *Black Narcissus* evoked this history of missionaries in India. Based on a 1939 novel by Margaret Rumer Godden, who grew up in India, and whose later novel *The River* (1946) Jean Renoir filmed in 1951, *Black Narcissus* was directed, written, and produced by Michael Powell and Emeric Pressburger for their company, the Archers.[39] Shot at Pinewood Studios and outdoors in Britain and Ireland, the film used hand-painted backdrops that stood in surprisingly well for the Himalayas. The story concerns a group of British nuns of the Order of the Servants of Mary who establish a hospital and school in the mountains above Darjeeling in an unspecified year. The site for their mission is the old Palace of Mopu, given to them by a local official, Toda Rai, known as the General (Esmond Knight). This Westernized potentate's invitation to British nuns to come and bring progress to his simple local villagers recalls the Anna Leonowens story, but it proceeds quite differently. Early on, the sisters learn two disconcerting facts: the palace had been the scene of debauchery when the General's father ran it, as frescoes of half-naked "dancing girls" who once lived here attest, and the villagers attend the school only because the General is paying them to do so. The very young but determined Sister Superior, Clodagh (Deborah Kerr), dismisses warnings from the General's local agent, an Englishman named Mr. Dean (David Farrar), that this convent, like a previous one, will fail by the time the rains begin.

Just what the nuns are up against takes some time to emerge. One conflict pits the nuns against the villagers' ignorance and superstition, and the film at first seems headed for the usual triumph of Western civilization. The sisters also confront the palace's past, of which the frescoes, Dean, and the old caretaker Angu Ayah (May Hallatt) constantly remind them; in one sequence, the camera pans from a lewd fresco to a crucifix, and in another Clodagh orders a subordinate to take down a disturbing painting. As the sisters begin to fall ill and become mentally unhinged—Sister Philippa (Flora Robson) plants flowers instead of the vegetables she was told to plant, and Sister Ruth (Kathleen Bryon) grows increasingly hysterical about nearly everything—it becomes apparent that they are struggling with enigmatic forces. Clodagh conjectures that the problem is the altitude and "this clear air and the wind always blowing," but the most sinister forces are within them, particularly the worldly desires they all became nuns to escape. While trying to keep her sisters in line, Clodagh struggles with her own memories, as flashbacks reveal that she joined the Order only after her true love jilted her. As she struggles with her past and her faith, a white-bearded Holy Man perpetually and silently sits contemplating nature on the convent's grounds, and when a perturbed Clodagh asks Dean to remove him, she learns he is the General's uncle, once a distinguished personage with multiple university degrees. What bothers Clodagh about him is that his amazing discipline and faith highlight the weakness of hers, for unlike her, he has fully mastered his past. The story resolves with Ruth finally going completely over the edge, literally and figuratively, and the thoroughly unnerved nuns withdraw in humiliating defeat just as the rains begin.

Black Narcissus defies conventional genres. In some ways a psychodrama, a tale of mental and emotional torment, of insanity and attempted murder, it veers into melodrama with Sister Ruth's hysterics. In its climax, the hyperdramatic music, lighting, and shots are worthy of a horror film. It is also a missionary picture with its theme of struggle against worldly temptation, but it departs from genre convention when these very flawed nuns fail to vindicate a superior faith and civilization. Finally, in its setting in the Raj and its theme of westerners trying to civilize the colonized, it is an empire film.

Determining what it says about empire is no easier than specifying its genre. Released in London in April 1947, four months before Britain's handover of power in India, this tale of Western failure and departure from India has led recent observers to read the film as a critique of colonialism and a commentary on decolonization.[40] Viewed today, the film may support such a reading, but it totally ignores resistance to colonialism, and although one might think that peasants in such remote areas were oblivious to politics, Gandhi's campaign against the British succeeded in large part because he and the Indian National Congress (INC) managed to mobilize the peasantry in places such as Darjeeling.[41] The British, in short, were not driven from India by the wind and the clear air. One might speculate that the film avoided politics to steer clear of British censors, but the novel contains nothing political that the film omitted, and neither the novel nor the film mentions British officials, tea plantations, or any other indication of British rule. (Politics are also strangely absent from Godden's The River.) The only ruling structures seen are indigenous ones—Dean is an agent of Toda Rai, not the British—so a viewer might be forgiven for thinking India was already independent and that Dean had simply "stayed on." The lack of any allusion to British rule (much less any condemnation of it) or to Gandhi and the INC makes it hard to see Black Narcissus as an anticolonialist film or a meditation on decolonization.

Also, given British rulers' attitudes toward missionaries in India in all but the early nineteenth century, one could just as easily read the film as endorsing the secular British colonialism that actually prevailed in India.[42] In a sense, it simply shows the failure of Christian missionaries (or one group of very flawed missionaries) in India, not British colonial rule as a whole, which actually left a very deep imprint on India. The film also indulges in many empire-film conventions. It depicts a dangerous place, where Ruth hears frightening animal noises in the jungle, where the nuns fear an attack by ignorant villagers after a baby in their care dies, and where "something in the atmosphere" makes the palace eerie and unsettling. It also perpetuates the old Western idea that civilized people deteriorate morally in the colonies. Not only do the nuns come unglued, but Dean has more or less gone native, sharing his house with monkeys, walking around half-naked, and living a carefree, hedonist life of drinking and cavorting with native girls. The villagers come off as superstitious, simple, and childlike, and their constant drumming recalls countless empire films. It is true that the most bigoted comments come from the unlikable Ruth, who calls the natives stupid, smelly, and black, but Dean, who seems to convey the film's point of view, also makes condescending remarks. Bringing to mind Richard Slotkin's concept of the "man who knows Indians" in American westerns, Dean tells Clodagh that these Indians are "primitive people and like children—unreasonable children," and he tells the nuns they really are in danger from the superstitious villagers after the baby dies in their care. And while it is Ruth who says the villagers all look alike, the film itself treats the villagers as an undifferentiated mass. A major theme contrasts the anxious, sexually repressed nuns and the happy natives' free, libidinous life, which it represents with the oversexed Kanchi (Jean Simmons) and her pursuit of the Young General (Sabu) as well as with repeated shots of lush, blooming vegetation and references to the palace's wild past.[43] It reinforces its noble savage outlook with its suggestion that the Young General's overeager attempts at Western learning are faintly ridiculous, and the picture repeatedly underlines cultural difference by contrasting the nuns' white robes with the locals' colorful costumes, and the convent's bells with the locals' horns and drums. The film may seem anticolonialist in suggesting that the sisters have no business here, but that is because the locals are irredeemably primitive.

Released through Rank's General Film Distributors (GFD), the film reportedly did good business in Britain.[44] In France it sold a respectable 1,379,264 tickets in 1948.[45] In the United States, it did not make *Variety*'s charts, perhaps because it was not what fans of missionary pictures wanted, and also because the Legion of Decency, perceiving an attack on religion and missionaries, launched protests that caused delays and cancelled bookings.[46] The film won several awards, including an Oscar and a Golden Globe for Jack Cardiff's cinematography and an Oscar for Art Direction/Set Decoration. Reviews were mostly positive in both Britain and the United States; of seventeen British reviews examined, nine were positive (53 percent), four negative, and four mixed or neutral, while among twenty American reviews, fourteen were positive (70 percent), five negative, and one mixed.[47] Nearly everyone praised the film's visual artistry, forgiving its other faults. Most reviews commented on the nuns' shortcomings, including the *New York Post*, which described their failure "to bring modern civilization and religion to Mopu." Some blamed that failure on the natives, calling them antagonistic, childish, primitive, half-savage, barbaric, and superstitious, though some also mentioned the air and the atmosphere.[48] The *Motion Picture Herald*, despite its conservative Catholic publisher's subsequent protests against the film, gave it a "very good" rating, but its critic complained that "just what causes their mental disturbance is never quite made clear," and Fred Majdalany of London's *Daily Mail* similarly felt that the directors "haven't wholly succeeded in suggesting the oppressiveness of the outpost." The *Manchester Guardian* saw "a faltering story," while the *London Times* faulted the film for drifting from one underdeveloped theme to another, and the *Sunday Times* called it "a work which has never quite decided on its mood." The liberal American Catholic weekly *Commonweal* praised the visuals and acting but wrote, "One also wonders what this movie is trying to say." Trade publications in both countries warned that viewers would be confused; the *Motion Picture Herald* wondered "whether Mr. and Mrs. Smith, USA, will be able quite to comprehend" the film's point, and Britain's *Kinematograph Weekly* wrote that "the industrial masses will, we fear, experience some difficulty in knowing what it is all about."

Despite readings of the film as a meditation on the end of empire, not a single one of the thirty-eight reviews examined here (twenty American, fifteen British, and three French) mentioned the Raj, colonialism, or Britain's departure from India. (Nor has any scholar shown evidence that the writers or filmmakers intended to comment on Britain's exit from India.) The closest anyone came was *Newsweek*, which wrote that the nuns, "having taken on an impossible assignment, execute a strategic withdrawal," but it made no connection to Britain's handover of power taking place the very week the review appeared. Several publications observed that the nuns' failure had taught them humility, but no one applied that lesson to the broader colonial project.[49] The film's relevance to decolonization may seem apparent now, but it eluded contemporaries, and this gap in perceptions attests to dramatic changes in Western sensitivity to issues of empire that took place well after 1947.

While many parts of Asia either gained their independence or were seeking it in the late 1940s, most of Africa seemed securely colonized. Egypt's 1952 revolution and various anticolonial movements in North Africa attracted attention from nervous colonialists, while south of the Sahara, riots in Accra in the Gold Coast in 1948 and the success of Kwame Nkrumah's Convention People's Party in local elections there in 1951 were exceptions to a general pattern of political calm.

Films set in Africa in these years gave little hint of trouble, and Hollywood in particular continued to make traditional jungle and safari pictures, comedies such as Abbott and Costello's *Africa Screams* (1949), and colonial-backdrop dramas about white people, including *The Macomber Affair* (1947) and *The Snows of Kilimanjaro* (1952). A few films set in Africa also featured the sorts of civilizing women seen in the Asia films. John Huston's *The African Queen* (1951) was a colonial-backdrop film with an "opposites attract" love story between an alcoholic boat pilot (Humphrey Bogart) and a prudish but feisty American missionary (Katherine Hepburn). It shows less of her work with Africans than of her efforts to civilize the down-and-out Bogart, recalling westerns in which women strive to civilize the rough-hewn white men whose semi-savagery qualified them for the arduous work of exploration and conquest.

One film that did examine relations between colonizer and colonized was Twentieth Century-Fox's *White Witch Doctor* (1953), directed by Henry Hathaway (*Lives of a Bengal Lancer*, *The Real Glory*, *China Girl*) and starring Susan Hayward and Robert Mitchum. Set in the Congo Free State in 1907, just before international condemnation of atrocities in King Leopold's personal fiefdom led the Belgian government to take over the colony, the story concerns an American widow, Ellen Burton (Hayward), who goes to work as a nurse at a missionary society's jungle clinic. Reluctantly escorting her beyond the last port of call on the Congo River is Lonni Douglas (Mitchum), a cynical animal trapper and man-who-knows-Africans. The two bicker over a woman being in such a place, and following them upriver is another white man, Huysman (Walter Slezak), who wants Lonni to help him conquer the Bakuba, a dangerous, isolationist tribe living on lands rich in gold. When Ellen learns that the clinic's doctor has died, she takes over the practice and uses her limited medical skills, angering local witch doctors but winning the hearts of the grateful villagers. The climax pits greedy white gold-hunters against the forces of good, who by then include not only Ellen and her African friends, but also Lonni, whose better nature has emerged under her civilizing influence.

White Witch Doctor follows many conventions of both empire films and westerns, starting with its depiction of the Congo's dangers. Lonni repeatedly warns Ellen not to wander far from camp, and the sound of drums reinforces his message. During the journey to the clinic, two African porters gaze at the shadow of Ellen undressing in her tent, perpetuating the old convention of the black man's threat to the white woman, as does another sequence in which a jealous witch doctor with stiletto fingernails creeps up to her tent at night. The porters' refusal to enter Bakuba territory highlights the dangerousness of one group and the cowardice of another, and when Ellen and Lonni arrive in the Bakuba compound, the camera captures her frightened reaction to skulls on poles and wild-looking men in garish costumes and face paint. The film underlines cultural differences, from an early scene in which giggling African women try on Ellen's clothing, to shots of native rituals and dancing that leave Ellen—and the audience—bewildered until Lonni explains them. Differences between civilization and savagery also appear in healing scenes that contrast African ignorance with Western medical knowledge. The good native/bad native dichotomy appears as well: a loyal African sacrifices his life to save Lonni, and the obedient patients at the clinic beam gratefully at Ellen for her good work, while the vengeful witch doctors and the menacing Bakuba reject Western ways and threaten Ellen. As in countless westerns and empire films, there are selfish white villains, and props such as elephant tusks and gold nuggets contrast their greed with the missionaries' benevolence. Expressing the film's plea for altruism are two character transformations: Lonni goes from abusing his porters and deriding missionaries to turning against his greedy partner and defending innocent Africans, while Ellen herself reveals to Lonni that she once selfishly kept her husband from working in Africa but is now here because, as she says, "I want to help somebody else for a change."

The film briefly turns critical of colonialism when the supposedly evil Bakuba turn out to be innocent victims of white exploitation. When Ellen helps to heal the chief's son, Lonni relays to Ellen the chief's grateful statement: "He said that you're the first white person who ever came here to try help his people. All the others came to rob, kill, destroy. He said that if all other white people were like you, the doors of the Bakubas wouldn't be closed so tight." Ellen's reaction—she bursts into tears—indicates that there are treasures greater than ivory and gold awaiting westerners in Africa: the emotional rewards of helping grateful, needy Africans. In short, the sentimental bonds bridging cultural chasms that mark Cold War fiction about Asia appear in this African setting as well. The doctor Ellen replaces, whom the natives had affectionately named Big Mama, had few possessions but "a heart that belonged to everybody," and when the chief bestows the title Big Mama on Ellen, she replies, "That makes me very happy." The film also shows how badly the ignorant Africans need white people to heal, protect, and civilize them; when Lonni suggests she go back where she belongs, she replies, "But what about the patients?" So like the Anna Leonowens films, this one argues not so much against colonialism as against a certain *kind* of colonialism—a selfish, rapacious colonialism rather than the currently fashionable liberal, humanitarian version that required and justified the whites' presence in Africa.

***

The female missionary and civilizer reappeared in 1958, in yet another Twentieth Century-Fox production, director Mark Robson's *The Inn of the Sixth Happiness*. Based on Alan Burgess's 1957 account of the life of English missionary Gladys Aylward, the lavish, 158-minute CinemaScope production filmed in Wales with a British crew starred Ingrid Bergman as a woman who devotes her life to bringing Christianity and civilization to China. In this tale of heroic sacrifice and missionary fervor, Aylward refuses to be discouraged by British missionaries who call her unqualified, and while working as a domestic servant for a missionary in London, she reads his books on China and saves her paltry wages for a transcontinental rail ticket. She then travels alone across Europe, the Soviet Union, and a war zone on the Soviet-Chinese border and arrives in Tientsin in 1932. Proceeding to a remote area in Shanxi province, she helps an elderly British woman, Jeannie Lawson (Athene Seyler) run an inn that spreads the gospel by telling Bible stories to dining muleteers. A model of Christian virtue, Aylward bears hardship, xenophobia, and danger with unflagging strength and cheer. She also shows limitless courage as she runs the inn after Lawson dies, shames the male villagers into abandoning foot-binding, single-handedly stops a prison riot, and finally, when the Japanese invade China and bomb her village, leads one hundred children to safety through icy rivers and enemy-occupied mountains. She is, in short, a saint. In this "hagiopic" overflowing with sentiment (and with the violinists working overtime), she forms enduring emotional bonds with the local Mandarin (Robert Donat), whose growing admiration and affection for her lead him to convert to Christianity. Aylward also falls in love with a Eurasian Nationalist general, Lin Nan (Curt Jurgens), though this love remains platonic. Most of all, she falls in love with China and its people—especially the children she adopts, protects, and teaches Western ways—and they reward her with their limitless love and devotion. Out of love for China, she learns the language, changes her name to Jennai ("the one who loves"), and adopts Chinese citizenship.

Made a decade after the Communist triumph in China—and the ouster of all foreign missionaries that soon ensued—the film is nostalgic about missionaries in that country. For late-1950s Western viewers depressed about China, *The Inn of the Sixth Happiness* offered a heartening tale of rousing victory, with Aylward succeeding brilliantly in every seemingly hopeless task she attempts.[50] When crises arise, the helpless Chinese turn to Aylward for guidance—"Tell us what to do!" one man begs her when the Japanese bomb the village—and she improvises solutions that never occur to any of the Chinese. Time and time again she gives orders to the Chinese, and they are all obeyed—by villagers committed to foot binding, mountain bandits, even a furious ax-wielding prison rioter. If ever a film merited the term, "imperialist nostalgia," certainly this one does. Its vision of pre-Communist China includes bucolic images of happy peasants toiling in the fields, and her main Chinese assistant, Yang, one of the few ordinary Chinese the film introduces, is a grinning, hunching character reminiscent of happy, obsequious blacks in old Hollywood films. Not that all of the images of China are positive, for Aylward loves China in spite of its sins, including polygamy, foot binding, inhuman prison conditions, savage public beheadings, the despotism of Mandarins—"If he say die, you die," Yang explains—and even a mother who does not care if her baby dies. (Aylward adopts the baby.) When the newly arrived Aylward expresses her alarm at conditions in China, Lawson replies, "There's much that *is* horrible in China, as in any country: babies left to die in ditches, the poor preying on the poor, many things. But they'll change. One thing at a time, with the help of the Lord." As Aylward begins cleaning up China, she enjoys the support of both the Nationalist General and the Mandarin, whose sponsorship of her modernizing campaign recalls both King Mongkut and the General in *Black Narcissus*, while the stubborn, spunky Aylward resembles Leonowens as she stands up to the Mandarin and teaches his wives to read and to question male domination. The tale presents a superhuman heroine—she is to missionary work what John Rambo is to soldiering—and the film, like the hagiographies Christian publishers churn out about Aylward, urge others to emulate her.[51]

For an ostensibly historical film about a real woman in a specific time and place, *The Inn of the Sixth Happiness* is strikingly oblivious to certain topics, most notably the Communists, whom the film never mentions, and imperialism, which made missionary work possible in China. The unequal treaties the Western powers imposed with gunboats in the nineteenth century had forced the Chinese to accept missionaries, and for the film to overlook that is disingenuous, though it certainly reflects the missionaries' own self-deceptions and self-images.[52] Aside from a couple of remarks about missionaries by the otherwise sympathetic Lin Nan, the film also ignores the vital topic of nationalist anger toward missionaries, whose presence underlined the West's humiliation of China.[53] Yet here Chinese nationalism amounts to nothing more than a campaign to modernize China and fight the Japanese, and the film neither critiques imperialism nor acknowledges its connection to missionary work.

When the film opened in the United States at Christmas 1958, the *Boston Globe* predicted "the general public will love it," and *Time*, despite panning the film, wrote that it "has just about everything the mass public is said to want."[54] Unlike *Black Narcissus*, this film gave fans of missionary films all they could want, while the print advertisements, which showed Bergman and Jurgens on the verge of a kiss, also lured romance fans.[55] The inclusion of the quotation, "Would it offend you to be loved by a man of another race?" added a third selling point amid a trend of film dramas of love across the color line. Finally, the usual faux-Chinese lettering for the title signaled the film's exotic appeal. This something-for-everyone approach took the film to number thirteen on *Variety*'s charts for 1959.[56] One person who did not like the film was Aylward herself. Objecting to the exaggerated love story with Lin Nan, which impugned her chastity, she also complained that the studio failed to send her a promised advance copy of the script, and her angry denunciation of Fox personnel as "a bunch of liars" and Bergman as a "wicked woman" suggested a nasty streak in the real Aylward whose use on screen might have made her character more believable and interesting.[57] Also unhappy with the film was Chiang Kai-Shek's Republic of China on Taiwan, which refused permission to shoot there, allegedly because of the film's foot-binding theme but perhaps also because of its portrayal of the helpless, backward Chinese.[58]

American reactions provide interesting evidence of attitudes toward overseas missionaries in the 1950s. Extensive evidence bears out images of the 1950s as a time of intense piety and public religiosity in the United States, but this film appeared on the eve of the 1960s, by which time some have argued that missionaries were losing their cultural legitimacy in the West.[59] Of twenty-four reviews examined here, thirteen were positive (54 percent), four negative, and seven mixed or neutral.[60] The critics who praised the film gushed, calling it "tremendously moving," "heart-stirring," "uplifting," "inspirational," and, in the words of the *Chicago Tribune*'s critic, "awe-inspiring to those of us who lead selfish lives." The *St. Louis Post-Dispatch* found it "so touching" it "qualifies as a four-handkerchief picture." While religious publications adored the film, so did many secular papers. The *Hollywood Reporter*'s Jack Moffitt called Aylward's work "a miracle" of "divine intervention" and exulted that it "will rekindle piety, hope, and comfort in the hearts of people of all faiths." Moffitt was also among those who lauded her work with the benighted Chinese, writing that "when local officials failed to halt the barbarous custom of binding little girls' feet until they were maimed for life, Gladys put a stop to it," and Martin Quigley's *Motion Picture Herald* noted that she "devotes her life to comforting and aiding some of the unhappy people of China." The same review added, stunningly, that "there is nothing that faintly resembles prosylitizing [sic] in the story," and the *New Orleans Times-Picayune* concluded that she "won the people by doing good." No favorable review raised the slightest doubt about the film's veracity, and *Variety* sounded a common theme in calling its rendering of China "completely authentic." Giving a hint of the coming culture wars and the feelings of persecution that religious conservatives would express toward Hollywood, the *St. Louis Post-Dispatch* explained that the Academy Awards overlooked Bergman because "this is merely an inspirational performance—Miss Bergman isn't playing a prostitute, an alcoholic, a dope-addict, a murderess, a psychotic, a neurotic, a hysterical shrew, a deaf-mute who is raped, a beautiful woman who is blinded, a screwball or a nymphomaniac."

American critics who gave the film negative or mixed reviews found it sentimental, even saccharine. The New York critics were hardest on it, with *Newsweek* complaining that it "totters from tedium to schmaltz and back again," and the *Saturday Review* called it predictable and "somewhat cloying." *Time* said it had "more sheer treacle than anybody has seen since the Great Boston Molasses Flood" and seemed "rather like a Cecil B. DeMille version of Now I Lay Me Down to Sleep." Regional papers also objected. The *Dallas Morning News* called it "a movie drama of some cheapness, gimcrack, and banality," and the *San Francisco Chronicle* felt it was "larded with unnecessary and sentimental details." Like several other papers, the *Philadelphia Inquirer* concluded that it "never quite succeeds in being either convincing or moving," and it called the film a "marathon" of "melodramatic mish-mash" that was "hard to believe on the screen." The paper was among those unconvinced by Curt Jurgens as a Eurasian, and *Time* questioned the cultural authenticity, calling it "the worst chinoiserie ever seen on screen." Most of the criticism targeted the film rather than the Aylward story or missionary work, but the *New Yorker* stated sarcastically that Aylward "was possessed by the notion that her destiny lay in bringing the story of Bethlehem and subsequent developments to the heathen Chinee." The *New York Times* similarly complained that Aylward "drips nobility" in a film that was "mainly for patrons of inspirational, non-interpretive stuff." These cynical comments provide some evidence for the notion that missionaries were losing their legitimacy—at least with film critics, if not audiences—but this was still a minority view among critics, most of whom liked the film and had no objection to missionaries.

The usually more cynical British critics liked the film even better, with twenty-one of twenty-seven (78 percent) praising it, two panning it, and four giving it mixed reviews.[61] The *Evening Standard* made a typical comment in calling it "faithful, believable, and above all heart-touching," and the *Daily Telegraph*'s Campbell Dixon reported that at the press screening, "there were tears in the eyes of critics rarely lachrymose." Echoing the St. Louis critic quoted above, Donald Zec of the *Daily Mirror* said it "cocks a snook at [the] current, overworked formula of success: horror, conflict, sex, or psychiatry," and the *Telegraph*'s Dixon, tired of films using "only violence & raw sex" to sell tickets, said that to win audiences, "the best bets are generally nobility and religion." Even Nina Hibbin of the *Daily*

Worker called it "a really great film" with "a mature feeling for the people" though "perhaps there is a little too much idealisation" in it. A few British critics disliked Jurgens as a Eurasian, but others praised him, and no one minded Sweden's Bergman playing Aylward. British critics reveled in their humble compatriot's successes; the *Daily Mirror* noted that "she makes a conquest" of both the Mandarin and the Nationalist General, while the *Daily Sketch*'s Harold Conway wrote that she "touches and charms herself into the Chinese people's trust." The *Evening Standard* wrote approvingly that she "teaches English spiced with Christianity" and "wins the affection of the people," and the *Reynolds News*'s Frank Jackson lauded her for saving children in "poverty-stricken, diseased, backward, [and] illiterate" China. A few critics who liked the film nonetheless found it too sentimental, and Majdalany of the *Daily Mail* felt that "one might be a little dubious about some of the more romantic overtones of the film and the presentation of the central character." Among dissenters, Peter Brinson of the *Financial Times* said it "sacrifices veracity to a false romanticism," and the *Glasgow Herald*'s Molly Plowright "wish[ed] it had a more documentary treatment ... instead of becoming vaguely reminiscent of the first 'Anna and the King of Siam.'" The most negative review appeared in the *Times Educational Supplement*, which complained of clichés and "music of purest saccharine" in "an oriental extravaganza with about as much connexion to China as *Chu Chin Chow*" (a 1934 musical). But while some found the film sentimental, manipulative, and unrealistic, no one raised the slightest objection to Western imperialism or missionaries in China.

The film did very well at the French box office, selling 3,457,438 tickets and finishing fourteenth on the box-office chart for 1959, but French critics gave it harsh treatment.[62] Of nineteen reviews examined here, five were positive (26 percent), eleven negative (58 percent), and three mixed, and three of the positive reviews were from right-wing or far-right-wing publications (the right-wing daily, *L'Aurore*, the monarchist/Pétainist weekly *Aspects de la France*, and the Pétainist weekly *Nouveaux Jours*).[63] Complaining of the salacious French films currently on offer, *Aspects de la France* welcomed *L'Auberge du sixième bonheur* for its "authenticity" and "exaltation of charity and missionary work," concluding happily that "here, we are far from Brigitte Bardot!" *L'Aurore* praised Aylward for taking on "the backward customs of the China of a few decades ago," and *Nouveaux Jours* lauded her "difficult and delicate missions, in which she succeeds for the good of all." The moderate *Le Figaro* also liked the film, but its statement that Aylward "wants to make a gift of herself to the wretched Chinese" paraphrased a famous line Pétain used in announcing the Vichy regime in 1940, suggesting a touch of sarcasm.

Among those who disliked the film, Grenoble's *Dauphiné Libéré* found "mildly irritating" the "preachiness of the good feelings, where it bogs down the most" while *France Catholique* called the film "dubious sentimental hodge-podge." The Catholic *La Croix* liked the story but felt the film "overdid, in our view, the idyllic side of Miss Aylward's work and life" and added, "To tell the truth, we did not really believe" in the Mandarin, the officer, the bandit, and the prisoner "continually uniting to facilitate her work." To *France Catholique*, "Miss Gladys's China is no truer than the Paris of Uncle Lachaille" (in MGM's *Gigi*), and "China, for us Europeans, is a very grave and serious subject on which it is not permissible to fool the public, even with good intentions." Among the secular critics, *Le Monde's* Jean de Baroncelli called the film "ridiculous at times" and reeled off Aylward's successes, which "Mark Robson's hyperbolic camera transforms into unconvincing miracles," and *Les Nouvelles Littéraires* complained that "the number of misfortunes that overwhelm this poor Gladys is not credible." Some also sneered at missionary work, with the left-leaning weekly *L'Express* noting that "she goes off to save the little Chinese" while *Libération* wrote that "God calls her irresistibly to China to convert the little Chinese." The Communist *L'Humanité* contended that "if you believe this film, China's future 'in those days' belonged to the Christian missionaries," but the film is a "perfectly ridiculous anachronism" now that "the Chinese people have since decided otherwise." The paper also charged that the film ignored British missionaries' ulterior motives, "such as the transformation of the country into a semi-colony of His Gracious Majesty," for "here everything is pure, everything is beautiful, everything is marvelous."

Why the differences between the film's reception in the United States, Britain, and France? For one, both France's political spectrum and its press corps were to the left of America's or Britain's. France's many left-leaning publications criticized the film and its subject as roundly as France's far-right magazines embraced it, and neither Britain nor the United States had any counterpart for either the Communist Party, which polled roughly 20 percent of the votes in the multiparty 1958 legislative elections, or *L'Humanité*, with a national readership in the hundreds of thousands in the 1950s.[64] Yet even Britain's *Daily Worker* praised the film and offered nothing like *L'Humanité*'s scathing denunciation of its colonialist attitude, while certain French Catholic publications viewed the film more skeptically than did even secular publications across the Channel or the Atlantic. Perhaps it mattered that the heroine was Protestant, but the whole topic of missionaries revealed a contrast between a heavily secular France and two countries with large evangelical and missionary communities and traditions. France, of course, had its own missionary tradition, but only the right-wing press still seemed proud of it. It also did not help that this was the sort of high-budget Anglo-American film that irked Parisian critics. Indeed, the more positive reaction in Britain than in the United States may have owed something to national pride, as the film featured a British heroine as well as a British crew for a film shot in Britain (as three reviews pointed out proudly).[65] Finally, the French skepticism that greeted Aylward's stunning successes raise the point that by 1959, the French, unlike the British and Americans, had already suffered a stinging defeat in Indochina and were bogged down in a nightmarish conflict in Algeria. The British, it is true, had been embarrassed in 1956 at Suez, but that was a political defeat at the hands of the Americans, not a military defeat by the Egyptians, and the closest the Americans had come to such humiliation was the standoff they reached after the Chinese entered the war in Korea. The experience of humiliating defeat in conflicts with third-world peoples, it seems, may have helped alter attitudes toward colonialism.

Less than a year later, white women civilizing the third world returned yet again with director Fred Zinnemann's *The Nun's Story* (Warner Bros., 1959). Audrey Hepburn played Sister Luke, a Belgian doctor's daughter in the 1930s who becomes a nun so she can serve as a nurse at a Congo mission station. Although it is mostly set in Belgium, a lengthy section in the Congo dusts off a slew of empire-film conventions, including ominous music at Sister Luke's arrival in Africa; happy, smiling villagers waving to her on her train ride to the mission; nuns teaching ignorant African women mothering skills; and the obligatory "bad African"—a savage who murders a nun on the orders of an evil witch doctor. *The Nun's Story* is a colonial-backdrop film about white people—in this case about Sister Luke's internal struggles and her clash with an atheistic white doctor (Peter Finch). The film reached number six on *Variety*'s 1959 charts, earning eight Oscar nominations and rave reviews in the United States (twenty-three of twenty five positive), but though the newspapers were then filled with reports of horrific violence and political upheaval in the Belgian Congo, critics, like the film itself, showed no interest in the country or its problems.[66] In Britain, the film earned five BAFTA nominations, with Hepburn winning Best British Actress, and in a sample of seventeen reviews, fourteen (82 percent) praised it.[67] British critics, like their American counterparts, either ignored the Congo altogether or praised what the *Daily Telegraph* called Sister Luke's "backbreaking work in Africa," and only Hibbin of the *Daily Worker* dissented, objecting to "the patronising and glamourised glimpse of 'native' life."

The Nun's Story opened in France in February 1960, just after news of Congo's impending independence, and it was a major triumph, selling 4,467,614 tickets—

the sixth most popular film of 1960.[68] As with *The Inn of the Sixth Happiness*, however, French critics were much harder on it than were American and British critics (eight positive, nine negative, and one mixed), and several of those panning the film objected to its treatment of colonialism and Africans.[69] "Belgian colonization works marvels here," complained *L'Express*, with the film depicting the mission station as "an earthly paradise" full of "such nice blacks." Equally sarcastically, *Les Lettres Françaises* noted that the "savages" and "*nègres*" (a derogatory term) are "big children, sometimes brutal and criminal, but not really bad at heart," just "simple souls" in a film about whites. Again, France's painful experiences with decolonization may have raised sensitivities about this topic, and its more leftist press also accounted for the national contrasts.

The impressive box-office performance of both *The Inn of the Sixth Happiness* and *The Nun's Story* suggests that audiences in all three countries remained quite receptive to tales of female missionaries at the end of the 1950s. Critics also welcomed these films, with the exception of the left-wing French writers, and indeed the reviews show great admiration for Western women's civilizing work and little hostility toward colonialism. Some of the films contained no indictment of Western colonialism at all, and the reviews of those that did—including the two Anna Leonowens films and *White Witch Doctor*—suggest little anticolonialism among critics. Instead, they saw the women's civilizing efforts as the films intended: as noble and altruistic rather than arrogant, condescending, and colonialist. In a period filled with news of decolonization, many in the West remained neither sensitive to nor keenly interested in colonialism, and judging from these films and reviews, any notion that Western revulsion toward colonialism was fueling the relinquishing of empires appears mistaken.

Given how badly Western colonizers wanted the colonized to love and appreciate them, these films may have succeeded because they provided the kind of gratification viewers desired. In all but *Black Narcissus*, third-world peoples shower the heroines of these highly sentimental films with love, affection, and gratitude, rewarding them for overcoming their fears and attempting arduous tasks in dangerous places. Richard Dyer has argued that in colonialist fiction, female protagonists suggest imperial defeat, but in all of these films but *Black Narcissus*, the heroines are triumphant.[70] Anna Leonowens succeeds in modernizing and westernizing Siam; in *White Witch Doctor*, Ellen defeats the witch doctors and opens Bakuba society to Western contact; in *The Inn of the Sixth Happiness*, Gladys Aylward triumphs in all her endeavors; and in *The Nun's Story*, Sister Luke overcomes African suspicion and helps cure the sick despite her own flagging faith.

In Western countries struggling to control the third world, these films offered emotional rewards and comforting fantasies of success. All of them simply ignored decolonization, and all but *Black Narcissus* qualify as colonialist nostalgia.

Aside from providing entertainment and emotional gratification, these films also served to encourage a continued Western presence in the third world, if only inadvertently, by mostly whitewashing colonialism and presenting it as beneficial and altruistic. Some films contrasted good and bad Western behavior (*Anna and the King of Siam, White Witch Doctor, The King and I*), while others ignored colonialism altogether (*Black Narcissus*) or showed only its noble side (*The Inn of the Sixth Happiness, The Nun's Story*). Crucial to their promotion of a liberal version of colonialism was their use of female protagonists. Not only did these films make women the face of colonialism, but following the usual practice, they cast beautiful, glamorous women such as Deborah Kerr, Susan Hayward, Ingrid Bergman, and Audrey Hepburn, making it even easier for audiences to sympathize with their work. But if telling stories of attractive women doing noble tasks made empire look valuable and just in an era of growing anticolonialism, could films with male protagonists manage the same task?

CHAPTER TWO

Heroes of Empire

The figure of the swashbuckling masculine hero had been a staple of the prewar empire film, but during the war, films about colonial action heroes gave way to war films. After World War II, a return to prewar conventions risked looking dated, but this did not stop filmmakers from bringing those heroes of empire out of mothballs. Tales of heroism, of course, suit adventure cinema, and the arrival of wide-screen technologies in the early 1950s made ample room for the colonial action hero. The new films once again focused on the early phases of colonization, on the reasonable assumption that explorers and conquerors made for livelier film fare than administrators, businessmen, and settlers. Yet pressures for decolonization did influence films about heroic men of empire, introducing new inflections to films about trailblazers and conquerors, as well as more emphasis on benevolent white protectors engaged in noble tasks such as civilizing natives and defending the helpless.

Trailblazers and Conquerors

The vast majority of Hollywood's forays into colonial history were set in the nineteenth and twentieth centuries, but one notable exception was Twentieth Century-Fox's *Captain from Castile* (1947), based on Samuel Shellabarger's best-selling 1945 novel about Hernán Cortés and the Spanish conquest of Mexico. Darryl F. Zanuck oversaw this superproduction, and he drew upon the advice and talents of a large team of writers and consultants—perhaps with unfortunate results for the film's coherence. Directed by longtime Zanuck collaborator Henry King, the film starred Tyrone Power as Pedro de Vargas, a young Castilian nobleman who marches with Cortés (Cesar Romero) in Mexico. In an opening act in Spain, Pedro's benevolent nature appears as he helps a runaway Mexican Indian slave named Coatl (Jay Silverheels, before his 1949 debut as Tonto in *The Lone Ranger*).

Pedro and his family run afoul of the Inquisition and the Santa Hermandad, an organization that helped police Spain and supported the Inquisition. After a fanatical leader of the Santa Hermandad, Diego de Silva (John Sutton), imprisons Pedro and his family—and tortures and kills his sister—Pedro manages to stab de Silva and escape. With his friend Juan García (Lee J. Cobb) and a pretty female servant, Catana Pérez (Jean Peters), he flees to the West Indies, where the three join Cortés's voyage to Mexico. There Pedro encounters Coatl, who has returned home, and he also bonds with the expedition's sympathetic priest, Father Bartolomé Romero (Thomas Gomez), confessing that he murdered de Silva. Pedro becomes an officer in the expedition, watching as Cortés receives precious gifts from envoys of Aztec Emperor Moctezuma, but rejects their admonitions to return home. De Silva, who survived his stabbing, turns up in Mexico, looking to arrest Pedro and establish the Inquisition, but he is murdered by his escaped slave Coatl. At the end, the Spaniards head off to conquer the Aztec capital.

Filming this long, sprawling novel posed numerous challenges, and though the film had striking production values—an impressive cast, stunning color cinematography featuring smoking volcanoes in Mexico, exciting swordfights and daring escapes, reconstructed Aztec pyramids, opulent costumes of the Spaniards and the Aztec envoys, and an Oscar-nominated Alfred Newman score—its story was politically ambiguous. Perhaps illustrating the pitfalls of both filmmaking by committee and of filming massive novels, the movie seems torn between two tales: one about the evils of the Inquisition and another about the conquest of Mexico, and though its condemnation of the Inquisition was clear, its position on colonialism was muddled.

Early in production, Father John J. Devlin of Los Angeles, who often advised the studios on Catholic issues, called the proposed film a "deliberate attempt to discredit Christianity in general and the Catholic Church in particular." In his view, "this story follows the common error of greatly exaggerating some of the evils associated with the Inquisition without giving proper credit as to the noble purpose of the Inquisition and the great good in reality it accomplished," and he advised Fox "to forget the story entirely."[1] In response, screenwriter John Tucker Battle advised Zanuck to add a good priest to the tale, to eliminate a burning at the stake, to make a lay person the villain, and to show no crucifix or rosary—all of which the film did. Battle, however, warned that "religious zeal was the projected excuse for barbarous treatment of the Indians by the Spaniards," and that fact "will react upon Catholicism as a faith in an extremely negative manner." Battle proposed that they "eliminate the aspect of the Conquistador as a soldier of Christ and make him what he actually was; primarily an adventurer after gold and new lands." He also proposed giving the good priest, Father Bartolomé (whose very name evoked the sixteenth-century defender of the Indians, Bartolomé de las Casas) "a desire to protect the Indians from the Spaniards," while showing him "counseling the Conquistadors against extreme and barbarous methods" and "warning them against confusing greed for zeal and gold for God." In dealing with "the abstract moral questions arising from the Spanish conquest of Mexico," Battle suggested the script "should be written from an impartial reportorial viewpoint" and should show "that the Aztecs themselves were a conqueror nation who invaded and enslaved the original inhabitants of Mexico and who were in their way equally as cruel and heartless as the Spaniards."[2] The film ultimately showed little of either the Aztecs' or the Spaniards' cruelties, limiting itself to a brief, easily missed shot of blood stains on an Aztec pyramid (an allusion to their human sacrifices) and a sequence in which Cortés has his cannons destroy a stone idol. The film contained no combat scenes and ended before the expedition reached the Aztec capital.

Given the enormous power the Catholic Church exercised over Hollywood, mainly through the head of the Production Code Administration, Joseph Breen, and the Legion of Decency, Fox had reason to tread carefully. It showed courage in raising the subject of the Inquisition at all and in rejecting Father Devlin's advice, but the studio nonetheless whitewashed the Church's integral role in the conquest and colonization of Mexico. Placating Catholics was not the studio's only concern. Zanuck also consulted with director and screenwriter Joseph L. Mankiewicz, who wrote Zanuck a long letter in July 1945 advising him, among other things, to emphasize the Spanish conquest. Mankiewicz called the event "one of the two or three most thrilling and famous exploits in history—Cortes and his accomplishments are to the Spanish and Portuguese speaking countries of the world what Washington, Lincoln, Frederick the Great, Joan of Arc, Nelson and Potemkin are to the rest," and he warned that "neither Cortes nor his conquest can be slighted without offending great numbers of greatly interested people."[3] Apparently unconvinced, Zanuck annotated a script by the film's producer and writer, Lamar Trotti: "Pedro must be against Cortez [sic] tyranny from the start! We hate conquerors."[4] This viewpoint, which certainly reflected many Americans' views of others' conquests, had gained new impetus from World War II, but the finished film did not reflect it, so perhaps Mankiewicz had convinced Zanuck after all. (Mankiewicz was probably wrong about the dangers of offending devotees of Cortés, who had no hero-cult in Spain and was certainly no icon in postrevolutionary Mexico.) Rather than make a clear statement either for or against colonialism, the film followed Zanuck's comments: "I want this to be a personal story, . . . laid against the background of the Inquisition and the conquest of Mexico."[5] In shifting its focus from history to romantic fiction, the film concocted a character Zanuck envisioned. "We want to get away from this standard hero in our picture," he wrote. "We don't want to tag him as a liberal or anything like that, but . . . as a man who has a sense of justice, who . . . feels that for one man to enslave another is wrong." The rather anachronistic conquistador Zanuck imagined simply "feels as does Father Bartolome about forcing Spanish beliefs and customs on Mexico."[6]

The finished film offered some mild criticism of colonialism. Cesar Romero's interpretation of Cortés as a cheerful, back-slapping entrepreneur who is good to Pedro makes the conquistador fairly likable, but the film draws a clear contrast between him and Father Bartolomé. Cortés rejects advice to accept Moctezuma's gifts and go home, declaring, "We came to settle, to colonize," and he asks, "Are we going to be content with trifles, when we could help ourselves to the whole treasury?" Bartolomé, on the other hand, advises the Spaniards, "Put this greed for gold out of your heart," and "go forward not as conquerors but as men of God." Even more noteworthy is a sequence in which Coatl, now imprisoned as a Spanish hostage and shown with the damaged Aztec statue over his shoulder, tells his friend Pedro: "This is my country, Señor. These my people. My gods. We not come tell you to stop loving your gods. We not come make you slaves. Why you do this, Señor?" Pedro hesitates, then counters that "it isn't right for men to worship idols. There's only one true God," to which Coatl replies: "Maybe your god and my god same god. Maybe we just call him by different names." And when Coatl says that despite their friendship, if "you hurt my people, I fight you," Pedro says, "I suppose that if I were in your place, I'd do the same." This device of asking the protagonist how he would like being colonized is an effective means of denouncing colonialism, and its presence in a 1947 film is remarkable.

Yet *Captain from Castile* undermined its own critique of colonialism in myriad ways. The choice of Spain and its setting in the early sixteenth century already weakened the film's potential to indict modern colonialism, and its Black Legend–view of Spain (Inquisition, slavery, cruelty, etc.) made it easy for Anglo-American viewers to miss any broader critique of their own relations with the third world. Also, the film distracts viewers from Spain's conquest of Mexico with its lengthy treatment of Pedro's conflict with Diego de Silva, the Santa Hermandad, and the Inquisition; Mankiewicz was right to advise focusing entirely on the conquest. Further distracting was a subplot about Pedro's romance with his social inferior, Catana, and the story resolves not with the conquest of Moctezuma's capital but rather with de Silva dying and Pedro ending up with Catana. Aside from the 4 minutes that this 141-minute film devotes to Coatl, it presents everything from Spanish points of view. And despite Pedro's sympathy for Bartolomé's perspective, he never quits the expedition or even criticizes it, and he rides off at the end with Cortés. The ending puts a triumphant flourish on the whole enterprise, with wide shots of the expedition advancing toward the capital and stirring martial music playing as Cortés declares: "Those who survive will one day return to their homeland, rich in wisdom and gold, exonerated by His Majesty, and forever secure in the knowledge that they have participated in the opening of a New World."

Pedro's flight to freedom in the New World adhered to typical American self-images of a contrast between the equality and opportunity of the Americas and the oppression and hierarchy of Europe, even if the basis of the film's utopian vision of a new society was not the society the Spaniards encountered in Mexico, but rather the one they would create through conquest and colonization. Nor should the film's contrast between greedy conquistadors and the noble Father Bartolomé be mistaken for anticolonialism (any more than Las Casas should be mistaken for an anticolonialist), for late in the film, the cleric revealingly tells a gathering of Spaniards, "The Lord has indeed blessed this land. In its richness it may yet out-value all the gold of Moctezuma. And in God's own time, it will yet blossom forth under the cross of Christianity." In other words, not only will the Spaniards impose their superior religion on the colonized, but they will also find wealth after all (as the Church did through its vast lands and enterprises in the New World). In reality, the spread of Christianity benefited from soldiers doing the dirty work of empire, so the film's ending, with its glorification of the conquistadors, makes a logical resolution to a liberal-colonialist (but nonetheless colonialist) film. That the film also contains a hint of real anticolonialism, nested within the larger work without affecting its conclusion or broader viewpoint, attests to the difficulties of adapting tales of imperial heroes to an era of changing political sensibilities.

Although the film lost money, it was the number ten picture of 1948 in the United States and number fourteen of 1949 in France.[7] Advertisements highlighted the romance angle, showing Jean Peters caressing Powers, with smaller images of a sword-wielding Powers, an Aztec in feathered headdress, and a helmeted Romero. Suggesting a positive view of colonialism, a caption read, "Conqueror of a New World . . . Here is the full surge of conquest of gold and empire!"[8] The American reviews—nine of twenty-three positive (39 percent), four negative, ten mixed—generally praised the film as visually stunning spectacle but questioned the content.[9] "The disappointment lies in the story," offered the *Boston Herald*, with "the only link" between "two good double features" being Pedro's personal story, and the *Los Angeles Times* lamented that the film bore "no particular message." Most of the reviews revealed American distaste for others' colonialism. The *Philadelphia Inquirer* called Cortés "a greedy, unscrupulous aggressor who makes some more modern plunderers of peaceful nations appear mild in contrast," while *Variety* denounced "the brutal, gunpowdered policy of Cortez toward the spear-armed Aztecs." The *San Francisco Chronicle*, calling the conquest immoral, observed that "an apologetic voice remarks on the soundtrack that the Spanish invasion was a wonderful thing for Mexico (a statement that three centuries of history have disproved)." The *Dallas Morning News* saw "the padre of the expedition spreading the gospel while others simply loot the vanquished," and the Catholic weekly *America* held that "there can never be any justification for using the sword to impose religious belief." Several reviews found the film anachronistic: *Time* complained that the priest's words about "the happy day when all men, even Indians, will be equal" sounded "a few centuries too soon, for a churchman of imperial Spain," and Richard Coe of the *Washington Post* wrote that it "tells history in terms of our present morality," with "parallels between today's intolerance (Nazi intolerance, not American intolerance—that would be too much) and the Spanish Inquisition." Far from making modern viewers question contemporary colonialism, Coe argued, "it gives one the comforting idea that, great as our present imperfections may be, we are far more civilized and more to be admired than the generations which came before us." These reviews suggest that the film might have been dramatically stronger and still commercially secure had it denounced Spanish colonialism less ambivalently, but Hollywood was still learning how to adapt empire films to a new political environment.

British filmmakers took their turn with Spanish explorers and conquistadores in the 1949 Gainsborough Pictures production, *Christopher Columbus*, starring Frederic March. It failed to reach the box-office charts in the United States, and it seemed even less sure of its viewpoint than *Captain from Castile*. A scene of the explorers' first contact with the people of the New World makes no discernible point, and in a subsequent sequence in which Columbus stops one of his men from swindling an ignorant Indian out of a gold nugget, the apparent message that Columbus protected the Indians is undermined when he himself pockets the nugget in exchange for a tiny bell. The Spanish come off well when Queen Isabella insists the Indians be converted, not enslaved, but overall this production shows no real interest in Spain's relations with the Indians, focusing instead on Columbus's battles with his detractors in Spain. The time when tales of Columbus could spark bitter debate in the West still lay far in the future.

Spain's conquest and colonization of the New World returned yet again with

Twentieth Century-Fox's *Seven Cities of Gold* (1955). Essentially a hagiopic about Father Junípero Serra (Michael Rennie), the film contrasts greedy Spanish soldiers with the heroic, selfless work of the Franciscan founder of the California missions, drawing the contrast between good and bad colonizers even more sharply than in *Captain from Castile*. As an expedition prepares to head north into California, Serra boldly denounces the soldiers to their faces, telling them, "You plan to pillage and plunder and loot and lust, and all because their tongue is strange and their skin is copper." He limps his way across California despite a painful leg abscess, and, ignoring a warning that the Indians will "split his head open," he shows no fear as he single-handedly dissuades a band of wildly painted, club-wielding savages from attacking the expedition. A compassionate civilizer as well as a heroic trailblazer, he heals and proselytizes, while also protecting what he calls "my Indians" from his fellow Spaniards. With God (or at least director Robert Webb) on his side, Serra even manages to make it rain after six months of drought, as a thunderclap arrives precisely when he rings a bell to proclaim the founding of his mission at San Diego—to the accompaniment of a heavenly string section. This pious film gives little hint of the ways in which the conquistador and the missionary made each other's work possible, and the film made a saint of Serra long before the Vatican beatified him in 1987. As with the 1949 Columbus film, it would still be years before Serra's name would provoke Native Americans, historians, and others to denounce the Franciscans' shackling and beating of their converts, their use of forced labor, and their refusal to let converts leave mission grounds.[10] The film missed the box-office charts, and it was the last in this cycle of films about Spain's conquest of the New World. The period did see several westerns about fur trappers, mountain men, and other trailblazers of empire in North America, but the following chapter will discuss those.

The "Opening" of Japan: *The Barbarian and the Geisha* (1958)

Although Hollywood's interest in the Far East in these years usually focused on recent times, one exception was John Huston's *The Barbarian and the Geisha*, a Twentieth Century-Fox release about the moment when the West, at gunpoint, had forced Japan open to international trade and contact. In a controversial bit of casting, Huston chose John Wayne to play Townsend Harris, America's first consul-general, who went to Japan in 1856 to follow up on Commodore Perry's visit and initial treaty. Explaining his choice of Wayne, Huston told the *Los Angeles Times*, "This huge figure in his innocence and naivete, with his edges rough, moving among these minute people and this exotic art work—I felt would symbolize the huge and awkward United States of 100 years ago."[11] The real Harris spent years as a merchant in Asia before securing his appointment and arriving at Shimoda, a fishing village near Edo, with Dutch interpreter Henry Heusken. The patient, persistent Harris eventually overcame Japanese reluctance and internal division and obtained a treaty that extended Western rights of residence and trade. Filming the story was not Huston's idea, but having enjoyed the Japanese films he had seen, he welcomed the studio's offer to make this film, and he insisted on shooting in Japan with a Japanese crew. Charles Grayson's screenplay followed the historical record on many points but embellished rumors of a romance between Harris and a geisha, Okichi (Eiko Ando), sent to spy on him.

The story begins as Harris and Heusken (Sam Jaffe) receive a frosty welcome from Governor Tamura (Sô Yamamura), who denies Harris's diplomatic status and prohibits the xenophobic but curious locals from trading with these "barbarians." In a scene that recalls King Mongkut offering Anna Owens a dilapidated hovel, Harris and Heusken are shown a broken-down temple, but Harris refuses to storm away and go home as the Governor had hoped. In a departure from Wayne's usual persona, Harris conquers not by force but by patient forbearance and rational argumentation; he also shows flexibility when his hosts order him to lower the U.S. flag—agreeing, but insisting he will fly it on special occasions. When an American ship arrives, Harris stands in front of the cannon to prevent its use. Amid a cholera epidemic brought by the American sailors, Harris and Heusken first help with the sick then end the outbreak by burning down the village. That act naturally horrifies the villagers, but it is the story's turning point, and the grateful survivors come en masse to thank Harris. When patience finally yields an invitation to meet the Shogun, those villagers escort Harris to the palace in one of many scenes making good use of Japanese extras and lavish costumes and sets. Inside the palace, a shot of a series of opening doors symbolizes the opening of Japan, after which Harris offers gifts to the teenage Shogun (then a figurehead for powerful lords).[12] The lad's amazement at a telescope, although a trope of empire films, raises the subject of Japan's fascination with Western technology, while Japanese interest in Harris's whiskey also has some basis in fact. The rest of the film shows the turmoil the Westerners caused, and though the lords approve the treaty, disgruntled xenophobes launch a rebellion and try to assassinate Harris. Betraying her lord, Okichi saves Harris, and the film ends with her tearful departure from the American she had come to love.

The Barbarian and the Geisha fits the pattern of Cold War fiction pleading for friendship across the Pacific. "The United States of America, your neighbor, stretches out its hand," Harris tells the Shogun's court. "It is the open hand of my countrymen, demanding nothing, asking no special favors, seeking only the common good." Harris says he has come, in what sounds like a marriage vow, "to pledge to you our friendship in peace, our help in trouble, and our strength in danger." The film first leads viewers to feel Harris's frustration in being kept at arms' length for so long, then delivers the gratification of seeing the Japanese warm to him. First, grateful villagers come to thank him for saving them, arriving just when his spirits were lowest; then Governor Tamura becomes fond of him and eventually cannot go through with orders to assassinate him; finally even a majority of the lords at Edo come over to his side. To 1950s viewers upset by news of anti-Americanism in Japan (where protests over nuclear testing broke out in 1954), the shot of a villager in Harris's procession to Edo enthusiastically waving an American flag must have been comforting.[13] And although Harris adopts no Japanese children, he does bond with them, first when they share a laugh over his bumping his head on a low beam (a convention of Hollywood's Japan films), and then in the palace, when he and a little boy playfully wiggle their ears at each other. Huston presents the romance between the two title characters sympathetically, though it is poignantly thwarted by cultural distance.

The film's central topic, the opening of Japan, seems innocent enough amid Harris's talk of friendship and neighborliness, and given Wayne's patriotic political views and screen image as a good guy, his casting as a simple, decent fellow who believes in American benevolence and righteousness makes perfect sense. But if the film's benign vision of American foreign policy in Asia exemplifies 1950s American self-images, it ignores certain historical realities that enabled Harris to succeed. Governor Tamura does tell Harris that the 1854 treaty "was made under the threat of Commodore Perry's guns, [and] such a treaty has no virtue," and Harris issues one threat, declaring that if Japan refuses to cooperate with China-bound sailors in need of assistance and coal, then "the world will treat Japan as it would treat a band of brigands infesting a highway." Mostly, Harris speaks in positive and peaceful terms, and the film shows neither the warships that had preceded Harris in 1853–54 nor those that came in 1864 to force Japan's compliance. The only hint of Western military force the film offers is the sound of the cannons on the ship that delivers Harris to Shimoda, and he quickly reassures the alarmed Japanese that it is a friendly salute. Nor does the film explain that the Japanese bowed to Western wishes in part because they knew of Britain's subjugation of China in the Opium Wars—the second of which was going on during Harris's visit. Like the "open door" concept in American policy in China from 1899 on, Harris's dream of trade without exclusivity or national spheres of influence fits Americans' anticolonialist self-image, but America's opposition to European designs was hardly anti-imperialist. If Asia's door was open, it was because

Americans and Europeans had broken it down. Also, given the West's Industrial Revolution, openness in Asia implied the creation of a classical colonial trade relationship in which the West imported raw materials and exported manufactures, undermining Asian artisans with mass-produced imports. An open world is generally not a world of equals, although Japan caught up rapidly.

The concept of openness in this historical film also has some interesting implications for its own time. By 1958, Japan and the United States had developed distinct models of capitalism, with Japan resisting American notions of free trade and investment—at least for American products and capital entering Japan.[14] The Americans and the Japanese, in a sense, were still having the same argument about openness in 1958 that they had had a century earlier, and that debate has gone on ever since. A certain presentism also appears in the scene in which Harris burns down the cholera-infested village, an unsettling image coming barely a decade after the Americans had firebombed Japanese cities. Harris, like the Americans in World War II, in essence sees himself inflicting harm for the ultimate good of the Japanese—freeing the village from cholera just as the Americans freed the Japanese people from a military dictatorship—and in both cases the Japanese themselves came to accept that vision. Finally, a scene in which Harris tries to retrieve Heusken's hat from a dwarf and a giant who have playfully stolen it evokes events both before and after 1958. Wayne briefly plays the action hero as he pounds the giant into submission with his fists, but when he takes on the dwarf—a martial-arts expert—he goes down to humiliating defeat, and the camera shows Wayne's shocked expression. This image of the tall American bested by the little Asian pugilist evokes a whole series of historical events, from Japan's defeat of the Russians in 1905, to the American defeats at Pearl Harbor and the Philippines in 1941–42, and America's setbacks in Korea in 1950.

Ads for the film played up the meager bit of action it contained, with images of Wayne holding a torch over his head and samurai warriors wielding swords, while a hyperbolic caption called it the "story of the first white man to open up the Far East!" If Wayne's fans saw these ads, some must have been disappointed by the lack of action, the pacific message, the casual pace, and the gentle images of Japanese beauty. In this sense, casting Wayne was indeed a mistake, and the ads' images of a partially disrobed Eiko Ando also raised hopes the film did not fulfill. The box-office performance—number thirty-three of 1958—was respectable if somewhat disappointing, given the film's sizable budget.[15] Yet contentions that this box-office failure resulted from poor reviews—one of Huston's biographers refers to "devastating reviews"—are overstated.[16] Of twenty American reviews examined here, ten were positive, five negative, and five mixed.[17] The critics who disliked the film singled out the casting of Wayne—*Commonweal* charged that he "seems ill at ease, as if he were looking for his gun and saddle"—and found the film slow; *Newsweek* called it "lamentably tedious" and "long on speeches on political neighborliness and brotherly love." On the positive side, the *Saturday Review*'s Hollis Alpert considered it "an unusually beautiful film, directed with spirit and remarkable taste," while the *Boston Globe*'s Marjory Adams described it as "a beautiful, touching and gorgeously hued production." No review hinted at any lingering hatred toward the Japanese, nor did any question the policies Harris served. The *Motion Picture Herald*, noting that Harris had to "overcome reactionary forces who wish to preserve Japan's isolationist attitude," said his mission "bears strong overtones of good will for Japanese-American relations, with an integrated plea for better understanding among all nations." Jack Moffitt of the *Hollywood Reporter* cautioned that this "eloquent plea for international friendship" overstated Harris's success by ignoring the military force the West used in 1864, "but after Pearl Harbor and Hiroshima, it's a good thing to restate a message of good will."

The reviews were indeed devastating in France, where in a sample of twelve reviews, ten were negative and only one positive, and where the film sold a paltry 334,644 tickets.[18] *Arts* lamented the lack of any "critical intent in this panegyric for a colonialist of the worst kind," while in the sarcastic words of *Les Lettres Françaises*, this "white man brings wisdom, progress (which he must define for these stupid natives), civilization, and the marvels of modern science." *France Observateur* felt that the film was made "to flatter the self-love of the Yankee spectator," while *L'Humanité* praised the film's visual beauty but complained that it "gives the American point of view on a historical event and honors the United States too much." So while American critics generally embraced the film's image of East-West friendship, critics in France detested its self-congratulatory view of a key chapter in U.S.-Japanese relations.

Trailblazers in Africa

As one of the last areas Westerners explored and colonized, the vast interior of Africa made an ideal setting for films about heroic trailblazers, and a new cycle of films took up where prewar productions such as *Trader Horn* (1931), *King Solomon's Mines* (1937), and *Stanley and Livingstone* (1939) had left off. The most influential film in this cycle was MGM's 1950 remake of *King Solomon's Mines*, based on H. Rider Haggard's 1885 novel. With effective performances from Stewart Granger and Deborah Kerr, impressive location footage in East Africa, a soundtrack with African drumming and chanting in lieu of the usual orchestral score, and

Watussis and Kipsigis as extras and actors, the film set new standards for adventure films. A major hit (it reached number three in Variety's charts for 1950, won Oscars for cinematography and editing, and was nominated for best picture), it was hardly advanced politically, as it mostly ignored current pressures on colonialism.[19]

Set in 1897, the film is a compendium of empire-film conventions. Despite its interest in local color, it is mostly about white people—the old battle of the sexes that develops into romance—while the dangerous setting gives Mrs. Curtis the opportunity to overcome her delicate Victorian upbringing and prove her mettle. She and her brother arrive in Africa in search of her husband, who disappeared seeking the legendary mines, and she struggles to persuade the jaded safari leader Allan Quatermain to help them find him in uncharted territory. The manly Quatermain fails to convince the stubborn Mrs. Curtis that Africa is no place for a white woman, but he is sure she will quit once faced with the hostile terrain and dangerous wildlife. Also dangerous are Africa's inhabitants, for although there are the usual good, loyal Africans who die serving the white man, there are also menacing, towering warriors in wild, exotic garb. Mrs. Curtis actually holds up well once she abandons her ties to civilization—symbolized by a shot of her reluctantly lopping off her impractical tresses—and she proves more courageous than the cowardly porters who flee as they near the fearsome Dark Region. In a classic village scene near the end, the three whites, down to their last two bullets, face down a village full of warriors through sheer courage and bluster and finally locate the mines.

Haggard's tale had done more than just entertain readers. It also encouraged them to explore and conquer unknown lands, luring them with images of fabulous mineral wealth and challenging them to abandon their easy lives and prove their worth in the wilds of Africa. By 1950 the tale had lost that function, but it still glorified the trailblazers of the past, and its image of primitive Africa catered to Western perceptions of a dark continent in need of Western tutelage. Like westerns about American Indians, films about Africa always seemed to take place in the past, and viewers might be forgiven for thinking Africans still lived this way. Yet the film also had certain liberal overtones. Quatermain, the man who knows Africans, also likes and cares about them; when an assistant dies during a hunt, he goes to console his widow and paternalistically pats her baby on the head as he leaves. His respect for Africans appears in his intimate knowledge of their languages and customs—including their elaborate handshakes—and he explains their ways to his countrymen. When Mrs. Curtis is surprised that they prefer gifts of salt over beads, he tells her, "They're not stupid, you know," and when he explains that the locals have replaced war with individual combat between political rivals because "they discovered it saves war and bloodshed," their ways probably seemed wise to war-weary Western audiences. Whether the film inspired anyone to learn more about Africa is hard to say, but it certainly inspired imitation by other filmmakers.

One of the first to follow *King Solomon's Mines* was *Bwana Devil* (1952), a rather inept 3D film from United Artists, starring Robert Stack as Bob Hayward, a foreman building a railroad line in eastern Africa. Loosely based on an ostensibly true account of man-eating lions that bedeviled a railroad-building crew in 1898 (remade in 1996 as *The Ghost and the Darkness*), the film depicts Hayward trying to protect his largely Indian crew from two man-eating lions who devour a railroad car full of British hunters sent to kill them.[20] A rather incompetent trailblazer, Hayward forgets his rifle as he pursues the lions at one moment and fails to make it work at another, but he does manage to avoid being eaten. Typical of countless mediocre Africa films of the 1950s, this clichéd story of Darkest Africa and the heroic work Europeans did there is notable mainly for its role in pioneering 3D.

John Ford's *Mogambo* (1953), a Loew's/MGM release starring Clark Gable as a white hunter in a love triangle (with Ava Gardner and Grace Kelly), was a remake of *Red Dust* (1932), another Gable empire film. The remake moved the action from Indochina to Africa and featured Gable as a manly white hunter who sells animals to zoos and protects two white women and a city-slicker anthropologist from the dangers of the jungle. A colonial-backdrop film, it focuses almost entirely on the love triangle and on wildlife shots while treating the African porters and servants more as props than human beings. *Mogambo* intends no specific message about colonialism, but it reflects colonialist mentalities by showing more interest in the animals than the people of Africa.

The French made a rare contribution to the African trailblazer cycle with *La Bigorne, Caporal de France* (1958). Robert Darène directed and cowrote this farce set in eighteenth-century Madagascar, adapted from Pierre Nord's 1957 novel. Although the French had yet to conquer and colonize Madagascar in 1750, they had a few trading posts along the coast, and the film shows elegantly dressed naval officers and ladies with parasols enjoying the perks of empire as blacks wait on them hand and foot. The film's "hero," Corporal La Bigorne (François Périer), a slacker and incurable womanizer, sleeps with the officers' wives, finally leading them to ship him off to fight local pirates in a barely seaworthy ship with one rickety cannon. Shipwrecked after a comical battle with the pirates, La Bigorne and three companions wash up on an apparently uninhabited island off the coast of Madagascar, Île Sainte-Marie. Soon La Bigorne meets a comely young woman, Bethi (Rossana Podesta), whose grandmother was French and whose African father is the local king, but the area is also full of pirates (true of Île Sainte-Marie then), and he and his companions wind up in their dungeon. Through La Bigorne's picaresque wits and audacity, they escape, and La Bigorne wins Bethi away from the English pirate Tom Wright, to whom the King had promised her. When Bethi's father foolishly drinks himself to death at a wild party—falling for Wright's plot to kill him and take over the kingdom—La Bigorne's maneuvering ensures that Bethi inherits the throne. Having won her love, Bigorne has her royal guards chase away the pirates, and he ends up in control of the island. This ne'er-do-well has managed to acquire a new land for his king and for France.

The film has been criticized for slandering Africans and celebrating the colonization of Madagascar.[21] This view is understandable today, and the sequence in which the King drinks himself to death is indeed insulting. Yet the film is a satirical farce, making it hard to question its taste or political judgment, and it makes the French look just as ridiculous as the Africans. Although La Bigorne shows a certain resourcefulness, many of the gags are about his cowardice and that of his goofy French pals (like the humor in Bob Hope films); rather than celebrating France's acquisition of an African colony, the film's main joke is the notion that France acquired it through the selfish philandering of a scoundrel like La Bigorne. In short, it satirizes the figure of the trailblazing hero of empire. The mock solemnity of the opening text's claim that Franco-Malagasy relations were "friendly, confident, indeed even sentimental" sets up the joke of La Bigorne romping in the sack with black women as well as white—friendly relations indeed. French censors, who did not explain their actions, likely approved this film not because it was useful colonialist propaganda, but rather because it was so evidently farcical that there was no reason to fear anyone taking seriously its unflattering image of both colonizer and colonized. The film, which sold a modest 1,165,131 tickets in 1958, contrasts sharply with American and British films about heroes of empire in Africa, which presented that work in earnest seriousness.[22]

By 1959, Ghana and Guinea were independent, and many other African colonies were about to be. Ignoring this inconvenient trend that threatened to make bwana-pics look hopelessly dated was *Killers of Kilimanjaro* (1959), from Warwick Films, a production company that Hollywood veterans Irving Allen and Albert Broccoli formed to make "runaway" films in Britain. Starring Robert Taylor as Robert Adamson, a rugged American railroad-builder in Kenya, the film recalls *Bwana Devil* in its setting and subject and *King Solomon's Mines* in its basic structure, as Adamson leads a white woman, Jane Carlton (Anne Aubrey) through uncharted territory in search of her fiancé. Finally, it recalls *White Witch Doctor* with its device of a fearsome tribe in the unexplored interior blocking progress;

in this case the "Warush," described as "the most treacherous tribe in Africa," block the projected railway and hamper Adamson's recruiting of laborers. The unflappable, no-nonsense Adamson ignores threats from the Arab slaver Ben Ahmed (Grégoire Aslan), who is building a rival line for his illicit traffic. Adamson thinks only of his work, but a grateful local tells him, "When you are done, you will realize what you have done for our country." Undaunted by the repeated attempts of Ben Ahmed's thugs to murder him, Adamson passes a test of bravery in the Warush village, calmly smoking a cigarette as warriors hurl spears closer and closer to his crotch. This manly hero saves Jane's life by felling a charging bull elephant with a single shot and wins over the hostile Warush chief (Orlando Martins) by proving his bravery and by dazzling the primitive, gullible Africans with tricks and trinkets. He also protects Ben Ahmed's young son, who has run away from his evil father and joined the expedition. The boy explains his flight, saying, "Since I go to school in England, I learn things my father does not understand. I learned good things: to be kind to people is a good thing, eh Bwana?" With the help of loyal Africans, Adamson finishes off the slavers, reaches Lake Victoria, and paves the way for civilization.

Killers of Kilimanjaro premiered in London in 1959 and the United States in 1960, by which time more than a dozen African countries were independent. Although it is hard to prove why this impressive-looking CinemaScope film with a major American star missed the box-office charts, perhaps by this time trailblazers of empire in Africa seemed dated. The *New York Times* called the film a "compendium of jungle clichés," while *Commonweal* found it "very sleazy indeed," and Britain's *Monthly Film Bulletin*, struck by the film's "antique morals," wrote that "anyone who has a conscience about Africa and takes the preposterous story seriously will be appalled."[23] Western filmmakers were not yet done with Africa, but as they entered the 1960s, they faced growing pressure to update their work.

The White Protector

Hollywood might have gotten pointers on updating the empire film from the British, who, unlike the Americans, were actually governing African colonies and were thus more sensitive to political trends. Their postwar films set in Africa focused less on heroic trailblazers than on benevolent civilizers and protectors, and their films took place after the conquest phase. The first of these was *Men of Two Worlds* (1946), a high-budget production from Two Cities Films. Thorold Dickinson directed and cowrote this Technicolor film from a Joyce Cary story, but the Colonial Office and the Ministry of Information first suggested making it.[24] Redolent of colonialist propaganda, it follows the fortunes of Kisenga (Robert Adams), an African who has become a successful composer and concert pianist after years of study in Britain. Telling his disappointed fans why he is returning to Tanganyika—"I'm needed in Africa, as an African, to teach"—he agrees to help British authorities combat a sleeping-sickness epidemic by persuading his people, the Litu, to relocate their village. His return highlights his differences from his family, as he wears a Western suit and tie while they all dress traditionally, but even deeper differences of outlook emerge when the Litu resist relocation and dismiss Western medicine as nonsense. The local witch doctor, Magole (Orlando Martins), has the superstitious villagers in thrall, and he keeps them that way by secretly murdering those upon whom he has placed curses. Kisenga convinces his own father to take a blood test for sleeping sickness, but this angers Magole, and when the old man catches malaria, the witch doctor breaks his will to live, then blames his death on the blood test. Kisenga's white mentors, District Commissioner Randall (Eric Portman) and Dr. Catherine Munro (Phyllis Calvert), encourage him to challenge Magole, which he does by letting the witch doctor take his blood and place a curse on him. Kisenga, however, already distraught at his failure to convince his people to relocate and wracked with guilt over his father's death, now descends into depression and self-doubt. "What's all my training worth?" he asks the D.C. "What's that against ten thousand years of Africa in my blood?" Randall, however, encourages him to press on, and overcoming his profound doubts about the Western path, he survives Magole's curse and turns the village against the witch doctor.

Despite its attempts to update Africa films for an era of colonial modernization and development, *Men of Two Worlds* partakes of many empire-film conventions, from its opening map shots to its Brits in pith helmets and its condescension toward Kisenga's people. "The Litu are a stone age people," declares one European, and their superstitions and endless drumming and dancing around bonfires support the point. Despite talk of Africa being in people's blood, the film is not biologically racist, as Kisenga proves Europeans can civilize Africans—even if that seems in doubt when he backslides. The film's sympathies for the civilizing mission are clearest in a debate that the D.C. and Dr. Munro have with a visiting British writer, Mrs. Upjohn. The audience is meant to dislike the arrogant Mrs. Upjohn, who insults Randall and Munro, sneers at trying to make the African "a cheap imitation of a wretched model of our so-called civilization," and declares that "the primitive African, yes even with hookworm, is nearer the great soul of things than any so-called scientist or education official." The script briefly turns relativist when Randall tells Dr. Munro that superstition, such as belief in astrology, exists in the West as well. But the condescension persists, and Randall, the man who knows Africans, explains the Litus' backwardness by telling Dr. Munro, "You won't find much initiative in these backwoods." For years, Britain's indirect rule had relied on chiefs, and *Men of Two Worlds* reflects a change in that model toward a reliance on Westernized Africans. "Use your Africa," the D.C. advises Kisenga. "Go back and dominate it. Put a bit in its mouth and ride it." The image of British rule fits what one would expect in a film the Colonial Office solicited. Even while growing frustrated with mindless resistance to his attempts to protect and help the Africans, the D.C. refuses to use force, and he and his protégé finally manage to save the villagers from the tsetse fly and their own superstitions.

British filmmakers returned to the subject with Ealing Studios' *Where No Vultures Fly* (1951), a fictionalized account of the work of Mervyn Cowie, who helped found Kenya's first national park. In the film, Bob Payton (Anthony Steel) tires of his government job culling wildlife and pursues his dream to create a park. He meets opposition from settlers, stingy bureaucrats, recreational hunters, ivory traders, and even a black man in glasses and a business suit who insists that "the interests of the African are paramount." Through a publicity stunt suggested by his wife Mary (Dinah Sheridan), he musters support for a park, and with meager resources and staff he sets out to protect its wildlife from hunters and ivory poachers. The film plays the underdog theme as Payton faces long odds and unscrupulous enemies, and it enlists sympathy for his work with shots of adorable baby animals. Enduring complaints from his wife about living in the bush, taunts from white hunters, hostility from African hunters, and even a spear through the leg, Payton finally prevails. Although set in 1947, the film rehearses various empire-film conventions, and it never really develops any African characters.[25] The loyal Africans—"they're such good boys," Mary says—call Payton bwana and risk life and limb to serve him, and he overcomes danger and hardship through singular courage and determination.

This liberal-colonialist film justifies Britain's presence in Africa by citing the threat from commercial operations supplying Europe and the world with ivory and zoo animals, so one form of colonialism justifies another. While the film seems to demonize black poachers, it shows that whites are putting them up to it, and one apparently villainous African poacher, "Scarface," turns out to be a decent chap who saves Bob's life. Representing the real villains is the British ivory poacher Mannering (Harold Warrender), who lambastes Payton for his work: "Why waste your time preserving wild animals? . . . As if anything mattered in this God-forsaken country. Oh, I know, you still think Africa's a fine place, a place to be saved." The film hints at decolonization as Mannering warns: "Someday that black scum is going to spread over the face of [Africa] and blot us out. The only thing to do is to take all you can as fast as you can." Payton's reply—"There is a new Africa, and there's no place for you"—contrasts rapacious colonialism with a more benevolent kind and depicts a historical transition from one to the other. So with its critique of white exploitation, the film followed the new outlines of British colonial policy.

If British films of the era generally supported empire, one notable exception was *The Heart of the Matter* (1953). Based on a Graham Greene novel, the film featured Trevor Howard as a depressed policeman in Sierra Leone mired in marital problems, diamond smuggling, blackmail, adultery, and Catholic guilt that will not allow him to commit suicide. Neither Greene nor the film really articulated a case against colonialism, but its dismal picture of life in the colonies was hardly the stuff of Colonial Office propaganda. Essentially a colonial-backdrop film, it followed many older films in using the colonies to establish an atmosphere of moral degradation that afflicts white people in the tropics.

More uplifting was Ealing's 1954 sequel to *Where No Vultures Fly*. *West of Zanzibar* (not a remake of the 1928 film of that title) used the same director and producer, and Anthony Steel again played Bob Payton, but this time he sought to protect people as well as animals in modern-day Kenya. A narrator explains that the story concerns the Galanas, "a simple, little tribe," and "a fine, happy people despite their struggle to exist," whose land has lost its topsoil. In the past they would simply have migrated, notes the narrator, but "now the white man must tell them where to go." Despite discussing the scarcity of land, the film makes no mention of white settlers farming prime lands in Kenya, and whereas *Where No Vultures Fly* had a white man represent Africa's exploiters, the sequel takes the safer path of blaming Arab traders. It briefly alludes to the former Arab slave trade (while saying nothing about Europe's version), but notes that the search for the "black gold of Africa" has given way to a quest for ivory, "the white gold of Africa." The film shows Bob discussing options with his friend, the Galana Chief Ushingo. The classic good native, Ushingo says, "You have looked after us for many years. What do you say?" Bob advises him to take his people to the hills, where good lands await, but although Ushingo agrees, he tells Bob that the young men prefer to go to Mombasa, as "they want to taste what you call civilization." A wary Bob replies that "they're not even ready for the beginnings of that kind of civilization," but he tells Ushingo, "You will vote in the traditional way of your fathers." This sequence evokes Britain's current experiment with greater measures of local-level democracy in Africa, and although it treats democracy as part of African culture, it also provides an unsettling message when the Galanas foolishly ignore the wisdom of the white man and the Chief and choose Mombasa. Sure enough, they soon fall into misery, as they get into drunken brawls in the streets, get swindled in the marketplace, and are lured into ivory poaching by sly Africans and Arabs. An anguished Ushingo tells Bob, "My people are sinful in the ways of the towns. . . . They starve in the slums or become thieves and bad men. They need your help."

The rest of the film resembles *Where No Vultures Fly*, as Bob and his loyal sidekick M'Kwongi (Orlando Martins) combat the ivory trade. Once again, the underdog Bob encounters British bureaucratic apathy, as one official asks, "Are we to blame because they became money-conscious?" The colony's judicial system is no better, as the courts acquit those Bob arrests. He and his wife Mary (Sheila Sim) confront the smugglers' well-dressed Arab lawyer Dhofar (Martin Benson, a British actor in brownface), who sounds like Mannering in *Where No Vultures Fly*. "Don't you think you are being, to put it delicately, a little starry-eyed about these so-called innocent tribes?" asks Dhofar. "The world cannot wait for civilization to catch up with the primitive black men." To Mary's charge that the ivory trade is turning the Galanas into slum savages, Dhofar replies, "That is what the black man is doomed to be: slum savages. Oh, it is regrettable, but inevitable. Perhaps you conveniently forget your Industrial Revolution and what it did to your people. Africa, Mr. Payton, is having its own industrial revolution. And no sentimental heart-burning is going to stop it." The reference to Britain's Industrial Revolution may have induced complacency about Africa's problems in British viewers raised on horror tales of that aspect of British history, but it leads nowhere, and the film does not suggest that ivory will bring Africa the kind of prosperity industrialization brought to Britain.

The film also seems to critique settler racism when Dhofar taunts Bob: "What are your innermost thoughts? 'I'd like to smack this little wog on the kisser,' or something like that?" Yet Dhofar is too despicable for anything he says to be taken seriously, and when Bob later catches him red-handed in a dhow full of ivory, the film gives the viewer the satisfaction of seeing Bob smack him on the kisser after all. After a chase scene in which the smugglers kill Ushingo, and in which Bob and the Chief's loyal followers apprehend the smugglers, Bob speaks with the deceased Chief's son and successor. It is clear that the Galanas are still in good hands—the young man, after all, is named Bethlehem. And in contrast to a hot-headed, rude young Galana who earlier had told Bob to go away, Bethlehem, an idealized colonial subject, tells Bob, "We are very thankful to you, Bwana," adding, "I think we must learn to walk before we can run." Having defended Britain's presence among a people unprepared for independence, the film lets

Bob bask in the gratitude of his charges, indicating the emotional rewards that lighten the white man's burden. *West of Zanzibar*, like *Where No Vultures Fly* and *Men of Two Worlds*, thus opposed decolonization in Africa without overtly acknowledging the subject, and all three films featured the benevolent white protector concerned about his African charges.

India

If making films that praised a new-and-improved brand of colonialism made sense about an Africa still under European rule, the production of films about India after independence raises questions about their motives and functions. Some have argued that decolonization made white people hunger for reassurance of their superiority, creating a need for nostalgic Raj films.[26] This intriguing theory calls for a closer look at the films and their reception.

One of the first post-independence Raj films was Twentieth Century-Fox's *King of the Khyber Rifles* (1953), from the old team of Darryl F. Zanuck, director Henry King (*Captain from Castile*), and Tyrone Power. If the film seems a throwback to the 1930s, it is partly because work on it began in the 1930s, and it makes an interesting case study in the adaptation of empire films to the decolonization era. Shortly after the success of Paramount's *Lives of a Bengal Lancer* (1935), Zanuck's new studio, Twentieth Century-Fox, began developing a script based on British novelist Talbot Mundy's *King of the Khyber Rifles* (1916). The project went through multiple scripts by 1936, and in 1938, John L. Balderston, writer of *Lives of a Bengal Lancer*, advised Zanuck: "We need a central idea . . . that will distinguish it and set it apart from other Sahib-native, Northwest-frontier, White Man's Burden productions."[27] Zanuck's team worked on the story while he produced another Raj film, the Shirley Temple vehicle *Wee Willie Winkie* (1937), and while RKO made *Gunga Din* (1939). The minutes from a March 1939 story conference reported: "Mr. Zanuck stated that we cannot hope to compete with a picture like GUNGA DIN from a spectacular viewpoint, the latter having cost two million dollars and every conceivable splash being contained in it."[28] The project was shelved with the arrival of World War II.

Zanuck never gave up on the story. In March 1951, Frank P. Rosenberg, who eventually produced the film, told him: "I am of the opinion that time and history have taken its toll of whatever qualities this particular story may have had eleven years ago."[29] Zanuck agreed on the need to update it, and he liked Rosenberg's suggestion that it concern an "aristocrat who learns that all men are basically the same in spite of the color of their skins."[30] Zanuck's interest in bigotry had produced two surprise hits—*Gentleman's Agreement* (1947) and *Pinky* (1949)—and he and his team pursued this angle. They first considered having the protagonist, Captain King, fall in love with a half-caste girl, then decided to made King a half-caste—the son of a British officer and a Muslim woman. An October 1951 script struck Zanuck as going too far in denouncing British racism. "I cannot understand how you can possibly hope to produce this picture without the cooperation of the British government," he told Rosenberg, adding that "the picture is bitterly and viciously anti-British from beginning to end." Also fearing that a tale of colonial heroism might seem dated, he added: "I just do not believe that you can make a military story about the Khyber Pass important or even exciting to an audience today unless the personal story is the main issue."[31] After more rewrites, Zanuck announced his satisfaction in July 1953: "The half-caste theme is worked out in a logical and adult fashion," he wrote, and "while this is an adventure story, it is also a racial story, and it has the flavor of being adult entertainment as well as an exciting melodrama."[32] This correspondence contains no hint of any urge to salve wounded Western egos or bolster whites' sense of racial superiority. What instead appears is a desire to make an action film relevant to the new struggle against racism.

With Fox having given up on securing British or Indian help, King shot the film in California, using the Sierras to stand in for the mountains of the Khyber Pass. Despite the urge to update the story, empire-film conventions abound, from a mountain ambush establishing the dangers of India to the courage of the dashing Captain King (Tyrone Power) and the usual Raj-film props—tiger's heads, elephant tusks, maps of India—in the office of General Maitland (Michael Rennie). Set in 1857, the story depicts the Mutiny through one regiment's fight with a scheming Muslim warlord, Kurram Khan (English actor Guy Rolfe, in brownface, turban, and beard). The brave Muslim sepoys under King's command are good, loyal natives, if undisciplined, unpredictable, and inscrutable even to King, despite his Muslim mother and his upbringing in India. King may be the man who knows (East) Indians, but he admits to his commander, "what goes on in their minds, only Allah knows." As for the villainous tribesmen, the film makes much of their atrocities, with references to tongues ripped out, skin peeled off, families tortured, and villages burned, but its only hint of why they were fighting was the megalomaniacal Kurram Khan's declared goal of "empire"—a term applied to the Muslims, not the British. King plays the protector when he saves the General's daughter from abduction, and he leads "the forces that would defend India against tyrants."

Nested within this colonialist framework is a subplot about King's struggle with British racism. Films about mixed-race characters were very common in the

1950s, and here the device served two purposes. By making King part white—and by casting the handsome Power to play him—the film encouraged Western viewers to identify and sympathize with him, and though it was a concession to Western ethnocentrism, this choice helped viewers rethink their racism. The second purpose was that King's ability to pass for white leads unsuspecting Britons to make racist comments in his presence. When Lieutenant Heath (John Justin) questions the natives' loyalty, King asks, "What about the natives in British uniform, Mr. Heath?" Unaware that King is half-Indian, Heath replies, "They're just better dressed. Between ourselves, a native doesn't change color when he joins up." Later, when Heath learns King is a "chee-chee," he moves out of the barracks. The film uses these situations to condemn racism and to dramatize King's pain, though he bears it stoically. Zanuck's reluctance to offend the British—owing to overseas box-office considerations as well as politeness toward friends—led the film to soften its indictment of British racism. It explains that when King's parents married, the Muslim and British sides of the family *both* disowned them, and it also follows a common pattern in associating racism with the lower ranks; the General, representing official British institutions, chides his subordinates for their attitudes. And when the General tells his daughter Susan (Terry Moore) why King was barred from an officers' ball—because "this is India and things don't change overnight"—the decision to say "India" rather than "the British army" spared British feelings and suggested that racism was only a problem in the colonies.

The film nonetheless takes polite aim at racism, and when Susan falls in love with King, her father's objections to their marriage expose the limits of his liberalism. The film also shows a long interracial kiss—though the actors were both white—and unlike many interracial-couple films, this one makes neither of the lovers pay for their transgression by dying. Susan also makes an impassioned speech urging King to defy society's prejudices and stand firm as his parents had done. The result is an odd mixture: a colonialist film with an antiracist streak of considerable vigor for its time—even if it takes on racism toward a half-caste officer rather than toward ordinary Indians. A text as hybrid as its protagonist, it resembles *Captain from Castile* in that progressive material appears alongside typically colonialist elements. The only real connection between the film's antiracism and King's heroic defense of the Raj comes in Susan's charge of hypocrisy in the British army: "You mean he's allowed to die for the Queen but a birthday party's out of bounds?" Perhaps *King of the Khyber Rifles* did help whites feel superior, but its critique of white racial arrogance undermined that function. The decision to highlight the heroism of a mixed-race character—and of the Muslim sepoys who win the climactic battle with no help from white troops—distinguishes this film from interwar productions, and the uneasy coexistence of regressive and progressive themes typifies 1950s efforts to update the empire film.

Ads for *King of the Khyber Rifles* ignored the progressive elements, showing Power on horseback with sword raised, against a background of elephants, thundering cavalry, and an inset of Power kissing Terry Moore. With the words "CinemaScope" in letters as large as the film's title ("you see it without special glasses!"), the posters were selling the new process more than the story. The ads also promised plenty of exotic material to fill the giant screen, assuring viewers that "CinemaScope engulfs you in the vivid Bazaars of Peshawar, the tumultuous Night of the Long Knives when Kurram Khan led his fanatic Afridi horsemen against the Khyber Rifles!"[33] Given all this sound and fury, the film's performance was mildly disappointing, ranking number thirty-four for the year.[34] Of thirty-four American reviews examined, twenty were positive (59 percent), eight negative, and six mixed, but many of the positive reviews were lukewarm and recommended the film for its impressive visuals and colorful action.[35] Nine reviews found the film old-fashioned: the *Washington Post* called it "old, flat wine in a shiny new bottle"; the *Christian Science Monitor* spoke of a "romantic retreat into the imperialistic past"; and the *Los Angeles Examiner* liked this "oldie" about the British Empire in India but added, "Dead, dead days they certainly are, as utterly lost as the dodo bird."[36] Nearly every review commented on the racial-prejudice theme, which led *America* to note that "Hollywood has begun to harbor reservations about the virtues of British imperialism." Edwin Schallert of the *Los Angeles Times* welcomed the prejudice theme as "the better part of the production," without which the film would have been "an intolerable bore." While welcoming this new twist, several critics used euphemisms for racism, calling it "snobbery" or "narrow-mindedness," and three reviews praised both King and the film for handling the theme with "commendable restraint."[37] Others, however, found the combination of themes jarring. The *Christian Science Monitor* felt that the film "makes no particular sense even on its own antique terms," and *Commonweal* added that King's interest in Susan "is not too clear. But neither is anything else in the picture."

British critics were even less impressed, with four of twenty reviews (20 percent) praising the film, ten panning it, and six giving mixed verdicts.[38] Even those who liked it found it old-fashioned, including the *Evening Standard*, which said it took place "when chaps were pukka sahibs and Nehru was never thought of." Roy Nash of the *Star* liked "the Kiplingesque heroics to bagpipe music, the punkah wallahs and the dancing girls, the Union Jack fluttering bravely over a lonely outpost of the Empire," and *Kinematograph Weekly* enjoyed the "compelling nostalgic sentiment." But while these reviews support the notion of Westerners yearning for the good old days of empire, most simply sneered or laughed. Derek Granger of the *Financial Times* wrote, "This is the kind of thing which might have entranced me at the age of nine," and the *London Times* scoffed that Power "saves India for the British Empire much as little Miss Shirley Temple once saved it in the dear dead days of long ago." Although the *Times* called it "a left-handed slap on the back for the British," few others seemed offended. Most of the complaints concerned the dated style and topic, as well as the American accents and Guy Rolfe's brownface makeup. No one, in short, really took the film seriously.

In France, where *Capitaine King* sold a respectable 2,381,943 tickets in July 1954—shortly after France's debacle at Dien Bien Phu—many critics either skipped the film altogether or gave it perfunctory notices.[39] A few critics liked it, praising the inclusion of the mixed-race Captain, but *Le Monde* called it "imagerie d'Epinal" (simplistic patriotic imagery) and wrote sarcastically of the racial problem being solved "with touching simplicity." *Combat* spoke of Britain's "army of occupation" and said it "no longer believed" in such films. In sum, few reviews bear out the image of westerners hungry for a reaffirmation of white supremacy or a vindication of their imperial deeds, as critics mostly viewed the film as a quaint, dated adventure fantasy with a modern subplot awkwardly grafted onto it.

Over the next few years, Hollywood made several films addressing Indian decolonization directly (see chapter 4), but in 1959 Rank tried one last time to recover the magic of the old Raj films with *North West Frontier* (U.S. title: *Flame over India*). The film's resemblance to American westerns was no accident, for it was based on a story by American writers Will Price and Patrick Ford (son of John Ford) and a script by longtime Ford collaborator Frank S. Nugent (*Fort Apache, She Wore a Yellow Ribbon, The Searchers*). Directed by Britain's J. Lee Thompson, who went on to make thrillers and action films in Hollywood, this tale set in 1905 concerns British efforts to extricate a six-year old Hindu prince from a fort besieged by Muslim rebels. Captain Scott (Kenneth More) plays the action hero and protector of a boy crucial to Britain's indirect rule through Hindu princes. After spiriting the boy out of the fort, a motley array of colorful characters journeys by rail through rebel territory—inviting unflattering comparisons to Ford's *Stagecoach*. Escorting the boy are Captain Scott; the train's engineer, Gupta (I. S. Johar); the headstrong American Catherine Wyatt (Lauren Bacall); the governor's wife, Lady Wyndham (Ursula Jeans); an amoral British arms dealer, Peters (Eugene Deckers); and a shifty, annoying journalist, Van Leyden (Herbert Lom). Escaping seemingly hopeless predicaments with feats of derring-do, Captain Scott and the others learn that Van Leyden is a half-Indian Muslim and a rebel sympathizer set on murdering the Hindu prince. Van Leyden finally bites the dust when, during a struggle with Captain Scott, Mrs. Wyatt shoots him, saving Captain Scott and the Hindu boy.

A thoroughly old-fashioned adventure film, *North West Frontier*'s conventions include the loyal, grinning Indian engineer reminiscent of Gunga Din; the faceless, fanatic Muslim rebels whose motives remain a mystery; and the heroic white protector who saves the Raj's helpless subjects with his courage, leadership, and quick thinking. It justifies British rule by depicting bitter communal hatreds, most strikingly when the party discovers a train full of Hindus massacred by Muslims, accompanied by the grisly sound of flies and shots of impatient vultures. Given that the film appeared in 1959, a device that had underlined the need for Britain's continued presence in India now seemed anachronistic, but perhaps diehard colonialists who had opposed Britain's withdrawal in 1947 felt vindicated by scenes that brought to mind the horrific Hindu-Muslim violence that followed independence. Indeed the film seems to address current tensions as it pleads for tolerance. A voice-over laments that India's people killed each other "because they worship God by different names," and Gupta tells the Captain, "Indian to kill Indian, not very good. . . . If other man has other religion, why should Gupta mind, Sahib?" Despite his embarrassing obsequiousness and his butchering of the English language—played for laughs—Gupta proves competent and resourceful under pressure, perhaps suggesting that independent India will be all right after all. Another bit of presentism appears in relations between the American Mrs. Wyatt and the British, symbolizing postwar Anglo-American collaboration in controlling the third world. The British characters sometimes resent Mrs. Wyatt's unsolicited advice on imperial affairs, while Mrs. Wyatt, like leaders in Washington, feels frustrated over British management of imperial affairs. "The British," she declares, "never seem to do anything until they have had a cup of tea, by which time it's too late," but like Washington shoring up Europe's empires out of Cold War concerns, she comes to the Captain's rescue when he needs it most. Wyatt and the Captain even develop their own "special relationship" by the film's end, when they march off arm in arm to martial music. If some Britons were still sore at Washington over Suez, the filmmakers were having none of it.

The film's presentism produced a few anachronisms. Van Leyden's plea "for a country that will be all Muslim" is, in 1905, rather ahead of historical demands for the creation of Pakistan, and his claim to sympathize with "small minorities fighting the aggression of big nations" sounds curiously like a statement of the 1950s. And although the film gives Van Leyden several anticolonialist lines, it hardly endorses his viewpoint. He is, after all, the film's villain and is thoroughly unlikable from the moment when he first barges into a room uninvited and refuses to leave. The film sympathizes instead with those who answer his anti-British quips, including Lady Wyndham, who tells him, "Half the world mocks us, and half the world is only civilized because we have made it so."

British critics divided evenly over *North West Frontier*, with eight positive, seven negative, and two mixed reviews.[40] Those who liked it qualified their praise, with the *Spectator* writing that it "stays on the schoolboy level" and the *Evening Standard* calling it "a well-made two hours of bang-bang adventure on the unashamedly unsophisticated level of a Boy's Own story." Though he liked this "film without any Message," Jympson Harman of the *Evening News* turned sarcastic, declaring, "I raise my white pith helmet and call 'Three Huzzahs' for 'North West Frontier' and let's all be boys and girls again at the pictures." Less indulgent were the left-wing papers. Derek Hill of the *Tribune* called it "appalling" and wrote, "Appearing at this time it can only be interpreted as a defence—and an encouragement of—the Suez mentality." Under the headline, "Ra-ra for the jolly Empire Builders!" the *Daily Worker*'s Nina Hibbin complained that it "has the impudence to discuss one of the worst periods of Colonial repression in terms of a game of 'pukka sahibs and Indians,'" and she called it "an absolutely flabbergasting burst of bare-faced jingoism." Van Leyden, she added, "seems to be talking sense," but "he turns out to be a fanatical Moslem with a machine-gun." Disdain for the film's colonialism was not limited to the left-wing papers. Dilys Powell of the *Sunday Times* said she could imagine the Captain saying, "There seems to be a spot of bother among the lesser breeds," and David Robinson of the *Financial Times* charged that "it seems a bit late in the day to be reviving the Empire in this style" and that "the jingoism of this film would have been reactionary even in 1905." Robinson also noted Van Leyden's anticolonialism but observed that "the only character who voices a few fairly liberal ideas on Indian nationalism . . . is chucked off the top of the train." He also quoted Kipling's "Gunga Din" in questioning the depiction of Gupta ("for all 'is dirty 'ide 'e was white, clear white inside"), and the *Monthly Film Bulletin* also disliked Gupta being "played for pidgin-English comedy." While most reviews found the film dated, the diehard-colonialist *Daily Telegraph* considered it too liberal. Objecting to Captain Scott's jokes and misgivings about soldiering, Campbell Dixon contended, "It's no use giving us another Bengal Lancer if you mock everything he stands for." Dixon lamented that "true-blue imperialism is out, of course, even if you temper its arrogance with the stoic virtues, and the sense of responsibility for the governed that so often accompanied it." His was the only review that took this position.

In the United States, the film did not make *Variety*'s box-office charts, but the critical reception was strongly positive (seventeen positive, three negative, and one mixed).[41] As in Britain, those who liked it praised it as exciting, if old-fashioned, adventure. *Time* snickered that it was "full of assorted jaws of death, nicks of time, hair's breadths, fell swoops, stiff upper lips, white man's burdens and whys not to reason." The *Boston Globe* called it "a melodrama of the old beloved 'Beau Gest' [sic] pattern in which a small group of courageous white men fight off whole armies of natives," but it also noted that its "scenes of enmity between Moslems and Hindus" evoke "today's newspaper headlines." Similarly, the *Motion Picture Herald* wrote, "The film's design is topical as well as melodramatic," with "oppressed brown-skinned peoples incited to war against each other and their colonial landlords." But whereas the *Hollywood Reporter* called the film "an unabashed paean to Empire," which, "considering how things have gone since independence, may not be undeserved," Philip Scheuer of the *Los Angeles Times* disliked the "clichés and obvious 'imperialistic' philosophy." Most of the American reviews simply saw it as old-fashioned entertainment rather than a serious examination of colonialism, and the *Miami Herald* observed that "the picture doesn't probe deeply into the political aspects" of a tale "right out of the boyhood literature of Novelist G. A. Henty." So while a few American critics felt that modern ethnic violence made the film's colonialist nostalgia understandable, most critics saw it as a throwback to a bygone era, not a serious defense of empire.

The French critics generally liked the film for its spectacle and excitement, but not for what *L'Express* called "nostalgia for the time of Kipling" and what *Arts* called "a racist, colonialist, ultrareactionary spirit."[42] Very few reviews, in short, bear out the notion of Westerners yearning for imperial nostalgia or reassurance of their racial superiority. Why anyone even made such a film in 1959 remains worth asking, but it may simply reflect unimaginative filmmakers reusing hackneyed formulas that had once brought rich rewards.

The South Seas Cycle

A popular locale for colorful outdoor films in the 1950s was the South Seas, a region that had long seen intense competition among Western colonizers. If that history made the region a prime site for films about heroes of empire, the West's traditional perceptions of the region as a pristine paradise had also led many films to criticize Western interference with a simpler, more natural way of life. Indeed, going back at least to the Enlightenment, Western texts such as Diderot's *Supplement to the Voyage of Bougainville* had used imagined versions of the South Seas to critique undesirable aspects of Western civilization—including greed and puritanical attitudes about nudity and sex—and to cast the locals as noble savages.[43] Westerners often felt conflicted: they took pride in their massive advantages of knowledge, wealth, and power, but the evident attractions of the local life invited them to question their desires to amass power and wealth and impose their customs on others—in short, to pursue empire. Even before World War II, films such as *White Shadows in the South Seas* (1928) and *The Hurricane* (1937) had criticized Western behavior there, and the growth of anticolonialism after 1945 only fueled that tendency. At the same time, however, the Cold War gave the Pacific new importance, and colonial competition now increasingly gave way to U.S. domination and military expansion.

In September 1953, just after the Korean War, United Artists released *Return to Paradise*, an independent production based on a short story by James Michener.[44] Directing was Canadian-born Mark Robson, who had already made two dramas about veterans and would later make other colonial films—*The Inn of the Sixth Happiness* (1958) and *Lost Command* (1966). *Return to Paradise*, filmed in Western Samoa, starred Gary Cooper as Mr. Morgan, an American drifter who in the early 1930s washes ashore on a fictional island under the iron grip of Pastor Corbett (Barry Jones). This hellfire-and-brimstone missionary rules Matareva through a goon squad of club-wielding native "wardens," and in a voice-over, an islander named Rori recalls that when Morgan arrived, "We were a people without joy." Over shots of the wardens marching everyone into church in orderly columns, Rori adds that "we were forced to attend prayer" twice a day; over a shot of a warden smashing a homemade ukulele, he states that "the old songs, the dances we knew were forbidden"; and over images of fully-clothed women bathing, he laments that "our young women, who once were proud of their bodies were taught to be ashamed" and "the natural laws of love were made a crime." The imperious Pastor immediately orders Morgan off Matareva, telling him, "White men are not welcome on this island. They corrupt the morals and people." But Morgan has nowhere to go and he tells Corbett, "I'm not taking orders from any two-bit Mussolini.... You leave me alone and I'll leave you alone." Set upon by five of Corbett's wardens, Morgan fights them off in front of the assembled people, using a club that an old woman tosses him, and his victory inspires the locals to imagine their liberation. Rori's father Tonga (Chief Mamea Matatumua) and his friends tell Morgan, "We have been waiting for a man like you. Will you help us fight against the wardens?" Morgan replies, "I just want to be left alone.... Anybody pushes me around I'll fight, but I'm not getting dragged into your squabble."

The cynical Morgan thus embodies American isolationism, which had abated in the 1940s but which postwar American cultural elites feared would reemerge.[45]

The film alludes to a different colonial arena when Morgan tells Tonga why he minds his own business: his father was an "Irishman fighting for the cause" who "ended up in a Dublin gutter with his head bashed in." Predictably, Morgan transforms as he reluctantly agrees to help the Matarevans resist tyranny. This conflict between Pastor Corbett and Morgan actually involves two white protectors—one who defends the islanders from sin and Western influences other than Christianity, and one who protects them from the overbearing, unwanted protector. Corbett sounds British (as was actor Barry Jones), and in pitting the American against him, it summons American resentment of European colonialism. At first the film is surprisingly hostile to missionaries—Morgan even shoots out the windows of the church after Corbett destroys his hut—but anyone aware of the Production Code and the Legion of Decency could have predicted a resolution less offensive to religious viewers. The film also tested Hollywood's boundaries in a subplot involving a rebellious young woman, Maeva (Roberta Haynes), who pursues the loner Morgan and eventually bears his child out of wedlock. It even builds sympathy for anticolonialist revolutions in a striking scene of the islanders, emboldened by Morgan's defiance of the wardens, staging a successful revolt that topples the Pastor's tyranny.

This subversive tone then gives way as the film changes direction and shows the emotionally aloof Morgan gradually accepting the affections of the natives, whose gratitude for their liberation turns into hero worship. The film personalizes his relationship with the locals first through Maeva, whom he is urged to love, but whom he refuses to marry out of distaste for commitment. Pastor Corbett, who mellows noticeably after his fall from power and who becomes a voice of wisdom, urges Morgan to act responsibly and marry Maeva. After she dies in childbirth, the film explores Morgan's relationship with his daughter Turia (Moira MacDonald), whom he abandons when he leaves the island. Returning (to paradise) years later, after the outbreak of World War II, Morgan meets Turia, now a rebellious teen; he keeps her at arm's length, then learns to embrace his obligations when amorous American GIs who have crash landed on Matareva romance her, awakening his paternal instincts. (The GIs are also protectors, defending the island from the Japanese.) In a sentimental climax, Morgan agrees to stay in Matareva and accept his paternal duties. The film thus urges Americans to overcome their isolationism, shoulder their obligations to protect the peoples of the Pacific, form emotional bonds with them, and reap the rewards of affection and gratitude.

The white hero in the South Seas returned in *His Majesty O'Keefe* (1954), an independent production from Burt Lancaster and Harold Hecht, directed by

Byron Haskin. Based on a 1950 book about an actual Irish American sea captain who made a fortune in Micronesia in the late nineteenth century, this colorful adventure tale filmed in Fiji starred Lancaster as David O'Keefe. A fortune-hunting captain thrown overboard by his mutinous Chinese crew, O'Keefe washes ashore on Yap, where Tetens (Andre Morrell), the agent of a German trading company, welcomes him. Tetens proves skeptical when O'Keefe speaks of harvesting the plentiful coconuts to make copra, much prized then as a source of coconut oil. The problem, as O'Keefe learns, is not the hostility of the local chief, Bugulroo (Archie Savage), whom O'Keefe bests in hand-to-hand combat, but rather the islanders' unwillingness to work. Images of lazy natives recall earlier colonialist works, which scholars have questioned.[46] Other conventions include images of a tropical island paradise; the dangerous, spear-wielding followers of the hostile Bugulroo; the friendly followers of the more welcoming Inifels (Lloyd Berrell) and his medicine man Fatumak (Abraham Sofaer); and the plentiful dancing and drumming. Rounding out the stock of stereotypes is the islanders' superstitious fixation on collecting *fei*, a stone they quarry on another island then carve into giant sacred rings. Contrasting with the lazy, superstitious natives is the robust, virile, enterprising O'Keefe, and not even a comely native girl, Kakofel, can distract him from building a copra empire.[47] After acquiring a ship in Hong Kong, O'Keefe figures out how to make the islanders work: he strikes a bargain with them, using his dynamite and ship to help them quarry and transport *fei* in return for their labor. Along the way, he meets and marries Dalabo (Joan Rice), the beautiful daughter of an English father and a mother from the islands. Leading loyal Yapese fighters, O'Keefe rescues islanders captured and enslaved by the American pirate and blackbirder Bully Hayes and the grateful Yapese reward their protector by proclaiming him king. Now running a thriving business, O'Keefe fends off both the hostile Bugulroo and various European rivals, so again one form of colonialism justifies another.

As this tale of empire building unfolds, however, it reveals misgivings about the whole idea. In posing ethical questions about O'Keefe's rise to power, it follows a Western literary tradition from Rudyard Kipling's "The Man Who Would Be King" to Conrad's *Heart of Darkness* and *Lord Jim* and Eugene O'Neill's *Emperor Jones*. Its denunciation of the greedy slaver Hayes and the equally greedy German colonialists recalls many films about whites protecting helpless South Sea islanders from cruel Western exploiters. It even begins to critique O'Keefe himself and his imperial dreams when Tetens, the grandson of a German philosopher who opposed worldly materialism, asks him why he risks his life in search of copra: "What are you trying to prove? Money? Power? This driving ambition to reach the top?" His island-raised wife also asks why copra is so important, and his reply seems designed to be unconvincing: "Men will kill to get it. Steal. Drive other men to their deaths. It's so important that nations will go to war with each other to get their share. Or more than their share." When Dalabo asks him what he will do with all his money, he has no reply, and in a later voice-over, she states: "I had become part of the O'Keefe legend. But was there really a place for me in it? Fame. Copra. Dreams of empire." When O'Keefe's relentless quest for wealth gets his friend Tetens killed, Dalabo, the voice of conscience, remarks sardonically that this should not stop His Majesty O'Keefe. As he sits disconsolate before his empty throne, he asks his friend and confidant Fatumak, "Where did I go wrong?" The medicine man replies, "The whale that swallows the dolphin chokes and dies, but the whale who lives without greed is king of the sea."

His eyes now open, O'Keefe decides to abdicate and invite Bugulroo to return and reunite the people. O'Keefe announces that Bugulroo was right all along—only *fei* gathered in the old way has any value—and he says he will give himself up to the Germans, who seek his arrest for the death of a German officer. But when the Germans return to reoccupy Yap and arrest O'Keefe, Bugulroo and his men come to O'Keefe's rescue—telling the Germans he is still their king. O'Keefe's reward for abandoning his dreams of empire is thus the gratitude of even the most hostile islanders—as well as a kiss from his happy, beautiful, mixed-race wife.

His Majesty O'Keefe follows the tradition of noble savage myths, with idyllic South Sea islands serving as a platform for Western self-criticism. In this case it was not Christianity and repressive Western sexual inhibitions the film questioned, but rather the West's heartless search for material wealth and power over others, and this old theme gained new relevance in the context of decolonization. Bugulroo, whose resistance to O'Keefe's modernizing rule at first makes him look like the usual empire-film villain, turns out to be a perfectly justified leader of resistance to colonialism, and by making audiences reconsider Bugulroo's supposed villainy, the film invites Western audiences to rethink their perceptions of demonized leaders of anticolonialist resistance movements.

Certain self-serving American messages nonetheless undermine the film's anticolonialism. Its critique of European colonialism erected an easy target, as it used domineering Germans with heavy accents to represent that force. A careful viewer of the convoluted ending might also have noticed that while Bugulroo returns as *chief*, he tells the Germans that O'Keefe remains their *king*. Of course O'Keefe has ceded to Bugulroo the right to administer Yap in his traditional way, but O'Keefe is staying on, and when the Germans threaten to return, O'Keefe, now a protector rather than an exploiter, replies, "We'll be waiting." The film, in short, sketches out a scenario replayed repeatedly in the postwar world, as the Americans, on the pretext of protecting vulnerable peoples, set themselves up as indirect rulers of former European colonies. It thus expresses American anti-imperialist imperialism, with O'Keefe enjoying the gratitude and affection of the people of a client state. And who knows? There could even be some copra in it for O'Keefe after all.

The film did moderate business, finishing in the number forty-four slot for 1954.[48] As with other films that nested anticolonialist material in conventional colonialist frameworks, the ads for this film ignored its anticolonialism. Most featured a bare-chested Lancaster kissing Joan Rice, against the backdrop of smaller images of spear-wielding islanders, with captions such as "The Fiery Love Story of the lost island trader from Savannah, Georgia who became ruler of 10,000 barbarous warriors!" Another showed Bugulroo in a loincloth and a large Afro flying through the air clutching a spear, with the caption "Sa Bula! Sa Bula! The White Man is Chief!" even though a memo in the publicity files said not to use that line.[49] Seventeen of thirty reviews praised the film (57 percent), while seven disliked it and six were equivocal, but everyone took it as light entertainment.[50] Like the ads, roughly half the reviews missed the critique of O'Keefe's imperialist folly.[51] The *Chicago Tribune* gave a typical misreading when it wrote that the film was about O'Keefe's "efforts to make the superstitious natives work for him." But while some critics seem to have left midway through the film, others at least got the noble savage theme, as *Time* noted that "the natives were happy until the white man came," and the *Boston Herald*'s Elinor Hughes observed that "the natives, happy, healthy and well fed, have no desire to work."

Among those who did get the film's critique of Western exploitation, *America*'s Moira Walsh noted "its ambivalent views on South Seas exploitation" as it sides with O'Keefe but "paint[s] a picture of the commercial methods of the day that is gruesome enough to underline the wisdom behind the natives' reluctance to work." Perhaps confused that the film criticized its hero, she called it "difficult to get an idea of what the script writer had in mind." Most who grasped the film's denunciation of Western encroachment focused on O'Keefe's rivals. *Film Daily* pointed out that "the Germans held control of the islands to exploit them for their copra wealth," and Edwin Schallert of the *Los Angeles Times* was pleased to see O'Keefe "turning against the exploiters from foreign countries and supporting ultimately native traditions." A few critics understood that the picture criticized O'Keefe, including the *San Francisco Chronicle*, which wrote that he "realized the evil of his greed," and *Cue*, which observed that he "learns the hard way that a mania for money can lead to murder, and true love blossoms best where peace and happiness—not business—prevail." A handful of critics even saw the critique not only of greed but also of O'Keefe's imperialist treatment of the Yapese. *Time* charged that O'Keefe "blackmails the poor natives into picking coconuts," while the *St. Louis Post-Dispatch* observed that "he bedevils the poor natives," and the *Denver Post* wrote that O'Keefe shows "the sort of megalomania that brought about the downfall of Napoleon, Mussolini, the Czar, Charles I and Humpty Dumpty." Suggesting why many critics misread the film, the *Post-Dispatch* noted that it "is told in terms of violence and action rather than of ideas," so that "what could have been a fine philosophical drama in an exotic setting, worthy of a Joseph Conrad, turns into merely a fairly diverting adventure romance."

British critics were even less perceptive than their American counterparts. Only three of thirteen British critics liked the film, and the *Evening Standard* made a typical comment in dismissing it as a "highly-coloured, old-fashioned picture."[52] Even the *Daily Worker* completely missed the anticolonialist theme— it denounced O'Keefe's exploitation of the natives without realizing that the film made that very point—and it concluded that it was "on the children's level." In France, where it sold just over 1.6 million tickets, few papers reviewed it, but while some dismissed it as a mindless adventure tale, *Le Figaro* praised it, saying, "One thinks of Conrad's novels," and *Paris-Presse*'s Robert Chazal argued that "these adventures, though simple, are no less exciting and contain a sort of philosophy, as Jean-Jacques Rousseau would say if he were a film critic."[53] So while a few American, British, and French critics understood the film's point, most did not, suggesting the difficulties postwar empire films faced in making serious points about colonialism. *His Majesty O'Keefe* demonstrated that as postwar filmmakers tried to explore and even critique colonialism, they had to overcome not only the constraints of a genre developed to defend colonialism but also the expectations of critics and audiences accustomed to that genre's conventions.

The early stages of Britain's colonization of New Zealand provided the setting for *The Seekers*, a relatively high-budget 1954 Rank film.[54] Directed by Ken Annakin in a lurid visual style, with intense colors accenting the film's exoticism, it tells the tale of English seaman Philip Wayne (Jack Hawkins), who comes ashore to explore with his Irish pal Paddy Clarke (Noel Purcell). *The Seekers* is both a trailblazer film, taking place very early in Britain's colonization of New Zealand, and a white-protector film. Its pairing of first-time visitor Philip with the whaler Paddy, a veteran of the area who speaks the Maori language, allows the viewer to experience the amazement of first contact through Philip while also having Paddy, the man who know Maoris, available to translate and explain what would otherwise be bewildering. After ignoring Paddy's advice to stay out of a cave and stumbling into a sacred burial site, Philip is captured by alarming-looking warriors with facial tattoos, brought to a village, and given a trial by ordeal—only to be spared at the last moment by the humane chief, Hongi Tepe (Inia Te Wiata, known to Britons as an opera singer). The Maoris, they learn, are tired of wars, and the chief's father prophesizes that Philip will return and put an end to the killing; he also gives Philip a plot of land. Philip then returns to England to marry his fiancée, Marion (Glynnis Johns), but he is arrested for unknowingly smuggling some human heads for the ship's captain, and after a nightmarish trial and the payment of a hefty fine, the shamed Philip flees England with Marion to start a new life in New Zealand.

The rest of the film focuses on the settler experience, an important topic for audiences in countries such as New Zealand as well as for countless Britons who knew emigrants. In recent debates over colonialism's impact on ordinary Britons' lives, there is wide agreement that emigration touched many, and a British critic noted in 1954 that "Britons and Europeans of all nations are leaving their homes every week for those same shores."[55] The few Americans who saw the film could also relate to a tale recalling America's pioneer mythology. Shots of settlers clearing and fencing the land, building log cabins, and farming and herding evoke countless westerns, while the contrast between virgin territory and an Old World filled with corrupt sea captains and tyrannical judges also sounds a familiar American theme. Evoking early Edenic descriptions of the New World, *The Seekers* sounds biblical themes, from an opening narration recounting Maori creation myths over shots of natural beauty, to later scenes in which Marion reads Hongi Tepe verses from the Genesis creation tale. Temptation also appears in this garden in the form of Moana (Laya Raki, of German and Javanese descent), Hongi Tepe's sexually aggressive wife, who leads Philip to betray both his own wife and his new Maori friend. As in many films set in the colonies—especially in the Pacific—the enchanting environment and supposedly libertine sexuality of the indigenous women present moral dangers even greater than any physical ones.[56]

Also recalling westerns are the settlers' relations with the Maoris. There are good natives—the chief and his followers, who yearn for peace, welcome the whites, offer them land, study Christianity, and help the settlers in a climactic battle—and bad—warlike Maoris who oppose Hongi Tepe and wish to expel the settlers. The film emphasizes Maori savagery with frightening close-ups of fierce warriors' tattooed faces, gruesome shots of preserved heads, and eerie chanting accompanying their exoticized rituals and dances. The film also features both a female civilizer—Marion teaches the Maoris Christian doctrine and morality—and a white protector, Philip. This settler-hero tries to keep the Maoris ignorant of firearms (in reality Maoris had muskets by this time), and he defends them from the exploitative head-trafficking Captain.[57] He also protects the Maoris from each other as he tries to broker peace among warring tribes. As in Spain's conquest of Mexico, superstition, in this case a prophecy of a peacemaker coming "on two legs," undermines resistance to colonization. The film shows the Maoris as troubled *before* whites arrived and thus disposed to accept new ways. In doing so, it ignores the prior history of white contact with the Maoris, for early European visitors, in bringing both the potato—which caused a population explosion—and the musket—which drastically raised the death toll in wars—actually helped create the miseries of war that the film shows the settlers resolving.[58] The film also puts a gloss on the whites' acquisition of land: it suggests that they received it as a gift from grateful Maoris and says nothing of other ways they acquired land.[59] Philip protects his fellow settlers, too, and as he rescues a foolish young lad who inadvertently shot a Maori's dog and then the Maori himself, Philip asserts the colonial doctrine of extraterritoriality, insisting that Britons must try Britons. When hostile Maoris, fed up with both the murder and the newcomers' growing numbers, unite and prepare to attack the settlement, Philip organizes the settlers' defenses. The film resolves with a climactic battle and the heroic sacrifice of all the settlers but the Waynes' baby, as both Philip and Marion die heroic deaths. The film offers a consoling hint of racial reconciliation as Hongi Tepe finds and adopts the white baby—followed by a final shot of more settlers arriving to carry on the martyrs' work.

Westerners viewing *The Seekers* today may be tempted to root for the Maoris as they attack the settlement, or may at least sympathize when Awarua exclaims, "You take the Maori's life. You take his land. Soon the Maori will be no more. Go away from here!" The film, however, made Awarua its villain, and though it humanized Hongi Tepe and acknowledged the settlers' human weaknesses, it did not really critique British colonialism. John Brodie, the New Zealand–born author of the novel, said he intended it to highlight his country's good racial relations, where "two races now live side by side, more happily and successfully than anywhere else in the world."[60] An opening title in some prints stated the film's liberal-colonialist intentions: "May our story serve as a tribute to the pioneers who transformed a wilderness into a fair and peaceful land—two races but one people."[61] Among those who welcomed this paean to settler colonialism, Britain's *Kinematograph Weekly* made the settlers sound like liberators, writing that they "sacrifice their lives to establish a British colony in Maori-occupied New Zealand,"

and it praised a film that "deals in a forthright manner with the hazards of Empire building . . . without whitewashing the natives or blackening the immigrants."[62] *To-Day's Cinema News* praised the film's "compelling atmosphere" full of "exotic pagan ritual," "tribal warfare," and a "topical message" of racial reconciliation.[63] Yet nine of eleven reviews panned the film as melodramatic and an unconvincing imitation of a western.[64] The *Guardian* complained that "when British film-makers take this imperialist path they do so with none of Hollywood's self-assurance," and it wrote that this film had "much of the California silliness but none of its grandeur."

The notion of the South Seas as an Eden endangered by Westerners reappeared in *Pearl of the South Pacific* (1955), an independent production from director Alan Dwan. Inverting the structure of *Return to Paradise*, in which a hard-bitten drifter protected the islanders and their way of life from a tyrannical missionary, this Jesse Lasky, Jr. script has Tuan Michael (Basil Ruysdael), an elderly white man reminiscent of an Old Testament patriarch, serving as the island's high priest and heroic protector from corrupting Western influence. Three unscrupulous white adventurers, two men and a woman, come seeking black pearls, and the woman, Rita (Virginia Mayo), poses as a missionary to win the islanders' confidence before making off with the loot. Tuan Michael ("tuan" is a Malay honorific) forbids the three to come ashore, and when Rita claims she brings the benefits of Christianity and civilization, Michael replies, "I know what . . . the blessings of civilization have brought to the other islands: sickness, drunkenness, greed, lust." To Rita's complaint about idol worship and her charge that "it's a sin to keep the savages in darkness," Michael insists, "My people are not savages, Miss Delaine. They're simple and honest, more so than most people I knew in the civilized world. . . . If the people are kind and decent, what does it matter what they name their God?" The film clearly sympathizes with Michael, who rules with the natives' consent, and it also embraces his paternalistic authority over the naive and vulnerable natives, including his own mixed-race son, who yearns to see the lights of Paris. A striking shot of native oarsmen paddling while Michael sits imperiously on a thronelike chair as he goes out to tell the unwelcome visitors not to come ashore offers a perfect visual representation of colonialism. Here, in short, is another example of anticolonialist themes in a liberal-colonialist film.

The films in this chapter all managed to ignore the current global phenomenon of decolonization, mostly by setting the action in the past, but while some told remarkably old-fashioned tales about heroes of empire discovering and conquering distant lands, others, particularly the white-protector films, injected new perspectives that reflected changing political realities. Even some of the trailblazer films included liberal elements, most notably Coatl's speech in *Captain from Castile*, asking how Europeans would like being colonized, Townsend Harris's plea for friendship with Japan, and Allan Quatermain's affection for and defense of the Africans and their cultures. Many trailblazers were protectors as well, as Harris saves the people of Shimoda from cholera, and Adamson in *Killers of Kilimanjaro* saves Africans from Arab slave-traders. The white-protector films are even more self-flattering, using that device to justify colonization and, in the case of the British films set in postwar Africa, to argue for the continued presence of the colonizer. The attempt to adapt the empire film to a new era led to some awkward juxtapositions and incoherent results, but even the films that went furthest in criticizing Western colonialism—*His Majesty O'Keefe*, *Return to Paradise*, and *Pearl of the South Pacific*—nonetheless made heroes of white protectors, establishing a basis for a Western presence. Nearly all of these films, in short, exemplified not anticolonialism, but rather the same kind of liberal colonialism seen in films about civilizing women.

CHAPTER THREE

Westerns

Many Americans, seeing themselves as an anticolonial nation, remain unaccustomed to thinking of their historical relationship with the American Indians as colonialist. The notion of American colonialism is certainly not news to historians, but many Americans have resisted it because their national identity was formed in opposition to British colonial rule and because colonialism seems incompatible with the concept of liberty that is so central to America's political identity.[1] Those who have noticed similarities between westerns about American Indians and empire films set elsewhere have usually stopped at observing similarities of cinematic genre and style without really seeing the unity of the history depicted. If the colonization of the American Indians is undeniably part of the history of Western colonialism, certain specificities of the North American experience stand out nonetheless. Above all, North America's colonizers never went home, so decolonization has distinct meanings in a settler colony such as the United States.

Discussing the relationship between colonizer and colonized in the United States presents certain problems of terminology. To speak of the colonizers as European or white is to ignore the role that African Americans, Asian Americans, and others played in this history, but white people dominated the multiethnic society that carried out this colonization.[2] To call the colonizers Americans may raise objections from others in the Western Hemisphere as well as from the continent's first inhabitants, even if they never thought of themselves as Americans before Europeans arrived. There is, however, no better term for the people of the United States than *Americans*. Indians today, of course, *are* Americans, as a result of a combination of coercive acculturation and assimilation, miscegenation, and the granting of citizenship. There are also drawbacks to terms such as

Indians or *American Indians*, but because so many American Indians use these convenient and familiar terms, this book will as well.

Films about the historical relationship between Americans and Indians have often emphasized warfare and stark differences between the two peoples. Historians, sharing the regret, disgust, and guilt that many Americans now feel about this history, have pondered whether some more equitable form of coexistence might have been possible, but for those Indians who followed migratory herds or raided farmers and herders—and who thus required vast stretches of territory—peaceful coexistence with ever-increasing numbers of white settlers was unlikely.[3] The growing imbalances of population and power gave whites little interest in compromising with peoples they considered obstacles to progress, and in light of significant differences in prevailing mentalities and ways of life, it is hard to imagine the two sides coexisting equally and peacefully.[4] None of this gave Europeans a right to seize the continent, but for historians, explaining the actions of the people of the past implies considering what realistic alternatives they did or did not have.

In this history of conflict, it is perhaps ironic that there were striking similarities between Euro-Americans and at least some of the Indian peoples. Those Indian societies that attracted the most attention from their conquerors—such as the Sioux, Comanche, Apache, and Cheyenne—could be warlike, violent, and expansionist, honoring military prowess while also valuing freedom and rejecting hereditary monarchy or dictatorship.[5] These similarities with aspects of Euro-American culture help explain why admiration has long been part of Americans' complex set of feelings about Indians, along with fear, hatred, and condescension. Perceptions of Indians as courageous defenders of their freedom help explain whites' inclination to make Indians into positive symbols, for example, on coins and stamps.[6] For many years, whites have proudly claimed partial descent from Indians (even falsely), "played Indians," and named sports teams after Indians— all of which it would be hard to imagine them doing with any other group they colonized.[7] These practices may seem condescending, insulting, antiquated, and hypocritical given how Euro-Americans actually treated Indians, but they suggest important things about whites' diverse perceptions and feelings. And the staggering number of films Americans have made about Indians—vastly greater than about any other colonized people—also attests to an enduring fascination.

The colonizers' mixed feelings about Indians were reflected in policies as well. The history of those policies is too vast to cover here, but it bears noting that while some Americans, usually settlers, were bent on exterminating the Indians in fulfillment of America's "Manifest Destiny" of spreading Christian civilization from sea to sea, other Americans, mostly "back East," staunchly opposed extermination. Ongoing debates about whether Americans committed genocide founder on the well-known lack of consensus about that term's definition, but if one defines it as an intentional policy of exterminating an entire people, then some Americans, including many settlers and *some* military officers and soldiers, tried to carry it out—including in a series of notorious massacres—while other Americans opposed it vehemently.[8] Opponents of extermination included humanitarians and religious leaders, and while many who wished to civilize and Christianize the Indians wished to erase Indian *culture*—a policy some call *ethnocide* to distinguish it from genocide—their opposition to extermination succeeded in shaping U.S. government policy.[9] Forcible acculturation and the placing of Indians on reservations may be morally indefensible, but only under the broadest definition of genocide would these policies qualify.

Defenders of the Indians often believed they were fated to disappear anyway in the face of advancing civilization, if only by blending into white society, but the famous myth of the vanishing American is, after all, a myth, and the survival of the Indians themselves—indeed their more recent demographic revival—contradicts notions of genocide.[10] Nor did attempts to eradicate Indian culture or "Indianness" succeed, despite the severe damage done.[11] Crucial to the survival of Indian culture were the reservations, which overcame years of official neglect (a frequent topic in films) and the 1950s termination policy, which envisioned closing them and ending government support altogether.[12] However one defines genocide, it is crucial to note the sharp divisions among the colonizers that existed during the years that westerns cover—divisions between liberal and conservative forms of colonialism.

Indians in the White Imagination

In drawing on a heritage of traditional images of Indians in American popular culture, Hollywood films naturally reproduced the twin stereotypes of the noble and ignoble savage, which go back to Europeans' arrival in the Americas.[13] In this imagery, the noble savage is courageous, wise, stoic, honest, pure, hospitable, strong, attractive, and dignified, living a simple, unchanging life of freedom in harmony with nature. The ignoble savage is bloodthirsty, cruel, vengeful, deceitful, thieving, superstitious, and may be either shrewd and cunning or ignorant and stupid. Both images were always present, and although there have been times when one or the other prevailed, they have tended to coexist in every period and in individual minds.[14] Rarely have Euro-Americans depicted individual Indians as complex and nuanced combinations of positive and negative characteristics, and westerns, with their penchant for simplistic good guys and bad guys, have certainly followed this bipolar tradition. Many of the complexities and contradictions of U.S. Indian policy have flowed from this structure of perceptions, with notions of the bloodthirsty, ignoble savage fueling pleas for extermination and subjugation while belief in the noble savage has produced calls for gentler policies. While some envisioned the successful assimilation of noble savages, others, doubting that was possible, thought more in terms of their disappearance. A civilized savage, after all, would be an oxymoron, and going back at least to James Fenimore Cooper's *The Last of the Mohicans*, the vanishing-American myth involved romanticizing noble savages who had to give way, for better and worse, to the march of progress.

From the earliest silent films, notions of civilization, savagery, and progress stood at the heart of the western genre. Not all westerns featured Indians, of course, but countless westerns depicted a fundamental struggle between whites and Indians—usually the most warlike nations.[15] Most westerns involving Indians took place amid the so-called Indian Wars of the second half of the nineteenth century, a choice that suited the genre's emphasis on violent action, and the constant repetition of certain themes and plots indicates the genre's mythic functions in American culture.

One of Hollywood's common departures from reality was the depiction of Indian tactics. Like villains in other empire films, Hollywood Indians often used suicidal or foolish tactics, compounded by implausibly poor marksmanship.[16] Historians have pointed out that Indians did not make suicidal attacks on forts and large troop concentrations, preferring hit-and-run tactics to the sorts of major assaults seen in countless films.[17] Rather than fighting battles, government troops carried out long, futile marches looking for warriors, and the U.S. Army eventually turned to more effective, if less glorious, tactics: destroying food supplies and luring warriors by attacking villages filled mostly with women and children.[18] And whereas films often highlight Western superiority by showing the army using modern rifles against Indians with lances, tomahawks, and bows and arrows, Congress's stinginess often left soldiers with poorer armaments than their opponents had.[19] Most troops never even saw combat, and instead endured a miserable existence of poor rations, harsh winters and summers, loneliness, and boredom—dubious material for the Saturday matinee.[20] The number of warriors the army killed in combat remained surprisingly low, and historians conclude that although the army helped to defeat the Indians, that defeat owed more to disease, the destruction of herds and food supplies, the building of the railroads, and the flood of European immigration.[21]

Many analysts of the western depict it as an inherently racist, triumphalist, and right-wing genre glorifying the conquest of the Indians.[22] Others, without denying that westerns have often glorified and justified that conquest, have questioned the genre's immutability, noting varied images of Indians in the silent era and increasingly positive imagery during World War II, when the demands of national security called for both national unity and images of American tolerance and brotherhood.[23]

These debates over the western's immutability and inherent racism, triumphalism, and conservatism often focus on the postwar period, when the genre occupied an enormous amount of Hollywood's output. The wartime imperative to improve America's image on racial issues carried over into the postwar years, but scholars and critics disagree on the significance of the "pro-Indian" films of the 1950s; many scholars now dismiss the trend and argue that in an increasingly conservative postwar environment in Hollywood, westerns changed very little.[24] This chapter seeks to clarify matters by undertaking both quantitative and qualitative analysis of westerns involving Indians made from 1946 through 1959. Its primary sample is a list of the fifty-one dramas about Indians that made *Variety*'s annual box-office lists in these years, but it also discusses a few films of particular interest that did not make those lists. It addresses the meaning and value of terms such as *pro-Indian*, asking how these films treated violence, what sympathies they sought to enlist in battle scenes, whose points of view they took, how fully they developed Indian characters and explained their motives, and what messages they conveyed about race relations and the conquest of the West.

Westerns of the Late 1940s

If postwar Hollywood aimed to improve its depiction of racial minorities and promote more harmonious images of relations with the Indians, it seems that no one told Cecil B. DeMille. The conservative filmmaker's 1947 Technicolor epic *Unconquered* honored the spirit of the pioneers, and it is a perfect example of an anti-Indian picture. Its central conflict pits Chris Holden (Gary Cooper), a Virginia planter who yearns for open country and heads west in 1763, against a shifty trader, Garth (Howard Da Silva), who has built a fur-trading monopoly by conspiring with the Indians to keep settlers out of the Ohio Valley. Garth not only blocks the march of civilization, but also buys white bond slaves, sells muskets to Indians, and has an Indian wife, Hannah (Katherine DeMille, the director's daughter), whom he married because she is the daughter of the Seneca chief, Guyasuta (Boris Karloff). Riddled with clichés about Indians, *Unconquered* has no noble savages, and though Hannah, the Indian princess, sacrifices her life to save a white man, she does so only to exact revenge on her cheating husband. When not grunting and whooping, the Indian characters speak a plodding, monosyllabic English that makes them sound dim-witted, and they are easily dazzled by tricks Holden does with gunpowder and a compass. They are cowardly, fleeing at the approach of white troops, and treacherous, massacring a fort full of whites who foolishly accept their peace offer. Among the clichés, several whites utter variations on the phrase, "You've seen what they do to white women," and when Holden's pal kills an Indian, he says, "That's one good Injun." When some Seneca women see the film's female lead, Abby (Paulette Goddard), they paw at her hair and dress and steal her jewelry, and a later scene lumps the squaws together with animals by showing them and their dog fighting ferociously over her dress. The pioneers, of course, are honest, decent, and courageous, and a voice-over states that they came "to build a nation, even at the price of their own lives" and to "push ever forward the frontiers of man's freedom." When Holden and Abby find a settler family slaughtered by Indians, he comforts her by telling her the settlers "will keep coming," because they "are the New World—unconquered, unconquerable, because they're strong and free, because they have faith in themselves, and in God."

Lines such as this exemplify the film's Cold War presentism. DeMille was a member of the Motion Picture Alliance for the Preservation of American Ideals, which helped bring the House Committee on Un-American Activities (HUAC) to Hollywood, and so were cast members Gary Cooper and Ward Bond; Howard Da Silva, on the other hand, was later blacklisted. Familiar claims that Cold War westerns use "red men" to stand for Reds seem to fit *Unconquered*, as sneaky Indians hiding in the forest recall anxieties about clandestine communists in America. This reading has its limits, for once they become visible, these half-naked, dark-skinned savages are obviously Indians, unlike "crypto-communists," who might be one's neighbors, coworkers, or friends.[25] Moreover, Indians had no sophisticated political ideology or plans for global revolution. American critics were divided—ten of twenty-two praised the film (45 percent), while seven panned it and five gave it mixed reviews—and even those who liked it found it hokey and old-fashioned.[26] The closest anyone came to protesting the image of Indians was Kate Cameron of the *New York Daily News*, who wrote that "only an Indian, and one could hardly blame him, would fail to thrill to the events" shown.

A new image of Indians came from an unexpected source with John Ford's *Fort Apache* (1948), made for his own Argosy Pictures. Ford's *Stagecoach* (1939) and *Drums along the Mohawk* (1939) had peddled familiar stereotypes of bloodthirsty savages attacking whites for no apparent reason, while *My Darling Clem-*

entine (1946) had featured a drunken Indian causing trouble. This script, loosely based on a James Warner Bellah story, was the first by former *New York Times* film critic Frank S. Nugent, who later wrote more scripts for Ford. When Indians first appear during the credits in *Fort Apache*, the music turns dark and ominous, but the film quickly shifts to establishing the thoroughly unlikable character of Colonel Owen Thursday (Henry Fonda). Riding through the stunning beauty of Monument Valley, the humorless, self-important Thursday grumbles to his daughter Philadelphia (Shirley Temple) about being posted to the boondocks, and upon his arrival at Fort Apache, he casts a pall over an officers' ball by his mere presence and by refusing to shake the hand of an old acquaintance. The central conflict between the Colonel and Captain Kirby York (John Wayne) begins when Thursday dismisses the Apaches as "a few cowardly digger Indians," raising objections from York—the man who knows Indians. Thursday's ultimately fatal flaw, underestimating the Apaches, follows an old pattern in westerns, in which neophyte easterners and pompous commanders ignore the wisdom of experienced subordinates. The Colonel's arrogance also reflects his disdain for the Irish—whose names he constantly confuses—and his class snobbery, which leads him to forbid his daughter's romance with the socially inferior Lieutenant O'Rourke (John Agar).

The film also seems to vilify the Apaches, as soldiers find a burned-out wagon and two troopers roasted to death over wagon wheels. But the image begins changing as an officer tells Thursday that Cochise (Mexican star Miguel Inclán, acting with strength and dignity) has "outgeneraled us, outfought us, and outrun us." More important, the film explains why the Apaches are fighting. "We made a treaty with Cochise," York explains to the Colonel. His people came to the reservation "to live here in peace, and did for two years" until the unscrupulous Indian Agent Meacham sold them "whiskey but no beef" and "trinkets instead of blankets." With "the women degraded, the children sickly and the men turning into drunken animals," he adds, "Cochise did the only thing a decent man could do. He left . . . rather than stay here and see his nation wiped out." York's speech expresses the film's viewpoint, and instead of Apache villains, it offers a second white villain: the corrupt merchant who represents the U.S. government.

When word arrives that Cochise wants to discuss a return to the reservation, York volunteers to meet him, taking along his translator, Sergeant Beaufort (Pedro Armendáriz). Colonel Thursday accepts Cochise's request for a meeting, but he orders the regiment to come along, provoking York to object that he promised Cochise the Colonel would meet him alone. "Your word to a breech-clouted savage?" asks Thursday. "An illiterate, uncivilized murderer and treaty breaker? There is no question of honor, sir, between an American officer and Cochise."

Thursday nonetheless relents, and Cochise explains movingly that his war-weary people will not return as long as Meacham runs the reservation. By spreading disease and vice, he says, "He not only killed the men, but the women and the children and the old ones. We looked to the great white father for protection, [but] he gave us slow death." When Cochise says that the alternative to peace is war, Thursday takes offense and barks at Beaufort to tell Cochise, "I find him without honor." A close-up of Cochise then lets the audience experience the Apache's anger and indignation. Having insulted Cochise when he was offering peace, Thursday prepares for war, ignoring York's warning that they are badly outnumbered. By the time Thursday relieves York of his command for calling his plan to ride into a canyon suicidal, *Fort Apache* has put the viewer into the unaccustomed position of rooting for the Apaches to defeat the cavalry in a climactic battle scene, if only to see the arrogant Thursday get his comeuppance.

The foolish Indian fighter leading his outnumbered men to ruin evokes Custer's Last Stand, and the film even mimics paintings and earlier Custer films through its staging.[27] For Americans, whose travails in Korea and Vietnam were still in the future, this film offered a rare lesson in the pitfalls of imperial hubris and the underestimation of enemies who fight unconventionally. Not that the film is anticolonialist: it faults whites for neglecting the Apaches on the reservation, not for taking their land and forcing them onto reservations. And as with the Custer story, viewers probably questioned the commander's strategic blunders, not the mission itself. The film's adoring view of the cavalry is clearest in a coda, in which newsmen viewing a heroic painting of Thursday ask York what kind of man he was only to hear York omit the truth and close ranks for the good of the regiment—to the sound of "Battle Hymn of the Republic" and a striking reflection shot of York gazing at troops riding out. Still, the film contains some fairly subversive notions for a 1940s western, and the coda invites viewers to question the film's glorification of the conquest of the West. For nested within a film about the winning of the West is a moving account of the injustices and suffering whites visited upon the Apaches on the reservation; a respectful depiction of a dignified Cochise and his people; a ringing denunciation of a condescending, hypocritical, and corrupt Indian agent; and a maddening depiction of a commander who insults worthy foes and acts dishonorably. The film remains within the framework of colonialist assumptions about the conquest of the West, but for its time, *Fort Apache* was remarkably ambivalent about that historical project.

Although the film did well at the box office, reaching number twenty-two on *Variety*'s annual charts, it confused some critics.[28] In a sample of twenty-eight reviews, fifteen praised it (54 percent), six panned it, and seven were mixed or noncommittal.[29] Several reviews noted the soldiers being tortured, while no one said much of the Apache grievances, and a few reviews missed the reversal of the usual good guys / bad guys scheme. "The local Indians are on the warpath," wrote *Newsweek*, giving no hint of why, and it announced that the film "succeed[s] in bringing back the time-honored business of making redskins bite the dust as first-rate entertainment." *Film Daily* summarized Thursday's meeting with Cochise with the bland statement that the "result is a breaking off of negotiations," saying nothing of Thursday's treachery or his insult to a peace-minded Cochise. And some who did notice the unusual goings-on seemed disoriented. "Exactly what Ford and Nugent were getting at here is not clear," wrote a baffled Richard Coe of the *Washington Post*, whose warning that it "almost smacks of un-Americanism" was a potent charge in the wake of the HUAC hearings. *Motion Picture Daily* informed exhibitors that "the outcome of the run probably will depend on the public's acceptance of a quite different treatment of the U.S. Cavalry and its dealing with the Indians than the subject has received heretofore." Explaining that "this time the Cavalry is the heavy," it called this "sharply enough at variance with cinema precedent to have thrown the Hollywood preview audience for a distinctly perceptible loss." The *Boston Globe*'s Marjory Adams grasped the story's innovations, writing that Thursday "insists upon treating the noble redman as if he were an unruly halfwit," but she seemed to view the twist as an unintentional blunder and concluded that "the film has smash and excitement, but it is due to Ford and his actors rather than to the script."

Others welcomed the film's role reversal. Bosley Crowther of the *New York Times* noted "a new and maturing viewpoint upon one aspect of the American Indian wars" and "a new comprehension of frontier history." Noting the coda, the *Philadelphia Inquirer* called the film "a wry exposé of historical myths," and *Motion Picture Daily* pointed out that the "press is shown to have glamorized the despicable Fonda as a hero." If some merely perceived one man's incompetence—*Cue* referred to Thursday's "bull-in-a-china-shop tactics," while the *San Diego Union* described "darn poor generalship on the part of whites"—others saw a broader indictment of America's treatment of the Indians and did not call the film un-American. The filmmakers, wrote *Motion Picture Daily*, "have undertaken to show, at great expense and considerable length, that the Indians, in at least this instance, and inferentially in general, received very shabby treatment at the hands of the Federal Government." Complaining that "practically every Indian I've come across in the movies has been a surly knave who would cut your scalp off as quick as look at you," the *New Yorker's* John McCarten declared, "I've always resented this harsh characterization of the red man," and he called it "a pleasure" to see it overturned.

British critics were even less perceptive than their American colleagues, and far less interested, and while four of eighteen reviews examined here were positive and three negative, eleven issued mixed judgments or none at all.[30] A few noted Thursday's flaws as a commander, but the mistreatment of the Indians raised a collective yawn. Among those who misread the film, the daily *Star* asked, "Who will not respond to the thrill of gallant adventure" and "shrieking hordes of Redskins on the warpath?" while the *Evening Standard* praised "a really superb half-hour of Indians biting the dust." The *Spectator* called it "an ideal film for children of every age who have a penchant for frontier fighting" and for "wild hawk-nosed scalpers who make such blood-curdling noises," but found it "extraordinarily difficult to distinguish *Fort Apache* from its predecessors," as Ford "keeps rigidly to traditional lines." The *Daily Telegraph* called it "a John Ford western that might have been made by Cecil B. De Mille" and pronounced it "good fun." The *Evening News*, upset about a flood of American films in Britain, complained that this film "dallies with a subject that, as treated, is of only national interest" and asked how Americans would like it if the British sent them a film about their soldiers in South Africa or "the massacre at Rorke's Drift" (as they would do with *Zulu* in 1964). The British critics, in short, saw no connection to their own colonial history, and no one noted that the commanders in the film were all of British descent. Nor did anyone remark on Thursday's disdain for the Irish or the irony of Irish Americans helping colonize others while Ireland remained an English colony.

In France, the film sold an impressive 2,293,565 tickets, and though many papers ignored the film, seven of nine reviews located here were positive (78 percent) and none negative.[31] These critics were quite perceptive, and no one mistook Ford's work for Cecil B. DeMille's. "The Indians are not evil savages," wrote *Combat's* Denis Marion, "but brave warriors," while "civilization is represented by a crooked trafficker" and a commander who "provokes a needless conflict with the Indians out of arrogance." Thursday's treachery interested *Le Monde*, which pointed out that he "even betrays a promise given . . . under the vain pretext that one does not give one's word to Apaches," while *Les Lettres Françaises* observed that "an American national hero was, according to John Ford's film, a stupid imbecile who betrays a promise." Georges Charensol of *Les Nouvelles Littéraires* called westerns "America's *chansons de geste*" and found the story "of exceptional interest" in that "for perhaps the first time we see the whites at fault, and the Indians, sure that they are in the right, inflict a stinging defeat on the American troops." He also speculated that Thursday might have "arrived with the order to carry out a policy of extermination," as "this is how the young American republic eliminated the red peril." Although no critic drew any parallel with France's current war in Indochina, *Libération*'s Jeander wrote that "this type of haughty, intransigent officer, ferociously attached to his caste, to a narrow nationalism, and to his military traditions is one we know very well here," for he is "arrogant, distant, authoritarian, and Pétainist." Calling Thursday "an absolute dictator," Jeander lamented that "in France we have never dared put an officer like Thursday on the screen." The mostly left-leaning publications surveyed here welcomed a film that questioned America's conquest of the Indians, even if they made no mention of French colonialism.

Ford left no record of his political intentions in *Fort Apache*, and although he claimed in 1969, "My sympathy was always with the Indians," the next two films in his "cavalry trilogy" undermined that assertion.[32] *She Wore a Yellow Ribbon* (1949), another Argosy/RKO film from a Bellah story and a Nugent script, again featured John Wayne as an Indian fighter, but this time the only explanation for the Indians being "on the warpath" was a statement that they sought "to drive the white man forever from the red man's hunting ground." The film gave no hint of miseries on the reservation or the corruption of government representatives, and in a gun-dealing scene, the Indians murder the white men and erupt in a savage orgy of violence. Another scene emphasizes Indian cruelty even more than *Fort Apache* had, in that children are among the traumatized survivors of an Indian raid. Balancing those negative images of Indians is a scene in which Wayne's character, Nathan Brittles, goes to see an old Indian friend, Chief Pony That Walks (Chief John Big Tree) to try to avert a war. The Chief desires peace but says it is too late and "young men do not listen to me." Here, then, is the old device of the good Indian who wants peace and the bad Indians who want war, and this good Indian is outnumbered and helpless. His character is also faintly comical with his overemphatic, high-pitched voice and his unsolicited declaration, "I am a Christian! Hallelujah!" Instead of *Fort Apache*'s white villain responsible for war, the heroic Brittles concocts a daring maneuver to prevent war. The figure of the good Indian, the film's brief allusion to the Indians' motives for fighting, and its refusal to end in a slaughter of Indians make *She Wore a Yellow Ribbon* more a mixed than a strictly anti-Indian film, but it closes with a narrator saying of the heroic cavalry, "Wherever they rode and whatever they fought for, that place became the United States." Indeed a statement Brittles repeats throughout the film—"Don't apologize: it's a sign of weakness"—could sum up the film's approach to America's treatment of the Indians.

The final entry in Ford's cavalry trilogy—*Rio Grande* (1950), another Argosy production from a Bellah story—was unambiguously anti-Indian. It omits even the brief explanation for the Apache attacks that *She Wore a Yellow Ribbon* gave, and the closest it comes to a sympathetic Indian character is a Navajo scout who earns a medal in the climactic battle, but whose heroism is never shown and who never speaks. While showing no Apache women or children, it does show Apaches attacking a convoy taking the soldiers' wives and children to safety. They kidnap the children, and by dwelling on the horrified reaction of the mothers, the film empathizes melodramatically with the settlers. It also establishes the Apaches' savagery with references to troopers tied face down on anthills, a sequence showing drunken Apaches imprisoning children in a church, and another showing Apache prisoners howling and wailing inexplicably, in stark contrast to the sweet harmonies of the Sons of the Pioneers, who appear in the film. No Indian character gets even a single sentence of dialogue.

Ford's transition from the pro-Indian *Fort Apache* to the mixed *She Wore a Yellow Ribbon* to the anti-Indian *Rio Grande* raises interesting questions. To some, *Rio Grande*'s hardline view of the Indians matches a rightward shift in public opinion about communism in the wake of Mao's victory in China and the Soviets' attainment of the atomic bomb, both in 1949.[33] *Rio Grande*'s disdain for Washington's constraints on the soldiers pursuing the Apaches across the Mexican border also seemed to reflect events in Korea, where General Douglas MacArthur chafed at Washington's refusal to let him pursue the enemy across the Chinese border, but a film released in November 1950 could only have a coincidental relationship to events occurring as the film came out.[34]

Many have argued that the Cold War and HUAC's arrival in Hollywood led filmmakers to shy away from liberal viewpoints, but Ford shot *Fort Apache* in June 1947, months after HUAC had held its first hearings in Hollywood.[35] Perhaps complaints about *Fort Apache* being "un-American" caused Ford to retreat, but he was not easily intimidated, and no one has presented any evidence that political criticism of *Fort Apache* led him to change course in the final two films. Ford disdained the whole idea of the blacklist, and he reportedly said of those blacklisted, "Send the commie bastard to me, I'll hire him."[36] Politically, Ford moved from liberalism in the 1930s and 1940s to conservatism and support of the Vietnam War in the 1960s—but this was far too gradual a transformation to explain differences among films released in 1948, 1949, and 1950.[37] Ford was not an overtly political filmmaker or a maker of message films, and all three of these films are primarily about whites. Just as many Americans had long perceived both noble and ignoble savages, Ford held a range of positive and negative views of both Indians and the conquest, and as a man of his time, he did not give much thought to the politics of his representations of Indians. So what looks like a sharp right turn may simply reflect the complexity and muddiness of much American thinking about Indians in those years.

The "Pro-Indian" Turn in the 1950s

The most famous of the "pro-Indian" films of this era was *Broken Arrow*. Based on Elliott Arnold's 1947 book *Blood Brother*, a fictional tale about army scout Tom Jeffords and his friendship with Cochise, this 1950 Twentieth Century-Fox film was directed by Delmer Daves and written by blacklisted screenwriter Albert Maltz (using writer Michael Blankfort as a front). The film was a major hit in 1950, reaching number nine on *Variety*'s charts (the third-highest ranking film about Indians between 1946 and 1959), and it later spawned a television show and influenced countless other westerns.[38] Yet despite its popularity and its renown as a pro-Indian film—or perhaps because of those things—scholars have leveled scathing criticism at it.

Since the advent of sound, films sympathetic to Indians have faced a dilemma, for having them speak English (as most of the movies chose to do at the time) leaves them sounding stupid, or at least unable to state their case, whereas having them speak eloquent English seems unrealistic. Having a character translate their statements, as in *Fort Apache*, is cumbersome and limits their dialogue. As for subtitles, Hollywood assumed, probably correctly, that they would annoy viewers, and it was not until 1990 and *Dances with Wolves* that a major Hollywood film about Indians used them extensively. *Broken Arrow* instead had Tom Jeffords (James Stewart) announce in an opening voice-over that "when the Apaches speak, they will speak in our language." By asking the audience to suspend disbelief on this point, the film was able to give the Apaches extensive dialogue and present them as intelligent, reasonable people.

Its story, set in 1870, begins when Jeffords, out panning for gold, comes across a lone wounded Apache boy undergoing a rite of passage. Despite his own fear and hatred of the Apaches, whom he calls "more dangerous than a snake," Jeffords decides to help the boy. The lad gradually overcomes his own mistrust of whites and tells Jeffords about his family and his mother, who must be crying over his long absence. When Apache warriors happen upon them, the boy stops them from killing Jeffords, whose voice-over explains, "I learned things that day:

Apaches' mothers cried about their sons. Apache men had a sense of fair play." The character transformation begun here serves the film's antiracist goals, for by having Jeffords start out sharing the whites' Indian-hating and then let go of it, the film marks out a path for white audiences to follow. When Jeffords returns to Tucson, the astonished settlers are skeptical at his story. After Ben Slade (Will Geer) says he should have killed the boy and suggests that "maybe he doesn't know what side he's on," Jeffords declares he is fed up with a war he insists whites started. Alluding to the 1861 Bascom affair, Jeffords tells a room full of settlers that the conflict began when a lieutenant betrayed a flag of truce, took Cochise hostage along with his brother and five others, and then hanged the hostages when Cochise escaped. Declaring, "I'm sick and tired of all this killin'," Jeffords asks a rather subversive question for a western: "Who asked us out here in the first place?" Determined to seek peace, Jeffords has Juan (Billy Wilkerson), an Apache who lives in town, teach him his language and customs to prepare him to meet Cochise. Ignoring Juan's warnings, Jeffords locates Cochise (Jeff Chandler), who spares him out of respect for his bravery in coming alone. Jeffords then impresses Cochise by his knowledge of his language and customs—a cinematic plea for Americans to learn more about foreign cultures and build bonds of friendship in the third world. As they discuss Tom's peace proposal, the two become friends, and the rest of the film relates their struggles against hatred and war-mongering on both sides.

Seeking to humanize the Apaches, Daves, who had lived on Navajo and Hopi reservations after working in the crew of *The Covered Wagon* (1923), devotes several sequences to showing and explaining Apache rituals and customs, and these images differ sharply from the wild war-dancing in films such as *Unconquered*.[39] Producer Julian Blaustein explained that they hired 375 Apaches from the White River Reservation to play themselves and to teach them about their culture.[40] And although the film was based on real people and events, one of its inventions was a romance between Jeffords and a young lass named Sonseeahray (Debra Paget), who fall in love despite their differences of age and culture. When they tell Cochise they wish to marry, the skeptical chief warns them of the hostility they will face from both peoples, but he reluctantly intercedes with her parents, and the two wed in an Apache ceremony.

When Jeffords returns to Tucson with word of Cochise's agreement to let mail riders pass through Apache territory, settlers angry over a recent Apache raid accuse him of spying for the enemy. As a mob tries to lynch him, General Oliver Howard (Basil Ruysdael) saves him with typical Hollywood timing. Howard, also a real historical figure known as "the Christian General," had come from Washington as part of President Grant's Peace Policy, and he declares to Jeffords that "the Bible I read preaches brotherhood for all of God's children" and "says nothing about the pigmentation of the skin." Here the film invokes the Christian values of brotherhood and peace instead of using Christianity to justify the conquest of heathens. With Washington behind his peace initiative, Jeffords takes Howard to meet Cochise (also a real event), and despite his skepticism, Cochise agrees to present the General's proposal to his people. The Apaches are divided: Geronimo (Jay Silverheels) leads a minority faction that mistrusts the whites, refuses to give up raiding for herding, and rejects peace. The fragile peace endures several tests, including an attack from Geronimo's renegades and a treacherous ambush by Slade's hard-liners that fails in its goal of murdering Cochise but results in a settler killing Sonseeahray. The grief-stricken Jeffords despairs of peace and wants revenge, but Cochise, recalling his own loved ones killed by whites, dissuades him, as does General Howard, who tells him, "Your very loss has brought our people together in the will to peace."

Broken Arrow contradicts claims that an inherently conservative, triumphalist genre cannot serve progressive purposes. For a revisionist film, it does have its share of clichés and conventions—such as a knife-fight between Jeffords and an angry brave jealous of his romance with Sonseeahray, which the white man naturally wins—and its adherence to genre conventions probably helped account for its success. It also rearranges historical facts, belying its rash claim that the tale "happened exactly as you'll see it." Scholars have pointed out that the Americans and Apaches began fighting long before 1861, that Cochise began seeking peace before he met Jeffords, and that it ignores the miseries the Apaches endured on the reservation after accepting peace.[41] Although some critics called this the first film to take the Indians' point of view, its protagonist is Jeffords, who often conveys the Apaches' viewpoints to his compatriots, even if Apache characters get extensive dialogue.

Telling the story from Jeffords's point of view and casting the popular Stewart to play him probably helped audiences sympathize with the film's politics.[42] Some of the Apache characters—and the casting of whites to play them—have raised objections. Sonseeahray certainly fits the stereotype of the Indian princess— the beautiful light-skinned girl who welcomes the white man and pays with her life for loving him—even if she is not the daughter of a chief.[43] (On this romance, see chapter 7.) Objections have also arisen over the contrast between good Indians who favor peace and bad ones who want war, with white actors playing good Indians and Jay Silverheels playing the warmongering Geronimo.[44] Any defense of Chandler's casting as an Apache on the grounds that Hollywood wanted an experienced actor and box-office draw is only half convincing, for although Chandler had acted in seven films, he was not yet a star, and Silverheels himself could have played Cochise. Several minor speaking roles did go to Indian actors, including Billy Wilkerson and Chris Willow Bird, and these were sympathetic characters, but a film that took on racism was not as bold in its casting. As for Geronimo, he is indeed a villain, if not quite as despicable as other Hollywood Indian villains, and the film takes seriously the choice the Apaches must make between peace and war. Cochise himself has grave doubts about the white peacemakers' sincerity, and the film lets Geronimo voice legitimate questions about the concessions the treaty demanded. His insistence on fighting for his freedom is something viewers probably understood, which is why many Americans have long admired as well as reviled Geronimo. A better example of a typical Hollywood Indian villain is Nahilzay (John War Eagle), who tries to murder Jeffords out of jealousy.

Other objections have concerned the film's apparent plea for Indian assimilation into white society, implying a desire to erase Indian identity.[45] The film does contend that the Apaches had to change some of their ways, but the effort this production made to research Apache culture and depict it sympathetically hardly supports claims that it favored the total erasure of Indian identity. If a flood of settlers inevitably forced the Apaches to give up raiding, it did not require them to abandon *all* aspects of their culture, and the only change the film actually discusses is the cessation of warfare, raiding, and violence. It is hard to see how the difficult process of preserving Indian identity and culture would have gained from the pursuit of a hopeless military struggle, and whether the film applauds the white conquest or simply takes it as a painful historical reality to which Apaches had to adapt, it could not simply rewrite this history. Peter Biskind suggests that if *Broken Arrow* were truly a left-wing film, we would have seen it "siding with Cochise and Geronimo, say, as they burned Tucson to the ground, slaughtering the Slades and Lowerys and sending the cavalry packing back to Washington with its tail between its legs."[46] As amusing as this suggestion is, it only underlines the lack of realistic alternatives. The notion that the film aimed to defend white conquest seems dubious in light of Jeffords's question, "Who asked us out here in the first place?," his admission that Americans started the war, and his statement to Cochise that "my people have done yours a great wrong." Even the claim that the film favored the Apaches' assimilation into white society seems questionable, as the peace deal it depicted involved creating what Jeffords calls "a clear territory that's Apache, ruled by Apaches." That vision of Apache autonomy on a reservation seems closer to multiculturalism than to assimilationism, and it contradicts suggestions that the film aimed to support the current termination policy of closing the reservations and integrating Indians into American society.[47]

Some observers have argued that films like *Broken Arrow* were really disguised statements about black civil rights, made when political repression in Hollywood prevented direct comment on that issue.[48] It may well be that Daves had broader issues in mind and that scenes such as the lynching evoked them for some viewers, but the film's central interest in war and peace had little relevance to relations between whites and African Americans, who were not fighting a war. Nor does the film's plea for peace have more than a coincidental relationship to the Korean War, which began just after the film previewed for critics. Above all, *Broken Arrow* concerns America's historical relationship with the Indians, a topic of particular interest to Daves and many other Americans. And while the film followed certain genre conventions, cast white actors as Indians, softened its critique of the conquest by including sympathetic white characters, and divided Indians into typical categories based on their attitudes toward whites, it merits the pro-Indian designation, given its ugly portrait of racist, treacherous settlers, the extensive opportunity it gives Apache characters to voice their grievances and concerns, its interest in their culture, and the way it leads viewers to side with Cochise, Jeffords, and Sonseeahray against devious, murderous settlers. Even the decision of the "bad Indians" to fight gets an understandable explanation, while those who favor peace clearly outnumber the die-hards. With Jeffords questioning the whites' very presence in Arizona, admitting that whites started the war, and acknowledging that "we murdered Indian women and kids," the film refutes notions of the western as an inherently conservative genre.

Despite claims that Americans were not ready for such revisionism, the film was a major hit.[49] Among its honors were three Academy Award nominations—for Chandler as supporting actor, Ernest Palmer's cinematography, and the screenplay. It also did very well with American critics: twenty-nine of thirty-seven (78 percent) praised it (some enthusiastically), four panned it, and four gave it mixed ratings.[50] Among the negative reviews, Bosley Crowther of the *New York Times* made clear that he liked the "honorable endeavor" to depict Indians sympathetically, but he objected to "red men who act like denizens of the musical comedy stage" and he found the love scenes "downright embarrassing." Political objections were more evident in the *St. Louis Post-Dispatch*'s complaints that "the whites are made responsible for much of the Arizona warfare" and that "the cards are stacked here just as much in favor of the redskins as they usually are for the whites." Suggesting that it was not genre conventions but rather viewers' expectations that resisted change, the *Christian Science Monitor* disliked the "long, friendly bull sessions," which "make one think nostalgically of the days when there wasn't any talk at all in Westerns." Among the far more numerous positive reviews, *Film Daily* called the picture "intensely moving"; the *Hartford Courant* considered it "one of the most compelling and brilliantly enacted and directed outdoor films to come this way in a long, long time"; and the *Hollywood Reporter* called it "an unusually fine motion picture" that "sticks in the memory." At a preview, Philip Scheuer of the *Los Angeles Times* heard an Indian boy tell an elder, "For the first time in my life I'm proud to be an Indian," and at a showing in downtown Los Angeles, Scheuer reported that viewers responded "with respectful attention and none of the giggles and imitative noises I had half-resigned myself to hearing."

If some critics missed *Fort Apache*'s revisionism, that did not recur with *Broken Arrow*. The *Miami Herald* found it "quite different from the early sagas of redskin-versus-pioneer in that it endeavors to give the Indian an even break," and *Life* wrote that it showed Indians "as proud people bravely defending their land against the white man." *Film Daily* told exhibitors that the film was "no ordinary tale about Indians and pioneers," and though it warned that "the audience has not been exposed to anything like this," it predicted that it "will be a standout film this year." Similarly, *America* observed that "according to the picture, the red man resorted to violence only to defend his homeland against unjust aggression," adding that the "only good Indian" idea had "so thoroughly permeated the American subconscious that this new and three-dimensional interpretation may come as something of a shock." Pleasantly surprised, the *Washington Post* called the film "something different in the way of western movies, a trick you may not have thought possible." While welcoming innovation, critics also embraced the positive image of Indians. New York's *Daily Worker* praised the film's "challenge to the imperialist expansion of the American government at the expense of the Indian nations," and its insistence "that all the right is on the Indians' side," but less radical papers also welcomed the revisionism. The conservative *Chicago Tribune* called it a "praiseworthy attempt to probe beneath the Redskin's war paint and discover his stern code of honor, the dignity and wisdom of a man worthy to be chief of the Apaches, and the beauty of the tribal worship of nature," and the *Wall Street Journal*, calling America's historical treatment of the Indians "shameful," wrote that here the Indian "is no longer the unprincipled savage" but is "drawn closer to his true mold." *Time* observed that "instead of the blood-lusting savages who whoop endlessly across the U.S. screen, its Indians are proud, dignified warriors with their own cultural tradition, a stern code of honor and a justified hatred of the white invaders." Several papers pointed out that Jeffords took the effort to learn the Apaches' language and ways, and the *Dallas Morning News* praised the film for showing "many appealing customs."

The dark picture of the pioneers raised surprisingly few objections. In the *Hartford Courant*'s view, the film showed that "the Indians have not been given a fair deal by the whites who have ruthlessly taken over their lands," and it described Ben Slade as "a fanatical Indian-hater." Indicting more than the settlers, the *Detroit News* explained that "Cochise is embittered over the repeated breaking of pledges by the white man and his government," while the *Milwaukee Journal* felt the Apaches had "reason enough not to trust the white man." The *Dallas Morning News* noted that "American hotheads break the armistice with a brand of treachery that should turn a white face red," and *Time* ventured that the film "works up such sympathy and respect for [Cochise] and his tribe, and such distrust of their ignorant, arrogant enemies, that most moviegoers will be delighted whenever another paleface bites the dust." The *Wall Street Journal* found the depiction of Cochise's "humanitarian qualities" overdrawn, but added, "Perhaps the exaggeration is needed to reverse . . . the distorted version already in existence." Among those who found the picture's treatment of the two sides equitable, the *New York Post* said it showed "decency on both sides, and villainy too," and *Motion Picture Daily* concurred, writing that "in showing good and evil on both sides, the picture is eminently fair." There were objections to the ethnic miscasting, but also praise for both Chandler and Paget, who both returned as Indians in future films.

These glimpses of Americans' feelings about their country's conquest of the American Indians suggest something rather different from the triumphal, white-supremacist view that years' worth of anti-Indian westerns and slanted textbooks supposedly produced. Among those who felt that the film could have gone even further, the *Wall Street Journal* pointed out that "eighteen months after the peace treaty was signed, the white men again invaded the Indian land and slaughtered them mercilessly," and the *Dallas Morning News* observed that the result of these events was that "the Indians get a reservation and the white men get Arizona." On the other hand, two conservative papers managed to reconcile the film with traditional outlooks, as the *Motion Picture Herald* praised this story of "the building of a great country," and the *Los Angeles Examiner* said the film proved "that the real American spirit cannot be broken" and "will make you prouder than ever of this land of ours." As for the notion that films used Indians to make indirect comments about black-white relations, the only critic who came close to drawing this parallel was *Commonweal*'s Philip Hartung, who said that the film showed "that in all racial problems there is something to be said for both sides."

In France, the film sold 2,339,101 tickets in 1951, but its Paris opening conflicted with the Cannes Film Festival, and few papers reviewed it.[51] British critics overwhelmingly praised it, with seventeen of twenty-one (81 percent) giving it positive reviews and only one panning it—the *Daily Telegraph*, which complained of "a genuine Hollywood starlet hiding her pretty features behind burnt cork."[52] The *Daily Express* called it "the first [film] I have seen in years to deal with the cowboy-Indian problem in an intelligent, adult way," and the *London Times* wrote, "At last a Western which puts the case from the Indians' point of view and states quite clearly that Americans were guilty of brutality and treachery in some of their dealings with the men whose land they invaded," though it added that it "does not go so far as to indict the United States Army." The *Times* also found it a "healthy corrective to the general American idea that it is only the British who go in for oppressing natives." Several papers expressed surprise: the *Sunday Pictorial* stated that "a Western with something to say is quite a novelty," while the *Daily Mail* found it "alarming how delighted we are whenever an arrow thuds into the back of an uncompromising roughneck from the saloons." The *Evening Standard* called it "all very bewildering but completely successful." Among those conflicted about the revisionism, the *Evening News* wrote that "good Indians are not as exciting as bad ones, but I think you will enjoy this if you're prepared for a film that has something to say," and the *Sunday Graphic* admitted that "on the whole I prefer my Indians bad, but this one is an honest and successful attempt to be different." Resisting the new approach were two papers that gave the film mixed verdicts: the conservative weekly *Time and Tide* found it "scrupulously fair but not nearly so much fun as the other kind [of western], without any really black-hearted primitives to come to justly violent ends," and the *New Statesman* described it as "a mild correction to some of the bad old Westerns that were so very much better." So while most critics welcomed the revisionism, a few dissented, suggesting again that it was not genre constraints but viewer expectations that stood in the way of new approaches to the western.

Completed at almost exactly the same time as *Broken Arrow* was MGM's *Devil's Doorway*. Directed by Anthony Mann in black and white from an original screenplay by Wyoming's Guy Trosper, it starred Robert Taylor as Lance Poole, a Civil War hero who returns to his native Wyoming hoping to run a ranch. The film opens with Lance, wearing his Union Army uniform and Congressional Medal of Honor, entering the local saloon to a warm welcome from the bartender and a cowboy, Zeke (Edgar Buchanan). The smiles quickly disappear when a man at the bar declares, "When I was in the army . . . we were a little particular about who wore those stripes," but the three say nothing. After Lance exits, the man at the bar mutters, "Notice how sour the air got? You can always smell 'em," and when Zeke goes outside, he tells Lance that the man is a lawyer named Coolan (Louis Calhern). The scene finishes revealing Lance's ethnicity when an elderly Indian rides up and Lance hugs him, saying, "Hello Father." As the two ride off, Coolan comes out, glares at Lance, and spits.

Lance and his father ride to Sweet Meadows, the family ranch in a beautiful, verdant valley. Lance dreams of building a thriving operation where there will be "plenty to eat, nothing but peace," and "no man red or white will ever be turned away from our door." His optimism evokes many Americans' postwar dreams of peace, prosperity, and racial harmony, as well as Indian veterans' hopes that their military service would bring acceptance in white society. "The war's over, all the wars, even yours," Lance tells his father. "They gave me these stripes without testing my blood. I led a squad of white men. Slept in the same blankets with them, ate with them, held their heads when they died. Why should it be any different now?" His father, however, informs his son—whom he addresses by his Shoshone name, Broken Lance—that he is dying, and when Lance says he will find a doctor, he replies, "Do you think the white doctor cares if I live or die?" The scene, shot with dramatic shadows, establishes a somber, elegiac mood as Lance's relatives sing a quiet dirge, and Lance's father tells him, "Our people are doomed. The white man knows great hate for us." Undaunted, Lance, clad in white men's clothing, rushes off to town. When it turns out that the doctor does not care about Lance's father—he continues playing cribbage with Coolan and suggests he get a Shoshone medicine man—the film underlines the futility of Lance's attempts at assimilation. When Lance's father dies, a funeral sequence treats the Indians' religion with unusual respect.

The film then develops the conflict foreshadowed earlier, as Lance clashes with Coolan and the settlers whom he encourages to seize Sweet Meadows. Lance learns that he can no longer drink in the saloon, as Wyoming has become a territory of the United States, whose law forbids Indians to drink. In a tense saloon scene staged while a thunderstorm rages outside, Lance endures the taunts of Coolan's pal, Ike, a vicious racist who draws his gun and loudly declares, "There's only one solution to the Indian problem." After Ike, grinning and lit from below, threatens to scalp Lance and empties his gun at the unflinching Lance's feet and hat, the film gives the viewer a bit of satisfaction when Lance, having counted six shots, proceeds to beat him up—as the film induces the audience to side with an Indian fighting whites. With homesteaders now on his land, Lance goes to see the town's only lawyer aside from Coolan, who, to Lance's surprise, turns out be a woman, Orrie Masters (Paula Raymond). Overcoming his own prejudices,

Lance seeks her help, but after she investigates, she informs him that he does not qualify under the Homestead Act, being a ward of the government rather than an American citizen. Zeke, now the marshal, puts the point more bluntly: "The law says that an Indian ain't got no more rights than a dog."

Mann brought to *Devil's Doorway* his skills as a maker of *film noir*, with its shadowy black-and-white cinematography and its penchant for tales of hard-bitten men heading slowly for defeat.[53] In this case, Lance realizes the futility of his legal situation and his rejection by a country he served, and to mark his transformation and disillusion with assimilation, he discards first his army uniform and then his cowboy garb for a headband and Indian clothing. He explains to his lawyer—and to the audience—how Indians felt about whites seizing their land and herding them onto reservations. "It's hard to explain how an Indian feels about the earth," he tells her. "My father said the earth is our mother. I was raised in this valley. I'm a part of it, like the mountains and the hills, the deer, the pine trees and the wind." Referring to Shoshones who have fled the reservation and taken refuge at his ranch, he tells her, "Their hearts are dying because they have no freedom. They have no milk and the children weep." And when her petition for a change in the law fails, he informs her, "We will die, but we will never go back to the reservation." In a climactic battle scene, Coolan leads the settlers in an assault on the Shoshones barricaded at Lance's cabin—a reversal of the usual scenario of whites taking refuge in a fort or other enclosure surrounded by Indian attackers. Once again the film induces viewers to root for the Indians, and it offers some satisfaction when Lance kills Coolan in combat. But when the cavalry arrives—summoned by Orrie, who wants Lance to surrender and go to the reservation—the Shoshones hold to their vow and fight to the finish. A mortally wounded Lance, now dressed in his army uniform, comes out, salutes the lieutenant, and falls dead at his feet.

Devil's Doorway offers the best example of a 1950s pro-Indian film, and it was even more daring than *Broken Arrow*. As in *Broken Arrow*, there are racist white villains, admirable Indian characters, sympathetic depictions of Indian ways, extensive explanation of Indian grievances, and fights that impel viewers to side with the Indians, but this film also features an Indian protagonist and no bad Indians. The few good white characters are helpless, like Orrie, or the barman who cannot stop whites taunting Lance, or Zeke, who must enforce unjust laws. And whereas *Broken Arrow* had a government representative rescue Jeffords and reach agreement with Cochise, Washington here is the root of the problem, as it uses Indians for military service then denies them citizenship and property rights. And while *Broken Arrow* urged Indians to adopt at least some of whites' ways, *Devil's Doorway* considered that hopeless, as whites were simply too racist to accept them in their society. The film underlines this point near the end, when Orrie tells Lance that she wants him to surrender and live because she has romantic feelings for him. The bitter Lance rejects her affections, convinced that she harbors racist attitudes. Finally, while *Broken Arrow* ends with hopes of peace, *Devil's Doorway* attempts no happy ending, leaving viewers with little but anger at the Shoshones' mistreatment.[54]

Could such a downbeat film succeed at the box office? This must remain unknown, as MGM, dubious about its prospects, first delayed its release and then gave it limited distribution. The *Motion Picture Herald* reported that it "played fairly well" at a preview, but *Variety*, whose box-office predictions could become self-fulfilling prophecies, called it a message picture that "doesn't set well as entertainment" and concluded that "the grossing possibilities do not appear good."[55] Unsure of how to market the film, MGM ran ads like those of an anti-Indian film: "SEE! A white girl run the gauntlet of cavalry fire to her Indian lover's side! The wild Shoshone tribesmen vs. U.S. Cavalry! Covered Wagons put to the torch!"[56] In many cities, the film ran with tiny ads or none at all, ending up as a second feature despite its noted star and director.

Of twenty-three American reviews located, nine were positive (39 percent), six negative, and eight mixed or neutral.[57] Several papers noted that Lance was losing his land because Indians lacked citizenship and property rights, an injustice for which Washington was responsible.[58] The film's larger point also came through, as the *St. Louis Post-Dispatch* noted that "most people at this stage will concede [that the Indians] got a pretty dirty deal," and *America* concluded that the film showed "the tragic reality of the injustice with which it deals." Among those sensing a pro-Indian trend in films, the *New York Post* observed that "the movies have been creeping up on the fact that the American Indian was not always treated in sporting fashion" as "his country was taken away from him." *Commonweal* said the film "points out who settled the land first and who was getting the raw end of the deal," and this was "not an action of which our historians can be too proud." Two of the reviews vaguely evoked current issues, as *Film Daily* claimed that the film "brings considerable material for modern thought" and the *Christian Science Monitor* stated that "its plea for live-and-let-live would apply today to any form of racial misunderstanding." The latter paper, however, reassured readers that such persecution of Indians "is no longer acute." Less convinced that everything was now fine, *Cue* wrote that the Indians "didn't get a fair deal seventy-five or a hundred years ago," and "there is some talk and question in Washington whether he's getting a fair deal now."

As for judgments of the film, most liked the action sequences, and though many praised Taylor's acting, his casting as an Indian raised objections. It did not help that Taylor, unlike Jeff Chandler, was already famous, and *Cue* complained that "dyeing Robert Taylor's face and hair, painting him up, and sticking a feather in his hair" did not make him a convincing Indian. *Time* was even more brutal, writing that Taylor "could pass only for a Cleveland Indian."[59] Doubts also arose over the film's entertainment value. *Variety* alluded to the "sense of guilt which seizes [the] spectator as he watches the noble Redman persecuted by the White," and the *New York Times*'s comment that the film "rattles some skeletons in our family closet," like the *New York Post*'s warning that "the picture has the power to jab some pretty sharp prongs into the white man's conscience," suggested that viewers might not enjoy their evening out. The *Boston Globe* complained that the film "has nothing in it but doom and destruction" and "too little to lighten the tragedy of the Indian hero" so that "everybody, including the audience, suffers considerably." In short, the film's power to elicit anger at America's treatment of the Indians was too much for some. The *New York Daily News* called it "much more serious and much less romantic" than *Broken Arrow*, and while scholars today prefer it for that reason, *Broken Arrow*'s immensely greater impact tends to vindicate its approach. And although the defiant, die-fighting attitude that *Devil's Doorway* glorified suits today's anticolonialist sensibilities, the compromise, resilience, and adaptation that *Broken Arrow*'s Cochise favors is closer to the path most American Indians took—one that permitted their survival and the preservation of much of their culture.

Whether inspired by *Broken Arrow*'s success or simply reflecting changing political outlooks, a series of liberal pro-Indian films followed in the early 1950s, despite the chilling effects of the HUAC campaigns and the country's conservative turn. One such film was *Tomahawk* (1951), starring Van Heflin as mountain man Jim Bridger. Its image of Indians is almost entirely positive, as it discards the usual good Indian / bad Indian dichotomy and shows Indian women and children as well as braves. It also cast Indian actor John War Eagle as the Sioux warrior Red Cloud. The film's villains are all white, most notably Lieutenant Dancy (Alex Nicol), who shoots an Indian boy unnecessarily and hankers for scalps—a marker of villainy in westerns. Even worse, Dancy proudly participated in the Sand Creek massacre of 1864, as he tells Julie (Yvonne De Carlo), "We really cleaned up that part of the country." Though the film does not show the massacre (as *Soldier Blue* would in 1970), Bridger describes it in detail, telling Julie that although the chief of the village was flying an American flag to show he had accepted a peace treaty, the Colorado volunteers "shot and hacked and killed until they'd had enough fun. Men, women, old people. And kids." When Bridger later confronts him about killing Indian children at Sand Creek, the Aryan-looking Dancy replies that he was only following orders, a transparent allusion to the Nazis, five years after the Nuremburg trials. Other white villains include Captain Fetterman, who wants to teach the Sioux a lesson but leads his men to their deaths. Not shy about depicting villainy among white officials, the film shows "representatives of the United States" lying to Sioux chiefs at a peace conference to get them to sign a bogus treaty. Bridger, however, reminds everyone that the government has repeatedly pushed the Sioux into smaller and smaller lands while breaking treaties and promises, and he translates Red Cloud's reply: "You're all a pack of liars and this peace conference is a fake."

Tomahawk softens its scathing attack on America's treatment of the Sioux with a few sympathetic white characters other than Bridger, including the Colonel in charge of the fort and his wife, who employs Jim's Cheyenne sister-in-law Monahseetah (Susan Cabot) as a servant and teaches her English. This brief passage suggests an optimistic assimilationism, though the rest of the film defends the right of the Sioux to maintain their way of life on their own lands. Bridger's attempts to mediate leads racist soldiers to accuse him of disloyalty to his country and spying for the enemy, a pointed comment in a film made in 1951. When asked, "What side are you on? . . . Your country's or its enemy's?" Bridger replies, "This is Red Cloud's country and yours and mine," summing up the film's vision that the two peoples could share the land if whites would stop acting greedily and dishonorably. The film loses its way at the end in a battle scene in which whites with new breech-loading rifles mow down the braves, a spectacle presumably offered for the audience's entertainment, and one shot from the whites' point of view. A closing voice-over declares blankly that Washington gave in and left the territory to the Sioux "for another thirty years," though in fact whites violated the 1868 Fort Laramie Treaty in less than a decade. Perhaps boosted by this uplifting ending, the film did far better than *Devil's Doorway*, reaching the number forty-four slot for 1951.[60] Critics questioned aspects of the filmmaking but not the pro-Indian perspective.[61] The *Hollywood Citizen News* wrote that "the seizing of the Indian territories by the white man is not one of the most praiseworthy chapters in our history," and the *Boston Globe*, which noted that when the Indian boy shoots the villain Dancy, "you forget all about white supremacy and cheer for the Red avenger." The *San Francisco Chronicle* noted that Hollywood "has been giving the movies back to the Indians and permitting them to say a good deal more than 'ugh,' " calling this "a fairness that comes about 85 years too late."

The Indian Bio-Pics

The pro-Indian turn included a series of bio-pics on American Indians, beginning with one set in the twentieth century: *Jim Thorpe—All American* (1951), a Warner Bros. production starring Burt Lancaster. The film traces Thorpe's rise to athletic stardom from his time at the Carlisle Indian School to his gold medals at the 1912 Olympics and his career in football and baseball. It merely hints at white racism as it shows his struggles—officials revoke his medals because he took money for playing baseball, his son dies, his white wife leaves him as he descends into depression, and he takes a humiliating job wearing an Indian costume in a marathon dance contest—but it certainly favors the full acceptance of assimilated American Indians into society. Most other films in this cycle were set in the nineteenth century, and all but *Taza, Son of Cochise* (1954) were pro-Indian. *Sitting Bull* (1954), despite the usual clichés and ethnic miscasting, showed the miseries inflicted on the Sioux at the Red Rock Agency, where a tyrannical Indian agent crowds starving men, women, and children into a stockade; calls them "dogs"; and gives them rancid food only once a day; and its villains include army officers, government officials, and white settlers, who, according to Major Bob Parrish, one of the film's leading characters, "go into Sioux territory and slaughter their game, foul their water, and shoot every Indian they see if he's old or harmless enough." *Chief Crazy Horse* (1955) offered more clichés and another white man (Victor Mature) playing an Indian, while also denouncing the whites' breaking of treaties, their seizure of what Crazy Horse calls "the sacred land of our fathers," and the miseries of the reservation. It also shows that it was a Sioux collaborator with the whites who murdered Crazy Horse, so like *Apache*, it reverses the usual scheme in which good Indians are those who side with the whites.

The most notable of these biopics was a young Robert Aldrich's *Apache* (1954), with Burt Lancaster again playing an Indian—Massai, the last holdout after Geronimo's surrender in 1886. Lancaster, fresh off his success in *From Here to Eternity* (1953), had just formed his own production company with Harold Hecht, so critics who objected to a blue-eyed Apache had the star himself to blame. (United Artists' press book claimed the real Massai had blue eyes, but sources on Massai are scanty.[62]) The film opens with Massai defiantly seeking to scuttle Geronimo's surrender ceremony, and he explains to Nalinle (Jean Peters), the Apache lass who loves him, that he refused to surrender because those who had were sent to Florida. Despite his heroics, Massai is captured by Al Sieber (John McIntire), who tells him, "You're not a warrior anymore; you're just a whipped Injun." The film's pro-Indian sympathies are clear in a somber scene depicting

Apache men, women, and children silently watching chained and numbered warriors, including Geronimo (Monte Blue) and Massai, being herded like cattle onto a train bound for Florida. On board, the film's main villain, Weddle (John Dehner), shows off his prisoners for reporters, who photograph them against their will, and in the commotion, Massai escapes. The rest of the film depicts his lonely war of resistance, while the Indian-hating Sieber pursues him obsessively like Javert tracking down Jean Valjean in *Les Misérables*.

On Massai's trek home, he first comes to St. Louis, and as he wanders in amazement through the streets, the film invites viewers to see white society through his eyes. Racists taunt Massai, call him Chief Rain-in-the-Face, and chase him when a man notices broken irons on his wrists—an action scene that induces the audience to pull for his escape from the ugly mob. In Oklahoma, he meets a farmer (Morris Ankrum) who turns out to be a Cherokee with his own farm and well-appointed house. Although Massai at first disdains this Indian who has surrendered and adopted the white man's ways—he even takes orders from his wife to fetch water—the Cherokee insists his people are no cowards, but after fighting and being driven from their homelands time after time, they have learned, as he says, that "we could live with the white man only if we lived like him." Over Massai's objections that Apaches are warriors, not farmers, the Cherokee gives him seed corn, planting an idea in the skeptical Apache's mind.

Massai finally reaches the reservation, where he observes Weddle bellowing insults at an Apache forced-labor gang. Still undetected, he goes to see Nalinle and her father Santos. Nalinle is intrigued by Massai's report of Cherokee farmers who "walk in peace and hold their heads high and work for themselves, not the white man," but the dispirited Santos is interested only in spirits—bottles of *aguardiente* stolen for him by his daughter's suitor, Hondo (Charles Bronson, then still called Charles Buchinsky). Santos turns Massai in, and as the reservation police lead him away, Aldrich again shows Apache women and children watching in sullen silence. After a second escape, in which Massai thwarts Weddle's plans to murder him, he begins a one-man war against the Americans, though one in which he only destroys property and kills no one. Believing that Nalinle had turned him in, he kidnaps her and treats her brutally until she finally convinces him of her innocence and love for him. The two marry (as the Production Code Administration insisted) and enjoy months of happiness and freedom on the run in the mountains, and as she prepares to bear their child, they settle in an abandoned cabin and plant their corn.[63] When Sieber and his Indian scouts finally find them, Massai prepares to die fighting, but in a final showdown with Sieber in his symbolic cornfield, he spares the white man when he hears the cry of his newborn baby.

Aldrich later complained that "a great deal of what I wanted to say about the Red Indians in *Apache* was lost."[64] United Artists, convinced that the original ending—the soldiers shoot Massai in the back—would cost the film at least a million dollars, pressured Lancaster into a new, ambiguous ending.[65] (The film does not state what happens after Sieber spares Massai.) The PCA also secured the removal of a statement that the Apaches are paid "half a white man's wages," which, it told Hecht, "could easily be offensive to members of your audience."[66] Even watered down, the film made a powerful point for its time about whites' injustices, and it leads audiences to view a tale through Apache eyes. Massai has his faults, but his reluctance to kill, which he does only in self-defense, may remind today's viewers of the first Rambo film, *First Blood* (1982)—as may Massai's amazing action-hero skills. And despite the unflattering portrait of Weddle and Sieber, it is not just evil individuals the film indicts, but also an entire system that turns Apaches into depressed, drunken captives on the reservation.

Like *Broken Arrow*, *Apache* has been the target of recent scholarly criticism for not going further and for favoring the erasure of Indian identity, though scholars exonerate Aldrich and blame the studio.[67] The *Broken Arrow / Devil's Doorway* debate thus recurs here, with laments that *Apache* did not allow Massai a glorious and defiant, if suicidal, final stand. It is true that the film's indictment of white conquest would have been even stronger that way, and that the film considers acculturation inevitable for the Apaches in 1886—at least the abandonment of raiding and warfare. And while it favors the Apaches farming, it fails to note that whites stuck Indians on lands no white farmer wanted. But if the film supports some measure of acculturation, the path the Cherokee farmer suggests to Massai does not involve living *among* whites and blending in with them; instead, he seeks to maintain independence from them by adopting *some* of their ways while preserving some traditional ways, as symbolized by his long hair. Selective borrowing from the colonizer in order to maintain as much independence as possible is a strategy virtually all decolonizing countries and peoples have used, often successfully, when further military resistance proved futile. The film thus defends the difficult decision most Indians made to accept some of the white man's ways (though some Apaches already farmed), and that decision neither required nor caused a total loss of Indian identity.[68] And unlike *Jim Thorpe*, it neither explores nor endorses Indians' efforts to live among whites. One might see in the film a defense of termination policies, given its dismal picture of life on the reservation and its attractive vision of the family farm, but this was not its intent. Despite its ending and its defense of farming, it embraces an outlaw's defiant struggle for freedom, a theme dear to many Americans.

Apache reached the number twenty-three slot in a year overloaded with westerns, and among twenty-nine American reviews, nineteen were positive (66 percent), six negative, and four mixed or neutral.[69] The harsh view of white society bothered two critics: the conservative Jack Moffitt of the *Hollywood Reporter* panned the film and said it was for "palefaces who love to believe Americans are always wrong and everyone else always right," and Myles Standish of the *St. Louis Post-Dispatch* seemed peeved that "the Indian agent and his assistant are cowards and murderers [and] the other white men are bullies." *Commonweal*'s Philip Hartung did not mind the film's politics, but he warned that it "runs relentlessly in one sullen key." Among the positive reviews, the *New Orleans Times-Picayune* called it a "powerful, authentic, and fascinating story" and "one of the all-time great Westerns," while the *Denver Post* described it as "powerful and important." And although the casting of Lancaster and Peters raised objections, many praised their performances.[70] Like previous pro-Indian films, *Apache* elicited many condemnations of American treatment of the Indians, as the *Boston Herald* said the film depicted "a chapter of which the Indian has more right to be proud than the white man," and the *Miami Herald* cited "the shabby deal the white man has handed out to the conquered braves who are shipped off to a place called Florida." Aware of the changed ending, Archer Winsten of the *New York Post* sided with Aldrich, saying that "the happy ending seemed too wishful to fit into the facts of Indian life in this country during the past century."

The British critics also questioned the casting, but four of seven liked the film, and only one panned it.[71] The *London Times* called it "a film that would seem to have a guilty conscience so far as Indians are concerned," adding that Massai "had his reasons" for resistance, while the *Daily Mirror* found it a "stirring story" and was pleased that "for a change Red Indians get a break." In France, where it opened in February 1955, three months into the Algerian War, it sold 1.2 million tickets, and most reviews were positive.[72] The noted analyst of westerns, André Bazin, wrote in *France Observateur* that it was "not a masterpiece" but was an "engaging and unexpected" film with "an agreeable ambition to venture off the beaten path." While objecting to "an unlikely conciliatory ending," *L'Humanité* stated that Indians had been "interned in concentration camps" and subjected to forced labor—two subjects familiar to the French from World War II—and it was pleased that "the atrocities committed by the American troops are shown very clearly and even criticized." *Franc-Tireur* also drew a parallel with French history by stating that Massaï's resistance "rather resembles a certain appeal of June 18," the date of Charles de Gaulle's 1940 radio broadcast urging resistance to the German occupation. No French critic alluded to the Algerian War at all, and if it was instead World War II that provided frames of reference, perhaps that was because that war affected the French much more directly than overseas colonial wars had. Nonetheless, the absence of parallels drawn between American actions against the Apaches and French actions in Algeria suggests French insensitivity to colonial questions in 1955.

A very different kind of revisionism appeared in MGM's *The Last Hunt* (1956), Richard Brooks's next film after *Blackboard Jungle*. Although it featured an Indian woman (Debra Paget) and a half-Indian boy (Russ Tamblyn), the film's purpose was less to show Indians in a positive light than to depict the conquest of the West as an ugly, grim act of violence. Personifying that point is Charlie Gilson (Robert Taylor), a sadistic killer who teams with veteran buffalo hunter Sandy McKenzie (Stewart Granger), who reluctantly returns for a "last hunt" of the nearly extinct buffalo even though he is "fed up on killing." Using footage of the shooting of buffalo from an annual culling that took place in the 1950s, the film uses violence to sicken and shock the viewer, long before Samuel Peckinpah's *The Wild Bunch* (1969). Charlie, the film's villain, is an Indian-hater who admits he knows little about them but declares that "Injuns ain't even human" and "ain't got no religion"—though he is not averse to using the Indian woman for sex—and the whites in the town are just as bad. Set just after the Indian Wars, the film demythologizes them, as Sandy explains why General Sheridan paid men to kill buffalo. "Every dead buffalo meant a starving Indian," he says. "The army couldn't lick the Indians, so he wanted to starve 'em back on the reservation." His conclusion on the slaughter of the buffalo is also the film's conclusion on the conquest of the West: "It ain't nothing to be proud of."

Although Brooks later said of the film that Americans "couldn't stand it because of their own guilt," this grim film placed number fifty-seven for 1956.[73] Fifteen of twenty-nine American reviews praised it (52 percent), while six disliked it, and eight were mixed or neutral, and critics easily grasped the implications for Indians of the slaughter of the buffalo.[74] Noting the "poverty and starvation" they faced because of the "wanton destruction of the buffalo by greedy white hunters," the *Dallas Morning News* described the subject as "an unflattering aspect of American history." *Film Daily* called it a "fascinating slice of American history" that "does not hesitate to portray the seedier side of frontier camp and town," and the *New York Post* found the film unsettling but "probably closer to frontier reality . . . than many a happier, pleasanter Western."

The British critics reacted much as the Americans did, with eight of seventeen praising it (47 percent), three panning it, and six giving it mixed or neutral ratings.[75] Among the naysayers, the *Observer* called it "gruesome business" and "a dreary film." The *Sunday Times* found it "bleak but sympathetic" and was pleased to "welcome a film which expresses a genuine disgust with the pursuit of extermination," while the *Evening Standard* wrote that "a harsh, unflattering light is beamed on the world of the pioneers" and that "the old Hollywood dream factory" has "retooled to turn out nightmares." In France, the film sold 1.2 million tickets, while twelve of thirteen reviews praised it (92 percent), and none panned it.[76] *La Croix* liked Brooks's "respect for human life and the fraternity of whites and Indians," while *Le Parisien Libéré* called it "a western of exceptional quality," even with a "script that is perhaps too full of intentions," including antiracism. *Les Lettres Françaises* noted that after Little Big Horn, the Americans saw "that there was only one way to defeat the Indians, which was to destroy the economic basis of their existence," and it concluded that the film "proves that there are decent people among American filmmakers" who can "speak firmly about what still causes them shame." Once again French critics drew historical parallels to Europe, as *Cinéma 57* called it an antiracist, antifascist film, "for one cannot help thinking of the exterminations perpetrated by the Nazis in the name of monstrously absurd racial theories." These positive reactions indicated that when filmmakers reworked the western for progressive ends, French critics understood and welcomed the effort.

The Holdouts: Anti-Indian Films in the 1950s

A few films made after *Broken Arrow* ignored or rejected such liberalism and adhered to staunchly negative depictions of Indians. *The Charge at Feather River* (1953) told a remarkably retrograde tale of heroic whites rescuing two white women from evil Indian kidnappers. Paramount's *Arrowhead* (1953) also ignored the new trend. Charles Marquis Warren wrote and directed this film about Ed Bannon (Charlton Heston), an army scout loosely based on Indian fighter Al Sieber. Bannon was raised by Apaches who murdered his father, but unlike the pro-Indian films in which men who know Indians use their knowledge to try to foster white understanding of them, Bannon tells a gathering of Apaches that they are animals and declares, "Whenever I am called an Apache, I grow sick with shame." *Arrowhead* fits the pattern of war films urging Americans to "become savage" to defeat savages, as Bannon advises an officer: "There's only one way to beat the Apache: Fight the way he fights."[77]

The film's depiction of Apaches is unrelentingly and passionately negative. There are no good Indian characters, and when an entire tribe comes into the fort in a surrender agreement, we see no children and only a few women briefly and from a distance. The bloodthirsty Apaches are superstitious, believing in an

Invincible One who will lead them in battle with the "white eyes." Bannon expounds on Apache ways, telling other whites of their cruelty to horses and to people, teaching their children "how to cut a man's throat so it takes him nearly a day to die." The film's main villain, Toriano (Jack Palance), "had a baby brother born sickly, and like a good Apache he took him out and bashed his head against a rock," Bannon explains. The film's racism is clearest in its treatment of a brother and sister of half-Apache and half-Mexican parentage. The sister, Nita (Katy Jurado), is attracted to Bannon, who hates himself for finding her alluring, and he tells her she is only pretty because of her Spanish blood. *Arrowhead* ridicules the notion of an Apache becoming civilized, and four characters who chose to live among whites (Toriano, Nita, Spanish, and Jim Eagle) turn against them and try to murder them. Fresh from his performance as the evil gunslinger in *Shane*, Palance shines as Toriano. After returning to his people from a school back East, he discards his suit and tie, and through an evil grin, announces to his people, "I am not a white man." Then in cold blood he murders a white boyhood friend and takes up the role of the Invincible One determined to "rid the earth" of white people.

Sneering at films such as *Broken Arrow*, *Arrowhead* calls the Chiricahuas "the most vicious Indians on earth," and whereas in pro-Indian films it was whites who lied and launched treacherous attacks under cover of white flags, here the Apaches do so. The depiction of rituals, instead of serving to humanize the Apaches and to educate Americans about them, regains its old function of horrifying white audiences; the only ones shown are savage war dances, drumming, and chants. A grim, cynical atmosphere pervades the film—novelist W. R. Burnett, on whose *Adobe Walls* (1953) this movie is based, specialized in gritty tales of hard-bitten men, including *Little Caesar*, *Scarface*, and *High Sierra*—and the unshaven, hard-drinking Bannon endures the scorn of everyone at the fort. The film sides with Bannon, as events repeatedly vindicate his warnings not to trust Apaches, and the starry-eyed fools who seek peace with Apaches either end up dead or tell Bannon he was right. *Arrowhead* thus rebuts 1950s liberals and pacifists as well as recent pro-Indian films. The CIA, alarmed at its image of Indian-hating, asked Paramount to tone it down, but the film leaves room to doubt the CIA's power over Hollywood.[78]

The film barely made *Variety*'s charts at number 109, despite good reviews, as fifteen of twenty-five (60 percent) praised it, and only three panned it.[79] The positive reviews lauded the filmmaking and acting and grasped without objection the point about not trusting Apaches. Few even noted that the film bucked the pro-Indian trend, but among the three negative reviews, *America* called Bannon "almost psychopathically committed to the view that the only good Indian is a dead one" in a "throw-back" that is "vigorous if hardly constructive." Bosley Crowther of the *Times* noted that it rejected recent westerns' "feelings of friendship for the American Indian" and clung to the view that "an Indian is still a treacherous dog," while William Hogan of the *San Francisco Chronicle* declared, "I found my sympathies with the Palance crowd, which is not what the makers of *Arrowhead* intended." These were minority views, suggesting that pro-Indian films still had work to do.

The Ambivalent Center

While many 1950s westerns were clearly pro-Indian and a smaller number were clearly anti-Indian, still others were essentially ambivalent, presenting contradictory and even incoherent messages. Typifying this stance were the "trapper" or "mountain man" films, set in the first phase of colonization. The most popular of these (number thirteen of 1951) was MGM's and William Wellman's *Across the Wide Missouri*.[80] It told the story of Flint Mitchell (Clark Gable), a trapper in Blackfoot territory around 1830, who marries a Blackfoot woman (Mexican actress María Elena Marqués). Framing the tale is a voice-over by their son, who looks back on the events of his childhood. The film depicts a nearly utopian moment when whites and Indians existed mostly harmoniously on the frontier, as the happy interracial marriage suggests. Kamiah, whom her son describes as "proud, strong, and beautiful" and who shows great courage in leading the trappers across a dangerous mountain pass, is one of several positive Indian characters. Recalling *Broken Arrow*'s opening voice-over, the narrator says his father "saw these Indians as he had never seen them before: as people with homes and traditions and ways of their own. Suddenly they were no longer savages; they were people who laughed and loved and dreamed." Like another character in this film who went native (Brecan) because he "liked the Blackfoot Indians and the way they lived," Flint chooses not to return to white society, for "he belonged to the Indian country now, heart and soul." The film also explains why the Indian villain, Ironshirt (Ricardo Montalban), fights the white men: he views them as "intruders and enemies" and "had the idea that this was his country."

This single line notwithstanding, Ironshirt is a classic Indian villain who smirks after shooting a white sentry, murders Kamiah, and even tries to kill Flint's baby with a tomahawk. Despite introducing several sympathetic Indian characters, the film also leads the audience to side with the trappers in its climactic battle scene. And at the same time that such films gazed nostalgically at a lost world, they also celebrated the heroic feats of the whites who began its destruction. Although their buckskin clothing, uncouth behavior, and intimate relations with the Indians all suggest a rejection of white civilization, they are in fact connected to it both by their means of making a living—selling pelts to white merchants—and by the intelligence information their trailblazing furnishes advancing white society. The narrator calls these men "giants who walked the West and became part of our history" and built "new outposts of civilization," and though he recalls his time on the frontier as "the happiest in my life," his father ends up sending him East for schooling, as in many previous books and films about white men who had children with Indians. These "giants" may have loved this pristine world of natural beauty and savages noble and ignoble, but they loved it to death, and the film cannot reconcile its conflicting images.

The same ambivalence also marked Howard Hawks's *The Big Sky* (1952), a nostalgic look at a band of trappers who "opened a new land for the future." In the film, an Indian-hater gradually lets go of his hatred and stays in Indian country to marry a Blackfoot woman, and despite its affectionate picture of the trappers, *The Big Sky* offers some sharp criticism of white civilization. One trapper explains the Indians' hostility to whites: "White men don't see nothin' purty unless they want to grab. The more they grab the more they want to grab. . . . [They] keep on grabbing until everything belongs to white men and then start grabbing from each other." Two later films on this phase of colonization, *Far Horizons* (1955), about the Lewis and Clark expedition, and *Yellowstone Kelly* (1959), were less critical of colonization, each featuring a single good Indian woman who helps the whites against hostile Indians.

While many films manifested such ambivalence, even anti-Indian films now made concessions to racial liberalism. In the low-budget *Apache Drums* (1951), an ordinary pioneers-versus-Indians picture filled with bloodthirsty Apaches, someone felt compelled to insert a pro-Indian opening monologue; an Apache narrator complains that his people were starving and states: "The white man from the north and the white man of Mexico have drawn a line across the middle of the land that feeds us . . . [to] thrust us away from the earth." Another low-budget 1951 film, *Cavalry Charge*, with Ronald Reagan as a Confederate captain fighting in Arizona, mainly deals with North-South reconciliation and white solidarity against the Apaches, but the film inserts one pro-Indian scene. When the Captain meets Chief Grey Cloud, he learns he is actually a white Union Army general who defected to the Apaches. "Who was it started the practice of paying bounties for Indian scalps?" asks Grey Cloud. "Who made treaties and promptly broke them?" He concludes, "I was compelled as a matter of pure ethics to side with the Indians."

The Searchers

Ambivalence about Indians also marks John Ford's *The Searchers* (1956), which has earned enormous respect from directors and film scholars as well as voluminous analysis and political critique. More complex than most westerns—Ford called it a "psychological epic"—the saga has more themes and layers of meaning than this brief treatment can examine, but its handling of the Indian question deserves a close look.[81] Frank S. Nugent's script, based on Alan LeMay's novel, tells the story of settlers in Texas in 1868, in remote territory still vulnerable to Indian raids. Ethan Edwards (John Wayne), a diehard Confederate veteran, returns after many years to the humble cabin his brother Aaron (Walter Coy), Aaron's wife Martha (Dorothy Jordan), and their two daughters share with Martin Pauley (Jeffrey Hunter), a young man, one-eighth Cherokee, adopted after Comanches killed his family. Drawn away from the homestead by a decoy cattle raid, Ethan, Martin, and their neighbors the Jorgensens realize too late that Comanches are raiding the Edwards homestead, and though this chilling scene leaves the details to the imagination, they return to find their worst fears confirmed. Realizing that the Comanches have kidnapped the two daughters, the men spend the rest of the film searching for them.

The search reveals that Ethan's knowledge of the Comanches is equaled only by his hatred for them. In a memorable sequence, he shocks his fellow searchers when he shoots out the eyes of a dead Comanche, explaining that to Indians this means he "has to wander forever between the winds." After everyone but Ethan, Martin, and Brad Jorgensen (Harry Carey, Jr.) abandons the search, Ethan discovers the body of the elder daughter, raped and murdered, which drives her sweetheart Brad into a suicidal charge at a Comanche war party. The obsessed Ethan prefers to continue alone, but Martin insists on going along, in part because he suspects that Ethan intends not to rescue but to kill Debbie, now defiled by her captors. The two spend years searching the vast Southwest, finally locating the war chief Scar (Henry Brandon) and his captive Debbie (Natalie Wood), now a young woman. Debbie at first refuses to be rescued—she shows no signs of mistreatment and tells Martin "these are my people"—and Martin only stops Ethan from shooting her by shielding her with his body. After the two escape Scar's village without Debbie, they return, joined by Texas Rangers and U.S. cavalry, and rescue her. This time, Ethan eludes Martin and chases Debbie down, but in a dramatic climax, he relents from killing her, telling her, "Let's go home, Debbie."

The film's complexity and Ford's refusal to spell things out leaves it open to many readings, but it is unwise to assume that Ethan expresses the film's political viewpoint. The first to make this mistake was the PCA, which objected to Ethan scalping Scar.[82] Among critics, Robert Hatch of the *Nation* made the same assumption; dismissing it as "a picture for sadists," he complained that Wayne's character "behaves like a dangerous lunatic" and "Wayne's behavior is presented as the heroic stuff out of which the West was made."[83] The casting of Wayne probably confused people, who did not expect him to play such a complex, morally ambiguous character.[84] Moreover, the film invites viewers to empathize with Ethan before it reveals his racist obsession—thus inducing viewers to confront their own racial animosities.[85] Further complicating the film's point of view is Martin, virtually a coprotagonist and a character with whom the audience empathizes as well. The title, after all, is plural, and the tension between the two men and their overlapping but distinct outlooks and agendas drives the story. Ford's own racial politics have provoked ongoing debate, with his biographers defending him against charges of hatred for Indians, and *The Searchers*, his most significant meditation on racism, stands at the center of that debate.[86] Indeed, the potential confusion between Ethan and Ford, as well as the film's dark subject matter and the way it draws the viewer into Ethan's mentality, may help explain why the Academy Awards snubbed it.

While some see *The Searchers* as a conservative, racist defense of extermination, Ford did not make the picture to endorse genocide.[87] A student of history, Ford offered a warts-and-all portrait of a time and place, unlike some of the more romanticized pro-Indian films made then and since. Both the Comanches and the Texas settlers could be brutal, and the realities of the conquest were not pretty.[88] Hardly a standard western hero, Ethan is a psychologically scarred, pathological Indian-hater who finally recovers his buried sense of humanity. While *The Searchers* explores and even critiques frontier racism, it is not its main purpose, any more than it was to demonize Indians. It is, instead, to explore the settlers' psychological and emotional experience, which it does brilliantly. A scene in which Ethan and Martin find some white women driven mad by their experience as Comanche captives, sometimes cited as evidence of Ford's own horror at miscegenation, conveys the settlers' terror at the prospect of rape by Indians, which was part of their mental world.[89] To depict a mentality, even to empathize with the women's suffering, is not necessarily to endorse all the characters' political values. Nor does the film approve of Ethan shooting the eyes of the dead Comanche, frantically slaughtering buffalo to try to starve the Indians, calling Martin a "blanket head," scalping Scar, or intending to murder Debbie. It presents such behavior as problematic, not heroic.

If *The Searchers* were an overtly political, antiracist film like *Broken Arrow*, it would indeed be a failure, for it is deeply ambivalent about Indians. On the one hand, its depiction of the horrors of a Comanche raid and the traumas captives endured encourage viewers to side with the whites, and its attempt at comic relief through Martin's inadvertent marriage to the Comanche woman they call Look (Beulah Archuletta) comes off as offensive, racist, and misogynist.[90] On the other hand, the film depicts Ethan's racial hatred as pathological and shows that Brad, Laurie Jorgensen (Martin's sweetheart), and others share some of his hatred for Indians, so the problem transcends one flawed individual.[91] Moreover, the film states that Scar had "two sons killed by white men," and it shows peaceful Indians who get along with whites. We also see the aftermath of a cavalry raid on an Indian village, where Ethan and Martin discover Look's body—prodding Martin to ask, "What did them soldiers have to go and kill her for, Ethan? She never done nobody any harm."[92] It also shows the army herding Indian women and children into an outpost after the massacre. Finally, it certainly endorses Ethan's decision to spare Debbie.

Yet despite the film's ambivalence, it ultimately leans toward the settlers, mainly because it tells the story from their point of view. The treatment of their point of view is complex because Ethan's relationship to the settler community is complex: he remains somewhat alien to the community that adores him. The ending emphasizes his distance, as he remains alone outside the Jorgensens' house after he brings Debbie back, heading off to wander, like the dead Comanche, in the winds.[93] His knowledge of Comanches sets him apart from everyone but his pal Mose (Hank Worden), placing him in an intermediate space between two rival communities, and he can never really return from the battlefield. He is the familiar white protector, but he remains aloof from those he protects—like Will Kane in *High Noon* (1952) and the title character in *Shane* (1953).[94] Although the film can be critical of Ethan and the settlers, it is hard not to see real affection in its treatment of them and their hardships, and in telling their story, it also tends to glorify the pioneers. "Someday this country's gonna be a fine good place to be," declares Mrs. Jorgensen, but "maybe it needs our bones in the ground before that day can come." In *Fort Apache* the glory of the regiment outweighed its colonel's flaws; here the greater good of the settlers' enterprise outweighs the faults of the individuals who carried it out. Despite acknowledging the harm this enterprise did to the Indians, the film is essentially colonialist in its overall vision of that enterprise, and it shows that in judging the politics of films about Indians, the depiction of Indians may matter less than the image of whites and their endeavors. Had the film been more balanced in presenting the whites' and the Indians' points of view, it would have suffered dramatically, and its purposes were more dramatic than political. If the film seems conflicted about racism and Indians, it reflects the thinking of many past and present Americans.

This unusually long, dark, and complex film reached number ten on *Variety*'s chart for 1956—the top western of twenty-one that year.[95] Despite claims that the film did poorly with critics, its American reviews were heavily positive.[96] Of thirty-four reviews located, twenty-two were positive (65 percent), five negative, and seven mixed or neutral.[97] Most complaints concerned the film's length, though six reviews disliked the comic sequences, and four found the ridicule of Look unfunny or objectionable, while no one praised those scenes.[98] A few critics mistook the film for a Saturday-matinee western, including *Cue*, which called it "first-rate, rousing entertainment" in which "hordes of howling Indians bite the dust." A few saw nothing wrong with Ethan, whom the *New Orleans Times-Picayune* described as a "rugged, straight-shooting hero whose integrity is never questioned." Others found him puzzling; *Variety* panned the film mainly because Ethan's motivations seemed unclear, but it explained them quite accurately.[99] Not everyone minded the film leaving things unexplained, and in a positive review, the *San Francisco Chronicle* called it "often exciting, sometimes mysterious, and occasionally downright baffling." Unlike scholars, who can watch films repeatedly over time and read others' analyses, critics had but a single screening and no time to reflect, and this film was unusually challenging.

Among the rave reviews, the *Hollywood Reporter* judged it "undoubtedly one of the greatest Westerns ever made." The *Los Angeles Examiner* declared that "the grandeur, the beauty, the sweep and the tragic horror" of the film "cannot, with justice, be detailed in mere words," while *Motion Picture Daily* called it "one of those rare pictures that the 'discriminating' audience can enjoy equally with the great mass of fans." Aware of Ethan's flaws, critics used terms such as "fanatic" and "obsession" to describe him. "He is driven by dark, relentless Furies" and "goaded by a blind hate of Comanches," observed the *New York Herald-Tribune*, and the *Hollywood Reporter* termed him a "vengeance seeking machine." Among those who noticed the pro-Indian elements, the *Boston Globe* wrote that "although the Indians are the villains of the plot, certain sequences show their side of the quarrel," including one showing that "Indian children are killed by white raiders with merciless indifference." The *Hollywood Reporter* pointed out, "We learn that the Chief ... has lost two sons in the wars with the palefaces who have taken their hunting grounds," adding that "the sight of the Indians trying to save their children from the avenging white men tugs at the heart." Perhaps by this time, three years after *Arrowhead*, pro-Indian films had begun to sensitize Americans to Indians' perspectives.

The film also did well with British critics, with thirteen of seventeen praising it (76 percent), two panning it, and two giving it a mixed judgment.[100] Some wished for clearer characters or found the film too long, but critic and director Lindsay Anderson's negative review in *Sight and Sound* added other objections. In addition to calling the Look sequence "an unnecessarily coarse touch," Anderson complained that Ethan "is an unmistakable neurotic, devoured by an irrational hatred of Indians and half-breeds" and his search is "inspired less by love or honour than by the obsessive desire" to kill Debbie. He also found Ethan's change of heart at the end unbelievable, unconvinced by subtle shots of Wayne that suggested a more human, emotional side. It would have been better, he suggested, "to make its hero not Edwards but Martin Pawley," for "at least here is a character who stands for something." Anderson, in short, assumed Ford was endorsing Ethan's behavior and making him a hero, and he misunderstood what Ford was doing. R. D. Smith of the socialist *Tribune* liked the film but complained that Ethan was "quite balmy as far as Indians are concerned," whereas "Indian fighters must be . . . good, they must be magnanimous, they must be noble." Like Anderson, Smith remained riveted to old notions of the western. More open to the film's innovations, Leonard Mosley of the *Daily Express* called it "the best Western I have seen in 10 years," one whose white characters "behave like human beings—some bad, some good, some stupid, some clever." *Time and Tide*'s Majdalany praised it for telling its story "slowly and atmospherically and with a poet's feeling," while the *Sunday Times*'s Dilys Powell wrote that the film's "contrast between the oases of human affection and the bloodstained world outside is exquisitely made." And the *Daily Worker* was pleased that "Ford's way with this primitive race hatred is not to pretend it didn't exist or to introduce a high-minded character to argue it away," but rather "to show it for what it was."

In France, where the film sold 2,255,352 tickets, eight of thirteen reviews (62 percent) praised it, and four panned it.[101] Although many critics echoed the American and British reviewers, some also likened it to Europe's own mythology: *Carrefour* compared Ethan and Martin to Lancelot and Galahad, while *La Croix* saw Ford as one of Hollywood's "modern troubadours who have written the *Chanson de Roland* of a nascent America." Some of the French also confused Ford's politics with Ethan's. In a positive review, *Radio Cinéma Télévision* wrote that "if hatred is a passion that is part of human nature, we have a hard time with it being presented as something acceptable, particularly at the present time." *Les Lettres Françaises* faulted the film "for not specifying how one should interpret certain ambiguities in the dialogue about the racial problem," while *Franc-Tireur* liked the film but found the Indians too stereotypical, and *L'Humanité* considered it "somewhat racist." The reviews from all three countries indicate that while some welcomed attempts to alter the western genre, others clung to expectations generated by years of previous filmmaking.

The vast number of westerns about Indians made between 1946 and 1959—more than fifty, including comedies, that made the box-office charts plus even more that did not—makes simple conclusions hazardous. Determining how many were "pro-Indian" depends on definitions, and it helps to distinguish between films' depictions of Indians and their broader messages about conquest and colonization. While one might expect pro-Indian films to oppose conquest and colonization, many westerns sympathized with Indians while generally endorsing colonization. The key to this apparent paradox is the notion of liberal colonialism, an outlook that saw the spread of Western civilization benefiting the colonized yet rejected extermination, forced relocation, and neglect. In judging depictions of Indians, this study considers the depth of character development and the amount and quality of dialogue Indian characters received; the effort made to explain Indian rituals, grievances, and motivations for using violence; the choice of whether to depict Indian women and children as well as warriors; the balance between "good" and "bad" Indians; and whether white characters familiar with Indian ways use their knowledge to advocate for their welfare or to gain strategic advantage over them.

By these criteria, twenty-four of the fifty-one dramas about Indians that made Variety's charts in these years were pro-Indian, while fourteen were anti-Indian, and thirteen were ambivalent or unclear (see appendix A). Within this period, anti-Indian films made up 43 percent of those released by 1953 (ten of twenty-three) and only 14 percent of those after that (four of twenty-eight), indicating a trend toward more positive treatment.[102] Hollywood nonetheless continued to make films of all three kinds, and the turn toward more positive images were part of a long-term transformation that began before 1946 and continued after 1959. This period also saw little improvement in the authenticity of Hollywood's representations of Indians, as ethnic miscasting and inaccuracies of representation persisted.

While it can be instructive to categorize films by their approaches to Indians, lines between the categories often blurred. Strikingly anti-Indian films might contain incongruously pro-Indian elements, suggesting some awkward, belated patching, and pro-Indian films included insulting and dated (if inadvertent) stereotyping. Moreover, individual filmmakers veered from making pro-Indian to mixed or anti-Indian films—as John Ford did in his cavalry trilogy and Delmer

Daves did in moving from *Broken Arrow* to *Drum Beat* (1954)—suggesting a shallow and uncertain commitment to new approaches. This diversity of views existed not just because there were both liberal and conservative filmmakers, but also because complex and changing blends of liberal and conservative ideas mingled within individual minds.

Indications of the films' position on conquest and colonization include whether they made a positive case for conquest, by praising pioneers or highlighting the superiority of Western ways; whether they showed white women and children or only gunmen, soldiers, miners, and the like; whether they depicted settlers and other whites as noble and heroic or greedy and racist—in short, whether they viewed conquest as desirable or merely inevitable. By such criteria, twenty-nine mainly supported conquest and colonization, seven took mostly negative views, and fifteen offered mixed views or none at all (see appendix A). Twenty-two of these films were "peace westerns," which featured protagonists—white, Indian, or both—seeking to stop warfare and violence and foster racial coexistence. The peace westerns generally featured one of three structures: roughly a dozen presented an alliance of moderates, in which peace-minded whites and Indians allied to defeat war mongers on both sides. Others either pitted good Indians and all whites against bad Indians, or good Indians and good whites against bad whites.

The proliferation of peace westerns—which still had plenty of violent action—illuminates Cold War culture and attitudes. Traditional, bellicose westerns reinforced self-confidence in the righteousness of Western ways and urged people to embrace the struggle. In these films, equating American Indians with communists had a certain logic despite basic differences between the two groups. But the peace westerns could also serve Cold War aims by uniting the home front and urging pride in tolerance and racial harmony. In these films, American Indians could stand for blacks and other minorities, and the films favored an end to internationally embarrassing racism.

However naive and incoherent it may seem to favor a combination of peace, western expansion, and concern for Indians, this liberal-colonialist outlook raises vital questions about the meaning of decolonization for people with no hope of their colonizers' departure. The peace westerns, of course, tell us nothing of how Indians felt about their options, but they tell us something of the colonizers' attitudes, and unlike the traditional westerns, with their vanishing-American assumptions, these films at least reminded viewers that Indians had a future after the wars. And though set in the past, they invited viewers to consider current policy toward Indians.

One form of internal decolonization to which films alluded was full assimilation, which required whites to abandon their racism, end discrimination, and accept acculturated Indians as fully equal members of society. This outlook corresponded to the prevailing integrationist outlook in the African American civil rights movement, while also appealing to proponents of termination, who envisioned Indians joining mainstream society. Despite scholarly criticism of films favoring assimilation, Indians found the adoption of some Western ways essential to surviving the conquest and retaining other aspects of their culture. Films that praised aspects of Indian cultures, called for peaceful coexistence, envisioned the survival of Indian communities, and urged decent treatment of Indians on reservations sketched out a multicultural model in which Indians could retain some measure of culture and community while living in the United States. Multiculturalism was not yet in vogue in the 1950s, but the films of these years contain some intriguing suggestions of its value. Opponents of termination in the 1950s in essence favored this model, with the reservations serving as bases of Indian identity and cultural preservation.

While these films showed real possibilities of reinscribing westerns with new content more favorable to Indians and more critical of American colonization of the West—undermining notions of an inherently racist and triumphalist genre— they still faced the challenge of convincing their viewers. The lack of comment in many reviews about the more depressing and critical images suggests the limits of that ability and the difficulties of getting new perspectives to register in viewers' minds. Yet reviews of the revisionist westerns displayed a range of reactions, and while some critics balked at the changes, most welcomed them, expressing the sort of guilt about Western dealings with third-world peoples that became familiar in the 1960s and after. On the whole, the reactions are complex, even incoherent: the same critic might praise a viciously anti-Indian, pro-conquest film such as *Arrowhead* then welcome a pro-Indian, anti-conquest film like *Apache*. This willingness to accept either view indicates that many people's thoughts on the subject remained fluid. In the absence of an ideology to make sense of the newer images, they did not yet translate into much real anticolonialism, though they prepared the way for significant changes in the next decade.

Revisionist westerns also faced constraints inherent in the medium as well as the genre, as the imperative to entertain hampered the presenting of new perspectives on conquest and colonization. In short, conveying Indians' experiences and views of conquest and colonization was likely to make for a depressing evening at the movies, as the makers of *Devil's Doorway* and *The Last Hunt* learned. Observers of films such as *Broken Arrow* may now chide them for omitting harsh realities, but such criticism overlooks the pressures filmmakers faced to please audiences. Those pressures produced some unrealistically rosy visions of the past; *Broken Arrow*, for example, leaves viewers thinking that Cochise's project of raising cattle will bring the Apaches prosperity, while *Comanche Territory* (1956) and *Drums across the River* (1954) offer happy endings in which white settlers pledge to pay Indians fair prices for minerals on their lands. By 1970, *Soldier Blue* could offer a depressing, unflinching picture of a massacre of Indians without a happy ending and succeed at the box office; in this era, the studios and producers were probably right that audiences were not ready for such films.

Yet despite the happy endings and upbeat tone of most of these films, quite a few presented the "winning of the West" in unflattering terms. Beginning with *Fort Apache*'s suggestion that some of America's mythic heroes were really racist scoundrels who dealt dishonorably with the Indians, the films of these years issued a long stream of messages of white malfeasance and cruelty. White racist villains appear in thirty-two of the fifty-one films on the charts, and viewers were bombarded with images of greedy, aggressive settlers, bull-headed, ignorant army officers, conniving politicians and Indian agents, broken treaties, illegitimate seizures of Indian land, and shameful mistreatment of Indians on reservations. Even films that seemed to celebrate conquest often had subversive currents that questioned how admirable and ethical the winning of the West had been, and though viewers probably struggled to reconcile these conflicting images, the accumulation of negative, self-critical images began to create fissures in the foundations of imperial pride.

PART TWO

COMING TO TERMS

Confronting Insurgency and Decolonization

After World War II, British and American filmmakers continued making colonialist films, while French filmmakers mostly avoided the subject until the late 1950s. Many British and American films basically ignored decolonization, carrying on interwar cinematic traditions by telling tales of civilizing women, heroic trailblazers, and white male protectors in the colonies. But each year brought new evidence of colonial change and unrest: the Philippines and Jordan became independent in 1946; followed by India and Pakistan in 1947; Burma, Ceylon, and Israel in 1948; and Indonesia in 1949. Riots, violence, and warfare also broke out in Algeria in 1945, Indochina in 1946, Madagascar in 1947, and in Malaya 1948, while the victory of Mao's Communists in China in 1949 marked the end of Western domination there. Western filmmakers, torn between their fear of political controversy and their desire to address these compelling events, began confronting the subjects of nationalist insurgency and independence in a growing body of work. The following three chapters examine these films, beginning with British and American films about decolonization and anticolonial movements in the British Empire.

CHAPTER FOUR

The British Empire and Decolonization

Given postwar British leaders' belief that economic recovery and new welfare state spending required revenue from the colonies, the loss of India and Pakistan in 1947 was a great disappointment. Determined to keep remaining possessions, leaders knew that the financial crisis made waging major military campaigns impractical, and a war-weary nation also yearned for peace.[1] In the first postwar decade, Britain did use military force in Palestine, Malaya, Kenya, and elsewhere, but its plan to regain control of the Suez Canal through an invasion coordinated with France and Israel in autumn 1956, while successful militarily, angered President Eisenhower, who used financial pressure to force an embarrassing withdrawal. After that, British colonial policy mostly followed the pattern of the peaceful handover of power used in India and Pakistan, with further colonial violence taking place only much later in Northern Ireland.[2] On the whole, Britain avoided the traumas, bitter internal divisions, and political disruption that decolonization caused in France and Portugal.

The picture of how the British reacted to losing their empire remains quite incomplete, and indeed the empire's meaning to ordinary Britons in earlier times has provoked vigorous debate among British historians. The notion that most Britons had little knowledge or interest about overseas colonies prevailed until the 1980s, when historians began emphasizing how thoroughly the culture and products of empire had pervaded people's lives in the classical age of imperialism. Identifying imperial content in leisure organizations, textbooks, mass-market books, ads, postcards, trinkets, paintings, music, plays, and eventually radio and cinema as well, revisionists insisted on the empire's importance in Britons' daily lives and national identity.[3] Others have questioned whether the imperial content in popular culture actually made people imperialists, and they have noted the difficulties of establishing what effects imperial products and propaganda had on people.⁴ The enormous efforts put into "selling" the empire suggest the imperialists' own doubts about their compatriots' support, and although sources such as soldiers' letters and working-class memoirs leave doubts about popular enthusiasm for empire, further evidence is certainly welcome.⁵

Although this debate has mostly focused on the late nineteenth and early twentieth centuries, evidence for the mid-twentieth century appears in surveys carried out by the research institution Mass Observation (founded in 1937). Those surveys suggested considerable ignorance and apathy about the empire, and a Gallup poll from 1939 found 77 percent agreeing that India should receive its independence "soon."⁶ Summarizing a series of polls the Colonial Office carried out in 1947–48, the *Manchester Guardian* wrote that it "reveals an ignorance which is remarkable even when one grants that most people are not much interested in the subject," as "only a quarter had any clear notion of the difference between a colony and a Dominion, and less than half were able to name a single colony."⁷ Closer scrutiny of these polls has revealed nuances and forms of knowledge that escaped survey questions, and people could certainly favor keeping British possessions even if they knew little about them.⁸ Indeed, some Britons staunchly opposed decolonization, including members of the League of Empire Loyalists, a pressure group founded in 1954, as well as settlers in the African colonies, who continued to arrive throughout the 1950s.⁹ The Suez debacle dealt the imperialists a serious blow without completely ending resistance to decolonization, and they increasingly looked to the Commonwealth as a new form of empire.¹⁰ On the other side, the Movement for Colonial Freedom, founded in 1954, had three million members, who struggled with the same widespread ignorance and apathy that troubled the imperialists.¹¹ The occasional opinion polls on the subject cannot really resolve the question of whether Britons reacted to decolonization mostly with indifference, as some argue, or with shock, as others contend.¹² A look at films about decolonization and anticolonial movements may cast further light on this topic.

The Malayan Emergency

One place where Britain fought to retain colonies was Malaya, a source of badly needed foreign-exchange earnings and resources such as rubber, tin, and timber, and the Malayan Emergency that began in 1948 led to two noteworthy films. Malaya, largely a British creation, comprised large Malay and Chinese populations and a smaller Indian population that labored on plantations. The roots of the Emergency lay in a combination of factors: the economic downturn of the 1930s and 1940s, hardships resulting from Japan's wartime plunder, the disruptions and internal migration those events caused, and anticolonialism encouraged both by Japan's defeat of Britain and by India's independence. The Japanese occupation had also spurred a resistance movement in which Britons fought alongside Malayans, mainly of Chinese descent. Although the Chinese-dominated Malayan Communist Party (MCP), linked to China's Communist Party, took control of the uprising that began in 1948, it was mainly the discontent of Chinese squatters and workers that initiated it, catching MCP leaders unprepared. The murder of three British planters in June 1948 naturally alarmed British settlers, who, though few in number, owned more than a million acres of land and who, along with Malay landowners, produced the resources Britain desired.[13] Throughout the Emergency, Britain enjoyed considerable cooperation from Malays and Indians, particularly the Malay-dominated United Malays National Organisation (UMNO). Rural populations in areas of heavy rebel activity, however, were caught between the extortion from rebels needing food and resources and the harsh tactics, including forced relocation, the British and their Malay police forces used. It took the British some time to grasp, or to admit, that they were facing more than "banditry," as officials often termed it.[14] The rebels did considerable damage in the first years, destroying rubber trees and killing planters—forty-nine between July and November 1951—until an economic recovery fueled by rising demand for Malayan exports during the Korean War and the appointment in 1952 of a new high commissioner who combined repression with an effective "hearts and minds" policy turned the tide.[15] Even more decisive was Britain's gradual transfer of power to an UMNO-led alliance of parties opposed to the MCP, culminating in independence in 1957. By 1960, the uprising was over.

The first of two British films to deal with these events was a 1952 black-and-white release from Rank's General Film Distributors: *The Planter's Wife*, directed by Ken Annakin. Shot mostly at Pinewood Studios, the film makes its agenda clear at the outset, with a dedication "to the rubber planters of Malaya, where only the jungle is neutral, and where the planters are daily defending their rubber trees with their lives." Hardly subtle, it opens with a jungle shot of two beady-eyed, slithering snakes, then fades to a shot of two beady-eyed, slithering Chinese guerrillas outside a planter's home. The film then introduces rubber planter Jim Frazer (Jack Hawkins) and his wife Liz (Claudette Colbert), awakened by a call from police informing them of the attack on their neighbor. Jim, Liz, and their young son Mike enjoy the life of colonial elites, complete with a handsome bungalow run by servants and social outings at the local club. The uprising forces them to turn their home into a fortress, and highlighting planters' sacrifices, the film shows Jim disturbing Liz's morning tea by practicing shooting in the front yard. One casualty of the Emergency is the Frazers' marital harmony: Liz, packing to take Mike to school in England, begs Jim to come along, but Jim is fixated on his work. His duties include searching his tappers, whom the guerrillas have coerced into smuggling food, driving saboteurs out of his groves, and shoring up the barbed-wire, floodlights, and machine gun nests around their bungalow. Liz, always dressed more for a soirée at the club than for jungle warfare, does her part as well, at one point whipping a pistol out of her dress just in time to gun down a guerrilla set on hacking her to bits on her front steps. A ferocious assault on the home by hordes of guerrillas—reminiscent of westerns—furnishes the story's climax, after which Liz resolves to stay with Jim.

Although the film never explains the politics of the uprising or the guerrillas' motives—like British leaders of the time, it calls them bandits rather than communists—it manages to convey political messages. The rebel leader, Ah Siong (Yah Ming), has a facial scar typical of movie villains, and his followers' unscrupulousness appears when Jim finds hand grenades that an infiltrator has hidden under the clothing of a young boy at the plantation. The film's insistence that the workers aid the guerrillas only out of fear underlines the rebels' lack of popular support and Britain's obligation to protect vulnerable subjects. Also demonstrating most Malayans' loyalty is their cooperation with security forces, who thank one man by telling him, "Without chaps like you coming forward as loyal citizens, we'd never catch a single bandit in this jungle of yours." Several scenes show harmonious relations between colonizers and colonized: Mike plays happily with Malayan children, Liz visits a Chinese girl wounded in a rebel attack, and Liz hands out sweets to children who mob her in town. Such scenes argue that the British belong here, as does Liz's statement to a friend: "I was born out here. I understand this country. For both of us planting is the only life we know." They also face danger stoically; a local commander (Anthony Steel) calls a fiery, fatal assault on one planter's home "a bit of trouble," and the Frazers take a pleasure jaunt to town, driving through rebel-infested territory in a car with retractable iron plates on the windows. In highlighting the settlers' sacrifices, the film dwells on threats to their homes—a theme in both fiction and news reports from Malaya and Kenya in these years.[16] The film emphasizes that theme in its climactic battle, as bullets shatter the china and other symbols of domesticity, and one rebel even penetrates the house itself.

Threats to the sanctity of the home were familiar to Britons from aerial bombing during World War II, and the film shrewdly enlisted British sympathies by connecting the Malayan Emergency to World War II through references to the Frazers' hardships under Japanese occupation. The film also connected with audiences at home through Liz, whose courage was designed to impress both men and women. Their hardships (including a cobra in the loo) cannot have done much to encourage emigration to Malaya, but that was not its purpose. It was, instead, to enlist sympathies for a struggle that required Parliament to spend money abroad—which British taxpayers were normally reluctant to do.

In Britain the film made *Kinematograph Weekly*'s list of 1952's top fifteen earners.[17] An advertisement in the *Times* showed a shirtless man with a bloody sickle, and its text described the battle that "the people of Malaya, the police, the military, the planter and the planter's wife" were waging against "a new enemy, cruel and fanatical, creeping from the jungle to murder and destroy." This "great new British film" honored "the heroes of this struggle [who] carry on, producing the *rubber* vital to the needs of the free world."[18] The British critics were mostly unimpressed, with nine of twenty-eight praising the film (32 percent), eleven panning it, and eight giving it mixed ratings.[19] A half dozen critics likened it to a western, including the *Evening Standard*, which mused that "the covered wagons have been converted into a rubber plantation and the Apaches have been deprived of their feathers and called Malayan bandits," while "the only thing missing is the horses."[20] The subplot about the Frazers' marital difficulties annoyed many critics, and among those who found the film poorly made, the *Observer* said it "treats of a grave subject in a comparatively artless and perfunctory way." The *Evening News*, while calling "the quiet heroism of the British in Malaya . . . a story that all the world (and America in particular) should know," said the film lacked "a script adequate to this important subject," and the *Evening Standard* welcomed "the attempt to portray something of the British struggle in Malaya" but felt it "made unbelievable the real trials and dangers of British planters and their families in this warmed-up area of the cold war." That reference to the Cold War indicates that the critics knew more about events in Malaya than the film conveyed, and the silence about politics bothered many. "By avoiding the use of the word Communist," wrote the *Evening Standard*, the film was like "a short-sighted ostrich with its head in the sand," and the *Manchester Guardian* charged that "the real issues of the Malayan problem have been quite ludicrously shelved." The *Daily Express*'s Leonard Mosley likened the omission of politics to "telling the story of Adam and Eve without mentioning the serpent," and he concluded that without any political context, the Frazers "might just as well be fighting back against Martians as against Reds." Noting that "nobody talks about Communism," the *Sunday Times*'s Dilys Powell conjectured that "the Americans would have been less discreet," but she was pleased that "for once we have not waited for America to tell us what is going on."

Expressing disdain for the film's politics as well as its artistry, the communist *Daily Worker* predictably derided what it called "propaganda in favour of Britain's bloodstained plundering of Malaya," and though it feared that "some may be swayed by the crude and shameless exploitation of small children to claim sympathy for a vicious colonial war," it also predicted that "millions of decent British people who thought the old imperialism was dead will be revolted by this attempt to enlist them on the wrong side." At least the film, it felt, showed the luxurious lifestyle of "a tiny minority of aliens" protected by a police state while "the people of that country are determined to rid their land of the oppressors and exploiters who are stealing their wealth at gunpoint." But the *Daily Worker* was alone in this view.

Among those embracing the film's imperialist politics, the pro-Labour *Daily Herald* called it "a fine and merited tribute to the courage and spirit most of us like to think is typically British," while the *Daily Mirror*, another Labour supporter, asserted that the picture "gives a grim and good idea of what is happening" in Malaya. The center-right *Daily Mail* called it a "tribute to some gallant men and women," and the populist *Star* praised its "laudable and patriotic aim" to publicize "a war that slips too often from our minds." Campbell Dixon of the pro-empire *Daily Telegraph* praised "the courage and devotion to duty of the planter in Malaya," who lives "with all war's horrors and none of its glamour and glory," even if "the Pinks and Little Englanders" misunderstand him. People imagine that these planters are "sitting round clubs all day, guzzling gin slings, while Malays do the work," but the film showed the real dangers they faced. Yet "their reward from stay-at-homes for their hazardous work to keep the Commonwealth solvent is usually a sneer." The *Evening News* printed a letter from a woman in Kensington who described herself as a planter's wife; she called the film "absolutely authentic," allowing for the condensing of events, and she urged others to see it because "in Malaya we often feel that people at home tend to forget us."[21] The *Picture Post*, however, ran a letter from a Mr. Leatham who saw the film in Kuala Lumpur and wrote that although he was "in no way trying to belittle the ordeal of the planter," he found the film inaccurate, for the "dangers lie in the unseen and unpredictable ambushes—not in major operations directed against their homes."[22]

Although the film targeted British audiences, a publicity memo said it also intended "to bring home to Americans the sacrifices in blood and effort which the British are making to keep Malaya free, and to ensure the continuation of the rubber supply in the Western world."[23] That document made no mention of communism, but producer John Stafford did in some of his public statements, and it is curious that a film seeking to enlist American support for this war ignored communism.[24] Retitled *Outpost in Malaya* in the United States, it did not make *Variety*'s charts for 1952, and it got a mediocre reception from the critics: six positive, six negative, and six mixed reviews in a sample of eighteen.[25] The *Hollywood Reporter* panned the film, "it never being quite clear what it is all about," and it reported that this "slow and silly story" was "so ludicrous as to draw hoots of derision from the audience" in Los Angeles. *Newsweek*'s sarcastic observation that "Miss Colbert proves that she can lug the white man's burden like a perfect little spitfire" suggests American resentment of British imperialism, and the term "plantations," which appeared in several reviews, had unfortunate associations for Americans.[26] The film was on safer ground with critics who mentioned communism, and helping make the connection, at least in Los Angeles, was the pairing of the film with an anticommunist documentary short.[27] But only four of eighteen American reviews spoke of communists, and the film might have done better in America had it mentioned them.[28] Instead, the *Boston Globe* likened it to westerns, calling it "a new kind of pioneer thriller with the Malayan rebels taking the roles usually assigned to savage Indians." It concluded that the film "makes you realize that our Indian-killing great-great grandmas . . . have their counterpart today." Few other American critics saw the parallel with westerns, and the film seems to have failed in its propaganda aims in the United States.

In France, *La Femme du Planteur* sold 1,386,306 tickets but did poorly with critics (three positive, six negative, and three mixed).[29] *Combat* liked it but called it propaganda "addressed mainly to the English" and said this conflict seemed "less spectacular than Korea or Indochina." Also praising it, and also mentioning Indochina, *Les Cahiers du Cinéma* pointed out that the British were facing "guerrilleros" seeking "a Malaya independent of European imperialisms." Though the conflict was "seen through the eyes of European settlers," theirs was "still a human perspective." Others on the left were cooler to the film's colonialism. Calling it "one of the most cynical and hateful displays of colonialism anyone has ever dared put on the screen," *L'Humanité* complained that a planter "is presented as a hero . . . [for] defending the colors of the British Empire and his own revenues from Malay partisans who fight to expel the exploiters from their country." With Malaya "burning under the feet of the English imperialists, like Indochina under those of the French," it called it "a duty of solidarity with colonized peoples to denounce and jeer this shameful work . . . aimed at stirring up racial hatred." "Rubber, how many crimes are committed in your name," wrote *Franc-Tireur*, adding that "obviously we are told nothing of the origins of the conflict (rich English colonists versus native 'terrorists')." The satirical *Le Canard Enchaîné* mockingly sympathized with the settlers in a country "infested with mosquitoes and terrorists," where "amusements are rare, aside from rubber and hunting natives." The lack of political context annoyed *Les Lettres Françaises*, which pointed out that though the rebels were fighting "foreign occupation," the film ignored their motives, "as if they did evil for the sake of evil." It also recalled that "terrorists" is what "the Germans called our resistance fighters." The film needed context, wrote *Les Nouvelles Littéraires*, because this war "is as unfamiliar to many Britons as our campaign in Indochina is to certain French people." *Le Figaro Littéraire*'s Claude Mauriac asked, "Who are these 'outlaws'? . . . Are they really 'bandits'? For whom or for what are they fighting (or do they think they're fighting)?" He cautioned that "Indochina is too close to Malaya for a French spectator not to wonder about these questions." So while unimpressed with the film, many French critics used it to raise the subject of Indochina.

Five years later, Rank's *Windom's Way* offered a very different look at the Malayan Emergency. By 1957, Malaya was independent and rebel activity was winding down, and this post-Suez revisiting of the subject reflected changed views of colonialism. Using a script adapted from American James Ramsey Ullman's novel, director Ronald Neame shot the film at Pinewood Studios and in Ceylon. Peter Finch starred as Alex Windom, a British doctor in a remote village in an unnamed country that most British critics spotted as Malaya. As Windom's estranged wife Lee (Mary Ure) arrives to try to revive their marriage, the doctor is tending to his grateful patients while also attempting to mediate a bitter labor dispute between the local rubber tappers and their British employer, Patterson (Michael Hordern). Speaking for the workers are Jan Vidal (John Cairney, a Scottish actor cast as a Malayan) and the group's spiritual leader, Father Amyan (Sanny Bin Hussan); when they convey the workers' desire to grow their own rice, Patterson refuses, suspecting communists are behind the demands. After Windom asks Patterson to hear them out, the imperious manager scoffs at "trumped-up grievances about rice," telling Windom, "This is the East," and "when you've lived in this country as long as I have, you'll know how to handle them." Jan's firing leads Windom to tell Patterson, "You can't sack people and have them injured just because they held a meeting. We're not living in the Middle Ages." And when Patterson has Father Amyan arrested, Windom informs him, "You've taken the most respected man in the village and put him in jail; you must be out of your mind." Matters worsen when Amyan dies in jail, provoking the workers to storm the jail and Patterson's bungalow. After a fighter jet strafes the workers, they decide to arm themselves, and with troops on the way, Windom persuades Jan to hide in the mountains while he reasons with the authorities.

With the arrival of the government's representative, Commissioner Belhedron (Anglo-Indian actor Marne Maitland), Windom, ignoring his wife's advice to mind his own business, states the workers' case, only to be accused of being a communist and the workers' ringleader. The film then delivers its message through an impassioned speech Windom makes to the Commissioner, Patterson, and the British Colonel Hasbrook (Robert Flemyng). Windom says he hates the communist leader, Semcar, too, "But are we not becoming so obsessed with what we're against that we've forgotten what we are for?" The workers "want freedom and dignity and independence. To them, the growing of rice is a symbol of that." They "have been on their knees for centuries.... Help them up and they'll thank you. If you don't, they'll go over to the enemy." The Commissioner accepts Windom's proposed deal, in which troops will leave the village and let the workers grow rice if they will resume tapping rubber. Just when it seems Windom has steered a course between Semcar and Patterson—between communism and colonialism—it turns out that the scheming Commissioner has summoned troops to arrest the workers, for his "instructions are quite clear: we're to make an example of these people to the whole country." Also rejecting peace by now are the workers, who have joined the communists in the mountains. The film hardly sympathizes with the ruthless communists, whose leader wears a uniform like Mao's and who has the hapless mayor (Gregoire Aslan) executed in cold blood, but it blames the workers' misguided defection to Semcar on their mistreatment by the British. The film ends with Windom hearing the sounds of war in the distance and realizing his wife was right: he should stay out of politics and treat his patients.

The film never specifies that this is Malaya, and like the American novel, it addresses the West's global struggle against communism. The novel's denunciation of hardline colonialists as well as communists reflected a typical American outlook, and one that scriptwriter Jill Craigie, a socialist and the wife of Labour Party politician Michael Foot, preserved. The film's depiction of its villains—the communists and the imperialist Patterson—was clearer than its treatment of the Commissioner and his government, and most viewers probably could not tell if Malaya was independent. It would have been hard for any film to capture the complex relationship between the country's British overseers and the Malayans to whom they were transferring power, and *Windom's Way* made no attempt. By casting Maitland, who looked possibly Malayan and wore Malayan garb, the film implied that it was Malayans, not the British, who reneged on the deal with the rebels. This British film was thus much harder on tyrannical plantation managers like Patterson than on British officials, and it also went easy on the duplicitous

Commissioner at the end. "If we are not altogether perfect," he tells Windom, "perhaps we are not such imbeciles as some people seem to believe," and he insists he regrets his harsh measures. In the end, it is Windom who appears the fool, and he must admit his naivete to the Commissioner.

Despite this ending and some pulling of punches about British colonialism, the film was not fundamentally incoherent. Its main message anticipated John F. Kennedy's famous line that "those who make peaceful revolution impossible make violent revolution inevitable," and its warning that colonialists' mistreatment of the villagers would drive them toward communism was a standard liberal notion in the Cold War. Condemning Windom for attempting to mediate was somewhat confusing, but his failure merely underlined the urgency of the film's warnings and did not contradict the condemnation of colonialist abuses. Indeed, had Windom succeeded, the film would have had its own colonialist overtones in suggesting that it took a white man to solve Malaya's problems. Instead, it criticized conservative colonialism while implying that Westerners might fail to solve the problems they helped to create.

The film did fairly well with the British critics: seventeen of twenty-nine (59 percent) gave it positive reviews, seven negative, and five mixed.[30] The main objections reflected confusion about the message. The *Guardian* found it "hopelessly muddled," and the *Monthly Film Bulletin* felt the filmmakers had been "betrayed by the uncertainty of their attitude and position," asking, "Does the complete failure of [Windom's] efforts to help the natives prove that he is wrong, or is it meant to express a wholly pessimistic and negative view of the situation?" The *Times* gave a mixed verdict, calling the script "a brave piece of work" while charging that "its thinking at moments appears to be muddled." It also asked in frustration, "Where exactly are we, geographically and politically, supposed to be?" Although Nina Hibbin of the *Daily Worker* liked the denunciation of the "rubber planter and his pals in the local police force," she was disappointed that all Windom learned "was to stick to doctoring and not to go meddling in politics." Derek Hill of the socialist *Tribune* (who noted Craigie's marriage to the magazine's editor) observed that the film's "suggestion that the way of the idealist is sure to be met with betrayal . . . is hardly a particularly cheering conclusion," but the film showed that "the individual who endeavours to follow a moral path . . . is not any less right if his advice and action do not produce fruitful results." *Kinematograph Weekly* saw no clear message and said it "wisely leaves its audience to draw its own conclusions," while the *Spectator* found it "politically uncommitted" and "intelligent enough to offer (which is gloomy, when you come to think of it) no solution." Conservative readings included that of the *Daily Sketch*, which disliked "the unsavoury light in which Colonial administrators are shown," and *Time and Tide*, which complained that the workers "are in a sad case on account of capitalism" and called it "an unfortunate film to publish at a time when the world situation is so tetchy."

Other critics welcomed a British film exploring political issues. Calling it "a fine film" about the spread of communism in the Far East, the *Daily Herald* said it "lays the blame squarely on dead-headed colonial administration," and for a studio that usually produced "silly whimsies and country-house comedies," it was good to see "a film which treats a vital modern problem seriously and courageously." The *Evening Standard* agreed but found it "a glum commentary on British studios that the fact should be thought at all extraordinary," and the *Sunday Express*'s Milton Shulman called it "almost unheard of" to find a British film that "tries intelligently to illuminate a serious social and political problem." It was, he added, "even more daring" that it "refuses to whitewash everything British and suggests that it is our own stupidity and intolerance that often drives Colonial and Asiatic peoples into the waiting arms of the Communists." Indeed, the criticism of British colonialism resonated widely. The *Glasgow Herald*'s Molly Plowright admitted that she had expected "some apologetic disclaimer for the British Empire . . . which will well suit a transatlantic audience" and was surprised to see a planter "stupid enough to send for the native police." Proclaiming it "one of the best British films of the year," the *Daily Mirror* said it "dares to suggest that not everything British is best—at least not in Malaya," including an "arrogant, brutish, [and] prejudiced" planter who is an "ancient relic of the British Raj." Despite panning the film, the *Monthly Film Bulletin* praised its "recognition of native rights and the suggestion that local people are exploited." Even on the right, the *Daily Telegraph* welcomed its warning of "how backward peoples come to turn towards Communism," and the *Spectator* also noted that "the agitators are treated as terrorists" until "they become terrorists." Such comments reflect misgivings about British colonialism by this time, and the conservative papers' reaction suggests that by outlining a pragmatic as well as a moral case against colonialism, the film found an effective way to criticize it.

Windom's Way did not make the charts in the United States, and many papers did not review it. Of thirteen that did, five praised it (38 percent), five panned it, and three gave it mixed ratings.[31] *Time*, a rare publication that understood the film, said it showed how "the Communist sickle reaped its impressive harvests in Southeast Asia," where the communists "are all too often the only alternative to economic exploitation, official corruption, [and] roughneck rule," but it found the plantation manager caricatured. Among the disoriented, the *Boston Herald* guessed that the action was taking place in Burma, and Hollis Alpert of the *Saturday Review* supposed it was in Indonesia. Alpert admitted, "I was always rather in the dark about just what was happening," but he did figure out that "the natives are all embroiled in some kind of social and political revolution." Only one of these critics, Archer Winsten of the *New York Post*, identified Malaya as its setting. The *New York Herald Tribune* concluded that the film's point was that "any attempt by a Westerner to meddle in native affairs is doomed," and *Cue* wrote that "the moral would seem to be Go home, white man, go home."

As *Alerte en Extrême-Orient*, the film sold a modest 572,040 tickets in France, where a meager batch of reviews included one positive, five negative, and three mixed verdicts.[32] French critics also had trouble locating the action (two of the nine named Malaya) or grasping the film's point. *Libération* mistook it for a patriotic defense of British colonialism in Burma, and *Combat* sneered that the British "made Victorian films amid the disorder of a world in revolt," a sort of "cinema of the ostrich." Closer to the mark, *Radio Cinéma Télévision* wrote that it dealt with "the birth of an anti-colonialist revolt" caused by "whites' incomprehension of the natives' mentality," and it praised its "lucidity and audacity." Samuel Lachize of *L'Humanité* gave the most thorough review, writing that it contained both "monumental errors" and "essential truths." The errors included showing rebels as "bloodthirsty fanatics no less despicable than the idiotic colonists and the governments in their pay," but it also showed that "peoples long accustomed to living in fear may awaken suddenly, and that old forms of colonialism are outdated." Lachize also called it "burningly topical for us in France." *Le Canard Enchaîné* drew the parallel with France's conflict in Algeria even more directly, through a prank review that pretended the film was set in Algeria and titled *Alerte en Algérie*. A whimsical "editor's note" then explained apologetically that the critic must have been drunk, as "it would never occur to anyone to give Algeria its independence." The film's reception in the United States and France, even more than in Britain, suggests the difficulties of making political films on complex colonial topics in unfamiliar places, and the film's ending, though not really inconsistent with its overall point, clearly confused many viewers. At least in Britain, *Windom's Way* did manage to invite critical reflection on the Cold War and colonialism in Asia.

Indian Independence

While Britain produced no feature films about India's independence in these years, several American films examined the subject. The first was Paramount's *Thunder in the East* (1952), officially an American film directed by Hungarian-born Charles Vidor from a script by Ukrainian-born Jo Swerling (and three other writers), based on Australian novelist Alan Moorehead's 1948 *The Rage of Vultures*. The film's dim view of Indian independence appears in opening titles proclaiming that "with it came many internal problems." The story begins as American pilot and arms dealer Steve Gibbs (Alan Ladd) lands in the small Indian state of "Ghandahar" (a fictional Kashmir site, not the Afghan province). Aware that tribesmen in the hills are massing to attack the town when the British leave, Gibbs hopes to sell machine guns to the Maharajah who governs the state, but barring him from meeting the Maharajah is his Prime Minister, Ram Singh (Charles Boyer). The pacifist Singh keeps a photo of Gandhi on his desk, and he assures Gibbs they have no interest in guns; when Gibbs hints at selling them to the leader of the tribesmen, Nawab Khan, Singh impounds his arsenal. At the local hotel, Gibbs meets some rich Europeans just beginning to realize the danger facing them; their immediate concern is that the hotel's native managers have taken down a sign reading, "Ghandahar British Club: Members Only." This symbolic act sends the Europeans into a tizzy; "We can't have our tea with outsiders gaping at us," one woman declares. Dropping that anticolonial theme for good, the film moves on to demonize the fanatical tribesmen, whose motives for attacking the town remain a mystery. (The book details the Muslim tribesmen's lust for loot and hatred for Hindus and Sikhs.) The film also mocks the naive Prime Minister, who still refuses to distribute Gibbs's weapons to the besieged hotel guests even after the rebels cut off his hand and warn him to flee. Coming off just as badly are the Maharajah, an idler who abandons his subjects and flees for the Riviera at the first hint of danger, and Gibbs himself, the kind of tough guy Ladd often played. The climax features two miraculous character transformations: Gibbs's love for a blind minister's daughter (Deborah Kerr) leads him to find his conscience and stay to help fight the rebels, and Prime Minister Singh finally abandons his silly belief in nonviolence. A final shot shows Gibbs and the one-handed Singh, side by side, firing away at the rebels.

The ridiculing of Singh's nonviolence suggests that buried under public admiration for Gandhi in the West was a current of resentment at a man who turned the tables on Western power, and whose principles indicted those of the West. Cold War overtones appear when the Yank must inform the Europeans of the danger they are in and—with his planeload of modern weaponry—organize their defense. Singh's statement, "I had every hope that I could contain the tribesmen without violence," uses a key Cold War term, and when the film shows how foolish he was, it vindicates violence against menaces like Nawab Khan. Despite Boyer's French accent, his costume and attitudes evoked Prime Minister Nehru, a thorn in the side of Western cold warriors, with his socialist policies and nonalignment. Concerned about the film's negative images of both Americans and Indians, the State Department protested the film and managed to delay its American release for more than a year.[33] An impressive cast helped the film reach number fifty-eight on *Variety*'s charts, but all eleven reviews in this sample panned it.[34] No one applauded the film's call to arms, and in discussing Singh's conversion to violence, the *Los Angeles Times* wondered "whether an East Indian would regard it as logic or libel." The film had a brief run in London, where few papers reviewed it, but the *Monthly Film Bulletin* complained that it shows "a man of high principles projected as an idealistic idiot" and "pokes cheap jibes . . . at international figures of exceptional integrity."[35]

Paramount also made *Elephant Walk* (1954), a lavish production set and filmed in Ceylon, and one that addresses Ceylon's decolonization only metaphorically. Elizabeth Taylor played Ruth Wiley, a Londoner who marries a wealthy planter, John Wiley (Peter Finch), and follows him to Ceylon. The colonial life looks attractive at first in a stunning mansion on an estate where obedient workers pick tea and an army of servants awaits them. But the colonial dream becomes a nightmare for Ruth, who learns that no women can stand the place and that John's friends are idlers, drunkards, and overgrown children who play indoor polo on bicycles in the middle of the night. John's power in this little empire has gone to his head, making him imperious even toward his wife—an important critique of colonialism's corrupting effects on the colonizer—and she soon regrets coming to Ceylon. John strains to live up to the image of his deceased father, a towering figure who, in another dig at colonialism, arrogantly and defiantly built this estate in a migratory route the local elephants refuse to abandon. Just as the Raj used an army of sepoys, the Wileys rely on natives to shore up the walls that keep the elephants from overrunning the estate, and intimations of impending doom finally culminate in a cholera epidemic, a fire, and the revenge of the elephants, who destroy the house. To those who saw decolonization as an irresistible, primal force that no European effort could withstand, the elephants' destruction of the Wiley estate made an apt metaphor. As the whites slink away in defeat, *Elephant Walk* evokes decolonization much as the departure of the nuns in *Black Narcissus* did, and it is noteworthy that Robert Standish's novel had been published in 1948, the year of Ceylon's independence.[36] Paramount's Head of Foreign and Domestic Censorship, Luigi Luraschi, wishing to avoid offending foreign markets, had worked to insert positive images of the Ceylonese and to tone down the slandering of Westerners, but it retains its skeptical view of colonialism and its sense of unstoppable decolonization.[37] The reviews, however, missed the metaphorical relevance to decolonization, and there is no evidence of the political intentions of Standish, director William Dieterle, or anyone else involved.[38]

A more direct look at decolonization appeared in MGM's *Bhowani Junction* (1956). George Cukor directed this superproduction, shooting in England and Pakistan; its script by Sonya Levien and Ivan Moffitt was based on the 1954 novel by John Masters, whose work reflected his years living in India.[39] Like *The Planter's Wife* and other films, it treats political events with little real interest, and Cukor, a specialist in "women's films," used the events of 1947 as a backdrop for a personal tale about the Anglo-Indian Victoria Jones (Ava Gardner).[40] The film also follows the efforts of Colonel Rodney Savage (Stewart Granger) to prevent the communist terrorist Darvey (Peter Illing) from sabotaging Britain's handover of power to the Indian National Congress, but the heart of the story concerns Victoria's identity crisis and her struggle to choose among three suitors: a fellow Anglo-Indian, Patrick (Bill Travers), a Sikh named Ranjit (Francis Matthews), and Colonel Savage. This racial melodrama reflects the concerns of novelist Masters, about whom long-standing rumors of his own mixed-race heritage were eventually confirmed.[41]

Victoria, back in India after military service in World War II, is the daughter of a British father and an Indian mother, and she immediately clashes with Patrick, having outgrown their relationship. Patrick, who wears a British suit and pith helmet and calls Indians "wogs," insists that "the British can't leave," for "what would happen to us Anglo-Indians?" His talk of going "home" to England if the British leave provokes an angry Victoria to tell him, "We can't become English because we're half-Indian, and we can't become Indian because we're half English." Her disdain for her own mixed-race status explains her declining interest in him. After she kills an English officer who tries to rape her, her Sikh friend Ranjit takes her home, where his politically radical mother, the Sandani (Freda Jackson), helps her out of her bloody army uniform; she also scolds her for working for the British, asking, "Why don't you see that you are an Indian and act like one?" Victoria then dons a sari and gazes at herself in the mirror. Soon, she is dating Ranjit, and her sari shocks her British superiors. Her dalliance with Ranjit ends when, after agreeing to convert to Sikhism to marry him, she gets cold feet at the wedding. Before long, her disdain for Colonel Savage ebbs, and the two fall in love, but when he proposes they marry and move to England, she replies, "I belong here, not as a phony Indian, not as a phony white, but as myself." The racially enlightened Savage then solves the dilemma by agreeing to stay in India with her.

This racial romance plot intertwines with the tale of Savage's struggle to keep the railway junction at Bhowani open despite the passive resistance of the local Congress leader, Surabhai (Abraham Sofaer), while he also pursues Darvey's communists. The film uses its lavish budget for impressive location crowd scenes, a major train wreck, and various riots and explosions. A scene in which Savage dislodges protesters from train tracks by having his men pour buckets of urine on them probably disgusted some viewers, and it led a Lieutenant Colonel Wakefield, who was advising Cukor during production, to protest the inclusion of this scene from the novel; Wakefield found it embarrassing to the army and unrealistic, in that it would have jeopardized relations with native troops.[42] Yet viewers who harbored resentments toward Gandhi and his followers may have chuckled at Savage's shrewdness, and the scene takes Savage's point of view. The film certainly intends viewers to root for Savage as he tracks down Darvey and prevents Gandhi's assassination.

The film's depiction of Indian characters ranges from wholly negative in the case of the communists (including Ranjit's domineering, British-hating mother) to mildly annoyed in the case of well-meaning but naive Surabhai and the passive resisters, to fully positive in the case of Govindaswami (Marne Maitland). The latter, a district official who wears tailored white suits and speaks with an Oxbridge accent, insists he is a nationalist, a wog (said ironically), and not "a lackey of British imperialism." The crowd scenes portray India as an overpopulated, chaotic place on the brink of anarchy. This image of India recalls older empire films, as do shots of white characters jostled as they make their way through seas of anonymous Indians. Despite painting India as a smoldering volcano, it refers to Hindu-Muslim tensions only once, in a line about the communists playing up "old religious differences." The British generally come off well, except for the officer who calls Patrick a "chee-chee" and tries to rape Victoria. The film downplays British racism when Savage, trying to persuade Victoria to live in England, tells her, "The English aren't going to eat you alive, you know." Though viewers today may see racism in the film's depiction of India's teeming hordes, Savage tells a fellow officer, "I never called the Indians wogs; I never hate in the plural," and he also declares, "It's about time the Lord started making all human beings the same on the outside as well as the same on the inside."

If Victoria's choice of Savage over the two nonwhite suitors can be read as racist, this was not the filmmakers' intent.[43] It turns out that MGM forced Cukor to change the book's outcome (in which Victoria married the Eurasian Patrick) and have her marry Savage instead after a California preview audience objected to Ava Gardner marrying a "black" man.[44] MGM's decision thus reflected the typical studio fears of controversy and made a concession to segregationism; ironically, this change led the film to strike a blow against color barriers by having the Eurasian Victoria end up marrying a white man. The film's image of the departing British as concerned about India's welfare and striving to minimize communal conflict has raised objections, but that image conforms to the historical record of these years.[45] The film also suggests that when the British depart, India will be in the good hands of men such as Gandhi, whose survival the film posits as India's salvation, and Govindaswami, a sensible, intelligent, well-educated product of British colonial rule. The film is thus colonialist not in the reactionary sense of digging in its heels against India's independence, but rather in the sense that prevailed among the British leaders who handed over power in 1947: that India's readiness for independence proved the success of Britain's enlightened rule there.

For such a lavish film, its performance at the American box office—number forty-three of 1956—was a disappointment.[46] The ads ignored Indian independence and played up the racial romance; they showed photos of a sari-clad Gardner with each of her suitors along with a caption that read, "The Three Loves of the Half-Caste Beauty!"[47] MGM could not blame critics for the poor box office, as twenty-four of thirty-two (75 percent) praised it, while five panned it, and three gave it mixed ratings.[48] Most critics seemed less interested in the soap-opera plot than in the crowd scenes. *Variety* wrote that "the milling, sweating, shouting crowds, egged on by Red agents, are almost frighteningly real," conveying an "India seething with discontent," while the *Washington Post* praised the film for capturing "that staggering impact which the visitor to India never forgets—people, hordes of bodies, mobs of humans." These reactions hint at Westerners' trepidation at the political awakening of India and other former colonies, and the film's depiction of communists manipulating those crowds only heightened their concerns. The *Detroit News* observed "a frightening quality to the anger spewed at the British by multitudes guided by the Communists," and the *San Francisco Chronicle* found "extremely exciting" the "turbulent Indian mobs" and the "seething quality of Indian destructiveness." Natural metaphors for decolonization appear in the *Atlanta Constitution*'s reference to "boiling nationalism" and the *Houston Post*'s comment that "the white-coated mob incited by Congress Party agitators surges through a railway depot like the tide." Support for decolonization appears in the *Boston Herald*'s description of India as a "newly freed land" and "a land in rebirth," in the *New York Post*'s characterization of India as "on its brink of freedom," and perhaps even in *Time*'s claim that the viewer "can experience the awesome fecundity of Asia, and can feel the blind power of the millions east of Suez who are now putting a shoulder to the wheel of progress."

And the *Christian Science Monitor*, while praising Govindaswami as "an intelligent and responsible man," complained that "the local Congress Party official is made ludicrous and pathetic." None of the thirty-two reviews regretted Britain's departure from India.

Welcoming the film's antiracism, the *Denver Post* quoted the line about God making people the same, and the *Saturday Review* applauded it for refusing "either Kipling's or Masters's conclusion" about "the incompatibility of East and West." The *New York Post*, announcing that here "the movies reverse their traditional fainthearted attitude towards interracial marriage," endorsed the film's rejection of the idea "that like should marry like and half-castes are fit only for each other or the inferior strain." It also called the film "particularly meaningful at this time in world history and in the history of racial conflict." Only one critic objected to miscegenation: the *Hollywood Reporter*'s Don Gillette wrote of Savage and Victoria that "perhaps because they are of a different caste—you never feel yourself rooting wholeheartedly for them." Among those who found the treatment of political issues too timid and superficial, *Variety* concluded that "it's doubtful that it will contribute much to Americans' knowledge of India and its people."[49] Once again, as Hollywood tiptoed through delicate ground, some critics wished it would stride more boldly.

The British critics were more divided, with nine of twenty-one praising it (43 percent), eight disliking it, and four undecided.[50] Political objections took various forms: whereas the *New Statesman* complained that "the English are shown as uniformly beastly," the *Daily Worker*'s Thomas Spencer chided the film's "slightly ridiculous" or "downright fiendish" Indians and its "traditional white attitude of superiority over the 'natives'" as well as its implication that "only a British colonel" can save India from "'Communist terrorists.'" Spencer added that "most dishonest of all is the attitude to violence, which is presented as practically a Communist invention, as if no British soldier or policeman had ever shot an Indian." Far more critics applauded the film's politics. The *Daily Herald* saw "an honest attempt to sum up the awful difficulties of the British troops leaving a land they looked after," and the *Sunday Express* claimed it "makes us feel something of the hate and helplessness of those urgent and troubled times." The *Evening Standard*'s Philip Oakes felt it "makes an honest bid to state the case as it was nine years ago," as "its reporting is realistic, cogent, and unbiased," and he marveled at the task Britain faced, as "rioting mobs swarm and boil across the screen like brown water." While sympathizing with their compatriots in India, no one suggested that Britain's departure was a mistake or that India was better off before 1947, and the *Daily Sketch*'s comment that "the Indians are booting the British out of their country" acknowledged that it is their country. Many also welcomed the film's antiracism. Both the *Evening Standard* and the socialist *Tribune* quoted Savage's statement about not hating in the plural, and the *Tribune* praised this "really courageous film" that "boldly and clearly speaks out against colour prejudice and race hatred." The critics' acceptance of India's independence likely owes something to the peaceful manner in which it happened, and a film that avoided criticizing British colonialism in India was unlikely to disturb this placid consensus.

In France, *La croisée des destins* sold 1,554,970 tickets, and French critics gave it seven positive (44 percent), five negative, and four mixed reviews.[51] Eric Rohmer, just starting his directing career, admired Cukor's crowd scenes and sense of space, and he wrote that "this India has such a striking truth and the riots are recreated with such breadth that it seems like reporting." André Bazin welcomed the break with Hollywood traditions concerning India, as the film "took on real current problems with a relatively impressive frankness" and shed the "exoticism, adventure, and mystery of most earlier productions." *L'Aurore* added that "one can criticize this film for its rather melodramatic story and for its various political tendencies," but it praised it for "taking on real issues," including "the problem of people of mixed blood, a problem the Western colonial powers created in their former colonies." Although critics reported that the subtitles translated "communists" as "terrorists," most understood who they were, and *L'Humanité* complained that "it is always the same pitiful scarecrow that reappears."[52] *Franc-Tireur* reported that the audience laughed when Savage's men threw urine on the caste-obsessed protestors, and it called it "odious" that the film "undertakes to ridicule 'native superstitions.'" The paper also scoffed at the image of the selfless British in India: "they alone could keep order there," it wrote ironically. Also sarcastically, *Les Lettres Françaises* said that "the valiant British Army plays a brilliant role," and "we go away saddened at the thought of the dark destiny of these poor Indians after the English depart." It objected that the film "aims to show us that a colonized people fighting for their liberty are but a gang of looters, arsonists, and butchers of innocent victims." Others brought up France's war in Algeria, as *Le Monde*'s Jean de Baroncelli noted that "certain scenes have a strange resonance for those of us in France," while Michel Mohrt of the conservative *Carrefour* saw "elements of a portrait of today's North Africa" in the film. And though he had long "believed it would be desirable if the two components of the population in Algeria managed to mix," this film warned that it "solves nothing." So while criticizing the film's politics, French critics praised it for confronting issues French films ignored.

Mau Mau and African Decolonization

Given people's fascination with violence—and thus its box-office power—it is not surprising that Western films on decolonization in British Africa focused on an atypically violent chapter: the Mau Mau uprising in Kenya in the 1950s. Although the revolt that began in 1952 was certainly anticolonialist in that it aimed to drive the British out of Kenya and regain lands whites had seized, it was not a national revolt pitting the Kenyan people against the British, as it took place only in part of Kenya and almost entirely among the Kikuyu, who made up roughly one-fifth of Kenya's population. Even the Kikuyus were divided: some, enjoying privileges under British rule and viewing the Mau Mau as undisciplined radicals, sided with the British, and most of those who actually tracked and fought the Mau Mau were Kikuyus with British military and police commanders.[53] The conflict began with attacks not on British settlers, but on a Kikuyu chief opposed to the Mau Mau and on Kikuyus who refused to take the Mau Mau oath of initiation. This violence and the killing of a settler in October 1952 led the British to declare a state of emergency.

Mass arrests, including that of nationalist politician Jomo Kenyatta, wrongly accused of being Mau Mau's leader, showed how poorly the British understood what they were fighting, and their methods, which included forced relocations, prison camps, and torture, resulted in both a victory and great suffering for those inside and outside the movement.[54] Both sides committed numerous atrocities, and the direct and indirect death toll—bitterly disputed, but probably in the tens of thousands—mostly involved Kikuyus killing each other, while roughly thirty settlers died.[55] The capture of Mau Mau leader Dedan Kimathi in 1956 helped finish off the revolt, and the emergency officially ended in 1959. The uprising's relationship to Kenya's independence in 1963 is complex; it contributed indirectly by spurring reforms and concessions, even though it ended in defeat, and though it was Mau Mau's rivals who came to power in the new state.

The first film to explore the crisis was Rank's *Simba* (1955), directed by Brian Desmond Hurst from a collectively written story credited to John V. Baines. The film opens with a black man on a country road finding a white man who has been injured in an accident. Instead of helping him, the black man looks around, then pulls out a panga knife and murders him for no apparent reason. After this sensationalist opening, the film introduces Alan Howard (Dirk Bogarde), who has come to Kenya to see his settler brother and is met at the airport by Mary Crawford (Virginia McKenna). Alan and Mary, former sweethearts, arrive at Alan's brother's house only to find him murdered by Mau Mau. Mary is among those settlers who resist letting their horror at Mau Mau atrocities make them hate all blacks, while the traumatized Alan is less understanding. As the film depicts the settlers' besieged lifestyle, complete with small arsenals in living rooms and pistols under pillows at night, it paints a picture not unlike that in *The Planter's Wife*, with the added difficulty that some of their own servants are in cahoots with Mau Mau. Scenes of Mau Mau initiations—spooky rituals in which men in garish costumes and face paint coerce initiates into taking a loyalty oath—underline the fanatical, unreasoning nature of this threat. Even more horrific is a scene in which Mau Mau murder Mary's parents and a loyal "boy" during dinner.

A key character is a black doctor, Karanja (Earl Cameron), who is caught in the middle—accused by whites of being the Mau Mau leader "Simba" and hated by Mau Mau for his Western ways. Karanja eventually realizes his own father, the local headman (Orlando Martins), is Simba. He informs Inspector Drummond (Donald Sinden) too late to prevent an all-out assault on Alan, stranded in his home with Joshua, a young African boy he adopted after Mau Mau massacred his family. In the climax, Mary and Karanja arrive at Alan's house just before the Mau Mau hordes. Karanja tries to reason with the mob, ignoring Alan's warning that "you can't talk to a bunch of howling savages." Stabbed by a tribesman just before the troops arrive—riding to the rescue like the cavalry in Arizona—a despondent Karanja dies in Mary's arms. Moderating this depressing conclusion is a shot of little Joshua, who steps symbolically over a gun and walks up to Alan and Mary, bringing hope that the next generation will rally to the whites as Karanja had.

During production, Director Hurst told the press that "every care must be taken to give both the European and African view," but while the film gives both white liberals and conservatives their say, its treatment of blacks is lopsided.[56] The black characters who get lines are mostly servants who express fear and hatred of Mau Mau, and while Karanja makes the case for cooperating with whites, no Mau Mau gets to express his motives or grievances. (Karanja tells a white man that his people "have their grievances" then fails to elaborate.) Instead, the film presents unexplained rituals—one oath-taker ingests flesh and blood, which the film hints are human—and when one man tries to flee, he is chased down and his screams are heard off camera. If the coerciveness of Mau Mau oathing and the price resisters paid were genuine enough, so were the grievances that fueled the revolt, including discrimination and land seizures, and omitting those facts undermined claims of balance. In depicting hanged cats and horrific rituals that intimidate superstitious blacks, and in suggesting that whites lived in constant terror, never knowing which of their "boys" were about to slaughter them in their beds, the film drifts from political drama into the horror, voodoo, and zombie genres. "Thousands of them really do hate Mau Mau," explains the Inspector, "but you can never be sure which they are," and by keeping viewers in the dark about which blacks are disloyal, the film impels them to share the settlers' suspicions of all blacks. While helping viewers empathize with the settlers, this approach makes a mockery of the claims of balance.

The film's empathy for the settlers includes Mrs. Crawford's uncontradicted statement that "when we came out here after the first war, there was nothing, nothing at all" (a common bit of settler mythology), as well as Mary's statement, "I was born here; Africa's my home." These statements recall similar ones in *The Planter's Wife*, *West of Zanzibar*, and *Bhowani Junction*. The threat to settlers' homes seen in *The Planter's Wife* also recurs, and the image of Mary's terrorized mother watching a panga knife slash through the locked kitchen door that separates her from a band of frenzied attackers conveys this violated domesticity.[57] The film does achieve some balance in its treatment of white liberals and conservatives, though it clearly intends audiences to reject some of the conservatives' statements. When Mary's father calls Kikuyus "Kukes" over Mary's objection, he comes off as racist, and he declares in the presence of his own servants that "sixty years ago, when the first white man came here, these Africans were hardly down from the trees." He also calls them "backward children" and complains, "We've given the Africans the wrong sort of toys—ideas of self-government, nationalism." At a settlers' meeting, another man bellows, "We've got to squash the blacks so flat they'll never dare raise their heads again or else we ought to clear out of Africa for good, and by thunder I'm not clearing out!" If these views are meant to seem excessive, other hard-liners get more sympathetic treatment, including Mary's mother, who answers a liberal's speech in a quivering voice, saying, "My husband and I have always done everything we could to help the Africans. . . . But you almost make us out to be heartless, cruel monsters." Despite opposing racial hatred, the film makes it understandable through close-ups of whites grieving over murdered loved ones.

The film also voices its main points through liberals, including Mary, who defends the kindness Alan's brother showed. "If every European behaved as he did," she says, "there would be no discontent. The Mau Mau wouldn't be able to exist at all." Also expressing the film's view is an elderly doctor who urges distinguishing between Mau Mau and other Africans: "You must make friends of these people or you'll find yourselves not fighting a few thousand fanatics, but five million angry people. . . . We must learn to live together, side by side, black and white, and make it a better world." The film also offers hope that whites can civilize the Africans, as they did with Karanja and the adopted boy. As Karanja speaks to the Mau Mau mob, the camera pans across black listeners in Western garb who seem persuaded until Simba and two of his fighters arrive—clad in traditional dress—and impel the mob to violence again. The first step in civilizing the Africans, the film argues, is to crush those who are leading the gullible astray, so while peddling a liberal-colonialist message of racial reconciliation and the civilizing mission, *Simba* also values a more conservative military approach to African unrest.

Critical reaction in Britain ran heavily positive, as twenty-three of twenty-eight critics (82 percent) praised *Simba*, while four disliked it and one gave it a mixed review.[58] The *Evening News* felt it was "as much as any audience could be expected to stand," and the *Sunday Times* praised the film but found it "too close at hand for realistic treatment in such detail." The *Daily Express* said it was "moving and serious" and "plays fair by everyone involved," and such praise spanned a wide political spectrum. The conservative *Spectator* called it "an extremely good film, a clear, fair exposition of the life and death problems which face both whites and loyal blacks in Kenya." To the *Manchester Guardian* it was "a British film to be proud of at this moment of our colonial history" and one that depicts "shades of opinion and feeling among the natives as well as among the European settlers." Like others, the *Financial Times* wrote that "one cannot but admire the scrupulous fairness" of the script, while the *Glasgow Herald* said a "complex situation [is] presented as fairly and objectively as possible." What qualified as fair, however, deserves a closer look. The *Spectator* only said the film gave the views of whites and "loyal blacks," not Mau Mau. In commenting that the Crawfords' murder was "heart-searing, while the aimless wanderings of a little piccaninny bereft of parents preserve[s] balance," *Kinematograph Weekly* actually cited two different Mau Mau atrocities (the boy having been orphaned in a Mau Mau massacre), and it saw balance because the film showed both white and black victims of Mau Mau. And though it admitted that "after all, the blacks were in possession of Africa long before the whites," it said the film explored "the Mau Mau problem" rather than the colonialism problem.

To some the film seemed so balanced that it had no viewpoint, and in Wales the *Western Mail* wrote that it "poses no solution." But if many reviews shared the film's politics while thinking it had none, three left-wing publications saw the film as deeply political and colonialist. The *Monthly Film Bulletin* charged that *Simba* "fails to acknowledge that the Mau Mau troubles are simply one extreme, particular issue of the wide colonial problem"; contending that "however extremist, Mau Mau represents *something*," it complained that "the native people never express any cause of grievance against the whites." The *Tribune* also objected to the film's silence about Mau Mau grievances, and in contrasting hard-line repression with "benevolent paternalism," it overlooked a third possibility: "to satisfy the Kikuyus' grievances." So while it "could have done a valuable job in informing public opinion on the worst troubled of Britain's colonies," it offered only "a gravely lopsided picture of the situation in Kenya." Finally, the *Daily Worker* called it Rank's "attempt to whitewash and justify Britain's war to crush the people of Kenya" and to "gain sympathy for the fight to protect Kenya's white colonists." The film, it added, gave "not a hint of the sickening torrent of blood poured out by the British security forces and Home Guard—of the hanging of thousands of Kikuyu, the torture and beating up of thousands more, and the detention of a sizable proportion of the population in concentration camps." So while most British reviews applauded the film's political fairness, a vigorous minority dissented.

In the United States, *Simba* had limited distribution and did not make *Variety*'s charts. Of fifteen reviews located, ten were positive, three negative, and two mixed.[59] *Variety* called it "grim, realistic entertainment" and warned that "as such, spotty returns loom," while the ads featured sensationalism that became standard for Mau Mau films. One showed a pistol-wielding Dirk Bogarde protecting Virginia McKenna while a running tribesman with face-paint, a giant Afro, and a loincloth clutches a pole with a skull on it in one hand and a huge panga in the other; a caption in giant letters screamed: "SIMBA, TERROR OF MAU MAU!"[60] The *New York Daily News*, calling the film "dramatic and moving," wrote that despite the progress Britain had brought to Kenya, "the suddenly organized Mau Mau started killing and disrupting the normal life of the community." Among those who grasped the film's message, the *New York Post* said it depicted hard-line settlers who want to attack all blacks, while "sensible whites point out that this forces all natives onto the side of the terrorists," and *Variety*, *Commonweal*, and the *St. Louis Post-Dispatch* agreed that the film preached peaceful coexistence.

Several papers questioned the film's balance, including the *New York Post*, which condemned Mau Mau violence but noted that "their justifications are never spoken," and "the mass of natives are viewed as passive spectators, or mentioned as victims themselves of the Mau Mau." *Variety* saw an attempt "to portray the anxious problems of the white farmer and loyal natives objectively," but "this treatment is not applied to the Mau Mau whose terrorist campaigns brook little sympathy." The *Saturday Review* also complained that "at no time are we given any clear-cut idea of what lies behind the terrorism," while "one is always aware of the bland assumption that the British belong in Kenya, that they have a God-given right to usurp the best grazing lands, and that their treatment of the natives is for the ultimate good." Even stronger words appeared in African American papers. Weary of films' inaccurate and biased images of Africa, the *Atlanta Daily World* called *Simba* "surely the most dangerously stupid of the lot," adding that "if the Europeans of Africa are as jittery and stupid as the film depicts them they should be evacuated at once." The *Chicago Defender* called the film "pro-British propaganda" and complained that "nowhere does the film tell why the Mau Mau was formulated or why the native wants to rule his own country." Instead, it portrays "the Mau Mau as insane murderers, and the white settler as a type of god." Most American reviews, however, followed the British pattern, praising the film's intensity and political balance.

Simba was the first film in a brief Mau Mau craze. After a low-budget exploitation documentary, *Mau Mau* (1955), which had little to do with Kenya, came *Safari* (1956), directed by Terence Young for Britain's Warwick Films and Columbia Pictures. Victor Mature starred as Ken Duffield, a professional hunter whose home is attacked by Mau Mau and whose young son is murdered by a trusted African servant, Jeroge (Earl Cameron). The rest of the film follows Duffield's attempts to track down and kill Jeroge, which he does by leading a hunting party into Mau Mau territory. *Safari* resembles *Simba* in ignoring Mau Mau's motives, in showing whites' fear of betrayal by trusted Africans, and in a climax in which whites and loyal Kenyans mow down hordes of crazed Mau Mau. But unlike *Simba*, it largely ignores the settlers and offers no defense of British colonialism. Indeed, the Mau Mau theme is grafted onto a standard safari-film plot, using natives to supply a dangerous background for a story about white people.

In *Beyond Mombasa* (1956), another Anglo-American production, American Matt Campbell (Cornel Wilde) arrives in Kenya to help his brother with a small uranium mine, only to find his brother murdered (recalling *Simba*). The killers, he learns, are not Mau Mau, but "leopard men," a religious cult that revived when Mau Mau arose, and one that also wished to drive white people out of Africa. Eventually, he journeys to the mine with a missionary, Ralph Hoyt (Leo Genn), Hoyt's anthropologist niece (Donna Reed), and others, and the film becomes a whodunit as bearers and members of the expedition die one by one. The culprit turns out to be the missionary, who has lost his mind in his obsession to protect his African flock, and who is prodding the leopard men to kill the white mine-hunters. "This land, the animals, and minerals in it belong to a simple people," Hoyt declares with a crazed look on his face. "You want to exploit these people for your own profit, your own material ends," but "somehow I had to protect these gentle people." The film thus treats the notion of favoring the Africans' right to control their own land and resources as the product of a deranged mind, and if it makes the familiar figure of the white protector an evil rather than a benign figure, it is firmly colonialist in defending the whites' right to African resources and in depicting African resistance as fanaticism.

Closing the Mau Mau cycle was MGM's *Something of Value* (1957), whose script director Richard Brooks (*Blackboard Jungle*, *The Last Hunt*) wrote from American novelist Robert Ruark's lurid 1955 bestseller. Brooks's liberal politics and Production Code Administration objections to excessive Mau Mau violence and to dialogue about "niggers" and Africans having just come down from the trees yielded a less sensationalist, more politically nuanced work.[61] An opening act set in 1945 focuses on a young settler, Peter McKenzie (Rock Hudson), and his friend Kimani (Sidney Poitier); the two are practically brothers, as Kimani's mother helped raise Peter. When the two accompany Peter's brother-in-law Jeff (Robert Beatty) on a lion hunt, Jeff overhears Kimani complaining to Peter, "Always when we hunt it is the same. You have all the fun; I do all the work." Jeff tells Peter to strike the uppity Kimani, and when Peter refuses, Jeff does. After a reaction shot of the shocked Kimani, Peter objects that "the world's changing," but Jeff replies, "Not in Africa it isn't." He tells Peter he must learn "to deal seriously with the wogs," an epithet that confirms the film's disapproval of his racism. An ensuing scene in a Kikuyu village shows the British putting Kimani's religious, traditionalist father on trial for murder after he orders a ritual killing of a baby born feet first. Peter's father protests to the judge—voicing the film's viewpoint—that "we take away their customs, their habits, their religion" and offer ways they cannot grasp, and he warns that tampering with African culture will prove dangerous if they cannot offer them something of value in return. Bearing out his warning, an exasperated Kimani flees to the mountains to join Kikuyus preparing for an uprising.

The film then advances to 1952, showing Kimani listening to a Mau Mau orator and undergoing the initiation ritual. His first assignment is to help attack the farm of Peter's sister Elizabeth, which he accepts reluctantly. Although he gladly helps kill Jeff, who had slapped him, his conscience leads him to save Peter's wounded sister, and in his guilt he gazes into a mirror then smashes it. As whites pursue the rebels, Peter tries to find Kimani and negotiate peace. When he finally persuades Kimani to bring in his fighters and seek justice peacefully, a hard-line settler, Joe Matson (Michael Pate) beats Peter to a rendezvous and opens fire on Kimani's people—killing his young wife but missing their baby boy. When Peter arrives, he cannot convince Kimani that this was not a trap, and after a furious struggle between the old friends, Kimani accidentally falls to his death. A disconsolate Peter picks up Kimani's baby and tells a loyal African he will raise the boy along with his sister's child. Like *Simba*, the film thus uses the adoption of African children to close on a hopeful note.

Something of Value resembles other Mau Mau films in showing harrowing attacks on settlers' homes and children, fears of betrayal by servants, and coercive Mau Mau blood-drinking. It also privileges whites' viewpoints, and though dialogue notes that most Mau Mau victims were black, it is the killing of whites the film actually shows, so like *Simba*, it leaves an exaggerated impression of white deaths. It also sympathizes with the whites' right to live in Kenya. "What are we supposed to do: pack up and get out because their grandfathers were here first?" asks Joe Matson. "I was born here, too. This is my country." While Matson is, admittedly, more a villain than a hero, Peter also states: "We belong here. This is our land; it was worked for and paid for." But *Something of Value* is more sympathetic to African resistance than other Mau Mau films. The loyal Lathela, despite helping track down Mau Mau, tells Peter, "I want the same thing for the African that Kimani wants," even if "Mau Mau is not the way to get it." The film also shows Kikuyu women and children in Mau Mau's mountain camps. Moreover, it makes Mau Mau grievances clear, in part through an articulate, rational African gentleman in a business suit (William Marshall) telling potential recruits, "We are beggars and slaves in our own land. The British allow us in their homes and hotels, yes, but how? As servants." He adds that "the whole colored world burns with the fever of revolt, with the fire for freedom." As shockingly primitive as Mau Mau rituals seem, the oath-giver Njogu (Juano Hernandez) explains them; he tells the initiates to grab a handful of dirt, saying, "Earth, hold it to your belly, that the land may feed us, and not the foreigners." And in Kimani, the film presents something no other film did: a sympathetic Mau Mau character with clear and reasonable motives.

Brooks's film goes beyond *Simba* in questioning colonialism, not just hard-liners on both sides. When Jeff declares, "If we don't make the African respect the law, the next thing you know, they'll be wanting to rule this country," Peter replies, "Imagine that. Whatever could give him that idea?" Peter's father also refers ironically to Jeff as "the perfect colonizer," for "what's his is his and what's theirs is his, too." The point that colonizing harms the colonizer appears in a discussion of torture (which British censors cut). Peter opposes torturing captives, warning a compatriot that "you might even grow to love it," and—following a scream from the next room—concludes, "We're not such a big jump away from being savages ourselves, are we?" Brooks also urges racial harmony, as he had in *Blackboard Jungle* and *The Last Hunt*, and Peter tells white officials Kimani is guilty only of "being born black." The film also pleads for racial harmony visually, with a shot of Peter carrying the injured Kimani on his back, a close-up of the two men's clasped hands, and the final shot of Peter cradling Kimani's son in his hands.

Yet this is rather paternalist liberalism. It is Peter who carries Kimani to safety on his back, not vice-versa, and an opening title card reads: "When we take away from a man his traditional way of life, his customs, his religion, we had better make certain to replace them with SOMETHING OF VALUE." This statement does not oppose taking away Africans' traditional ways; it simply underlines the obligation to bring Africa something better. Showing what this is are several shots over the opening credits: a farmer on a tractor plowing a field, black children filing into a classroom in neat columns as a white man looks on, and a black teacher in the classroom, symbolizing the successful enlistment of Africans to carry on the task. This "something of value," in short, is the product of the old civilizing mission, so although it criticizes colonialism and shows more sympathy for Mau Mau than any other film of its era, it remains more liberal-colonialist than anticolonialist.

Something of Value reached number forty-five on *Variety*'s charts—a respectable mark for its topic.[62] The ads used the usual sensationalism, with an image of Poitier and Hudson struggling over a panga, superimposed on a map of Africa; two captions read, "THE MOST DANGEROUS BIG-GAME IN AFRICA ... MAN!" and "filmed under military protection in Africa's Mau Mau country!"[63] Of thirty-seven reviews located, twenty-two were positive (59 percent), seven negative, and eight mixed or neutral.[64] In Atlanta, where the film opened at the whites-only Loews Grand Theater, the *Atlanta Constitution* panned it, writing that "the social aspects tend to take it out of the world of entertainment," and the monologues "sound very much like propaganda." Myles Standish of the *St. Louis Post-Dispatch* also had political objections, charging that it unfairly condemns "the apparently necessary brutal retaliation of the white settlers against the Mau Mau," and he called the film a "preachment, with apologies rippling unctuously out for atrocities on both sides." Among the positive reviews, the *Chicago Tribune* called it "a painful, violent, but deeply moving film," while the *New York Post* found it "profound, eloquent, and exciting" and "a courageous pictorial plea for freedom." The *Los Angeles Examiner* recommended it, "if your nerves—and conscience—can take it." In segregated New Orleans, the *Times-Picayune* offered a slanted description of it as "a saga of white people in Kenya, Africa, beset by the uprising and subsequent slaughter brought on by the Mau Maus." Most others, however, saw it as a tale about both blacks and whites, and among those who explained Kimani's motives, the *Detroit News* cited his "mistreatment by arrogant colonials and the jailing of his father for practicing an ancient tribal rite," while *Time* said he was "outraged by white tyranny and black suffering." Stanley Kauffmann of the *New Republic*, though admitting the film showed Kimani facing injustice and being "robbed of his land and his traditions," asked why, if "Poitier has to be sacrificed . . . to atone for the several years of Mau Mau brutality," Hudson is not "sacrificed for a century of Negro enslavement?" Like others, *Life* felt the picture showed "that fault for blood-letting lies with both races," and the *Los Angeles Examiner* praised it for indicting both "the human degradation of the Mau Mau initiation ritual and the sadistic violence of white colonist."

What gave *Something of Value* its power, for many American critics, was its relevance to ongoing racial conflicts in the United States. Although it took place in Kenya and dealt with a violent black uprising unlike anything in America, it cast two American actors in the lead roles. The *Dallas Morning News* described it as "the latest attempt via film to touch the raw sore of race relations," while *Variety* warned that some "may be offended by the outspoken dialog about the yearning for equality and the rights of man." Welcoming the theme, the *New York Post* called it "a plea for the equality of black and white" that is "outspoken in the cause of justice and understanding." African American papers reported that southern theaters were boycotting the film, because, in the words of the *Pittsburgh Courier*, "Negroes are shown in roles of dignity and on the same level as whites" and also because it "shows a Negro striking a white man and a white woman receiving a blood transfusion from a Negro man."[65]

Others denied any relevance to America. "There may be analogies made between the African problem and other racial situations," noted the *Hollywood Reporter*, "but this is a superficial comparison," and it suggested that "a truer parallel is with the Indian wars." Calling the Mau Mau struggle a "far-distant sort of conflict" that "has no particular parallel with life around us," the *Los Angeles Times* nonetheless felt it necessary to make that point, and though the *New Republic's* Kauffmann insisted that "the picture does not, of course, mirror the American situation," he added that "it cannot help but reflect a few of the changes that have taken place in our attitude." While the problems of Kenya, in short, were distant enough for Americans to feel comfortable in criticizing British colonialism, even those who emphasized differences between America and colonial Africa worried that others might miss them.

British critics were less receptive: in a sample of fourteen British reviews five were positive (36 percent), seven negative, and two neutral.[66] Philip Oakes of the *Evening Standard* found it a "powerful, sober, and painful film," and though he said, "I would not call it entertainment," he felt "it should be seen." The pro-empire *Daily Telegraph* termed it "painfully absorbing" and a "searing film [that] shows how hatred and suspicion can drive natives to the obscene horrors of Mau Mau, and some white men to acts of violence of which the great majority are ashamed."

At the other end of the spectrum, the *Daily Worker*'s Robert Kennedy also praised it as "the first film with the honesty to show some of the real reasons behind the Kikuyu revolt." Kennedy added that while it depicts Mau Mau methods as "primitive and brutal," it also "shows Kikuyu leaders as men of courage and integrity" and admits that the whites' actions "'make us look like savages too.'" Some of those unimpressed found it oversimplified. The *Financial Times* denounced it as "a sentimental fantasy about hands clasping across the racial barrier," and the *News Chronicle* wrote that "its sermonizing on the subject of intolerance is emotional and sentimental, and its final solution is mawkish." Others simply disliked the subject. The *London Times* said it would have been good if fictional, but it "becomes impermissible when the film insists that this is Kenya and this is 1952," and it concluded that "it is doubtful whether the idea of making a film out of the Mau Mau terror in Kenya is a good one." Objections to Hudson's American accent were common, and some wished the Americans would mind their own business. "Wise onlookers always keep out of private fights," insisted the *Evening News*, and the *Daily Sketch* added that "coming from Hollywood, this film is either tactless, ironical, or impertinent," and "perhaps a little of all three."

French critics saw *Something of Value* at the 1957 Venice Film Festival. It then opened in France in spring 1958 under the odd title *Le carnaval des dieux* and sold 1,016,461 tickets.[67] Of twenty-two reviews from Venice and the French release, twelve were positive (55 percent), four negative, and six mixed.[68] Several reviews voiced anticolonial opinions, including *Les Lettres Françaises*, which said the Africans "worked, struggled, and died without profit on a land that had belonged to them for eternity and which had been purely and simply stolen from them."[69] Defending the film against leftists in Venice who found the film too liberal and bourgeois, *Cahiers du Cinéma*'s critic argued that it was not realistic to expect a truly radical film from Hollywood, and he concluded, "For my part, I salute its honesty and courage."[70] *France Observateur* saw "a typically liberal, clearly antiracist American point of view" but lamented the film's "simplistic schemes" regarding "problems that are more complex than it is wise to take on in the current state of the 'spectacle industry.'"[71] The conservative *L'Aurore* expected the film to anger the British, "some of them being presented as torturers," and in reminding readers of America's own racial problems, it found it hypocritical for Americans to make anticolonialist films. *Radio Cinéma Télévision* similarly wrote, "We are a bit annoyed at the Americans seeming to teach other countries lessons on this subject."[72]

Others welcomed the critique of racism. *Combat* noted that the film "takes on racial questions with a courage that is all the greater in coming out of Hollywood," while for *Libération*, the fact that "the viewer comes away sickened by the whites ... and filled with pity for the blacks shows how far Richard Brooks dared go in taking on his country's racial prejudices."[73] *Libération* also wrote that it "poses the question not only of Kenya, but of all of Africa as well," and thus, "had it been made in France, it would certainly have been banned or mutilated." Indeed, *Les Lettres Françaises* also predicted that it would be banned, as "its situation presents too many analogies with the war in Algeria not to catch the censors' attention" in France, where "even the mildest criticism of colonialism attracts the harshest penalties."[74] Nearly half these reviews alluded to Algeria, and *L'Humanité Dimanche* went even further, praising the film for examining torture and writing that "in Nairobi as in Algiers, an obsolete system is teetering before it falls."[75] To those eager for public discussion of French misdeeds in Algeria, *Something of Value* provided a welcome pretext.

In 1958, Mau Mau was near defeat, and Ghana had just won its independence without a war. The choice between violent and peaceful methods was the basis for the independent *The Mark of the Hawk* (1958), starring Sidney Poitier as Obam, a labor leader seeking independence for his fictional African country. Financed by the Board of Foreign Missions of the Presbyterian Church and the Methodist Church, the film was shot in Britain and Nigeria, with an inexperienced director, producers, and screenwriters. Despite Poitier's efforts, the result was amateurish, with long static shots, a plodding story and direction, and interminable speeches. Also starring were Eartha Kitt as Obam's wife; Juano Hernandez as an African preacher, Amugu; John McIntire as American missionary Bruce Craig; and empire-film regulars Marne Maitland and Earl Cameron in bit parts. The story used the familiar alliance of moderates against extremists of both races. On the white side, racist settlers act as vigilantes against native fighters, while missionaries and British authorities represent legalism, reason, and decency. Among the Africans, the devoutly Christian Amugu tries to keep the masses from following Obam's brother, who resembles the hotheaded young braves of countless westerns. Caught between the extremists, Obam vacillates: his position on the Legislative Council gains him no concessions from dilatory white authorities, while his church education makes him resist the radicals and their *juju* rituals. Although sympathetic to Africans, the film never shows their mistreatment, leaving only dialogue to make the case for independence. Meanwhile Amugu reminds blacks of the fine things whites had done for them—building schools and hospitals, fighting the tsetse fly, and, above all, bringing the word of Jesus Christ. The fruits of Western civilization include shiny new churches, hospitals treating black patients, modern mines providing mass employment, and multiracial democratic institutions. If the film repeats the common warning that extremist whites may push frustrated Africans into violence, it amounts to a liberal-colonialist sermon on the superiority of Christianity over African superstition and the benefits of Western civilization for backward Africans.

The film bore out *Variety*'s prediction of "spotty returns."[76] It did not play in many American markets, though it had special screenings for clergy and educators; the *Dallas Morning News* reported that local churches were distributing discount coupons and that theaters were donating a share of ticket sales to local churches.[77] Eight of fifteen reviews were positive (53 percent), three negative, and four mixed, but even critics who liked the film complained about the endless speeches.[78] For the *New York Times*, "The trouble is simply that Africa speaks—incessantly." More receptive, the Catholic weekly *America* asserted that "only the wholehearted practice of Christianity can provide a peaceful solution to African turmoil," calling that insight "important enough to be worth saying, even badly." The *Pittsburgh Courier* reported that Martin Luther King, Jr. called the film "the most captivating and moving production that I have ever seen." Even the *New York Times*'s Howard Thompson claimed he had "yet to hear a better suggestion on the subject: simple adherence to the teachings of Christ"—a sentiment one no longer finds in *New York Times* film reviews. Support for Christian missionary work in the third world remained strong enough to create sympathy for this film's liberal colonialism.

The inclusion of blacks in colonial legislatures—part of Britain's attempt to save its empire as well a measure to prepare the colonized for self-government—also figured in Darryl F. Zanuck's *Island in the Sun* (1957). Zanuck's first film for the production company he founded after leaving Fox was based on British novelist Alec Waugh's 1955 bestseller; set in a fictional British island in the Caribbean, it was shot in London, Grenada, and Barbados. Its treatment of interracial relationships is examined in chapter 9, but the film deserves mention here for its consideration of Britain's transfer of power in the West Indies. Harry Belafonte plays David Boyeur, a popular labor leader who, like Obam in *The Mark of the Hawk*, is torn between cooperating with British authorities and seeking power by mobilizing the black majority. At a party at the governor's mansion, Boyeur meets Maxwell Fleury (James Mason), the son of a plantation owner, who tells Boyeur he recalls his father working on the plantation. When he adds that the man was well cared for, Boyeur replies, "That was charity. What we want is equality." After a journalist reveals that Maxwell's father had a mixed-race mother, Maxwell decides to run for the Legislative Council, on the assumption that his mixed ethnicity will endear him to black voters. But when Fleury holds a rally to launch his campaign, the all-black crowd drowns out his speech in noise and steel-band music. Despite a police presence and a public-address system, Fleury is powerless—a new feeling indeed for the scion of a family of wealthy planters. Boyeur then strides to the podium, easily secures the crowd's silence, and makes a speech of his own that mocks Fleury's invocation of his mixed ancestry. When Fleury tries to rebut Boyeur, the crowd shouts him down, and he exits in humiliation. This scene suggested that any British attempt to institute real democracy in a crown colony such as this would doom white political domination, and for white viewers still harboring hopes of clinging to power, it offered a rude awakening.

The Ireland Cycle

Britain's mostly peaceful approach to decolonization after World War II may have owed something to memories of Ireland's bloody struggle for independence. The willingness to fight a prolonged war against the Irish Republican Army (IRA) during and after World War I reflected a common English and Irish-Protestant view that Ireland was no more a colony than Scotland and Wales were. Geographical proximity shaped this outlook, as did the 1800 Acts of Union, which had merged two formerly separate kingdoms and parliaments. For most of Ireland's Catholic majority, of course, it was indeed a colonial relationship. From this perspective, the 1921 Anglo-Irish Treaty, which ended the Irish War of Independence and created the Irish Free State—while allowing Protestant-dominated Ulster province to remain part of the United Kingdom—was the century's first case of decolonization. The topic remained sensitive in Britain after 1945 because of memories of the War of Independence and the atrocities of the British paramilitary Black and Tans as well as the unresolved Ulster question. The presence of Ulster Protestants in Parliament and Irish Catholics in England made the subject even touchier, but several British and American films examined it in these years.[79]

A few interwar films had dealt with Ireland's struggle for independence, though they sidestepped sensitive political questions by using the independence struggle as a backdrop for personal stories.[80] After World War II, the first film on the subject was *I See a Dark Stranger* (1946; U.S. title: *The Adventuress*). Frank Launder wrote and directed this black-and-white spy comedy starring Deborah Kerr as Bridie Quilty, a naive but headstrong Irish lass who grew up on her father's tales of fighting the British alongside Michael O'Callaghan (an allusion to Michael Collins). In an opening scene in a village "deep in the west of Ireland" in 1937, her father regales a pub full of Guinness-clutching listeners with old war stories, and the fourteen-year-old Bridie is transfixed even though she has heard the tales so often she can mouth along with her father's words. The film then leaps to 1944, when, at twenty-one, she heads for Dublin to join the IRA. Sharing a rail compartment with a well-dressed gentleman, she finds him attractive until she learns his name is Miller. Realizing he is English, her admiration turns to disgust, and she thinks to herself, "You could mistake him for Cromwell" (the hated conqueror of Ireland in the seventeenth century). Once in Dublin, she seeks out O'Callaghan, now an official at an art museum. After she gazes in awe at his portrait among Irish heroes, she meets the man himself. Crestfallen to learn that her father's war stories were pure blarney, she still asks to join the IRA.

The scene, like the film, is tongue in cheek, but the joke is on Bridie and those foolish enough to keep fighting for Ulster. The veteran patriot, who now goes by Callaghan and has an English accent, tries to dissuade her, noting that "we're not at war with Britain" and that in the 1921 treaty, "We got a good deal of what we wanted." When Bridie brings up Ulster, he says it is better dealt with by constitutional means, and he assures her that "when England and Ireland come together and discuss it on a friendly basis, partition won't last very long." He calls her outlook "very romantic and very remote," and while admitting that "we all lose something as we grow older," he adds that "if we're very lucky, we gain a little wisdom on the way."

Undeterred, Bridie heads off to pursue her career as a revolutionary, and when she stops at a bookshop to buy a German-language instructional manual, she runs into Miller, who turns out to be a German spy. Remembering Bridie and her anti-British views, he recruits her for a mission to free a German spy from a jail in an English village (where she vandalizes a statue of Cromwell). Asked to distract a British intelligence officer, Lieutenant Baynes (Trevor Howard), by romancing him, she obeys reluctantly, and soon she cannot rid herself of the smitten Baynes. Her fervor abates when she realizes she may get British and Irish lads killed in the war, and as her political feelings soften, so does her resistance to her English suitor. After confessing to Baynes, she abandons her foolish crusade and her hatred of the English and marries him—though her old feelings resurface when he foolishly books a honeymoon suite at the Cromwell Arms.

Analyzing political comedies risks taking seriously what is "all in good fun," but unlike films that lampoon everything and everyone, *I See a Dark Stranger* pokes fun mainly at Irish nationalists. Even the German villains are not ridiculed, and though the film has a comical pair of English army bureaucrats, it makes no political critique of the British. By having a ingenuous lass raised on barroom blarney represent Irish nationalism while the mature Callaghan is the voice of wisdom, the film takes a condescending view of Irish anticolonialism. The laughs come at Bridie's expense, even if nothing was more naive than Callaghan's claim that friendly discussion could easily end the partition. Ever since London partitioned Ireland into the Irish Free State and Northern Ireland—an act of gerrymandering that created a new country with a Protestant majority inside a Catholic-majority island—completing Ireland's decolonization "by constitutional means" has proven impossible, and despite the IRA's abandonment of violence in the 1990s, the island remains partitioned.

British filmmakers returned to the Irish question the following year. Producer-director Carol Reed's *Odd Man Out* (1947) starred James Mason as Johnny McQueen, an IRA leader in Belfast (though the film names neither the city nor the IRA). The script, which British author F. L. Green helped adapt from his own 1945 novel, involves a robbery gone awry, as McQueen is shot and slowly bleeds to death while eluding a police manhunt. The film mainly avoids politics, stating at the outset, in scrolling titles just after the credits, that "it is not concerned with the struggle between the law and an illegal organisation, but only with the conflict in the hearts of the people when they become unexpectedly involved." Reed and cinematographer Robert Krasker created a visually stunning film noir that won BAFTA's award for Best British Film. It creates a rich tableau out of ordinary people's reactions to the fugitives, which range from sympathy for the fighters to outright betrayal for the basest of motives—and much fence-sitting in between. So despite raising universal issues of justice and mercy, integrity and opportunism, sin and redemption, images of reactions to the IRA raise the vital issue of the movement's popularity. *Odd Man Out* questions that support by showing Johnny and his comrades repeatedly betrayed and rebuffed in Belfast's Catholic neighborhoods, and if, as Mao argued, "the guerrilla must move amongst the people as a fish swims in the sea," this film suggests the IRA men were swimming in shark-infested waters. It also briefly turns political when a comrade doubts Johnny's commitment; having escaped a British prison, Johnny affirms his loyalty and then says, "This violence isn't getting us anywhere." Explaining that "in prison you have time to think," he now wishes "we could throw the guns away [and] make our cause in the parliaments instead of in the back streets." He also remains racked with guilt for shooting a man during the robbery. Like Michael Callaghan in *I See a Dark Stranger*, Johnny has come to question political violence, and once again British filmmakers have Irish characters express opposition to anticolonial violence.

That theme appeared yet again in *The Gentle Gunman* (1952), from Michael Balcon Productions and Ealing Studios. Basil Dearden directed from Scottish screenwriter and playwright Roger MacDougall's adaptation of his own 1950 play. Set in London, Belfast, and a village on the Ireland–Northern Ireland border in

1941, it follows disillusioned IRA fighter Terry Sullivan (John Mills) and his efforts to persuade his younger brother Matt (Dirk Bogarde) to quit the violent campaign for Ulster. In an opening act in London, when Matt learns from two IRA bomb-makers, Tim and Patsy, that his older brother has betrayed the cause, he volunteers to replace him, and he takes a bomb into a crowded underground station where civilians are taking refuge from German bombardment. By chance Terry sees Matt enter the station, and when Matt botches the operation, Terry intervenes to save some children. As the two escape, the police follow Matt back to the safe house, where they arrest the bomb-makers. The brothers return to Northern Ireland, where Terry tries to persuade the IRA men that he is not a traitor. An operation to free Tim and Patsy during their transfer to Belfast allows Terry to prove himself and help the cause in his new, nonviolent way, but although he succeeds, the local IRA chief, Shinto (Robert Beatty), doubts his story and orders a summary trial. Just as Terry is about to be executed, the two prisoners arrive, proving Terry's claims, and Matt walks away from the IRA with his brother.

The Gentle Gunman intends an even-handed view of the Ulster debate, presenting the two sides' views through a friendly debate between an Irish doctor and his English chess partner, Henry. When Henry attacks the IRA for bombing tube stations in wartime, the doctor explains that "Northern Ireland is occupied territory: exploited [and] unhappy," adding that Britain had used force against the Irish for three centuries. Henry's reply that "there's a difference between using soldiers in uniform to keep the peace and gunmen to break it" and his contention that the law-abiding Irish had nothing to fear from British guns leads the doctor to ask, "How can any self-respecting Irishman be law abiding when he can't abide the laws you make?" The scenes with these two bickering friends have a comical tone, trivializing the debate and inviting viewers to roll their eyes at the whole squabble. Also played for laughs is a scene in London, where the bomb-makers chat with their English landlady, who has come to collect coins for the war against Germany. "They say Hitler's going to invade England," Tim tells her, "occupy six of the northern counties and found a new kingdom, and you know what he's going to call it? The United Kingdom of Great Germany and Northern England. Isn't it shockin'?" The oblivious landlady misses the joke and expresses her confidence in their support for the war, telling them, "I know you're all really British at heart." This joke is on the silly English landlady and her patronizing view of the Irish, so the film makes a rare pro-Irish political point.

The film's main goal is to oppose violence, which it does through the sympathetic Terry's conversion to nonviolence.[81] Insisting that he remains committed to the cause, Terry tells Matt, "I've just begin to think there are better ways of serving your country than dying for it" and "better ways of getting what you want than at the point of a gun." He also expresses a universal humanism learned from living among ordinary Britons.[82] "An Irishman is the same thing as an Englishman or a Frenchman," he says. "It's the way we're all separated out into different countries that causes the trouble." Despite this internationalism, the film only questions *Irish* nationalism and its dreams of decolonizing Ulster. It reinforces its message through Molly (Barbara Mullen), whose loss of her husband Joe in an IRA action makes her resist Shinto's recruiting of her son Johnny. But when she tells Shinto, "Joe was happy enough until you told him he was unhappy, and he was free, too, till you told him he wasn't," she goes beyond condemning violence, as she and the film scoff at Irish discontent over Ulster.

In moving the London bombings, which mostly took place before the war, to 1941, the film makes the IRA look even more ruthless.[83] And despite Shinto's historically accurate statement that Ireland secured its independence through violence, the film paints IRA violence as futile, as symbolized by Shinto getting two of his men killed in a plot to free two men who had already escaped. Nonviolence, of course, did work in India and elsewhere, but the film never suggests how it might have succeeded in Ulster, and it dismisses the Irish case for regaining what Britain kept in 1921. "It's peace we want and security and a decent life," Terry declares, voicing the film's plea to forget about Ulster. It would be one thing for an Irish film to make this point; it was quite another for a British film to do so.

The last 1950s film in this cycle was *Shake Hands with the Devil* (1959), an Anglo-American film shot in Ireland and based on a 1933 novel by Irish writer Rearden Conner. Marlon Brando's Pennebaker Productions coproduced it with a company owned by Britain's Michael Anderson, who directed it from a script by Ben Roberts, an American, and Ivan Goff, an Australian who emigrated to the United States.[84] With an equally multinational cast, this black-and-white film offered a relatively frank treatment of a politically sensitive topic. The story, set in 1921, concerns Irish American Kerry O'Shea (Don Murray), a student at the College of Surgeons in Dublin and the son of an Irish revolutionary killed by the British. Kerry's professor Sean Lenihan (James Cagney) is a distinguished surgeon and also a clandestine leader of "the organization." Kerry, a veteran of the Great War, favors independence but is tired of violence and refuses to join the IRA. He is gradually drawn into the struggle when he must flee the Black and Tans after helping a friend gunned down in the streets. Arrested, Kerry endures a brutal interrogation, and when the rebels free him, he joins the IRA. The rest of the film deals with the IRA's kidnapping of a British official's daughter, Jennifer (Dana Wynter), seized to exchange for Lady Fitzhugh (Sybil Thorndike), an

Irish aristocrat arrested for helping the IRA. When Lenihan learns of the imminent Anglo-Irish Treaty, he opposes it because Ireland will be only a "Free State" tied to the British Crown, not a republic. Word of Lady Fitzhugh's death from a hunger strike convinces Lenihan that Jennifer must die, leading Kerry, who has fallen in love with her, to try to stop him. In a final showdown, Lenihan draws his gun, but the American beats him to the draw and kills him, then throws his gun away in disgust.

Shake Hands with the Devil is fairly sympathetic to the IRA, and an opening voice-over explains that the Irish had often "risen to fight for their freedom, only to be crushed." The notorious Black and Tans make an easy target whose actions (such as the 1920 Bloody Sunday massacre at an Irish football match) provoked outrage even in Britain. In the film, the Black and Tan leader Colonel Smithson is cartoonishly evil, and the film views the "Tans" from the republicans' point of view. Director Anderson shot the scene of Kerry's beating at police headquarters with a point-of-view close-up of Smithson's fist coming straight at the camera, while graphic sound effects conveyed Kerry's experience. And instead of depicting the Tans as a rogue element beyond London's control, the film underlines the close connections between the two in a scene showing Smithson meeting British officials. The film also invites sympathy for the rebels in a series of tense action scenes. Finally, at Lady Fitzhugh's sentencing, her statement poses the most pointed of anticolonial questions: "What is an English judge doing in an Irish court?" If the film only consisted of these views, it would have been a remarkably bold anticolonialist film.

Clouding the issue, however, is the film's opposition to violence, which offsets its hostility to British rule in Ireland. Lenihan's image darkens drastically as the film unfolds, but this is not a character transformation. Instead the film simply changes its mind about him: he starts out as a courageous, humorous, charismatic Irish patriot then becomes a fanatical, misogynist psychopath reminiscent of Cagney's gangster roles. Using the old empire-film device of depicting good and evil natives—the former open to reconciliation with the colonizer, the latter mindlessly bloodthirsty—the film sides with the American, who fights reluctantly and sees the humanity of his foes, and Lenihan's fighters all side with Kerry at the end. Although one character points out that America secured its independence through violence, the film qualifies its anticolonialism, and from its title (a warning of the soul-corrupting consequences of violence) to its final shot of Kerry flinging away his gun, it opposes the bloodshed that actually secured Ireland's independence.

The film deals with the IRA's division into pro-treaty and anti-treaty camps through a debate between Lenihan and his superior, "the General" (Michael Redgrave). "Both sides must bend a little," the General contends. "We'll be ruling ourselves at last, after seven hundred years." He also calls it "a fair treaty" that provides a general amnesty and an Irish parliament, while "the republic will come later." Lenihan replies that Ireland will remain "tied to England's apron strings," but the script makes no mention of either Britain's retention of Ulster or the hated oath of loyalty to the king that the treaty required of Irish parliamentarians. Instead, the script limits Lenihan to arguing that violence has been working and that they had all vowed to fight for a republic "to the last man." To this seemingly suicidal view, the General asks, "What good is the Republic if there's no one left to enjoy it?" and the film clearly favors the pro-treaty camp, as the 1996 film *Michael Collins* would do. So while *Shake Hands with the Devil* contains a strong indictment of British colonialism and clear sympathy for the Irish independence struggle, it tempers that outlook by its rejection of violence and its demonizing of Lenihan, and in opposing both colonialism and anticolonial violence, it risks naivete and self-contradiction.

Although the film did not make the box-office charts in the United States, it did well with the critics; of twenty-two reviews examined, fifteen were positive (68 percent), four negative, and three mixed.[85] *America* said the film "squanders a notable opportunity by using a melodramatic and trivial approach to a serious subject," particularly with the romance subplot. Even some who liked the film objected to its treatment of Lenihan, whom they described with terms such as "fanatic," "zealot," and "psychopath." The *Boston Herald* found it "a bit bewildering" that "a strongly sympathetic and courageous man is gradually transformed into a ruthless, maniacal fanatic," and *Commonweal* concurred, writing that an otherwise strong script "fail[s] to prepare us for the near-psychopath this man becomes." The *Los Angeles Examiner's* Ruth Waterbury saw the film in Dublin, where "three quarters of the audience adored it" while "the other quarter hated it," and though she liked the film, she complained that "it minimizes the Cagney character to write him off at the end as a mad-dog killer." The *New York Times* and the *Dallas Morning News* lamented the absence of English points of view, while the *Chicago Tribune* called the IRA's violence "senseless slaughter." Others sympathized with the Irish struggle. In heavily Irish American Boston, the *Globe* called the IRA fighters "men who hid in cellars and fought the brutal Black and Tans with all their courage and what weapons they had," while Jack Moffitt of the *Hollywood Reporter* wrote that "after 700 years of indomitable courage, bushwhacking, and terrorism, the Hibernian people, in their fight for freedom, had all but brought the British Empire to its knees." The *Examiner's* Waterbury also quoted Lady Fitzhugh's question about an English judge in an Irish court. These reviews suggest pervasive American sympathy for the Irish cause as well as a basic disdain for European colonialism.

Critical reaction was cooler in Britain, where ten of twenty reviews were positive, seven negative, and three mixed.[86] Suggesting that some Britons preferred not to dredge up this painful history, Jympson Harman of the *Evening News* alluded to the "tricky business of stirring up old memories," but he clarified whose memories concerned him when he wrote that the film crew in Dublin had "to make sure that excitable Irish memories were not aroused." The *Times* contended that "the Black-and-Tan war in Ireland—for such it was—in 1921 makes sad reading for an Englishman, and it is hard to bear when a film of American origins rubs an audience's nose into a fictional version of it." For the *Daily Mail*'s Fred Majdalany, it was not "sufficiently clear that the security forces (the 'Black and Tans') were not the British Army," making it "unjustifiably one-sided in its anti-English bias." *Kinematograph Weekly* put this even more strongly, calling the film "a long, loud, and lusty hymn of hate [that] will, no doubt, be sweet music to Southern Irish folk and certain Irish-Americans, but the possibility of it jarring on many British audiences cannot be entirely ignored." It added that "the Black and Tans appear more ruthless than the Irish rebels, despite the ugly fanaticism of Sean, and bias frequently debases its drama."

While some resented the Yanks' meddling or found the film anti-British, the *Daily Telegraph* judged that it "holds the balance pretty fairly," and Margaret Hinxman of the *Daily Herald* praised the "savagely outspoken" film for pointing "an accusing finger at a shameful episode in British history," insisting that it "doesn't overstate its case against the Black and Tans." The *Times* felt the film "must be commended for making the point that it was not British regular soldiers the Irish were fighting," and on the Tans' brutality, the film "has here a case to argue." The *Daily Worker*'s Nina Hibbin quoted Lady Fitzhugh's question about the English judge, and she welcomed the Americans' making the film, as "no *British* production could maintain this pitch of national feeling in a film about a suppressed people." Although she complained that Lenihan "is depicted as a homicidal maniac"—when in reality "thousands of Irishmen" and "nearly half the members" of the Irish parliament opposed the treaty—she praised the film for showing "the cruelty of British rule [and] the solid fight of the Irish for their freedom." Some critics wished the film had been bolder still. The *Monthly Film Bulletin* maintained that "when it comes to voicing an issue, as it should do in the scenes between Lenihan and the general, the film has all too little to say," and the *Financial Times*'s David Robinson complained that "Ireland is no more than a background for a rather violent adventure piece" with "no comment on the times and the troubles." Cautious as it was, the film revealed a wide range of British feelings about a dark chapter in Britain's colonial history. Overall, British critics seemed less colonialist than British films were on the Irish question.

These English, American, and Anglo-American films on decolonization in the British Empire offered views ranging from staunch defenses of empire to relatively bold denunciations of colonialism. *The Planter's Wife* was the most plainly colonialist, but *Thunder in the East, Bhowani Junction, Simba, Safari,* and others also supported violence against anticolonial movements. The way these films presented the rival forces, telling the story from the colonizers' point of view and depicting the anticolonial rebels' atrocities in grisly detail without letting them state their case, reinforced their sympathy for the defense of threatened colonies.

Some of the films did recognize legitimate grievances of the colonized, despite questioning their methods. *Something of Value* dramatized Africans' mistreatment and allowed a Mau Mau spokesman to state his case; *Windom's Way* sympathized with oppressed workers while showing collusion between tyrannical planters and unscrupulous officials; *The Mark of the Hawk* supported Obam's pleas for African self-rule; and *Shake Hands with the Devil* supported Ireland's struggle for independence. Yet all of those films also condemned anticolonialist violence, and their endorsement of the grievances of the colonized did not always imply real opposition to colonialism. In Malaya, after all, the British developed the hearts-and-minds concept while waging a war against communist rebels, and the Mau Mau films all suggest that whites should fight the rebels while treating other Africans better. This outlook, in short, amounts to liberal-colonialism rather than true anticolonialism.

Despite the scarcity of bonafide anticolonialism in these 1950s films, several did present sharp criticisms of colonialism—or at least conservative colonialism. Examples include the snobbish Britons sputtering at the closing of their exclusive club in *Thunder in the East*; the boorish behavior of childish, drunken planters in *Elephant Walk*; the racial arrogance of *Island in the Sun*'s Maxwell Fleury; and the settlers' demands to teach the natives a lesson in *Simba, Something of Value, The Mark of the Hawk,* and *Windom's Way*. These negative views of colonialism grew more prominent throughout the 1950s, suggesting that British and American attitudes were slowly changing. Rank's staunchly colonialist *The Planter's Wife* appeared in 1952, whereas the same studio's return to the subject in *Windom's Way* (1957) took a much more liberal view. *Something of Value* was more liberal than *Simba* had been two years earlier, and though that may primarily have reflected a difference in national perspectives, it may also have indicated changing outlooks. The film most critical of colonialism, *Shake Hands with the Devil*, which favored independence rather than more liberal colonial rule, appeared at the end of the decade (and also concerned a fait accompli).

These films also offer glimpses of how the Americans and the British envisioned the new nations' futures. In *Bhowani Junction*, the defeat of the communists leaves hope, and *The Mark of the Hawk* seemed content with power going to the well-educated, politically moderate Obam. In *Shake Hands with the Devil*, the elimination of the fanatical Lenihan left Ireland in the hands of reasonable men such as the General. Yet some of the films convey more anxious visions, and to die-hard colonialists they communicated a dispiriting sense of decolonization's historical inevitability. *Windom's Way* seems to support the good doctor's mediation efforts until it ends with his failure, and *Elephant Walk*'s image of the elephants as a primal, native force overrunning the plantation house has symbolic import. Similarly, in *Island in the Sun*, Maxwell's anxiety as Boyeur used his control of the black masses to silence him underlined this message of white helplessness. Nor did colonialism have any future in *Thunder in the East*, where whites merely manage a brave last stand, in *Bhowani Junction*, where Savage's victory merely allows Britain to leave gracefully, or in *Shake Hands with the Devil*, where the British agree to leave. These films, in short, helped accustom Western audiences to the idea of decolonization.

While filmmakers tiptoed through controversies in the 1950s, many American, British, and French critics welcomed films on colonial politics and wished they had been bolder. Some critics clearly knew little about the political settings—especially American critics viewing films about Malaya. Critics in all three countries showed considerable sympathy for colonized peoples wanting their freedom, if not for their use of violence. It was always easiest to criticize others' colonial policies, and the French and the Americans were the warmest to critiques of British colonialism, while some Britons bristled at American meddling in what they saw as their affairs. The most serious anticolonialism, including a willingness to countenance violence, remained confined to the far left, which was practically absent from film reviewing in the United States, confined to small-circulation papers in Britain, and comparatively common in France's press. But if many critics disliked violent insurgencies, even though they sympathized with desires for independence, there may have been more than mere naivete and inconsistency at work. Reactions to these films evoke the "fait accompli" phenomenon noted in opinion research, in which survey respondents prove less receptive to a proposed action than to a completed one. Films about Malaya and Kenya made during the wars generally supported counterinsurgency, whereas films about Indian and Irish independence made after the fact showed rather different attitudes. As students of public opinion also point out, it makes a difference whether people's opinions have settled into firm patterns, and it appears that attitudes about decolonization in the 1950s had yet to do so. The many ambivalent reactions seen here suggest that decolonization took place against a background of rather fluid Western attitudes.

CHAPTER FIVE

The French Empire and Decolonization

For years, scholars have contrasted the turbulent history of "the contentious French" with the more peaceful evolution of the British, and that contrast appears in studies of decolonization. In this view, just as France's violent eighteenth-century revolution initiated two centuries of revolutions and regime changes while Britain gradually and peacefully became more socially and politically inclusive, France waged traumatic colonial wars that fueled internal political crises while the British avoided such problems through a series of prudent, peaceful transfers of power. Although there is some truth to this picture, it is oversimplified and misleading. We have seen that the British waged wars in their colonies after World War II, and although the French fought bitter wars in Indochina and Algeria, they also transferred power peacefully elsewhere. And although no colonial crisis ever triggered a British regime change, as in France in 1958, the conflict with the IRA brought violence to England. In terms of cinema, however, while the British made films on imperial topics throughout the late 1940s and 1950s, French filmmakers—constrained more tightly by political censorship and apparently less inclined to make pro-imperial films—largely avoided that subject. Hollywood certainly did not, and this chapter looks at a series of American films about unrest in France's empire. It then examines three early French fiction films about the war in Indochina.

The Fractious French and the Ambivalent Americans

Hollywood films suggest that Americans have long been both horrified and attracted by France's history. In films based on classics from French literature such as *The Three Musketeers* and *The Hunchback of Notre Dame*, Hollywood made historical adventure tales of heroes battling French tyranny and injustice. A contrast between tyranny and liberty naturally pervaded interwar films on the Old Regime and the French Revolution, including *Orphans of the Storm* (1921), *Scaramouche* (1923), *Voltaire* (1933), *Madame Du Barry* (1934), *A Tale of Two Cities* (1935), and *Marie Antoinette* (1938). Particularly in the Great Depression, audiences enjoyed lavish costume dramas depicting the glamorous and decadent lives of French monarchs and aristocrats. Although these films ended up inviting some measure of sympathy for doomed royals and nobles by telling their stories, depictions of the lives of the idle rich at a time when millions were struggling to get by carried overtones of moral and political condemnation. These films also allowed the studios to show off opulent costumes and sets, and these images of Old World splendor lured American viewers in the same way the Palace of Versailles has long attracted American tourists. Like Hollywood films about the decadent Roman Empire, films about the Old Regime offered audiences the pleasure of gazing at luxury while having the moral superiority of their own, more austere existence confirmed. Hollywood's conflicted populism did not extend to endorsing the Revolution or the Reign of Terror, and both American and British films typically argued that the Revolution's cure was worse than the disease. This message that revolution worsened rather than solved the problem of tyranny took on added significance in Cold War era films such as Anthony Mann's *Reign of Terror* (1949), in which Robespierre brought to mind communist dictators.

The liberty versus tyranny theme recurred in films on other topics from French history, including *The Life of Emile Zola* (Warner Bros., 1937), which showed both the best of France, in the writer's crusade to liberate the falsely imprisoned Alfred Dreyfus, and the worst of French tyranny, in the army's false accusations and the notorious penal colony, Devil's Island. Similar contrasts between good and evil French forces also figured in wartime films such as *Passage to Marseille* (1944), which presented the clear moral and political opposites of the Free French and the Vichy regime. The most famous wartime film, *Casablanca* (1942), also presented both French collaboration and resistance, with Captain Renault (Claude Rains) coming over to the side of liberty at the end.

Prewar Empire Films

Casablanca, despite its colonial setting, ignored the Moroccans and their feelings about foreign occupation while sympathizing with France's struggle against German occupation. Other films, however, did show interest in French colonialism. Perhaps the most negative prewar depiction was John Ford's *The Hurricane* (1937). Reflecting a typical noble-savage view of the South Seas as a paradise spoiled by Western intrusion, *The Hurricane* depicts a heartless martinet, Eugene DeLaage (Raymond Massey), the absolute ruler of a tiny French island, Manukura.

DeLaage represents the France of the Bastille, sentencing natives to hard labor for minor infractions such as "stealing" a canoe for a moonlight tryst. Equally tyrannical authorities in Tahiti sentence Terangi (Jon Hall), to six months' hard labor for striking a belligerent white racist who ordered him and his fellow Polynesian seamen out of a waterfront saloon. When the newlywed Terangi escapes from the local version of Devil's Island to rejoin his pregnant wife in Manukura, he is captured, and further escape attempts extend his original sentence to sixteen years, to the delight of a sadistic warden (John Carradine). Both DeLaage and Tahiti's governor dismiss other whites' pleas to pardon Terangi, and this melodrama urges sympathies for the colonized, who fear and detest their inhuman French overseers. The film softens its anticolonialism with a bit of liberal colonialism in the person of Father Paul (C. Aubrey Smith); in the climactic hurricane, images of the islanders taking refuge with him and joining him in prayers suggest a benign side to French colonialism. Though the hurricane wipes out the church and nearly everyone in Manukura, it also gives the audience the satisfaction of seeing DeLaage's little empire destroyed, and it even causes DeLaage, the Javert of the Pacific, to abandon his obsessive pursuit of Terangi.

A more ambivalent look at French colonialism appears in *Algiers* (1938), a United Artists' remake of Julien Duvivier's *Pepe Le Moko* (1937). Once again, a French gangster, Pepe (Charles Boyer), hides from the law in the Casbah and falls for a beautiful Parisian visitor, Gaby (Hedy Lamarr). It sympathizes with French colonialism in depicting the Casbah as a squalid, racially impure "anthill" that France sought to cleanse. In this sense, *Algiers* treats France's empire much as Hollywood handled Britain's empire in these years, embracing the civilizing mission while getting entertainment value out of exotic locales and people. But if *Algiers* officially supports the French authorities, its heart is really with the outlaw Pepe and his motley entourage. Pepe, after all, is a charming rogue, and his motive for walking into the final trap is not greed or criminal instinct, but rather *l'amour*—or Lamarr, at least. This femme fatale also reminds Pepe of Paris and the liberty he lost in fleeing to the Casbah. And if Pepe and liberty must come to a tragic end, images of the pompous, self-deluding Parisian police inspector hardly flatter French authority.

Also highlighting French colonialism was William Wellman's *Beau Geste* (1939), made for Paramount. Like many interwar empire films, *Beau Geste* shows little real interest in either the North Africans or their relationship with the colonizers, and it uses Arab attackers to create a backdrop of tension for a drama about white people. *Beau Geste* focuses on three English brothers who run away to join the Foreign Legion, and though they find themselves under the authority of a sadistic sergeant, the film avoids offending the French by making him Russian.

The Postwar Era

As the task of winning World War II gave way to that of crafting a postwar order, Washington had new reasons for ambivalence about French colonialism. While war aims and principles conflicted with the reestablishment of an inherently undemocratic colonial system, growing American concerns about communism complicated matters. Americans feared that colonized peoples seeking their freedom might turn to the Soviets (or the Chinese, after 1949), so when Europeans were fighting leftist rebels, as the French were in Indochina by November 1946, the temptation to support colonial regimes proved irresistible. Concerns about communism in western Europe also led the United States to back European colonialism, given assumptions that the French and others needed their colonies to recover economically and avoid the desperate conditions in which communism thrived. Of course, American filmmakers did not have to follow Washington in backing French colonialism—though they did hope to export films to France— and their postwar films continued the tradition of viewing French imperialism ambivalently.

Hollywood's love for the French empire was never clearer than in *Outpost in Morocco* (1949), made by the production company of the film's star, George Raft, for United Artists. Raft played Foreign Legion Captain Paul Gerard, a stereotypical French ladies' man who romances the local emir's daughter, Cara (Marie Windsor), while also fighting a desert uprising whose leader turns out to be the Emir himself. Shot partly in Morocco with official French cooperation, the film takes a reverent view of French imperialism, opening and closing with shots of the French flag flying over a fort. It is riddled with empire-film conventions and clichés, such as the rallying of the loyal natives to their kindly French protectors and the ill-fated romance between Gerard and Cara. It even gives French imperialism religious overtones when a lieutenant and the Captain pray to Jesus inside their besieged fort, followed by a miraculous rainstorm that saves the garrison from dying of thirst. The Emir's revolt gets little explanation, nor does the film give any hint of the Istiqlal Party's growing nationalism or its recent declaration of independence.

Far less flattering to French colonialism was *Sirocco* (1951), an independent production released by Columbia Pictures that strove to recapture the magic of *Casablanca*. Humphrey Bogart starred as Harry Smith, a cynical American adventurer, this time in Syria in 1925, amid a revolt against the French military occupation that a League of Nations mandate had authorized. This film noir evokes *Casablanca* in countless ways, while giving much more attention to the Syrians than *Casablanca* gave the Moroccans—including allowing the resistance leader, Emir Hassan, to state his case. The Emir is a civilized gentleman—he speaks excellent English and wears a Western business suit with his Arab headdress—and he tells one English and one American reporter, "We fight because they have invaded our country. They want to govern us, tell us what to do. We want to govern ourselves" and "recapture our freedom." The film also differs from *Casablanca* in that there are no Germans—only grim French soldiers struggling to control a hellish, chaotic Damascus, where it always seems to be night.

After giving the Emir the floor, the film cuts to General LaSalle, a stern figure briefing reporters on why the French are in Syria—though he simply cites the League of Nations mandate. In a subsequent scene, the scowling General orders that because of rebel attacks, the French will henceforth execute five Syrians in public for every French soldier killed. The script did not invent this scenario, which hints at the collective punishment and draconian violence France used against Syrian rebels.[1] The film does not show such French actions, but even the threat brought to mind Nazi tyranny, and the General addresses his men beneath a portrait of Marshal Pétain—a symbol in 1925 of France's costly victory in World War I, but one that by 1951 evoked French dictatorship. The film reinforces its dim view of French colonialism with a scene in which a distraught Arab complains to two French soldiers that their curfew is ruining his business, only to be roughed up and sent packing.

After this anticolonialist opening act, the film shifts its attention to Harry Smith and his attempts to elude French authorities while selling guns to the rebels and romancing the girlfriend of Colonel Louis Feroud (Lee J. Cobb). Once again, a cynical American gradually rediscovers his morality and idealism, and as in *Casablanca*, he lets his lover get away and accepts the tragic fate of the film noir protagonist. Meanwhile, the dour but upstanding Colonel Feroud redeems France's image somewhat as he dissuades the General from massacring civilians, warning him that the rebels "consider themselves patriots" and that people will call him a butcher. Feroud also proposes a cease-fire to the Emir, telling him, "We can try to settle our differences according to the dignity of man." The Emir, however, views Feroud's plea as a call for surrender and replies that "there is dignity in men who are willing to give their lives for what they believe in." Indeed, the film never comes down clearly on either side, and it observes that both the French and the Syrians wade in blood while believing they have God and justice on their side. And while the film is hardly flattering either to the Arabs or to dark, dirty

Damascus, where much of the action takes place in the Roman-built catacombs, it joins the ranks of those postwar films that questioned colonial rule. Syria hardly seems worth the trouble, as a French envoy has his throat slit, officers are blown up by grenades in a café, and soldiers on patrol are mowed down by rebel machine guns—all without any apparent compensation such as lucrative commodities or success in spreading civilization. *Sirocco* thus reflects American ambivalence about French colonialism, with its mixture of admiration for Colonel Feroud and disdain for General LaSalle and his repression of a people desiring freedom.

A far more flattering image of French colonialism appears in MGM's *Saadia* (1953), which director Albert Lewin wrote and shot in Technicolor in Morocco. In 1953, France, resisting demands for independence in its protectorate, exiled Sultan Mohammed V to Madagascar, but the film, based on a 1950 French novel, ignores those developments. The tale concerns a selfless, young French doctor, Henrik (Mel Ferrer), and his work in a village where the superstitious locals are in thrall to a sorceress, Fatima (Wanda Rotha). Representing French colonialism's success in spreading modern ways is the French-educated Caid, Si Lahssen (Cornel Wilde), a beloved ruler who, a narrator explains, "has brought his Western knowledge to the service of his country." Most of the story concerns Henrik's competition with the sorceress over a beautiful young Berber, Saadia (Rita Gam), whom Fatima desires as a protégée and surrogate daughter—though the film also indicates lesbian desire when a supine Fatima fondles a statuette of Saadia and holds it to her heaving bosom. After Henrik saves Saadia with an appendectomy, the grateful young woman, repelled by Fatima's advances but still afraid of her black magic, goes to work at the doctor's clinic. During an outbreak of bubonic plague, when a plane carrying serum crashes in the territory of the feared bandit Bou Rezza (Michel Simon), Saadia heroically ventures into the bandit's camp, resists his attempt to rape her, kills him, and escapes with the serum. So while the doctor is both a civilizer and a protector, so is Saadia, who protects her people and embraces Western ways, pointing to a successful colonial partnership.

While the doctor and Fatima carry on their struggle between ancient indigenous and modern French ways, the doctor and the Caid also compete for Saadia's love, which ultimately goes not to the handsome doctor, but, in an anti-miscegenation twist, to her fellow Moroccan, with whom she rightly belongs. After an action climax in which Henrik, Si Lahssen, and Saadia are besieged in a mountain cave by bandits bent on avenging their leader's death, only to be rescued with impeccable Hollywood timing by loyal tribesmen and Moroccans serving in France's army, the doctor saves the badly injured Caid while the worried villagers stage a prayerful vigil. Though he has lost the competition for Saadia, Henrik announces he will stay in Morocco, telling the wise Muslim cleric Khadir (Cyril Cusack), "I can't turn my back on these people."

This colonialist, Orientalist film uses locations effectively, filling the screen with quaint souks, minarets, brightly-clad dancing women, and the striking colors of the desert. Undermining its authenticity, however, is its ethnic miscasting, resulting in jarring accents: French officers who sound British, a Caid and a French doctor with American accents, and tribesmen with French accents. Although just as condescending toward indigenous popular religion as old zombie and voodoo films, it depicts Islam more positively through the cleric, Khadir, suggesting that if French colonialism rightly eradicated absurd superstitions, it was tolerant toward legitimate faiths. Like *Outpost in Morocco*, it opens with a shot of the French flag, as titles thank "the authorities of the Protectorate of Morocco." The film failed to make *Variety*'s charts, and its few American reviews dismissed it as silly, if visually striking.[2] In France, it sold a modest 834,442 tickets when it finally arrived in August 1955; by then the war in Algeria had begun, making it seem even more dated and irrelevant, and it received very few reviews.[3]

Also in 1953 came another desert adventure set in French North Africa: *Fort Algiers*, an independent black-and-white film distributed by United Artists. Directed by Lesley Selander, a maker of low-budget westerns, the film starred Yvonne De Carlo as Yvette Delmar, a French spy. Apparently set in the present, the film opens with rifle-waving Arabs shouting triumphantly inside a fort littered with the bodies of French soldiers, as their leader, the Amir (Raymond Burr in full Arab dress), instructs them to finish off the prisoners and lower the French flag. When next seen, the debonair Amir wears a tuxedo with his turban as he romances Yvette in an elegant nightclub. A character describes him as "the richest man in North Africa," though it is unlikely that an Arab could have been wealthier than French Algeria's *grands colons*, such as Henri Borgeaud, Laurent Schiaffino, and Georges Blachette, who presided over vast agricultural and commercial empires.[4] Having bugged the Amir's palace, Yvette overhears him telling several sheikhs of his plan to seize the local oil fields, after which "we'll have the sympathy of the entire world." Yvette and Jeff Nelson (Carlos Thompson), an American serving in the Foreign Legion, manage to inform headquarters before rushing to the oil fields to improvise hasty defenses against the Amir's onslaught. Using dynamite and small arms, they fend off the Amir's multitudes until French forces ride to the rescue, to the sound of bugles Selander knew well from his cavalry westerns.

This run-of-the-mill empire film follows genre conventions by contrasting evil natives—the scheming Amir and his primitive fighters—and good—the loyal sheikhs who warn the French about the Amir's revolt. The French come off as benevolent defenders of order and civilization, and when the sheikhs express their concerns that the Amir covets "the oil lands that now belong to our tribes," a French major reassures them that "France will see to it that your rights are protected." France did no such thing when a French company discovered oil in Algeria three years after the film's release, but the oil issue updates this otherwise old-fashioned picture. The Amir's calculation that the world would back him once he seized the oil fields calls to mind international sympathy for Iranian nationalist Prime Minister Mohammed Mossadegh's efforts to free his country's oil industry from British and American domination in 1951–53.

Fort Algiers also reflects the Cold War concerns about revolutionary forces such as Egypt's Free Officers' Movement, which brought Gamal Abdel Nasser to power after the Egyptian Revolution of 1952. When the Amir, angry at the loyalist Haroon (Robert Warwick) for opposing his revolt, calls him a paid French agent, Haroon replies, "I wonder whose money you've been spending so freely, . . . possibly that of some nation that would like to see fire and bloodshed sweep over our land for its own selfish aims." After this allusion to the Soviets, the Amir echoes third-world nationalists by responding, "I am free to accept help from whomever I choose." The film also has unintended relevance today, as it ends with a war over oil in which Western forces use superior weaponry to defeat Arab nationalists. The victorious Western forces even include female combatants, as Yvette detonates the improvised explosives and picks up a rifle to help mow down the Arab attackers in a terribly lopsided war.

The cheering for French colonialism continued in 1959 with *Timbuktu*, though with minor concessions to changing times. French-born director Jacques Tourneur, who made horror films such as *Cat People* (1942) and *I Walked with a Zombie* (1943), and who spent years in America, shot this independent, United Artists–released, black-and-white film in Utah, which stood in for French West Africa. Set in 1940, the story concerns an uprising of Tuareg tribesmen against French forces depleted by the transfer of units to fight in Europe. The figure of the cynical, selfish American arms dealer in the French colonies recurs yet again with Victor Mature playing Mike Conway, and as in *Sirocco*, the Yank divides his time among selling guns to the rebels, evading arrest by the French, and romancing the wife of the local French commander, Colonel Dufort (George Dolenz). The film's colonialist attitudes are clearest in its portrait of the natives, starting with an attack on French troops by Tuareg warriors led by a swarthy, bearded ruffian with the largest facial scar any makeup department ever devised. Maneuvering the Tuareg fighters is another articulate, educated Emir (John Dehner), but here he is unambiguously evil, gunning down his own men to test out machine guns and taking sadistic pleasure in killing French prisoners with his pet tarantulas—a horror-film touch that Tourneur handles deftly.

In blaming the unrest on the scheming Emir, the film exonerates his followers, if condescendingly. The Emir tells Conway that his people "need a crusade to rouse them from their lethargy," but "first they must have a taste of blood." He adds that "to be truly civilized one must have a slave caste, and the French have spread ideas about equality that must be destroyed." Once he has stirred up his people's bloodlust and xenophobia, he informs the American, "We'll sweep north and engulf Tunis and Morocco." Although set in 1940, the film was made during France's war in Algeria, and it seems to evoke French frustrations in fighting enemies they could not find; a French officer, for example, says of their foe, "His camps move like the drifting sands. He strikes and he's gone. We're fighting a phantom."

Timbuktu softens its denigration of the locals through the figure of a holy man, Mahomet Adani (Leonard Mudie), whom the Emir tries to use to help stir up anti-French hatred. Resisting the Emir's cynical use of religion, Adani insists his is a "voice of peace," and the film thus joins *Saadia* in depicting Islam positively. The holy man also rejects the Emir's anticolonialism, declaring that "there is no more slavery in the Sudan; the village council govern themselves without interference. This the French have done. And much else: they brought doctors, teachers." His love for French colonialism is robust, but not unlimited, as he adds, "The Sudan is not theirs and never will be. Someday, as they come, so must they go. When my people are ready to take their place in the world, then I will preach independence." At the film's climax, when a French force arrives and finishes off the Emir's revolt, the holy man tells a crowd, "These people are our friends—lay down your weapons and let us seek independence with honor"—a line evoking President de Gaulle's 1958 plea for a *paix des braves* (peace of the brave) in Algeria. *Timbuktu* thus follows empire-film conventions by dividing the natives into simplistic categories of good (peaceful, cooperative) and evil (cruel, bloodthirsty, and rebellious), while depicting the French in wholly positive tones—even if the Colonel is a cold husband who could learn a thing or two about love from the American. Once again a cynical American rediscovers his idealism, risking his life to help save the French Empire, and again a story set in wartime highlights Franco-American cooperation. When the French officer dies while the American survives to ride (literally) into the sunset with the Colonel's wife, the film symbolically suggests that the Americans shall inherit the earth—or at least France's colonies.

Timbuktu did not make the charts in the United States, where Victor Mature's box-office power was waning. Neither did it secure distribution in France, despite a famous French director and a wholly positive image of French rule in Africa. Perhaps the French, now bogged down in the Algerian War, were in no mood for Hollywood desert fantasies.

French Empire in the Pacific

If Hollywood's desert films, with their harsh landscapes and primitive, camel-borne bandits and tribesmen, invited positive appraisals of civilizing colonizers, films in the gentler climes of the South Seas more often depicted the French as intruders. One such example was *South Sea Woman* (1953), a Warner Bros.–First National black-and-white release from comedy and fantasy specialist Arthur Lubin (*Ali Baba and the Forty Thieves*, 1944). This comedy-adventure shot in Fiji starred Burt Lancaster as Marine Sergeant Jim O'Hearn, facing court-martial for desertion in 1942. The film unfolds in flashback, gradually revealing O'Hearn's innocence. After fleeing a barroom brawl with fellow marine Davey White (Chuck Connors) and Davey's fiancée, Ginger (Virginia Mayo), the three wash up on "the French colonial island of Namou." When the French Gouverneur-Général, Pierre Marchand (Leon Askin, straining to sound French) informs them about Pearl Harbor and arrests them as enemy soldiers, they regain their freedom by declaring that as deserters, they are on Vichy's side. After a farcical sequence in a French brothel, O'Hearn frees a dungeon full of Free French prisoners, massacres Vichy troops with a machine gun (a jarringly violent sequence for a comedy), commandeers a German yacht in the harbor, and sails off to fight the Japanese. The film shows little interest in relations between the French and the natives beyond a brief shot of tin-horn tyrant Marchand reclining while a native woman waves a fan over him. The natives mostly remain in the background, dancing about in bizarre costumes, and the only "South Sea Woman" in this mistitled film is the American bar girl, Ginger. It does carry on the American tradition of contrasting good, freedom-loving French—here the Free French whom O'Hearn releases, and who fight the Japanese alongside their American brethren—and bad, tyrannical French—the Vichy forces. Though the film reached the number fifty-seven slot on the American charts for 1953, it was not released in France until 1962, perhaps because the French seemed unready for a comedy about Vichy collaboration.[5]

France's relations with its colonial subjects in the South Pacific figured more centrally in Columbia's *Drums of Tahiti* (1954), shot in 3D. An opening voice-over sounds anticolonial themes as it recounts Tahiti's nineteenth-century history, stating that "men, women, and children rushed to defend their island against the powerful arms of France, until finally a treaty was forced upon the tribes." The local tyrant of this tale, set in 1877, is the portly Police Commissioner Duvois (Francis L. Sullivan), whose men keep busy intercepting arms the Tahitians are importing for a revolt. The condescending Duvois refers to the Tahitians as "such playful children," and the film emphasizes his Frenchness as the English Sullivan manages a decent French accent and interjects occasional French words. It also links Duvois with France's less-desirable history, as he sarcastically tells his men who have arrested some Tahitian rebels, "*Maintenant*, confiscate the guns and make our friends happy in the Bastille." Instead of letting Tahitians articulate their own grievances, the film has Duvois's American chess partner Mike Macklin (Dennis O'Keefe) state them. To Duvois's claim, "I protect these islands for France," Mike replies, "You're going to protect the Polynesians even if it kills them, huh?" and to Duvois's claims that the French have brought civilization to Tahiti, Mike skeptically retorts, "If you go half a mile out of town you're back in the jungle again." Mike plays the usual American arms dealer meddling in French colonial affairs, but rather than condemning him for his amorality and cynicism, this film invites the audience to sympathize with his efforts to arm the Tahitians and evade Duvois's stifling surveillance.

Yet the film's anticolonialism turns out to be shallow indeed. It indulges in colonialist imagery and attitudes—native men drum, girls dance, and Mike advises Duvois to hire a native girl to operate the fan over his hammock—and it undercuts its anticolonialism when it reveals that the Tahitians wish to oust the French not to rule themselves, but to seek English rule. When Mike visits Queen Pomare, who is behind the effort to import English guns, he tells her, "The French have always treated Tahiti well," and asks, "What makes you think the English would do any better?" Instead of seizing the opportunity to voice complaints about French colonialism, she simply explains that she is half English. And when the Queen's conspiracy finally collapses, she easily accepts the futility of resisting French rule, saying, "The end comes so quickly that all the years of fighting seem ridiculous." The latter term occurred to those few critics who bothered to review this film. The shortcomings of the filmmaking aside, the ambivalence—or incoherence—of its treatment of French colonialism typifies American outlooks at the time.

France's Mexican Adventure

If Americans ultimately had few real objections to France's presence in the South Pacific, the same could not be said of France's nineteenth-century foray into Mexico, when Emperor Napoleon III took advantage of America's Civil War to invade

Mexico in 1861. The preoccupied Americans could not enforce the Monroe Doctrine as French troops took the capital, overthrew Benito Juárez's republic, and installed Emperor Maximilian as a French puppet. When the Civil War ended, Americans sent troops and helped arm Juárez's forces, and by 1866, the French adventure in Mexico was crumbling. Having dealt with this history in *Juarez* (1939), Hollywood revisited it in the Hecht-Lancaster / United Artists release *Vera Cruz* (1954). Robert Aldrich directed the film just after *Apache*, working with most of the same team and shooting on location in Mexico. In this story, two apparently amoral American mercenaries, Ben Trane (Gary Cooper) and Joe Erin (Burt Lancaster), come to Mexico to sell their services to Emperor Maximilian, while Juarista revolutionaries try to dissuade them. The Juarista leader, General Ramírez (Morris Ankrum), tells Joe, "Certainly as an American you can appreciate our fight for independence." When the Americans refuse to switch sides, the Juaristas surround them, telling them, "We are not savages, . . . but we cannot permit you to serve with Maximilian." The unscrupulous Americans escape by taking some Mexican children hostage, and they head off to meet the Emperor, escorted by the Marquis de Labordère (Cesar Romero).

Like the old French Revolution films, this one makes a transparent moral point by contrasting the poverty of the peasants with the luxury of the aristocrats in their palatial headquarters. Next to the lavishly attired Maximilian (George Macready) and his entourage of European nobles, the uncouth Americans seem to have more in common with the peasants—except for Ben, who despite his rough edges is a French-speaking Louisiana plantation owner ruined in the Civil War. The cultured Europeans are happy to hire these gunmen to escort Countess Marie Duvarre (Denise Darcel) to Vera Cruz—ostensibly for a visit home, but in fact to smuggle out $3 million worth of Mexican gold to secure more French troops. On a climactic journey to Vera Cruz, the villainous French rob peasants and monks and sadistically execute captured Juaristas. The rebels are pursuing the convoy because they, like the mercenaries, know the carriage is full of gold. The ruthless French Countess covets the gold, and after much double-dealing, Ben agrees to help the Juaristas seize the treasure in exchange for a hefty cut. Although Ben's demand for $100,000 makes him seem as greedy as everyone else, he reveals noble motives when he tells Joe he wants the money to restore his plantation and save his dependents. Ben is thus yet another apparently cynical American adventurer in a dangerous land who turns out to be moral after all, while the French characters are brutal, corrupt imperialists in a land where they do not belong.

Vera Cruz did well at the American box office, reaching number twenty for 1955, but critics were less impressed, as twelve of twenty-six (46 percent) praised it while eleven panned it, and three issued mixed judgments.⁶ Many of the positive reviews qualified their praise, treating it as a mindless action film, while the negative reviews mostly focused on its violence and the unattractiveness of the American mercenaries. Although the film is really a conventional western morality play, not everyone grasped Ben's decency; indeed, many critics found the story confusing and were put off by the harsh, cynical tone that pervades the film's surface until the end. *Vera Cruz* foreshadows Aldrich's fondness for the amoral, violent characters later seen in *The Dirty Dozen* (1967) and *Ulzana's Raid* (1972), but in 1954 he still accepted the prevailing cinematic morality and its demand for the triumph of righteousness. The critics focused on the American characters, barely explaining what the French were doing in Mexico.

Despite its disdain for French imperialism, the film did very well in France, where it sold 4,501,021 tickets in 1955, placing it seventh on that year's box-office charts.⁷ French critics mostly ignored it, leading François Truffaut to write in *Cahiers du Cinéma* that "it is a shame that many of my colleagues have overlooked *Vera Cruz*, some not really having understood it at all." Enjoying a film in which "everybody betrays everybody and his brother, everybody lies and knows how to divine and decipher facial expressions," Truffaut maintained that "each scene would justify a film of its own."⁸ No one used the film to bring up the Algerian War, then in its seventh month, but in the *Parisien Libéré*, film scholar André Bazin signaled his sympathy for the film's dim view of French imperialism in referring to "Napoleon III's war against Mexico," to "the French occupier," and to Ben's having "enough moral fiber to end up on the side of liberty." *Radio Cinéma Télévision* also sympathized with the Juaristas, calling them "partisans" and writing that "the Mexican people rose up against their emperor, installed by the French." *Les Lettres Françaises* did not mind that Maximilian "comes off as a total cretin" who had "the unfortunate sympathies of Napoleon III." In *Combat*, R.-M. Arlaud, noting "the tendency to laugh at the expense of the French," did not take the film seriously, and he admitted, "It is true that Maximilian's adventure . . . was rather tragic, a dreadful farce."

Others were touchier about France's image. "*Vera Cruz* is a troubling film for us French," wrote *La Croix*. "Our soldiers, those of Maximilian, were not, perhaps, angels, but they were worthier than the portrait we are shown here." Claude Garson of the conservative *L'Aurore*, while granting that the Juaristas were "fighting for their country's independence," rejected "the portrait we are shown of French soldiers," who "appear worse than the Gestapo executioners" and "amuse themselves diabolically with the poor Mexican prisoners." Garson "deplore[d] that such regrettable anti-French propaganda should be made in a film by our friends and allies." But if nationalist reflexes caused some to take umbrage while others shrugged off the film's denigration of the French, no one really defended French imperialism in Mexico.

America's Indochina Films

If France's adventures in Mexico were ideally suited to bring out American hostility to French imperialism, France's more recent endeavors in Indochina were another matter. Indeed, communism's ability to make Americans embrace French colonialism was clearest in a handful of films about France's war with the Vietminh. Some of these minor productions, including *Rogue's Regiment* (1948) and *A Yank in Indo-China* (1952) appeared during the war, lending an ideological hand to the French cause, and they continued to appear even after France's defeat in 1954. A good example of these films is *Jump into Hell* (1955), a Warner Bros. production directed by David Butler, whose career highlight was directing fifty-eight episodes of *Leave It to Beaver*. This black-and-white film about Dien Bien Phu, made with the approval of the American and French governments and featuring both French and American actors, offered an unabashed tribute to the French, and its opening narration was hardly subtle in denouncing "the Vietminh reds, who were trying to conquer their country for international communism."[9] The film combines the clichés of the empire film—waves of faceless Vietnamese besiege a fort full of courageous white men—with staples of anticommunist films such as *The Shanghai Story* (1954), including an overly insistent close-up of a Chinese infiltrator's pistol implausibly marked with the giant letters "U.S.S.R." Its enthusiasm for French rule even led the film to laud Louis Napoleon's Mexican imperialism; it likened the troops' heroism at Dien Bien Phu to the Foreign Legion's legendary defeat at Camarone, Vera Cruz in 1863, and it evoked Anglophone viewers' sympathies by recalling the last stand at the Alamo and Britain's defeat at Dunkirk. French filmmakers had long ignored the Camarone episode, and it would be nearly four decades before a French film, Pierre Schoendoerffer's *Dien Bien Phu* (1992), revisited that battle, so in these years it was up to anticommunist Americans to wave the *tricouleur* over France's colonies. The film did not make the American box-office charts, and it did not even play in France, despite its pro-French stance, for reasons that a report to Warner Bros. from the firm's French sales office explained. Pointing out that there were 105 Communists in the Chamber of Deputies and five million Communists in France, the report stated that "French opinion as a whole has been and is still extremely divided concerning the Indochina war," and it warned that the war "has been the object of extremely violent discussions." Given that the film "could only reawaken painful memories," and that "the accentuated anti-communist nature of the picture risks to provoke in France certain troubles or rough quarrels in theatres," it considered it "nearly certain that no exhibitor will in France take the risk of playing the film."[10]

Far better known today is Samuel Fuller's *China Gate* (1957). Fuller, a World War II veteran, pulp novelist, and former crime reporter, broke through as a film director with his gritty Korean War drama, *The Steel Helmet* (1951); several films later he directed, produced, and wrote the low-budget, black-and-white *China Gate* for his own production company, distributing it through Twentieth Century-Fox. Fuller's anticommunism, already seen in *The Steel Helmet* and *Pickup on South Street* (1953), pervaded this story of American Sergeant Johnny Brock (Gene Barry) fighting in the French Foreign Legion in Indochina in 1954. The plot follows two intertwined threads: in one, a French Captain (Paul Dubov) leads Brock's unit into enemy territory near the Chinese border to blow up a hidden arsenal; in the other, Brock encounters his estranged wife, Lea (Angie Dickinson), a mixed-race saloon girl (nicknamed "Lucky Legs") he abandoned when their son was born looking fully Asian. Fuller's films often attacked racism, and here he does so by having the entire unit, most notably the African American Goldie (Nat "King" Cole), chide Brock for his racism and his abandonment of Lea, who goes along on the mission and proves useful because she knows all the local communist troops (biblically and otherwise). Also intertwined are the film's anticommunism and its enthusiasm for French colonialism. Fuller emphasizes Soviet and Chinese involvement in Indochina through countless references to Moscow, through enemy villagers' photos of Stalin and Mao alongside Ho Chi Minh, through communist soldiers who resemble Mao, and through its insistence that Soviet and Chinese arms are crucial to a Vietminh victory. The usual cinematic devices convey the communists' villainy: they emerge from the jungle like the reptilian rebels in *The Planter's Wife* and Fuller also sounds the familiar Cold War theme of communist hostility to religion. At the communists' headquarters, we see a Buddha statue with its head blown off; a Hungarian in the Legion explains that he joined up out of anger at communists taking over his church; and a one-legged French priest (Marcel Dalio) tells Brock the communists sawed off his leg and pinned a sign reading "capitalist spy" into his flesh.

In *China Gate*, Fuller as usual wrapped idealistic messages in a gritty film filled with tough, cynical characters. Unlike typical cinematic Legionnaires, these battle-scarred veterans are not fleeing the law or failed marriages; instead they are bent on saving the world from communism. The film congratulates the Americans for their material assistance to the French and to beleaguered peasants whose only sustenance comes from American airdrops, but given that France had already lost the war long before Fuller made the film, *China Gate* amounts to a plea for greater American involvement in Indochina.[11]

Its sympathies for French colonialism actually go beyond its anticommunism. Over newsreel footage, a narrator proclaims, "This motion picture is dedicated to France," then explains, in what sounds like a press release from France's Ministry of Colonies:

> More than three hundred years ago French missionaries were sent to Indochina to teach love of God and love of fellow man. . . . Despite many hardships, they advanced their way of living, and the thriving nation became the rice bowl of Asia. Vast riches were developed under French guidance. . . . [In 1945] a Moscow-trained Indochinese revolutionist who called himself Ho Chi Minh began the drive to make his own country another target for Chinese Communists. . . . France was left alone to hold the hottest front in the world that became the barrier between communism and the rape of Asia.

The homage to the French continues when a hungry, knife-wielding villager eyes the pet dog Lea's son is cradling. The boy takes shelter with two French soldiers— white protectors—and when Lea and the soldiers come upon villagers listening to a captured record of the "Marseillaise," Lea tells them it is "the music of the people" and teaches them the words. That anthem returns, played on a lonely trumpet at the end of the film, when the French Captain has died saving two Americans. Fuller thus glossed over the anger, tensions, and recriminations the war in Indochina provoked in Franco-American relations, offering instead a romantic paean to French colonialism and its struggle for liberty and civilization in Indochina.

The film was never released in France. Years later Fuller claimed in his memoirs that his friend Romain Gary, a writer and France's consul-general in Los Angeles, told him after viewing a rough cut that his prologue was "too harsh toward his country"; Gary's objections, Fuller suggested, convinced the French government to bar the film's release in France. Writing in the 1990s, Fuller insisted he had always disliked French colonialism and refused to change the prologue, which is why the French shunned the film.[12] There is one problem with this story: there is nothing remotely critical of French colonialism in that prologue. Perhaps Gary's objections led Fuller to revise the prologue after all, or perhaps by the time he wrote his memoirs, Fuller's memory had faded, but his explanation of why it never showed in France makes no sense.

In the United States, it did poorly with both audiences and critics: of nineteen reviews, six were positive (32 percent), ten negative, and three mixed.[13] While a few found it impressively realistic and exciting despite its low budget, the *Chicago Tribune* wrote that "its construction is sleazy, its acting varies from mediocre to atrocious, and it seems to go on forever." The *Philadelphia Inquirer* called the subplot about Brock and Lea "incredible twaddle" and complained of "endless gabble about sex, sin, patriotism and the evils of the Red ideal." The topic of the war in Indochina, however, led several critics to praise the French effusively. "The recent history of Indo-China," declared the *Christian Science Monitor*, "has contained heroic chapters that stagger the imagination, . . . as for example the siege at Dien Bien Phu," while Bosley Crowther of the *New York Times* said the film was "dedicated to a just and honorable cause." The *New York Daily News* similarly noted that the film was "dedicated to the French who fought so valiantly in Viet Nam," and such comments showed how Cold War concerns could lead Americans to abandon any qualms about French colonialism. That Americans had a hazy grasp of what happened in Indochina appeared when Crowther said of the characters that "recent history is on their side." Perhaps he was misled by advertisements that referred to "the Heart, Hope and Heroism that turned the tide in Indo-China!"[14] Fuller's film, with its triumphant, heroic conclusion, cast a fog over the failure of the French and their American benefactors in Indochina.

In Hollywood's contradictory messages about French colonialism, communism obviously made anticolonialist inclinations disappear. Support for French colonialism also marks the North Africa films (*Outpost in Morocco*, *Fort Algiers*, *Saadia*, and *Timbuktu*), in which communism barely figured, while *Sirocco*'s image of the French in Syria is mostly negative. Negative images of French colonialism also mark *Vera Cruz* and the South Seas films *Drums of Tahiti* and *South Sea Woman*, even if the latter is more ambivalent, as it includes Free French as well as Vichy forces. In chronological terms, most of these films appeared by 1955, and the two films made after that date (*China Gate* in 1957, *Timbuktu* in 1959), both favored French rule. No film made during the Algerian War alluded to it, and the only exception to a pattern of depicting archaic forms of anticolonial resistance was the allusion to oil nationalism in *Fort Algiers*. So even where communism was absent, American films might be either critical or supportive of French colonialism. Americans were of two minds when it came to France's imperial endeavors.

Historically, Hollywood had embraced Britain's empire more consistently than France's, though the postwar years did see swipes at British colonialism in *Thunder in the East*, *Elephant Walk*, *Something of Value*, and *Shake Hands with the Devil*. If fears of offending customers led Hollywood to soften critiques of others depending on their importance as markets, then it stands to reason that Britain, as Hollywood's largest overseas market, would get more deferential treatment than France, even if France remained an important market.[15] Hollywood generally devoted bigger budgets to films about Britain's empire, and many of these second-rate productions about France received little or no distribution there. In the absence of evidence about why certain films were *not* distributed, one may speculate that the oft-cited French reluctance to explore painful imperial topics played some role. The cultural distance between the French and the Americans was greater than that between the British and the Americans, and there were more individuals from Britain and its empire working in Hollywood, though Jacques Tourneur, Marcel Dalio, Denise Darcel, and others helped to make these American films. In addition, there were far more Anglo-American than Franco-American productions and more Hollywood films made in Britain than in France in these years. Finally, Hollywood films had more leeway for creating negative images of the French, given France's history of internal divisions; there was, in short, no British counterpart for the Vichy French, who made such convenient villains. Despite their cinematic shortcomings, these American films offer useful insights into American views of France's empire in this era.

French Films on Indochina: Breaking the Silence

Distributors' assumptions that French moviegoers did not want to watch films about their empire fits a common view that the French preferred to avoid painful or controversial imperial topics.[16] This notion pervades studies of French cinema, as scholars, noting the abundance of American films on Vietnam, have wondered why the French have not engaged in a similar process of cinematic catharsis and autocritique. While French censors—more sensitive about politics than sex, unlike their Hollywood counterparts—certainly helped keep colonial topics off French screens in these years, scholars have suggested that censorship restricted the supply of something for which there was no demand, given France's preference for *l'oubli* (deliberate forgetting) regarding colonial controversies and defeats.[17] Although in recent decades French films began to explore colonial issues and to reflect on the debacles in Indochina and Algeria, it is widely assumed that in the 1950s French filmmakers simply avoided such subjects.[18] Periods of public silence commonly follow national traumas, but in the 1950s the French actually did make films about that war.

The first was *Le Rendez-vous des quais*, a low-budget, black-and-white film completed in 1955. Paul Carpita, son of a Marseille longshoreman, became a schoolteacher, freelance filmmaker, and communist militant; he wrote and directed the film, working with amateur actors and shooting without official permission on the docks of Marseille.[19] The film tells the story of two young workers, Robert (André Maufray) and Marcelle (Jeanine Moretti) who fall in love and marry during the turmoil of the longshoremen's refusal to load war materiel for Indochina. Much of the film concerns the couple's personal life, and its treatment of the Indochina War is earnest but restrained. One brief shot shows a large artillery piece being loaded by crane—accompanied by ominous music—and the workers sneak out one night to paint "Peace in Vietnam" in large letters on a jetty, but the film's critique of the war is limited to a reference to coffins returning from Indochina, complaints about the high cost of the war, a subplot about an informer, and a militant's speech denouncing war profiteers.

As a glimpse of life among Marseille's workers and labor activists of the time, the film is a valuable historical document, but as anticolonialist propaganda, it is mild indeed, making antiwar statements that could apply to any war rather than specific arguments against colonizing Indochina. Nevertheless, the French government banned the film, and after its premiere in August 1955 at the Rex Theater in Marseille, a second showing the next day was interrupted when the police burst into the theater and seized the reels.[20] The film was presumed lost, and only in 1989 did Carpita learn of a surviving copy. While in retrospect the censorship hardly seems necessary given the mildness of the film's accusations, it offered an unusual look at labor politics from the workers' perspective, which may have sufficed to get it banned. With France's war in Indochina having ended by 1955, concerns about the film inspiring similar action against the current war in Algeria may have motivated the censors. The entire episode suggests that the paucity of French films on colonial themes owed less to the skittishness of French filmmakers than to that of French authorities.

The next French film about Indochina was Marcel Camus's *Mort en fraude*, based on Jean Hougron's 1953 novel of the same title. Camus, best known for his Oscar-winning *Black Orpheus* (1959), made his directorial debut with *Mort en fraude*, released in May 1957. Following the book fairly closely, the black-and-white film shot in Cambodia tells the story of a Frenchman named Horcier (Daniel Gélin) who arrives in Saigon in 1950, during France's war against the Vietminh. Deliberately elusive about Horcier and the purpose of his visit, the film begins as a noirish tale of a nervous man involved in illicit dealings with shady waterfront characters. Horcier has been enlisted to deliver a suitcase full of cash, and French viewers would likely have spotted the allusion to the *piastres* scandal that made the news in 1950. (That scandal, involving black-market transactions of an overvalued currency subsidized by French taxpayers, reinforced suspicions that colonialism was really about illicit profiteering.) Unfortunately for Horcier, he must inform his contact that the money was stolen. On the lam from gangsters, he stumbles into the hotel room of an attractive young Eurasian, Anh (Anne Méchard), who accepts his offer of money to let him hide in her room. For five thousand *piastres*, she also agrees to take him to hide in her village.

Horcier's arrival in the village takes the film in a very different direction. At first ill-tempered and rude to his hosts, he is ignorant of Vietnamese culture; he cannot handle chopsticks, for example, and the film makes a point of his arrogance toward these colonial subjects. Although the village endures both French shelling and periodic Vietminh harassment, what really bothers this Frenchman is the inferior local cuisine, which includes bugs and giant lizards. As he gets to know Anh, her Vietnamese grandparents, and her village, however, Horcier undergoes a character transformation as he begins to sympathize with the plight of poverty-stricken villagers caught in the crossfire between the French and Vietminh. When Anh falls ill with the malaria that plagues the village, Horcier decides to risk a perilous voyage in search of quinine, which he finally steals from a French military post. He also buys the villagers a large quantity of rice, which is promptly blown up by a French artillery shell that lands in the village. Horcier eventually wears out his welcome after Anh's grandfather is murdered by the Vietminh for refusing to reveal Horcier's whereabouts, and he agrees to leave.

The argument that love affairs sometimes helped bridge the racial divide in European colonies finds illustration in *Mort en fraude*.[21] Horcier only begins to pay attention to Anh after he accidentally walks in on her showering and realizes she is sexually attractive, but his growing romantic interest in her leads him to see the villagers as people. The romantic interest is mutual, and when Horcier leaves the village, Anh goes with him. For the rest of the film, Horcier tries to help the village by begging French authorities to destroy a dike that makes the village vulnerable to attacks. As Horcier and Anh arrive in a French town, an innkeeper assumes Anh is a prostitute or concubine and turns her away. Horcier angrily leaves, having now experienced French colonial racism. Walking through the streets together, they hear French settlers insulting them, as one complains that Frenchmen like him are eroding French prestige by crossing the color line. The film, in short, attacks French racism and allows its audience to experience it through characters with whom it has come to sympathize. Toward the film's end, it reconnects with its noirish beginning by having Horcier come to ruin, for just after blowing up the dike himself, he is gunned down by French troops.

The film thus presents a rather grim portrait of the French, who—apart from Horcier—are racists and are indifferent to the villagers' plight. French authorities are more interested in Horcier's papers and his presence in Vietnam than in his attempts to help the people whom French colonialist rhetoric claimed they were there to protect. Despite its grim image of the villagers' lives, the film is remarkable for its interest in their culture and daily lives, and it humanizes them through several sympathetic characters, including Anh, her family, and a young boy who befriends Horcier. *Mort en fraude* is hardly sympathetic to the Vietminh, who remain a rarely glimpsed menace who make life miserable for the villagers, but given the film's poor image of French colonialism, it is noteworthy that government censors approved it.

Belying notions of the French people's dislike for films about painful colonial topics, the film received national distribution and sold an impressive 1,411,723 tickets, including more than 1.1 million in the provinces.[22] Most critics were also impressed, and of twenty-five reviews examined here, twelve were positive, seven negative, and six mixed.[23] While most of the negative comments had to do with artistic aspects and a lack of clarity about the dike's importance, some also found the film too impartial about events requiring a clear political stance. In the left-wing *France Observateur*, Jacques Doniol-Valcroze first said the film was right to be objective, showing equally "the atrocities of the Vietminh, the criminal stupidity of the French, and the villagers' total inability to grasp the historical evolution of their time," then he changed his mind mid-paragraph and declared that "objectivity is not good enough, [for] a story must lead somewhere." The left-wing film magazine *Positif* complained that "to refuse to take sides and to put everyone in the same boat is a dangerous position, permitting the most dubious interpretations," and it also objected that "it is a white man who saves these poor yellow people, who are incapable of saving themselves." A letter from a Vietnamese reader to *Les Lettres Françaises* took issue with the film's rendering of relations between the Vietminh and the villagers. In reality, he wrote, "The Vietminh, which is to say the Resistance, was inside each village," and "the Vietnamese people were not at all passive during this war of liberation," but were "the 'soul' of the Resistance."[24] *L'Humanité* agreed that the Vietnamese people "hated their oppressors" and "gave unconditional support to the soldiers of the liberation army," though if Camus "had shown a village favorable to the Vietminh, he could never have made his film." It called *Mort en fraude* "an exceptional film, . . . which, for the first time, dares to tear away the cynical and bashful veil that covers colonialism," and it welcomed its denunciation of French racism.

This French *autocritique* appeared in other reviews. *Témoignage Chrétien* noted the image of "whites set in their superiority complexes," and *La Croix* similarly praised the film for displaying "the disdain the French showed toward the natives." The latter review expressed mixed feelings, for it also objected that though "traffickers there certainly were, there were also engineers, doctors, in short, decent men," making it unfair to show only the worst of the French in Indochina. But many reviews praised the film's impartiality, and ten papers surveyed here praised the courage it took to make it. *Combat* spoke for papers across the political spectrum when it wrote that Camus "has treated a particularly delicate subject with singular vigor." Moreover, with the film appearing in the midst of the Algerian War, several publications noted its timeliness. As Marcel Martin wrote in *Cinéma 57*, "Today, when colonial wars have shown their true face," the film has "a burning relevance, as a new conflict has erupted at our doors. And as the analogy between this sad past and the sad present directly calls for comparison, Marcel Camus's courageous film may provoke useful reflection." So although the film struck some on the left as insufficiently critical of colonialism, while right-wing papers mostly ignored the film's politics, it is noteworthy that papers from left to right applauded it for breaking the silence on the Indochina War.

Just two months later came another black-and-white drama on Indochina, also set in 1950 and also a director's first feature. Claude Bernard-Aubert, who later revisited the Indochina War in the satire *Le facteur s'en va-t-en guerre* (1966) and the combat drama *Charlie Bravo* (1980), was twenty-six when he wrote and directed *Patrouille de choc*, which he shot in South Vietnam. He had made army newsreels in Indochina, and his connections evidently helped him get support from the French army, albeit with strings attached. As many newspapers reported, French authorities disliked the film's original title, *Patrouille sans espoir*, suggesting the more uplifting *Patrouille de l'espoir*. Bernard-Aubert balked at that and managed to secure the compromise title actually used. He explained his intentions to *Les Lettres Françaises*: "I would like to shoot a true film about the real war in Indochina, a film dedicated to the French who really fought there, a simple film in which the enemy soldiers would not be ridiculed. Not an optimistic film, no. A film for people who did not show much interest in that faraway war."[25]

Although an ad in the right-wing *L'Aurore* claimed that the film might remind viewers of their own experiences or those of a relative, France did not use draftees in Indochina, and for many of the French the war had seemed remote.[26] In an opening designed to connect with viewers' memories, *Patrouille de choc* begins with an excerpt from a newsreel, moving from footage of an ice hockey game to a report from Indochina. A soldier then begins to narrate the events as the images fade into flashback, and the film proceeds with its tale of thirty-seven soldiers from France and its colonies at an isolated post in northern Vietnam. The main difficulty the unit encounters later became familiar in various colonial wars and Cold War counterinsurgencies, as the Vietminh infiltrate the village and blend in with the locals. Also recalling other colonial wars, the French hold the terrain only during the day, and more than once the soldiers awake to find the Vietminh flag planted inside the post as a warning.[27] The Vietminh also leave a more detailed message in a leaflet urging the troops to "give up fighting for the imperialists and colonialists" and to demand their repatriation, as "France does not like this war."

The film shows the French befriending the villagers, and they build a school, a bridge, and a dispensary for the smiling locals. These images must have placated French censors, but Bernard-Aubert showed a hint of the anticolonial sarcasm that would mark his later films on the subject, as a Senegalese soldier teaches the Vietnamese children that "our ancestors the Gauls had blond hair and blue eyes." Despite their efforts, the soldiers eventually find themselves betrayed by villagers and killed off one by one. When the Vietminh launch a climactic nighttime attack, the troops radio for help, only to be told no reinforcements are coming. Just as the Vietminh begin pouring through the barbed-wire defenses, a French column miraculously rides to the rescue. This happy ending was obviously another concession forced on Bernard-Aubert, and one inconsistent not only with the entire previous story, but also (like *China Gate*), with the real ending of the war in Indochina.

Patrouille de choc offers an interesting example of how a filmmaker with anticolonialist views—which became clearer in his later works—coped with censorship. Indeed, one could read the film as right-wing, in that it seems to praise the *mission civilisatrice*, and its image of brave soldiers abandoned to their fate by apathetic officials and civilians reflects the bitter resentment many veterans and French conservatives felt after the country's defeat in 1954. (The same attitude existed among American conservatives and some veterans after America's war in Vietnam.) And though the film humanizes several Vietnamese characters, it never explains the Vietminh's motives; it simply presents the enemy as a menacing, shadowy force. Yet the film also paints a picture of a hopeless war in a place where the French do not belong and are not welcome. Using a brief shot of a newspaper a soldier is reading, Bernard-Aubert even managed to insert a fleeting reference to the *piastres* scandal, indicating either the censors' lenience or their inattention. The extensive publicity that newspapers gave the forced title change and the cut-and-paste ending made the government look rather clumsy. Censorship, after all, works best when it remains unnoticed.

Despite coming so soon after another film on the same war, *Patrouille de choc* did even better than *Mort en fraude*, selling 1,847,864 tickets and winning an audience referendum at a festival in Vichy.[28] Two Parisian papers reported that audiences watched attentively and applauded at the end.[29] Critics also applauded; of twenty reviews examined here, fifteen were positive, two negative, and three mixed or neutral.[30] More than half the papers praised the film's sober realism, including *France Observateur*, which wrote, "no noisy patriotism, then, and no *Marseillaise*." The *Nouvelles Littéraires* noted, "We were expecting one of those films celebrating sweet and joyous war, like those the Americans make"; *Combat*'s critic (having missed *Jump into Hell*) was similarly relieved that the Americans "did not get the idea to make a film about Indochina, with feats of derring-do at Dien Bien Phu," concluding, "One shudders to think." *Libération* felt it showed "the pointlessness of a bloody, absurd war," and *Témoignage Chrétien* agreed, writing, "It is clear that war is absurd, and this one more than any other." Again, even making a film on Indochina struck observers as courageous. *France Observateur* called it "a rare, sincere, and original attempt to mark the memory of this sad war," and *Cahiers du Cinéma* praised it for "putting its finger on a wound instead of averting its gaze." Watching a French unit slowly wiped out led both *Radio Cinéma Télévision* and *Téléciné* to remark that it reminded them of Dien Bien Phu.

One reason why *Patrouille de choc* did so well was that it appealed to people across a wide political spectrum, and while left-wing papers praised it for showing the absurdity of the war in Indochina, right-wing papers lauded it for honoring the men who fought there. *L'Aurore*, for example, felt it showed "the grandeur of our fighters." In its words, "while the Viets prepare their exterminating action, our soldiers find the energy and patience to build schools and dispensaries, transforming a Vietnamese village into a temporary bastion of French civilization." *Le Parisien Libéré* charged that the Vietminh, seeing France's good works winning over the villagers, used "terrorism" to intimidate the civilians. *Paris-Presse / L'Intransigeant* articulated the right's bitterness in writing of "the hopeless struggle of those who fought over there, abandoned with nothing but their courage and their sense of duty." Indeed, less conservative voices made similar points, as *La Croix* held that "independent of any political consideration—which would be out of place here—the film shows that the French Army of Indochina did the fatherland proud," and even the left-wing *France Observateur* felt that despite "an absurd cause" the men "did indeed do their ignorant and ungrateful fatherland proud."

A sharply dissenting view appeared in the one paper that disliked the film: *L'Humanité*. Critic François Maurin complained that the film's "bogus realism" "shows the combatants of the popular army in the most abominable light," while "presenting the instruments of colonialist domination as victims." Maurin added that it "ignores the basic reasons for the war" and "the struggle the Vietnamese people as a whole waged for their independence and freedom." At least, he concluded, the film proved "that it is impossible to keep an entire people under domination when it aspires to liberty," and that "should cause fervent partisans of the war in Algeria to reflect."[31] *Les Nouvelles Littéraires* also noted the film's relevance to Algeria, for the drama it depicted "is still being experienced every day, not in Asia this time, but in Africa."

In light of such comments, the censors' decision to approve the film seems curious, and indeed one paper reported that the Defense Ministry quietly pressured the Gaumont theaters not to show it.[32] Perhaps fears of a public outcry over censorship restrained the authorities, and indeed the changes forced upon Bernard-Aubert drew scathing comments. *Libération* noted that the film originally "included a real—which is to say tragic—ending," and *Le Monde* added that "we can guess the real ending: no reinforcements arrive." *Le Monde* also charged that "the false victory reflects a singularly puerile policy," for hope cannot be "bought with miserable lies," and "it is not with such crude measures that one preserves ... the morale of those who are still fighting." Similarly, *France Observateur* wrote that "our governments" wish "to obstruct as much as they can the cinematic record of their errors," and *Radio Cinéma Télévision* found the film "hard on those who condemned our 'boys' to a hopeless struggle." *France Observateur*'s comment on the false ending—this "poor little ruse changes nothing of the meaning or the impact of the work"—suggests that the government incurred a political cost for its actions without even preventing the damage it feared the film would do.

The strong box-office performance and largely positive critical reactions for both *Mort en fraude* and *Patrouille de choc* call into question several familiar arguments about French cinema and colonial memory. Although censors kept some works from appearing at all and altered the works that did appear, these two films show that it was possible for filmmakers to confront colonial topics and to criticize French racism and policy in Indochina. That French filmmakers had to engage in the sort of subterfuge and innuendo familiar to artists in dictatorships says much about French democracy in the 1950s, and the government surely paid a price for its clumsy intervention into the cultural realm. Perhaps even more significantly, these films and their reception undermine images of a willfully amnesiac French public unwilling to revisit painful colonial memories. The films' reception suggests that by 1957, literally millions of French people wanted to see films on this topic—even relatively low-budget films lacking major stars or publicity campaigns—and critics across the political spectrum welcomed the films even when they questioned aspects of their artistry or politics. *Mort en fraude* and *Patrouille de choc* may be obscure today, but these largely forgotten films and their reception in 1957 suggest a need to rethink some familiar notions about the history of French cinema and colonial memory.

CHAPTER SIX

Americans in Postwar Asia

While the British and French were coping with decolonization, Washington was dealing with both the Cold War and decolonization. The Cold War certainly affected the Europeans' management of colonial affairs, but for the Americans, Cold War concerns dominated foreign policy, taking precedence, as we have seen, over misgivings about European colonialism. Washington was engaged in its own process of decolonization, granting independence to the Philippines in 1946 as well as offering greater measures of self-government to Puerto Ricans, pondering the termination of the reservation system for American Indians, and proceeding cautiously with new policies toward African Americans. Yet it was also moving in the opposite direction, expanding its presence in much of Asia, Europe, and the Middle East. World War II had left America's military in control of unprecedented expanses of land and sea, and its occupations of Japan and West Germany had colonial overtones. Also in this period, the Americans acquired new obligations and influence in others' former colonies and client states such as Indochina, Korea, Pakistan, Iran, and Egypt. In short, while the Europeans were decolonizing, the Americans were both decolonizing and expanding.

How did Americans, long inclined to isolationism, feel about their new global role? Providing valuable evidence to supplement the findings of opinion polls and other sources were the many films Hollywood now made about an especially important area for postwar U.S. foreign policy: East Asia. Unlike many other parts of the world, East Asia—especially China—had long attracted interest from American missionaries and business people, but the war with Japan brought the region to the attention of a much wider public. The lessons in Asian geography, politics, and culture continued with a series of wars and revolutions beginning soon after World War II, including the French war in Indochina, an uprising in the newly independent Philippines, the Communist victory in China, and the war in Korea. Publicizing and dramatizing these crises was an outpouring of new films about the region.

Hollywood and "the Loss of China"

Supporting an "open door" policy in China from 1899 onward, Americans claimed to oppose Western and Japanese colonialism there. Belying those claims were American gunboats helping to enforce a system of unequal treaties forced on China in the nineteenth and early twentieth centuries, so it was disingenuous for Americans to deny their role in the country's subjugation by imperialists. As multilateral Western and Japanese meddling in China's affairs increasingly gave way to unilateral Japanese domination by the 1930s, Washington aspired to protect China from Japanese imperialism but was unwilling to confront Japan militarily. In the 1930s, Hollywood's considerable attention to China rarely included imperialism, instead highlighting China's myriad internal problems, such as warlords and civil war (*Shanghai Express*, 1932; *The Bitter Tea of General Yen*, 1933; *The General Died at Dawn*, 1936; *West of Shanghai*, 1937); disease (*The Painted Veil*, 1934); opium and vice (*Charlie Chan in Shanghai*, 1937; *The Shanghai Gesture*, 1941); human trafficking (*Daughter of Shanghai*, 1937); and poverty (*The Good Earth*, 1937). The cumulative effect of these images of Chinese misery seemed to justify Western intervention in a helpless land, and after Pearl Harbor, American impulses to aid and protect the Chinese grew even stronger—even if Washington never made China a high military priority. During the war, Hollywood rallied to the Chinese cause, often dramatizing Chinese suffering at Japan's hands. After the war, the studios continued to make films about wartime China while ignoring the civil war that ended with the Communist victory in 1949. After 1949, Republicans' charges that President Truman had "lost China" reflected proprietary attitudes toward the country, and the shock of Mao's victory—soon compounded by the war in Korea, where China turned an apparent American victory into a frustrating stalemate—gave Americans a taste of the defeat and humiliation that decolonization was bringing the Europeans.

Starting in 1951, Hollywood began digesting China's decolonization with a series of captivity tales set just after the Communist victory. The first of them, *Peking Express* (1951), from Paramount and director William Dieterle, was a remake of *Shanghai Express* (1932) updated for the Cold War, with Corinne Calvet playing a role modeled on Marlene Dietrich's Shanghai Lil. For the left-wing Dieterle, this crudely anticommunist film was an embarrassing contractual obligation.[1] Joseph Cotten starred as Dr. Michael Bachlin, a World Health Organization physician in China ostensibly on a humanitarian mission, in fact there to do surgery on the ailing leader of the Nationalist underground. On a train from Shanghai to Peking, Dr. Bachlin meets his old flame Danielle (Calvet), and the two share a dining table with a zealous Communist journalist, Mr. Wong (Benson Fong), and a shady Chinese trader, Mr. Kwon (Marvin Miller, in one of his many yellowface roles). Bachlin and Wong debate communism and democracy, with Wong quoting Marx and Bachlin replying, "It's fortunate that we're not all disciples of Marx." The film refutes Wong's ridiculous claims about the new China's eradication of corruption and the unity of the Chinese people. Kwon, however, proves the more dangerous one, as he leads a gang of bandits who hijack the train and imprison the Westerners. Yellow-peril motifs recur in the cruelty of Kwon and his men and in his lecherous interest in Danielle, who tolerates his advances to save her true love, the Doctor. At the climax the Doctor becomes an action hero, engineering a daring escape for himself, Danielle, and a kindly Catholic priest, and then gunning down a Jeep full of Chinese pursuers. Nearly every scene takes place at night, suggesting that darkness has descended on China, and though it alludes to Nationalist resistance and shows the Westerners' escape, it presents a gloomy vision of a new China filled with ideological fanatics and corruption. This heavy-handed propaganda film may have placated the House Committee on Un-American Activities (HUAC) and its supporters, but it barely made *Variety*'s charts at the number 119 position.[2]

The following year came *Hong Kong*, starring Ronald Reagan as Jeff Williams, an American veteran and adventurer fleeing Communist China for Hong Kong. After Jeff helps an American missionary, Victoria Evans (Rhonda Fleming), lead a group of refugees to safety in Hong Kong, the film's disdain for communism gives way to praise for British colonialism. In Hong Kong, Jeff and Victoria fall in love, and after they rescue a Chinese orphan from kidnappers—with the help of kindly, competent British policemen—they adopt him, sounding the familiar theme of the West's concern for Asian children. The film missed the box-office charts.

In 1954 came *The Shanghai Story*, a low-budget, black-and-white affair from Poverty Row survivor Republic Pictures shortly before the studio's demise. Scottish-born Director Frank Lloyd, two-time Oscar winner and director of *Mutiny on the Bounty* (1935), had not directed since 1945. After an opening monologue that described Shanghai as "a city of shame behind the bamboo curtain, its jails already filled with those condemned," the film shows Chinese soldiers herding a group of Westerners into a hotel, over the indignant protests of a mink-clad American woman. When a little girl's pet pooch, Bootsy, harasses the soldiers, one pulls out his gun and executes the imperialists' running dog, sending the poor girl into hysterics. At the hotel are Major Ling (Korean-American actor

Philip Ahn) and several of his captives: Dr. Daniel Maynard (Edmond O'Brien), cut and bruised from a run-in with Communist thugs; "Knuckles" Greer (Richard Jaeckel), a hoodlum who befriends the doctor and urges resistance; Rita King (Ruth Roman), an elegant Westerner who speaks Chinese and is allowed to come and go freely (a reward for sleeping with the local Colonel); as well as an artist, an elderly American missionary, and an arms dealer indignant at his Communist customers for arresting him. In a bit of doublespeak, the Chinese tell their captives, "The new government of China has until now graciously permitted you all to continue your residence." The Major announces that one of them is a spy sending radio messages to the Americans, and when Dr. Maynard learns it is the artist, he and Knuckles plot to help him escape. The spy gives Maynard a copy of his coded messages and then sneaks out, only to be gunned down in the streets. The Doctor then plans his own escape with the help of Rita, who has fallen in love with him and whose friendship with anti-Communist Chinese proves vital. He and Knuckles finally escape to a rendezvous with an American patrol boat.

Lloyd borrowed heavily from film noir for this picture. With all but one brief sequence set at night, the film, like *Peking Express*, makes a political point about the new regime through its dark shadows and dim lighting (while also saving on the penurious studio's electric bill). Shanghai, historically the main site of Western imperialism in China, makes a logical setting, and there is a proprietary sense to the Westerners' protests at their homes and luggage being searched. Orders that the guests must keep their doors unlocked for inspections day or night evoke Orwell's *1984* (the 1956 film version of which would also star Edmond O'Brien). Although the arms dealer, the hoodlum, and the dissolute Rita give Westerners a poor image, the film aims squarely at the Communists. "But Daddy, why did they have to kill Bootsy?" pleads the little girl, and the film continues to lay it on thick. In an old yellow-peril convention, Major Ling attempts to rape a married American woman. Disrespect for property rights appears as Chinese soldiers steal chickens from peasants and as a man tells an interrogator that his friend, a restaurant owner, had probably been shot, as "property owners don't live long in the new China." Communist guards torture an American (shown through a reaction shot of the horrified internees) and execute a captured Chinese Nationalist with a gunshot to the head, in full view of the captives. Under interrogation, a Norwegian with a heart condition calls the new regime an "octopus, reaching out arms to enslave the free peoples of the world" then dies as the guards beat him. And when the Colonel is asked to let a little girl go to the hospital, he refuses, replying, "What is one human life worth?" The film also shows Russians in positions of high authority, making a transparent Cold War point.

The film's failure to make the box-office charts was common for Republic's releases. It strives to be uplifting with its ending and its depiction of a Nationalist who tries to assassinate the arms dealer, declaring that "the Nationalist underground movement in Shanghai numbers thousands." But the failed escapes, the relentless darkness, and the drumbeat of sadistic incidents risks demoralizing Western viewers about the new China, and the main hope the film offers is simply that a few individuals might escape this enormous prison.

The next captivity narrative about Red China was *Soldier of Fortune* (1955), from Twentieth Century-Fox. Director Edward Dmytryk, an immigrant of Ukrainian descent, had been one of the Hollywood Ten, and after spending months in jail, he was able to resume his career by changing his mind and naming names.[3] *Soldier of Fortune* certainly reflected his political conversion as it hewed closely to anticommunist orthodoxy. Clark Gable starred as Hank Lee, a U.S. Navy veteran who runs a shady commercial empire in Hong Kong and lives in a mansion overlooking the city. Susan Hayward played Jane Hoyt, a devoted wife who has come to Hong Kong in search of her photojournalist husband, Louis (Gene Barry), now missing after sneaking into Red China in search of a story. When British Police Inspector Merryweather (Michael Rennie) tells Jane that Louis was unwise to enter China without a visa, she naively asks, "What's wrong with wanting to do a picture story on life in China as it is today?" The film reiterates Louis's foolishness in entering Red China—apparently he and Jane had missed *The Shanghai Story*—when Jane goes to ask the well-connected Hank to help free her husband. "It wasn't very bright" to go to China, he tells her. Though too rich to care about the money she offers, bachelor Hank instantly falls for Jane, and he offers to help because he wants to win her from her husband in a fair competition, with Louis present. The loyal wife proceeds without Hank's help, but her search through the rough quarters of Hong Kong and Macau gets nowhere, and she returns to Hank in desperation. The film then shifts from romantic drama to action as Hank goes upriver to Canton, into the heart of darkness, frees Louis from jail, eludes a pursuing Chinese patrol boat, and reaches freedom in Hong Kong.

Hank resembles countless American movie characters in colonial settings: a tough, apparently amoral, selfish adventurer whose better nature finally emerges. After the Inspector calls Hank "a disgrace" to his country and "a gangster," Jane is surprised to find two cute Chinese children at his mansion; the two are orphans Hank has adopted, a sure sign of his decency. Praising this white protector is a Chinese woman in a curio shop calls him "the most wonderful man in the world" because he "put up the money for this shop," and he frees Jane from captivity in Macao and Louis from a Communist dungeon. He even tells Jane, "Lady, you need a protector," but his offer comes with strings attached, like the protection colonial powers offered the colonized.

Other Westerners in Hong Kong and Macao come off poorly—a sordid batch of waterfront drunks, skirt chasers, thugs, and con men. The only decent white character aside from Hank is Inspector Merryweather, a representative of British colonial authority, who shows affection and paternalistic concern for his Chinese charges—even patting a sampan girl on the head after questioning her. The film briefly gives the Communists a break, as a prison interrogator answers one of Louis's flippant remarks by saying, "As an American, you of all people should know that building a new nation is no joke." Given Dmytryk's past, it is understandable that the film's sympathy for the Communists ended here, and everything else in the film follows Hollywood's typical vilification of Red China. Louis's interrogator shows him a photo of his wife with Hank at a Hong Kong restaurant—taken by a smiling Communist spy—and then tortures him verbally to get him to confess to absurd accusations. "You will notice that Mrs. Hoyt is not exactly grieving at your absence," he tells him. "I suggest you visualize her ... in that man's arms; see him caress her; listen to the quick breathing." Communist disdain for religion also emerges when a Christian missionary tells Hank that his mission in Canton has been turned into a prison.

Soldier of Fortune also shows the good Chinese who live in the freedom of British colonial rule in Hong Kong, and it arouses sympathy for the Nationalists through the kindly General Po Lin (Richard Loo), now unemployed in Hong Kong. Po Lin tries to escort Jane to Macao, but the omniscient Communists intercept the ferry and arrest him in Chinese waters. "Do not think all Chinese are barbarians," he pleads with Jane (and the audience) as Communists lead him away. The love of the good Chinese for Western culture appears in Po Lin's quotations from Keats, and in less erudite fashion, when the curio-shop owner tells Jane that she speaks English because she had been a cheerleader at UCLA. As in *The Shanghai Story*, toppling the Communists seems hopeless, with escape being the only recourse.

The film dramatizes Western impotence in the new China when Hank's junk does battle with a Chinese patrol boat; as the junk endures a pounding from the better-armed Chinese boat, Hank's shells fall frustratingly short of their target. They manage to escape, however, when a flotilla of sailboats from Hong Kong forms a protective barrier blocking the patrol boat. Although the Hong Kong sailors' assistance suggests that ordinary Chinese revile communism, the film indicates baser motives when it shows them wearing watches Hank had given them as bribes. Nevertheless, as the junk crosses into Hong Kong's waters, Louis asks Hank, "Is this free air?" and then takes a deep breath when he learns it is.

Hollywood's next broadside at Communist China, *Blood Alley* (1955), came not surprisingly from John Wayne's Batjac Productions. Director William A. Wellman, near the end of an illustrious career, launched the project after reading Sid Fleischman's 1955 novel with same title, and arranging for him to write the script. Wayne then produced and starred as merchant marine Captain Tom Wilder. Yet another captivity tale, the story begins with Wilder in a Communist prison, where he has spent two years resisting brainwashing by talking to an imaginary girlfriend he calls "Baby." For reasons he does not understand, someone bribes the guards to free him and gives him a Soviet army uniform as a disguise—surely the only time Wayne was ever so attired. Wilder soon learns that the local villagers paid the bribe because they need his skills and knowledge of the coastal waters for their plan: to commandeer a decrepit paddlewheel steamer to take the entire village, livestock and all, three hundred miles to freedom in Hong Kong. Also residing in the village is Cathy Grainger (Lauren Bacall), the daughter of a surgeon the Communists seized for his skills and then murdered after a party bigwig died in surgery. The bulk of the film follows the shrewd villagers' elaborate preparations and getaway; against all odds, Wilder and the villagers elude a patrol boat, endure a violent thunderstorm, and survive an artillery barrage from a Chinese destroyer. Compounding their difficulties, the Feng family, die-hard Communists brought along to keep them from informing the authorities, first poison the boat's food supply and then attempt to seize the bridge during the storm, beating Wilder mercilessly. After countless feats of heroism, the intrepid little boat arrives safely in the British colony.

Long before Wayne played the plucky underdog in flag-wavers such as *The Alamo* (1960) and *The Green Berets* (1968), he played it to the hilt in *Blood Alley*.[4] In order to raise the odds before beating them, the film has Wilder, upon first hearing the villagers' plan, remind them that there are "five hundred million" Chinese, and he tells them, "I don't intend to play David to China's Goliath." In casting the humble villagers as David—alongside the quirky American—the film challenges communism on the very point that supposedly justified it: the people abhor communism so passionately that they vote with their feet, abandoning their ancestral home, risking their lives in a crazy plan, and choosing, as the trailer put it, to "run the gauntlet from slavery to freedom." Wilder shares their hatred of communism, and as soon as they embark, they burn the boat's Communist flag and scrape off its political slogans. Despite lampooning a Chinese servant girl's fractured English—"You likee," she says, and Wilder mocks her struggles with the English "r"—the film depicts the villagers as intelligent and courageous.

The Communist mendacity seen in *The Shanghai Story* recurs here when Western telegrams spreading news of the escape report Peking's response that the story is "completely unfounded" and "an invention of foreign propaganda." *Blood Alley* also follows *The Shanghai Story* in having a Communist officer attempt to rape a white woman (Cathy), and once again a white man thwarts him. Embodying the evils of communism are the Fengs, and as the camera focuses on the face of the instigator of the poisoning, it invites viewers to hate this demon. At the end, however, when Wilder offers the Fengs a choice of disembarking with their Communist patriarch or staying on the boat for Hong Kong, they all opt for freedom. Even seemingly devoted Reds, the film is saying, would reject communism if given half a chance. The film also subtly backs American support for Taiwan with its references to the Straits of Formosa at a time when news reports on clashes between the Communists and Nationalists had made the islands of Quemoy and Matsu famous. And while the film supports Washington's defense of Taiwan (articulated in Congress's Formosa Resolution of January 29, 1955), the news reports probably helped the film's ticket sales in return. Finally, it displays lingering colonialist attitudes toward China with the construct of a white protector saving the Chinese, and with the notion that ordinary Chinese would rather live in a British colony than in a country the Communists had finally freed of Western domination.

Although *Blood Alley* did not appear on *Variety*'s box-office charts, the American critics mostly applauded it, with fifteen of twenty-three praising it (65 percent), one panning it, and seven giving it mixed or neutral ratings.[5] Hollywood's current fascination with Asia drew comments in *Variety*, which noted that "the Orient is having its day in films," and the *Boston Herald*, which said it was "designed to take advantage of the current interest in matters Oriental." In a typical formulation, *Time* wrote that an entire village "flees from Communist tyranny to democratic freedom"; indeed disdain for what the *Motion Picture Herald* called "Red-ridden China" was universal. Two reviews treated communism as temporary in China: the *Boston Herald* referred to "Communist-occupied China" while the *Los Angeles Examiner* said the film was "set in China, red-controlled."

The flight from China also figured in Twentieth Century-Fox's *Love Is a Many-Splendored Thing* (1955). The film primarily concerned an interracial romance between American journalist Mark Elliott (William Holden) and Eurasian physician Han Suyin (Jennifer Jones), and chapter 8 analyzes that aspect of the film, but its handling of international politics deserves mention here. The real Han

Suyin (a pen name for Rosalie Chow) published her autobiographical tale in 1952, and playwright John Patrick adapted it for the screen. Director Henry King (*Captain from Castile, King of the Khyber Rifles*) shot it in CinemaScope in Hong Kong and California. The story takes place in 1949, just as the Communists have taken Shanghai, and at a Hong Kong hospital, Dr. Han treats a little girl hit by a car. The girl, she learns, is "a refugee from China, one of 3000 new ones [who] pour in every day." She then meets a desperate mother who offers to sell her son to pay for her sick husband's treatment, a pathetic illustration of China's abject poverty and need for Western assistance. The image of Red China becomes even clearer when Suyin meets an elderly white missionary at a cocktail party. Father Low (Herbert Heyes) explains that he was just "thrown out" of northern China even though he loved the people and "knew them as I knew the back of my hand." When Suyin says she is heading for China to help her people, Father Low tells her, "You'll be shot," but she dismisses the warning, saying she is neither a politician nor a missionary. Her willingness to return to China reflects her courage and devotion to her people, not her naivete; she is only too aware of China's realities, as we learn that her deceased husband was a Nationalist "captured and shot by the Communists." Not wishing the point to elude viewers, the film repeats it when she goes to Chungking to visit her relatives, who expect to be shot when the Communists take over.

Apparently oblivious to all the flying bullets, a Chinese doctor at the hospital in Hong Kong, Dr. Sen (Kam Tong), sneers at the refugees' exodus, and he cannot understand why more than a million have come to Hong Kong. When Suyin later decides to stay in Hong Kong, having fallen in love with Mark, Dr. Sen chides her. "China has been reborn, Suyin," he declares. "Our people are free at last." During the Cold War, of course, Americans could not resist gloating over people voting with their feet in their desperation to escape communism, and here Suyin notes that thousands arrive every day. She asks her colleague, "As a man who believes in this new order, doesn't it disturb you that so many flee from freedom?" The film permits Dr. Sen no reply, and given the political atmosphere in America and Hollywood, there was no reason to expect one. So despite mild allusions to "race snobbery" in Hong Kong, *Love Is a Many-Splendored Thing*'s contrast between the tyranny of Communist China and the freedom of British Hong Kong illustrates how anticommunism trumped anticolonialism in films as well as in U.S. policy.

The religious case against communism was the principal charge in a long section about China in *The Mark of the Hawk* (1958), discussed in chapter 4. Missionary Bruce Craig urges the angry African nationalist Obam not to turn his back on Christ over the church's lamentable failure to support his people's independence. Hoping to rekindle Obam's Christianity, he recounts his experiences in China in a flashback. Craig begins by telling Obam about his work in China and how he and his wife adopted an orphan named Ming Tao (David Goh). They stayed after the Communist takeover, and he tells Obam, "For three years I saw this [pause] 'People's Government' at close quarters." The tale then morphs into a captivity narrative as soldiers arrive at their home at night to arrest him and his wife. The scene conveys their alarm as soldiers pound loudly on the door—recalling a scenario in films about Nazis—then storm in, barking orders, and haul them away. Prison scenes of Craig's endless interrogation—the passage of time indicated by his long beard—also recall the Nazi films, and a zealous interrogator with a bright spotlight over his shoulder makes ridiculous accusations about Craig working for the FBI.

His ordeal worsens one day when he sees his son, a guard in a Red Army uniform. "The change in him was incredible," Craig explains as the camera shows an imposing Ming Tao, lit and shot from below, staring icily at him and clutching a rifle with a gleaming bayonet. Later, Ming Tao comes to his adoptive father's cell to urge him to confess to the imaginary charges, mouthing the party line: "You cannot deny that you've always been an agent for American imperialism and white superiority." This image of children turning on their parents for the good of the state was a staple of Cold War images of totalitarianism, whose disregard for familial love and loyalty was its gravest fault. As Ming Tao berates his father for his missionary work, he lays out the charges: that he preached of a white God, that whites controlled the church hierarchy and funds, and that white missionaries enjoyed social privileges based on race. Those charges are hardly ridiculous, but they get no further discussion, and Ming Tao never voices the common Chinese nationalist complaint that missionaries, as part of the Western power structure, promoted Westernization under protection of gunboats.

It turns out that Ming Tao's indoctrination has failed to extinguish his love for both his father and Jesus Christ. Ming Tao tells his father, "I can no longer put faith in the bright policies of the People's Government. I've seen too much violence, too much oppression, too much bloodshed." Like *Blood Alley*, in which the Fengs decide to abandon their Communist patriarch and head for Hong Kong, this plot twist raises Western hopes of deprogramming the indoctrinated masses. Yet in this totalitarian state, a guard is monitoring Ming Tao's conversation with his father, and after the guards lead the lad away, the camera shows the father's face as he hears a gunshot in the hallway. The film then cuts back to the present, giving no clue of how Craig managed to escape this nightmare.

Among these films, *The Mark of the Hawk* and *The Shanghai Story* offer the most chilling images of Red China, presenting a grittier, more vivid case than the high-budget films. Yet all of them depict China as a giant prison and a daunting new enemy of the West. They raise hopes that clever, courageous whites and Chinese can outwit their captors and escape, and they temper their demoralizing tone with suggestions that the Chinese people detest their new regime and would rather live under Western rule. This dismal portrait of the new China managed to obscure almost entirely the history of the Western imperialism that helped the Communists come to power, and if the films helped Western audiences to absorb the reality of decolonization in China, they did little to explain why it had occurred.

The Philippines

Given how few formal overseas colonies the United States has had, it is striking how rarely Hollywood examined U.S. rule in the Philippines. The Americans seized the Philippines in the Spanish-American War of 1898 and then fought a brutal war against Philippine rebels seeking independence, a conflict in which more than two hundred thousand Filipinos died. Those events took place in the early days of cinema, and although pioneer filmmaker J. Stuart Blackton recreated the navy's conquest of Manila in *Battle of Manila Bay* (1898), few such films followed.[6] In 1926, Warner Bros. made *Across the Pacific*, about Americans fighting Filipino rebels, and in 1939, Samuel Goldwyn produced *The Real Glory*, with Gary Cooper as an army doctor fighting Moro rebels in Mindanao. Interest in the Philippines suddenly grew with Japan's conquest of the country and America's war to recover its colony. Films such as *Manila Calling* (1942) *Bataan* (1943), and *Back to Bataan* (1945) highlighted Filipino-American brotherhood, and such World War II films appeared occasionally after 1945. The advent of Philippine independence in 1946 did not interest Hollywood, and aside from the war films and occasional South Seas adventures and fantasies set or filmed in the Philippines, Hollywood continued to overlook the country. The Filipinos themselves continued to adore American movies, but it was unrequited love.

Philippine independence actually changed very little in America's relationship with the country.[7] Throughout the first half of the century, the United States had colonized the country, put down rebellions, built military bases, invested in cash crops such as sugar and copra, established a monopoly for American exporters, sent teachers to educate and Americanize the people, and flooded the country with its culture, language, and products. In short, the relationship featured the occupation, exploitation, discrimination, and acculturation that define colonialism. For years, Filipino leaders publicly called for independence while quietly reassuring the Americans they were in no hurry to see them leave. Americans were divided over keeping the colony—domestic sugar interests wished to be rid of competitors with access to U.S. markets, while military strategists and investors prized the islands. In 1933–34, Congress worked out a compromise that promised independence within a decade, then followed through in 1946. The ceremony—on the Fourth of July—attested to the continuing amity between the two nations, and perhaps for American dignitaries in Manila that day, the sounds of "The Star-Spangled Banner" and the stifling heat and humidity made them think they were home in Washington.

Massive American aid helped ensure continuing influence over the new government—not that its leaders actually wished to end relations—and before long the two countries worked out ninety-nine-year leases for the military bases. Congress also passed the 1946 Philippine Trade Act, which in classic colonial fashion granted U.S. exporters a monopoly in the Philippine market, pegged the peso to the dollar, and prevented the country from selling to the United States manufactures or other products competing with American ones. The act also granted Americans "parity" in the Philippines, giving them the same rights to own mines and natural resources that Filipinos had—a provision that violated the country's new constitution. In order to secure the supermajority in the legislature needed to amend the constitution, President Roxas disqualified newly elected opposition representatives (though his accusation that they had been elected fraudulently was a case of the pot calling the kettle black). The ouster of those representatives, elected mostly by peasant voters, then triggered a major rural uprising that would finally attract enough attention to yield one American film on the subject.

Huk! (1956), from the obscure Pan-Pacific Productions, was the only American film about the postwar rebellion of the ragtag peasant force known as the "Huks," whose roots lay in the worsening conditions for peasants in Central Luzon in the early 1900s.[8] Amid a population boom and the increasing commercialization and mechanization of agriculture that American colonial rule promoted, traditionally paternalistic landlords had proven less and less willing to help their peasant workers with loans and "rations" to tide them over in hard times. As a new generation of absentee landlords relied on the police and their own "civilian guards" to enforce increasingly harsh contracts, the peasants sought employment elsewhere, organized politically, and tried negotiation, strikes, and demonstrations. When Japan invaded in 1941, peasants secured arms and formed the People's Anti-Japanese Army (Hukbalahap), which resisted the occupation and helped defeat Japan in 1945. Hoping for American gratitude, the Huks were denounced as communists and bandits by Philippine elites, shunned by the Americans, and subject to arrest and harassment. President Roxas's disqualification of peasant representatives elected in 1946 and the murder of peasant leader Juan Feleo led tens of thousands to launch the revolt. Contrary to accusations, the Huks received no aid from the Soviets, and the tiny Philippine Communist Party did not endorse the revolt until 1948. Rather than seeking changes in land ownership, the Huks mainly wished to restore more equitable terms between landowners and workers and to end the violence that the government and the landowners' thugs used against peasants. Roxas's vow to crush the Huks in sixty days proved unrealistic, and into the early 1950s the Huks held their own against Philippine forces and their American suppliers and advisers. The Americans backed the landed elites, and the provision of airplanes and other modern weaponry against rebels armed with rifles helped wear down the Huks. By the early 1950s, the exhausted, hungry rebels were essentially defeated, though a handful fought on a bit longer.

The 1956 film *Huk!* originated with a novel and screenplay by Stirling Silliphant, who later wrote scripts for *In the Heat of the Night* (1967), *Charly* (1968), and *The Liberation of L. B. Jones* (1970). No one else involved ever reached that level; director John Barnwell, who had made short films for the State Department in 1951, made only one other feature in his career, and the cast was filled with B-film veterans.[9] George Montgomery, a burly ex-boxer who made several westerns, played Greg Dickson, an American raised in the Philippines who returns after a long absence to sell the family's island sugar plantation after the Huks kill his father. The usual cynical American in the third world, Greg shrugs at the death of a father who neglected him while "building an empire," but he is glad to see the elderly Stephen Rogers (James Bell), a schoolteacher at the plantation who had been his surrogate father. Greg also follows cinematic stereotypes by lusting after Cindy Rogers (Mona Freeman), the wife of Stephen's son Bart (John Baer), whose obsession with killing Huks makes him neglect his wife. Recalling other films urging Americans to overseas involvement, Greg overcomes his selfishness and cynicism. Stephen, declining Greg's plea to return to the United States with him, reminds Greg why he had come to the Philippines: "To help the people with quinine and clean drinking water and the three Rs." Adding that the Americans did "a job to be proud of," he recalls their successes: "Got the illiteracy rate down below 50 percent, cleaned up cholera and the plague, and taught folks to hold up their head and look a man straight in the eye." Echoing Kipling's "The White Man's Burden," which had warned Americans that civilizing the Philippines would be a thankless, if noble, task, the skeptical Greg asks, "Do you think anyone appreciates what you did? Remembers?" Stephen believes they do and explains, "Americans have a wonderful ability to win friends. They have a nice smile. They're simple and honest." American colonialism, in this view, was a matter of decent people's selfless devotion to the needy, earning rewards of affection and loyalty.

Greg has little time to ponder these words as he fends off several brazen Huk attacks, including a knife-wielding assassin and fanatics who swarm over the plantation's fences, burning and murdering as they go. Their leader is Kalak (Mario Barri), whose speeches give no hint of the rebels' motives, and the film never shows the fighters' families or living conditions. Balancing this image of fanatic savages is Major Balatbat (Teddy Benavedes), an upstanding Philippine Army commander who embodies Filipino love and loyalty toward America. When the Major hears of Greg's intention to sell his land and leave, he asks, "Who will defend the people who live here, who worked your land all these years?" He also asks Greg if he is familiar with Ramon Magsaysay (who oversaw Manila's defeat of the Huks first as defense minister and then as president). Embodying the American ignorance the film aims to remedy, Greg says he has heard of Magsaysay, but "he hasn't knocked the World Series off the front page." This gives the Major an opportunity to inform him (and the viewers) that Magsaysay "teaches what I first learned in your country, when I took my training at Fort Benning: that all free men are brothers." The Major also politely chides Greg's concern about the rebellion's effects on real estate values. "On this side of the world," he explains, "we are all playing for larger stakes than your plantation. Your country and mine, we have been together a long time. We're going to stay that way." The Major's speech contributes to Greg's change of heart, as does his grief over the death of Stephen, gunned down in his classroom by laughing, torch-wielding rebels. The film's climax is a Huk assault on a ferry boat taking the plantation's workers to safety, and though the endless waves of rebels kill Bart and sink the boat, Greg and Cindy help the peasants to safety. To the sounds of the Philippine national anthem, Greg, Cindy, and a peasant girl wade ashore in a shot reminiscent of General MacArthur's return to Leyte in 1944. Informed that his plantation was destroyed, the transformed Greg declares, "We'll start all over again."

Cinematically, *Huk!* owes much to old-fashioned westerns, from its shots of warriors emerging over a ridge to the convention of outnumbered whites mowing down hordes of attackers. Whites aiming at Huks never miss, while dozens of Huks surround Greg and Bart during their railway escape and fire at them point blank without hitting them. Silliphant's knowledge of the revolt seems dubious, as the action takes place not in the plains and mountains of Central Luzon, where the Huks actually operated, but rather in fictional islands, and the film simply invents the rebels' killing of Americans. And whereas in reality Philippine troops and civilian guards often burned villages suspected of aiding the Huks, in the film it is the Huks who burn the villages. Finally, whereas the mechanization of Philippine agriculture helped cause and fuel the revolt by putting Filipinos out of work, when Greg urges his peasant laborers to help defend the plantation, he asks them, "Where would you earn money for your families if it weren't for these machines?" Strangely absent are accusations that the Huks were communists, for while Kalak and a few other Huks wear red headbands, no character ever mentions communism. As for the film's purpose—aside from the entertainment value of watching brave Americans slaughter waves of savage attackers—*Huk!* justified in retrospect U.S. support for the counterinsurgency and continuing aid to a pro-American regime. This terribly self-congratulatory colonialist film also reminded Americans of their noble deeds in the Philippines while urging isolationists to follow Greg Dickson's example, overcome their cynicism, and bear the white man's burden.

This United Artists release drew little attention. The *New York Times* complained that "paying customers who go in wondering just what the title means, and what prompted a terrible conflict, will leave the same way," and *Variety* wrote that the Huks were "given over to a not-clearly-expressed fanaticism."[10] The *Motion Picture Herald* explained that the Huks were "guerrilla fighters who turned against their native Philippine land to become ruthless desperadoes." The film sold 608,366 tickets in France, and a rare review revealed seething anger at Washington's criticism of France's war in Algeria.[11] Jean Dutourd of the conservative *Carrefour* referred to the Huks as *fellaghas*, as the Algerian rebels were known, and he noted sarcastically that the Americans in the film "whose ancestors taught them fine lessons in exterminating the Redskins," respond to the rebels "with absolute, complete, total carnage, after which they return to their little colonial enterprises that serve the prosperity and happiness of the Philippines." He added that the audience broke out in laughter at the line, "Americans have a wonderful ability to win friends," and he concluded that "the moral of all this is, I imagine, that *fellaghas* have a perfect right to kill Frenchmen, but not American citizens."[12]

The Americans and the Japanese

In the years since American ships first visited Japan, the relationship between the two countries has gone through many phases. Commodore Perry's expeditions in 1853 and 1854, following several unsuccessful attempts to establish trade, began a period of Western imperialism, as the United States and other European powers used the military advantages the Industrial Revolution had given them to force Japan to abandon its isolation. When Japan reacted to this shock by learning from the West, modernizing rapidly, and launching its own imperial expansion, the United States and Japan became imperial rivals, culminating in World War II. The American occupation of Japan from 1945 to 1952 in some ways meant a return to imperialism, but by the 1950s the relationship was becoming more equal and friendly, and it has remained so despite lingering disagreements.

Historians have noted the colonialist aspects of America's occupation of Japan after World War II, but if colonialism consists of occupation, exploitation, discrimination, and acculturation, the relationship in this period fits the definition only imperfectly.[13] Occupation there certainly was, as the Americans moved in a quarter of a million troops after the war, established numerous military bases, and began remaking Japan. Supreme Commander for the Allied Powers (SCAP) General Douglas MacArthur wielded immense power, and the Americans largely imposed a new constitution and refashioned Japan's institutions in their own image.[14] As for acculturation, although Japan's love of American baseball, movies, and music had begun long before 1945, it reached new levels after the war.[15] This acculturation had its limits, as the Japanese proved adept at selecting aspects of Western culture that suited them while rejecting others and preserving essential traditions. During the occupation, and especially in its first years, discrimination included Jim Crow–style segregation of public facilities, but hiring decisions, for example, were largely left up to the Japanese.[16]

Exploitation looked likely in 1945, when the Americans' briefly considered hamstringing Japan—disarming it, restricting its heavy industry, breaking up the *zaibatsu* (conglomerates) that had dominated the economy, and purging business leaders complicit with the military regime. Although doing so would have benefited U.S. firms and constituted economic exploitation, several American leaders objected, and with the advent of the Cold War, Washington's containment strategy required a prosperous Japan to lead capitalist growth throughout East Asia.[17] So unlike U.S. policy in the Philippines, where restrictions on the exports of manufactures followed classic colonial patterns, the Americans encouraged Japan's rapid industrial revival. Proof of exploitation seems easier to find in military matters, as the United States still retains military bases in Japan, and Article IX of the 1946 constitution, limiting Japan's military capabilities, remains in place. Many Japanese actually supported disarmament, and Japanese leaders refused or resisted later American pleas to rearm, so it would be misleading to depict defense arrangements as something Washington imposed on an unwilling nation. Considering that those arrangements leave America bearing much of the cost of defending Japan, it is not even clear which country has been exploiting the other.[18] Far easier to demonstrate than economic and military exploitation was the sexual exploitation of Japanese women, whose poverty forced them into humiliating sex work and other relations with the occupiers (see chapter 8). The postwar relationship thus fits only some of the components of the definition of colonialism outlined in the introduction, but at least during the formal occupation period it merits inclusion here, and it was certainly an important case for American reflections on how to treat those they ruled.

Although the postwar evolution of Hollywood's images of the Japanese awaits a comprehensive study, that evolution was rapid and profound.[19] World War II films continued to dominate Hollywood's postwar output about Japan, but a rare early film about the occupation was *Tokyo Joe* (1949), which Stuart Heisler directed for Humphrey Bogart's Santana Pictures. Bogart starred as Joe Barrett, a veteran who had run a gambling joint in prewar Tokyo, and who returns to see if it is still standing. He finds the club intact and his friend and business partner Ito (Teru Shimada) running it; he also learns that his wife Trina (Florence Marly), a White Russian he had left in 1941 and whom he thought had died in the war, is alive and married to an American lawyer for SCAP. Joe now wants her back despite her having divorced him *in absentia*, and he also meets his daughter, born after he left. In order to remain legally in Japan, Joe must enlist the help of Ito's acquaintance, Baron Kimura (Sessue Hayakawa). The Baron, former head of the Imperial Secret Police, now runs a shady export business, and Joe partners with him in a freight airline that gives Joe the right to stay in Japan. When the Baron uses his intelligence files to blackmail Trina over her wartime collaboration with the Japanese government, he forces Joe to cooperate in his illegal activities. These involve a plot to smuggle three fugitive war criminals from Korea back into Japan to start an uprising against the Americans, and when U.S. authorities discover the Baron's plans, a bloody showdown thwarts the conspiracy.

The film paints a very positive image of the American occupation, aside from SCAP's stifling bureaucracy, while its image of the Japanese is mixed. Joe's friend and partner Ito is a humble, deferential fellow (whose friendly judo match with Joe may remind viewers today of Inspector Clouseau sparring with Kato in the *Pink Panther* films), and he expresses the war guilt American viewers probably wanted to hear when he tells his American pal, "I still feel very bad about everything" and "We are ashamed because you [Americans] treat us decently." But Ito and his henchman Kanda are in cahoots with the Baron, a die-hard militarist whose work with the ultranationalist Black Dragon Society (a real organization) makes continuing U.S. rule seem necessary. As an American officer tells Joe, the Baron hopes to "build up hatred and fanaticism among disgruntled Japanese veterans" and launch "a bloody uprising that the vast majority of the Japanese people knows to be against its own best interest."

The script confuses the far left and far right when the Officer calls the Baron's plot "communist inspired" and "communist directed," but if the Americans' grasp of Japanese politics is weak, the army's competence is reassuring, as the Americans come to the rescue repeatedly. Lest the pro-occupation message elude audiences, Joe tells a dying Ito, who has just stabbed himself after being caught collaborating with the Baron, "You think we're the real enemy because we're occupying Japan. But do you know why we're doing it? To help the Japanese people stand up on their hind legs like men and women have a right to in this world." This line expresses the American view that the occupation was freeing ordinary Japanese from elite oppressors who had led them astray, even if in reality SCAP had by 1949 abandoned its initial New Deal sympathy for Japan's unions and working classes and had helped restore the power of the upper classes (as in the Philippines). Ito's dying admission that Joe is right offers the encouraging message that most Japanese can be persuaded to abandon their nationalist fantasies and embrace the American way. The film, which contains fine performances from Bogart and Hayakawa and some rare street scenes shot in postwar Tokyo, reached the number fifty-six slot on the 1949 box-office charts.[20]

Aside from Samuel Fuller's *House of Bamboo* (1955), a noirish, apolitical tale about American criminal gangs in postwar Japan, few other films examined the occupation. The most significant film on the subject in the 1950s was MGM's *Teahouse of the August Moon*, a 1956 comedy based on the 1951 novel by Vern J. Sneider and John Patrick's Pulitzer- and Tony-winning 1953 Broadway play. Director Daniel Mann and cinematographer John Alton shot the CinemaScope film mostly on location in Japan. Set in Okinawa in 1946, it opens with a heavily made-up Marlon Brando addressing the camera. His character, Sakini, interpreter for blustering bureaucrat Colonel Wainwright Purdy III (Paul Ford), signals the film's interest in colonialism when he explains that Okinawa has been conquered and subjugated repeatedly—by the Chinese, English missionaries, the Japanese, and now the Americans. "Okinawa very fortunate," he explains, tongue in cheek. "Culture brought to us. Not have to leave home for it." This ironic tone gives a clue to the character of the disingenuous Sakini and his fellow villagers, who seem childlike at first but prove adept at resisting the designs of busybody conquerors such as Colonel Purdy. Frustrated to find Sakini napping during work hours, the Colonel asks him, "Where's your get up and go?" and observes, "No wonder you people were subjugated by the Japanese." When his new assistant, Captain Fisby (Glenn Ford), arrives, the Colonel states his mission: to establish a democratic government and a school in Sakini's village, Tobiki. Warning Fisby that the locals "lack the capacity for sustained endeavor," he tells him, "Don't hesitate to build a fire under them." When Fisby, a former professor of humanities, questions his own qualifications, the Colonel scoffs at his timidity. "What did I know about foreigners?" he asks. "But my job is to teach these natives the meaning of democracy, and they're going to learn democracy if I have to shoot every one of them." Handing Fisby a massive tome titled "Plan B"—Washington's detailed instructions for reconstruction—he sends him off with Sakini.

Outfoxed by the Okinawans before he even gets to Tobiki, Fisby fails to interest the locals in the pentagon-shaped schoolhouse he must build. He is also terribly uncomfortable with a gift from one of the villagers: a geisha named Lotus Blossom (Machiko Kyô, Japan's leading film actress of the 1950s). Facing the villagers' polite resistance, Fisby gradually gives in, agreeing to build a teahouse instead of a school—which is, after all, the will of the majority. He also fails to bring American capitalism to the village by having the people make souvenirs for sale to American GIs, but the discovery that they make a very potent sweet-potato brandy quickly has Fisby's phone ringing off the hook with orders from GIs. Tobiki's versions of democracy and capitalism do not match the Pentagon's plans, and as the Colonel realizes that Fisby is disobeying orders and going native, he sends army psychiatrist Captain McLean (Eddie Albert) to check on him. The psychiatrist, even odder than Fisby, soon goes native, too, forcing the Colonel to come to Tobiki, where he finds a new teahouse but no school. When the exasperated Purdy learns that the villagers have pooled their earnings, on the principle of "share and share alike," he exclaims, "That's communism!" The Colonel orders the stills destroyed and the teahouse dismantled, then learns that an American senator, having heard of the village's booming brandy business, is coming to see the local success story. Purdy despairs until it turns out that the wily villagers only pretended to destroy the stills and the teahouse.

Politically sensitive viewers today may find *Teahouse of the August Moon* offensive, or at least dated, with Brando in yellowface. It also takes aim at Western feminism through the geisha, a common object of white-male fantasy in films of this era. Lotus Blossom knows how to please a man—unlike Western women ruined by notions of sexual equality—and within the context of an occupation, such sexual inequality has colonialist overtones, even if the conscientious Fisby resists her affections. Although Sakini protests Fisby's assumption that a geisha is some sort of sex slave, many viewers undoubtedly preferred their own concepts, and a comic sequence in which Lotus Blossom attempts to remove Fisby's clothing derived its humor from sexual suggestiveness. The film's image of the apparently primitive villagers may seem condescending now, and like traditional empire films, this one often treats the villagers as a faceless group; even Lotus

Blossom, the next most important Asian character after Sakini, gets little character development. Yet most of the film's humor comes at the expense not of the Okinawans but of the Americans. Just what the film satirizes, and thus what it says about America's remaking of Japan, requires a closer look.

In one possible reading, the film is merely a service comedy taking the usual potshots at the foibles of the higher ranks and the mindless bureaucracy of the armed forces. Colonel Purdy believes firmly in the Pentagon's instructions, which, he tells Fisby, make thinking unnecessary, and he is a rube who confuses Dickens and Hugo and mangles Kipling's "East is East" line. Yet given the army's role in remaking Japan, ridiculing Purdy and his pentagon-shaped schoolhouse inevitably raises questions about that overall project. For Purdy embodies anti-American stereotypes: he is powerful but ignorant, and his dismissal of Fisby's proposal to study Japanese—"there's no need: we won the war"—lampoons Americans' lack of interest in other languages and cultures. In ridiculing an army bureaucrat, who measures the progress of his civilizing mission in terms of Okinawans memorizing the English alphabet and learning to sing "God Bless America," the film also calls into question the entrusting of nation-building to soldiers. Indeed, the film uses Sakini's wry cultural-relativist observations to question the whole idea of remaking Japanese culture, and in the tradition of noble-savage narratives of the South Seas, it suggests that Okinawan ways are not just different but better. When Fisby, seeking a new source of income for Tobiki, suggests they use machines to mass-produce lacquered cups and sell them to GIs, an elderly gentleman responds, "I take pride in making one cup at a time." The film also sympathizes with local ways in showing the villagers' custom of ending each day by sipping tea in a pine grove and watching the sunset, a custom Fisby quickly adopts.

So unlike films such as *Anna and the King of Siam* and *The Inn of the Sixth Happiness*, in which Western civilizers learn virtually nothing from their pupils, *Teahouse of the August Moon* reverses the teaching relationship as the colonizers learn things of true value from the colonized. As he prepares to leave Tobiki late in the film, Fisby tells Sakini and Lotus Blossom, "I'll never forget this village. . . . I'll remember what was beautiful, and what I was wise enough to leave beautiful." He also adds, "Now I'm not sure who's the conquered and who's the conqueror. . . . See, I don't want to be a world leader. I've made peace with myself somewhere between my ambitions and my limitations." While the film's plea for Americans to form emotional bonds with Asians has colonialist overtones, it also stakes out anticolonialist positions and breaks with those films that urge Americans to embrace world leadership and spread their ways throughout Asia. And whereas anticommunism often trumped American anticolonialism, this film's only allusion to communism amounts to a satirical poke at Americans' overreactions to it—suggesting that by this time, HUAC's hold on Hollywood was weakening.

Despite the film's noble-savage notions, these villagers are not the innocents they wish to appear. When Fisby asks Sakini to announce that he comes as their friend, "to lift the yoke of oppression from their shoulders," Sakini replies, "Oh, they like that Boss; that's their favorite speech"—one they heard from the Japanese. "Now when friends come," he adds, "we hide everything as quick as Dickens." Their naivete, in short, is an illusion, part of the defenses that prior conquests taught them to erect, and they adopt only those aspects of modernity they find attractive. "They want teahouse like big city," Sakini explains to Fisby, and they use the Americans to get it. The choice of Okinawa as the film's setting is somewhat misleading in that the reforms and cultural reprogramming applied in the rest of Japan were largely absent in Okinawa, which the Americans treated merely as a military base, but the choice of Okinawa and the attention drawn to Japan's historical conquest of it help invite sympathy for resistance to colonization.[21]

The film also reflects certain truths about the occupation of Japan, in that the conquerors came in with grand plans to remake a society in America's image but soon scaled back those ambitious schemes and then left, while the Japanese took what seemed useful from the conquerors and rejected the rest. The humor of Purdy's threat to teach his subjects democracy at gunpoint also reflects the absurdity of an American project repeated elsewhere in the ensuing years.[22] Even the drastic discrepancies in power, knowledge, and economic sophistication that supposedly justify colonization—which this film questions—did not endure for long in reality, and by the time this film came out, Japan was already exporting manufactures successfully enough to provoke complaints from American firms.[23] So despite some dated ethnic and gender imagery, the film critiques the colonialist tendencies of America's postwar mentality, using humor to help Americans accept that criticism.

Teahouse was a major hit in the United States, reaching number six on the annual charts, and the *Motion Picture Herald* reported that at a New York sneak preview, "audience reaction indicated a profound impression had been made."[24] It did equally well with critics, as twenty-eight of thirty-four (82 percent) praised it—including many raves—while four critics (three from New York) panned it, and two split their judgments.[25] While two critics disliked the casting of Brando, far more extolled his performance.[26] Condescension toward the Okinawans appears in several reviews: the *Chicago Tribune* calls them "a childish, pleasant people," while the *St. Louis Post-Dispatch* referred to their "childlike, innocent craftiness," and the *Boston Globe* noted that "the mighty can be flattered and fooled into doing just what their inferiors plan." But many critics followed the film in questioning Americans imposing their ways on others. For the *Boston Herald*'s Elinor Hughes, the film showed "the desirability of helping people to be happy in their ways, not yours," and Kate Cameron of the *New York Daily News* welcomed Fisby's decision to "give them what they want rather than what the Army decrees they should have." Roughly half the papers noted the reversal of the teaching relationship, including the *Philadelphia Inquirer*, which wrote that "a much-conquered people given to sitting in a fir grove, sipping tea and watching the sun set quietly teach their conquerors 'the wisdom of gracious acceptance.'" Many critics also saw *Teahouse* as more than a comedy. The *Los Angeles Times* found in the film "material for serious thought," and the *Denver Post* noted that this comedy "has its serious side, as well, and the picture treats with a certain dignity the way of life of an alien people for whom materialism is second to spiritual values." The *Motion Picture Herald* found the film's insights "profound and yet understandable," adding that it has "meat for the analytical and contemplative and milk for those who seek only to laugh and cry their cares away." The film got similar reactions in Britain, where twelve of fourteen reviews were positive and two mixed.[27] Both the *Evening News* and the *London Times* commented on how the film showed Americans doing the sort of empire-building often seen in films about the British. The *Daily Worker* also identified the film's funniest line as Colonel Purdy's statement, "That's communism!" The film had a brief run in France and received few reviews.[28]

Indochina in the 1950s

Long before the 1970s and the flood of films about the Vietnam War, a handful of films gave Americans a glimpse of an area few knew. For years Americans had paid French Indochina little attention, but after World War II it became a prime site for the conflict between America's fears of communism and its distaste for European colonialism. When Ho Chi Minh's Vietminh launched its revolt against France in November 1946, the initial American reaction was to let the French deal with it and provide indirect financial assistance. U.S. interest grew with Mao's victory in China in 1949 and the war in Korea in 1950, both because of domino-theory fears and because Washington's Cold War strategy required Japanese access to Southeast Asian raw materials.[29] Despite paying most of France's war expenses, Washington gradually abandoned hope of France defeating the Vietminh, and its decision not to rescue the French at Dien Bien Phu in 1954 worsened existing tensions between these allies.³⁰ After the 1954 Geneva Accords in effect split Vietnam into two zones, Washington took over from the French in the south, and it soon settled on Ngo Dinh Diem to lead a new American client state, South Vietnam. The late 1950s were a crucial moment in America's long descent into the quagmire of Vietnam, as Washington put increasing economic and military resources into South Vietnam.³¹ During this period, Diem consolidated his dictatorship against all rivals, while the southern Vietminh remained demoralized and inactive. Only between 1957 and 1959 did North Vietnam decide to aid its southern affiliates.³²

By the time of the May 1957 U.S. release of Samuel Fuller's *China Gate*, France's defeat had made its vigorous tribute to French colonialism obsolete, but its image of the Communists remained relevant, and the film encouraged U.S. involvement in Vietnam. A French soldier in Brock's unit declares that "America's our friend. . . . She's helping us where we need it most. War costs money, . . . [and] it's cost her a lot." The film invited concern through images of hungry villagers dependent on American airdrops and through its insistence on Soviet and Chinese involvement in Vietnam. Indeed, the film virtually effaced the Vietnamese from the tale. At one point, Lea explains that her mother was a "Moi," which she defines as "Vietnamese for savage," and is indeed a derogatory term for the country's ethnic minorities living in the northern highlands where the film takes place. This brief statement aside, the film presents the fight as a struggle between the West and the Chinese, backed by the Soviets. Major Cham (Lee Van Cleef) tells Lea he hopes to become a general, "stationed in Peking, or perhaps even Moscow," and "the day I can report directly to Moscow, instead of through Peking, that's the day I'll be in line to command a Vietminh Politburo." Portraits of Stalin and Mao reinforce the point, as do shots of enemy soldiers wearing caps like Mao's. The film's lack of interest in the Vietnamese and their grievances reflect American ignorance of local realities, and while *China Gate* may have served to encourage American involvement, it did little to educate its audience about Vietnam.

The following year saw the release of Oscar-winning director, producer, and writer Joseph L. Mankiewicz's adaptation of a 1955 Graham Greene novel, *The Quiet American* (1958), which Mankiewicz's own Figaro, Inc. made for United Artists. While the film delved more deeply into Vietnam's politics than *China Gate* had, it did so misleadingly, and its allusions to the competing groups in Vietnam were also probably too complex for most viewers to follow. Those complexities are in the novel, but the film also reflected the visions of the American director and writer, the Production Code Administration, and even the CIA's Edward Lansdale, who advised Mankiewicz during production.

Shot in black and white in South Vietnam and at Rome's Cinecittá, the film, set during France's war with the Vietminh in 1952, opens with street scenes of revelry at Chinese New Year in Saigon. Rapid cuts give the impression of a chaotic place; shots of heavily armed soldiers suggest danger as well, and a panning shot settles on a body face down on a riverbank. French Police Inspector Vigot (Claude Dauphin) then questions a British journalist, Thomas Fowler (Michael Redgrave), who knew the deceased, a young American, whom Greene named Pyle to reflect his annoyance with his type, but whom the film never names. Vigot knows that the American (Audie Murphy) was courting Fowler's mistress, a bar hostess named Phuong (Italian actress Giorgia Moll), who, like the American, is years younger than Fowler. Most of the film takes place in flashback, as Fowler answers Vigot's questions by recounting in voice-over his troubled acquaintance with the American.

Asked what the American did for a living, the uncertain Fowler replies that he belonged to "one of those American groups—there seem to be hundreds of them—that stretch helping hands around the world, holding out packages of hope." The group, called "Friends for Free Asia," brings to mind America's anticommunist "Vietnam lobby," which formed the influential American Friends of Vietnam three years after this tale takes place.[33] Like Fowler, the novelist had served as a correspondent in Saigon in the early 1950s, and the character also resembles Greene when he denounces the meddling of starry-eyed young Americans ignorant of local realities.[34] Fowler tells Vigot of their rivalry for Phuong and of his disdain for the American's promotion of a "third force" of Vietnamese opposed to both French colonialism and communism. The American's very politeness—he is unlike the loud-mouthed Yanks in Saigon's bars—and his candid intentions to steal Phuong fairly from Fowler (whose wife refuses to divorce) only irritate him more. When a Communist agent in Saigon informs Fowler that the American is importing plastic explosives for General Thé, leader of a local sect and a prospect for the third-force strategy, Fowler suspects that the American is a CIA agent, and when Fowler witnesses a deadly street bombing, he becomes enraged enough to help the Communists murder him. Fowler also wishes to rid himself of a rival for Phuong, who wants to see the skyscrapers of New York. Vigot finally tells Fowler that the American was innocent and was importing plastic for toys, not plastic explosives. The jaded correspondent who sneered at the American's naivete has thus been duped by the Communists, and though his collaboration in the murder falls short of grounds for arrest, he is left with a burden of guilt.

Discussion of the film has long focused on Mankiewicz's changes to the novel, rumors of which led Greene to protest while the film was still in production, and which infuriated him long afterward.[35] Although the film preserved the book's characters, most of its plot, and even some of its dialogue, it made a profound change in blaming the bombing on the Communists, whereas in the book General Thé carried it out with explosives the American had given him. (A real January 9, 1952, bombing was likely the work of a militia led by Trình Minh Thê, a former member of the Cao Dai sect in contact with Lansdale.)[36] This change, which has dominated many scholars' judgment of the film, raises the issue of evaluating films made from novels. Those who demand fidelity to the essence and spirit of a novel have understandably excoriated Mankiewicz's changes. There is a certain irony in those changes given the story's focus on an act of betrayal, and both the ingenuousness and the Anglo-American tension that lie within the story are strangely reproduced in accounts of its adaptation. Greene, of course, had enough experience to know that in selling the film rights, he was relinquishing control over the resultant work, and he was naive to sell a bitterly anti-American novel to an American film company—even one partly owned by the urbane, Europhile Mankiewicz.

Others prefer to judge a film as an independent work rather than by its fidelity to its source material. As with other Mankiewicz films such as *A Letter to Three Wives* (1949) and *All About Eve* (1950), this film's strengths lie in its sophisticated dialogue, even if Robert Krasker's shots of Saigon street life and the brief bombing scene occasionally enliven it. Mankiewicz explained that he found the book a "terribly distorted kind of cheap melodrama in which the American was the most idiotic kind of villain," and he called it "without humor, . . . bitter, and dominated by an absurd anti-Americanism."[37] What drew him to the novel was "how the emotions of a man can affect his political convictions," and despite the title, it was Fowler, not the American, who really interested him.[38] Fowler gets all the wittiest lines, and despite Mankiewicz's dismissal of Greene's anti-Americanism, he apparently shared some of Fowler's views.[39]

While mainly interested in Fowler's psychology, Mankiewicz apparently took suggestions from others regarding the politics. In April 1956, Arthur G. McDowell of the Council against Communist Aggression advised UA's Arthur Krim that "it would be a simple thing to simply reverse Mr. Graham Green's [sic] bias and turn it into a pro-American and pro-freedom plea," which is exactly what the film did.[40] Also in 1956, the PCA complained that Fowler, an adulterer and opium user, came off too well, and it did not want the film "open to the criticism that it represents unfairly a prominent institution such as the Foreign Service of the United States or any branch of it." Reassuring the PCA that he considered Fowler "as unsympathetic a character as I have ever chosen to portray," Mankiewicz insisted he would "make Pyle a thoroughly attractive young man" and would "remove him, of course, from any branch of the United States government service."[41] Lansdale also helped shape the film, as he encouraged Mankiewicz to blame the Communists for the bombing and exonerate Colonel Trình Minh Thê, who, he admitted to Mankiewicz, was likely the culprit.[42] Some have charged that Mankiewicz ended up making a propaganda film for the government, but the director, who served on the board of the International Rescue Committee, an organization favoring overseas involvement, needed little prodding to praise Americans such as Pyle.[43]

In the conflict between Fowler and the American, the latter quite transparently represents the idealism, optimism, and ignorance with which many Americans approached Vietnam; what Fowler stands for is less clear. He is annoyed at everything about Americans, including their language (saying "hi" instead of "hello"), their consumption of frozen and canned food, and their tendency to flaunt their wealth, and when the American responds to Fowler's request for a cigarette by offering him a whole pack, Fowler remarks, "I asked for one cigarette, not economic aid." Even if Mankiewicz sympathized with some of these anti-American cracks, he adds a comment by Vigot to critique Greene's clichéd, simplistic view of a country he never visited: "Strange country, America," observes the Frenchman. "What one thinks of it depends on which American one has in mind at the moment." More politically significant are Fowler's criticisms of the quest for a third force. When the American asks him rhetorically if it matters how the Vietnamese live, he replies, "If you mean does it matter whether they stay alive under French colonialism or Chinese communism, the answer is no." Using Phuong as an example of Vietnamese mentalities, Fowler admonishes the American, "Don't ask her to separate the concepts. Don't expect her to understand ideas. She's far too busy fighting for existence in a world far too full of people." He later adds that the Vietnamese "don't believe in anything either. They just want enough rice. . . . They *don't* want our white skins around, telling them what they want." Fowler, in short, offers a critique of American imperialism, if hardly a sophisticated one. He suggests, contradictorily, that the Vietnamese resent white people's presence but are indifferent to the struggle between French colonialism and Chinese communism, and his view that ideas are beyond the Vietnamese has condescending, colonialist overtones.

In the years since America's war in Vietnam, Greene's novel has struck many readers as a prescient and politically insightful warning, but Greene was hardly the anticolonialist some imagine, and Fowler, in both the novel and film, expresses more a plea for isolationism than a serious critique of colonialism.[44] In rewriting Greene's ire at Washington, Mankiewicz answered several statements Fowler made in the book with replies defending U.S. policy. In a voice-over, Fowler says of the American, "He moved like a hero in a Boys' Adventure story, wearing his heroism like a scout's badge, quite unaware of the absurdity and improbability of his adventure"; to that line from the book Mankiewicz adds: "But the absurd and the improbable, like the Boy Scouts and the Marines, win more often than we like to think."[45] And to Fowler's claim that the Vietnamese have no interest in ideologies and care only about their next meal, the American replies, "Isn't that a frightening assumption: that twenty-two million people are content only to stay alive" and that "what they don't know won't hurt them?" His vision of a third force—"twenty-two million Vietnamese deciding for themselves how they want to live"—sounds reasonable, even if the realization of that vision in South Vietnam fell pathetically short. Finally, Fowler's remark that the Vietnamese resent white people telling them what they want, also taken from the book, sets up the American's reply, which is not in the book: "You're telling them what they don't want, which is the same thing," and "the skins in Russia are still white, too."[46]

The romantic rivalry over Phuong also takes on a different meaning in the film. In critiquing the American's idealism, Greene had Fowler answer Pyle's statement that they both have Phuong's best interests at heart by saying, "I don't care about Phuong's interests. . . . I want *her*. . . . I'd rather ruin her and be with her than worry about her interests." In a pro-American film, this exchange takes on new meaning, contrasting selfish, cynical European colonialism with American sincerity. The competition between the middle-aged Fowler and the young American also recalls the familiar American contrast between a vigorous New World and a tired Old World. Yet such contrasts are misleading, for Fowler's sneering cynicism hardly reflects the equally idealistic and altruistic rhetoric of British and French colonialism in this era. In both the novel and the film, Phuong remains an inscrutable, passive character of little interest.

The film's inversion of the book's politics and its optimistic view of Americans' ability to reshape Asia through sentimental people-to-people contacts display the mentality that led to U.S. involvement in Vietnam. The film even premiered in Washington as a benefit for the American Friends of Vietnam, but while it pleased the Vietnam lobby, it did poorly at the American box office, failing to make *Variety*'s charts and disappearing quickly from theaters.[47] The poor results are understandable: it was a long, loquacious, black-and-white film that surely disappointed Audie Murphy fans; its setting and subject were obscure; and 1950s anticommunist films often flopped.

Scholars have argued that poor reviews also took their toll.[48] It is true that influential early reviews in *Variety*, the *Hollywood Reporter*, and the *New York Times* were negative, while *Time* gave it a mixed judgment, but the American critical response was better than some suggest. In a sample of thirty-one reviews, seventeen were positive (55 percent), seven negative, and seven mixed.[49] *Commonweal*'s Philip T. Hartung called it "an unusual and penetrating film," that was "beautifully photographed" and whose dialogue "is often brilliant." Philip Scheuer of the *Los Angeles Times* proclaimed it the best film since *Bridge on the River Kwai*, describing it as "brilliantly intellectual" and "a complex and disquieting drama of conflicting philosophies," while the *San Francisco Chronicle* praised it as "a superior and adult picture, sparkling with amusing and intelligent dialogue." "If this is the kind of picture there isn't room for any more," declared Arthur Knight of the *Saturday Review*, "the movies might just as well close up right now." Perhaps in using terms such as "philosophies," "literate," "intelligent," and "brilliantly intellectual," these reviews inadvertently harmed the film's box-office prospects.

Accounts of the poor reviews blame the changes Mankiewicz made to the novel, as well as Audie Murphy's poor acting.[50] The *Detroit News* did indeed pan Murphy's performance, and the *New York Post*'s Archer Winsten wrote that he seemed "amateurish in comparison" with Redgrave, but he also admitted that Murphy "has much in common with the character he is supposed to portray." Others echoed that point, and more papers praised than panned Murphy's performance.[51] Although *Time* and *Variety* objected to Mankiewicz's changes, few other American critics did. "Only rabid Graham Greene fans will object strenuously to the changes," predicted *Commonweal*, and the *Hartford Courant* applauded them, writing that "the book's slant was more debatable than the film's." Explaining that Mankiewicz was "not going to throw his picture down the American drain," the *New York Post* maintained that "his story is as possible and legitimate as Greene's," while the *St. Louis Post-Dispatch* speculated that although Greene must have "choked when he saw this picture," he should have expected changes to "this diatribe against Americans," and it called the changes "poetic justice." Even the *Nation*'s Robert Hatch, who called the plot switch "ridiculous" and a "travesty of the story," nonetheless wrote that Mankiewicz's alteration "doesn't bother me." In his words, "Greene's anti-Americanism is too simple," being based "more on a refined distaste for our wealth, pious vulgarity and sunny mediocrity than on the real shortcomings of our foreign relations." Hatch also questioned the book's politics: "Considering the various and dubious roles played out there by French, English, Chinese and Russians, it is absurd to suggest that some kind of gentlemanly accord would prevail if only the Yankees would go home."

The most common theme in the negative reviews was, instead, that the film was too talky and confusing. The *Detroit News* bemoaned "a lack of melodramatic action and an excess of philosophical debate," while the *Miami Herald* complained about "the very involved politics" in "one of the most loquacious movies of the year." *Variety* called it "a picture that stimulates thought," but its warning that "mass audiences will get restless" in this "overlong, overdialogued" film may explain why the film did not even play in some markets.

Most American critics welcomed the film's positive view of American efforts in Vietnam. To the *Christian Science Monitor*'s Ben Crisler, the film's point—that "so-called intellectuals who collaborate with a murderous system, such as communism, are unintelligent dupes" and "moral imbeciles"—was "well taken." He also praised the message that "the democratic idea . . . will inevitably triumph because it lives in the hearts of the people." So the film's sunny optimism about the righteousness and universal appeal of American ideals turns up in the reviews as well, and neither the film nor the reviews warned of a chasm between lofty ideals and the realities of an unfamiliar country. A few critics, however, seemed to get Greene's isolationist message rather than the film's plea for involvement; as *Cue* put it, "The internecine civil wars in Asia, it is suggested, are a private affair and outsiders mix in at their own peril," while the *Beverly Hills Citizen* felt that the film showed the foolishness of "Uncle Sam's sucker generosity in forcing economic aid upon self-respecting peoples who do not want charity."

Such statements indicate the challenge facing interventionist films such as *The Quiet American*, and the reviews also show how little Americans knew about Vietnam. Getting the opposing forces wrong, the *Hartford Courant* spoke of the "struggle between Communists and Nationalists" rather than between the Communists and French colonialists, and the *Los Angeles Times* described the third force as "something between democracy and Communism." The *New York Daily News* took refuge in vagueness, speaking simply of "the two belligerent factions in the country," and *Time* was similarly imprecise in referring to "the local right and left." Other mistakes included the *Houston Post*'s reference to Fowler's "Chinese mistress" (recalling *China Gate*'s conflation of the Chinese and Vietnamese), and the *Philadelphia Inquirer*'s allusion to "British colonial policy" in Indochina. The *Hollywood Reporter*, missing altogether the film's political inversion of the novel, predicted the film would "do better abroad than in the USA" because its "basic point of view is hostile to us." Also confused was the *Motion Picture Herald*, which wrote that "Redgrave is led to believe that Murphy is working for the Communists," and the usually astute Archer Winsten of the *New York Post* explained that the American is "playing footsie with the Indo-Chinese Communists." Frustration with the complexity of the plot—or perhaps of Vietnam itself—turned up even in positive reviews; *Cue*'s referred to "an intensely interesting if sometimes difficult exercise in plot comprehension" and the *Philadelphia Inquirer*'s spoke of "an exciting, frequently bewildering drama." For the *Los Angeles Examiner*'s Ruth Waterbury, the film was "almost impossible to understand," and Bosley Crowther of the *New York Times* wrongly charged that Mankiewicz "permits it to go vague as to what finally occurs off screen" and "just leaves you wondering at the end." If Americans needed things spelled out more simply, it is partly because they knew so little about Vietnam. The price of their eventual education would be steep indeed.

Attributing negative reviews to Mankiewicz's changes applies better to Britain. After the *London Times* ran a partially inaccurate story about the upcoming film—claiming, for example, that it would show "the triumphant emergence of the democratic forces" and the "downfall of the British and French imperialists"—Michael Redgrave complained in a letter to the *Times* that its report was based on gossip and that people should issue their judgments "when the film is completed and released, which is after all the normal time for such assessment."[52] Whether or not the adverse advance publicity influenced critics, British critical reaction was unfavorable; of twenty-two reviews examined, five were positive (23 percent), eleven negative, and six mixed.[53] The film did earn some strong praise; one trade paper, the *Daily Cinema*, found it "notably intelligent and literate without ever getting so high-flown that ordinary audiences will not be able to follow it," and the *Evening Standard*, despite noting the changes to the novel, called it "an exciting, intelligent, and very well-acted film." The *Sunday Express*'s Derek Monsey described it as "absorbingly thrilling" and "intelligent film-making: articulate, dramatic and adult," though in a postscript written after someone apparently informed him of the changes, he added that it was "also totally dishonest."

Most British critics faulted the film's infidelity to Greene's novel. For Molly Plowright of the *Glasgow Herald*, "where the film is objectionable—and I do not think that too strong a word—is in changing the whole implication of the story," and both the *Daily Herald* and the *Tribune* saw the film "whitewashing" the American. The *New Statesman*'s William Whitebait charged that it "exceeds all bounds of re-shaping," calling it "malpractice," and Dilys Powell of the *Sunday Times* wrote that "though I deplore the habit of expecting a film to be a replica of a book or a play, I look for adaptation, not assassination." In her view, "to turn Graham Greene's acid study of a dangerous meddler in Indo-Chinese politics into a tribute to a saintly all-American boy is going too far." The reviews also suggest wounded nationalism. Campbell Dixon of the *Daily Telegraph* was upset that "the

Englishman seems rather a symbol of our age's cynicism, self-pity and corruption," while Monsey's postscript complained that Mankiewicz chose "to show the Briton as a sneering, ludicrously jealous inferior fool loaded with anti-American sentiment" in "one of the most expert pieces of anti-British propaganda I have ever seen." Similarly, the *Daily Mail* grumbled that the film takes "a passing swipe at the impotent, intellectually snobbish, colonially constipated English" and offers "a stirring tribute to the American way and purpose." This British resentment of an American film turning a British novel from anti-American to pro-American is certainly understandable, especially given Hollywood's dominance of Britain's film industry and cultural life (as well as America's recent displacement of Britain in world politics), but missing from these objections was any real discussion of colonialism. What truly rankled, then, was not what Western colonialism had done to Vietnam; it was what an American film had done to a British novel.

In France, the film sold a mere 316,446 tickets.[54] Of twenty-one reviews examined, seven were positive (33 percent), eleven negative, and three mixed, a marginally better result than in Britain.[55] Writing in *Cahiers du Cinéma*, Eric Rohmer, whose own films would rival this one in verbosity, admired the quality of the dialogue and defended the amount of it on the grounds that these characters happened to be talkative. Rohmer also felt that Mankiewicz had improved on Greene's treatment of the characters' relationships and psychology, and he called it "one of the few great *political* films that the history of cinema has known." *Radio Cinéma Télévision* applauded "the richness of the dialogue and its constant inventiveness," while *Cinéma 58* found it "a work of unparalleled subtlety" but wondered, "Will Mankiewicz pay for being too intelligent?" *Libération* called it "a success" that "benefits from an extraordinary atmosphere" while regretting that "such a rich and intelligent film has been given a poor, illogical ending by some sort of censorship."

Greene had far fewer defenders in France than in Britain, and many French critics found the novel excessively anti-American. *Carrefour* applauded the changes made to a novel marked by "a facile, rather crude, anti-Americanism," and *Radio Cinéma Télévision* sympathized with American disdain for the book, given its "rather puerile oversimplification" and its "totally un-nuanced contrast between the laudable, phlegmatic, and skeptical Englishman and the ridiculous, criminal, naive self-assurance of the American." *Le Monde*'s Henri Pierre called the novel's anti-Americanism "rather systematic, unjust, and exasperating," even if the film erred in the other direction, ending up "in the style and spirit of [John] Foster Dulles." As in Britain, several critics spoke of "betrayal" in the changes to the novel, and *Le Monde*'s Pierre wrote that "we deplore them all the more because the film is interesting, well directed, and remarkably acted." More French than British critics objected to the film's defense of American policy, including *France Observateur*, which referred to "the Americans' stupid intrigues" in Vietnam, and *L'Express*, which applauded Greene's condemnation of Americans who "take themselves for good little soldiers of God fighting the communist devil." *L'Express* also complained that "the American insists on saving humanity, which had not asked him to," and it agreed with Fowler that "asking a colonized people to fight communism in the name of liberty" is both "highly comical" and "tragic." Anticolonialism also appeared in *Le Canard Enchaîné*'s reference to "that murderous and imbecilic war that we waged for seven years," and in *L'Humanité*'s allusion to "the war that a people waged for their independence," though that paper noted that Greene was hardly an anticolonialist and "had no sympathies for the Vietminh."

The film's rapid exit from theaters in all three countries seems to support Greene's prediction that his book would outlive the film.[56] In recent years, scholars have agreed with Greene, noting the film's obscurity and the lack of a VHS release, but films can have peculiar life cycles.[57] In this case, a 2002 remake, followed by MGM's 2005 DVD release of the 1958 film—in addition to the ever-growing body of writing about it—suggest that it is still too soon to judge Greene's prediction. Historical interest in America's war in Vietnam largely accounts for this revived interest, and no other American film of that era offers such a valuable glimpse of American attitudes and perceptions of Vietnam on the eve of the country's ill-fated intervention.

America's often-professed opposition to colonialism appears only rarely in Hollywood's postwar films about Asia. *Teahouse of the August Moon* most directly questions the wisdom of one society imposing its ways on another, but coercive acculturation is only one aspect of colonialism, and the film does little to question other aspects such as exploitation. Moreover, while its use of humor allowed it more leeway to critique American policy, that humor probably also blunted the force of its arguments. The film's Okinawans are simply too good-natured to convey the angry resentment of America's presence that had by then surfaced in Japan.

American opposition to European colonialism appears in *The Quiet American*, but the American never explains why he opposes French colonialism, and the film's positive image of the French Inspector—unlike its depiction of the scheming Communists—gives no reason to resent France's presence. Aside from a few lines supporting the concept of self-rule, the film does little to dramatize anticolonialist grievances and limits its critique of French rule to the strategic point that the French are failing to protect the country from communism. *The Mark of the Hawk*'s flashback in China gives only a single hint of contrition about Western imperialism in the minister's unexplained reference to "mistakes we made in China." A mild rebuke of colonial snobbery appears in *Love Is a Many-Splendored Thing*, in which Mrs. Palmer-Jones voices the wishes of the British of Hong Kong to retain their cheap servants and racial purity. Overall, the criticism of colonialism seen in 1950s American films about British and French colonies (including *Sirocco, Vera Cruz, Something of Value*, and *Shake Hands with the Devil*) was rarely seen when American filmmakers examined their own country's actions in Asia.

Although pro-Indian westerns and films denouncing bigotry in America showed that American films could be self-critical, when Hollywood depicted U.S. actions in Asia, anticommunism consistently trumped anticolonialism—as it did in American policy. In this case, the HUAC investigations and the blacklist undoubtedly constrained filmmakers, and partisan accusations about Truman's "loss of China" also made the topic too sensitive for Hollywood's tastes. This political atmosphere discouraged serious exploration of the nationalist and anticolonialist anger that helped communism grow. Filmmakers were naturally more interested in making money and entertaining audiences than in educating them, but these films missed an opportunity to enlighten Americans in even small ways about the grievances and motives of the people they were fighting. Of course filmmakers were not foreign-policy experts, and they often knew little more than their audiences did about Asian history and politics. Nevertheless, as policymakers understood, backing European colonialists against communists in places such as Indochina meant ceding the nationalist high-ground to insurgents. These films thus illustrate certain fatal flaws in American views of Asia in this period.

Films help shape as well as reflect popular outlooks, and several of these films in effect encouraged Americans and others to support the country's policies in Asia. The films about China all dealt with captivity in the People's Republic, and although they painted a demoralizing picture of the power and oppressiveness of the new regime, they boosted morale somewhat by showing ordinary Chinese "voting with their feet" (*Blood Alley, Love Is a Many-Splendored Thing*), resisting Communist rule (*The Shanghai Story, The Mark of the Hawk*), or helping Westerners escape (*Soldier of Fortune*). Several films also urged American involvement in Asia, including *Huk!*, which showed the apathetic Greg Dickson resolving to stay on and fight the rebels, while employing and protecting his workers. The film's image of the pro-American Philippine military also encouraged support for U.S. aid to the Philippines. *The Quiet American* similarly urged Americans to take an interest in Vietnam and to support America's efforts there, while *Jump into Hell* and *China Gate* lauded past U.S. support for the French and urged America to fill the void. *Tokyo Joe*'s warnings about resurgent Japanese militarism underlined the importance of the American occupation, while implying that the tasks of reconstruction and crime-fighting also required America's presence.

Why many of these films did poorly at the box office can only be a matter for speculation.[58] While some were low-budget films facing long odds, those with larger budgets and big stars, such as *Blood Alley* and *The Quiet American*, fit the pattern of overtly anticommunist films that flopped in 1950s America. Nor did Europeans welcome such fare, and the British and French critics certainly showed little love for patriotic American films. American critics rarely objected to these films' colonialist attitudes (whereas French critics often did), and their reviews suggest little American sensitivity to perceptions of U.S. imperialism in Asia.

As groups such as the American Friends of Vietnam illustrate, the friendship and the sentimental personal bonds these films highlighted had ulterior motives. The films mostly ignored historical and political contexts, while emphasizing, as films generally do, personal stories and relationships. While Americans adopting Asian children turned up frequently, no film showed Asians adopting white children, and that double standard indicates the colonialist overtones of these parental relations. East-West emotional bonds could take the form of friendships between individuals, as in *Tokyo Joe*, or between lone whites and whole villages of Asians. Examples of the latter include the affection that develops in *Blood Alley* between Tom Wilder and the villagers he guides to freedom; the fondness between Fisby and the people of Tobiki in *Teahouse of the August Moon*; Dickson's eventual bonding with his laborers at the end of *Huk!*; and the fondness of various Chinese characters toward Hank Lee in *Soldier of Fortune*. To American viewers tired of news images of angry foreigners waving "Yankee Go Home" signs, these fantasies must have boosted morale, even if they did little to explain that troubling anger at America. And by pointing to the emotional gratification available to Americans who shouldered the white man's burden in Asia, these films also functioned to encourage involvement, to build support for U.S. policies in Asia, and to dismiss any notion that those policies constituted imperialism.

PART THREE

DANGEROUS LIAISONS

Interracial Couples in Films

In the late 1940s and 1950s, movies about miscegenation in the colonies or the metropole were so numerous that they indicated a kind of cultural obsession. Miscegenation, the term used by Hollywood's Production Code Administration, has faintly negative connotations; its root, however, is not *mis-*, but rather *misce-*, from the Latin *miscere* (to mix), and the suffix derives from *genus*, in this case meaning race.[1] So the term simply means race mixing, a practice about which attitudes have changed enormously in recent years. Postwar films about miscegenation between colonizer and colonized dealt with many kinds of relationships, including rape, seduction, prostitution, casual sex, cohabitation, platonic romance, and marriage, either temporary (common in colonies) or permanent. Some films examined miscegenation through mixed-race characters, while others featured potential or suggested relationships that failed to develop because of taboos against crossing color lines. Including all of these variants, at least one hundred American, British, and French films released from 1946 to 1959 dealt with miscegenation in some way (see appendix B). Some of these films used cross-racial relationships and mixed-race characters to make a point; others seem merely to have followed a trend in empire films and had no clear point, even if they still revealed assumptions and mentalities.

One common reading of interracial relationships in empire films takes them as metaphors for relations between colonizing and colonized nations, and if lovers represent nations, then assumptions of male dominance help explain why most of these films paired white men with women of color.[2] While one can certainly read films this way, it is hard to show that contemporaries did, or that filmmakers intended that. Even if individuals do not represent nations, tales of interracial couples still explore the nature of colonial relations in concrete terms.[3] Films about colonial miscegenation evoke all the aspects of this study's definition of colonialism: they highlight a significant aspect of occupation; they may either support or question racial discrimination and the colonizer's insistence upon difference; they raise the topic of exploitation, given the inherent inequalities of the colonial situation; and they highlight interracial relationships' ability to promote acculturation—potentially in both directions.

Miscegenation in the Metropole

Although colonizers might view interracial relationships differently at home and in the colonies, they inevitably brought with them attitudes learned at home, and especially for Americans, those attitudes varied by ethnicity. Whites' tolerance toward miscegenation with American Indians, for example, certainly exceeded acceptance of black-white miscegenation.[4] That tolerance rested in part on beliefs that mixed-race offspring were heartier and hopes that miscegenation would gradually solve racial tensions.[5] Given how greatly whites outnumbered Indians and how fully they controlled the continent by the late nineteenth century, many whites also felt safe enough to accept a bit of red-white miscegenation and even to take pride in Indian ancestors. Black-white miscegenation was quite another matter, and in their informal rankings of other races, whites had long placed blacks at the bottom. In the postwar United States, racism remained strongest toward blacks, and a 1958 opinion poll found 96 percent of whites opposing black-white marriages.[6]

In explaining variations by ethnicity, one cannot ignore visual racism and its simple reasoning that if dark is bad, darker is worse—reflecting historical Western associations between black and evil—but the "one-drop rule," by which Americans classified people with any African ancestry at all as black, calls for additional explanations.[7] In the United States, blacks, the largest racial minority, were numerous enough in some areas for whites to feel threatened, while in areas where Indians were a tiny fraction of the population, Indian-hating was weaker than in frontier regions.[8] Attitudes varied depending on gender as well, as seen in the familiar question, "Would you want your daughter to marry one?"

One manifestation of white hostility toward miscegenation in the United States was legislation against interracial marriage, with twenty-nine states still outlawing it in 1959.[9] Far fewer states outlawed interracial sex, a discrepancy that suggests, among other things, concerns about property passing from whites to people of color.[10] Alongside laws against miscegenation stood other penalties, including police harassment, dismissal from employment, the disowning of children, and diagnosis of it as a symptom of mental illness.[11] Yet if whites abhorred miscegenation because they really feared loss of material privilege, they also opposed desegregation and racial equality because they feared miscegenation would follow—a central anxiety in *The Birth of a Nation* (1915). The two fears thus coexisted in a circular, semirational outlook. World War II, decolonization, and the Cold War put increasing pressure on racism in the United States, and miscegenation became the subject of intensive postwar discussion.[12]

British attitudes look more lenient, and a 1943 poll found that only one in seven Britons stated opposition to interracial marriage.[13] The racial climate in Britain seemed far better to African Americans, including Paul Robeson, who moved there in the 1920s; a scene in the British film *Song of Freedom* (1936), starring Robeson, reflects that point by showing whites and blacks living harmoniously in a working-class neighborhood of London.[14] Many white Britons associated racism with the United States, South Africa, and their own colonies, and in World War II, British authorities enforced color bars and discouraged interracial couples mainly to placate Americans.[15] But Britain had its own history of racism, especially directed at black sailors in British ports, and one cause of race riots in Liverpool and Cardiff in 1919 was white hostility toward black men dating white women.[16] Cardiff's Chief Constable proposed a ban on interracial sex in 1927, and though none was enacted, the ensuing 1930 Fletcher Report expressed anxieties about miscegenation and mixed-race children.[17] In general, the critical-mass argument applies well to Britain, as racial tensions rose with the arrival of black GIs in World War II and again with growing immigration from the colonies in the late 1940s and 1950s. Amid growing white consciousness and concern over miscegenation, a survey from 1954—still early in the postwar wave of immigration—suggested that one-third of Britons were racially tolerant, one-third mildly prejudiced, and one-third extremely prejudiced.[18] Continuing immigration fueled race riots in 1958, and in 1962 Parliament's Commonwealth Immigrants Act restricted nonwhite immigration.[19] In short, the more Britain came to resemble America in its racial composition, the more racial attitudes converged.

France seemed even more tolerant of interracial couples, and African American soldiers and civilians in Paris during and after World War I remarked on the better racial atmosphere.[20] Yet attitudes in the nightclubs of Jazz Age Paris probably differed significantly from those in the rest of France, and even in Paris the motives for crossing color lines included exotic desires and fantasies.[21] French authorities in World War I sought to prevent contact between white women and black troops from the colonies, and a French magazine's 1920 reader survey about marrying a man of color found 1,060 out of 2,040 respondents saying they would not do so, in part because they feared the mistreatment of mixed-race children; even the positive responses reflected racial prejudices, such as women stating that "their physical repugnance at black people would soon wear off once they became used to them."[22] Interwar French empire films such as *Princesse Tam-Tam* treated *métissage* quite negatively, and Muslims in France often faced racism and segregation.[23] The worsening of the problem amid growing immigration from the colonies after World War II further supports the critical-mass concept.

Miscegenation in the Colonies

As historians have paid increasing attention to colonial sexuality, they have often noted colonial officials' opposition to miscegenation.[24] These policies reflected in part the Puritanism and racism colonizers brought with them, and although attitudes toward sex changed throughout the twentieth century, that evolution took time.[25] Given entrenched Western perceptions of the tropics as a sexual playground, the regulation of sexuality that existed at home seemed even more necessary to colonial officials.[26] Colonial theorists such as Benjamin Kidd expressed concerns about Europeans becoming morally corrupted in the tropics; the white man living there, he wrote in 1898, does not "tend so much to raise the level of the races amongst whom he has made his unnatural home, as he tends himself to sink slowly to the level around him."[27] Moral corruption included giving in to sexual temptation, which caused anxieties because of beliefs that mixed-race children would, like mules, prove infertile or would inherit the weaker traits of each parent.[28] Even if mixed-race offspring were neither inferior nor infertile, their mere existence blurred the boundary between colonizer and colonized, and in the United States, where whites faced the consequences of having brought colonized Africans to the metropole, the need to maintain difference helps explain the one-drop rule.[29] Given that colonialism usually required the few to rule the many, maintaining the ruler's prestige and image of superiority demanded social distance, which miscegenation threatened.

Complicating this picture of white opposition to colonial miscegenation, however, were voices openly defending it. To some extent, the defenders made a virtue of necessity, as it was simply unrealistic to stop something as widespread as sex between colonizer and colonized, and some whites working in the colonies saw sexual opportunities as compensation for living abroad.[30] Some officials considered interracial unions a necessary evil, preferable to homosexuality or prostitution, while some white men preferred native or mixed-race women, viewing them as more uninhibited, beautiful, or exotic.[31] In his 1890 poem "Mandalay," Rudyard Kipling captured this European sexual fascination with the exotic, contrasting "beefy face an' grubby" English girls with "a Burma girl" he calls "a neater, sweeter maiden in a cleaner, greener land" where "there aren't no Ten Commandments."[32] On more pragmatic grounds, some found concubinage useful to colonization. Dr. Louis Barot, author of a 1902 guide for Frenchmen bound for the colonies, recommended "a temporary union with a well-chosen native woman" because it was healthier than prostitution and would help them learn the local language and customs and form alliances with local chiefs.[33] Officials of the British East India Company also valued such relationships as a means of gathering knowledge of India and of helping build up the company's army.[34] Concerns about Europeans falling ill in the tropics led officials of the Dutch East India Company to place their hopes in mixed-race children, who would be better suited to the tropics but still reliably Dutch.[35] And even if literary defenses of interracial love amounted to rhetorical justification for Western rule, writers such as Pierre Loti added their voices to the defense of miscegenation.[36]

Given the fundamental inequalities of the colonial situation, there is good reason to consider all interracial sex in colonies inherently exploitative. Some settings were so coercive—slavery, above all—that all sex amounted to exploitation, but elsewhere colonized women could refuse unwanted overtures, and unless one denies all possibility of agency to the colonized, one must consider the possibility that individuals chose to enter into relationships for a combination of strategic and romantic reasons.[37] Insofar as discrimination limited opportunities for the colonized, the notion of consensus remains deeply problematic, but within that unequal system women could indeed improve their personal situation through liaisons with colonizers. Of course, class and gender inequalities existed in the metropole as well, and women using sex to rise socially—a favorite topic in classical-era Hollywood—was hardly limited to the colonies. As for miscegenation's effects, interracial relationships—often the only significant personal contact colonizers had with the colonized—could alter perceptions and humanize colonial subjects, even softening attitudes and behavior.[38] Indeed fears of such outcomes were a major reason why colonial officials sought to prevent miscegenation. Colonial miscegenation, in short, took many forms and generated diverse reactions and consequences.

Film and Colonial Miscegenation

Historically, cinematic depictions of colonial miscegenation often mirrored official attitudes and policies. Although relationships between governments and film industries varied over time and by country, governments' concerns about films' impact on overseas interests sometimes brought pressures on filmmakers, whose desire to shoot on location, secure financing, or avoid censorship compelled cooperation. Hollywood's desire to avoid offending viewers and clashing with censors in crucial markets such as Britain and France also led filmmakers to treat colonial topics delicately.[39] Government censors and colonial administrations did not always need to pressure filmmakers, whose own racist and colonialist attitudes often made them willing collaborators, and who fashioned mostly cautionary tales about interracial sex and romance. Empire films' tendency to deal in stark opposites of heroism and villainy made the figure of the native rapist irresistible, catering to white audiences' racial fears and anxieties.[40] Although horror tales about rape might inadvertently discourage white settlement, they also exhorted whites to control dangerous populations of color and to restrict nonwhite immigration to the metropole.

The unhappy endings in cautionary tales usually had the woman of color come to ruin: in *Bird of Paradise* (1932), Luana (Dolores del Rio) leaps to her death in a volcano, while in *Lady of the Tropics* (1939), Manon (Hedy Lamarr) shoots herself. A common variant had the woman sacrifice herself to save her white lover, as in tales of Pocahontas and Madame Butterfly.[41] Yet in *La Bandera* (1935) it was a white man (Jean Gabin) who died, while in *The Bitter Tea of General Yen* (1933), a man of color died. Even when whites suffered only the sadness of a failed romance, these films about ill-fated couples sent a clear "East is East" message. The pre-code *Cimarron* (1930) was a rare film in which an interracial relationship ended well.

Films made before 1946 also dealt with interracial couples through their mixed-race offspring, and these characters made it less ridiculous to cast white actors as people of color. Here, too, cautionary tales prevailed, as most mixed-race characters were either tragic or villainous figures whose very existence defied taboos.[42] The mulatto film villain goes back at least to Silas Lynch in *The Birth of a Nation*, often illustrating the theory of hybrid degeneracy.[43] In *Call Her Savage* (1932) and *Lady of the Tropics*, mixed-race women struggled to live in white society and to tame the savage half of their nature. Tragic characters such as Manon in *Lady of the Tropics* and Peola in *Imitation of Life* (1934) were caught between two worlds, unsatisfied to live among people of color and unwelcome among whites.

Calls for censorship affected Hollywood's treatment of miscegenation even before enforcement of the Production Code began in 1934, as a June 1927 resolution of the Motion Picture Producers and Distributors of America had added miscegenation to an earlier Hays Office list of taboo subjects.[44] The code, in force until 1968, certainly affected films on miscegenation, but it has generated misunderstandings. For one thing, attention to the Production Code Administration often overlooks state and local censors, who could ban films in specific markets or compel costly edits. It was the censors' power, along with threats of federal government intervention and a boycott by the Legion of Decency, that persuaded the studios to create the PCA. As zealous as PCA head Joseph Breen was for his conservative, Catholic vision of decency, his power ultimately derived from forces in society, and the studios created the PCA as a breakwater to shield themselves from external groups.[45] Misunderstandings also concern the code's operation; it did not, for example, ban depictions of either rape or adultery, demanding only that those subjects be treated carefully and not shown explicitly, humorously, or positively.[46] The absence of depictions of plantation owners raping their slaves was not a matter of the PCA blocking the studios from filming that topic, for the studios did not wish to touch it in the first place, and that cinematic silence long predated the code's adoption. The code's treatment of miscegenation has also fueled misunderstandings; whereas scholars and critics have often claimed it applied to all images of miscegenation, it only banned black-white miscegenation.[47] Films could even explore black-white miscegenation indirectly through mixed-race characters such as Peola in *Imitation of Life*. With mixed-race characters, films could cast white actors, and audiences were more tolerant of onscreen physical affection when both actors were white.[48] In short, it is mistaken to argue that the code banned all depictions of miscegenation into the 1950s, and even its ban on black-white miscegenation was occasionally evaded.[49]

As for the PCA's operation, its comments on scripts were starting points for negotiation, not diktats, and the negotiations went on through multiple script revisions. In responding to a 1950 PCA report on a planned remake of *Bird of Paradise*, Darryl F. Zanuck accepted some of the PCA's proposed changes but told his colleagues that the PCA "can go to hell" about another and that "the rest of the [PCA] note seems pure nonsense."[50] In general, enforcement slackened over time, and by the 1950s, some films played without a PCA seal of approval while others carried the seal despite containing material the PCA disliked.[51] In 1955, Breen's successor Geoffrey Shurlock explained that brutality was the PCA's main concern, though nudity was certainly another. Operating within a social and cultural environment, the PCA showed increasing tolerance of films about miscegenation in the postwar years, culminating in a 1956 revision of the code that removed the miscegenation clause altogether.[52]

In Britain, France, and the United States, cinematic treatments of miscegenation in the 1940s and 1950s took place amid growing public support for racial justice and harmony. France's wartime experiences with Vichy anti-Semitism and the Holocaust, followed by the triumph of the Resistance and the Left in 1944, energized antiracist forces, and in all three countries, pressure to live up to principles proclaimed during the war and to reward people of color for wartime contributions also fueled this trend. The desire to seem racially enlightened grew with pressures for decolonization and with the Cold War struggle for the allegiance of third-world peoples. Showing uncharacteristic courage, Hollywood took on anti-Semitism in Warner Bros.' *Crossfire* (1947) and Fox's *Gentleman's Agreement* (1947).[53] Emboldened by their success at the box office and by President Truman's reelection in 1948, Hollywood proceeded to explore prejudice toward blacks and black-white miscegenation in several late-1940s films (see chapter 9).[54]

The proliferation of miscegenation films had several possible motives, in addition to cashing in on a demonstrably profitable trend. For those alarmed at growing racial equality, the need for cautionary tales to help police color lines probably seemed more urgent than ever. Yet a growing number of filmmakers, critics, and viewers sincerely opposed racism, and even staunch colonialists might concede that racially liberal images could help empire survive. The Cold War had complex effects on racial-themed films, for while liberal images could burnish the West's image in the third world, the State Department feared that exposing racism in the United States provided fodder for communist propaganda.[55] These were complex times, in short, and the meanings, functions, and reception of films about miscegenation in these years require careful analysis. The following chapters inquire what points those films made and how they were received. Although old conventions persisted, standard situations could take on new meanings in new times. Were films about rapists of color still common? Did films continue to show interracial relationships ending badly? If so, what point did the outcomes make? Did films challenge the taboo on romance between white women and men of color? How did films depict mixed-race characters? Did British and French filmmakers share Hollywood's interest in these subjects? What was the impact of the 1956 Production Code revision that removed the ban on depicting black-white miscegenation? Were filmmakers ahead of or behind society on these issues, or did their outlooks seem to mirror social attitudes? What do the films and their reception suggest about attitudes toward colonialism and domestic race relations?

Treatments of Rape

Although colonialism complicates distinctions between consensual and coercive sex across color lines, it remains worthwhile to try to distinguish between cinematic depictions of rape and consensual relations. Films make very different points depending on the question of consensus, and they typically use rape to contrast extremes of villainy and innocence.

Old devices still appeared after World War II. DeMille's *Unconquered* emphasized the danger Indians posed to white women by having characters refer to it with horror three times, and although Abby is not actually raped, Chris Holden must rescue her from Indians who have tied her to a stake. Three more westerns—*The Charge at Feather River*, *The Searchers*, and *Trooper Hook* (1957)—also dealt with the rape of white women captured by Indians, though the latter film is ambiguous about how coercive the sex was between Cora (Barbara Stanwyck) and Nanchez (Rodolfo Acosta). While several films hinted at Indians raping white women, it is striking that of the fifty-one dramas about Indians on *Variety*'s charts in these years, only four raised the subject directly.[56] Films set in Asia also evoked the yellow peril to white womanhood, including *The Shanghai Story*, in which Major Ling assaults a married white woman; *Blood Alley*, in which Captain Wilder saves Cathy Grainger from a rape attempt; and *Five Gates to Hell* (1959), a yellow-peril captivity tale of white and Asian nurses and missionaries becoming sex slaves of a xenophobic Vietnamese warlord. Aside from these anticommunist films, depictions of rape by Asian men were rare after 1945. In films set in South Asia, the South Pacific, and Africa, men of color raping white women was quite rare, as it was in postwar films about African Americans.

At the same time, films were beginning to break the silence about white men raping women of color. David O. Selznick's *Duel in the Sun* (1946), discussed in chapter 7, features a predatory white man, Lewt McCanles (Gregory Peck), forcing himself on the semi-willing half-Indian Pearl Chavez (Jennifer Jones). *The Last Hunt* implies that the villain, Charlie Gilson (Robert Taylor), has his way with his very unwilling Indian captive (Debra Paget). No such ambiguities appear in *Last Train from Gun Hill* (1959), which opens with horrifying images of white men raping and murdering the Indian wife of Marshal Matt Morgan (Kirk Douglas). The white rapist also appears in *Bhowani Junction*, in which Victoria (Ava Gardner) fends off a rape attempt by the racist Lieutenant McDaniel (Lionel Jeffries). Films even began to break the cinematic taboo on depicting white men raping African American women, beginning in 1949 with Darryl F. Zanuck and Elia Kazan's *Pinky* and continuing in *Band of Angels* (1957) and *Tamango* (1958), a French production (see chapter 9). In this period, the white man threatening or raping women of color became as common as the older image of the rapist of color (see appendix B), indicating a significant shift in cinematic practice.

CHAPTER SEVEN

Miscegenation in Westerns

Westerns featuring miscegenation had been relatively common from the silent era through the 1930s, and the tradition persisted after World War II. John Ford's Wyatt Earp yarn, *My Darling Clementine* (1946), included a troubled romance between Doc Holliday (Victor Mature) and Chihuahua (Linda Darnell), a floozy who seems to be part Apache and part Mexican. Chihuahua's role as the racial other follows empire-film traditions, as her fiery temper, her complicity with shady gamblers, and her sexual infidelities contrast with the virtues of the white, civilized easterner, Clementine (Cathy Downs), who wants to found a school in Tombstone. The love triangle involving Doc and the two women recalls *Pepe le Moko* (1937), in which a white fugitive from civilization must choose between a proper white woman and a dark-skinned embodiment of the sordid world into which he has descended. But whereas Pepe ultimately rejects his Gypsy girlfriend and the multiethnic Casbah for the upper-class Parisian Gaby and the impossible dream of returning to Paris, Doc, who has inexplicably left a respectable life back home, rejects Clementine for a life of drinking, gambling, and interracial sex with Chihuahua.[1]

Miscegenation figured even more prominently in *Duel in the Sun* (1946). King Vidor received the director's credit despite quitting late in production after clashing with producer David O. Selznick, and at least five others helped direct.[2] *Duel* was Selznick's film, as he produced it in his typically overbearing fashion and helped write the screenplay from a novel by Niven Busch.[3] An odd blend of epic, psychological western, melodrama, romantic tragedy, grand opera, and soap opera, this Technicolor blockbuster tells the story of the "half-breed" Pearl Chavez. Playing Pearl was Selznick's future wife, Jennifer Jones, in dark makeup, and making a sharp departure from her role as a saint in *The Song of Bernadette* (1943). Chavez is the daughter of the feckless aristocrat Scott Chavez (Herbert Marshall) and his wild Indian wife (Tilly Losch), who dances lewdly for men in a raucous cantina and cheats on her husband; in the opening, a fed-up Scott murders his wayward wife and her lover. Just before his hanging, Scott advises Pearl to become a lady, and he sends her to live with old flame and distant cousin Laura Belle (Lillian Gish) and her husband, Texas Senator Jackson McCanles (Lionel Barrymore). At the million-acre McCanles ranch, Laura Belle welcomes Pearl, but the Indian-hating Senator sneers at the dark-skinned girl.

The rest of the story revolves around Pearl's tortured relationship with the two grown McCanles sons, Jesse (Joseph Cotten), an upstanding lawyer who treats her decently, and Lewt (Gregory Peck), a sexual predator who scoffs at his brother's moral decency and immediately pursues her. Pearl, young, beautiful, and insecure, tells Laura Belle, "I want to be a good girl" and "I want to be like you," but Lewt's animal magnetism and sexual aggressiveness awaken the "savage" side she inherited from her mother. Aware of Pearl's struggles, Laura Belle summons a self-appointed preacher, "the Sinkiller" (Walter Huston), who warns the girl she was "built by the devil to drive men crazy." Sure enough, Lewt enters her room at night and essentially rapes her, and though fingernail scratches on his cheek suggest attempted resistance, she gives in to Lewt and her own savage passions. After finding Lewt and Pearl together, a disgusted Jesse tells Pearl he loved her but is finished with her, and she resigns herself to Lewt, imagining he will marry her. After Jesse's falling out with his tyrannical father over a railroad the government wishes to build through the ranch, the good son departs, and Pearl turns to a new suitor, the foreman Sam Pierce (Charles Bickford), whom the jealous Lewt guns down. Pearl's only remaining protector is the slowly dying Laura Belle, and when she dies, the film proceeds to its notorious climax, in which Lewt and Pearl's love-hate relationship culminates in their fatally shooting each other.

Discerning the film's point about race and miscegenation is difficult in part because, unlike many contemporary films on that topic, this was not a message picture. While a few observers take the film seriously as fine art, most view it as kitsch deserving of its nickname, "Lust in the Dust."[4] With a budget well over $5 million, it was extraordinarily expensive cheapness, a glossy forerunner of later "exploitation" films and lurid television melodramas such as Dallas.[5] Complicating the reading of the film are the concessions made to placate the head of the Production Code Administration, Joseph Breen, who later regretted approving the film.[6] Whereas in the novel Pearl kills Lewt in self-defense and goes off to marry Jesse—a more optimistic view of interracial relationships—Selznick changed the ending both for dramatic reasons and because he knew the code would not allow Pearl to get away with murder. Scholars disagree over the film's jumbled politics, the key to which is the issue of civilization versus savagery.[7]

The traditional dichotomy in westerns, in which whites represent civilization against Indian savagery, fits *Duel* imperfectly. The film takes a conservative line in that Pearl's Indian blood makes her hard to civilize, and it rejects the wartime trend toward kinder depictions of American Indians.[8] It also perpetuates the tragic-mulatto tradition, as Pearl's savage side makes her a misfit in white society. The film's racial conservatism also appears in the McCanleses' witless African American servant Vashti (Butterfly McQueen), a reprisal of McQueen's role in Selznick's *Gone with the Wind* that looks even more retrograde after the racial progress of the war years.[9] Laura Belle's frustration with Vashti—"I'll never be able to train her properly," she complains—reinforces the implication that nonwhites simply cannot be civilized. In stark contrast stand decent whites, most notably Laura Belle and Jesse, as well as Jesse's kind wife, Helen, and Pearl's suitor, Sam Pierce. The film's embrace of Western civilization also emerges in the railroad subplot, which trumpets the progress whites are bringing to the West.

Complicating the picture are some very uncivilized whites, principally the villainous Lewt and his equally dislikable father, an opponent of progress, as well as Lewt's henchman, Sid, and the boisterous men in the wild cantina. Uncivilized whites are a staple of westerns, while films about Indians often contrast good whites who wish to protect and civilize them with villainous whites who wish to murder them or sell them whisky and guns. *Duel*'s main white villain, Lewt, scoffs at morality, shoots unarmed men, and derails trains, and his corrupting effects on Pearl bring to mind South Seas films about greedy, lecherous whites spoiling paradise and corrupting noble savages. The film also condemns the Senator for his Indian-hating, as reaction shots of Pearl show her pain when the malevolent old man calls her Minehaha and taunts her for having a name unsuited to her dark skin. Also conveying this dim view of whites are shots at the McCanles barbecue—a man wipes his mouth on a linen tablecloth and an ignorant woman drawls, "Wouldn't surprise me none if that Indian girl didn't massacree the whole lot." The Sinkiller, enlisted to civilize Pearl, twice forces the half-naked girl to kneel before him in sexually suggestive poses, and comes off as so bombastic and ridiculous that the film pre-empted protests by stating that he was not an ordained minister. So although the film dabbles in notions of racial superiority, it undercuts that image with negative white characters and their ugly racist attitudes.

The opening scene with Pearl's parents gives a traditionally negative view of miscegenation. At his trial, Scott says his downfall began the day he married

Pearl's mother, and their violent end suggests the typical cinematic punishment of those who cross color lines. Although the demise of Pearl and Lewt seems to confirm the point, with this couple, the white man leads the woman of color astray, for Lewt was already rotten before Pearl arrived. Pearl, moreover, had to die as punishment for killing Lewt, not because of PCA rules against miscegenation, which did not apply to American Indians. Nor does the film really dismiss the possibility of happy marriages across color lines or of whites successfully civilizing Pearl. Either Jesse or Sam seemed up to the task, and Jesse expresses the notion when he asks Lewt to "leave this one alone," telling him, "She may do nicely if given half a chance." What makes the tale tragic is not Pearl's yearning for an impossible goal, but rather the intervention of an evil white man who ruins her dreams.

Although making Pearl's Indian side the source of her flaws and miseries is indeed racist, the film's indictment of savage whites and its sympathies for Pearl reflect liberal colonialism, not conservatism. The film, after all, values progress and the replacement of men like the Senator and Lewt with decent types such as Jesse and Sam, who treat Pearl with respect and have no objection to miscegenation, at least on the white man's terms. *Duel in the Sun* is ultimately for, not against, assimilation, suggesting that it will become possible once the first wave of white men in the Wild West gives way to more qualified civilizers, a process already under way in this story. And although certainly not anticolonialist, it dramatizes the damage colonialism did to the colonized. Pearl's pathetic self-flagellation—"I'm trash," she keeps declaring—expresses her self-hatred over her sexual undiscipline as well as her internalization of white racism. In underlining the price Pearl pays for lacking pride in her Indian side, it unwittingly indicates an escape route from the mental colonization that makes her so miserable. Solving social problems was hardly Selznick's purpose, and like so many Hollywood films, *Duel in the Sun* lacks ideological clarity, but that lack of clarity about race and miscegenation says much about white Americans' attitudes at that time.

Duel in the Sun did very well at the box office, finishing behind only *The Best Years of Our Lives* on *Variety*'s box-office charts for 1947.[10] Later studies adjusting for inflation ranked the film as the most popular western of all time; that point needs qualification, given that film attendance was at an all-time high, and given that Selznick, fearing bad reviews, allocated massive amounts for promotion and used a saturation releasing strategy. In New York City, for example, it opened simultaneously in thirty-eight theaters, giving regular moviegoers few alternatives.[11] A few critics, mostly from the trade papers and the Los Angeles press, were quite indulgent, and eight of twenty-four reviews examined here were positive (33 percent), while twelve were negative and four mixed.[12] *Time*'s review was uncharacteristically lenient, perhaps the result of a letter Selznick had written to his friend, publisher Henry Luce, lobbying for positive coverage.[13]

Reviews elsewhere were brutal, particularly in New York. *Cue* called it "the biggest and emptiest thing since the Grand Canyon" and an "absurdly overblown emotional steam bath" aimed at "the peanut-munching, gum-chewing level of moviegoers." Pronouncing it "spectacularly disappointing," Bosley Crowther of the *New York Times* scoffed at "the ultimate banality of the story and its juvenile slobbering over sex," while Kate Cameron of the *New York Daily News* warned that its ending, "meant for high tragedy, comes very close to being low comedy." Yawning at the attempt to shock, John Hobart of the *San Francisco Chronicle* charged that the problem with this "old-fashioned, corny melodrama" was not "its moral offensiveness, but its pretentiousness." The racial themes barely interested the critics, most of whom simply mentioned that Pearl was a "half-breed," and *Life* called her past "as dark as her cocoa-stained complexion." And although Richard L. Coe of the *Washington Post* praised "a delightful performance by Butterfly McQueen as a dusky servant," the *New York Post*'s Archer Winsten wrote that this "dim-witted and complaining servant role should draw pickets from the NAACP."

Most of the British critics panned the film and focused on its faults rather than the issues it raised.[14] In France, as in America, box-office performance and critical reactions diverged, as it sold 3.7 million tickets and reached number nine for 1949, despite a drubbing from the critics, who showed less interest in the film's treatment of race than in its artistic failures and its budget—larger than the entire French film industry's budget for one year, noted *Les Lettres Françaises*.[15] If the film's flaws kept it from eliciting serious consideration of the political and social issues it raised, that was, in fairness, never Selznick's purpose.

Go Left, Young Man

If negative images of red-white miscegenation in early postwar films such as *My Darling Clementine*, *Duel in the Sun*, and *Unconquered* gave the impression that wartime racial liberalism had vanished quickly in Hollywood, things began to change in 1950, with *Broken Arrow* and its positive view of red-white miscegenation. Film scholars who reject *Broken Arrow*'s progressive reputation often cite the unhappy ending of the marriage between Tom Jeffords (James Stewart) and Sonseeahray (Debra Paget), arguing that the film punished the two for breaking the miscegenation taboo.[16] Yet if Sonseeahray's death seems to fit old patterns, events may have different meanings in different films, so one must consider a film's overall politics. In this case, the film's demonizing of white racists, its sympathetic portrait of Apache culture, and the adoring tone it took toward the two characters and their touching romance do not support a reading that the blacklisted, leftist writer Albert Maltz and the film's liberal producer and director wished to punish violators of racial segregation. Equally unconvincing are claims that the PCA forced the film to punish the two, as the authorities never objected to this romance and had no rule against depicting miscegenation between whites and American Indians.[17]

What purpose, then, did Sonseeahray's death serve? The circumstances answer the question: white racist villains concoct a lie to lure Cochise and Jeffords into an ambush and then treacherously open fire on them. It makes no sense to suggest that the film suddenly switched sides and endorsed Sonseeahray's murder, for the scene elicits grief over the death of a sympathetic character, outrage at her killers, and solidarity with Jeffords. The murder also tests Jeffords's commitment to peace, which only the empathy and support of his friends Cochise and General Howard salvage. So in this film a familiar cinematic event takes on a new meaning: Sonseeahray is a martyr in the cause of peace and racial harmony, not a transgressor or a villain, and *Broken Arrow* is not hostile to interracial marriage at all.

Devil's Doorway features another interracial romance that ends badly, as Broken Lance dies fighting U.S. troops shortly after telling Orrie that their love could not succeed. The notion that his death is punishment for miscegenation does not apply here either. Broken Lance breaks off the romance, as the film explores the hidden racism of whites who claimed to be friends of Indians. "The color of my hide means just as much to you as it does to them out there," he tells her, then taunts her by embracing her and asking, "Would you let an Indian put his arms around you?" Given that he has just defended a separatist vision of the Shoshone living freely on their own land, speaking their own language, and maintaining their own religion, his snubbing of Orrie dramatizes his rejection of the white culture he once served. His death thus reflects his complete break with a colonial conqueror, and his martyrdom differs substantially from Sonseeahray's. Nevertheless, like *Broken Arrow*, *Devil's Doorway* showed that unhappy endings of interracial relationships could take on new meanings.

Comparing *Broken Arrow* and *Devil's Doorway* underlines the complexity of the relationship between films' views of colonialism and miscegenation. Unlike traditional empire films, which opposed miscegenation in defending cultural barriers essential to colonialism, *Devil's Doorway* criticized miscegenation from an anticolonialist viewpoint. Broken Lance does not reject Orrie out of concerns that marrying whites will endanger Indian identity, but rather out of bitterness at his treatment by whites, and the film addresses present-day concerns in implying that white liberals still harbor deep-seated prejudices. His statement that their romance might have worked "a hundred years from now" suggests that the film does not oppose miscegenation in principle or consider it impossible forever; it simply insists that whites must first overcome their racism. *Broken Arrow* also suggested that white racism obstructed cross-racial romance, albeit in a very different way, in that it was the settlers, not Tom, whose attitudes ended an otherwise idyllic marriage. Whereas the anticolonialist *Devil's Doorway* viewed miscegenation skeptically, the liberal-colonialist *Broken Arrow*—which accepted white conquest as a fait accompli but urged peace, tolerance toward the colonized, and the removal of barriers between the two peoples—viewed miscegenation positively and optimistically. So while *Devil's Doorway* undermined assumptions that opposition to miscegenation implied support for colonialism, *Broken Arrow* undermined assumptions that support for miscegenation implied opposition to colonialism.

Other films favored both white colonization and intermarriage. Although the marriage between Flint and Kamiah in *Across the Wide Missouri* (1951) ends when the Indian villain kills her, the film depicts a happy marriage and a happy mixed-race child who is proud of both his parents and their cultures. Sensing the film's sympathy for miscegenation, *Time*'s critic proposed a different explanation for Kamiah's demise, writing that a "Blackfoot arrow, guided by the Production Code's antimiscegenation line, cuts down Gable's bride," and scholars have echoed that explanation.[18] In fact, PCA representatives neither objected to the interracial couple nor required her death, and they conferred with MGM about how best to correct such erroneous views of the code.[19] The real function of Kamiah's death was, as in *Broken Arrow*, to dramatize the sacrifices of peacemakers, even if here it was an Indian who murdered her. Ironshirt's act raises the important topic of how Indian men felt about Indian women in romances with whites; she is, in his eyes, a collaborator with invaders. The film was hardly anticolonialist, as it glorified the winning of the West, but it is another liberal-colonialist western that favored miscegenation.

Support for both colonialism and miscegenation also marks two Kirk Douglas films, *The Big Sky* (1952) and *The Indian Fighter* (1955), in which white trappers and pioneers colonize the West while falling in love with Indian women. Howard Hawks's *The Big Sky* features a character transformation as Boone (Dewey Martin), an Indian-hater who believes Indians killed his brother, clashes with Teal Eye (Elizabeth Threatt), a Blackfoot Indian woman guiding the white traders upriver. Gradually, Boone and Teal Eye stop fighting, and romance develops despite the language barrier. When they finally reach Teal Eye's people, Boone ends up, through a misunderstanding, unintentionally marrying her, but when the white men head home, Boone decides to accept the marriage and stay with her. *The Big Sky* thus takes the same positive view of the first wave of white colonizers that *Across the Wide Missouri* took while allowing the interracial couple a happy ending. Like *Broken Arrow* and other films, *The Big Sky* uses the transformation of a white Indian hater to invite white viewers to reconsider their prejudices.

Also proving that interracial couples did not have to end badly was *The Indian Fighter*, the tale of a white man, Johnny Hawks (Kirk Douglas), who knows Indians well from years of fighting them but does not hate them and uses his knowledge of them to foster peace. He ultimately talks his Indian friend Red Cloud (Eduard Franz) into accepting peace and abandoning his quest for revenge against two white murderers. Johnny, who fears that white settlers will ruin the pristine wilderness he shares with the Indians, also romances a defiant Onahti (Elsa Martinelli)—he wins her over with the same affectionate force the pioneers used to conquer the wilderness—and at the end he looks forward to their son living in peace between the two peoples. Like *Broken Arrow*, *Across the Wide Missouri*, and *The Big Sky*, this film endorses interracial marriage as part of a vision of coexistence between colonizer and colonized.

The ranks of Hollywood westerns with liberal views of race and miscegenation continued to grow in the 1950s. *Tomahawk* (1951) kept the interracial couple off screen, though white racists mistake Jim Bridger (Van Heflin) and his sister-in-law Monahseetah (Susan Cabot) for a couple and call him "squaw man." He later explains that his Cheyenne wife was the victim of Colonel Chivington's massacre at Sand Creek, so the film joins *Broken Arrow* in eliciting viewers' anger at white racists for killing an innocent Indian woman. Fred Zinnemann's *High Noon* (1952), with a script by blacklisted writer Carl Foreman, presents a strikingly different picture of the Mexican woman from that in *My Darling Clementine*. Not only did the role of Helen Ramirez go to a Mexican actress (Katy Jurado), but this former girlfriend of Marshal Will Kane (Gary Cooper) is a far more admirable character than Chihuahua in *My Darling Clementine*: a strong, wise, and independent business owner, she urges Will's bride (Grace Kelly) to show courage and support her husband. Although the film did not explain why Will and Helen had separated, for once a western refrained from contrasting a virtuous blonde and a villainous woman of color.

Budd Boetticher's *Seminole* (1953) introduced a twist: a white woman, Revere (Barbara Hale), in love with a man of color, the mixed-race Osceola (Anthony Quinn). When Osceola, like Broken Lance in *The Devil's Doorway*, abandons life in white society out of pride in his Indianness and a desire to help his people, he tells Revere that they should part, asking rhetorically, "Will your people accept me in their society, as your husband?" Revere's love for him—she initiates the physical affection—makes her willing to live among the Seminoles, in effect conceding that white society is too racist to accept them, but Osceola doubts she can "live in a muddy Indian village as my squaw." Osceola ends up betrayed by both unscrupulous, war-mongering white racists who sabotage the good whites' efforts at peace and by a fellow Seminole who kills him for seeking peace. Although it is the Indian, not his white partner, who dies, the film is not punishing Osceola for miscegenation; it is instead following a new pattern of blaming prejudice for ending such relationships. Positive views of interracial couples continued to appear in other films, including *Captain John Smith and Pocahontas* (1953), *Broken Lance* (1954), *White Feather* (1955), *Apache Woman* (1955), *The Last Hunt* (1956), *Mohawk* (1956), *Gunman's Walk* (1958), *Yellowstone Kelly* (1959), and *Last Train from Gun Hill* (1959), and eight of those nine films also featured happy endings for interracial couples. Only one of them, *The Last Hunt*, was anticolonialist, and the prevailing pattern was to combine racial liberalism with the acceptance or endorsement of whites' conquest of the West.

Films with frankly negative views of both Indians and love across the color line did not disappear. *The Charge at Feather River* (1953) used the whole gamut of anti-Indian clichés and stereotypes (war-mongering, massacres of settlers, torture, scalping). It also contrasted two white sisters kidnapped by the Cheyenne—the good sister, who hates her captors and welcomes her rescue, and her evil sister Jennie (Vera Miles), who loves her Indian fiancé and betrays her rescuers. This film punishes miscegenation and offers the audience the satisfaction of seeing Jenny fall to her death. The vehemently anti-Indian *Arrowhead* (1953), whose hero, Ed Bannon (Charlton Heston), hates the Apaches who raised him, also hates himself for being attracted to the half-Mexican, half-Apache Nita (Katy Jurado). When Bannon stops her from stabbing him, he explains to a soldier, "The Apache Indian in her finally came out," and after she kills herself to avoid imprisonment, Bannon tells the soldier, "There's a dead Apache in here. Get it out." Bannon's hatred may seem excessive, but the film vindicates his warnings to naive whites who envision peace with Indians.

Other films showed less animosity toward Indians while still rejecting interracial romance. In *War Arrow* (1953), a young Seminole woman, Avis (Suzann Ball), unsatisfied with the poverty of her people after their defeat and relocation to the Great Plains, yearns to be more like the white Elaine Corwin (Maureen O'Hara), who attracts the romantic interest of Major Howell Brady (Jeff Chandler). After the Major shows some interest in Avis, he ends up choosing the white woman over Avis, who resigns herself to a Seminole suitor in an East-is-East conclusion. *Far Horizons* (1955), a retelling of the Lewis and Clark expedition, resembles *The Big Sky* in featuring a white pioneer undergoing a character transformation. William Clark (Charlton Heston) overcomes his initial hatred for Indians by falling in love with Sacajawea (Donna Reed), but after he declares his desire to marry her and takes her to meet the president in Washington, she decides to return home without him. "I have met your people, and they were very kind to me," she announces, "but it is not my country and they are not my people."

Standing between films either clearly endorsing or opposing miscegenation were several ambivalent ones. *The Searchers*, which deals with red-white miscegenation in a range of relationships, does not endorse Ethan's obsessive hatred of Indians, and instead supports his decision to welcome Debbie back despite her marriage to Scar. Martin's inadvertent marriage to Look, however, is played for laughs, suggesting that the very idea of a marriage between an Indian woman and the mostly white Martin would be preposterous—a view closer to the real feelings of most white Texans in the 1870s than those seen in pro-miscegenation westerns. Contemporaries' horror at the prospect of the Indian rapist appears in the rapes of Martha and Lucy as well as in the scene in which Ethan and Martin discover some traumatized white women rescued from captivity, but whether the film is endorsing the attitude it depicts is open to interpretation, and neither the film nor any character in it objects to the mixed-race Martin marrying the blonde Laurie Jorgensen.

In *Seven Cities of Gold* (1955), a Spanish soldier in the expedition in California, José Mendoza (Richard Egan), falls in love with an Indian woman, Ula (Rita Moreno), at the mission of Father Serra (Michael Rennie). When the soldiers abandon the ill-fated outpost, Ula wants to accompany José, but he tells her that her brother, the Chief, would not permit it. Just as it appears that another film is blaming Indians for obstructing an interracial marriage, Ula secures her brother's permission to marry. Having shifted attention to whites' attitudes, the film has José oppose her coming with him, explaining, "Things are different in Mexico City and Madrid. You just wouldn't get along with my people. . . . They'd never let you belong." Then, having broached the subject of white hostility to interracial marriage, the film abruptly ducks any further exploration of a controversial topic by having distraught Ula accidentally fall to her death.

Similar evasiveness about miscegenation appears in *Walk the Proud Land* (1956), starring Audie Murphy as Indian agent John Clum. Combating the prejudices of white settlers and soldiers as well as the resistance of the die-hard Geronimo, Clum wins over most of the Apaches on the reservation by defending their interests. Before his wife arrives partway through the film, Clum inadvertently attracts the romantic interest of an Apache widow, Tianay (Anne Bancroft). Because Clum is already married, this liberal-colonialist film uses the subplot not to explore interracial marriage, but rather to allow Clum to expound the Christian principle of monogamy to his puzzled pupil.

In *Run of the Arrow* (1957), director Samuel Fuller seemed intent upon denouncing racial prejudice. In this western about a Confederate veteran, Private O'Meara (Rod Steiger), who turns his back on the United States and "goes native" with the Sioux, Fuller inserts transparently presentist lines critical of the Ku Klux Klan and white racism. The film drifts at the end as O'Meara abandons the Sioux and his marriage to a Sioux woman after realizing that he has no stomach for Sioux brutalities. An apparently antiracist film thus concludes on an East-is-East note. If filmmakers seemed conflicted, they undoubtedly reflected the thinking of the society as a whole, and despite their relatively undeveloped and contradictory ideas on the subject, their films still provoked consideration of interracial love and marriage in a society just beginning to rethink its attitudes toward those issues.

Miscegenation in Modern-Era Westerns

Two mid-1950s films, *Foxfire* (1955) and *Giant* (1956), raised the subject of miscegenation more boldly by setting their tales in the contemporary West. *Foxfire*, starring Jane Russell, seems an innocuous bit of fluff from Universal-International, but it actually explores interracial marriage with some seriousness. In addition to taking place in the present, it reverses the usual pattern by pairing a white woman with a man of color. Russell plays Amanda Lawrence, a New York heiress who, while vacationing in Arizona, meets the handsome Jonathan Dartland (Jeff Chandler in yet another Apache role). Her encounters with Apaches get off to a rocky start when her car breaks down on a highway and a poverty-stricken Apache family declines to help her. She then flags down a passing Jeep driven by Jonathan, manager of a local copper mine. When they catch up with the Apache family, "Dart," as Jonathan is known, speaks with them in their language; Amanda misses this clue that he is half-Apache, and she soon makes racist comments about Indians. Dart, the stereotypical stoic Indian, lets the comments pass and accepts her invitation to a party she is giving. That evening, when he mentions in passing that his mother lives on a reservation, an embarrassed Amanda apologizes for her comments. Her racism, it turns out, is only skin-deep, and his ethnicity does not bother her in the least; indeed romance quickly leads to an engagement.

Having set up this opportunity to explore racism, the film then turns timid. Amanda's wealthy mother, flustered at the news, objects not to Dart's race but to her "living in this God-forsaken town," and the hesitant Dart similarly wonders only about a socialite marrying a miner and living in a small town. Despite a hint of tension at the wedding as Amanda's mother meets Dart and his more Indian-looking cousin Nediate, everyone is cordial. The film finally confronts white racism after the wedding, when Mrs. Mablett, the busybody wife of Dart's boss, arrives to give Amanda some unsolicited opinions. Telling Amanda, "You're very brave to marry him," she explains that Apaches are "cruel and dangerous" and "can never rise above their background." She also sneers at Dart's mother, who after the death of her white husband, went back to "living like a savage on that horrible reservation." Ignoring the annoying Mrs. Mablett's advice and Dart's own discouragement of her interest in his heritage, Amanda takes a tourist bus to the reservation in hopes of meeting Dart's mother. Amanda thus follows the well-trodden path of the white character whose pursuit of romance leads from initial hostility and racism to curiosity and then affinity for Indian ways, and despite some tensions between Dart and Amanda that highlight the challenges cultural differences pose to such a marriage, the film grants them a happy ending.

Despite perpetuating a few cinematic stereotypes and criticizing traditional Apache treatment of women and children, *Foxfire* questions certain Hollywood conventions. Dart reacts to Amanda's delight at learning that his godfather was a chief by asking, "You mean his royal blood makes me more acceptable?" It also pokes fun at whites during Amanda's bus tour of the reservation, as a dim-witted white woman tells her son, "Look here, real Indians!" The film is overly reassuring about white racism, which only the Mabletts harbor, and the interracial marriage encounters suspiciously little opposition in rural Arizona. It is also evasive at times, particularly when Amanda's miscarriage removes an opportunity to explore reactions to the birth of a mixed-race child. And though shots of the couple contrast the rather dark-skinned Chandler with the very pale Russell, the casting of a white actor as a person of color once again softened a challenge to viewers' readiness to view interracial affection. Nevertheless, this run-of-the-mill production exemplified popular cinema's new progressiveness, with its foregrounding of miscegenation in a tale set in the present, its pairing of a white woman with a man of color, and its support for interracial marriage. And by looking favorably on both Dart's desire to assimilate and his mother's choice of a more traditional Apache life, the film in effect endorses the notion of multiple options for American Indians' pursuit of happiness in the aftermath of colonization. The film reached the number sixty-five slot on the charts for 1955, and critics split evenly among mildly positive, mixed, and negative judgments, while saying little about interracial marriage.[20]

A far more ambitious modern-era western, director George Stevens's epic, *Giant* (1956), was adapted from an Edna Ferber novel and released by Warner Bros. The film traces Texas's history in the first half of the twentieth century through a single family, the Benedicts. In the opening act, Jordan "Bick" Benedict, Jr. (Rock Hudson), the young heir of the family's 595,000-acre cattle ranch, travels to Maryland to buy a racehorse, and returns with a bride as well—Leslie (Elizabeth Taylor), the daughter of a wealthy family. Taming this bride, however, proves harder than taming the horse: shortly after Leslie and Bick meet, she reads up on Texas history and upsets him by asking, "We really stole Texas, didn't we Mr. Benedict? I mean away from Mexico." The sequence establishes her feisty, politically liberal persona and begins the film's exploration of its principal theme: the rebellions of race, class, gender, and generation that confront a cattle tycoon in an era of rapid historical change.

Giant explores gender rebellion through Leslie's refusal to accept the submissive role assigned to Texan women, while ranch hand Jett Rink (James Dean) represents class insubordination by clashing repeatedly with his employer. When Jett suddenly inherits some land from Bick's sister—then discovers oil on it—Bick must come to terms with his uncouth subordinate growing richer than him. The film's interest in racial politics begins with Leslie's anticolonialist reading of Texas history, and upon arrival in Texas, she violates local customs and exasperates her husband by treating the ranch's Mexican peons as human beings and calling attention to their dire poverty. Afraid that her consorting with the peons will undermine their deference and the social distance necessary to an essentially colonial relationship, Bick repeatedly but ineffectually orders her to stop. As the years pass and the couple's three children mature, the prospective heir, Jordan "Jordy" Benedict III (Dennis Hopper), rebels by planning to study medicine instead of managing the ranch, and even more subversively, by falling in love with Juana Guerra (Elsa Cardenas), the black-haired, dark-skinned daughter of a local Mexican American physician. In place of a Texas-style extravaganza, they marry in a simple ceremony in a Mexican chapel, and Jordy later informs his shocked parents of the marriage by telling them and their backyard party guests in an announcement over the band's public-address system. Leslie quickly regains her composure and gives Juana a warm welcome, but Bick struggles to cope with this latest blow to his patriarchal authority.

The white racist's transformation recurs here, though with more nuance, as Bick struggles to accept his son's marriage. Although *Giant* sympathizes with both Bick and the rebels who challenge him, it leans toward the rebels. It humanizes the Mexican characters by showing the peons' shameful treatment and by depicting movingly the funeral of young Angel Obregón (Sal Mineo), a ranch hand's son who died in World War II for a country that considered him inferior. A saddened Bick hands the grieving mother his own Texas flag in consolation, a symbolic act that illustrates how the war helped alter whites' attitudes toward their nonwhite compatriots. When Jordy and Juana's son is born at the same time that daughter Judy and her white husband also have a boy, a simple but effective sequence shows Bick smiling at the little blond baby, then frowning at his black-haired, dark-skinned grandson. Later, in a clear indictment of white racism, the hair salon in a luxury hotel refuses Juana service, provoking husband Jordy to a fit of rage. Near the end of the film, the Benedicts stop at a roadside diner, where the white owner and waitress make racist comments about Juana and the boy, and where a fed-up Bick takes offense at the owner's throwing a Mexican family out of the diner. The aging Bick gets into a brawl with the burly owner and loses, but he earns Leslie's praise for his effort. Rather than present a miraculous transformation, however, the film has Bick complain to a perturbed Leslie, "My own grandson don't even look like one of us. He looks like a little wetback." The eradication of racism, the film suggests, would not be simple. Although some audience members undoubtedly sympathized with Bick, the final shot reveals the film's sympathies visually. The camera dwells on the two grandsons standing in the same crib—with a white sheep and a black calf behind them—then pans from the blond to the dark-skinned boy, eliciting audience sympathies with a close-up of the adorable Mexican American heir to the Benedict fortune.

Filming Ferber's 1952 novel had aroused concerns about furnishing material that communist propagandists could use against America, and Paramount's head of foreign and domestic censorship, Luigi Luraschi, assured a contact in the CIA that he would prevent his studio from filming the novel. He detailed the dangers, citing its generally "unflattering portrait of rich, uncouth, ruthless Americans," and their "racial denigration of Mexicans in Texas," and the "implication [that the] wealth of Anglo-Texans [was] built by exploiting Mexican labor." Luraschi warned, however, that he could not stop other studios from filming it, and although it took three more years, the Warner Bros. release contained all the themes Luraschi disliked. As disturbing as the CIA's involvement in Hollywood may be, *Giant* suggests the limits of its ability to control filmmaking. Moreover, Eric Johnston, head of the Motion Picture Association of America, told its board of directors in 1958 that foreign audiences liked American films' self-criticisms, and he paraphrased foreign audiences' view that Hollywood films "don't try to hide the faults in your society. . . . That's why we respect your films."[21]

Giant was an enormous hit, reaching the number three slot for 1957.[22] It also received ten Oscar nominations, losing out to *Around the World in Eighty Days* and *The King and I* for all but a directing Oscar for Stevens. The film tested very well—with less than 3 percent rating it "fair" or "poor"—at studio previews in San Diego, home to a large Mexican-American population. A few comment cards from the audience disliked the racial theme—one lamented the "overemphasis of [the] wetback issue" and another called it "unfortunate that the problem of discrimination [was] so often over-emphasized in films"—but more viewers embraced the message. One teenage girl, for example, "liked the honesty and frankness about the treatment of the Mexicans," and a young man praised the film for showing that people "should weigh their prejudices and realize it is no good."[23] Enthusiastic fan mail soon poured in from around the country, including a letter from a white shop owner in Sumter, South Carolina, who explained that his recent efforts to organize bi-racial discussions of local problems had provoked threatening phone calls from whites. Calling *Giant* "the most inspiring picture produced in Hollywood for a long time," he contended that "after the picture was shown here you could tell a difference in the people," and he said that the film "gave me courage and strength to face anyone anywhere."[24]

Despite complaints about the film's length, American critics were nearly unanimous in praising it, with twenty-two positive (88 percent), one negative, and two mixed reviews in a sample of twenty-five.[25] Nearly all of the reviews lauded the treatment of racial discrimination, including a positive review in the *Dallas Morning News*, which noted "some nauseating examples of anti-Mexican race discrimination along the Texas border." Aware that Ferber's novel had angered many Texans, the *Morning News* called the film "one of the most successful motion picture ventures in decades," and in an article titled "Texans Can Take It," the paper quoted a theater manager who said, "I haven't heard anybody say that 'Giant' misrepresents Texas. It tells of a class and of situations that are part of our life [and] our politics."[26] The film played in the South, but although the *Atlanta Constitution*'s Paul Jones liked it and informed readers that it "deals with human emotions and racial prejudices," he complained that "the social theme got too much attention, especially in the closing episode in the café," and in the *New Orleans Times-Picayune*, Jack Boyd, Jr. said nothing about the film's exploration of racial discrimination and intermarriage.

A few critics drew parallels between anti-Mexican attitudes and racism toward blacks: both Mildred Martin of the *Philadelphia Inquirer* and Bosley Crowther of the *New York Times* alluded to "Jim Crow" attitudes, and in the African American *Chicago Defender*, George Daniels remarked, "I have seen Texans persecute Mexicans and Negroes alike, and 'Giant' brought back those memories." Despite finding a racially liberal Marylander "somewhat hard to believe," Daniels said the film "strikes hard at racial intolerance and injustice." *Newsweek* was impressed, given that "expensive productions like this usually stand clear of controversy," and the *St. Louis Post-Dispatch* wrote that "the film dispenses no mercy in its relentless jabs at racial intolerance." *Time* was effusive in calling *Giant* "probably the most effective declaration against racial intolerance ever shown on the screen." Amid the chorus of support for the film's antiracism, Archer Winsten of the *New York Post*, the sole critic in this sample to pan the film, called it "popular wish-fancy that'll take some time yet to come true in Texas." *Commonweal*'s Philip T. Hartung also found the film too optimistic about racism, writing that Stevens "does make it clear that it's a big problem and will in time be solved—though hardly by the next generation as the film suggests." As for interracial marriage, most critics noted Jordy's marriage to Juana with little comment, but in the *Hollywood Reporter*, James Powers sympathized with Bick, writing that "a grandfather wants his progeny to look like him."

British critics were much harder on *Giant*, and in a sample of eighteen reviews, seven were positive (39 percent), seven negative, and four mixed.[27] Its length, which drew minor complaints from American critics, struck their British counterparts as outrageous. Perhaps the film felt so much longer to the British because racial discrimination and miscegenation did not interest them nearly as much. While a few critics noted the interracial marriage, several others summarized the film without mentioning racial issues at all. The *Sunday Express* concluded sarcastically, "Moral: racial intolerance is a bad thing," and Peter Burnup of *News of the World* wrote that "the cinema shouldn't be turned into a pulpit."

Among those who welcomed the racial theme, the *Daily Worker* praised the "genuine attempt to show the gross exploitation of the Mexican Indians" and noted "the slow grinding away of [Bick's] own violent colour prejudices by his liberally minded wife." Harris Deans of the *Sunday Dispatch* stated that "the treatment of the unhappy Mexicans, from whom the land was 'acquired,' is sickeningly shown." Others liked the miscegenation issue but judged the treatment of it implausible. The *London Times* complained that "the comparative calm with which [Bick] takes his son's marriage to a Mexican girl is irreconcilable with much that has gone before," and the *Monthly Film Bulletin* wrote that the film's "sentiments are irreproachable but its exposition naïve," for "one is sceptical that the dear son of a prejudiced Texan should fall in love at sight with a Mexican girl." Perhaps these skeptics would first have to witness changing attitudes about race and miscegenation in their own society, something yet to happen in a Britain barely beginning public discussion of those issues.

The film did very well in France, where it sold more than 3.7 million tickets, reaching the number eight slot for 1957.[28] French critics often had their knives sharpened for lavish Hollywood films like this one—*Le Monde* noted its 3.5 billion franc budget and called it a "super-superproduction"—and as in Britain, the film's length upset numerous critics.[29] Nevertheless, French critics liked the film a bit better, giving it seven positive (41 percent), four negative, and six mixed or neutral reviews in a sample of seventeen.[30] Panning it, François Truffaut saw in it "everything that is despicable about the Hollywood system," and he charged that "racial questions are met with the usual hypocrisy." Of the black calf and white sheep at the end he wrote, "It is by such crude symbols that this film advances so laboriously." *Libération* noted that "a little child of color will henceforth bear the sacrosanct Benedict name," but it scoffed at the film's "silliness and phony antiracism," and *Le Monde*'s Jean de Baroncelli, in a mixed review, wrote that "the highly moralistic conclusion ('the Americans may have racist inclinations but they can reform themselves') leaves us indifferent."

L'Humanité's Armand Monjo also doubted that "the 'good Americans' are not racist, or at least can correct themselves," but he applauded the film for showing "the poverty of the shantytown next to the luxury of the bosses" and for highlighting "the reactionary and racist prejudices of the first colonizers of this Texas, grabbed from the Mexican people." He also lauded the "critical attitude toward certain problems Hollywood rarely confronted honestly: racism and the omnipotence of the big capitalists." Both pleased and puzzled, Georges Sadoul of *Les Lettres Françaises* called it "one of the richest and most courageous works Hollywood has given us in ten years" and "an antiracist attack that surpasses *Crossfire*." Drawing parallels with French colonialism, he wrote that Bick "makes the sarape sweat as the North African colonists make the burnoose sweat," while wondering "how the devil a rude, feudal southerner grown rich by exploiting Mexicans can suddenly become a champion of antiracism." In the *Nouvelles Littéraires*, Georges Charensol also questioned "Bick's liberal transformation," suggesting that the film would have been truer had it "shown us the persistence of prejudices and the complete triumph of money." All the same, he welcomed the film's antiracism and highlighting of poverty, adding that normally, "it is only outside their country that our American friends are opposed to colonialism." Less ambivalently, *Le Canard Enchaîné* considered the film's "intellectual and political honesty" and its antiracism "quite rare in grand American productions," and *La Croix* added that "all the antiracist scenes are treated with a force and audacity that are very rare in Hollywood." The conservative *L'Aurore* called it "very hard on Texans, showing them to be vulgar, poorly educated nouveaux riches full of racial prejudices" and found it odd that "America enjoys inflicting blame upon itself." In a mixed review, André Bazin wrote that Hollywood's "sociological backgrounds . . . constitute one of the decisive components of its greatness, if not to say its superiority," and he wished that "Soviet cinema would bring us an eighth of Hollywood's social testimony on America."

American westerns of the late 1940s and 1950s dealt extensively with miscegenation—at least forty-seven films depicted relationships involving whites and either American Indians or Mexicans—and in expressing everything from traditional hostility to enthusiastic endorsement, they reflected the diversity of society's views on the subject. Given the hostility to miscegenation seen in opinion polls and other evidence from these years, Hollywood was generally well ahead of public opinion on this issue, and pro-miscegenation films vastly outnumbered films with frankly hostile outlooks. The hostile films were most numerous in the 1940s, and a "left turn" beginning with *Broken Arrow* in 1950 produced a flurry of positive depictions of miscegenation in the American West. Most American critics accepted or welcomed the new outlook, and many of the films did outstanding business as well. Their reception was also generally positive in Britain and France, though some British critics seemed bored with a theme they considered irrelevant in Britain. As with the pro-Indian westerns of the 1950s, films exploring miscegenation in the West suggested a broad desire for racial harmony, at least between whites and American Indians. Of course, the total dominance of white society over the small remaining populations of Native Americans afforded the luxury of generosity toward a people who no longer posed any threat, so exploring attitudes about miscegenation requires a look at the issue in other contexts.

CHAPTER EIGHT

Romance across the Pacific

In the late 1940s and 1950s, while the British and the French were leaving many of their colonies in Asia, the Americans were expanding their presence there, in some cases replacing formal European colonial rule with less formal American oversight. And while Europeans were just beginning to look back on their colonial experiences in Asia, Americans were still getting to know much of the region and coming to terms with their new role. In both cases, films played an important role, often addressing historical and political issues through tales of sexual and romantic relationships between Asians and Westerners.

Among the thirty-four American, British, and French films from this period that deal with miscegenation in Asia, Oceania, and the Pacific, only nine are hostile or deeply skeptical. Old yellow-peril fears of Asian rapists turn up in four American films made after the Communists' victory in China in 1949: *Peking Express*, *The Shanghai Story*, *Blood Alley*, and *Five Gates to Hell*, all of which flopped at the box office.

Negative views of miscegenation also appear in two British films. In Carol Reed's 1952 adaptation of Joseph Conrad's *Outcast of the Islands*, set in an unnamed land that resembles Malaya, ne'er-do-well Peter Willems (Trevor Howard) works for Captain Tom Lingard (Ralph Richardson), who monopolizes rubber and tin exports from a remote native settlement. When Captain Lingard learns of the locals' desire to bring in a rival Arab trader, the paternalistic Lingard reminds them, "This is a peaceful place, a thriving place because I made it so," and he warns them, "I am your friend. Take care not to make me your enemy." The surly natives remain unconvinced, and one of them asks, "Does the white man know what is best for us?" Such lines bring to mind the insurgency going on in Malaya, which gave Conrad's 1896 story of colonial unrest new relevance. When Lingard departs, he unwisely leaves Willems to assist his local agent, Elmer Almayer

(Robert Morley). The trouble begins when Willems becomes smitten with the chief's daughter, Aissa (Kerima, an Algerian in her film debut), a steely, mysterious young woman whose aloofness only makes Willems want her even more. The two can barely communicate, and the locals resent his interest in her, but he is obsessed. In this cautionary tale of interracial lust, Willems betrays the man who has protected and employed him by showing the Arab trader the Captain's secret sea route to the village, which he does as part of a deal for the right to see Aissa. He also betrays Almayer by helping stir up rebellion, and in a nightmarish scene suggesting colonialist anxieties in the decolonization era, the natives overpower Almayer and torture him by binding him in a hammock and swinging him over a fire. When the Captain returns, he restores order and shames Willems into obedience, letting him live only so that he can wallow in his misery. As Aissa spurns him out of disgust at his refusal to murder the Captain, the white man sees that his foolish passion has brought him to ruin.

The native temptress appeared in another British film, *The Seekers*, set in New Zealand (see chapter 2). The lust of British settler Philip Wayne (Jack Hawkins) for Moana (Laya Raki), the sexually aggressive wife of the local Maori ruler, leads him to betray both his own wife and his new friend, the chief. Although the film glorifies the British pioneers, it acknowledges their flaws through Philip's sexual dalliance with Moana, and it propounds a model of settler colonialism that expected white people to live a righteous life among the heathens and to civilize them but not mix with them sexually.

Other films opposed colonial miscegenation by carrying on the narrative tradition of Westerners corrupting noble savages in the South Seas. Discarding the defense of miscegenation he had made in *Broken Arrow*, Delmer Daves pursued a different kind of liberalism in *Bird of Paradise* (1951), which he wrote, produced, and directed for Darryl F. Zanuck at Twentieth Century-Fox. In this remake of King Vidor's 1932 film, Frenchman André Laurence (Louis Jourdan) arrives in an unnamed Pacific island with his friend Tenga (Jeff Chandler). The two had met in college in the United States, and when Tenga chose to abandon civilization for his island paradise, André decided to accompany his friend for a brief visit. Smitten with Tenga's comely sister Kalua (Debra Paget, transformed, like Chandler, from Apache to Polynesian), André resolves to settle there. The attraction is mutual, and Kalua chooses André in a mating ritual, much as Sonseeahray chose Jeffords in *Broken Arrow*. Unfortunately, the local priest, the Kahuna, remembering the diseases and corruption other whites brought, forbids the marriage.

The Kahuna is not alone in opposing the marriage. "We are of two different worlds," Tenga tells André, doubting that a European can live here. "What is in us has been born in us; it cannot be changed." An unconvinced André replies, "I think it can, if the wish is strong enough—if the love is great enough." Despite the purity of his love, the film sides with Tenga and the Kahuna, reaching an East-is-East conclusion. Daves wished to present Polynesian culture sympathetically, and the film even asks the audience to believe that the local volcano really stops erupting when Kalua leaps into it, but Zanuck urged Daves to darken the Kahuna's image: "Whether accurate or not, we should reach for an evil and spooky representation of this character" and make him "a more or less reasonable fanatic."[1] The film, hardly Zanuck's or Daves's finest moment, questioned interracial marriage in making the anticolonialist point that whites should simply leave the islanders alone.

That point recurred in *Pearl of the South Pacific* (see chapter 2), in which the scheming white woman (Virginia Mayo) seduces the half-native George to discover where his people hide the island's black pearls. It even turned up in a film about India: *The Rains of Ranchipur* (1955), a remake of *The Rains Came* (1939). In this story of an adulterous romance between a naive Indian physician, Dr. Safti (Richard Burton in brownface and turban), and a self-centered, jaded, and abrasive Lady Esketh (Lana Turner), the Englishwoman finds just enough decency to accept others' advice to leave him and not ruin his life. "My going away," she tells him, "may be the one unselfish act of my life." Some Westerners had been criticizing themselves as morally corrupt and noxious to non-Western peoples for centuries, and these films carried that tradition into an era when decolonization gave such narratives new significance.

Other films took ambivalent or evasive positions on miscegenation in Asia and the Pacific. *King of the Khyber Rifles* presented a debate between the white General's daughter Susan (Terry Moore) and her half-caste sweetheart Alan (Tyrone Power). Susan urges him to defy society's prejudice and emulate his parents, asking, "Are we going to admit that we have less courage than your father and mother? Wasn't the love they had for each other big enough to make up for everything?" Alan replies that "everything you said was right, but this is not the time" and "it just wouldn't work," and after this exchange the film drops the subplot for good.

Equally evasive was *The Inn of the Sixth Happiness*. When Gladys (Ingrid Bergman) and Lin Nan (Curt Jurgens) begin to fall in love, they discuss the obstacles to their love—including the prejudice they would face and her devotion to her work—but after a departing Lin Nan tells her, "Let's leave it this way till I come back," they never discuss their relationship again. And in *Love Is a Many-Splendored Thing*, Mark's death in Korea ends any further probing of the issues that his and Han Suyin's love would have raised in colonial Hong Kong. In this case, the film neither makes Mark a martyr for antiracism nor conveys a disapproval of miscegenation; it is simply following the real events of Han Suyin's autobiography. Although the tragedy also serves the film's tear-jerking aims, this movie, like many others, raises the subject of interracial romance and then gives it short shrift.

Even films frankly supporting miscegenation sometimes skirted the subject. Joshua Logan's 1958 film of the Michener tale and Rodgers and Hammerstein musical *South Pacific* examined miscegenation through two romances involving white characters struggling with prejudices learned in the United States. When Lieutenant Joe Cable (John Kerr) falls in love with Liat (France Nuyen), no one objects to their relationship, but he fears taking her back to New Jersey, and his own prejudice surfaces when Liat's mother alludes to their future children (followed by an ominous orchestra chord). Joe struggles with his racism, and he seems to be overcoming it—he even sings the famous Rodgers and Hammerstein number with the line, "You've got to be taught to hate and fear"—when he suddenly dies in combat. If the story thus foregoes an opportunity to pursue the subject, it hardly means to punish him for crossing racial barriers, and it returns to the subject through the romance between Nellie Forbush (Mitzi Gaynor) and a Frenchman, Emile de Becque (Rossano Brazzi). The racism Nellie has brought to this island paradise from her hometown of Little Rock, Arkansas—which had gained new notoriety in the September 1957 school desegregation showdown—surfaces when she learns Emile had been married to a Polynesian woman and has two mixed-race children. Like Joe, she struggles to overcome her ingrained hatreds, and in a love-conquers-all ending, her affection for Emile's irresistible children helps her to see the error of her ways.

Films such as *South Pacific* illustrate an overlooked way in which World War II contributed to decolonization. For Americans, military service in the Pacific theater created new opportunities for interracial romance, while the distance from home made white Americans more forgiving of what would have been scandalous at home. The idyllic setting of the South Seas also played a part, with the stunning tropical scenery and the imagined lack of inhibitions in local cultures making the prejudices and taboos of home seem cold, unnatural, and unnecessary. Such films may have given unrealistic impressions of an environment free of racism—in *South Pacific*, no one, not even military authorities, objects to miscegenation—but they helped audiences visualize a world without prejudice. And in questioning cultural differences and taboos, while also presenting likable individuals to represent unfamiliar peoples, such films eroded important foundations of colonialism.

The tendency of antiracist films to downplay hostility to intermarriage also appeared in *His Majesty O'Keefe*, in which the white protagonist marries a mixed-race woman in the South Seas without encountering so much as a dirty look from anyone. Such films may simply reflect the old colonialist attitude of winking at the peccadilloes of white men far from home, which recalls the lenience slave-owning societies of the Americas showed toward the liberties plantation owners took with their slaves, or they may be read as helping viewers to envision a post-racist world. Taking the cinematic erasure of racism even further than usual was Samuel Fuller's *The Crimson Kimono* (1958), which tested the limits more than usual by setting its story in the present-day United States and pairing a man of color with a white woman. Los Angeles police detective Joe Kojaku (James Shigeta) loves Chris (Victoria Shaw), a white woman and artist whom his buddy and fellow detective Charlie Bancroft (Glenn Corbett) also desires, and when Joe tells Charlie of his love for her, he mistakes Charlie's pained reaction for racism. Chris later scoffs at Joe's belief in Charlie's racism and tells him, "You only saw what you wanted to see." In the end, Joe, who claims he had never sensed any racism in his years in the army and the police, admits he was merely imagining things. Given that Joe was old enough to have lived through the era of the Japanese internment, his claim strains credibility and denies the existence of the very problem the film combats.[2] So despite Fuller's desire to envision a society free of racism and to encourage the crossing of racial barriers, his film offered a terribly unrealistic image of American society.

While some films opposed colonial miscegenation and others treated it evasively, a majority—twenty of thirty-four—frankly favored it. The pro-miscegenation films could be condescending and colonialist; many, for example, purveyed white men's fantasies about eager Asian and Polynesian women and old notions of the colonies as sexual playground. In *Return to Paradise*, Maeva throws herself at a resistant Morgan, giving him leis and kisses, and she cleans his hut while he relaxes. In *South Pacific* comely young women in Bali Hai greet the GIs with smiles, flowers, and alluring looks, and Bloody Mary leads Joe through a jungle paradise bathed in golden light to meet her beautiful daughter Liat. Although such images were most common in the South Seas films, the tellingly titled *China Doll* (1958) used them as well. In that World War II film, an embittered Captain Cliff Brandon (Victor Mature) first rejects a saloon girl's overtures then unwittingly buys the daughter of an impoverished peasant. Like Morgan in *Return to Paradise*, Cliff at first ignores Shu-Jen (Li Hua Li) when she comes to his home to be his maid; soon, she undresses him when he comes home drunk, scrubs his floors, serves him coffee, nurses him in sickness, and finally nestles up to him in bed, breaking his resistance. Her love even rescues him from depression, giving him a reason to live. In *The Quiet American*, the beautiful young

Phuong is a compliant, undemanding partner—first for Fowler, then for Pyle—though objections from the Production Code Administration removed the novel's references to her filling Fowler's opium pipe and offering him her body.

Films set in Japan also followed this pattern, often with geisha characters. In *The Barbarian and the Geisha*, Okichi explains, "I was a geisha and I knew men. I was to please Harris San in every way." In Samuel Fuller's *House of Bamboo* (1955), set in occupied Japan, army investigator Eddie Spanier (Robert Stack) moves in with Mariko (Shirley Yamaguchi), who bathes him, cooks his meals, massages his shoulders, and shares his futon. *Teahouse of the August Moon* uses the geisha image for comic effect when Lotus Blossom, whom Sakini tells Captain Fisby is "trained to please you," tries to undress him, and later she falls in love with him and wants to marry him. These films—all made by men—expressed male resentment of Western feminism in an era hardly noted for it, but several also unwittingly raised the subject of sexual exploitation, given the highly unequal environments depicted. Despite their condescending tone, they also showed love's potential to bridge cultural barriers, and they helped humanize the West's subject peoples for millions of Western viewers.

Scholars have suggested that miscegenation films set in Asia use the figure of the "white knight," a white protector who strips women of their independence, dominates them, and removes them from their culture.[3] In *China Doll*, it is true, the money Cliff pays for Shu-Jen rescues her family from poverty, and their mixed-race daughter eventually makes it to safety in the United States. In *Mort en fraude*, Horcier risks his life trying to help Anh's village, but he does not dominate Anh or destroy her independence. The white-knight concept also seems unconvincing for *Love Is a Many-Splendored Thing*.[4] Far from wishing to tear Suyin away from her culture or career, Mark is disappointed when she wears Western clothing, and he volunteers to live with her in China to allow her to continue practicing medicine. These two professionals respect each other, and she gives up no more independence than he does in entering into a serious relationship.[5] Indeed, the white-knight concept fits few of these films, and while some show white men saving women of color, others show women of color saving white men. In *Mort en fraude*, Anh saves Horcier twice by hiding him: first from the gangsters pursuing him and then from the Communists who search her village. In *The Purple Plain* (1954), a British film starring Gregory Peck as a depressed, self-destructive Canadian pilot in World War II Burma, the love of a young Burmese woman, Anna (Win Min Than), rescues him, much as Shu-Jen's love rescues Cliff from depression in *China Doll*.

Reading miscegenation narratives as metaphors for relations between colonizing and colonized nations has particular interest for films that urged white men who slept with Asian or Polynesian women to marry them. Such films were common: *China Gate* condemns Brock for abandoning Lea; *Return to Paradise* sides with Pastor Corbett when he urges Morgan not to abandon Maeva; and *The Quiet American* sides with Pyle, who, unlike Fowler, can marry Phuong. These stories in effect urged Westerners to treat their political relationships with the peoples of Asia and the Pacific as long-term commitments. Colonialist overtones also mark films that highlight white men's parental responsibilities toward their mixed-race children, including *China Gate* and *Return to Paradise*, while other films approve of whites adopting or protecting children, including *Anna and the King*, *The King and I*, *Pagan Love Song*, *The Inn of the Sixth Happiness*, and *China Doll*. The paternalist and colonialist overtones of such relationships are particularly clear in *China Doll*; after Cliff and Shu-Jen both die in a Japanese air raid, an epilogue set in 1957 shows Cliff's old war pals gathering at the Los Angeles airport to welcome their daughter, Shiao-Mee Brandon, who was found in a Hong Kong orphanage. These images urge Americans to do their duty, protecting and nurturing a region vital to the West's postwar strategic designs.

For Americans, their expansion in Asia and the Pacific after a war against empires with frankly racial ideologies called for affirmations of their differences from fascist imperialists.[6] Films fulfilled this role, while those that minimized the real extent of racism reassured Americans of their national virtues and moral fitness to lead postwar Asia. Many of these pro-miscegenation films used the backdrops of recent and current wars, but a few looked back to the early days of Western expansion in the region, and if the interracial relationships remained stymied in *Anna and the King*, *The King and I*, and *The Barbarian and the Geisha*, the sadness the films elicited as potential couples faced separation underlined the need to "open" Asia and erode cultural barriers.

Japan: The Occupation and the Cold War

Crucial to Washington's Cold War strategies in Asia were solid bonds with Japan, and cinema played a vital role in turning wartime enmity into friendship. An early example of this was King Vidor's *Japanese War Bride* (1952), a relatively obscure black-and-white independent film distributed by Twentieth Century-Fox. The film appeared amid growing attention to Japanese war brides, reaching theaters just before a 1952 revision of American immigration law that, while preserving national quotas for Asians, let Asian spouses move to the United States.[7] In calling attention to immigration from occupied or colonized countries, the film highlighted something both Europeans and Americans were just beginning to confront. Vidor's film, from a script Catherine Turney based on an Anson Bond story, tells a simple tale of an American, Jim Sterling (Don Taylor), who is wounded fighting in Korea and falls in love with his Japanese nurse, Tae Shimizu (Shirley Yamaguchi). Tae takes Jim to meet her parents, who grudgingly approve their marriage and relocation to the United States, and as they arrive at Jim's home in the farming community of Salinas, California, he introduces her to his family. The rest of the film examines the range of reactions their marriage elicits, and unlike so many evasive films about interracial couples, this one addresses crucial issues directly. Set in the present and mostly in the United States, it highlights the hostility the couple encounters, and it pursues the issue by their having a baby. The film has a keen eye for awkward little moments: Tae bows when people reach to shake hands with her; she tries to win over her frosty mother-in-law by helping dry dishes on her first evening in Salinas but is mortified when she breaks a dish; the family's friends laugh at Tae when Jim teaches her to dance. The film follows a convention by highlighting one racist villain, Jim's former girlfriend and now sister-in-law Fran (Marie Windsor), who detests Tae and schemes to turn Jim against her. In the scenes with Fran, the film briefly turns melodramatic and uncharacteristically evasive, as a subplot about Fran's enduring desire for Jim changes the subject from racism to jealousy. Nearly everyone, however, shows some degree of prejudice or ignorance. A friend at a party insults Tae by assuming Jim must have met her "at a geisha house"; Jim's father refers to her as a "Jap," then corrects himself; and Jim's mother complains, "I don't know how any of them think."

The film depicts American racism unblinkingly, and its characters remain human and believable as their memories of the war make their reactions understandable. When a friend of Jim's mother is rude to Tae, Jim's father reminds him that the woman's son was killed on Bataan, and though the woman's daughter insists, "We can't carry hatred and grudges the rest of our lives," the mother vows never to set foot in the Sterlings' house again. An elderly Japanese neighbor, Mr. Hasagawa, is equally bitter and refuses to enter the Sterling house, but not out of hostility toward the marriage; his anger comes from his internment during the war and locals' efforts to take his land, and though the film was bold in raising the subject at all, it claims that the government returned the Hasagawas' land after the war. The tensions finally take their toll on Tae, who runs away, and although the tale seems headed for a tragedy, it ends encouragingly.

The film invites viewers to sympathize with the likable Jim and Tae, and while confronting problems squarely, it suggests that people can learn from and overcome them. Tae assures Mr. Hasagawa's son that "time will heal the wounds of memory," and Jim's father tells him, "We all made our mistakes, but if we see them in time it isn't too late." The hardships Jim and Tae endure and the strains placed on their marriage and family relations may have made this seem more a cautionary tale than a defense of intermarriage, but for its time it showed courage in confronting prejudice. It also insisted that while overcoming prejudice would be slow and painful, Americans could indeed manage it. The film did not make the box-office charts, in part because it was a low-budget, poorly advertised picture with an obscure cast, and in part because it probed too soon and too deeply into painful issues. Most critics overlooked it, but in a sample of fourteen appraisals, it received eleven positive (79 percent), one negative, and two mixed reviews, with most applauding the film's plea for tolerance.[8]

Interracial relationships' ability to bridge cultural distance, foster understanding, and dissolve racism figured prominently in *Three Stripes in the Sun* (1955), which Richard Murphy cowrote and directed for Columbia Pictures. Based on a real story that seems tailored for Hollywood, this black-and-white film stars Aldo Ray as Sergeant Hugh O'Reilly, a World War II veteran whose combat experiences left him filled with hatred of the Japanese. The film begins with his arrival in Japan in 1949 on a mission to train American troops, and while his pals are eager to enjoy the nightlife and date Japanese women, O'Reilly broods and scowls. He starts a street brawl when he pushes a pesky Japanese would-be tour guide into a street vendor's stand and then goes after a man who shouts, "Yankee, Go Home!" After the military police bring him in, a Colonel explains that the Japanese will judge America by the individuals they meet, and "when we leave this occupation we'd like to leave them as friendly allies." In seeking to build support for a crucial Cold War alliance, the film urges Americans to abandon their hatred of the Japanese, whom the Colonel insists are "about the same as anybody" and who "take pride in their own civilization." The anti-American heckler, he informs O'Reilly, "wasn't Japanese to begin with," allowing the film to elide the troublesome topic of the anti-American protests that had flared up in Japan in 1954. O'Reilly remains unconvinced, but his transformation begins when he falsely accuses a Japanese man of stealing his wallet, only to learn that the man is a Catholic priest who found the wallet and was returning it. The Colonel orders the embarrassed O'Reilly to drive Father Yoshida to his orphanage, where he is shocked at the harsh conditions. Connecting with a little boy who reminds him of his own childhood spent shuffling from home to home, O'Reilly decides to start raising money from other GIs, and he embarks on a project to build a new orphanage.

O'Reilly's transformation proceeds as he falls in love with his interpreter,

Yuko (Mitsuko Kimura). Yuko's father objects to their romance by pointing out that when GIs fall in love with Japanese women, the army sends them home, and this film follows others in urging Americans to make serious commitments to the women they meet—much as Washington was making serious commitments to its Asian client states. It also hints at sexual exploitation of the poverty-stricken Japanese when Yuko notes that "since the occupation, many things change, Japanese girls change, many American soldier with much money." Although favorable to interracial marriage, the film sounds a note of caution when O'Reilly's commander, now a General, reacts to his intent to marry Yuko by telling him, "The army's opposed to these marriages for good and sufficient reasons, the chief one being that a large percentage of them end up unhappily." Yuko explains her own reluctance to marry Hugh by expressing concerns about how their children will be treated, and she worries about her fate should they move to America.

The film generally downplays American racism. The General dismisses O'Reilly's fears about Yuko's treatment in the United States, asking, "Do you really believe the American people are like that?" While the film highlights Japanese opposition to intermarriage through Yuko's parents—her father tells her, "You are of different races. It is not right you be together"—the only American racism depicted is O'Reilly's. In a brief moment of jealousy, he snaps at Yuko, "You want to marry a stinking Jap, it's your business," and though she is wounded by this outburst, she forgives him, certain that he carries no real hatred in his heart. As part of its flattering picture of Americans, the film highlights the soldiers' noble efforts for Japan's orphans, and in an era of angry anti-Americanism around the world, it must have been soothing to behold Japanese gratitude for the Yanks' kindness. The film's positive tone may well have won audience sympathies for its political messages, and while its suggestion that Yuko had nothing to fear in America was unduly sanguine, its sentimental depiction of the love between Hugh and the charming Yuko probably persuaded some viewers to think twice before giving dirty looks or worse to American-Japanese couples they encountered. The film's optimism culminates in a happy ending, a passionate kiss, and the completion of O'Reilly's transformation. A hit with the Defense Department and the State Department, which helped arrange its showing overseas, it did not make the box-office charts in the United States.[9]

In 1957, a far more successful, expensive, high-profile production revisited the subject: a film version of James Michener's 1953 novel, *Sayonara*. Marlon Brando's own company produced the film for Warner Bros., with Joshua Logan directing from a script by Paul Osborn (*Teahouse of the August Moon*). Brando starred as Major Lloyd "Ace" Gruver, a war-weary fighter pilot in Korea in 1951 who is brought to Japan by General Webster (Kent Smith), ostensibly for rest and recuperation but really because the General hopes Gruver will marry his daughter Eileen (Patricia Owens). Though the two go back many years, he now associates her with a humdrum military life like that of his father, and he begins drifting away from her. Asked by another officer to dissuade a subordinate, Airman Joe Kelly (Red Buttons), from marrying his Japanese sweetheart Katsumi (Miyoshi Umeki), Gruver fails, and out of frustration at Kelly's threat to give up his U.S. citizenship if need be, he tells Kelly in his thick southern accent, "Go ahead and marry this slant-eyed runt if you want to." Kelly gets Gruver to apologize for the slur, and he even convinces him to be his best man. Later, when Gruver sees the General and his abrasive, racist wife (Martha Scott) dressing down Captain Bailey (James Garner) for bringing a Japanese woman to an officers' club—"it degrades the uniform," Mrs. Webster insists—he says little. His transformation proceeds when he meets Kelly's endearing bride, and he also takes offense when an American bureaucrat who weds the two sneers at mixed marriages and treats the couple rudely.

When Bailey takes Gruver to a spot where the female members of a theatrical troupe parade by each day, Gruver is smitten upon glimpsing the star of the troupe, Hana-ogi (Miiko Taka). After watching her perform, Gruver—ignoring warnings that her troupe does not allow its members to date—gets Kelly and Katsumi to invite her to dinner at their house, and soon a clandestine romance develops. From this point on, General Webster; Colonel Crawford (Douglas Watson), a fanatically racist southerner; and the entire U.S. military establishment in Japan ban all "fraternization" with Japanese women, coming down hard on both Kelly and Gruver. To punish Kelly for his marriage, the Air Force announces his transfer home, knowing that U.S. immigration law prevents Katsumi—who is now pregnant—from accompanying him. The distraught couple, inspired by a Bunraku play about lovers committing suicide, carry out a suicide pact. Furious and grieving for his friends, Gruver, who has just learned of new legislation that will let GIs bring their brides home, proposes to Hana-ogi, who yearns to marry him and have children but explains her lifetime obligation to her troupe. In a twist from the novel's ending, in which Gruver and Hana-ogi part, the film ends happily with Gruver and Hana-ogi deciding to marry. The book's title, which conveyed the sadness of the lovers' separation, acquires a new meaning as Gruver and Hana-ogi ask reporters to tell all of those who opposed this marriage, "Sayonara."

The film is at times evasive in its treatment of miscegenation. Kelly, for example, says he has no family, so the film cannot examine their reactions, and it omits a subplot from the novel in which Gruver's father, a general, arrives in Japan and opposes the mixed marriage. When Eileen meets a Kabuki theater star, Nakamura (Ricardo Montalban), the film shows romantic interest developing but then abruptly drops the subplot, foregoing an opportunity to show General and Mrs. Webster faced with miscegenation in their own family. Although the film notes Japanese hostility to intermarriage, the main obstacle Hana-ogi faces is her atypical obligation to a troupe that rescued her when her father planned to sell her into prostitution. Like other films, *Sayonara* indirectly criticizes Western feminism and indulges white men's fantasies about servile Japanese women, showing Katsumi lovingly scrubbing Kelly's back in the bath.[10] Yet the white-knight syndrome does not apply to Kelly's marriage to Katsumi—he neither saves her from any danger, nor ends any career of hers, nor even wants to take her home, preferring instead to stay in Japan. Although Gruver's relationship with Hana-ogi has drawn charges that he forces her to abandon her career and her independence, Gruver offers to quit the Air Force despite knowing no other trade, and he does not want her to quit the theater.[11] The problem is that both face unjust restrictions on their personal freedom: Gruver from the military's policies against miscegenation (as well as racist U.S. immigration policies), and Hana-ogi from her membership in a troupe that binds her to a lifetime of celibacy and loyalty. The film still does not write off Hana-ogi's career; "I hope I can continue as a dancer," she tells the press after she and Gruver announce their marriage, "and I hope when I'm old I'll be able to teach children to dance." Gruver, in short, does not force her to retire, and she makes her own choice to marry him.

Despite its evasions, the film remains a bold indictment of racism, ethnocentrism, and hostility to miscegenation. Giving Gruver a southern accent was Brando's idea, and when he calls Katsumi a "slant-eyed runt" in that drawl—and when the racist Colonel Crawford speaks in a similar accent—the film makes a rather transparent point.[12] Gruver's transformation, which recalls those of O'Reilly in *Three Stripes in the Sun*, Horcier in *Mort en fraude*, Jeffords in *Broken Arrow*, and Boone in *The Big Sky*, invited viewers to rethink their own racism. Some have suggested that Gruver abandons Eileen out of a disdain for Western feminism and a crisis of masculinity, and that he prefers Hana-ogi—who wears pants and plays male roles on stage—out of latent homosexuality, but there are other ways to read his choice.[13] Although his views on miscegenation change in part because he is impressed with how "cute" and subservient Katsumi is, he spurns Eileen not because he has lost interest in women. Instead he resents her parents pushing him into a marriage that (as the novel explains more fully) reminds him of his own parents' emotionally barren marriage. He also finds something missing in his own life, and his transformation involves his discovery of attractive aspects of Japanese culture. For a man unfulfilled by his world of military bases and wars, his visits to theater performances and his delight at discovering sake, the tea ceremony, and the beauty and grace of Japanese homes and gardens are part of his awakening and transformation. His pal Kelly is clearly happier when wearing his kimono, and he takes great pleasure in teaching Gruver Japanese ways; the working-class Kelly, in effect, civilizes his social and military superior, and the film also reverses colonialist conventions as Asia teaches and civilizes the West. Both men fall in love with Japan as well as Japanese women.

The film's boldness extends to its criticism of the U.S. military, which contrasts with *Three Stripes in the Sun*. A military doctor who sends Gruver to Japan for a furlough suggests he "tangle with one of those beautiful Japanese dolls," and the juxtaposition of this semi-official encouragement of casual sex with the cruelty the Air Force shows in separating Kelly and his pregnant wife amounts to an indictment of American exploitation of Japanese women.[14] Eileen also complains to her father, "The army lets them marry then forces them to desert their wives and babies," and in the grim scene in which Colonel Crawford tells Kelly he must leave Japan and abandon his pregnant wife, two props—a portrait of General MacArthur and an American flag on the Colonel's desk—link this racist Colonel with the United States and its military. During production, American military authorities in Japan wrote to studio head Jack Warner to complain that "the *Sayonara* story reflects far from favorably on the Air Force and its personnel" and to warn that the Air Force would not cooperate.[15] The filmmakers stood their ground, and the film's credits include no thanks to U.S. military authorities. As with *Japanese War Bride*, the film shows the hostility facing interracial couples so frankly that it may have unintentionally dissuaded people from such relationships, but the film urges defiance of prejudice. When Gruver first warns Kelly, "Even your friends are going to put you down if you marry this girl," Kelly replies, "The friends I got of that kind, they won't be friends of mine much longer." When Hana-ogi voices doubts about their marriage by asking Gruver, "What would happen to our children? What would they be?" he replies calmly, "They'd be half Japanese, half American; they'd be half yellow and half white; they'd be half you, they'd be half me." And when Hana-ogi and Gruver tell the press of their intention to marry, she tells a reporter whom she knows, "my people will be shocked," then adds, "I hope they will learn to understand, and someday approve. We are not afraid, because we know this is right."

To some, the unhappy ending that befalls Kelly and Katsumi signifies the film's conservative outlook and disdain for miscegenation.[16] As in *Broken Arrow*, however, this is a case of martyrdom designed to elicit anger at those who harmed an interracial relationship presented entirely sympathetically, not a conservative device in a cautionary tale opposing miscegenation. The film (unlike the book) gives the other relationship a happy ending, and both outcomes are consistent with the film's sympathy for miscegenation. *Sayonara* demonstrates once again that not all unhappy endings for interracial relationships mean the same thing.

Despite its allusion to Americans' exploitation of Japanese women, and to official acquiescence in it, the film does not try to explore the entire range of sexual relations during and after the occupation. It does briefly acknowledge Japanese men's resentment of GIs dating Japanese women when a mob of Japanese nationalists in matching headbands attacks Gruver and Bailey. Despite offering this whiff of anticolonialist nationalism, the film does not sympathize with it at all, and it reassures viewers about Japanese-American friendship by having locals rescue the Americans from the mob.[17] Like *Three Stripes in the Sun*, it also obscures Japanese anti-Americanism when General Webster explains that these were "professional troublemakers" sent by "those who hate us." The story notes understandable Japanese anger at America, as Hana-ogi initially resists Gruver's affections because, as Kelly explains, "We shot her brother and killed her father with our bombs." But Gruver later tells her "there were an awful lot of Americans killed, too, but I think it'd be best if we forgot about that." Indeed Hana-ogi gradually overcomes her prejudices against Americans just as Gruver sheds his hostility toward intermarriage, and these twin transformations invite both Japanese and American viewers to follow their path.

If claims that *Sayonara* frowns on interracial marriage are unconvincing, arguments that it reflects colonialist thinking stand on somewhat firmer ground. The pairing of American men with submissive Japanese women may indeed be read as a metaphor for U.S. domination of Japan, but whereas Katsumi seems submissive, Kelly studies Japanese and is happy to live in her country and by her customs, and the relationship between Gruver and Hana-ogi is even more egalitarian.[18] Instead, what gives the film certain colonialist overtones is its promotion of emotional bonds with a crucial country in Washington's Cold War strategy in Asia, and like many romantic films in politically sensitive settings, *Sayonara* essentially ignores that broader political context. As the U.S.-Japanese relationship evolved, however, from the total domination of the early occupation years into a more mutual relationship that served both countries' interests, it became less and less colonialist, and *Sayonara* did little to urge American domination of Japan. Indeed its attacks on the U.S. military's policies on "fraternization," on Washington's anti-Asian immigration policies, and on the sexual exploitation of Japanese women took direct aim at racial discrimination, a defining trait of colonialism.

Sayonara was the number three film of 1958, received ten Oscar nominations (winning four), and impressed American critics, as twenty-seven of thirty-four praised it (79 percent), two panned it, and five gave it mixed or neutral reviews.[19] Not everyone welcomed its message: *America's* Moira Walsh denounced "a flat-footed glorification of Oriental-Occidental marriages" that "stacks the cards outrageously in making the Army and military regulations the villain," and the *Hollywood Citizen News* praised the filmmaking but charged that the "ethical and social values are not acceptable to our Western customs." In the conservative *Los Angeles Times*, Edwin Schallert noted that while one interracial relationship ends in suicide, the other "takes the happier turn, if it can really be called that," and that paper's Philip K. Scheuer considered the ending happy "at least for the picture's purpose," while warning that it "will certainly not meet with universal approval." Noting that interracial love was "outside the frame of reference for most of us," James Powers of the *Hollywood Reporter* also feared that the film and its ending "may be considered controversial in some areas," but he found it an "extraordinary picture" with a "piercing and shattering story."

Such praise was common, and most reviews endorsed the film's views on interracial marriage. Calling it "one of the great pictures of the last two decades," Marjory Adams of the *Boston Globe* noted that "intolerance gets a blow in the solar plexus," and she praised it for showing "the ugly side of the situation," including "American disdain for Oriental manners, the Army refusal to allow 'fraternizing,' and the manner in which men who married Japanese women were callously and brutally sent home" alone. Nisei journalist Larry Tajiri of the *Denver Post*, pleased that "times have changed" since the days of Madame Butterfly and of Kipling's "East is East" warning, wrote that the filmmakers "have told their story well" in "one of the year's important films." The New York critics were especially warm toward its politics; Kate Cameron of the *Daily News* found it "a persuasive argument for the ultimate integration of the races," while *Cue* called it "about as poignant and moving a plea for universal brotherhood as we have had yet, in any movie." In the *Post*, Archer Winsten described it as a "profoundly moving" and "beautiful picture which also has something to say," adding that "it does not blink at facts an American need not be proud of." Sharing its Cold War aims, Winsten wrote that it "spurns the national and racial prejudices that so handicap this country in its dealings with the world and its competition with Russia." Even southern critics—in Dallas, New Orleans, and Atlanta—praised the film without protesting its view of miscegenation.

British critics were more skeptical, with four positive, six negative, and eleven mixed reviews in a sample of twenty-one.[20] Although a few resented a massive publicity campaign, most complaints concerned the film's length and Marlon Brando's southern drawl, which many critics found unintelligible. In the *Daily Herald*, Harry Weaver called it a film with "something worth saying," and the *Daily Telegraph*'s Campbell Dixon wrote that "it really is, in its romantic, glossy way, a highly expert job," and he pronounced himself "agreeably surprised." The *Sunday Express*, noting that "the Americans are depicted as naïve social barbarians," remarked that "there is no nation than can beat itself harder over the head than the United States." Although puzzled by its intentions, Nina Hibbin of the *Daily Worker* felt it showed "the brutal racial policy of the American military authorities," adding that "at its peak it is deeply disturbing, and that is its special quality." The *Sunday Dispatch*, however, complained that it "leans over backwards in its glamorisation of slant-eyed women and the Japanese way of life" as it shows an American "marrying a Jap girl," while the *Reynolds News* resented its defense of interracial marriage and felt that Hana-ogi "asks all the important questions," such as, "What about the duty we owe to our people, to our differing cultures?" and "What about our children?"

Sayonara sold 1,641,646 tickets in France, where critics divided roughly evenly among positive, negative, and mixed judgments.[21] Critics generally welcomed the film's antiracism and saluted its courage for criticizing the military's policies, even if some found the treatment of the racial issues superficial. André Bazin, who reviewed the film in three publications, praised its intentions and moral courage but felt that its critique of racism had, for Americans, "an interest and an edge that it lacks for us."[22] Bazin hastened to add that "it is not, alas, that we have nothing to learn on this subject, but because the crystallization points of our own racist reflexes are different from the Americans' we can scarcely connect with the film's heroes." He also found the conflict between the lovers and racist authorities less compelling than a theme he wished it had explored: "the real difficulties of love between two beings shaped by different civilizations." Because of that cultural distance and the problems mixed marriages encountered, he even sympathized with the army's opposition to them. Such pessimism about love's ability to bridge cultural differences contrasts with the attitudes of those French colonialist authorities and writers who had believed that bonds of love would strengthen France's hold over its colonies.[23] Still, no French critic voiced suspicions of the film's ulterior political motives.

The pessimism about East-West romance that Bazin expressed also marked Alain Resnais's *Hiroshima, mon amour* (1959), based on Marguerite Duras's screenplay. Although the Franco-Japanese relationship was not a colonial one, the film remains noteworthy for its suggestion of insurmountable East-West differences. In the story, an unnamed French woman (Emmanuelle Riva) visiting Hiroshima to make a film for the peace movement has an affair with an unnamed Japanese man (Eiji Okada), and while the two find common ground in their painful memories of the war, he insists she can never really grasp the tragedy of Hiroshima. As she recounts the trauma of an affair she had with a German from the occupying forces in her hometown of Nevers, he sums up his own inability to understand by saying, "I was not in Nevers," and despite their bonds of suffering and wounded memory, the two struggle to connect. Although the camera lingers on their bodies as they touch, their ongoing conversations highlight a void between them, and the film conveys a powerful and deepening sadness when she returns to France. Resnais's purpose was hardly to oppose interracial relationships, and the brief but passionate affair between the two certainly allowed each a merciful moment of happiness. The film contrasts sharply with Hollywood message pictures, and Resnais was more interested in abstract, poetic explorations of the intricacies of human grief, memory, and stymied healing than in facile political points, but the film nonetheless looks skeptically at interracial romance's power to bridge cultural gulfs.

The experience of World War II and the wars that followed in Indochina and Korea raised Western people's awareness of Asia and the Pacific and shaped their attitudes toward the inhabitants of the region. For the hundreds of thousands of Westerners who went there for the first time in these wars, their personal encounters, including sexual and romantic liaisons, affected their perceptions of these peoples, and even people at home became more familiar with the region through news reports and conversations with veterans. Films made during and after these wars also dramatized the experience of the soldiers and other Westerners who went there and conveyed them to millions of movie viewers at home. Just over half of these thirty-four films about interracial relationships in Asia and the Pacific either took place in one of the recent wars or concerned veterans of those wars. Wars, of course, create a wide range of emotions, and they have the potential to poison relations for many years. And much as wars could generate a wide range of feelings about the peoples involved, films took many different positions about cross-racial sex, romance, and marriage. Familiarity, in short, could breed contempt, but it could also build sympathy, understanding, and respect.

A significant minority of these films, whether war-related or not, took wholly or largely negative views of miscegenation. Old yellow-peril fears of Asian rapists appeared in several films about Communist China and Indochina; equally old notions of Westerners' corrupting effects on noble savages figured in others; and a few, such as *The King and I* and *Hiroshima, mon amour* simply questioned love's ability to bridge cultural differences. A majority of these films, however, viewed interracial relationships optimistically and sympathetically. Some purveyed images of these lands as sexual playgrounds for white men and offered fantasies about eager and servile women of Asia and the Pacific. Others, more numerous, urged Westerners to treat their partners with respect and to commit to serious, lifelong relationships, and intentionally or not, those films served to build support for America's postwar role in Asia and the Pacific. They did so by teaching the uninitiated about the region, by humanizing the peoples depicted, by insisting on their need for Western protection and assistance, by urging Western viewers to abandon their racial prejudices and opposition to miscegenation, and by giving Western policies a benign image. These films thus fit the patterns of liberal colonialism, favoring the West's basic aims in Cold War Asia through sentimental narratives urging fair and humane treatment of the people of the region. Yet while they may have served imperial purposes, these films, by questioning rather than highlighting and stigmatizing differences and by attacking notions of racial superiority that colonialism ultimately requires, also helped Western audiences to reimagine their relations with racial others in more equal terms.

CHAPTER NINE

Black-White Couples and Internal Decolonization

Any claim that Western filmmakers wished to challenge the miscegenation taboo in these years meets its stiffest test with black-white relationships. Attesting to the particular sensitivity of this issue for Americans was the Production Code's specific ban on miscegenation between "the black and white races," and images of both romantic black-white relationships and relations between masters and slaves remained missing from movie screens while depictions of other forms of miscegenation were fairly common. Nor were things much different in Europe, for aside from a few interwar French films pairing Josephine Baker with white men, neither French nor British filmmakers explored that topic before the late 1950s. There were, of course, far fewer black people in Britain or France than in the United States, but those two countries ruled over large black populations in Africa and the Caribbean. Cross-racial relationships were not part of the formula in African jungle and safari films in the 1940s and 1950s, and overtly political films set in the present featured black-white friendships, not miscegenation. Two 1950s films set in Africa that did depict miscegenation—*Saadia* (1953) and Britain's *The Black Tent* (1956)—featured Arab or Berber women played by white actresses.

Many white Americans were not—and are not—accustomed to seeing black-white relations as part of the history of colonialism. While the belief that colonialism only existed overseas helped to produce this blind spot, in the decolonization era that misconception drew growing criticism from African Americans. As postwar filmmakers began to explore black-white miscegenation, they faced a choice between setting tales in the past or present, with each option having certain didactic advantages and disadvantages. Those set in the past were likeliest to illuminate the colonial dimensions of American race relations, but viewers might consider them remote and irrelevant. Stories set in the present, while more evidently topical, were less likely to indicate a historically colonial relationship. And whether set in the past or present, no films illuminated connections between slavery and current problems.

The box-office success of two 1947 films on anti-Semitism—Edward Dmytryk's *Crossfire*, made for RKO, and Elia Kazan's *Gentleman's Agreement*, made for Darryl F. Zanuck at Fox—inspired Hollywood to examine other forms of prejudice. A handful of films about African Americans released between 1949 and 1951 included three about black-white miscegenation, eluding the Production Code by focusing mainly on the mixed-race offspring of previous relationships not depicted. The first to arrive was *Lost Boundaries* (1949), a low-budget, independent production that B-film specialist Alfred L. Werker directed for producer Louis De Rochemont, known for the *March of Time* documentaries. Based on journalist William L. White's *Reader's Digest* story and his subsequent 1948 book about a real African American physician who passed for white in a New Hampshire town, the film starred the half-Cuban New Jersey native Mel Ferrer in his first credited role, as Dr. Scott Carter.

The film opens with Scott's graduation from medical school in Chicago in 1922 and his wedding with Marcia Mitchell (Beatrice Pearson), also a "Negro" who looks white. Rejected for an internship at a black hospital in Georgia because he looks white, and unable to find work in white hospitals because he is open about his ethnicity, Scott gets nowhere, and a montage sequence shows a slew of rejection letters. Like a medical school classmate who spoke of working as a Pullman porter, Scott contemplates working for a railroad in Boston, musing that "if a passenger faints, my medical training will be invaluable"; he turns instead to making shoes. The film thus resurrects the tragic-mulatto convention while clearly blaming racism for it. He reluctantly accepts his black friends' advice to get started in medicine by temporarily passing for white, and he accepts a position in the fictional New Hampshire town of Keenham. He gradually overcomes the all-white town's wariness toward outsiders, and he and Marcia happily raise two children, telling them nothing of their ethnic heritage. Years pass, and with the arrival of World War II both Scott and his son Howie (Richard Hylton) enlist in the navy, but background investigators discover the truth, and the navy's racial policies force Scott to resign his commission. When he informs Howie of their dark secret, the lad suffers an identity crisis as he stands before the mirror in disbelief, has nightmares about white friends morphing into blacks, and runs away to Harlem. After Howie's mistaken arrest in a minor incident involving a gang fight, a wise, sympathetic black police officer, Lieutenant Thompson (Canada Lee, shortly before his blacklisting), helps him come to terms with his situation and understand his parents' actions. Although the town's discovery of the

Carters' secret leads old acquaintances to shun them, at the end the pastor reminds his flock that "we are all God's children," and a narrator closes the film on a positive note by stating that Scott is still the town doctor.

Despite retaining a sober, semidocumentary feel, *Lost Boundaries* reveals its colors, so to speak, in denouncing racism and in affirming people's common humanity. Scott, for example, answers a navy investigator's routine question about having Negro blood by saying, "We all have the same blood in our veins." A denunciation of racism informs the film's indulgence of passing: Marcia's father urges the newlyweds to pass, telling Scott that when he and his family were living as Negroes in the South, they "had nothing, absolutely nothing," and now, living as a white man in the North, he has "a good job—a white man's job." Lieutenant Thompson reminds Howie of the poverty and crime he had just seen in Harlem and asks him, "Can you honestly blame anyone for trying to cross the boundary into the white man's world?" Indeed, the film dramatizes the privileges white Americans enjoy because of past and present racial discrimination.[1] It even shows how white-dominated society harms itself through discrimination, as medical school graduates working as railroad porters and shoemakers indicate a waste of talents and educational resources. In wartime, racism in the military was responsible for the turning away of doctors like Scott and the loss of potential fighting men like Howie's black friend "Coop" (William Greaves), who tells Howie he will not join the navy because "serving meals to officers just isn't my idea of war."

The costs of racism also emerge when a nurse deliberately drops a bottle of blood donated by "somebody's chauffeur," leading an angry Scott to snap that "some fighting man may lose his life because of this." That nurse is but one of the racists presented for condemnation. When Howie brings Coop home from college to a party at his parents' home, a white neighbor sneers to a friend that "no one with any background invites darkies to their home," and even the Carters' daughter Shelly (Susan Douglas) objects to Coop's presence, complaining to her parents, "With all the boys at college, my brother's got to bring home a coon." Her crisis upon learning of her own ancestry again recalls the tragic-mulatto convention, and in the final church scene an anguished Shelly walks out during the antiracist sermon. Screenwriter Charles Palmer explained that he used this device to avert "any peaches-and-cream feeling of a completely happy ending on a problem which is still unsolved generally."[2] In the church, a white man shakes Scott's hand, Shelly's boyfriend gives Howie a wink and a smile, and the pastor pats Howie on the shoulder and smiles, but it remains unstated whether this means that the whole town or simply a few individuals have rejected prejudice.

So although the film denounces racism and offers hope of progress, it suggests that change may take time.

Like other films about racism, Lost Boundaries has incurred criticism for timidity and false progressivism. The charges include the claim that the film makes black people the villains, but the argument fits only the black doctor and nurses who turn Scott away for being too light-skinned.[3] The positive black characters include Scott's mentor, Dr. Charles Howard, Howie's friend Coop, and the police Lieutenant, and the film primarily indicts white characters and institutions (including the Navy). Claims that the film pities the Carters for having Negro blood and blames them for fooling people might be more compelling if the film did not highlight the discrimination that compelled the Carters to pass—though it does fault them for deceiving their children.[4] Another source of criticism, reflecting resentment over Hollywood's history of racist hiring practices, is the casting of white actors to play the Carters; in this film, however, using actors who looked at all African American would have undermined the story, which requires everyone to believe the Carters are white.

The attention the film gave to the problems of "white Negroes" has also provoked charges that it avoided issues relevant to most African Americans, while defending passing—a choice unavailable to most African Americans.[5] Yet if it defends the Carters' passing, it is hardly sanguine about it, and they chose this path only in reaction to racist injustice. The film's main point is to critique racism, not to recommend passing. It also underlines a crucial drawback even for those who can pass: the need to live in fear of discovery. The film, it is true, does little to emphasize other drawbacks to passing, such as the difficulty of taking pride in one's ethnicity or fighting to change a nefarious system rather than simply surviving it individually. On the other hand, Scott speaks out against prejudice when possible, and he travels to Boston regularly to treat patients of all races; he could not have done much more to combat racism without arousing suspicions and sacrificing his career. So although this film might have been even bolder, there are limits to what one movie can accomplish, and this pioneering work, by leading viewers to put themselves in the Carters' place, offered a persuasive critique of racism.

A certain measure of historical empathy is in order in assessing this film, which was made before the victories of the civil rights movement in the 1950s and 1960s and was one of the very first films to criticize racism toward blacks. The concept of cinematic empathy also applies in light of complaints of timidity.[6] Although a more radical film might be more pleasing to viewers today, it bears recalling the challenges of making such a film in 1949, of securing distribution, and of getting audiences to watch and embrace it. Several writers struggled to fashion a script that was neither too inflammatory nor too timid, and MGM, which had originally accepted the script, got cold feet and dropped the project after testing audience reactions to the story.[7] De Rochemont had to invest his own money, and with no studio willing to make or distribute the film, he and others took considerable risks. Moreover, a box-office failure would have discouraged further films on racial issues, so there was more than his own money and future in the film industry at stake. The need to draw audiences also helps explain the casting of white actors and the restraint of its criticism of racists.[8] While the film did disappoint some black intellectuals and leftist film critics at the time, a film that pleased them would likely have died at the box office. If the point was to get people to rethink their prejudices, it made little sense to cater to people already staunchly opposed to racism. Perhaps it was pandering to whites' prejudices to evoke their sympathies for characters who looked like them, but given the film's political aims, the strategy made sense.

That strategy was vindicated when this low-budget, independent film reached the number forty-eight slot for 1949, despite a meager promotion budget, exclusion from the studios' distribution system, and what *Variety* called "the pic's virtually guaranteed tabus in large sectors of the south."[9] Censors in the South did indeed ban it, and de Rochemont even tried to buy television time to air it in Atlanta and Memphis.[10] Many newspapers ran only tiny ads, and larger ones used a sensationalist tone out of keeping with its sober approach. Despite claims that it received "mixed reviews," it did extremely well with American critics: twenty-one of twenty-two reviews examined here were positive.[11] Bosley Crowther of the *New York Times* found it a film of "extraordinary courage, understanding, and dramatic power," while Archer Winsten of the *New York Post* described it as "a profoundly stirring emotional experience" that "could also move the hearts of men to historic change." Nor was such praise limited to national magazines and New York critics. In the *St. Louis Post-Dispatch*, Myles Standish described it as "an intelligent, dramatically sound, engrossing, and touching work," and the *Detroit News*'s John Finlayson claimed that "few motion pictures have tackled the problem of racial intolerance with such forthrightness and compassion." Critics in New England raved: the *Hartford Courant* felt it showed "what the movies might be," while the *Boston Herald* called it "a film to make you think and feel, as well as be proud of the men and women who produced it." Calling it "a great and important picture," the *Boston Globe* noted the town's acceptance of the Carters and added, "Praise to New England, the place where the abolitionists preached the equality of all races." One paper after another lauded the film's restraint and lack of preaching while attesting to its emotional power.

Some critics did express reservations. Lillian Scott of the African American *Chicago Defender* contended that "the reaction of most Negroes to 'passing' is one of disapproval," and she charged that Scott's rejection at the black hospital in Georgia "didn't ring true" in a region filled with "light skinned southern Negroes." Though Scott admitted "we went to 'Lost Boundaries' prejudiced against its casting of white actors and actresses," she gave it "credit for courage and imagination" and concluded that it "will never be forgotten by white or black." At a rare southern booking in Dallas, the *Morning News* praised it as entertainment but complained that "there are many bits of subtle propaganda worked into the screen play which is heavily overlaid with the crusading spirit" and warned that "neither films like this one nor legislation will bring the solution." The *Post*'s Winsten suspected that "Negroes might well object to the picture's graphic sequence of the son's nightmare horror as he realizes his new condition." Regarding the focus on passing, Crowther wrote, "To be sure, this film is not a picture of the whole complex problem of race and racial discrimination," and *Commonweal* said that while it did not "tackle all the problems connected with Negroes in the United States" it remained "a tremendous step forward in the fight against prejudice."

As for charges that the film faulted the Carters' deceptions rather than the racism that provoked it, it bears noting that no critic blamed the Carters, while many defended their passing. *Film Daily* wrote that "circumstances and prejudices force them to do so," and *Commonweal* pointed out that though they deceive people, "the preceding scenes make very clear the difficulty that a Negro doctor has in getting a position." The problem, the *Boston Globe* concluded, is "the fault of society," and *Time* called Carter "a decent man caught in an indecent dilemma." Indeed, the indictment of racism resonated strongly with American critics. Winsten called the Carters' plight "a near crucifixion on the cross of America's color psychosis," which was "the shame of our nation," and *America* said the film revealed "the weakest link in American democracy." Noting the spotlight on institutional racism, the *New York Daily News* observed that "the hospitals and the U.S. Navy are the villains of the piece." St. Louis's Standish liked the focus on the North, where "racial injustice is too smugly thought of as an offense only of the South." Nor did the happy ending engender complacency. To Standish, "the recording of one small victory for humanity emphasizes, by its very minuteness, the vastness of the problem," and the *Detroit News* lamented "the meagerness of tolerance among well-intentioned white people." Declaring that *Lost Boundaries* had paved the way for more such films, *Variety* said it "shows that the U.S. film industry, having once decided to tackle the most explosive issue in the U.S., is capable of extraordinary courage, intelligence, and human sympathy."

De Rochemont had far less success getting distribution overseas. Despite winning the prize for the best screenplay at the 1949 Cannes Film Festival, it received scant coverage and few bookings in France. In Britain, it had a brief run in London and got few reviews. Two papers on the left praised it: the *Manchester Guardian* wrote that "Hollywood is building up a good reputation in its exploitation of the colour bar theme, and human stories like this will have a much wider influence than reformist preaching," and the *Daily Worker* found it "a sincere and moving film."[12] But the *London Times* yawned at "yet another in the cycle of American films on the question of racial discrimination," calling it "very slow." The *Times* also misread the film, claiming it said "everything would be all right if only black were not really black."[13] Dilys Powell of the *Sunday Times* also found the subject uninteresting and the film "well-meaning, slow, and dull," admitting that she preferred a good musical.[14] Perhaps because Britain's colonialism took place overseas, and because most immigration from the Caribbean and Africa was still in the future, few British critics showed interest in films about racism.

Pinky (1949)

Three months after *Lost Boundaries* came out, Twentieth Century-Fox released a much higher-budget tale of miscegenation and passing in *Pinky* (1949). After director John Ford quit the picture early on, Zanuck replaced him with Elia Kazan, director of *Gentleman's Agreement*; Philip Dunne, Dudley Nichols, and others based the script on Mississippi novelist Cid Ricketts Sumner's 1946 book, *Quality*.[15] Rising young star Jeanne Crain played Patricia "Pinky" Johnson, who looks white but whose grandmother Dicey (Ethel Waters) is black. As the film opens in a small southern town, it shows Pinky arriving, and because it does not reveal her ethnicity at first, it leaves viewers to wonder what a white woman is doing in a black neighborhood. Her Granny does not recognize her at first, as she has been away at nursing school in Boston. She has returned, we learn later, because of misgivings about her engagement to a white man, Dr. Thomas Adams (William Lundigan), who is unaware of her ancestry. Accustomed to the privileges of whiteness up North, Pinky enjoys respect only until people discover her race, and she also struggles to cope with her Granny's poverty.

When Pinky goes to see Jake (Frederick O'Neal), a black man who owes Dicey money, she ends up in an argument in the street with Jake's ill-tempered girlfriend Rozelia (Nina Mae McKinney), who is also of mixed race but visibly so. When two white policemen break up the argument, they address Pinky as "Ma'am" until Rozelia tells them, "She's nothing but a low-down colored gal," at which point the officers manhandle and arrest her along with Rozelia and Jake. After the kindly Judge Walker (Basil Ruysdael) releases her, she is walking home at night when two drunken white men offer her a ride, telling her, "We can't let no white girl walk by herself in this nigger section." When she tells them she lives there, their attitude changes, and after their headlights reveal her body through a translucent dress, she barely escapes a rape attempt. That trauma leads her to ponder her own ancestry and the probability that it involved a similar incident.

Pinky's travails continue when Dicey pressures her to serve as nurse to Miss Em (Ethel Barrymore), a crotchety, dying white woman who lives alone in the big house of the old plantation. The house and all it represents horrify Pinky, who resents Dicey's devotion to Miss Em and does not wish to work for her. "I've known another kind of life," she explains. "I've been treated like a human being." Pressured by her grandmother, she takes the unpaid job, putting up with the imperious Miss Em, who comes to respect her when she stands up for herself. When Pinky's former fiancé Tom arrives unexpectedly, she informs him of her Negro ancestry. Despite his shock, Tom wishes to resume their engagement on the condition that they live in the North with Pinky passing for white; Pinky is skeptical but undecided. (The film, by the way, shows Tom and Pinky kissing, in clear violation of the Production Code.) Meanwhile, Miss Em is visited by her annoying cousin, Melba Wooley (Evelyn Varden), who keeps insulting Pinky and accusing her of pilferage. Mrs. Wooley expects to inherit the house and property, but when Miss Em dies, a will she had just written bequeaths the house and land to Pinky. When Mrs. Wooley contests the will on the grounds that Pinky drugged Miss Em and made her rewrite her will, Pinky rejects everyone's advice to abandon a case against whites in a southern court, and she finally persuades Judge Walker to be her lawyer. Although the case goes badly, it is not a jury trial, and the judge implausibly rules in Pinky's favor. Facing a choice between marrying Tom and passing for white up North or staying and putting the house and property to some use, she decides to stay, bidding Tom farewell. After struggling to figure out what Miss Em meant when her will expressed "confidence in the use to which she will put this property," Pinky finally turns the house into a clinic and nursing school for blacks. At the end, Pinky busily oversees her creation, and for the first time her mood has finally brightened.

Scholars, citing Pinky's decision to reject Tom and stay in the South, have called the film conservative, reactionary, and segregationist, and they have argued that it sought to criticize blackness and passing and to keep blacks in their place.[16] Other criticisms concern the casting of a white actress to play Pinky and, as with *Lost Boundaries*, a distracting focus on the atypical problems of "white Negroes."[17] To evaluate these claims, it helps to consider the filmmakers' intentions, as well as the pressures facing them in a country overwhelmingly opposed to miscegenation and an industry forbidding images of black-white miscegenation.

In 1948, as Zanuck was overseeing rewrites, South Carolina Governor Strom Thurmond was running for president from a Dixiecrat splinter party opposed to President Truman's civil rights agenda. Films were just beginning to examine bigotry, and though *Crossfire* and *Gentleman's Agreement* had drawn well, it was unclear how a film on bigotry against African Americans would do. Moreover, *Pinky* was bolder than *Home of the Brave* (1949) and *Lost Boundaries* in scrutinizing racism in the South. In a business in which even moguls lacked job security, Zanuck feared boycotts and censorship. "There is a grave danger," he told a colleague in October 1948, "that a large part of the southern market may be lost," making the film "a doubtful venture."[18] Zanuck pressed on, hoping that northern and foreign markets would compensate, and believing it might even play in the South.[19] The Production Code Administration also feared losing the southern markets, and it warned that the film might spur the creation of new state and local censorship boards, fuel recruitment for the Ku Klux Klan, and create perceptions that Hollywood was siding with Truman on civil rights.[20] There were also fears that a backlash against *Pinky* could damage current efforts to get the Supreme Court to grant films First Amendment rights.

Zanuck's motives were political as well as commercial, though he disingenuously claimed otherwise.[21] His antiracist agenda is visible in a note to the NAACP's Walter White—who himself could pass for white, and who wanted a bolder film; Zanuck wrote that "if the picture is not shown and seen in those regions where injustice and racial prejudice are strongest, no good can be accomplished."[22] In order to persuade those who needed it, Zanuck wanted a film they would actually go see, so the picture "must be above all things non-propagandist."[23] This reluctance to alienate white viewers led Zanuck and his writers to remove the character of Arch Naughton—in the novel, an abrasive, light-skinned civil rights activist from New York—but the film added various racial incidents that help to awaken Pinky's racial consciousness and defiance.

As for casting Crain, Zanuck called her "the biggest box-office attraction on the lot today," and with so much at stake, his choice is understandable. Although the decision cost a black actress a starring role, the production did provide work for numerous black actors and extras.[24] Kazan's wish for Dorothy Dandridge to play Pinky foundered when the studio's New York office, relaying pressure from distributors, vetoed the idea.[25] Indeed, any actress who looked at all black, including Dandridge and Nina Mae McKinney, would have been problematic for a character everyone assumes is white.[26] Although the casting of a white actress has drawn charges that the film pandered to racists, the decision made sense given Zanuck's goal of altering the attitudes of prejudiced whites.[27] As Zanuck told White, he sought "to make the white majority experience emotionally the injustice and daily hurts suffered by colored people."[28] As for the film's intentions regarding interracial marriage, Kazan told *Ebony*, "I'm worried because people might think we're saying Negroes and whites shouldn't marry," when in fact it was only that "this particular boy and girl shouldn't get married."[29] In earlier versions, the two did marry, but a Zanuck associate recommended "something that will jolt and outrage the racists," and they settled on a Negro woman snubbing a white man.[30]

The film does contain some dated imagery and stereotypes of blacks.[31] Benevolent whites such as Judge Walker and Miss Em also bear out complaints about the film's paternalism, and it takes a woman who looks white to provide leadership for the black community.[32] As for the treatment of passing, it is true that we see no discrimination before Pinky's decision to pass, so the picture does less than *Lost Boundaries* had done to justify passing as a rational act.[33] But it does allude to a less-than-perfect racial situation up North, where Tom insists Pinky must resume passing if they are to marry. And although it is true that Pinky's invisible blackness horrifies white characters—Mrs. Wooley declares that it "just gives me the creeps"—this does not warrant confusing the film's viewpoint with that of its most unsympathetic character.[34]

Whether the film endorses segregation hinges on concepts of racial identity and on interpretations of Pinky's choices. While it may appear that the film chides Pinky for passing, insists on her blackness, and urges her to know her place, her decision to stay in the South is highly circumscribed by social pressures, constructs, customs, and taboos. It was neither Pinky nor the film's producers who invented the "one-drop rule"; it was instead whites who opposed miscegenation and wished to protect their privileges from mulatto infiltration.[35] Even African Americans have long accepted the one-drop rule, viewing people with almost any degree of African ancestry as African American and resenting passing.[36] Zanuck himself criticized the idea "that having Negro blood somehow sets one apart, that it makes one *internally* as well as *externally* different, that the possession of a trace of Negro blood makes one feel a mystic identity with the race."[37] The film makes that point when Pinky tells Miss Em, "You're the ones who set the standards, you whites."

What realistic alternatives did Pinky have? Only very recently have Americans begun to affirm mixed-race identities, and in 1949, a person such as Pinky had but two options: try to pass for white, or identify with blacks.[38] Criticism of her decision thus implies that moving North with Tom was a better option. But was it? Tom informs her that because of publicity in Boston about her court case, "too many people in Boston know, or they might find out." Through Tom the film probes the superficiality of northern liberalism; despite denouncing "the mythology of superior and inferior races," he admits that "you never know what exists deep down inside yourself," and he insists that Pinky resume passing. His proposal to abandon Boston for Denver does not sway her: "You and me running away from it, Tom, this time to Denver, running away for the rest of our lives." What she was rejecting, then, was not really integration; it was dissimulation (the *Lost Boundaries* scenario) and marriage to a man uncomfortable with her ethnicity. Moreover, subsequent history has borne out the film's implied questioning of the reality of integration in the North, where schools and neighborhoods remain heavily, if informally, segregated.

Accusing the film of segregationism without recognizing Pinky's limited options brings to mind later charges that black separatists favored segregation. "Segregation," explained Malcolm X, "is that which is forced upon inferiors by superiors. But separation is that which is done voluntarily, by two equals—for the good of both."[39] Pinky and the whites who ran the town—and the country—were hardly equals; nor was her decision truly voluntary. Segregation was certainly something superiors forced upon inferiors, so having a character try to make the best of a bad situation is hardly endorsing segregation. Indeed, the belief that African Americans should stop expecting whites to help them or to offer full integration and should instead look to themselves to improve their situation within their own institutions such as the black colleges has a long history in the United States. In the interwar years, Marcus Garvey's United Negro Improvement Association exemplified the self-help mentality, and after the film's release, figures from Elijah Muhammad and Malcolm X to Spike Lee continued to pursue variants of this philosophy, while multiculturalist conceptions of society increasingly displaced doctrines of assimilation and integration.[40] In that light, Pinky's decision to decline the sort of marriage and life Tom offered and to use her newly acquired resources to found an institution to help southern blacks improve their own lives is, especially for its time, more progressive than reactionary. With its call for black pride, property ownership, and education, the film raises topics that would receive far more attention in the future.

The reading of *Pinky* as a conservative film that seeks to keep blacks in their place cannot account for many of its scenes. The attempted rape, the abuse by white police, the humiliation Pinky endures in the general store (where she arrived first but is forced to step aside and then pay double after Mrs. Wooley informs the owner she is a Negro), and the hostile stares of the white crowd at the courtroom all indict racism powerfully and invite viewers to experience it through a sympathetic character. The rape scene in particular breaks Hollywood's taboo against depicting southern white men's sexual exploitation of African American women. Far from urging blacks to accept their place humbly, the film favors defiance of racism through a character who is hardly passive. Under Kazan's direction, Crain's restrained performance conveys a smoldering anger as she defies injustice. Pinky challenges the police who arrest her, asking what charges they have against her, and she defies Miss Em, telling her, "I'm a trained nurse and I won't be spoken to like that"; later, she asks rhetorically, "What should I do? Dye my face, grovel and shuffle, say yas'm and no'm?" Above all, she defies the entire town and its racist power structure when she defends what is rightfully hers. That decision put the film in line with current civil rights strategies that focused on legal battles, as did her decision to confront racism in the South instead of simply fleeing North.[41]

In a 1949 essay on films in this cycle, Ralph Ellison derided *Pinky* for losing its focus on interracial marriage. He also objected that "Pinky decides that to marry [Tom] would 'violate the race' and that she had better remain a Negro."[42] But Ellison misread Pinky's motives for rejecting this marriage, and despite the presence of the interracial couple in this film, *Pinky* is not primarily about interracial marriage, any more than it is primarily about passing. The film, after all, never shows her trying to deceive anyone about her ethnicity (as she had in Boston), and it largely ignores social reactions to the interracial relationship. It is, instead, a film about racial identity, pride, and rebellion in the face of prejudice and injustice. It is true that Miss Em advises Pinky to take pride in her race— though so does her black grandmother—and there is certainly an air of paternalism in white filmmakers crafting a film with this message.[43]

If the assistance Pinky gets from a few benevolent white southerners gives the film paternalist overtones, it also underlines the colonialist nature of American race relations, and understanding the film requires viewing it in the historical context of decolonization. Whites such as Miss Em are, in effect, like those colonialist powers that took eleventh-hour steps to prepare colonized peoples for independence. Pinky's indecision reflects her mental colonization, most strongly indicated by Miss Em's influence over her, so her resolution to take pride in her ethnicity, to defy her oppressors, and to create her own educational institution amount to steps toward decolonization. Perhaps the film's compromises make it, like its protagonist, something of a hybrid, as it blends undeniably progressive ideas with elements that are less so, but that is no reason to apply a kind of one-drop rule to it and judge it reactionary or segregationist because it made certain compromises. Although dated in some ways, *Pinky*, if viewed with historical empathy, hardly expresses the political outlook of real segregationists such as Strom Thurmond.[44] It was, for its time, a significant critique of racial injustice.

Zanuck's strategizing, collaboration, and consultation paid off, as the film secured Oscar nominations for Crain, Waters, and Barrymore and reached *Variety*'s number two slot for 1949.[45] (That it came in behind the ode to the blackface musical *Jolson Sings Again* says something about its era.) The film did secure a few southern bookings, and newspapers reported long lines of both black and white patrons in Atlanta, where the Roxy Theater suspended its whites-only policy and opened its balcony to blacks.[46] Atlanta censor Christine Smith approved *Pinky* just after rejecting *Lost Boundaries*, though she cut a total of thirty-four seconds.[47] "I know this picture is going to be painful to a great many Southerners," Smith admitted. "It will make them squirm, but at the same time it will make them realize how unlovely their attitudes are."[48] Smith's comments, and reports that when Pinky won her case, a cheer went up in both the white and black sections of the Roxy, indicate that not all white southerners thought alike.[49] The most racist southerners (and northerners) undoubtedly skipped the film, but in an era when many Americans still went to the movies habitually, some probably wandered into theaters knowing little about it. Unlike ads in the North, which referred to her passing for white, one in the *Atlanta Constitution* gave little clue of the film's racial themes (aside from a photo of Ethel Waters in the background). Its text read cryptically, "Does he know?" and "Pinky knew that her whole life of deception had brought her to this."[50] Other southern markets banned it, and in Marshall, Texas, an exhibitor was jailed for showing it despite a local ban.[51] In Macon, Georgia, a cross was burned at a drive-in theater that screened it.[52]

Despite the usual scholarly claims that the film received mixed reviews, American critics overwhelmingly applauded, with twenty-six of twenty-seven film critics (96 percent) in this sample praising it, often effusively.[53] Robert Hatch of the *New Republic* panned the film for its "standard soap romance" and its "Jim Crow stereotype" of Dicey, and he derided Pinky's decision to stay in the South, but he misunderstood why she made it. The film attracted an unusual amount of press coverage, including criticism from several black intellectuals, activists, and celebrities. The NAACP's Walter White, who was battling for integration, resented Zanuck's ignoring his advice and criticized the film in the *Chicago Defender*. He contended that it "accepts without visible objection the philosophy that the Negro has his 'place,' that he accepts that place, and that all white people are united in agreement that colored people must forever stay in a position of inferiority," and he concluded, "I seriously doubt it will do much good."⁵⁴ Ralph Ellison disliked the situation *Pinky*'s writers had concocted: "Should Negro girls marry white men or—wonderful *non sequitur*—should they help their race?" Nevertheless, in appraising this and other new films, he wrote that "despite the absurdities with which these films are laden, they are all worth seeing, and if seen, capable of involving us emotionally," and he concluded that "the thinking of white Americans is undergoing a process of change."⁵⁵ Bandleader Cab Calloway wrote about *Pinky* and *Lost Boundaries* in the *Chicago Defender*, where he complained that "neither picture treats the Negro problem as such"—only "a very specialized problem" irrelevant to most Negroes. Although he called the films "steps in the right direction," he felt that "all to [sic] few white people will realize the purpose, understand it, or sympathize with it."⁵⁶

If American critics' reactions are any indication, Calloway was worrying unnecessarily. The *Detroit News* described it as a "poignant, moving drama"; the *Hartford Courant*'s labeled it "a great film" and "deeply moving"; and the *New York Herald Tribune* called it a "courageous and powerful screen drama" that "attacks the racial question directly and with tremendous impact." Numerous reviews spoke of the film's impact on viewers; the *Los Angeles Times* claimed that "it holds its audience under a singular spell," while the *Hollywood Reporter* said it "draws the spectator in, rooting for the good people and scorning the evil." Several trade papers praised Zanuck's courage in making the film, which, in *Variety*'s words, "meets the problem head-on" and "truly moves the American film medium a desirable notch forward." Warning of "almost impossible sledding" down South, *Variety* predicted that a few "courageous theater owners will play it, . . . [but] undoubtedly a majority will choose to skip the picture." In the *Times*, Crowther noted that the filmmakers "have barged right into that area of most conspicuous racism, the Deep South," and the *San Francisco Chronicle* said it "boldly sets its locale in the place where the evil of race prejudice flourishes most."

No review treated blackness as horrifying, and none thought the film sought to criticize passing. It was, instead, racism and injustice that drew most critical comment. The *Boston Globe*'s Marjory Adams called the film "a revealing, pitiless denunciation of the racial prejudices that exist in this democracy," adding that Pinky "learns what it means to be a Negro, to live in a broken-down and dirty neighborhood, to be fair game for the white youths who are liquored up and ready for deviltry, to be treated as a menial by the white people." The *San Francisco Chronicle*'s John Hobart wrote that Pinky "finds herself subjected to all the degradations and humiliations that are implicit in the Jim Crow system," and the *New York Post*'s Winsten praised "several beautifully drawn portraits of degrees of prejudices." The *Boston Herald* also remarked on the "poor housing, slurring remarks, police insults, and Jim Crowism in its meanest and nastiest form," while *Time* concluded that the film "leaves a strong impression that racial discrimination is not only unreasonable but evil."

Some critics, especially in New York, did register complaints. The *New York Daily News*'s Kate Cameron felt that "it doesn't attempt to go very deeply into the problem," but she called it "a stirring dramatic film" and "a moving human document of one of our most poignant social problems." Winsten said it was "not a perfect picture," with its "falsely, prettily, happy ending that must be ignored," though he considered it "a picture of major proportions" on "our peculiarly American ground of race prejudice." Suspecting that some would think the film opposed interracial marriage, he noted "the reason why the girl made the decision," namely, "the slow realization of what is vital to self-respect" and "an affirmation of Negro pride." Crowther derided the "'old mammy' sentiment" and "passion for paternalism," but he praised its "vivid exposure of certain cruelties and injustices" rendered "with moving and disturbing force." To Mildred Martin of the *Philadelphia Inquirer*, "if the ending is slightly on the side of compromise, the picture as a whole is never less than completely absorbing, painfully and disturbingly honest, emotionally affecting."

While some objected mildly to the film's concessions, many others lauded its restraint. *Commonweal*'s Philip Hartung believed "Zanuck deserves credit for not attempting to cover the entire racial question" and he judged it "all the more effective because the movie has gone out of its way to avoid melodrama." Though he hoped future films would "go the whole way in blasting the false notions of white supremacy," he found the current films "an encouraging start along the right lines in condemning anti-Negro prejudice." *Time* was pleased that it "puts entertainment above soap-boxing," and the *Hollywood Reporter* was impressed that its "devastating indictment of bigotry and prejudice" is "accomplished without preachment and without sacrifice of entertainment." Others welcomed the absence of "propagandizing," "sensationalism," and "melodramatics," and the *Washington Post* was pleased "that neither race is pictured as either all virtuous or all evil."[57]

As for the African American press, Lena Brown of the *New York Amsterdam News* felt "the picture doesn't go far enough" as it "treats the race problem most delicately," but she admitted it "will not be to the liking of bigots anywhere," and she pronounced it "worth an evening and a fee." She also understood why the role went to a white actress, given the "great deal of kissing and hugging, which simply could not have been permitted under present Hollywood codes if the principals had been of different races." The *Pittsburgh Courier* defended the casting on the grounds that it helped whites experience what blacks routinely endured. The *Atlanta Daily World* called the film "a moving drama, packed with emotions and superb acting," while the *Chicago Defender*, despite running critical statements from Walter White and Cab Calloway, called the film "excellent and 'meaty' entertainment." That paper also wondered if this "unusual picture" would play "in certain sections where it might do most good."

Among critics in the South's mass-circulation dailies, Paul Jones of the *Atlanta Constitution*, in an article titled "'Pinky' Recommended Despite 'Social' Theme," found it "an outstanding movie, both dramatically and otherwise," which does not "antagonize the majority," and "builds sympathy and understanding for the minority." Cautioning that "I do not recommend that social topics be continued on the screen," he recommended this film as "an editorial—and a good one—on intolerance." John Rosenfield of the *Dallas Morning News* praised the film, calling it "one of screendom's honest dramatic jobs," though he sounded sarcastic in calling Pinky "a victim of the careless, brutish master race," and he also averred that "the world is not ready for intermarriage." The *New Orleans Times-Picayune* termed it "a heart-warming story" in which Pinky "encounters prejudice at its worst," and it pronounced it the best of the new films about racial prejudice "because it is more easily understood from the Southern standpoint."

To some, this southern praise may seem to confirm its reactionary, segregationist politics, but more likely, these reactions indicate that changes in America's racial attitudes extended beyond the North, and that not all white southerners thought alike. Even if these urban critics were in the minority among southern whites, the publishing of such views in southern papers remains significant. This praise also suggests that Zanuck calculated fairly accurately what he could get away with, crafting a film that criticized racism powerfully while still securing bookings and drawing crowds and warm reviews in the South. The African American *Atlanta Daily World* observed that "possibly the greatest feature about the entire performance is that it has been allowed to be shown this far South of the Mason-Dixon line without any signs of disturbance," which suggests "that prejudice and hate among us is a rapidly fading evil," and the *Pittsburgh Courier* argued that "reception in the South is the biggest headliner of all, with so little friction caused that one would begin to think traditional attitudes must be changing."[58] Prejudice, of course, also existed in the North, as the film suggested. In Boston, the *Globe* called it "almost incredible" that *Pinky* was breaking attendance records, for ten years earlier such a film "would never have been made, let alone shown to huge audiences in metropolitan movie palaces," and it called this "a commentary both on the quality of the film and on the attitude of its audience."[59]

The film had far less impact in Britain. Critical response was heavily positive—eighteen of twenty-one reviews were positive (86 percent), none negative, and three mixed—but positive reviews often expressed reservations.[60] The conservative *Time and Tide* found the film "mercifully free of overstatement" and judged it "one of the two or three great films of the year," even if "to expose the unjust lot of the Negro is, of necessity, to imply the guilt, or at least the indifference, of white people." The *Daily Worker* disliked the film's paternalism and sentimentality while finding it implausible that Pinky wins her case, but it applauded the depiction of racist incidents and declared it "a valuable and often moving film." The socialist *Tribune* also objected that "white supremacy is left undisturbed" as Miss Em directs Pinky's actions, but it wrote that "in spite of its phoney patches, *Pinky* remains a film with some moving and disturbing moments." It also welcomed the film, asking, "Where are the equivalent English films which try to discuss a social problem or which contain even moments of genuine social documentation?" The *Monthly Film Bulletin* was pleased that "the film never assumes that the colour question can be smoothed over with a few easy platitudes," and "for this, and for the absence of sensation—the undercurrent of feeling is more impressive than a lynching would have been—the film deserves great praise." C. A. Lejeune of the left-leaning *Observer* found it "an adroit attempt to treat a highly controversial subject in a discreetly uncontroversial way," but she wished for something stronger and complained it "has about as much daring as a cheese mite." Her contention that it "is careful to affront no particular section of the public" revealed a certain ignorance about the depth of American racism, and her suggestion that it should have cast a "coloured girl" and had her marry the white doctor overlooked the Production Code as well as American attitudes.

The entire topic seemed remote to several British critics. With a tinge of pity for the Americans, the *Times* remarked that "the problem of racial discrimination is one that would appear to weigh heavily on their conscience," and the *Evening Standard* called it a "magnificent film whose message must needs sound only an echo in British hearts." Jympson Harman of the *Evening News* admitted, "I am not much moved by the [color] problem, . . . but I was deeply affected by this picture." The *Daily Herald* urged people to see the film "even if the subject and treatment do not attract you," and Dilys Powell of the *Sunday Times*, who had yawned at *Lost Boundaries* and wished for a good musical, found *Pinky* an "extremely moving" film "not because it has a praiseworthy subject," but because it examines "the courageous human figure." Virginia Graham of the conservative *Spectator* also considered the issue of racial discrimination "mainly an American one," but added, "It is not wholly so" as "no white peoples living can truthfully deny their insistence on the superiority of their colouring."

In France, *Pinky* sold a paltry 244,619 tickets, and many papers ignored it.[61] Of eight reviews located, four were positive, three negative, and one mixed.[62] Claude Garson of the conservative *L'Aurore* observed that "obviously for us this film seems less relevant" than for Americans, for "in France blacks are not on our minds," and he found the film "slow and uneventful." On the far left, Georges Sadoul of *Les Lettres Françaises* penned a scathing review that called *Pinky* propaganda for "southern slave-owners" and a film conveying the views of "racists, colonialists, slave-owners, Hitlerites, and American southerners." He also likened the black characters, who "fit the worst conventions of racism," to those in *The Birth of a Nation* and described Jake as "one of the most odious caricatures of a black that the screen has ever given us." Sadoul's memory of *The Birth of a Nation* may have been a bit hazy, and his plot summary contained several mistakes, but he offered an interesting theory for the inclusion of depictions of white racism. In his view, the film "contains 90 percent lies, and it tries to disguise them as true by mixing in 10 percent truth," a technique of crafty propagandists. Though less apoplectic, Georges Charensol of the *Nouvelles Littéraires* also panned the film and complained that "the southern blacks leave the task of defending their cause to whites or half-whites." *Libération* felt that Pinky should have been black, and to the objection that a black woman inheriting property would have led "the general public in America, less enlightened than the French public, to leap in horror," it replied, "So, too bad!"

Others were more sensitive to the difficulties of making such films in the United States. "One cannot doubt the audacity" of the filmmakers, wrote Guy Marester in *Combat*, as the film shows "the stupidity, cruelty, and hypocrisy of the whites," even if blacks must "decline to cross the line and accept racial divisions." While admitting that "to us Europeans the film will seem timid," *Ce Soir* called the United States "a country where the problem it evokes still unleashes passions," and it praised the "intelligent, broad-minded film" for "putting its finger on one of America's most hideous wounds." J. G. Pierret of *Radio Cinéma Télévision* alluded to "prejudices that we in Europe probably cannot fully appreciate" and thought the film must have been made for export only, "as one finds it hard to imagine it succeeding in the United States outside of southern theaters reserved for people of color!" Pierret understood Pinky's decision not to flee north, writing that "she comes to realize that such an 'escape' would be the greatest of betrayals," and in *Franc-Tireur*, Jean Néry agreed, writing that it would bring only "a happiness based on lies." Néry also expected "someone in France to declare that such a problem is irrelevant" here, but he recalled "the outbursts of joyful anti-Semitic sadism that attracted quite a few enlightened Europeans when laws and public opinion made them safe." He concluded that "we will never see too many films like this one."

American reactions to *Pinky* showed considerable receptiveness to films about racism, and although the critics' support for the film's antiracist aims obscured the private opinions of countless white Americans, the film's remarkable ticket sales and the domination of the public sphere by antiracist opinions nonetheless made this a significant moment. American critics did not, however, draw parallels between this topic and colonialism elsewhere. Some Europeans, meanwhile, showed how little they understood the American situation, and they generally considered these issues irrelevant to them. This lack of interest reflects the smaller number of people of color in Britain or France, but if Americans failed to see colonialism on their own soil, the British and the French seemed to forget racism in their colonies. And if Americans showed little historical awareness of how colonialism and the slave trade had produced the current racial situation, the British, in viewing these issues as irrelevant to them, seemed to have forgotten who had founded a society based on African slavery in North America. Despite British and French involvement in transatlantic slavery, and despite their ongoing rule over the descendants of slaves in Africa and the Caribbean, the Europeans seemed relieved to be free of racial problems.

This cycle of films about black-white miscegenation came to a close with two 1951 releases. One was British: *Pool of London* (1951), from producer Michael Balcon of Ealing Studios and director Basil Dearden. A heist picture set among the docks of London—a historically appropriate setting for an exploration of British racism and attitudes toward black-white miscegenation—the film features a subplot in which a black Jamaican seaman, Johnny Lambert (Earl Cameron), meets a blonde woman named Pat (Susan Shaw) and spends a few hours on the town with her. The extent of the film's interest in racism consists of Johnny's encountering a few bits of mild rudeness, and though Johnny and Pat exchange a couple of lengthy looks, the two never touch. The film drops that subplot entirely midway through.

The second release was a new version of *Show Boat*, based on Jerome Kern and Oscar Hammerstein's 1927 Broadway hit, which had been derived from Edna Ferber's 1926 novel. Ava Gardner played Julie LaVerne, an African American member of a floating theater troupe who passes for white, and she has a white boyfriend. When a spurned suitor informs authorities of a miscegenation case on board, Julie avoids arrest but loses her job, and she later turns up as a single, depressed alcoholic in Chicago—the tragic mulatto. Because the film purveys dated images—notably the happy blacks who greet the showboat's arrival—one can overlook the ways in which it was progressive for its time. As in *Pinky*, the film got away with violating the Production Code by casting a white actress to play a woman of mixed race. William Warfield's rendition of "Ol' Man River" certainly gave a gloomier picture of blacks' lives than the scene of their greeting the boat had, and if the notion that poor Southern blacks' lives were difficult was hardly news, it was still rare for Hollywood to make that point. The film played widely in the South, where reviews ignored the miscegenation issue.[63]

The Second Cycle, 1957–1959

After *Show Boat*, Hollywood stopped making films about black-white miscegenation for several years, and even films on "the Negro question" became rare. Although the Supreme Court finally granted films First Amendment rights in 1952, the Production Code Administration's black-white miscegenation ban remained. Hollywood had evaded the ban in *Pinky* and *Show Boat* by casting white actresses as light-skinned Negroes, but by 1951 it had exhausted that subject and device. Also discouraging films on black-white miscegenation was the intensification of the Cold War, spurred by the Communist victory in China (1949), the Soviet acquisition of nuclear weapons (1949), the outbreak of the Korean War (1950), the Alger Hiss verdict (1950), the start of Senator Joseph McCarthy's communist witch hunt (1950), and the trial of Julius and Ethel Rosenberg (1951). The House Committee on Un-American Activities (HUAC) also returned to Hollywood in 1951 for a second round of investigations, and historians depict the early 1950s as a period of even greater political timidity than normal in American film.[64] This point should not be overstated, as racial liberalism could serve Cold War aims, and skilled screenwriters (including blacklisted ones using pseudonyms) crafted liberal films about miscegenation in these years, including *Across the Wide Missouri* (1951), *Japanese War Bride* (1952), *Return to Paradise* (1953), and *King of the Khyber Rifles* (1953).

If Hollywood's interest in the "Negro question" seemed to flag after 1951, it revived with new developments in the civil rights struggle such as the 1954 *Brown v. Board of Education* ruling on school segregation, the 1955 arrest of Rosa Parks, and the ensuing Montgomery, Alabama, bus boycott. In 1956, rising American impatience with movie censorship led to a revision of the Production Code that removed the black-white miscegenation ban. Hollywood's skittishness about political and racial controversy endured, and most whites still opposed miscegenation, but a new cluster of films on black-white miscegenation soon appeared.

The first, *Island in the Sun* (1957), was Zanuck's first for his own Paris-based company, though Fox distributed it. Directing this high-budget film was Robert Rossen, an ex-Communist who had cooperated with HUAC. An Anglo-American "runaway" production—both screenwriter Alfred Hayes and novelist Alec Waugh were British, as was much of the cast, and interiors were shot in Britain—it used the fictitious British Crown Colony of Santa Marta to comment indirectly on the U.S. South.[65] This timely tale of impending decolonization probed fears that the advent of political and racial equality would bring a flood of miscegenation.

As an American journalist arrives to examine Santa Marta's transfer of power to the black majority, a complicated soap opera unfolds about four couples, each raising the miscegenation question. In the first, a happy romance between Margot Seaton (Dorothy Dandridge) and Denis Archer (John Justin) proceeds at lightning pace. The PCA's miscegenation ban was still in place when Columbia Pictures first submitted the story in 1955, but even after the 1956 revision, the film remained terribly skittish in showing cross-racial affection. In a scene in a summerhouse, Denis confesses his love for Margot, and although the two are alone and sharing a moment of passion, they embrace without kissing, as Margot turns her mouth away at the last moment. Margot and Denis fear the locals will oppose their marriage, so they leave for the more enlightened terrain of England.

Another romance pairs black union leader and politician David Boyeur (Harry Belafonte) with Mavis Norman (Joan Fontaine), whose ancestors had owned a plantation. This subplot was daring in featuring a black man and a white woman—and a blonde at that—and Belafonte's character also broke with the deferential, grinning, emasculated image Hollywood had long given black men. Although the politically radical Belafonte later denounced the film, the fire he brought to the role of a black man who challenges and intimidates the white rulers and reminds them bluntly about slavery gave the film a much-needed edge. By today's standards, shots of his taking Mavis to see where he grew up look timid, but at the time, images of a black man putting his hands on a white woman to help her off a bus and drinking out of the same coconut with her were quite bold, and this was the first Hollywood film to show a black man dating a white woman. The image of Mavis among dozens of blacks and a later scene with the two alone by the sea discard old anxieties about the black rapist. The romance ends when David tells Mavis his people would never understand it and would "feel I'd betrayed them." Although it was politically timid to avoid an interracial marriage—while blaming black people's prejudices—David's decision, like Pinky's snubbing of a white suitor, expresses his belief in black independence and solidarity. Once again, an unhappy end to an interracial romance took on a new meaning.

With the third and fourth couples, the film approaches miscegenation very differently. When the American journalist prints a report that Julian Fleury (Basil Sydney), head of a rich and powerful family, had a mixed-race mother, the two grown Fleury children must suddenly rethink their identity. Maxwell (James Mason), whose combination of arrogance, racism, and insecurity illustrates the situation of the colonizer facing decolonization, mistakenly believes his wife is cheating on him. The news of his African ancestry sends the already unbalanced Maxwell over the edge, and when he goes to see the man he suspects of sleeping with his wife, he ends up murdering him out of rage over a taunt about the "tar brush."

His sister Jocelyn (Joan Collins) is also traumatized by the news. Engaged to the governor's son, she breaks the engagement, asking her father, "Can you picture a black man sitting in the House of Lords if we had a son?" Her mother then informs her that she is not of mixed race, as her father was a white man with whom she had an affair. The film thus presented one couple that turned out to be interracial and another that turned out not to be, and in both cases it made people's racial anxieties seem overwrought. Expressing the film's disdain for these racial anxieties is the journalist, whose exposé of the Fleurys' ancestry states, "For 300 years there's been marriage and intermarriage with nobody sure of their precise ancestry. But a veil of secrecy, whispers, and innuendo has been drawn across this problem." Although Boyeur's rejection of Mavis seems to suggest limits to the film's belief in interracial marriage, it is really people's anguished reactions to it, not miscegenation itself, the film criticizes.

As with *Pinky*, Zanuck faced various pressures, and in launching his new company he was determined to avoid a flop.[66] Fox, which provided financing and distribution, became alarmed when news of the impending film provoked protests and boycott threats of *all* Fox pictures, and it pressured Zanuck to make changes.[67] Earlier, Geoffrey Shurlock of the PCA had expressed doubts about "whether or not this story constitutes an unfair portrayal of the Negro race," and when Fox bought the rights, Zanuck consulted with Truman K. Gibson, Jr., a Chicago attorney who had advised the Roosevelt administration on racial issues.[68] Noting that he could not speak for all Negroes, Gibson told Fox, "The development of Boyeur as a cynical exploiter of his people diverts attention from some of the basic reasons why people in that area now are actively and rapidly pushing towards dominion status; and also why the Caribbean world has so radically changed in the last few years." Gibson felt that Fox "is due tremendous credit for courage," and he found the story "not objectionable from a racial point of view," as it was "not used for the purpose of portraying all natives as being stupid, singing Calypso-dancing dwellers of a beautiful semi-tropic paradise."[69] Viewers today might disagree, as Freddie Young's cinematography includes postcard shots, scenes of carnival, limbo dancing, and blacks contentedly cutting cane and harvesting bananas. But if the shots of blacks working recall happy-slaves images, they appear mostly in the scene in which Boyeur gives Mavis a tour of his home region. As the workers greet Boyeur warmly, the film gives an optimistic vision of life after decolonization, suggesting that social and political harmony will prevail under black leadership and the economy will function properly. In a memo on an early treatment, Zanuck specified that "Boyeur, despite the role he plays in this story, is not a heavy; it would be unfortunate if the story should emerge with a West Indian as the drama's villain," and although white characters call Boyeur a demagogue, he is an intelligent, principled, and determined advocate for his people.[70]

During production, Zanuck expressed doubts about the film's direction. "I can't figure out what we are trying to say in this story," he complained in October 1955, and he called it "foolish to get into a so-called controversial story and then try to white-wash it or avoid the controversy." The film's emphasis on personal relationships, he feared, was overshadowing the political issues, and he reminded his team, "I thought we would tell our personal stories in the foreground, while in the background would be this seething mass of black people straining against the domination of these few whites."[71] Several rewrites later, he wondered, "What is our theme? What do we advocate? . . . Are we saying that we do or do not advocate marriage between blacks and whites?" Further discussion yielded the trite conclusion that "what is good for one person or one couple may not be good for another one."[72] Zanuck later avowed that he disliked the film because "they made me compromise the book," but the diffuse narrative was also part of the problem.[73]

While Belafonte made his dissatisfaction clear to the press, Dandridge expressed hers more discreetly.[74] She complained of Denis and Margot's not being allowed to kiss, which she found silly given how common interracial relationships were in the West Indies.[75] Zanuck, however, was less concerned with West Indian than with American realities, fearing trouble in the South and elsewhere for a film that, despite its timidities, went well beyond any previous film in depicting black-white romances. Those fears proved real enough: the film secured bookings in some areas of the South and was banned or simply not shown in others, despite the Supreme Court's having undermined local censorship. The South Carolina legislature considered a bill to fine theaters for showing it; a cross was burned at a North Carolina drive-in; a man with a shotgun prevented patrons from entering a drive-in in Alabama; protesters picketed outside theaters and launched petition drives and boycott campaigns in many locations—including Minneapolis.[76] Joan Fontaine received hate mail for her role, and a sample of letters written to Virginia's censorship authorities suggest the virulence that those written to Fontaine must have contained.[77] C. C. Stockton of Richmond wrote to complain to Virginia's censors that Belafonte and Dandridge "are cast opposite Joan Fontaine and John Justin, who call themselves white people." Claiming that "Communists, the NAACP, radicals, hoodlums, foreigners and various subversive elements in this country and thruout [sic] the world are out to destroy the white race," he urged banning "this disgraceful picture anywhere in the Commonwealth of Virginia."[78] Landon B. Lane of Altavista called the film "an insult to any and all members of the white and negro races who retain any semblance of racial self-respect." He felt it would please only "would-be racial perverts" serving "the Communist Party's avowed determination to destroy racial integrity in the United States generally, and in the South particularly."[79] A representative of the Dixiecrats called it "pernicious propaganda and an attempt to foster integration on [sic] the minds of young Americans," while the American Nationalists warned that "if successful at the box office, it will open the floodgates for a deluge of similar interracial filth."[80] Perhaps unaware that Zanuck was a gentile, Randolph McPherson of Norfolk claimed that "this picture was sent out by Hollywood Jews, who are members of NAACP, and doing everything in their power to break down racial barriers in the South."[81]

The Virginia authorities replied that they no longer had the legal right to ban the film. The state's attorney general tried to console one citizen by writing that the authorities found it "much less objectionable and not nearly as favorable propaganda for integration as most critics and national magazines had portrayed it as being."[82] Another Virginia official averred that "the conclusion reached in the story is that where integration has been tried, it does not work."[83] This dubious reading overlooks the happy ending for Margot and Denis, and it also shows that if a film depicted the problems interracial couples encountered, segregationists could cite them to confirm their views. Also illustrating some whites' ability to tune out the film's viewpoint, a Memphis critic who saw the banned film in a private showing reassured readers that he was "unoffended by the film's interracial romances because I was perfectly aware that they were taking place, not in our own South, but in the British West Indies."[84] As students of propaganda have argued, people may be impervious to messages that fall too far outside their cone of visibility. Southern whites' anxieties also illustrated the "third-person effect," in which a person is not swayed by a message but fears others will be.[85] One can imagine how these letter writers felt upon learning that the Supreme Court had undercut state censors, and the film likely contributed to the embittering and demoralizing of segregationists.

Their discontent likely grew with news of long lines and extended runs all around the country—the South included. The film finished at number nine on the 1957 box-office charts, not far behind *Giant* and *Teahouse of the August Moon*, which also featured interracial couples.[86] That success came despite rough handling from American critics: in a sample of thirty-five reviews, twelve were positive (34 percent), seventeen negative, and six mixed or neutral.[87] Among the positive reviews, the *Detroit News* judged it "powerful, provocative drama of inter-racial passions and hates," and the *Miami Herald* considered it an "exciting treatise on integration and-or the mixing of the races" though "its entertaining value will depend in some measure on the depth of the individual's attitude toward the Negro-white situation." Many reviews praised the filmmakers' courage. *Variety* quipped that in the South, "blood vessels will pop like popcorn" as "racist taboos are trod upon heavily," and it called it "a milestone in courageous picture-making."[88]

Some who praised the film's courage questioned its execution. Robert Hatch of the *Nation* wrote that "it is always gratifying when the movies whack away at a taboo," as Hollywood is "so crabbed by prohibitions that mere iconoclasm is a positive virtue," but he added that "iconoclasm is about all this picture has to offer." Like others, *Time* criticized a "disjointed welter of plots," and the *New Yorker* wrote that it "sprawls all over the place." Many also disliked the film's timidity about interracial romance. While judging the film "a step in the right direction," the African American *Chicago Defender* found it "incredible" that it presents "a pair [of] love romances without a single kiss." *Cue* wrote that "in an attempt to depict interracial prejudices and passions without stirring up too much resentment, the over-edited, disconcertingly truncated film too often douses its dramatic fire before it has been fully kindled." *Newsweek* added that "the problems of mixed marriages and mixed love affairs are neither debated with anything resembling authoritative wisdom nor resolved with any sort of conviction."

The film's racial politics provoked conflicting assessments. The *Post*'s Archer Winsten felt it "attacks the evil of color prejudice," and the *Hartford Courant* perceived a disdain for racists' anxieties, writing that Jocelyn Fleury is "beating her brains out with worry over her mixed parentage." In *Commentary*—not yet a conservative magazine—Henry Popkin quoted a moviegoer in North Carolina who found it "a pro-segregation picture," but Popkin judged its view of miscegenation "inconsistent, haphazard, and aimless." Showing how a film with antiracist intentions might leave segregationists feeling vindicated, the conservative *Chicago Tribune* said it dealt with "murder and miscegenation and the problems created by both."

Ten reviews pointed out that Boyeur spurned Mavis's romantic interest.[89] To Kay Proctor of the conservative *Los Angeles Examiner*, the film "says times and mores are changing and like it or not we are going to live with what's coming," and she warned that "it will make you violently angry, uncomfortable, or sad," but "it will make you ponder—which I am sure was Zanuck's purpose." In Hollywood, the *Citizen News* declared that "intelligent, thinking people will not accept the breaking down of accepted conventions," and it also objected that "the white residents of the island are made the aggressors, guilty of terrible crimes and mistreatment, while the black people are shown as fine and upright." Not wishing to provide the film publicity, several papers that reviewed most major releases skipped this one, including *America* (whose Moira Walsh would soon denounce *Sayonara* for glorifying miscegenation). Despite an extended run in New Orleans, the *Times-Picayune* did not review it. It did report hostility to it and quoted the American Legion's statement that director Rossen "has admitted being a one-time member of the Communist party." In these reviews, the miscegenation issue almost completely obscured the colonialism issue. American critics' references to blacks in the Caribbean as "the natives" also showed little historical awareness—blacks were no more native to the region than were the whites who brought them there—and despite news of Puerto Rican nationalism in these years, decolonization in the Caribbean did not seem to interest Americans in 1957.

British critics were even harder on the film, as two of eighteen reviews were positive (11 percent), fifteen were negative, and one neutral.[90] The *Monthly Film Bulletin* found the script "muddled and confusing" and "the motives and actions of the characters . . . bewildering." The film's intentions divided critics; in the *Daily Express*, Leonard Mosley said it "sets out, with the sincerest and most decent intentions, to show up the colour bar for the hateful thing it is," but Reg Whitley of the *Daily Mirror* wrote, "I do NOT see this film as a profound contribution to a controversial subject. And I don't think it was intended to be." The *Daily Herald* believed it "sets out to shock" and "to sell tickets at the box office by exploiting the sad problem of the colour bar," and the *Daily Worker* charged that it "has tried to commercialise the box office properties of the colour bar." The *Observer* lamented that it "toys nervously with problems of miscegenation and politics," and the *Evening Standard* wrote that it "buries its brightly coloured head in the sand whenever the problem looks like becoming at all unruly." Milton Shulman of the *Sunday Express* contended that it "bangs on the colour bar with the abandon of a mad xylophonist in a Negro band" but "strikes every note of the problem but the authentic one." Denis's romance with Margot bothered no one, though the *Star* referred to "that lovely piece of chocolate Dorothy Dandridge." The *Daily Telegraph's* Campbell Dixon found the British governor "a pleasant change from Leftist caricatures," but he disliked the image of other whites, "an ineffectual lot" who sit "nursing cool drinks on terraces, watching the rising tide of Colour."

In France, where the film sold just over a million tickets, four of sixteen reviews were positive (25 percent), seven negative, and five mixed.[91] Despite faulting this "superproduction" for its sprawling narrative and superficiality, French critics showed more interest than the British had in the treatment of colonialism and race relations. Two reviews insisted that films about race had little relevance to France: *France Soir* wrote that "the sentimental relations between blacks and whites . . . do not have for us the explosiveness they may have elsewhere," and *Le Parisien Libéré* added that "for us the film is far from shocking." Others, while not disagreeing, found the film interesting, given events in America, including the Little Rock crisis unfolding as the film played in France. *Le Parisien Libéré* called it "an insanely audacious work on this burning subject in the U.S.," and *La Croix* applauded "the courage of its intentions" if not the clarity of its exposition. "The Ku Klux Klan," declared *Les Lettres Françaises*, "was not wrong to mobilize its troops, its banners, its crosses, and its clubs to get the film banned in the old South," as it is "a blow struck against racism, this affirmation that love is possible between beings of different colors." *L'Humanité Dimanche* saluted "its courage and its novelty, which is almost revolutionary for American cinema in the era of MacCarthy [sic] and the Ku Klux Klan," while in that paper's daily edition Samuel Lachize wrote that "the hotheads of the Ku Klux Klan must have blanched under their hoods when this film was shown." Lachize regretted "a certain confusion and some serious flaws" but found it "one of the most courageous and appealing American films of the last few years" and "one of the best films on view in Paris."

Among those interested in the decolonization theme, Marie Perrot of the Communist *France Nouvelle* explained that "it implicitly raises the question of the independence of black peoples," and "one senses the memory of Bandung passing over the work." She also enjoyed the electoral rally, where "one feels the force of the crowd of blacks" who help Boyeur thwart "the reign of the planters." Lachize also liked the "black leader of the plantation workers' union" who "fights for the total liberation of his brothers of color," while *La Croix* added that Boyeur "proves to the white candidate that he has the population firmly in his grip, and that the English have no more business here." *Franc-Tireur* saw a bitter lesson for all colonists: "Those who do not wish to return home can only resign themselves" to a new order in which "now, at the eleventh hour, it is no more possible to change camps than to change the color of their skin." Those embracing the film's anticolonialism also understood Boyeur's rejection of Mavis. La Croix said such a marriage would be "a betrayal of his racial brothers," and L'Humanité Dimanche saw Boyeur "totally devoting himself—and sacrificing his love—in the cause of his brothers of color and their struggle for liberation." On the far right, Rivarol used the epithet nègres and dismissed the film as a plea for "universal intermarriage." But in a country where left-wing publications far outnumbered those of the right, Rivarol was in the minority.

Despite its flaws, Island in the Sun spurred discussion of miscegenation, and it broke new ground by casting black actors in interracial romances. The film's shortcomings certainly distracted from the issues raised, and its treatment of interracial relationships was too cautious to say anything definitive. Although Boyeur's snubbing of Mavis suggested an intriguing anticolonialist case against intermarriage, the hasty exposition of his motives suggested blind ambition more than a clear ideology of black separatism. Given that integration was then the civil rights movement's dominant concern, there was little reason to expect a clear exposition of black separatism from Hollywood films. That the film went too far for some and not far enough for others reflected the difficulties of making movies on such controversial topics at that time, so the film and its reception afford useful insights into American and European opinions on miscegenation and decolonization in 1957.

While slavery metaphors pervaded Cold War depictions of life behind the Iron Curtain, Western filmmakers rarely addressed the slavery in their own countries' past.[92] Show Boat alluded to it, as did dialogue in Pinky and Island in the Sun, but Hollywood still generally steered clear of the subject. One significant exception was the Warner Bros. release Band of Angels (1957), which examined both slavery and sex between masters and slaves. A few older films had depicted slavery or the slave trade, with some emphasizing the happiness and loyalty of the slaves (Birth of a Nation, Gone with the Wind), while others underlined the miseries of slavery (Uncle Tom's Cabin, Slave Ship), and still others managed to do both (Way Down South). The first major production on slavery in many years, Band of Angels illustrates the difficulties Hollywood faced in rethinking the subject, and if it ultimately failed, its flaws and the reactions it produced remain instructive.

Raoul Walsh directed Band of Angels from a script based on Kentuckian Robert Penn Warren's 1955 novel. In a film emulating Gone with the Wind, Yvonne De

Carlo played Amantha "Manty" Starr, a Scarlett O'Hara knock-off. The pampered daughter of a liberal Kentucky planter, this Southern belle rushes back home from finishing school upon learning of her father's grave illness. Arriving at the Starrwood plantation just in time for his funeral, she protests when a slave-dealer, Mr. Calloway (Ray Teal), to whom her father owed a fortune, announces to the white and black mourners that he will sell off the plantation's slaves. Manty declares that her father never sold or abused his slaves, but her plan to save the plantation collapses when Calloway delivers the shocking news—punctuated by an orchestra chord—that Manty's mother was a slave, and that as a Negress, she will be sold, too.

Calloway imprisons Manty in his room on a boat to New Orleans, and after she attempts both escape and suicide, she manages to fend off his rape attempt only because the slaver does not wish to damage his merchandise. At a New Orleans slave auction, a humiliated Manty waits helplessly as the wealthy and dashing Hamish Bond (Clark Gable) strides in, bids $5,000, and takes her away to his mansion in town. The rest of the film relates their evolving relationship against the backdrop of the Civil War and the Yankee invasion of Louisiana.

At first a surly and bitter Manty shuns Hamish, whom she expects to rape her, but he instead showers her with privileges and treats her respectfully as he seeks to win her heart. During a thunderstorm, Hamish visits Manty's bedroom, and a code-placating ellipsis leaves the audience to deduce that they slept together. Revealing to Manty his guilt over his past as a slave trader in Africa—for which he insists the Negro part of her will always hate him—Hamish decides they have no future, so he plans to free her and send her to Cincinnati. When Hamish gets off the northbound riverboat at his Louisiana plantation, Pointe du Loup, and bids her farewell, she chooses love over freedom and disembarks to join him. Hamish curiously allows an arrogant neighbor, Charles de Marigny, to romance Manty against her will, and when Charles tries to force himself on her, Hamish's black overseer, Rau-Ru (Sidney Poitier), bursts into the room and strikes Charles—an unpardonable act for which he must flee. Rau-Ru escapes justice when Union troops invade, and he enlists in a black regiment. Like Manty, who feels a mixture of love and disdain for Hamish, Rau-Ru, whom Hamish has educated and given extraordinary privileges, deeply resents his master. Rau-Ru, seeking a Union reward for Hamish's capture, finds him on his plantation, but when Hamish reveals to Rau-Ru that he rescued him as a baby during a slaving raid in Africa, the adoptive son relents and helps Hamish escape with Manty.

The difficulties of discerning this film's point originate with the novel, which reflects Robert Penn Warren's own evolving outlook as he distanced himself from his segregationist past.[93] The film follows the first half of the novel closely, though it condenses a passage in which Hamish describes Africans as brutal savages. While the film contains certain progressive elements, it also follows some cinematic conventions regarding slavery, and the result is a half-hearted updating of the genre. Given the film's obvious debt to *Gone with the Wind*—with its casting of Clark Gable as a rich adventurer who scoffs at the Confederacy's grand illusions and tries to tame a strong-willed woman in the South just before and during the Civil War—it is not surprising that *Band of Angels* fails to effect any real transformation of the genre.

The film's regressive elements include a rosy image of slavery conveyed by two kindly, benevolent slave owners: Manty's father and Hamish. Acknowledgment of the cruelties of other plantation owners appears only in the dialogue, and the film never shows any planter mistreating his slaves. A sequence in which happy, loyal slaves gather on the riverbank to greet Hamish with joyous song and dance is even more regressive than the similar scene in *Show Boat* in that they are greeting their master, not a boat full of entertainers. Hamish regrets his slave trading and mentions its horrors, but the attention he calls to Africans' complicity in that trade weakens the plea for white atonement. The film also invokes old fears of the black rapist; on the riverboat, Calloway threatens Manty by telling her, "I'm gonna chain you to a post down there with those hot-natured blacks and I ain't gonna care what happens to ya." Offensive images of blacks include two female slaves who taunt Manty about what white masters will do to her. Taking a Confederate viewpoint, the film depicts Union troops as a cruel, greedy, racist "band of angels" who intend to re-enslave blacks, as Manty learns when boorish soldiers harass her in the street.

The casting of a white actress to play a woman of mixed race—nearly a decade after *Pinky* and in the same year in which *Island in the Sun* cast black actors in interracial relationships—also seems regressive, but once again, it makes sense in that Manty had to look completely white: even she had no idea of her mixed ethnicity, her father having lied about her deceased mother. Although the code's miscegenation ban had just been rescinded, Warner Bros. engaged in a lengthy exchange with the PCA, which objected to Manty's romance with Hamish not just because they are unmarried, but also because "they are master and slave."[94] Given the diminished powers of the PCA and state and local censors, persistent social hostility to interracial romance was the main reason for the studio's timidity, and it likely went ahead with the film only because the story allowed for a white actress to play opposite Gable.

More objectionable than the casting is Manty's decision to get off the boat at

Pointe du Loup, abandoning her resistance to Hamish and giving up freedom in the North. Her decision differs in several ways from Pinky's decision to remain in the South: Manty chooses to stay in a slaveholding society; she expresses no concerns about "living a lie" in the North; she shows no interest in racial pride; she does not stay to deny white racists a victory; and she does not stay in order to own an institution providing her professional and personal fulfillment. She stays, instead, because she has fallen for her master. So whereas the film breaks an old taboo by highlighting sex between masters and slaves, it weakens the critique by presenting this relationship as consensual. On the other hand, Calloway's attempted rape of Manty gave audiences a very different picture, even if the film allows her to preserve her virtue. Once again, telling the story of a woman who looks white panders to white audiences' ethnocentrism, but it also likely induced white viewers to imagine the experience of slavery more effectively than if the actress and character had been black. The narrative structure also had a certain shrewdness, first inviting white viewers to identify with what they believe is a white woman then shocks them with her sudden sale into slavery, followed by the traumas of the attempted rape and the slave auction. Although it was hardly news that it was undesirable to be a slave, the film conveys it effectively and deserves credit for breaking Hollywood's long silence about the miseries of slavery.

Another important difference from films such as *Gone with the Wind* was the character Rau-Ru. A decade later, black radicals would assail Poitier as a black man whom white liberals could love, but his performance gives Rau-Ru an angrier, more powerful edge than he had in the novel, and he breaks with the old cinematic tradition of the smiling, obsequious black man. Whereas Manty learns to love Hamish, Rau-Ru hates him despite his privileges. "This kindness," he warns Manty, "it's a trap that can hold you in bondage forever," and his hatred for Hamish foreshadows 1960s black radicals' disdain for white liberals. Given that white audiences tended to focus on the ethnicity of the actors rather than the characters, it must have shocked many viewers when Rau-Ru slapped Manty for wanting to pass for white, perhaps even more than when he struck Charles. Nevertheless, the dialogue barely explains Rau-Ru's disdain for Hamish, and he finally relents and helps Hamish escape. The film also hints at Rau-Ru's romantic interest in Manty, but neither the book nor the film developed it.

In the heated racial atmosphere of 1957, the film predictably stirred up controversy. "Negro Market Specialist" Charles Williams sent Jack Warner a telegram on July 11, warning that "recent developments indicate possible national Negro boycott," though none materialized.[95] Warner also heard from a dean at Southern University, a black college in Baton Rouge, complaining that students who had been extras in the film could not see it at the city's whites-only theater.[96] The film played in the South, even in Memphis, where censors barely approved it, despite the contact between Poitier and De Carlo, because Manty was not purely white.[97] Once again, angry southerners protested; in Virginia, one wrote to chide the censors for approving "this picture of racial propaganda that is intended to popularize miscegenation and interracial love-making in the eyes of the nation's youth"; the writer was especially upset that "Sidney Poitier is shown slapping a white woman across the room in a tantrum of rage."[98]

Despite this controversy and its major stars, the film did mediocre business in the United States, finishing at number thirty-three for 1957, a result that probably owed something to its flogging by critics.[99] In a sample of twenty-nine reviews, three were positive (10 percent), eighteen negative, and eight mixed or neutral.[100] For once, lurid ads reflected a film's true content, proclaiming: "And then they told her . . . 'your mother was a negro!'" and "He bought her . . . she was his!"[101] Despite panning the film, *Cue* was pleased that it gave "a somewhat more unvarnished version of slave days than is usually exhibited via the magnolia approach to the Old South," but more critics questioned the film's politics. Like others, Henry Popkin of *Commentary* complained of the slaves "jumping for joy" and "burst[ing] into song when they see old massa." The film seemed so pro-southern to the *Philadelphia Inquirer*'s Mildred Martin that she wrote, "It wouldn't have been surprising to find the South winning the war." These Confederate sympathies won the film few friends among southern critics, as some ignored it altogether while others gave only bland plot summaries.[102] One exception was the *Miami Herald*, which predicted southerners would enjoy the film's skewering of northern "bleeding hearts who yelled for 'equal rights' and then exploited the victims of their so-called emancipation," even if the romance amid slavery "may sound corny in this day of civil rights fights." The African American papers showed less interest in the film than in censorship efforts, but the *Los Angeles Sentinel*, while charging that it "comes no nearer being an 'airtight' picture on the racial issue than others we have seen," nevertheless added: "We must admit progress is being made," and "Hollywood is on the job and one day it will come up with the whole loaf."

Among those discussing miscegenation, the *Milwaukee Journal* noted it was the summer's second film on the "delicate movie subject" of "Negro-white love affairs," even if "neither movie really comes to grips with the problem." James Powers of the *Hollywood Reporter* found the treatment of the Poitier-De Carlo relationship timid. "Whether or not such romances should be explored on the screen is not the point," he wrote, but "once you start to tell such a story you have to go all the way with it," and here "the result is a half-told and vitiated story." In the *Los Angeles Examiner*, Ruth Waterbury wrote that this film on "one of the most important problems in American life . . . comes out namby-pamby and frequently foolish," while predicting that "someday someone is going to do the theme of miscegenation with courage and dignity." Voicing a common view, *Commonweal* called it "such a cheesy melodrama that one cannot consider it seriously at all," so once again a film that ventured into dangerous terrain provoked more discussion of its faults than of the issues it raised.

The British censors, like the Virginians, cut the line about the "hot-natured blacks" and also removed Rau-Ru's slap of Manty.[103] British critics were hard on the film—three of nineteen praised it (16 percent), ten panned it, and six gave split judgments—and the comments echoed American ones.[104] In France, *L'esclave libre* sold 1,279,129 tickets, and though many critics ignored the film, it received four positive, four negative, and two mixed reviews in a sample of ten.[105] *Combat*, observing that race "continues to obsess American souls and filmmakers," complained that "all the slave owners are good and generous," while the liberators are "racist, hypocritical, and crude." *Les Lettres Françaises* wrote that "such a pile of nonsense makes us forget that in sum, the film's purpose is not so bad," for "in the time of Governor Faubus and Little Rock, it is no small thing that a film tells us that a white man could marry a mulatto woman." Though claiming it would "make the Ku Klux Klan jeer," *L'Humanité* said it lacked the power of *Giant* and "drowns laudable sentiments in romantic hodgepodge."

In the aftermath of the Production Code revision, Western filmmakers' fascination with black-white romances and their mixed-race progeny reached a peak with the appearance of seven films between June 1958 and November 1959. The films are too numerous to examine in detail here, but a brief survey will indicate some patterns. Delmer Daves's *Kings Go Forth* (1958), set in World War II–France, starred Natalie Wood and Frank Sinatra in a romance between the mixed-race daughter of Americans who fled racism in the United States and a racist GI whose love for her initiates his transformation. Despite its progressive intentions, it had yet another white actress playing a mixed-race character who can "pass," and it showed typical evasiveness and timidity in its vague ending, its lack of interracial kissing, and its total lack of black characters or actors.[106]

Night of the Quarter Moon (1959) also featured a white actress (Julie London) as Ginny, a mixed-race woman who looks white, telling the story of her troubled marriage to the white scion of a rich San Francisco family. The story highlights both plebeian racism, in the form of hostile neighbors, and the racism of the upper crust, as Ginny's mother-in-law sues to annul the marriage. The film encourages defiance of racism and defends interracial marriage, granting the couple a happy ending after a traumatic court case.[107]

On its surface, Douglas Sirk's 1959 remake of *Imitation of Life* appears surprisingly regressive. This ultramelodramatic remake of the 1934 film retains its antiquated racial outlook, as Sarah Jane, the mixed-race daughter of a black maid, is the usual tragic mulatto, breaking her poor mother's heart by trying to pass for white. When a white boyfriend, irate to learn her dark secret, beats up Sarah Jane, the film shifts attention—and blame—from the racist lad to Sarah Jane and her dissimulation. The images of the miserable girl warn against miscegenation as well as passing, and the film treats racism as immutable. Film scholars have argued that Sirk's melodramas intended a sardonic critique of American ways and attitudes, but if it aimed to criticize America's racial situation, it did so unfairly, as it simply ignored the changing racial situation and the struggles of both blacks and whites to combat racism.[108] Although the film reached the number five slot, the reviews were brutal, and critics saw it as dated and racially offensive.[109]

An unconventional look at black-white miscegenation appeared in Ranald MacDougall's *The World, the Flesh, and the Devil* (1959), a racially inverted Robinson Crusoe tale set in the aftermath of a nuclear holocaust. A black man, Ralph (Harry Belafonte), who thinks he is the lone survivor, meets a young blonde woman, and when romance stalls because of Ralph's internalized misgivings— "people might talk," he warns her in a totally deserted New York City—the film highlights both the absurdity of racism and the difficulty of eradicating its effects from the deep recesses of people's psyches. Belafonte later complained that nervous MGM executives bowdlerized the film, whose opaque ending was typically evasive.[110] Nevertheless, its treatment of race, like its stance on nuclear war, insists that people must wake up and learn from their mistakes, by overcoming the burdens of memory and ingrained habit.

Also in 1959, actor John Cassavetes made his directorial debut in the low-budget *Shadows*, which also dealt with interracial romance. This largely improvised black-and-white film about bohemians in New York cast a white actress as an African American who passes for white and enters into a failed interracial relationship. Cassavetes denied any interest in racial issues, but his explanation of how they chose the topic indicates the intensity of interest in black-white relationships at the time: while experimenting with skits, he explained, "one particular improvisation exploded with life. It was about a black girl who passes for white."[111]

Europe and Black-White Miscegenation

By 1958, Europeans began making their own films on race and black-white miscegenation. The first was *Tamango* (1958), adapted from an 1829 short story by Prosper Mérimée, and starring Curt Jurgens as the captain of a slave ship and Dorothy Dandridge as his mulatto mistress, Aiché.[112] Technically a Franco-Italian production, its director and cowriter was New York–native John Berry, who ran afoul of HUAC in 1951 and fled to Paris.[113] Although made in Nice, safely outside the PCA's jurisdiction, hopes of an American release constrained the film, as did French censorship. A French version opened with an explanation that "it is the honor of France to have been one of the first nations to pass laws against slavery" in 1794, a self-congratulatory statement that passed over France's long involvement in the slave trade and its reinstatement of slavery in 1802. Both versions showed the slave ship pursued by a French ship enforcing the ban on slave trading, even though it was mainly the British who policed that ban.[114] Mérimée's story about a revolt on a slave ship was hardly an abolitionist tract, despite a few digs at Europeans and the slave trade.[115] Indeed, it was quite insulting to Africans, as the revolt's leader, Tamango, was himself a slave trader hoodwinked into captivity, and the successful rebels ended up in a drunken stupor, fighting among themselves, and unable to figure out even the most basic principles of sailing.

The 1958 film altered the story considerably, making Tamango (France's Alex Cressan) a heroic figure and altering Mérimée's unflattering ending. After the ironically named *Esperanza* (Hope) loads its human cargo and eludes a French warship, the film focuses on the slaves' mistreatment and a revolt that ends with the Captain massacring them. Aiché enjoys her privileges and advises Tamango not to rebel, but when she learns that the Captain intends to marry a white woman and abandon her, she turns against him. When he frees her, hoping she will stay with him, she declares her true feelings. "I've always hated you," she says, "hated your hands on me, hated that bed," and she insists she is "telling the truth to a white man for the first time in my life." Taken hostage by Tamango, who had told her, "Your place is with us," she eventually declines his offer to rejoin the Captain and chooses to die with the rebels. The film thus updates Mérimée's tale for the decolonization era by siding with the colonized.

Although *Tamango* went beyond any Hollywood film of the 1950s in its frank depiction of a white man in a sexual relationship with a black woman—played by an African American actress—Dandridge called the script "a shipboard sex drama, tawdry and exploitive" and pushed Berry to make her role more confrontational.[116] It sought neither to defend miscegenation nor to promote integration, instead opposing colonialism's sexual exploitation. Unlike Manty in *Band of Angels*, who stays with Hamish out of love, Aiché spurns the Captain, having slept with him only reluctantly. It also sounded the important theme of the solidarity of the colonized through her defection to the rebels. Tamango, whom Cressan played with strength and dignity, continued the new cinematic type of the angry, defiant black man, going beyond David Boyeur in *Island in the Sun* by using violence, and beyond Rau-Ru in *Band of Angels* by pursuing resistance to the bitter end. A happy ending would have weakened the film's angry denunciation of slavery, so it endorsed even futile revolt—two years before *Spartacus* did so. Although hardly a masterpiece, *Tamango* remains a historically significant, bold statement for its time.

The film had limited distribution in the United States, though claims that it was banned until 1962 are incorrect.[117] The obscure Hal Roach Distribution Corporation released it in late 1959, nearly two years after it opened in France, with minimal advertising (of the usual sensationalist sort); it did not play in many southern markets or make the box-office charts. Quite a few critics reviewed it, however, and eight of twenty reviews located were positive (40 percent), eight negative, and four mixed or neutral.[118] The dubbing annoyed critics, and *Film Daily* wrote that the film had "an art house quality to it" while *Variety* warned of poor prospects in the South. The *Los Angeles Times* dismissed it as a "low-grade new race melodrama" and mocked it, writing that Tamango is punished by being "tied down on the deck in the sunshine, which is something most tourists do voluntarily." The *St. Louis Post-Dispatch* also panned it as "a trashy and rather lurid melodrama" using miscegenation "for box-office sensationalism."

The African American papers showed less interest in its treatment of slavery than in the interracial romance; the *Chicago Defender* mistakenly wrote that the French government had banned it in most of France (it was only banned in the colonies) and that the interracial romance was the reason. (The real reason was its depiction of a violent uprising of blacks at a time of pressures for decolonization.) The *Pittsburgh Courier*'s Darcy DeMille argued that it "presents a good and wonderful argument AGAINST racial discrimination" but "should never have been filmed" because it would fail at the box office. She warned that whites would shun the film "because what they see in their brother-whites will make them squirm" and that "Negroes from the South and from the North will intensely dislike" it as well, as "they too go to the theatre to be entertained."[119] Several white critics questioned examining slavery at all. Marjory Adams of the *Boston Herald* suggested that the tale "seems out-of-date in these days when the Negro problem has ramifications having nothing to do with stolen Africans and men thrown to the sharks," while Wanda Hale of the *New York Daily News* declared that "the significance is considerably weakened by a story that goes back to the early 19th century."

Not everyone considered slavery irrelevant history. Although he panned the film, *Commonweal*'s Philip Hartung called it "an effective reminder of a period which saw the origins of many of today's woes," and in the *Los Angeles Examiner*, Ruth Waterbury maintained that "for all those who feel superior because of the tint of their skin, it's a good corrective to remember our own national guilt." The *Dallas Morning News* added that "present social undertones naturally update this age-old controversy," and it welcomed a film that "will help us remember" slavery's harm "to both slave and master." The *Chicago Tribune* also applauded the making of a film on slavery and suggested that someone make a film about the *Amistad* revolt.

The film did far better in France, where it sold 2,174,246 tickets despite heavily negative reviews; five of twenty reviews located were positive (25 percent), eleven negative, and four mixed or neutral.[120] Many criticized the directing and acting, praising only Cressan while giving Dandridge rough treatment. François Truffaut called it a stupid and "racist film," explaining that charge only by saying that the ending placated American viewers. Despite panning the film, critics on the left praised its courage and relevance; *La Croix*'s Jean Rochereau noted it had "multiple resonances" for current issues, and *Libération* called it "a cry to which one must pay heed." *L'Humanité* praised the revision of Mérimée's insulting image of Tamango, making him "free and proud, aware of his dignity," and pronounced it "a courageous film that evokes, for the French viewer, several burningly relevant problems." *France Observateur* specified its relevance to "a France officially engaged in the war in Algeria," writing that it "portrays different attitudes toward the colonial problem," including collaboration and resistance. *Témoignage Chrétien* found it rare "that a French film shows such courage."

On the right, Jean Dutourd of the Gaullist *Carrefour*, insisted, "I am neither pro-slavery nor hostile to the emancipation of peoples of color," but he sneered at "a rather inept story of black patriots" who spoke like graduates of the University of Dakar and concluded, "I felt as if I was at the Bandung Conference." The far-right *Aspects de la France* lamented that Africa was now filled with "all the ferment of hatred against the civilizing nation, stirred up by our own democratic errors" and "the resurgence of age-old tribal rivalries that a wise colonial administration thought it had abolished." Objecting to the alteration of Mérimée's tale, *Rivarol*'s Gilles Martain complained that "all the people on the bridge, the whites, are ignoble and degenerate," while "all below, the blacks, show a moving nobility, purity, and moral beauty."

In May 1959, Rank released Basil Dearden's *Sapphire*. The impetus for the film came from race riots in London's Notting Hill neighborhood in August 1958 and growing racial tensions as whites beheld an influx of immigrants from current and former colonies.[121] This color film shot in London opens with the discovery of a young blonde murder victim, Sapphire Robbins, leading Police Superintendent Bob Hazard (Nigel Patrick) and his assistant, Inspector Phil Learoyd (Michael Craig) to begin investigating. Learning that Sapphire was a student at the Royal College of Music, they visit her rented room, where they discover garish, sexy lingerie in a locked drawer; their next surprise comes when they meet her brother, Dr. Robbins (Earl Cameron), and the sight of a black man entering—punctuated by a jazz-orchestra chord—leaves the Superintendent momentarily stunned. The police learn that Sapphire had been seeking to rise socially by passing for white, having abandoned her black circle of friends; she had also become engaged to—and pregnant by—a young white student, David Harris (Paul Massie).

The investigation yields an interesting look at London's ethnic neighborhoods and racial attitudes in 1959. It shows white working-class racism: a group of "Teddy Boys," street toughs notorious for their anti-immigrant racism, beat up a fleeing black suspect, Johnnie Fiddle. It also shows middle-class racism through the respectable Harris family and landladies who reject colored tenants—Sapphire's landlady slams the door in her brother's face. Even more boldly, it shows racist policemen, as Phil tells his boss, "These spades are a load of trouble. I reckon we should send them back where they came from." The wise Superintendent redeems the image of the police as he gently chides his partner for his ignorant views, and he represents the film's viewpoint, along with an enlightened doctor who also challenges Phil's racist views. Additionally criticizing racism is Sapphire's brother, who tells the Superintendent, "I see all kind of sickness in my practice, Superintendent. I've never yet seen the kind you can cure in a day."

While exposing racism, the film purveys some racist stereotypes of its own. Although there are positive black characters, including Sapphire's brother and two West Indians who tell the fleeing Johnnie Fiddle it is "your kind that gets us respectable folk a bad name," other black characters live in dirty slums, dance wildly in seedy nightclubs, and live by crime. When Phil visits Horace Big Cigar, a room full of idle, grinning, wisecracking black lowlifes make Phil's urge to deport all West Indians understandable. The film also insists on blacks' primal attraction to drumming and rhythm. A black bartender in a seedy dive (Orlando Martins) tells the Superintendent "you can always tell" if someone who looks white is really colored "once they hear the beat of the bongo." The camera then zooms in on the feet of a woman who looks white but cannot resist a jazzy dance beat. The film also assuages white guilt about racism by insisting that blacks are just as racist, and a young black barrister who drives a flashy Jaguar convertible—an image liable to elicit white resentment—tells the Superintendent that his father would not let him marry the partly white Sapphire. Finally, the murdered Sapphire is the usual tragic mulatto, unwilling to live in the black world but unwelcome among whites.

British critics applauded *Sapphire*, giving it seventeen positive (81 percent), two negative, and two mixed reviews.[122] Although some praised it simply as fine entertainment and said little or nothing about the racial theme, others shared the *Daily Cinema*'s verdict that it was a "first-rate whodunit ... with a salutary moral of tolerance." Most reviews discussed race relations, which the *Sunday Times* called "a division comparatively new in English society." The *Guardian* wrote that "we still tend to think cosily of this as something to be read about in the news from Africa or America," so the film "came as a bit of a shock." John Waterman of the *Evening Standard* declared that "after the Notting Hill riots" and after "seeing for myself accommodation notice boards that announce: 'No Coloured,'" ... I must conclude that the happenings in *Sapphire* can be certified as a true likeness." In an increasingly cosmopolitan London, he added, most people know prejudice exists but "have no defined attitude," and he applauded a film that "brings every member of the audience face to face with the appalling revelation."

Others were more indulgent of the racism depicted. The *Observer*'s C. A. Lejeune was pleased that the film "has fair arguments to advance on both sides," and the *Daily Mail*'s Fred Majdalany praised it for showing "the attitudes of landladies" quite "understandingly." This objectivity, however, bothered Nina Hibbin of the *Daily Worker*. "You can't fight the colour bar merely by telling people it exists," she charged. "You have to attack it, with passion and conviction." Complaining that black characters "have been put on the shady side of life," and fearing that "a colour-baiter among the audience could well find himself in complete sympathy with the racialism expressed," she had "an uneasy feeling that it will do more harm than good," for this "objective exposure" is "perilously near to becoming a justification." Curiously, the only other critic who shared the *Daily Worker*'s outlook was the conservative *Spectator*'s Isabel Quigly, who found the film "exaggerated, confusing and slightly patronising." She noted that the black barrister "is turned into the familiar spade figure by a flashy car and girl," while throughout, "coloured = tomtoms, slums, rackets, zooty suits, [and] taffeta petticoats." She also complained that "we might have been shown a coloured family as respectable as David's." Nonetheless, she concluded (speaking as if Britons were all white) that "there is room for a British film on our present ... attitude to coloured people" and not just those "tyrannised in Little Rock or Johannesburg." Few others derided the film's racial blind spots, and both the film and the reactions to it reveal a society just beginning to grapple with this aspect of decolonization.

In 1959, the French revisited black-white miscegenation in Michel Gast's film of a 1946 Boris Vian novel, *J'irai cracher sur vos tombes* (released in New York in 1963 as *I Spit on Your Grave*). Gast cowrote the low-budget black-and-white revenger with Vian and two others. It opens with a barely explained lynching of a black man by a white southern mob angry over his dating a white woman. The victim's brother, Joe Grant (Christian Marquand), who looks completely white, burns the body and then heads north to "Trenton," where he takes random revenge on the white race by sleeping with racist white women unaware of his ethnicity. Taking on Stan Walker, heir to the family that dominates the town, Joe faces down Stan's goon squad, sleeps with his sister, and gets his fiancée, Elizabeth, to fall in love with him. By the time the police track down the fugitive lovers, Joe has had his revenge in white women's beds. The film's depiction of America is weird and unrealistic, but at least the handful of Americans who saw it learned for once how foreigners felt watching Hollywood try to depict their societies. Its problems as a revenger began with its failure to create emotional impact in the hasty lynching scene, and despite a certain novelty in Joe's way of taking revenge on white people, the lack of realism weakened its critique of racism. And while French filmmakers were certainly free to critique American racism, examining someone else's racism took little courage. French censorship, of course, would have blocked any film about French racism toward North Africans, and it would be another decade before Michel Drach explored that issue in *Elise, ou la vraie vie* (1970).

The black-white miscegenation films of this period may now seem dated and timid, perhaps even conservative and hostile to racial progress, as some contend.[123] While some viewers at the time certainly found them timid, others found them shocking and offensive, and despite the war's influence on racial attitudes, ample evidence indicates the depth and breadth of hostility toward black-white miscegenation, principally in the United States. The old litmus test about permitting one's daughter to marry a Negro expressed something very real in many white people's attitudes. In exploring romance between blacks and whites, filmmakers focused on the most sensitive of racial questions, and assessing those films requires recalling how dramatically racial attitudes have changed since then. In addition to judging the films for their time, one needs a sense of the realities of the film industry and the conflicting pressures filmmakers faced in an art form in which nearly everything seen on screen represented compromises, in an industry in which failures could end careers, and in an era when declining ticket sales made it risky to alienate large sectors of an audience. Securing financing and distribution for such films was challenging, and as Zanuck explained in making *Pinky*, attracting the people who most needed to see such pictures demanded compromises. Keeping these caveats in mind, very few of these films are the reactionary, segregationist works some suggest.

One striking characteristic of these films is their interest in "white Negroes," who appear in eleven of the fourteen films examined—all but *Pool of London*, *Tamango*, and *The World, the Flesh, and the Devil*. Filmmakers' copying of successful formulas—in this case the surprise hits *Lost Boundaries* and *Pinky*—help account for this phenomenon, as do Hollywood's racist hiring practices and preference for white characters (though the European films also featured "white Negroes"). Casting whites allowed the films to avoid the inflammatory sight of black and white actors kissing and touching, a key issue given audiences' tendency to perceive the ethnicity of actors more than characters. Telling tales of white Negroes also helped white viewers empathize with racism's victims, even if doing so pandered to their ethnocentrism and made the films less compelling to black viewers. Casting white actors made sense in that the narratives required the characters to fool everyone, and characters who looked white also ferreted out hidden racism, as others made racist comments or became involved in interracial romances in ignorance of their mixed heritage.

Despite their many compromises and blind spots, these films provoked reflection about racism and the nature of the differences whites used to justify discrimination. Calling attention to the one-drop rule did more than just demonstrate how extreme racism could be. Behind the often-decried irrationality of racism stood a quasi-rational system of discrimination that benefited white people, and the one-drop rule helped prevent infiltration of a reserved domain by the many African Americans with white ancestors. From this perspective, far from dwelling on an insignificant issue, these films scrutinized and threatened a cornerstone of segregation and discrimination. The fury with which certain white southerners protested the films and the dire warnings they issued about their consequences attest to the issue's importance. By 1960, this cycle of films may have exhausted the subject of miscegenation between whites and "white Negroes," but these films remain important in the history of race relations and decolonization.

Also historically significant is these films' replacement of the obedient, grinning black characters of prewar films with new characters—proud, angry, defiant, and rebellious. In an era when the civil rights movement was gaining strength, the films both reflected and encouraged boldness with characters such as Pinky, standing her ground against southern racists and taking pride in her ethnicity; David Boyeur, challenging the white power structure in the West Indies and shunning Mavis in the interest of the cause; Rau-Ru, detesting his liberal master for his paternalist kindness; Tamango, courageously leading a slave revolt against hopeless odds; Aiché, finally joining the revolt; Ginny, refusing to surrender her husband to a rich and powerful mother-in-law in *Night of the Quarter Moon*; and Joe Grant, in *J'irai cracher sur vos tombes*, pursuing his vendetta against the white race. A few of the films also showed that one might reject miscegenation not out of colonialist concerns to preserve racial hierarchies, but rather out of anticolonialist motives of racial pride (Pinky), racial solidarity (David Boyeur), and rejection of sexual exploitation (Aiché). Films also broke an old taboo by highlighting whites' sexual exploitation of blacks, as seen in the attempted rape scene in *Pinky*, the slave dealer's attempted rape of Manty in *Band of Angels*, and the Captain's sexual imprisonment of Aiché. Finally, nearly all the films featured white racist villains, and all indicted racism in some way. Far from carrying on prewar "business as usual" or seeking to put blacks in their place, these films reflected and promoted changes in race relations and attitudes toward miscegenation.

Film, Miscegenation, and Decolonization

Postwar films on miscegenation in the American West, in Asia, and between blacks and whites in Europe and America reveal an extraordinarily diverse array of issues, messages, concerns, and approaches. Deciding what even constitutes a film about miscegenation is nettlesome, but excluding off-screen relationships, this study has identified more than one hundred American, British, and French films from the period that deal with miscegenation, whether through rape, consensual or semiconsensual relations, or mixed-race characters. Ten of the films present rapists of color threatening white women—a strikingly low number— while white rapists threatening women of color appeared in nine films. This parity suggests an era in which new, more anticolonialist or racially liberal attitudes overlapped with persistent colonialist and racist tropes.

A similar picture emerges from examining the outcomes of these tales. The common notion that films reinforced colonialist taboos with cautionary tales of interracial lovers meeting bitter ends has some validity in that forty-six of eighty-nine consensual couples ended up separated, often by violent death. Yet thirty-five of these relationships ended happily, while eight were left unresolved, so once again new attitudes became common while old ones persisted. And while nearly all the films with happy endings for interracial couples viewed miscegenation positively, unhappy endings did not always signify opposition, as films often made martyrs of lovers killed or separated by racist villains. Although many films were evasive or ambiguous, films frankly opposing miscegenation were now in a distinct minority.

With some films opposing miscegenation from anticolonialist perspectives, it was impossible to assume either that films opposing miscegenation favored colonialism or that films favoring miscegenation opposed colonialism. Indeed most pro-miscegenation films took a liberal-colonialist view, favoring a tolerant, racially inclusive vision of the spread of Western rule. In most of those films, either the interracial couples themselves or their offspring ended up living happily not in indigenous societies, but in Western societies whose inclusiveness helped legitimize their dominance. Also suggesting the limits of change was the persistence of the double standard that tolerated white men's relations with women of color more than the inverse: only twenty-two of the eighty-nine consensual couples featured men of color, and those relationships were less likely to end well.[124] Resistance remained stronger to seeing white women with men of color.

Depictions of mixed-race characters in this period did not always follow familiar patterns. The figure of the tragic mulatto does fit roughly a third of the mixed-race characters, while roughly the same number seem happy, even in the face of mistreatment by racist whites. Some of the unhappy characters suffer simply for being nonwhite as opposed to being mixed, while quite a few, such as Pinky, the Carters in *Lost Boundaries*, and Victoria Jones in *Bhowani Junction*, suffer at first but ultimately find happiness. The figure of the evil mulatto or mixed-race character nearly disappeared in this period, as only three of the sixty-five (Nita in *Arrowhead*, Armand in *Apache Woman*, and Major Cham in *China Gate*) were clearly villains. Many mixed-race characters were children, and films such as *Giant*, *China Gate*, and *Trooper Hook* invited sympathy for miscegenation by showing adorable little children, though never children of black-white couples.

Critics mostly praised messages of tolerance, with only a small minority openly opposing miscegenation, and none stated anything like the vitriol white southerners expressed to censors. Already by this time, if critics held white supremacist or segregationist views, they mostly kept them silent. There were probably big differences between private and public opinion on miscegenation, but the domination of the public sphere by voices favoring tolerance was a significant historical development in this period. Attitudes certainly varied by country; the French seemed generally more open to miscegenation, though no French film took on the sensitive topic of relations with North Africans in France. France, in short, combined the most racially enlightened views and the strictest movie censorship.

The films might have provoked more hostility about miscegenation had they presented it more boldly. Most avoided showing actors of different colors kissing, told tales of white men rather than women in interracial relationships, dropped miscegenation subplots abruptly, and set tales in the past and/or overseas. These timidities and evasions provoked complaints, particularly in liberal or left-wing papers, but while some critics felt the films did not go far enough, many viewers likely felt they went too far. In short, this was an issue where the opinions of critics and many audience members likely diverged somewhat. Many miscegenation films proved unsatisfying as entertainment—in part because filmmakers were treading so cautiously and in part because the subject made people uncomfortable—and their shortcomings distracted critics from discussing the issues they raised.

Despite this timidity, filmmakers were mostly ahead of the general public on this issue—expressing more liberal views and calling attention to issues others preferred to ignore. Many of the films illustrate interracial love's ability to bridge the distance between colonizer and colonized, as sexual exploitation gradually led to more serious relationships and fostered familiarity and mutual understanding. Racist whites gradually lost their hatreds in *Broken Arrow*, *The Big Sky*, *Three Stripes in the Sun*, *Sayonara*, and other films, gaining insight and sympathy for another culture by falling in love. While this was an actual experience for some Westerners, films transmitted that experience to millions of others, and though watching a film about someone's transformation through a love affair means less than experiencing it personally, films' ability to capture people's emotions and remain in their memories for years suggests how influential they can be. As unfortunate as it may be that people can only begin to see others' humanity and cultural worth through finding them sexually attractive, things often worked that way. Films made this easier by casting good-looking people to play romantic parts, and viewers' tendencies to find actors and movie characters attractive—even to fall in love with them—helped them rethink their perceptions of peoples under forms of colonial rule.

Although the casting of white actors weakened the effect, many films did cast attractive actors of color in romantic roles, including Harry Belafonte, Earl Cameron, Armando Silvestre, James Shigeta, Dorothy Dandridge, Katy Jurado, Elsa Cardenas, Rita Moreno, Maria Elena Marques, France Nuyen, Li Hua Li, Miiko Taka, Shirley Yamaguchi, Machiko Kyô, Eiko Ando, and Miyoshi Umeki. If these films indeed led viewers to think more about people of color and to reconsider their assumptions of racial difference, then cinema played a significant role in undermining one pillar of colonialism. At the very least, this avalanche of films about miscegenation accustomed Western filmgoers to the sight of interracial couples, and when people actually saw an interracial couple for the first time, they probably thought of films they had seen.

CONCLUSION

If movies can serve as even a rough indicator of popular attitudes, then it appears that fundamental changes in Western thinking about colonialism took place in the twentieth century. To some, popular cinema's treatment of colonialism and race relations has always been conservative and has never really changed, and indeed the films of the 1940s and 1950s may not seem progressive today. But if we contrast, say, *Gunga Din* (1939) and *Gandhi* (1982), or *Unconquered* (1947) and *Dances with Wolves* (1990), or *The Birth of a Nation* (1915) and *Malcolm X* (1992), it seems clear that significant changes have occurred.

Although the discrediting of colonialism was a long-term process, the late 1940s and the 1950s were a critical moment. The massive number of films from these years saw the overlapping of traditional colonialist views and newer, more critical views. Retrograde outlooks in films such as *Unconquered* (1947), *The Planter's Wife* (1952), *Arrowhead* (1953), and *The Inn of the Sixth Happiness* (1958) persisted, despite the proliferation of films with anticolonialist or progressive views, including *Devil's Doorway* (1950), *The Last Hunt* (1956), *Giant* (1956), *Mort en fraude* (1957), *Tamango* (1958), and *Shake Hands with the Devil* (1959). Between the most colonialist and anticolonialist films stood an even larger number of movies blending the two outlooks. This diversity of views existed because filmmakers themselves ranged from staunch conservatives, such as Cecil B. DeMille and John Wayne, to liberals or progressives, such as Richard Brooks, Robert Aldrich, John Berry, and Albert Maltz. Yet it was more than a question of individuals with different political views. The collaborative nature of filmmaking and the extensive process of rewriting scripts, as well as the compromises made to placate studios, financiers, pressure groups, censors, and government officials combined to yield pictures with curious and even incoherent blends of political perspectives. Moreover, in an era when people's ideas about these issues were still fluid, conservative, liberal, and even radical ideas often coexisted within a given filmmaker's mind. Filmmakers, in short, were often of two minds, and from one picture to another a director might express strikingly different views. An "overlap thesis," in which older perspectives on colonialism persisted while newer views became more common, thus provides a useful framework of analysis.

Was a transition to newer outlooks evident *within* these years? Treatments of interracial couples did change between the 1940s, when films had white actors play people of color, and the late 1950s, when the end of the Production Code Administration's ban on black-white miscegenation let Darryl F. Zanuck cast Harry Belafonte and Dorothy Dandridge in interracial romances. The late 1940s saw some very retrograde films (*Duel in the Sun, I See a Dark Stranger, Unconquered*) as well as "colonial backdrop" films whose indifference to the colonized reflected racist and colonialist attitudes, and the figure of the white racist villain was still fairly rare in the 1940s. A few progressive films, including *Fort Apache, Pinky, Broken Arrow,* and *Devil's Doorway* appeared by 1950, and despite the chilling effects of the Cold War and the House Committee on Un-American Activities investigations, filmmakers continued to make racially liberal films in the early 1950s. Significant changes then became even more apparent, even if a few retrograde pictures such as *North West Frontier, Five Gates to Hell,* and *Killers of Kilimanjaro* still appeared in 1959. A fundamental transformation thus took place in the 1950s, and in the gradual discrediting of colonialism and racism, the entire period from the end of World War II to the end of the 1950s was a complex but crucial period of transition, laying foundations for the changes of the 1960s and after.

Many postwar empire films ignored decolonization, either by telling tales of the early stages of colonization, or simply by overlooking historical resistance to colonial rule. Even those films often made tacit concessions to new perspectives, striving to make colonialism look altruistic and beneficent by spotlighting kindly female civilizers and male protectors of needy, vulnerable peoples. Whether or not these filmmakers consciously hoped to save colonialism, their films adhered to colonialist mentalities through force of habit and the rigidities of genre conventions. For a so-called creative industry, the film world is not always so creative, and its adherence to genre conventions and its reliance on tried-and-true plots, character types, and imagery led many postwar empire films to perpetuate old mentalities. As correspondence among moguls, producers, writers, and directors indicates, filmmakers often wished to update their tales of empire, and they nested progressive arguments and sequences in dated colonialist frameworks. If these insertions seemed awkward and confusing even to contemporaries, the confusion and incoherence of the film world probably reflected the confusion and incoherence of the societies themselves confronting political change. Societies' myths must evolve to retain their power, but the empire films of these years suggest that refashioning myths is not easy.

Of course, nations do not exist in isolation, and given the international nature of filmmaking, the recasting of national mythologies in this period reflected foreign influences. In these years, "runaway" productions blurred lines between national cinemas; writers, directors, and other film people migrated across borders; novels from one country were filmed in another; filmmakers in each country influenced others; and hopes for foreign revenues shaped films' content. These issues all complicate national-level analysis and comparisons between national cinemas, but with those caveats in mind, we can see the emergence of some national differences.

Americans emerged from World War II less isolationist than ever, and the Cold War then accentuated that change. Internationalist elites feared a reemergence of isolationism, and many postwar films encouraged Americans to bear the burdens of international leadership, as seen in Hollywood's frequent recourse to the device of the cynical, materialistic, selfish American man who learns to embrace his obligations to others. Examples of such transformed characters include Tom Jeffords overcoming his hatred of Indians to become a peacemaker in *Broken Arrow*; Harry Smith risking his life to broker peace in Syria in *Sirocco*; Steve Gibbs staying in India to help fight Muslim rebels in *Thunder in the East*; Mr. Morgan returning to be a proper father in *Return to Paradise*; David O'Keefe abandoning his dreams of a copra empire and helping to defend Yap in *His Majesty O'Keefe*; Ben Trane agreeing to help the Juaristas in *Vera Cruz*; Greg Dickson abandoning plans to sell his Philippine plantation and deciding to stay and fight the rebels in *Huk!*; Sergeant O'Reilly overcoming his hatred of the Japanese to oversee an orphanage and marry a Japanese woman in *Three Stripes in the Sun*; Mike Conway accepting his duties to the French who are fighting Tuareg rebels in *Timbuktu*; and Robert Adamson saving a young boy and helping Africa to modernize in *Killers of Kilimanjaro*. This device appeared in only one of the thirty European films examined here: *Mort en fraude*. Characters who were altruistic from the outset appeared in numerous other American films, as well as one French film (*Patrouille de choc*) and several British ones (*Where No Vultures Fly*, *West of Zanzibar*, *North West Frontier*), but there was something characteristically American about the hard-bitten, selfish cynic learning to help others, and the self-flattering image of American men as tough guys with hearts of gold proved a staple of Hollywood's postwar empire films.

If American films could be self-flattering, they could also be self-critical. Historians have noted that tendency, and numerous British and French critics made similar observations about American films of this period, while few European films showed contrition about colonial crimes. While American films about American misdeeds often featured happy endings and provided reassurance that Americans ultimately right their wrongs, they also showed a great deal of "dirt" from America's past. And while some westerns of these years were indeed triumphalist, a larger number painted an ugly picture of ruthless, culturally ignorant soldiers; corrupt, heartless Indian agents; and greedy, violent settlers grabbing land, breaking treaties, and slaughtering Indians and buffalo. In addition to much serious criticism of the "winning of the West" and the treatment of Indians, Hollywood cast a harsh light on American racism in general. Anyone accustomed to the notion that empire films pitted white good guys against villains of color may be surprised at how pervasive the white racist villain became in these years. That type was not unknown in British and French films (or in older empire films, for that matter), and four of the seven French films and three of the twenty-two British films examined here featured white racists—though only one of these films (*Where No Vultures Fly*) appeared before 1957, and only one French film depicted French racists. Meanwhile, nearly half of the American films—58 of 120 (48 percent)—included white racist villains, and the trend was under way by the late 1940s. In only one American film, *Arrowhead*, was the white racist clearly a hero. The rest of the fifty-seven films depict racists, usually Americans, as villains or at least present racism as a problem. The Indian-hater was the most common racist villain, followed by whites who hated blacks or the Japanese.

In addition to America's penchant for cinematic self-criticism, national differences in censorship also explain American films' attention to white racism. The U.S. Supreme Court's 1952 granting of First Amendment rights to films gave filmmakers' new freedom, and the PCA was in retreat, standing its ground more on matters of sex, nudity, and brutality than on treatments of racial prejudice or black-white miscegenation, which it stopped prohibiting altogether in 1956. In France and Britain, on the other hand, no major changes in censorship regimes took place in these years, and it seems likely that more filmmakers, particularly in France, would have explored the problem of racism if given more freedom.

Differences between these countries' experiences with colonial rule also seem pertinent, in that humiliating defeats bring more soul-searching and contrition than victories do. Britain had certainly experienced defeats in colonial settings, but the loss of the American colonies in the eighteenth century and most of Ireland in 1921 were far in the past, and the loss of Singapore to the Japanese in 1942, while certainly humiliating, came at the hands of a rival imperial power, not a colony in revolt. The Suez debacle of 1956 also resulted from a political defeat at Washington's hands, not a military defeat by the Egyptians. Britain's other recent withdrawals from colonies took place peacefully—allowing British leaders to put a positive "spin" on them—and when Britain used force in Kenya and Malaya, it succeeded.

The French had also experienced defeats, both at home to Germany in 1940 and in Indochina, where a colonized people vanquished them. The remoteness of Indochina and the fact that France had not used draftees for that war limited the shock of defeat; the war in Algeria would prove far more traumatic, but well into that war one could harbor illusions of victory, and the digestion of defeat in Algeria only began in earnest in the 1960s. The Americans, meanwhile, had risen to superpower status, and although Pearl Harbor and other early setbacks in World War II administered a shock, they were soon redeemed by victory. Other setbacks in the Cold War came from the rise of the Soviets, a rival imperial power. The "loss of China" came closer to being an imperial defeat, though the Americans had not fought the Communists in the field. The embarrassing retreat after China intervened in Korea gave Americans a clearer sense of the limits of their own power, yet that war ended in a draw rather than a defeat. Like the French, the Americans' real experience with humiliating defeat would come later, in Vietnam. In sum, all three countries had significant but limited experience with humiliating defeat by the 1950s.

A more promising explanation for Hollywood's greater interest in racism concerns the location of the three countries' colonial endeavors. Only one British or French film featured a white racist villain in the mother country—*Sapphire* (1959)—while most of the American films on the topic took place in the United States and highlighted racism toward American Indians or African Americans. With so much of their colonial history taking place inside the United States, more Americans than British or French lived alongside people of color, and though few Americans had much contact with American Indians, the countless westerns made over the years had no counterpart in either British or French cinema. As for African Americans, millions of whites came into contact with them in their daily lives, but that contact did not necessarily generate any real familiarity, so again cinema helped white Americans to think in new ways about a people they had colonized. The scarcity of colonial subjects in Britain and France began to change only with large-scale migration of former colonial subjects to Britain and France toward the end of the 1950s. In short, both the location of much of American colonialism and the considerable attention Hollywood had long paid to certain colonized peoples help explain the national differences. British and French films rarely explored the issues of internal decolonization that many American films of the late 1940s and 1950s raised—especially films about African Americans in the present (*Lost Boundaries, Pinky, Night of the Quarter Moon*) and about American Indians after the conquest (*Walk the Proud Land, Foxfire*). If American films proposed few concrete solutions for the colonized who lived inside the United States, that is not really cinema's role, and Hollywood did its part by inviting reflection on issues of internal decolonization.

Films and Public Opinion

The issue of films' role in shaping Western attitudes about colonialism—in effect, whether films were ahead of or behind public opinion's evolution—raises fundamental questions about the nature of the film industry and its relationship with public opinion. While some argue that film industries, particularly Hollywood, value profits above all and thus cater to audiences' perceived tastes, concerns, and political outlooks, others see filmmakers using their extraordinary power to advance their own views and alter public opinion. The evidence considered here suggests that there is some truth to both theories, and that things vary from film to film, studio to studio, and moment to moment. All films and filmmakers exhibited some inclinations in both directions. Darryl F. Zanuck, for example, left an ample record of his interest in conveying his political and social principles, but he was always careful to temper such impulses and to keep in mind that he was in the business of popular entertainment.

Assessing whether films were ahead of public opinion requires distinguishing between two relationships: one between filmmakers and their public and one between film critics and audiences. Many studio heads and filmmakers came out of the same social circles as their audiences, even if they became much wealthier. In terms of class or social background, regional origins, educational level, and political outlooks, discrepancies between filmmakers and audiences were not so great, and on the specific issues of foreign policy and the treatment of colonies and subject peoples, filmmakers had no expertise or experience that really distinguished them from audiences. The same holds for film critics: some knew much more than their readers did about movies, but few had any real advantage in terms of knowledge or experience with issues of colonialism. There were important differences between film criticism in the United States, Britain, and France; regional newspapers, for example, had larger market shares in the United States than in Britain and France. France also had more newspapers and magazines on the left and far left—in part because France had more such voters—and both left-wing film critics and French Communists were generally more hostile to and aware of colonial questions than were others. For the most part, however, critics' reactions to films about colonialism often revealed considerable ignorance, and while no evidence permits a careful comparison of the views of critics and their readers on these questions, it seems plausible that the two held roughly similar views. In the absence of direct evidence of viewers' reactions to these films, film reviews constitute a valuable historical source.

So were films ahead of or behind the evolution of public opinion on colonial issues? A relatively small group of films with very conservative views on colonial issues did well at the box office and raised few objections from critics. Hardly any critics, for example, objected that *Duel in the Sun, Unconquered, Charge at Feather River,* or *Arrowhead* insulted American Indians, or that films on Africa purveyed dated colonialist mentalities. In films about communism, such as the China films, Cold War concerns trumped misgivings about Western imperialism, though blatantly anticommunist films generally flopped at the box office. Many of the more conservative films appeared by the early 1950s, and by 1959, the Raj adventure film *North West Frontier* seemed dated to many critics.

While a few films lagged behind changing political views about colonialism and got away with it, others were well ahead of most people's thinking and paid a price for it. *Devil's Doorway* missed the box-office charts despite a compelling story, a major star (Robert Taylor), and a skilled director (Anthony Mann), and *The Last Hunt* reached only the number fifty-seven slot despite three stars and a director (Richard Brooks) fresh off a major hit (*Blackboard Jungle*). Such films also show how intermediaries between film artists and the public complicate the analysis of reception. The studios seemed wary of films too critical of traditional attitudes, and when films nested disparagements of colonialism within otherwise colonialist frameworks, their advertisements ignored such critiques. Films such as *Devil's Doorway* and *Tamango* struggled for distribution, and French censors simply banned *Le Rendez-vous des quais*. Films that criticized someone else's colonialism might do better: *Tamango* did well in France, for example, while many Hollywood films critical of European colonialism did well at home. No one can say how some of the most self-critical films would have done if given a proper chance, but when strongly anticolonialist films did play, reviews illustrated another danger in getting too far ahead of people's mentalities: critics seemed confused and disoriented. Anticolonialist films also risked depressing audiences and critics, particularly when, as in *Sirocco, Tamango,* and *Devil's Doorway*, they used a somber tone and ended with the protagonist's death.

A far larger number of films sought out a middle ground, by blending conservative and liberal viewpoints and by being timid and evasive. Films used all sorts of evasions when dealing with controversies, such as leaving interracial relationships unresolved and casting white actors to play people of color. This timidity did not go unnoticed, as many critics derided the hedging and lack of courage, but it likely dampened angry reactions from viewers and pressure groups. Films that included both positive and negative perspectives on colonialism probably matched viewers' and critics' own mentalities.

The most successful films calibrated their critiques of racism and colonialism carefully, nesting them in uplifting narratives with happy endings and staying barely ahead of existing outlooks. Examples of hit films critical of colonialism and racism include *Pinky* (number two of 1949), *Broken Arrow* (number nine of 1950), *Giant* (number three of 1957), *Teahouse of the August Moon* (number six of 1957), *Island in the Sun* (number nine of 1957), *Sayonara* (number three of 1958), and *South Pacific* (number seven of 1958), and most of these did well with critics. That these films generally criticized aspects of colonialism without questioning the entire system helps explain their success. At least by the mid-1950s, liberal-colonialist films that defended or accepted Western domination while urging better treatment of the colonized did better with critics and audiences than conservative-colonialist or anticolonialist films. The films and their reception provide some support for notions of the 1950s as an era of centrism and political consensus rather than a deeply conservative era, but there is some danger of overstating the consistency of people's views, as both films and their reception show the overlapping of older and newer outlooks.

The reception of films, of course, has more to do with their qualities as entertainment than with their politics, and a close look at individual critics shows that the same person might like or dislike films in any political category. In other words, only critics from staunchly left-wing or right-wing publications showed much political consistency; most others might applaud a very liberal film, then a very conservative one. Reception thus mirrors production, for as noted above, the same director might make a liberal film, then a conservative one. In retrospect, people from this era may seem ignorant, insensitive, or naive about colonialism and race. In all three countries, politics was still taboo in both films and reviews. Ethnic miscasting, about which people have since become keenly sensitized, was less controversial then, and objections were less about culturally insensitive or insulting images than about unconvincing filmmaking.

This seemingly inconsistent blend of views on colonialism should not be surprising, for colonialism had always provoked mixed feelings among the Americans, British, and French. Moreover, breaking colonialism down into its component elements makes their outlooks seem less incoherent. A pervasive belief in the superiority of Western ways led many to support spreading them to the colonized, as long as the effort seemed altruistic and neither brutal nor coercive. Although missionaries did not come off well in *Black Narcissus* and *Return to Paradise*, missionaries and teachers got very positive treatment in *Anna and the King of Siam*, *The King and I*, *White Witch Doctor*, *Three Stripes in the Sun*, *Pillars of the Sky*, *Mark of the Hawk*, *Patrouille de choc*, *The Inn of the Sixth Happiness*, and *The Nun's Story*. Most films also urged welcoming culturally assimilated colonial subjects into Western society. Doubts about the superiority of Western civilization did surface, especially in films about the South Seas, but these films were in the minority. And the notion of an obligation to defend, adopt, cure, and otherwise help colonized peoples pervaded many films, while resonating strongly with critics; examples would be too numerous to name, but doctors and nurses, for example, figure prominently in *Black Narcissus, Saadia, White Witch Doctor, The Command, Giant, Windom's Way*, and *The Nun's Story*.

Far less accepted were greedy fortune-hunters, miners, land grabbers, and overzealous soldiers, all of whom made convenient villains. So did anyone who seemed racist or abused the colonized. In terms of the components of colonialism, exploitation and discrimination were roundly rejected, whereas acculturation enjoyed more support under proper conditions. Attitudes toward occupation depended on how films handled the other issues; despite underlying misgivings about going to distant lands and meddling in the lives of the indigenous peoples, films and their critics were willing to support occupation under certain conditions. Colonial policymakers and officials of this era knew that saving colonialism required giving it a more benign image, and the reception of these films suggests that colonialism's legitimacy in the postwar era depended more than ever on fashioning a benevolent and beneficent image.

The Significance of Empire Films in the Decolonization Era

The empire films of these years and the reactions they encountered reveal much about public opinion on colonialism and decolonization, but did they also alter those attitudes? No definitive answer to this tantalizing question is possible, for any changes in people's attitudes could have had other causes. Nevertheless, it seems likely that films had some effects on viewers, especially the large numbers who lacked both knowledge and well-formed, deeply rooted opinions. Films that adhered to old colonialist mentalities may have bolstered colonial rule, while the few anticolonialist films may have planted seeds of doubt in some minds. Those that went beyond what most people could understand or accept probably had little effect (or none at all, if people did not see them). The films likeliest to induce questioning of colonialism were those that calibrated their critiques very carefully while meeting people's expectations of good entertainment. This body of movies was larger than either the traditionally colonialist or staunchly anticolonialist films, and though their compromises now draw sharp criticism, analysis of their reception suggests that those compromises made them persuasive.

While some American films still praised European imperial rule, many others criticized aspects of it. Many American films also criticized America's own past and present actions, and a bit of self-criticism even appeared in a few French and British films. The films of these years launched a sustained assault on racism, and a substantial number also defended miscegenation, inviting audiences to sympathize with the characters in interracial relationships and casting attractive actors and actresses to play them. The old notion that films had to punish interracial couples persisted, but happy endings for such couples also became very common, and unhappy endings acquired new meanings, such as martyrdom in the struggle against intolerance. If nothing else, the flood of films featuring interracial couples helped accustom viewers to them. In defending miscegenation, films seemed to be ahead of public opinion; in the 1960s, laws and attitudes about miscegenation began changing dramatically, and the films of the previous decade most likely helped foster those changes.

Even liberal-colonialist films, which accepted or endorsed a continued Western presence in colonies and supported acculturation and Westernization, nonetheless hammered away at certain aspects of colonialism. In doing so they raised awareness of and sensitivity to the concerns and perspectives of the colonized; most important, they humanized them for large numbers of viewers who had never visited the colonies or gotten to know any of the colonized at home or abroad. Examples of likeable, reasonable characters with legitimate grievances against Western imperialism include King Mongkut in *Anna and the King of Siam* and *The King and I*, Coatl in *Captain from Castile*, the Carters in *Lost Boundaries*, the title character in *Pinky*, Red Cloud in *Tomahawk*, Massai in *Apache*, the title characters in *Sitting Bull* and *Chief Crazy Horse*, Sakini and his fellow villagers in *Teahouse of the August Moon*, Anh in *Mort en fraude*, Kimani in *Something of Value*, Obam in *Mark of the Hawk*, and Jan Vidal in *Windom's Way*. There were still numerous pictures that continued old traditions of ignoring the colonized or treating them as a faceless mass, but they overlapped with dozens of films that introduced individuals, including women and children, allowed them extensive dialogue, told their stories, and made their grievances clear and emotionally compelling. To say that films encouraged viewers to consider the concerns and perspectives of the colonized is not to say that they conveyed them accurately; these were Western artists' mythic, imagined versions of the colonized, and only when those people made their own films would cinema convey their (already semi-Westernized) perspectives.

One major flaw in Western attempts to speak for the colonized was their inclination toward happy endings, rosy scenarios, and grateful colonial subjects repaying the work of civilizers and protectors with love and affection. As a rule, films did a poor job of preparing Western viewers for the rage that fueled anticolonialist liberation movements during and after this period. But some films did introduce a character type virtually absent from older empire films: the angry, defiant, and dignified colonial subject engaged in active resistance. Such characters included the title character in *Pinky*, Broken Lance in *Devil's Doorway*, Massai in *Apache*, Kimani in *Something of Value*, David Boyeur in *Island in the Sun*, Rau Ru in *Band of Angels*, Tamango and Aiché in *Tamango*, Joe Grant in *J'irai cracher sur vos tombes*, Ginny in *Night of the Quarter Moon*, and Kerry O'Shea and the Irish rebels in *Shake Hands with the Devil*. Breaking with the old convention of depicting anticolonialist resistance as irrational and inexplicable, these films presented positive, rational characters, conveying the point that reasonable people might dislike being colonized and be ready to do something about it. If films conveyed that notion, then they did something substantial to help Western audiences come to terms with decolonization.

There are thus good reasons to doubt that all Western films were conservative and that Hollywood's politics never change. Viewed today, after years of dramatic political changes and new insights contributed by political leaders, scholars, and artists, it is easy to see political flaws in those films, but for their time many were indeed progressive. Even films that seemed evasive and timid to some people at the time included material that helped to build a case against colonialism and racism. Judging films requires cinematic as well as historical empathy, taking into account the conflicting pressures and difficulties of making films on controversial topics in any era. There is a certain irony here: film scholars often criticize works that were trying to propound (admittedly milder) versions of the same political and social values they hold dear. Revolutions, it has been said, devour their children. They also devour their ancestors.

Liberal-colonialist films also threatened colonialism inadvertently and unintentionally. The very concept of liberal colonialism is, after all, a rather unstable construct, perhaps even an oxymoron. In attacking racism and discrimination, films were taking on a pillar and defining trait of colonialism, even if they adhered to assumptions of cultural superiority. History shows that colonialism could endure for years while it slowly "civilized" colonial subjects, a project that generally rested on a rejection of biological inferiority. But as colonialist skeptics of the civilizing mission warned, the more the colonizers made the colonized resemble themselves, the more they undermined the very basis of the colonial relationship. As postwar policymakers learned, trying to save colonialism by making it more benign did not really work, any more than tyrants facing revolutions can save their regimes with eleventh-hour reforms and liberalization.

If fervent opposition to colonialism remained rare in these years, these films and their reception indicate that the growth of Western anticolonialism in the 1960s had its roots in the 1940s and 1950s. Despite films' diverse and contradictory roles—simultaneously bolstering and undermining colonialism—films both raised awareness of colonial issues and helped people come to terms with new realities, and no other source invited so many people to think about these issues at that time. In order for many people to proceed from their poorly formed and conflicted views of colonialism to a more coherent and consistent anticolonialism—in other words, for colonialism to become discredited—it would take the formation and spread of a proper ideology to bring together scattered doubts and misgivings about aspects of the colonial endeavor. It would also take further humiliating defeats at the hands of imperial subjects and more time for their implications to help erode Western arrogance. These things would come to pass in the 1960s, with events such as France's defeat in Algeria and America's defeat in Vietnam, but the films of the late 1940s and the 1950s helped to lay the foundations for those changes.

APPENDIX A

Attitudes toward Indians and U.S. Conquest in Westerns

The following dramas about Indians appeared on *Variety*'s annual box-office charts. Some films released late in the year appeared on the charts in the following year. The list does not include comedies or films such as *My Darling Clementine* (1946) or *Winchester 73* (1950), which featured only brief appearances by Indians.

Film (year) / chart ranking	Position on Indians	Position on conquest
Duel in the Sun (1946) #2	anti	n/a (post-conquest)
Unconquered (1947) #5	anti	positive
Fort Apache (1948) #22	pro	mixed
She Wore a Yellow Ribbon (1949) #25	mixed	positive
Broken Arrow (1950) #9	pro	mixed (inevitable)
Comanche Territory (1950) #68	pro	positive
Rio Grande (1950) #34	anti	positive
Across the Wide Missouri (1951) #13	mixed	positive
Apache Drums (1951) #93	anti	positive
Jim Thorpe—All American (1951) #76	pro	n/a (post-conquest)
Last Outpost / Cavalry Charge (1951) #108	mixed	positive
Tomahawk (1951) #44	pro	negative
Warpath (1951) #106	anti	positive
Battle at Apache Pass (1952) #41	pro	positive
Big Sky (1952) #61	pro	mixed
Distant Drums (1952) #20	anti	positive
Flaming Feather (1952) #93	anti	positive
Pony Soldier (1952) #62	mixed	positive
Arrowhead (1953) #107	anti	positive
Charge at Feather River (1953) #12	anti	positive

Film (year) / chart ranking	Position on Indians	Position on conquest
Escape from Fort Bravo (1953) #51	anti	positive
Great Sioux Uprising (1953) #87	pro	no judgment
Seminole (1953) #86	pro	mixed
Apache (1954) #23	pro	negative
Broken Lance (1954) #20	pro	n/a (post-conquest)
The Command (1954) #42	anti	positive
Drum Beat (1954) #31	mixed	positive
Drums across the River (1954) #102	pro	positive
Garden of Evil (1954) #26	anti	positive
Hondo (1954) #16	mixed	positive
Sitting Bull (1954) #77	pro	negative
Taza (1954) #100	mixed	positive
War Arrow (1954) #87	mixed	positive
Chief Crazy Horse (1955) #71	pro	negative
Far Horizons (1955) #78	anti	positive
Foxfire (1955) #65	pro	n/a (post-conquest)
Smoke Signal (1955) #107	pro	negative
White Feather (1955) #77	pro	negative
Comanche (1956) #93	pro	positive
Indian Fighter (1956) #33	pro	mixed
Last Frontier (1956) #105	mixed	positive
Last Hunt (1956) #57	pro	negative
Last Wagon (1956) #69	pro	mixed
Pillars of the Sky (1956) #70	mixed	positive
The Searchers (1956) #10	mixed	positive
Walk the Proud Land (1956) #73	pro	positive
Guns of Fort Petticoat (1957) #88	mixed	mixed
Westward Ho the Wagons (1957) #29	mixed	positive
Last Train from Gun Hill (1959) #38	pro	n/a (post-conquest)
Tonka (1959) #40	pro	mixed
Yellowstone Kelly (1959) #56	anti	mixed
Total: 51	pro-Indian: 24 anti-Indian: 14 mixed: 13	positive: 29 negative: 7 mixed / no judgment: 15

APPENDIX B

Outcomes of Interracial Romance in Miscegenation Films

Consensual Couples (77 films, 89 couples)

An asterisk (*) after the characters' names indicates a "reverse" interracial couple (man of color with white woman). Of the relationships listed below, forty-six end badly, thirty-five end well, and eight remain unresolved. Of the twenty-two "reverse" couples listed, eight relationships end well.

Film	Characters	Ends well
Duel in the Sun (1946)	Scott & Mrs. Chavez	no
"	Lewt & Pearl	no
My Darling Clementine (1946)	Doc & Chihuahua	no
Unconquered (1947)	Garth & Hannah	no
Colorado Territory (1949)	Wes & Colorado	no
Lost Boundaries (1949)	Andy & Shelly	unresolved
Outpost in Morocco (1949)	Paul & Cara	no
Pinky (1949)	Tom & Pinky	no
Broken Arrow (1950)	Tom & Sonseeahray	no
Pagan Love Song (1950)	Hazard & Mimi	yes
Across the Wide Missouri (1951)	Flint & Kamiah	no
Bird of Paradise (1951)	Andre & Kalua	no
Jim Thorpe—All American (1951)	Jim & Margaret*	no
Show Boat (1951)	Steve & Julie	no
Big Sky (1952)	Boone & Teal Eye	yes
High Noon (1952)	Will & Helen	no
Japanese War Bride (1952)	Jim & Tae	yes
Outcast of the Islands (1952)	Peter & Aissa	unresolved
Arrowhead (1953)	Ed & Nita	no
Captain John Smith & Pocahontas (1953)	John Smith & Pocahontas	no
"	John Rolfe & Pocahontas	yes
Charge at Feather River (1953)	Thunder Hawk & Jennie*	no
Hondo (1953)	Hondo & Angie*	yes

Film	Characters	Ends well
Return to Paradise (1953)	Morgan & Maeva	no
"	Harry & Turia	no
Broken Lance (1954)	Matt & Sra. Devereaux	yes
"	Joe & Barbara*	yes
His Majesty O'Keefe (1954)	David & Dali	yes
King of the Khyber Rifles (1954)	Alan & Susan*	unresolved
Purple Plain (1954)	Bill & Anna	yes
Seekers (1954)	Philip & Moana	no
Seminole (1954)	Osceola & Revere*	no
Apache Woman (1955)	Rex & Anne	yes
Far Horizons (1955)	William & Sacajawea	no
Foxfire (1955)	Dart & Amanda*	yes
House of Bamboo (1955)	Eddie & Mariko	yes
Indian Fighter (1955)	Johnny & Onahti	yes
Love Is a Many-Splendored Thing (1955)	Mark & Han Su-yin	no
Rains of Ranchipur (1955)	Dr. Safti & Edwina*	no
Seven Cities of Gold (1955)	José & Ula	no
They Rode West (1955)	Indian Husband & Manyi-ten*	no
Three Stripes in the Sun (1955)	Hugh & Yuko	yes
View from Pompey's Head (1955)	Garvin & Lucy*	yes
White Feather (1955)	Josh & Appearing Day	yes
Bhowani Junction (1956)	Rodney & Victoria	yes
"	Mr. and Mrs. Jones	yes
Black Tent (1956)	David & Mabrouka	no
Burning Hills (1956)	Trace & Maria	yes
Giant (1956)	Jordy & Juana	yes
Last Hunt (1956)	Sandy & "Indian girl"	yes
Mohawk (1956)	Jonathan & Onida	yes
Reprisal (1956)	Neola & Catherine*	yes
Searchers (1956)	Martin & Laurie*	yes
Teahouse of the August Moon (1956)	Fisby & Lotus Blossom	unresolved
Band of Angels (1957)	Hamish & Manty	yes
China Gate (1957)	Sgt. Brock & Lea "Lucky Legs"	no
Island in the Sun (1957)	Denis & Margot	yes
"	David & Mavis*	no
"	Maxwell & Sylvia*	unresolved
Mort en fraude (1957)	Horcier & Anh	no
Run of the Arrow (1957)	O'Meara & Yellow Moccasin	no
Sayonara (1957)	Lloyd & Hana-ogi	yes
"	Joe & Katsumi	no
Barbarian and the Geisha (1958)	Townsend & Okichi	no
Fort Bowie (1958)	Thompson & Chanzana	yes
Gunman's Walk (1958)	Davy & Clee	yes
In Love and War (1958)	Alan & Kalai	yes

Outcomes of Interracial Romance in Miscegenation Films

Film	Characters	Ends well
Inn of the Sixth Happiness (1958)	Li Nan & Gladys*	unresolved
Kings Go Forth (1958)	Sam & Monique	unresolved
"	Britt & Monique	no
La Bigorne, Caporal de France (1958)	La Bigorne & Bethi	yes
The Quiet American (1958)	Fowler & Phuong	no
"	The American & Phuong	no
South Pacific (1958)	Joe & Liat	no
Tamango (1958)	Captain & Aiche	no
Touch of Evil (1958)	Mike & Susie Vargas*	yes
"	Manolo & Marcia*	no
Crimson Kimono (1959)	Joe & Christine*	yes
Five Gates to Hell (1959)	unnamed white man, Asian woman	no
Hiroshima, mon amour (1959)	Lui & Elle*	no
Imitation of Life (1959)	boyfriend & Sarah Jane	no
J'irai cracher sur vos tombes (1959)	Joe & Lisbeth*	no
"	Joe & Sylvia*	no
Last Train from Gun Hill (1959)	Matt & Catherine	no
Night of the Quarter Moon (1959)	Chuck & Ginny	yes
Sapphire (1959)	David & Sapphire	no
Shadows (1959)	Tony & Lelia	no
World, the Flesh, and the Devil (1959)	Ralph & Sarah*	unresolved
Yellowstone Kelly (1959)	Yellowstone & Wahleeah	yes

Stalled Romances (14)

Film	Characters
Anna and the King of Siam (1946)	Mongkut & Anna
Devil's Doorway (1950)	Lance & Orrie
Pool of London (1951)	Johnny & Pat
Saadia (1953)	Henrik & Saadia
War Arrow (1953)	Howell & Avis
Drum Beat (1954)	Johnny McKay & Toby
White Orchid (1954)	Juan & Kathryn
Pearl of the South Pacific (1955)	George & Rita
King and I (1956)	Mongkut & Anna
Walk the Proud Land (1956)	John Clum & Tianay
Sayonara (1957)	Nakamura & Eileen
War Drums (1957)	Fargo & Riva
Windom's Way (1957)	Alec & Ana
Yellowstone Kelly (1959)	Anse & Wahleeah

White Rapist (9)

Duel in the Sun (1946), Pinky (1949), Wagon Master (1950), Bhowani Junction (1956), Last Hunt (1956), Reprisal (1956), Band of Angels (1957), Tamango (1958), Last Train from Gun Hill (1959). Alluded to in dialogue: Half-Breed (1951), War Paint (1953), Last Wagon (1956).

Rapist of Color (10)

Unconquered (1947), Peking Express (1951), Charge at Feather River (1953), Shanghai Story (1954), Blood Alley (1955), Last Wagon (1956), The Searchers (1956), Trooper Hook (1957), Touch of Evil (1958), Five Gates to Hell (1959). Alluded to in dialogue: Drum Beat (1954), Pillars of the Sky (1956).

Mixed-Race Characters (53 films, 65 characters)

Film	Characters
Duel in the Sun (1946)	Pearl Chavez
My Darling Clementine (1946)	Chihuahua
Colorado Territory (1949)	Colorado
Lost Boundaries (1949)	The Carters (4)
Pinky (1949)	Pinky
Pagan Love Song (1950)	Mimi
Across the Wide Missouri (1951)	Narrator (Mitchells' son)
Half-Breed (1951)	Charlie Wolf
"	Nah Lin
Jim Thorpe—All-American (1951)	Thorpes' son
Show Boat (1951)	Julie
Distant Drums (1952)	Quincy's son
Japanese War Bride (1952)	Jim, Jr.
Arrowhead (1953)	Nita
Hondo (1953)	Hondo
Return to Paradise (1953)	Turia
Broken Lance (1954)	Joe Devereaux
His Majesty O'Keefe (1954)	Dali
King of the Khyber Rifles (1954)	Alan King
Seminole (1954)	Osceola
Apache Woman (1955)	Anne
"	Armand
Chief Crazy Horse (1955)	Commissioner
Foxfire (1955)	Dart
Love Is a Many-Splendored Thing (1955)	Han Su-yin
Pearl of the South Pacific (1955)	George
View from Pompey's Head (1955)	Garvin
Bhowani Junction (1956)	Victoria
"	Patrick
Burning Hills (1956)	Maria
Giant (1956)	Jordy, Jr.
Last Hunt (1956)	Jimmy
Last Wagon (1956)	Jolie
Reprisal (1956)	Neola
The Searchers (1956)	Martin
Band of Angels (1957)	Manty
China Gate (1957)	Brock & Lea's boy

Film	Characters
Island in the Sun (1957)	Julian Fleury
"	Maxwell Fleury
Mort en fraude (1957)	Anh
Trooper Hook (1957)	Quito
China Doll (1958)	Shiao-Mee Brandon
Fort Bowie (1958)	Chanzana
Gunman's Walk (1958)	Clee
In Love and War (1958)	Kalai
Inn of the Sixth Happiness (1958)	Li Nan
Kings Go Forth (1958)	Monique
La Bigorne, Caporal de France (1958)	Bethi
South Pacific (1958)	Emile's daughter
"	Emile's son
Five Gates to Hell (1959)	Chen Pamok
"	Ming Cha
Imitation of Life (1959)	Sarah Jane
J'irai cracher sur vos tombes (1959)	Joe Grant
Last Train from Gun Hill (1959)	Matt & Catherine's son
Night of the Quarter Moon (1959)	Ginny
"	Maria
Northwest Frontier (1959)	Van Leyden
Sapphire (1959)	Dr. Robbins
"	Sapphire
"	woman in bar
Shadows (1959)	Lelia

NOTES

The notes below refer the reader to pertinent primary sources and the secondary literature that proved most helpful in researching and writing this book. For a complete alphabetical listing of the published sources, please refer to the Johns Hopkins University Press website at www.press.jhu.edu.

Introduction

1. Colin Legum, *Pan Africanism: A Short Political Guide* (Westport, CT: Greenwood, 1962), 25.

2. Bernard Porter writes that "imperialism became deeply unfashionable in the last forty years of the twentieth century"; see *The Absent-Minded Imperialists: Empire, Society, and Culture in Britain* (Oxford: Oxford University Press, 2004), 4. In *Colonialism in Question*, Frederick Cooper cites three different decades as the time when colonialism lost its legitimacy; see *Colonialism in Question: Theory, Knowledge, History* (Berkeley: University of California Press, 2005), 33, 54, 232. Ella Shohat and Robert Stam merely say that the change took place "recently"; see *Unthinking Eurocentrism: Multiculturalism and the Media* (New York: Routledge, 1994), 33.

3. Macmillan gave the speech to the Parliament of South Africa on 3 February 1960.

4. A pioneering work in treating film as modern myth is Richard Slotkin, *Gunfighter Nation: The Myth of the Frontier in Twentieth-Century America* (New York: Atheneum, 1992), 5. Also emphasizing film's value for examining collective mentalities was Siegfried Kracauer, *From Caligari to Hitler: A Psychological History of the German Film* (Princeton, NJ: Princeton University Press, 1947), 5. See also Susan Courtney, *Hollywood Fantasies of Miscegenation: Spectacular Narratives of Gender and Race, 1903–1967* (Princeton, NJ: Princeton University Press, 2005), 12; Dina Sherzer, ed., *Cinema, Colonialism, Postcolonialism: Perspectives from the French and Francophone Worlds* (Austin: University of Texas Press, 1996), 229.

5. On film's power to influence, see Jean-Pierre Jeancolas, *Le cinéma des français: La Ve République (1958–1978)* (Paris: Stock, 1979), 8; Lary May, *The Big Tomorrow: Hollywood and the Politics of the American Way* (Chicago: University of Chicago Press, 2000), 2.

6. See Pierre Bourdieu, "Opinion Polls: A 'Science' without a Scientist," in *In Other Words: Essays Towards a Reflexive Sociology*, trans. Matthew Adamson (Stanford, CA: Stanford University Press, 1990), 173.

7. George Gallup and Saul Forbes Rae, *The Pulse of Democracy: The Public-Opinion Poll and How It Works* (New York: Simon and Shuster, 1940).

8. See May, *The Big Tomorrow*, 122–23. Critic Michael Medved cites a 1991 survey in which one-third of Americans said they never went to the movies; see his *Hollywood vs. America* (New York: HarperCollins, 1992), 7.

9. On violence and colonialism, see Frantz Fanon, *The Wretched of the Earth*, with a preface by Jean-Paul Sartre, trans. Constance Farrington (New York: Grove Weidenfeld, 1968), 36, 40.

10. Discussing such claims is Romain Bertrand, *Mémoires d'empire: La controverse autour du "fait colonial"* (Broissieux: Croquant, 2006), 13.

11. Ronald Robinson, "The Excentric Idea of Imperialism, with or without Empire," in *Imperialism and After: Continuities and Discontinuities*, ed. Wolfgang J. Mommsen and Jürgen Osterhammel (London: German Historical Institute; Boston: Allen and Unwin, 1986), 271. On the dangers of using force, see Jürgen Osterhammel, "China," in *The Oxford History of the British Empire*, vol. 4, *The Twentieth Century*, ed. Judith M. Brown and William Roger Louis (Oxford: Oxford University Press, 1999), 651.

12. On the term's multiple meanings, see Bernard Porter, *Empire and Superempire: Britain, America and the World* (New Haven, CT: Yale University Press, 2006), 44.

13. Adam Smith, *An Inquiry into the Nature and Causes of the Wealth of Nations*, ed. Edwin Cannan (New York: Modern Library, 1937), chap. 7. D. K. Fieldhouse uses the phrase "exploitative British neo-mercantilism" in *The West and the Third World* (Oxford: Blackwell, 1999), 97. On anticolonialism, see Jean-Pierre Biondi, *Les anticolonialistes (1881–1962)* (Paris: Robert Laffont, 1992); Stephen Howe, *Anticolonialism in British Politics: The Left and the End of Empire, 1918–1964* (Oxford: Clarendon, 1993); Bernard Porter, *Critics of Empire: British Radical Attitudes to Colonialism in Africa, 1895–1914* (London: Macmillan, 1968); Nicholas Owen, "Critics of Empire in Britain," in Brown and Louis, *Twentieth Century*, 188–211.

14. Catherine Hall and Sonya O. Rose, "Introduction: Being at Home with the Empire," in *At Home with the Empire*, ed. Catherine Hall and Sonya O. Rose (Cambridge: Cambridge University Press, 2006), 18; see also Cooper, *Colonialism in Question*, 23.

15. Richard Dyer, *White* (London: Routledge, 1997), 18–19. Ann Laura Stoler, *Carnal Knowledge and Imperial Power: Race and the Intimate in Colonial Rule* (Berkeley: University of California Press, 2010), 24.

16. David Fitzpatrick, "Ireland and the Empire," in *The Oxford History of the British Empire*, vol. 3, *The Nineteenth Century*, ed. Andrew Porter (Oxford: Oxford University Press, 1999), 499.

17. Robert M. Utley, *The Indian Frontier of the American West, 1846–1890* (Albuquerque: University of New Mexico Press, 1984), 270. For a fuller treatment of this issue, see Francis Paul Prucha, "Scientific Racism and Indian Policy," in *Indian Policy in the United States: Historical Essays*, ed. Francis Paul Prucha (Lincoln: University of Nebraska Press, 1981), 180–97.

18. Andrew Thompson notes that missionaries needed prospective converts to be "redeemable," so they "rarely indulged in pseudo-scientific racism"; see *The Empire Strikes Back? The Impact of Imperialism on Britain from the Mid-Nineteenth Century* (Harlow: Pearson, 2005), 111.

19. B. Porter, *Absent-Minded Imperialists*, 78.

20. See Robert Stam and Louise Spence, "Colonialism, Racism, and Representation: An Introduction," in *Movies and Methods: An Anthology*, vol. 2, ed. Bill Nichols (Berkeley: University of California Press, 1985), 635–36; see also Shohat and Stam, *Unthinking Eurocentrism*, 22–23.

21. Wolfgang J. Mommsen, "The End of Empire and the Continuity of Imperialism," in Mommsen and Osterhammel, *Imperialism and After*, 336–37; see also D. K. Fieldhouse, *The Colonial Empires: A Comparative Survey from the Eighteenth Century* (New York: Delta, 1965), 377; Susan Bayly, "The Evolution of Colonial Cultures: Nineteenth-Century Asia," in A. Porter, *The Nineteenth Century*, 467; B. Porter, *Empire and Superempire*, 59.

22. Bayly, "The Evolution of Colonial Cultures," 447; see also Ronald Hyam, *Empire and Sexuality: The British Experience* (Manchester: Manchester University Press, 1990), 196; Fieldhouse, *Colonial Empires*; Ronald Robinson and John Gallagher, *Africa and the Victorians: The Climax of Imperialism on the Dark Continent* (New York: St. Martin's, 1961), 7; B. Porter, *Absent-Minded Imperialists*, 15; Ashis Nandy, *The Intimate Enemy: Loss and Recovery of Self under Colonialism* (Oxford: Oxford University Press, 1983), 32; Dennis Judd, *Empire: The British Imperial Experience from 1765 to the Present* (London: Fontana, 1996), 10. Richard Stubbs reports that only about 1,500 British planters and miners lived in Malaya during the 1950s insurgency; see *Hearts and Minds in Guerrilla Warfare: The Malayan Emergency, 1948–1960* (Singapore: Oxford University Press, 1989), 85.

23. Albert Memmi, *The Colonizer and the Colonized*, introduction by Jean-Paul Sartre, trans. Howard Greenfeld (Boston: Beacon Press, 1967), x, 121. See also Octave Mannoni, *Prospero and Caliban: The Psychology of Colonization* (New York: Praeger, 1956).

24. Memmi, *Colonizer and the Colonized*, 121, 87, 93.

25. On Francophone African elites using their education for their own purposes, see Catherine Atlan and Jean-Hervé Jézéquel, "Alienation or Political Strategy? The Colonized Defend the Empire," in *Promoting the Colonial Idea: Propaganda and Visions of Empire in France*, ed. Tony Chafer and Amanda Sackur (Houndmills: Palgrave, 2002), 114; see also Eric Savarese, *L'ordre colonial et sa légitimation en France métropolitaine: Oublier l'autre* (Paris: L'Harmattan, 1998), 274; Rudolf von Albertini, *Decolonization: The Administration and Future of the Colonies, 1919–1960*, trans. Francisca Garvie (New York: Africana, 1982), 288–89.

26. Edward Said, *Culture and Imperialism* (1993; repr., New York: Vintage, 1994), 5. See also Philip D. Curtin, "Introduction: Imperialism as Intellectual History," in *Imperialism*, ed. Philip D. Curtin (New York: Harper and Row, 1971), ix; Robert Malley, *The Call from Algeria: Third Worldism, Revolution, and the Turn to Islam* (Berkeley: University of California Press, 1996), 84; B. Porter, *Absent-Minded Imperialists*, 8.

27. Said, *Culture and Imperialism*, 9.

28. H. L. Wesseling, "Imperialism and Empire: An Introduction," in Mommsen and Osterhammel, *Imperialism and After*, 8.

29. John Gallagher and Ronald Robinson, "The Imperialism of Free Trade," *Economic History Review*, 2d ser., 6:1 (1953): 3.

30. For criticism of Gallagher and Robinson's arguments, see the essays in William Roger Louis, ed. *Imperialism: The Robinson and Gallagher Controversy* (New York: New Viewpoints, 1965).

31. Fanon, *Wretched of the Earth*, 35, 37.

32. The Third All-African Peoples Conference of March 1961 addressed neocolonial-

ism; its resolution appears in *The Age of Neo-Colonialism in Africa: Essays on Domination and Resistance after Independence*, ed. Ehiedu E. G. Iweriebor (Ibadan: African Book Builders, 1997), 137–41.

33. Kwame Nkrumah, "Neo-Colonialism: The Last Stage of Imperialism," in *The End of European Empire: Decolonization after World War II*, ed. Tony Smith (Lexington, MA: D.C. Heath, 1975), 199–201.

34. Bethwell Ogot and Tiyambe Zeleza argue that within fifteen years of Kenya's 1963 independence, the country had rid itself of the settlers' influence; see "Kenya: The Road to Independence and After," in *Decolonization and African Independence: The Transfers of Power, 1960–1980*, ed. Prosser Gifford and William Roger Louis (New Haven, CT: Yale University Press, 1988), 425.

35. Nkrumah, "Neo-Colonialism," 200.

36. In Bernard Porter's words, "you can't control a Shah like you can a viceroy" (*Empire and Superempire*, 92); see also Mommsen, "End of Empire," 354; B. R. Tomlinson, "The Contraction of England: National Decline and the Loss of Empire," *Journal of Imperial and Commonwealth History* 11:1 (1982): 61; Albertini, *Decolonization*, xxiii; Robinson, "Excentric Idea," 284–86. On the Commonwealth, see Judd, *Empire*, 385–86; D. A. Low, *The Eclipse of Empire* (Cambridge: Cambridge University Press, 1991), 330; John Darwin, *Britain and Decolonisation: The Retreat from Empire in the Postwar World* (New York: St. Martin's, 1988), 306.

37. Edward Said wrote in 1993 that third-world nations were still "as dominated and dependent as they were when ruled directly by European powers" (*Culture and Imperialism*, 19).

38. Cooper, *Colonialism in Question*, 29, notes that calling all forms of international inequality "empire" constrains our tools of analysis.

39. Fieldhouse, *Colonial Empires*, 401; Owen, "Critics of Empire in Britain," 210; see also Judith M. Brown, "India," in *The Oxford History of the British Empire*, vol. 4, *The Twentieth Century*, ed. Judith Brown and William Roger Louis (Oxford: Oxford University Press, 1999), 444; Mommsen, "End of Empire," 342; Fieldhouse, *Colonial Empires*, 406; Darwin, *Britain and Decolonisation*, 128; Owen, "Critics of Empire in Britain," 209–10; Christopher Flood and Hugo Frey, "Defending the Empire in Retrospect: The Discourse of the Extreme Right," in *Promoting the Colonial Idea: Propaganda and Visions of Empire in France*, ed. Tony Chafer and Amanda Sackur (Houndmills: Palgrave, 2002), 208.

40. See James Chapman and Nicholas J. Cull, *Projecting Empire: Imperialism and Popular Cinema* (London: I. B. Tauris, 2009), 7; Caroline Eades, *Le cinéma post-colonial français* (Paris: Cerf, 2006), 138; Kathleen A. McDonough, "Wee Willie Winkie Goes West: The Influence of the British Empire Genre on Ford's Cavalry Trilogy," in *Hollywood's West: The American Frontier in Film, Television, and History*, ed. Peter C. Rollins and John E. O'Connor (Lexington: University Press of Kentucky, 2005), 99–114.

41. Calling for a transnational approach are Benjamin Stora, *Imaginaires de guerre: Algérie, Viêt-Nam, en France et aux Etats-Unis* (Paris: La Découverte, 1997), 10; B. Porter, *Empire and Superempire*, 13.

42. On the saltwater fallacy and American empire-denial, see B. Porter, *Empire and Superempire*, 64–65.

43. Among historians who view the American West in these terms, see Patricia Nelson Limerick, *The Legacy of Conquest: The Unbroken Past of the American West* (New York: W. W.

Norton, 1987), 26; Jay Gitlin, "On the Boundaries of Empire: Connecting the West to Its Imperial Past," in *Under an Open Sky: Rethinking America's Western Past*, ed. William Cronon, George Miles, and Jay Gitlin (New York: W. W. Norton, 1992), 72.

44. William Roger Louis and Ronald Robinson, "The Imperialism of Decolonization," *Journal of Imperial and Commonwealth History* 22:3 (1994): 466–72, 487; Niall Ferguson, *Empire: The Rise and Demise of the British World Order and the Lessons for Global Power* (New York: Basic Books, 2004), 299; on U.S. aid for France's war in Indochina, see Marianne Sullivan, *France's Vietnam Policy: A Study in French-American Relations* (Westport, CT: Greenwood, 1978), 42–43; George McT. Kahin, *Intervention: How America Became Involved in Vietnam* (New York: Anchor, 1987), 7–8, 36; on Washington's role in France's war in Algeria, see Irwin M. Wall, *France, the United States, and the Algerian War* (Berkeley: University of California Press, 2001), 4, 9, 23.

45. Memmi, *Colonizer and the Colonized*, 149–50; Cooper, *Colonialism in Question*, 27.

46. See Brenda Gayle Plummer, *In Search of Power: African Americans in the Era of Decolonization, 1956–1974* (Cambridge: Cambridge University Press, 2013).

47. On empire's effects on English identity, see Wendy Webster, *Englishness and Empire, 1939–1965* (Oxford: Oxford University Press, 2005).

48. On the empire's role in World War II and its importance to the French people, see Tony Chafer and Amanda Sackur, "Introduction," in *Promoting the Colonial Idea*, 9.

49. On these influences in the 1950s and 1960s, see Mark Harris, *Pictures at a Revolution: Five Movies and the Birth of the New Hollywood* (New York: Penguin, 2008), 7–11.

50. On France, see Alastair Phillips, "People, 1930–60: Migration and Exile in the Classical Period," in *The French Cinema Book*, ed. Michael Temple and Michael Witt (London: British Film Institute, 2004), 103–17.

51. On runaway production, see Drew Casper, *Postwar Hollywood, 1946–1962* (Malden, MA: Blackwell, 2007), 50–53.

52. Ruth Vasey, "Foreign Parts: Hollywood's Global Distribution and the Representation of Ethnicity," in *Movie Censorship and American Culture*, ed. Francis G. Couvares (Washington, DC: Smithsonian Institution Press, 1996), 212–36; Richard Maltby and Ruth Vasey, "The International Language Problem: European Reactions to Hollywood's Conversion to Sound," in *Hollywood in Europe: Experiences of a Cultural Hegemony*, ed. David W. Ellwood and Rob Kroes (Amsterdam: VU University Press, 1994), 68–93; Paul Swann, "The Little State Department: Washington and Hollywood's Rhetoric of the Postwar Audience," in *Hollywood in Europe*, 176–95.

53. Interwar market-share figures for various countries are in Maltby and Vasey, "The International Language Problem," 69–70; see also Vasey, "Foreign Parts," 221–24. On American films' favorable views of European empire, see Shohat and Stam, *Unthinking Eurocentrism*, 113. For a discussion of Hollywood's seeking prior approval from European censors, see Kenneth M. Cameron, *Africa on Film: Beyond Black and White* (New York: Continuum, 1994), 60.

54. On interwar empire films, Marcia Landy, *British Genres: Cinema and Society, 1930–1960* (Princeton, NJ: Princeton University Press, 1991), chap. 3; Brian Taves, *The Romance of Adventure: The Genre of Historical Adventure Movies* (Jackson: University Press of Mississippi, 1993), chap. 8; Chapman and Cull, *Projecting Empire*; Prem Chowdhry, *Colonial India and the Making of Empire Cinema* (Manchester: Manchester University Press, 2000); David Henry Slavin, *Colonial Cinema and Imperial France, 1919–1939: White Blind Spots, Male*

Fantasies, Settler Myths (Baltimore: Johns Hopkins University Press, 2001). Jeffrey Richards discusses films about the British Empire from the interwar years through the 1960s in part 1 of *Visions of Yesterday* (London: Routledge and Kegan Paul, 1973).

55. Memmi, *Colonizer and the Colonized*, 3.

56. On Western images of the South Seas, see Alan Moorhead, *The Fatal Impact: The Invasion of the South Pacific, 1767–1840* (New York: Harper and Row, 1966); Michael Sturma, *South Sea Maidens: Western Fantasy and Sexual Politics in the South Pacific* (Westport, CT: Greenwood, 2002); Matt K. Matsuda, *Empire of Love: Histories of France and the Pacific* (Oxford: Oxford University Press, 2005).

57. Stam and Spence, "Colonialism, Racism, and Representation," 638, 637.

58. Tom Engelhardt, *The End of Victory Culture: Cold War America and the Disillusioning of a Generation* (New York: Basic Books, 1995), 41.

59. See Shohat and Stam, *Unthinking Eurocentrism*, 139.

60. See Cameron, *Africa on Film*, 79–80.

61. See, for example, Courtney, *Hollywood Fantasies of Miscegenation*, 10; Christina Klein, *Cold War Orientalism: Asia in the Middlebrow Imagination, 1945–1961* (Berkeley: University of California Press, 2003), 7; Slavin, *Colonial Cinema and Imperial France*, 3; Sherzer, "Introduction," in Sherzer, *Cinema, Colonialism, Postcolonialism*, 4; Martine Astier Loutfi, "Imperial Frame: Film Industry and Colonial Representation," in Sherzer, *Cinema, Colonialism, Postcolonialism*, 21; Odile Goerg, "The French Provinces and 'Greater France,'" in Chafer and Sackur, *Promoting the Colonial Idea*, 96.

62. On the malleability of modern myth, see Richard Slotkin, *The Fatal Environment: The Myth of the Frontier in the Age of Industrialization, 1800–1890* (Norman: University of Oklahoma Press, 1985), 19; Chapman and Cull, *Projecting Empire*, 11; see also Steven C. Caton, *Lawrence of Arabia: A Film's Anthropology* (Berkeley: University of California Press, 1999), 15.

63. See Stam and Spence, "Colonialism, Racism, and Representation," 644–45.

64. For a survey of the field and its past, see John E. O'Connor, "Framework 2: The Moving Image as Evidence for Social and Cultural History," in *Image as Artifact: The Historical Analysis of Film and Television*, ed. John E. O'Connor (Malabar, FL: Krieger, 1990), 108–18.

65. Edward Buscombe refers to a "pedantic listing of errors" and "exercises in tedious point-scoring." See *Injuns! Native Americans in the Movies* (London: Reaktion, 2006), 17. For an example of the tendency, see Allen M. Ward, "*Gladiator* in Historical Perspective," in *Gladiator: Film and History*, ed. Martin M. Winkler (Oxford: Blackwell, 2004), 31–44. Among those urging historians to take films seriously are Robert Brent Toplin, *Reel History: In Defense of Hollywood* (Lawrence: University Press of Kansas, 2002), 9, 4, 61. Frank Manchel, "Cultural Confusion: *Broken Arrow*," in *Hollywood's Indian: The Portrayal of the Native American in Film*, ed. Peter C. Rollins and John E. O'Connor (Lexington: University Press of Kentucky, 1998), 93.

66. See Shohat and Stam, *Unthinking Eurocentrism*, 214.

67. John E. O'Connor, "Framework 4: The History of the Moving Image as Industry and Art Form," in *Image as Artifact*, 218; see also Toplin, *Reel History*, 177.

68. Toplin, *Reel History*, 177.

69. Shohat and Stam, *Unthinking Eurocentrism*, 7, describe Hollywood as "ideologically reactionary" without specifying any period, implying that its political outlook has never

changed. M. Elise Marubbio's study of more than ninety years' worth of films about Native American women concludes that Hollywood films "romanticize imperialism and nationalism" and that "all the films reinforce American myths of the frontier [and] manifest destiny"; even today "the film industry remains committed to replicating mainstream cultural and social concerns regarding interracial love"; see *Killing the Indian Maiden: Images of Native American Women in Film* (Lexington: University Press of Kentucky, 2006), 21; see also Gina Marchetti, *Romance and the "Yellow Peril": Race, Sex, and Discursive Strategies in Hollywood Fiction* (Berkeley: University of California Press, 1993), 114.

70. Elliot Silverstein, letter to Clyde Dollar, 21 December 1968, Elliot Silverstein Papers, Margaret Herrick Library, Academy of Motion Picture Arts and Sciences (hereafter AMPAS).

71. John E. O'Connor, "Historical Analysis, Stage One: Gathering Information on the Content, Production, and Reception of a Moving Image Document," in *Image as Artifact*, 10.

72. On auteur theory, see François Truffaut, "Une certaine tendance du cinéma français," *Cahiers du Cinéma* 31 (January 1954), reprinted in Nichols, *Movies and Methods*, 224–37; Andrew Sarris, "Notes on the Auteur Theory in 1962," in *Film Culture*, 27 (Winter 1962–63): 1–8; Pauline Kael, "Circles and Squares," in *I Lost It at the Movies* (Boston: Little, Brown, 1965), 292–319. See also Thomas Schatz, *The Genius of the System: Hollywood Filmmaking in the Studio Era* (New York: Metropolitan Books, 1988), 5–8. On researching production, see O'Connor, "Historical Analysis," 17–19; Harris, *Pictures at a Revolution*, 4. See also John H. Lenihan, *Showdown: Confronting Modern America in the Western Film* (Urbana: University of Illinois Press, 1980), 8.

73. See Thomas Andrae, "Adorno on Film and Mass Culture: The Culture Industry Reconsidered," *Jump Cut* 20 (1979): 34–37; Robert Sklar, "Moving Image Media in Culture and Society: Paradigms for Historical Interpretation," in O'Connor, *Image as Artifact*, 125–28.

74. Medved, *Hollywood vs. America*, 293–96, 32; see also Stephen Powers, David J. Rothman, and Stanley Rothman, *Hollywood's America: Social and Political Themes in Motion Pictures* (Boulder, CO: Westview, 1996), 67.

75. On Zukor, see Susan Ohmer, *George Gallup in Hollywood* (New York: Columbia University Press, 2006), 1. On William Fox, see Neal Gabler, *An Empire of Their Own: How the Jews Invented Hollywood* (New York: Anchor, 1988), 67. On Walt Disney doing sneak previews, see Ohmer, *George Gallup in Hollywood*, 208–9. On early audience research, see John Izod, *Hollywood and the Box Office, 1895–1986* (New York: Columbia University Press, 1988).

76. See Slotkin, *Gunfighter Nation*, 659; John E. O'Connor, "The White Man's Indian: An Institutional Approach," in *Hollywood's Indian: The Portrayal of the Native American in Film*, ed. Peter C. Rollins and John E. O'Connor (Lexington: University Press of Kentucky, 1998), 30. J. Hoberman calls the films of the 1960s "movies that America could be said to have given itself, films that emanated from, and returned to shape, the nation's dream life." See his *The Dream Life: Movies, Media and the Mythology of the Sixties* (New York: New Press, 2003), xvii.

77. MGM's Irving Thalberg pioneered the use of previews; see Schatz, *Genius of the System*, 37. In the 1950s, MGM's Louis B. Mayer and Dore Schary disagreed about making message pictures; see Gabler, *Empire of Their Own*, 412. Only some studios used opinion polling for audience research; see Ohmer, *George Gallup in Hollywood*, 149, 163.

78. Welles quoted in May, *The Big Tomorrow*, 56; Dunne quoted in ibid., 140. Eric Johnston, head of the Motion Picture Association of America, also spoke of movies' powers; see May, 176.

79. For an epigraph to his *Pictures at a Revolution*, Mark Harris quoted filmmakers David Newman and Robert Benton: "When you talk about films, nobody agrees with any body. Guys get mad at each other and the air is full of screaming."

80. See Janet Staiger, "The Handmaiden of Villainy: Methods and Problems in Studying the Historical Reception of a Film," *Wide Angle* 8:1 (1986): 19–28; Stam and Spence, "Colonialism, Racism, and Representation," 646; Pierre Bourdieu, *Distinction: A Social Critique of the Judgment of Taste*, trans. Richard Nice (Cambridge, MA: Harvard University Press, 1984); Peter Dahlgren, "What's the Meaning of This? Viewers' Plural Sense-Making of TV News," *Media, Culture and Society* 10 (1988): 285–301.

81. For skepticism about box-office figures, see Izod, *Hollywood and the Box Office*, x–xi; Sklar, "Moving Image Media," 120.

82. *Variety*'s charts reported domestic rental income, the money that distributors collected from theaters, which is roughly half of domestic ticket sales. Films released late in a year were usually tallied in the following years. The charts, usually published in the first week or two of January, often included explanations of the process.

83. Simon Simsi, *Ciné-Passions: 7e art et industrie de 1945 à 2000* (Paris: Dixit, 2000).

84. Izod, *Hollywood and the Box Office*, 114.

85. In 1951, when the population of greater London was about 8 million, the combined circulation of the ten highest-circulation dailies was well over 20 million; for Sunday papers it was greater than 27 million; see David Butler and Anne Sloman, *British Political Facts, 1900–1975*, 4th ed. (London: Macmillan, 1975), 388–89. On national and provincial dailies and Sunday papers, see Colin Seymour-Ure, *The British Press and Broadcasting since 1945*, 2d ed. (Oxford: Blackwell, 1996), 17, 28–31.

86. On French audiences, see Gregory Sims, "Spectators: The Golden Age of Spectatorship," in *The French Cinema Book*, ed. Michael Temple and Michael Witt (London: British Film Institute, 2004), 163.

87. Thomas Cripps cites a U.S. Army study from the 1940s that reached that conclusion; see his *Making Movies Black: The Hollywood Message Movie from World War II to the Civil Rights Era* (New York: Oxford University Press, 1993), 161.

88. Sue Harper and Vincent Porter, for example, argue that "reviewers and critics in the period rarely represented any views but their own"; see *British Cinema: The Decline of Difference* (Oxford: Oxford University Press, 2003), 2.

Part I · The Persistence of Empire

1. See Ole Holsti, *Public Opinion and American Foreign Policy* (Ann Arbor: University of Michigan Press, 1996), 17. The percentage of poll respondents agreeing with the statement that "the United States should join a world organization with police power to maintain world peace" rose from 26 percent in 1937 to 81 percent in 1945; see "The Quarter's Polls," *Public Opinion Quarterly* 9:2 (Summer 1945): 253.

2. William Louis and Ronald Robinson, "The Imperialism of Decolonization," *Journal of Imperial and Commonwealth History* 22:3 (1994): 468.

3. Ibid., 480; Dulles's comments appear in "Memorandum of Discussion at the 302d Meeting of the NSC, Washington, Nov. 1, 1956," Document 455, United States, Depart-

ment of State, *Foreign Relations of the United States, 1955–7: Suez Crisis, July 26–Dec. 31, 1956*, vol. 16, ed. Nina J. Noring (Washington: USGPO, 1990), 906.

4. William Inboden, *Religion and American Foreign Policy, 1945–1960: The Soul of Containment* (Cambridge: Cambridge University Press, 2008), 227, 36, 105–7, 261.

5. Quoted in Stephen J. Whitfield, *The Culture of the Cold War* (Baltimore: Johns Hopkins University Press, 1991), 87. On church membership, see ibid., 83; on bible sales, see Douglas T. Miller and Marion Nowak, *The Fifties: The Way We Really Were* (Garden City, NY: Doubleday, 1977), 85.

6. Larry Ceplair and Steven Englund, *The Inquisition in Hollywood: Politics in the Film Community, 1930–1960* (Berkeley: University of California Press, 1979), 209–15; Neal Gabler, *An Empire of Their Own: How the Jews Invented Hollywood* (New York: Anchor, 1988), 351–86; Mark Wheeler, *Hollywood: Politics and Society* (London: British Film Institute, 2006), 106–16.

7. On the moguls' sensitivity about their Jewishness, see Gabler, *Empire of Their Own*, 2–4.

8. Lary May argues that the demonizing of big business essentially came to end in these years; see *The Big Tomorrow: Hollywood and the Politics of the American Way* (Chicago: University of Chicago Press, 2000), 204, 263.

9. On the CIA and Hollywood, see David N. Eldridge, "'Dear Owen': The CIA, Luigi Luraschi, and Hollywood, 1953," *Historical Journal of Film, Radio and Television* 20:2 (June 2000): 149–98; Frances Stonor Saunders, *The Cultural Cold War: The CIA and the World of Arts and Letters* (New York: New Press, 2000), 284–98.

10. Whitfield, *Culture of the Cold War*, 188.

11. Drew Casper reports these figures for weekly American movie attendance: 90 million in 1946, 64 million in 1951, and 46.5 million in 1956; see *Postwar Hollywood, 1946–1962* (Malden, MA: Blackwell, 2007), 43. Similar declines took place in the number of theaters and films produced; see ibid., 88, 43.

12. Ibid., 43, 53.

13. See John Izod, *Hollywood and the Box Office, 1895–1986* (New York: Columbia University Press, 1988), 120–29.

14. Thomas Schatz, *The Genius of the System: Hollywood Filmmaking in the Studio Era* (New York: Metropolitan Books, 1988), 412; Dennis McDougal, *The Last Mogul: Lew Wasserman, MCA, and the Hidden History of Hollywood* (Boston: Da Capo, 2001), 152–53.

15. Izod, *Hollywood and the Box Office*, 126; Paul Monaco, *The Sixties, 1960–1969* (Berkeley: University of California Press, 2001), 26; Thomas Cripps, *Making Movies Black: The Hollywood Message Movie from World War II to the Civil Rights Era* (New York: Oxford University Press, 1993), 177; Calvin Pryluck, "Front Office, Box Office, and Artistic Freedom: An Aspect of the Film Industry," in *Movies as Artifacts*, ed. Michael T. Marsden, John G. Nachbar, and Sam L. Grogg, Jr. (Chicago: Nelson-Hall, 1982), 52.

16. Richard S. Randall, "Censorship: From *The Miracle* to *Deep Throat*," in *The American Film Industry*, ed. Tino Balio (Madison: University of Wisconsin Press, 1976), 433–35; Casper, *Postwar Hollywood*, 122, 129; Izod, *Hollywood and the Box Office*, 130.

17. Casper, *Postwar Hollywood*, 137.

18. Randall, "Censorship"; Garth Jowett, "'A Significant Medium for the Communication of Ideas': The *Miracle* Decision and the Decline of Motion Picture Censorship, 1952–1968," in *Movie Censorship and American Culture*, ed. Francis G. Couvares (Washington, DC: Smithsonian Institution Press, 1996), 258–76.

19. William Roger Louis, "Introduction," in *The Oxford History of the British Empire*, vol. 4, *The Twentieth Century*, ed. Judith M. Brown and William Roger Louis (Oxford: Oxford University Press, 1999), 12.

20. Louis and Robinson, "Imperialism of Decolonization," 465.

21. On the 1940 bill, see Howard Johnson, "The British Caribbean from Demobilization to Constitutional Development," in *The Oxford History of the British Empire*, vol. 4, *The Twentieth Century*, 610–14.

22. Quoted in Rudolf von Albertini, *Decolonization: The Administration and Future of the Colonies, 1919–1960*, trans. Francisca Garvie (New York: Africana, 1982), 182.

23. See D. K. Fieldhouse, "The Metropolitan Economics of Empire," in *The Oxford History of the British Empire*, vol. 4, *The Twentieth Century*, ed. Judith M. Brown and William Roger Louis (Oxford: Oxford University Press, 1999), 88–113. 103; B. R. Tomlinson, "The Contraction of England: National Decline and the Loss of Empire," *Journal of Imperial and Commonwealth History* 11:1 (1982): 67.

24. Wendy Webster, *Englishness and Empire, 1939–1965* (Oxford: Oxford University Press, 2005), 59–60.

25. Ibid., 7–8, 26.

26. Philip Corrigan, "Film Entertainment as Ideology and Pleasure: A Preliminary Approach to a History of Audiences," in *British Cinema History*, ed. James Curran and Vincent Porter (Totowa, NJ: Barnes and Noble, 1983), 26.

27. Robert Murphy, "Rank's Attempt on the American Market, 1944–1949," in Curran and Porter, *British Cinema History*, 171; Patricia Perilli, "Appendix: Statistical Survey of the British Film Industry," in ibid., 372–82.

28. Richard Pells, *Not Like Us: How Europeans Have Loved, Hated, and Transformed American Culture since World War II* (New York: Basic Books, 1997), 217.

29. On Hollywood's ties with Washington, see Gian Piero Brunetta, "The Long March of American Cinema in Italy: From Fascism to the Cold War," in *Hollywood in Europe: Experiences of a Cultural Hegemony*, ed. David W. Ellwood and Rob Kroes (Amsterdam: VU University Press, 1994), 144–45; Paul Swann, "The Little State Department: Washington and Hollywood's Rhetoric of the Postwar Audience," in Ellwood and Kroes, *Hollywood in Europe*, 179; Reinhold Wagnleitner, "American Cultural Diplomacy, the Cinema, and the Cold War in Central Europe," in Ellwood and Kroes, *Hollywood in Europe*, 203, 207. Swann (p. 195) argues that Hollywood was not a tool of Washington, and perhaps even the reverse. Yet Washington did not always do Hollywood's bidding either; see Ian Jarvie, "The Postwar Economic Foreign Policy of the American Film Industry: Europe 1945–1950," in Ellwood and Kroes, *Hollywood in Europe*, 157, 173–74; Swann, "Little State Department," 178, 181, 186, 195.

30. Webster, *Englishness and Empire*, 15, 81.

31. Sue Harper and Vincent Porter write that the boycott caused "chaos in the cinemas and a consequent fall in revenues from entertainment duty" (*British Cinema: The Decline of Difference* [Oxford: Oxford University Press, 2003], 5).

32. Ibid., 6; Jarvie, "Postwar Economic Foreign Policy," 171.

33. Harper and Porter, *British Cinema*, 6, 30, 114; Jarvie, "Postwar Economic Foreign Policy," 172; Thomas H. Guback, "Hollywood's International Market," in *The American Film Industry*, ed. Tino Balio (Madison: University of Wisconsin Press, 1976), 400–402.

34. Harper and Porter, *British Cinema*, 17; see also 8, 30.

35. Ibid., 16, 22; see also Izod, *Hollywood and the Box Office*, 160; Harper and Porter, *British Cinema*, 2; Pells, *Not Like Us*, 218.

36. See Henry Rousso, *The Vichy Syndrome: History and Memory in France since 1944*, trans. Arthur Goldhammer (Cambridge, MA: Harvard University Press, 1991).

37. See Robert O. Paxton, *Vichy France: Old Guard and New Order, 1940–1944* (New York: Columbia University Press, 1972).

38. See "*Le Rang*" in his *Mémoires de guerre: Le salut, 1944–1946* (Paris: Plon, 1959).

39. *Les états-généraux de la colonisation française*, quoted in Jean-Pierre Biondi, *Les anticolonialistes (1881–1962)* (Paris: Robert Laffont, 1992), 248.

40. Robert Aldrich, *Greater France: A History of French Overseas Expansion* (New York: St. Martin's, 1996), 90. See also Henri Grimal, *La décolonisation de 1919 à nos jours*, rev. ed. (Brussels: Editions Complexe, 1996), 14; Charles-Robert Ageron, *France coloniale ou parti coloniale?* (Paris: Presses Universitaires de France, 1978), 269, 272–73, 283; Biondi, *Les anticolonialistes*, 239.

41. See Denise Bouche, *Histoire de la colonisation française*, vol. 2 (Paris: Fayard, 1991), 372–74; Ageron, *France coloniale*, 269.

42. Aldrich, *Greater France*, 280; Raymond F. Betts, *France and Decolonisation, 1900–1960* (Houndmills: Macmillan, 1991), 59–61; Biondi, *Les anticolonialistes*, 238; Bouche, *Histoire de la colonisation française*, 378, 390.

43. Aldrich, *Greater France*, 284–85, 293; Bouche, *Histoire de la colonisation française*, 415; Biondi, *Les anticolonialistes*, 247.

44. Bouche, *Histoire de la colonisation française*, 395; Betts, *France and Decolonisation*, 60–61.

45. Quoted in Aldrich, *Greater France*, 281.

46. Bouche, *Histoire de la colonisation française*, 404–5; Betts, *France and Decolonisation*, 70; Grimal, 199.

47. Aldrich, *Greater France*, 282.

48. In his war memoirs, de Gaulle details the damage in 1945: more than six hundred thousand killed, five hundred thousand buildings completely destroyed, 1.5 million seriously damaged, and a million hectares of land rendered unusable; see de Gaulle, *Mémoires de guerre*, 272–73.

49. See the annual charts in Simon Simsi, *Ciné-Passions: 7e art et industrie de 1945 à 2000* (Paris: Dixit, 2000). See also Patricia Hubert-Lacombe, "L'accueil des films américains en France pendant la guerre froide (1946–1953)," *Révue d'Histoire Moderne et Contemporaine* 33 (April–June 1986): 301–313. For a survey of France's film industry in these years, see Jean-Pierre Jeancolas, "Le cadre," in *D'un cinéma à l'autre: Notes sur le cinéma français des années cinquante*, ed. Jean-Loup Passek (Paris: Editions du Centre Pompidou, 1988), 12–24.

50. Simsi, *Ciné-Passions*; polls suggested French viewers' preference for French films; see Hubert-Lacombe, "L'accueil des films américains," 310–11.

51. Jacques Portes, "Les origines de la légende noire des accords Blum-Byrnes sur le cinéma," *Révue d'Histoire Moderne et Contemporaine* 33 (April–June 1986): 328, 325.

52. Ibid., 318.

53. Victoria de Grazia writes that French production "collapsed" during the Blum-Byrnes period and that "by 1947, American movies had overrun the country"; see her "Mass Cul-

ture and Sovereignty: The American Challenge to European Cinemas, 1920–1960," *Journal of Modern History* 61:1 (March 1989): 82. Susan Hayward's figures for these years also appear incorrect; see her *French National Cinema*, 2nd ed. (London: Routledge, 2005), 25.

54. Simsi, *Ciné-Passions*, charts for 1946 and 1947.

55. Portes, "Les origines de la légende noire," 321.

56. Jeancolas, "Le cadre," 18. Rémi Lanzoni calls France "unquestionably the European country that best protected itself against an American cinematographic hegemony"; see his *French Cinema from Its Beginnings to the Present* (New York: Continuum, 2002), 150. On why the threat was overstated, see Portes, "Les origines de la légende noire," 328.

Chapter 1 • The White Woman's Burden

1. On empire films going out of fashion in World War II, see James Chapman and Nicholas J. Cull, *Projecting Empire: Imperialism and Popular Cinema* (London: I. B. Tauris, 2009), 26.

2. Melani McAlister, *Epic Encounters: Culture, Media, and U.S. Interests in the Middle East since 1945* (Berkeley: University of California Press, 2001), 45, 79; Christina Klein, *Cold War Orientalism: Asia in the Middlebrow Imagination, 1945–1961* (Berkeley: University of California Press, 2003), 15–16, 42–43.

3. Wendy Webster, *Englishness and Empire, 1939–1965* (Oxford: Oxford University Press, 2005), 92.

4. Richard Stubbs, *Hearts and Minds in Guerrilla Warfare: The Malayan Emergency, 1948–1960* (Singapore: Oxford University Press, 1989), 1.

5. Raymond F. Betts, *France and Decolonisation, 1900–1960* (Houndmills: Macmillan, 1991), 67–68. Matt K. Matsuda, *Empire of Love: Histories of France and the Pacific* (Oxford: Oxford University Press, 2005), 8.

6. See "Jules Harmand on the Morality of Empire and the Policy of Association," in *Imperialism*, ed. Philip D. Curtin (New York: Harper and Row, 1971), 293.

7. Albert Sarraut, *La mise en valeur des colonies françaises* (Paris: Payot, 1923), 123.

8. Benjamin Batson, *The End of the Absolute Monarchy in Siam* (Oxford: Oxford University Press, 1984), 6.

9. See David K. Wyatt, *Thailand: A Short History*, 2nd ed. (New Haven, CT: Yale University Press, 2003), 170.

10. Jean Heffer, *The United States and the Pacific: History of a Frontier*, trans. W. Donald Wilson (Notre Dame, IN: University of Notre Dame Press, 2002), 72.

11. Batson, *End of the Absolute Monarchy in Siam*, 10; Wyatt, *Thailand*, 169.

12. On Mongkut's interest in learning before Leonowens's arrival, see Wyatt, *Thailand*, 161.

13. Abbot Low Moffatt, *Mongkut, the King of Siam* (Ithaca, NY: Cornell University Press, 1961), 222–23.

14. *Philadelphia Inquirer*, 28 August 1946.

15. *Variety*, 8 January 1947.

16. Favorable reviews: Thomas J. Fitzmorris, *America*, 29 June 1946; Marjory Adams, *Boston Globe*, 19 July; Elinor Hughes, *Boston Herald*, 19 July; Mae Tinee, *Chicago Tribune*, 4 October; Philip T. Hartung, *Commonweal*, 5 July; Jesse Zunser, *Cue*, 22 June; John Finlayson, *Detroit News*, 31 August; Jack Moffitt, *Esquire*, September 1946; *Film Daily*, 3 June; Hubert Roussel, *Houston Post*, 2 August; *Hartford Courant*, 18 July; Jack D. Grant, *Holly-*

wood Reporter, 3 June; Ruth Waterbury, *Los Angeles Examiner*, 19 July; Harrison Carroll, *Los Angeles Evening Herald and Express*, 19 July; Edwin Schallert, *Los Angeles Times*, 19 July; Marion Atchison, *Miami Herald*, 8 August; William R. Weaver, *Motion Picture Herald*, 8 June; C.S., *New Orleans Times-Picayune*, 6 September; *Newsweek*, 24 June; Kate Cameron, *New York Daily News*, 21 June; Archer Winsten, *New York Post*, 21 June; Mildred Martin, *Philadelphia Inquirer*, 15 August; John Hobart, *San Francisco Chronicle*, 19 July; *Time*, 24 June; Brog., *Variety*, 5 June; Nelson Bell, *Washington Post*, 1 August.

Negative: John McCarten, *New Yorker*, 6 July; Jack Balch, *St. Louis Post-Dispatch*, 30 August.

Mixed or neutral: John Rosenfield, *Dallas Morning News*, 18 July; Bosley Crowther, *New York Times*, 21 June; D.S., *San Diego Union*, 24 July.

17. The nine: *America, Boston Globe, Chicago Tribune, Cue, Detroit News, Newsweek, Philadelphia Inquirer, San Diego Union, Washington Post.*

18. Objecting to ethnic miscasting were the *Boston Globe, Boston Herald, New York Post, New Yorker*, and *San Francisco Chronicle*.

19. Positive reviews: Paul Holt, *Daily Express*, 9 August 1946; Paul Mannock, *Daily Herald*, 9 August; *Evening News*, 9 August; *Kinematograph Weekly*, 4 July; K.F.B., *Monthly Film Bulletin*, 31 August; I.H.C., *Manchester Guardian*, 10 August; C. A. Lejeune, *Observer*, 11 August; A. E. Wilson, *Star*, 9 August; *Tribune*, 9 August; *Time and Tide*, 17 August.

Negative: Fred Majdalany, *Daily Mail*, 9 August; Richard Winnington, *News Chronicle*, 12 August; *Reynolds News*, date illegible in British Film Institute (BFI) clippings copy; Basil Wright, *Spectator*, 16 August.

Mixed or neutral: Noel Whitcomb, *Daily Mirror*, 9 August; Campbell Dixon, *Daily Telegraph*, 12 August; *Daily Worker*, 9 August; Ian Coster, *Evening Standard*, 9 August; *London Times*, 12 August; Dilys Powell, *Sunday Times*, 11 August; William Whitebait, *New Statesman*, 17 August; *Sunday Dispatch*, 11 August; Stephen Watts, *Sunday Express*, 11 August.

20. Caren Kaplan, "'Getting to Know You': Travel, Gender, and the Politics of Representation in *Anna and the King of Siam* and *The King and I*," in *Late Imperial Culture*, ed. Román de la Campa, E. Ann Kaplan, and Michael Sprinker (London: Verso, 1995), 47.

21. Claude Lazurick, *L'Aurore*, 28 May 1947, gave it a positive review. The negative reviews were *Combat*, 24 May; Pierre Laroche, *Franc-Tireur*, 28 May; and Jeander, *Libération*, 3 June. Louis Chauvet, *Le Figaro*, 25 May, gave it a mixed review.

22. *Variety*, 2 January 1957.

23. Kaplan, "'Getting to Know You,'" 42.

24. Margaret Landon, *Anna and the King of Siam* (New York: HarperPerennial, 2000), 22, 199.

25. Klein, *Cold War Orientalism*, 206. Klein also notes Thailand's importance to Washington's containment strategy in Asia, 197.

26. Kaplan, "'Getting to Know You,'" 49.

27. Klein, *Cold War Orientalism*, 217–18.

28. The positive reviews: Thomas J. Fitzmorris, *America*, 29 June 1956; John William Riley, *Boston Globe*, 30 June; Elinor Hughes, *Boston Herald*, 30 June; Mae Tinee, *Chicago Tribune*, 2 July; Philip T. Hartung, *Commonweal*, 20 July; John Beaufort, *Christian Science Monitor*, 30 June; Jesse Zunser, *Cue*, 29 June; John Rosenfield, *Dallas Morning News*, 19 July; Al Weitschat, *Detroit News*, 8 July; Mandel Herbstman, *Film Daily*, 29 June; M.O.S., *Hartford Courant*, 26 July; *Hollywood Reporter*, 29 June; Edwin Schallert, *Los Angeles Times*,

29 June; Dorothy Manners, *Los Angeles Examiner*, 29 June; George Bourke, *Miami Herald*, 19 July; Charles S. Aaronson, *Motion Picture Herald*, 7 July; *Newsweek*, 9 July; Wanda Hale, *New York Daily News*, 29 June; Bosley Crowther, *New York Times*, 29 June; Mildred Martin, *Philadelphia Inquirer*, 13 July; Paine Knickerbocker, *San Francisco Chronicle*, 29 June; *Saturday Review*, 21 July; Holl., *Variety*, 4 July.

Mixed reviews: John McCarten, *New Yorker*, 14 July; *Time*, 16 July; Richard L. Coe, *Washington Post*, 30 June.

29. Positive reviews: Leonard Mosley, *Daily Express*, 12 September; Anthony Carthew, *Daily Herald*, 14 September; Fred Majdalany, *Daily Mail*, 14 September; Robert Tee, *Daily Mirror*, 14 September; Harold Conway, *Daily Sketch*, 12 September; Campbell Dixon, *Daily Telegraph*, 15 September; Thomas Spencer, *Daily Worker*, 15 September; Dilys Powell, *Sunday Times*, 16 September; *Manchester Guardian*, 15 September; Paul Dehn, *News Chronicle*, 14 September; C. A. Lejeune, *Observer*, 16 September; Milton Shulman, *Sunday Express*, 16 September; Isabel Quigly, *Spectator*, 21 September; Fred Majdalany, *Time and Tide*, 22 September.

Negative: *Monthly Film Bulletin*, no. 272, September 1956.

Mixed: Patrick Gibbs, *Daily Telegraph*, date illegible in BFI clippings file; Felix Barker, *Evening News*, 13 September; Derek Granger, *Financial Times*, 17 September; *London Times*, 12 September.

30. *Manchester Guardian*, 15 September; Shulman, *Sunday Express*, 16 September.

31. Simon Simsi, *Ciné-Passions: 7e art et industrie de 1945 à 2000* (Paris: Dixit, 2000), 131.

32. Heffer, *The United States and the Pacific*, 121; Susan Thorne, "Religion and Empire at Home," in *At Home with the Empire: Metropolitan Culture and the Imperial World*, ed. Catherine Hall and Sonya O. Rose (Cambridge: Cambridge University Press, 2006), 153; on Indochina, see Jacques Dalloz, *La guerre d'Indochine, 1945–1954* (Paris: Seuil, 1987), 9; on Syria, see J. P. Daughton, *An Empire Divided: Religion, Republicanism, and the Making of French Colonialism* (Oxford: Oxford University Press, 2006), 15.

33. Daughton, *Empire Divided*, 11.

34. Andrew Porter, "Religion, Missionary Enthusiasm, and Empire," in *The Oxford History of the British Empire*, vol. 3, *The Nineteenth Century*, ed. Andrew Porter (Oxford: Oxford University Press, 1999), 239.

35. John Cell, "The Imperial Conscience," in *The Conscience of the Victorian State*, ed. Peter Marsh (Syracuse, NY: Syracuse University Press, 1979), 187.

36. A. Porter, "Religion," 245; see also Thorne, "Religion and Empire at Home," 153; Charles-Robert Ageron, *France coloniale ou parti coloniale?* (Paris: Presses Universitaires de France, 1978), 36.

37. Benjamin Disraeli, in Great Britain, *Parliamentary Debates (Hansard)*, House of Commons, vol. 147 (July–August 1857), column 447; Queen Victoria's Proclamation of 1 November 1858 to the Princes, Chiefs, and People of India: http://en.wikisource.org/wiki/Queen_Victoria's_Proclamation.

38. A figure of five to six million Christians out of 300 million in 1921 is cited in Judith M. Brown, "Who Is an Indian? Dilemmas of National Identity at the End of the British Raj in India," in *Missions, Nationalism, and the End of Empire*, ed. Brian Stanley (Grand Rapids, MI: William B. Eerdmans, 2003), 113; see also Jeffrey Cox, *Imperial Fault Lines: Christianity and Colonial Power in India, 1818–1940* (Stanford, CA: Stanford University Press, 2002).

39. Margaret Rumer Godden, *Black Narcissus* (Boston: Little, Brown, 1939).

40. See critic Dave Kehr's 2001 review, at http://www.criterion.com/current/posts/94, and Sarah Street, *Black Narcissus* (London: I. B. Tauris, 2005), 29, 57, 88. Tony Williams says the film "at least recognizes that repression and colonialism are dangerous for the British character"; see his *Structures of Desire: British Cinema, 1939–1955* (Albany: SUNY Press, 2000), 134.

41. The Communist Party was also active on tea plantations; see Atis Dasgupta, "Ethnic Problems and Movements for Autonomy in Darjeeling," *Social Scientist* 27:11–12 (November–December 1999): 58–60.

42. Street makes a similar argument; see *Black Narcissus*, 59.

43. Ibid., 41.

44. Ibid., 63.

45. Simsi, *Ciné-Passions*, chart for 1948.

46. *Variety*, 7 January 1948, 5 January 1949; Street, *Black Narcissus*, 70–73.

47. Positive: Leonard Mosely, *Daily Express*, 26 April 1947; Reg Whitley, *Daily Mirror*, 25 April; Campbell Dixon, *Daily Telegraph*, 28 April; Jympson Harmon, *Evening News*, 24 April; K.F.B., *Monthly Film Bulletin*, 31 May; C. A. Lejeune, *Observer*, 27 April; Stephen Watts, *Sunday Express*, 27 April; C.A.W., *To-Day's Cinema News*, 23 April; Helen Fletcher, *Time and Tide*, 26 April.

Negative: *Kinematograph Weekly*, 24 April; *London Times*, 24 April; *Manchester Guardian*, 26 April; William Whitebait, *New Statesman*, 3 May.

Mixed: Fred Majdalany, *Daily Mail*, 25 April; John Thompson, *Evening Standard*, 25 April; Dilys Powell, *Sunday Times*, 27 April; Basil Wright, *Spectator*, 2 May.

For the United States, the positive reviews were: Marjory Adams, *Boston Globe*, 26 January 1948; Elinor Hughes, *Boston Herald*, 26 January; Mae Tinee, *Chicago Tribune*, 11 December 1947; *Film Daily*, 17 July 1947; Jack D. Grant, *Hollywood Reporter*, 8 July 1947; Philip K. Scheuer, *Los Angeles Times*, 19 September 1947; Ruth Waterbury, *Los Angeles Examiner*, 19 September 1947; Fred Hift, *Motion Picture Herald*, 12 July 1947; *Newsweek*, 18 August 1947; Kate Cameron, *New York Daily News*, 14 August 1947; Irene Thirer, *New York Post*, 14 August 1947; T.M.P., *New York Times*, 14 August 1947; John Hobart, *San Francisco Chronicle*, 17 September 1947; Gane., *Variety*, 7 May 1947.

Negative: Moira Walsh, *America*, 6 May 1947; Philip T. Hartung, *Commonweal*, 22 August 1947; Jesse Zunser, *Cue*, 27 December 1947; John Rosenfield, *Dallas Morning News*, 3 April 1948; *Time*, 25 August 1947.

Mixed: Richard L. Coe, *Washington Post*, 6 March 1948.

48. See *New York Post*, *Boston Herald*, *Chicago Tribune*, *Cue*, *Newsweek*, *New York Post*, *New York Times*, *Daily Mail*, and *Evening Standard*.

49. *Boston Globe*, *Boston Herald*, and *To-Day's Cinema News*.

50. Emphasizing the paucity of conversions is John K. Fairbank, *The Missionary Enterprise in China and America* (Cambridge, MA: Harvard University Press, 1974), 1. Given the growth of China's Christian population after 1949, the undertaking was not a complete failure.

51. See, for example, Catherine Swift, *Gladys Aylward: The Courageous English Missionary Whose Life Defied All Expectations* (Bloomington, MN: Bethany House, 1989).

52. Warren I. Cohen, *America's Response to China: A History of Sino-American Relations*, 4th ed. (New York: Columbia University Press, 2000), 21. Fairbank, *Missionary Enterprise in China*, 2.

53. Cohen, *America's Response to China*, 44; Jessie Gregory Lutz, *Chinese Politics and Christian Missions: The Anti-Christian Movements of 1920–28* (Notre Dame, IN: Cross Cultural, 1988), 88.

54. Marjory Adams, *Boston Globe*, 26 December 1958; *Time*, 22 December 1958.

55. See *Philadelphia Inquirer*, 24 December 1958.

56. *Variety*, 6 January 1960.

57. *Newsweek*, 15 December 1958; "Woman in Row over Bergman Film," *Evening Standard*, 15 September 1958; Philip K. Scheuer, "Director Declares Charges Unfounded," *Los Angeles Times*, 11 December 1958.

58. Scheuer, *Los Angeles Times*, 11 December 1958.

59. Klein, *Cold War Orientalism*, 90, writes that by the 1950s, the missionary cause "had lost much of its cultural legitimacy and was increasingly seen as an outmoded figure of cultural intolerance, if not outright racism."

60. For the United States, the positive reviews were: Marjory Adams, *Boston Globe*, 26 December 1958; *Boston Herald*, 26 December 1958; Mae Tinee, *Chicago Tribune*, 25 December 1958; Philip T. Hartung, *Commonweal*, 19 December 1958; Jesse Zunser, *Cue*, 13 December 1958; Larry Tajiri, *Denver Post*, 25 December 1958; *Film Daily*, 21 November 1958; Jack Moffitt, *Hollywood Reporter*, 18 November 1958; Philip K. Scheuer, *Los Angeles Times*, 26 December 1958; James Jerauld, *Motion Picture Herald*, 29 November 1958; Sim Myers, *New Orleans Times-Picayune*, 2 January 1959; Myles Standish, *St. Louis Post-Dispatch*, 6 March 1959; Rich., *Variety*, 19 November 1958.

Negative: *Newsweek*, 15 December 1958; Bosley Crowther, *New York Times*, 4 January 1959; Mildred Martin, *Philadelphia Inquirer*, 25 December 1958; *Time*, 22 December 1958.

Mixed or neutral: John Beaufort, *Christian Science Monitor*, 26 December 1958; John Rosenfield, *Dallas Morning News*, 30 January 1959; Al Weitschat, *Detroit News*, 1 January 1959; John McCarten, *New Yorker*, 20 December 1958; Paine Knickerbocker, *San Francisco Chronicle*, 1 January 1959; Hollis Alpert, *Saturday Review*, 13 December 1958; Richard L. Coe, *Washington Post*, 1 January 1959.

61. For Great Britain, the positive reviews were: Anthony Carthew, *Daily Herald*, 21 November 1958; Fred Majdalany, *Daily Mail*, 21 November 1958; Donald Zec, *Daily Mirror*, 21 November 1958; Harold Conway, *Daily Sketch*, 19 November 1958; Campbell Dixon, *Daily Telegraph*, 22 November 1958; Nina Hibbin, *Daily Worker*, 22 November 1958; Jympson Harman, *Evening News*, 18 November 1958; John Waterman, *Evening Standard*, 20 November 1958; *Kinematograph Weekly*, 20 November 1958; Dilys Powell, *Sunday Times*, 23 November 1958; *Manchester Guardian*, 22 November 1958; *News Chronicle*, 22 November 1958; Peter Burnup, *News of the World*, 23 November 1958; C. A. Lejeune, *Observer*, 23 November 1958; Ernest Betts, *The People*, 23 November 1958; Frank Johnson, *Reynolds News*, 23 November 1958; Philip Oakes, *Sunday Dispatch*, 23 November 1958; Derek Monsey, *Sunday Express*, 23 November 1958; Isabel Quigly, *Spectator*, 28 November 1958; Ivon Adams, *Star*, 20 November 1958; Charles MacLaren, *Time and Tide*, 29 November 1958.

Negative: William Whitebait, *New Statesman*, 29 November 1958; *Times Educational Supplement*, 12 December 1958.

Mixed or neutral: Leonard Mosley, *Daily Express*, 21 November 1958; Peter Brinson, *Financial Times*, 24 November 1958; Molly Plowright, *Glasgow Herald*, 26 January 1959; *London Times*, 20 November 1958.

62. Simsi, *Ciné-Passions*, chart for 1959.

63. For France, the positive reviews were: Georges Hellio, *Aspects de la France*, 13 March 1959; Claude Garson, *Aurore*, 1 March 1959; Elsa Casals, *Dauphiné Libéré*, 4 March 1959; Louis Chauvet, *Figaro*, 3 March 1959; D. de F., *Nouveaux Jours*, 6 March 1959.

Negative: Jacques Chastel, *Combat*, 4 March 1959; *Express*, 5 March 1959; André Besseges, *France Catholique*, 19 March 1959; Claude Mauriac, *Figaro Littéraire*, 5 March 1959; Samuel Lachize, *Humanité*, 4 March 1959; *Humanité Dimanche*, 1 March 1959; *Libération*, 8 March 1959; Martine Monod, *Lettres Françaises*, 5 March 1959; Jean de Baroncelli, *Monde*, 5 March 1959; Georges Charensol, *Nouvelles Littéraires*, 5 March 1959; Michel Aubriant, *Paris-Presse-L'Intransigeant*, 3 March 1959.

Mixed or neutral: Jean Rochereau, *Croix*, 3 March 1959; Robert Chazal, *France Soir*, 28 February 1959; Claude Casa, *Juvenal*, 6 March 1959.

64. See Philip M. Williams, *French Politicians and Elections, 1951–1969* (Cambridge: Cambridge University Press, 1970), 142; on *L'Humanité*'s circulation, see Philip M. Williams, *Crisis and Compromise: Politics in the Fourth Republic* (London: Longmans, 1964), 77.

65. *Daily Sketch, Kinematograph Weekly, Sunday Times*.

66. *Variety*, 6 January 1960. Positive reviews (all in 1959): Moira Walsh, *America*, 27 June; Marjory Adams, *Boston Globe*, 28 June; Elinor Hughes, *Boston Herald*, 27 June; Mae Tinee, *Chicago Tribune*, 6 July; Philip T. Hartung, *Commonweal*, 17 July; Jesse Zunser, *Cue*, 20 June; John Rosenfield, *Dallas Morning News*, 5 August; Al Weitschat, *Detroit News*, 25 June; *Film Daily*, 6 May; Jack Moffitt, *Hollywood Reporter*, 6 May; Philip Scheuer, *Los Angeles Times*, 31 May and 26 June; Richard Gertner, *Motion Picture Herald*, 9 May; *Newsweek*, 29 June; Kate Cameron, *New York Daily News*, 19 June; Archer Winsten, *New York Post*, 19 June; John McCarten, *New Yorker*, 27 June; Bosley Crowther, *New York Times*, 19 June; Mildred Martin, *Philadelphia Inquirer*, 26 June; Paine Knickerbocker, *San Francisco Chronicle*, 1 July; Hollis Alpert, *Saturday Review*, 27 June; Myles Standish, *St. Louis Post-Dispatch*, 10 July; Powe., *Variety*, 6 May; Richard L. Coe, *Washington Post*, 24 and 29 July.

Mixed: Melvin Maddocks, *Christian Science Monitor*, 27 June; Stanley Kauffmann, *New Republic*, 29 June.

67. Positive reviews (all in 1959): Leonard Mosley, *Daily Express*, 25 July; Fred Majdalany, *Daily Mail*, 23 July; Campbell Dixon, *Daily Telegraph*, 25 July; Jympson Harman, *Evening News*, 23 July; *Evening Standard*, 23 July; *London Times*, 27 July; Dilys Powell, *Sunday Times*, 26 July; D. H., *Monthly Film Bulletin*, no. 308; C. A. Lejeune, *Observer*, 26 July; Ernest Betts, *People*, 26 July; Allen Wright, *Scotsman*, 2 September; Derek Monsey, *Sunday Express*, 26 July; Isabel Quigly, *Spectator*, 7 August; Ivon Adams, *Star*, 25 July.

Negative: William Whitebait, *New Statesman*, 8 August.

Mixed or neutral: Nina Hibbin, *Daily Worker*, 25 July; *Manchester Guardian*, 25 July.

68. Simsi, *Ciné-Passions*, chart for 1960.

69. Positive reviews (all 1960): *Aux Ecoutes*, 12 February; Michel Duran, *Canard Enchaîné*, 17 February; André Besseges, *France Catholique*, 12 February; Robert Chazal, *France Soir*, 5 February; Jean de Baroncelli, *Monde*, 13 February; Pierre Laroche, *Noir et Blanc*, 4 March; D. de F., *Nouveaux Jours*, 12 February; Michel Aubriant, *Paris Presse/L'Intransigeant*, 5 February.

Negative: *Arts*, 15 February; Pierre Marcabru, *Combat*, 9 February; François Maurice, *Croix*, 25 July; Bruno Gay-Lussac, *Express*, 11 February; Samuel Lachize, *Humanité*, 10

February; Simone Dubreuilh, *Libération*, 11 February; P. L. Thirard, *Lettres Françaises*, 11 February; C.-M. Tremois, *Radio Cinéma Télévision*, 14 February; d'Yvoire, *Radio Cinéma Télévision*, 14 February.

Mixed: Louis Chauvet, *Figaro*, 8 February.

70. Richard Dyer, *White* (London: Routledge, 1997), 184.

Chapter 2 • Heroes of Empire

1. John J. Devlin, letter to Clarence Hutson of Twentieth Century-Fox, 14 December 1945, in Joseph L. Mankiewicz Papers, Herrick Library, Academy of Motion Picture Arts and Sciences (AMPAS), Beverly Hills, CA.

2. John Tucker Battle, memo to Darryl F. Zanuck, 19 January 1945, Special Collections, Doheny Library, University of Southern California (USC), Los Angeles.

3. Joseph L. Mankiewicz, letter to Darryl F. Zanuck, 16 July 1945, Joseph L. Mankiewicz Papers, Herrick Library, AMPAS.

4. Handwritten note on title page of a script dated 21 March 1946, Special Collections, Doheny Library, USC.

5. Darryl F. Zanuck, comments on memo of 20 January 1945, Special Collections, Doheny Library, USC.

6. Unsigned minutes of conference with Mr. Zanuck on outline of 22 May 1946, Special Collections, Doheny Library, USC.

7. Rudy Behlmer's liner notes for the soundtrack album quote Zanuck's 20 October 1949 memo about the film losing money. Ned Comstock of USC's Doheny Library kindly brought the liner notes to my attention. For the U.S. box office, see *Variety*, 5 January 1949; on France, see Simon Simsi, *Ciné-Passions: 7e art et industrie de 1945 à 2000* (Paris: Dixit, 2000), chart for 1949.

8. Advertisement in production files for *Captain from Castile*, Herrick Library, AMPAS.

9. Positive: Marjory Adams, *Boston Globe*, 26 December 1947; John Rosenfield, *Dallas Morning News*, 30 January 1948; Al Weitschat, *Detroit News*, 26 December 1947; *Film Daily*, 26 November 1947; Kay Proctor, *Los Angeles Examiner*, 26 December 1947; Archer Winsten, *New York Post*, 26 December 1947; Gene Peach, *San Diego Union*, 1 January 1948; John Hobart, *San Francisco Chronicle*, 26 December 1947; Herm., *Variety*, 26 November 1947.

Negative: Howard Watson, *Boston Herald*, 26 December 1947; Bosley Crowther, *New York Times*, 26 December 1947; Mildred Martin, *Philadelphia Inquirer*, 26 December 1947; Richard L. Coe, *Washington Post*, 7 February 1948.

Mixed: Moira Walsh, *America*, 3 January 1948; Mae Tinee, *Chicago Tribune*, 26 December 1947; Jesse Zunser, *Cue*, 27 December 1947; *Hollywood Reporter*, 26 November 1947; John L. Scott, *Los Angeles Times*, 26 December 1947; Red Kann, *Motion Picture Herald*, 29 November 1947; *Newsweek*, 5 January 1948; Kate Cameron, *New York Daily News*, 26 December 1947; *St. Louis Post-Dispatch*, 16 January 1948; *Time*, 5 January 1948.

10. See Edward D. Castillo, "The Impact of Euro-American Exploration and Settlement," in *Handbook of North American Indians*, ed. William C. Sturtevant (Washington, DC: Smithsonian Institution, 1978–2008), vol. 8: *California*, ed. Robert F. Heizer (Washington, DC: Smithsonian Institution, 1978), 88–107; Sherburne F. Cook, *The Conflict between the California Indian and White Civilization* (Berkeley: University of California, Press, 1976). On Serra's canonization, see James A. Sandos, "Junípero Serra's Canonization and the Historical Process," *American Historical Review* 93:5 (December 1988): 1253–69.

11. Cecil Smith, "Back from Japan, Hustling John Huston Flies to Africa," *Los Angeles Times*, 16 February 1958.

12. John McMaster, *Sabotaging the Shogun: Western Diplomats Open Japan, 1859–1869* (New York: Vantage, 1992), 2.

13. On the 1954 protests, see Walter LaFeber, *The Clash: A History of U.S.-Japan Relations* (New York: W. W. Norton, 1997), 311.

14. Ibid., xviii, 303–4.

15. *Variety*, 7 January 1959. The film's budget is reported as $3.5 million on IMDb.com, and *Variety* reports that it made $2.5 million in domestic rentals in its theatrical release.

16. Axel Madsen, *John Huston* (New York: Doubleday, 1978), 172.

17. All reviews are from 1958: Positive: Moira Walsh, *America*, 18 October; Marjory Adams, *Boston Globe*, 23 October; Elinor Hughes, *Boston Herald*, 23 October; John Rosenfield, *Dallas Morning News*, 30 October; Larry Tajiri, *Denver Post*, 15 October; *Film Daily*, 30 September; Samuel D. Berns, *Motion Picture Herald*, 11 October; Bosley Crowther, *New York Times*, 3 October; Hollis Alpert, *Saturday Review*, 11 October; Richard L. Coe, *Washington Post*, 9 October.

Negative: Philip T. Hartung, *Commonweal*, 17 October; Stanley Kauffmann, *New Republic*, 3 November; *Newsweek*, 6 October; John McCarten, *New Yorker*, 11 October; *Time*, 6 October.

Mixed or neutral: Mae Tinee, *Chicago Tribune*, 17 October; M.O.S., *Hartford Courant*, 17 October; Jack Moffitt, *Hollywood Reporter*, 30 September; John L. Scott, *Los Angeles Times*, 16 October; Powe., *Variety*, 1 October.

18. Simsi, *Ciné-Passions*, pt. 3, p. 5. The reviews are all from 1958: Positive: Robert Chazal, *France Soir*, 15 November.

Negative: Charles Bitsch, *Arts*, 20 November; Jean Dutourd, *Carrefour*, 21 November; Henry Rabine, *Croix*, 16 November; Louis Chauvet, *Figaro*, 16 November; Jacques Doniol-Valcroze, *France Observateur*, 21 November; *Libération*, 24 November; Georges Sadoul, *Lettres Françaises*, 21 November; Pierre Laroche, *Noir et Blanc*, 28 November; *Paris-Presse/L'Intransigeant*, 14 November; André-S. Labarthe, *Radio Cinéma Télévision*, 25 November.

Mixed: Jacques Deltour, *Humanité*, 15 November.

19. *Variety*, 3 January 1951.

20. J. H. Patterson, *The Man-Eaters of Tsavo* (London: Macmillan, 1919). The book can be found online: http://robroy.dyndns.info/tsavo/tsavo+pics.html.

21. Susan Hayward, *French Costume Dramas of the 1950s: Fashioning Politics in Film* (Bristol: Intellect, 2010), 146–49.

22. Simsi, *Ciné-Passions*, 87.

23. Eugene Archer, *New York Times*, 7 July 1959; Philip T. Hartung, *Commonweal*, 6 May 1959; *Monthly Film Bulletin*, no. 310 (November 1959).

24. Rosaleen Smyth, "Movies and Mandarins: The Official Film and British Africa," in *British Cinema History*, ed. James Curran and Vincent Porter (Totowa, NJ: Barnes and Noble, 1983), 135. See also Michael Paris, "Africa in Post-1945 British Cinema," *South African Historical Journal* 48 (May 2003): 64.

25. Marcia Landy, *British Genres: Cinema and Society, 1930–1960* (Princeton, NJ: Princeton University Press, 1991), 113.

26. Prem Chowdhry, *Colonial India and the Making of Empire Cinema*. (Manchester: Manchester University Press, 2000), 251, 253–54.

27. Memo from John Balderston, 8 January 1936, *King of the Khyber Rifles* files, file 2552, Warner Bros. Archives, USC.

28. Notes on conference with Mr. Zanuck, 23 March 1939, *King of the Khyber Rifles* file, file 2552, Warner Bros. Archives, USC.

29. Frank P. Rosenberg to Zanuck, 29 March 1951, file 2551, Warner Bros. Archives USC.

30. Darryl F. Zanuck to Frank P. Rosenberg, file 2551, 6 April 1951, Warner Bros. Archives, USC.

31. Zanuck to Frank Rosenberg, 1 October 1951, file 2552.21B, Warner Bros. Archives, USC.

32. Zanuck memo of 18 July 1953 on revised script of 16 July 1953, file 2552.36, Warner Bros. Archives, USC.

33. See ads in *Los Angeles Herald and Express*, 6 February 1954; *Philadelphia Inquirer*, 25 December 1953.

34. *Variety*, 5 January 1955.

35. Positive: Moira Walsh, *America*, 9 January 1954; Paul Jones, *Atlanta Constitution*, 3 January 1954; Marjory Adams, *Boston Globe*, 26 December 1953; Elinor Hughes, *Boston Herald*, 26 December 1953; Mae Tinee, *Chicago Tribune*, 2 February 1954; Steele Hooper, *Dallas Morning News*, 18 February 1954; Alex Murphree, *Denver Post*, 10 January 1954; *Film Daily*, 22 December 1954; M.O.S., *Hartford Courant*, 22 January 1954; Milton Luban, *Hollywood Reporter*, 22 December 1953; Ruth Waterbury, *Los Angeles Examiner*, 6 February 1954; Harrison Carroll, *Los Angeles Herald & Express*, 6 February 1954; Mandel Herbstman, *Motion Picture Herald*, 26 December 1953; *Newsweek*, 11 January 1954; Kate Cameron, *New York Daily News*, 23 December 1953; Archer Winsten, *New York Post*, 23 December 1953; Bosley Crowther, *New York Times*, 23 December 1953; Mildred Martin, *Philadelphia Inquirer*, 26 December 1953; Edwin Martin, *San Diego Union*, 13 February 1954; Brog., *Variety*, 23 December 1953.

Negative: John Beaufort, *Christian Science Monitor*, 26 December 1953; Jesse Zunser, *Cue*, 2 January 1954; B.J.P., *Milwaukee Journal*, 22 January 1954; Kermit Tarleton, *New Orleans Times-Picayune*, 15 February 1954; Hollis Alpert, *Saturday Review*, 16 January 1954; Myles Standish, *St. Louis Post-Dispatch*, 20 March 1954; *Time*, 11 January 1954; Richard L. Coe, *Washington Post*, 23 January 1954.

Mixed: Philip T. Hartung, *Commonweal*, 29 January 1954; Al Weitschat, *Detroit News*, 20 February 1954; Gene Miller, *Houston Post*, 1 January 1954; Edwin Schallert, *Los Angeles Times*, 6 February 1954; John McCarten, *New Yorker*, 2 January 1954; Luther Nichols, *San Francisco Chronicle*, 3 February 1954.

36. The others calling it old-fashioned were the *Boston Herald*, *Chicago Tribune*, *Denver Post*, *Los Angeles Herald & Express*, *Milwaukee Journal*, and *New York Post*.

37. *America*, *Dallas Morning News*, *Houston Post*.

38. The British reviews (all from 1954): Positive: Thomas Spencer, *Daily Worker*, 10 April; *Kinematograph Weekly*, 8 April; Roy Nash, *Star*, 9 April; L.H.C., *To-Day's Cinema News*, 7 April.

Negative: *Daily Herald*, 9 April; Fred Majdalany, *Daily Mail*, 9 April; Harold Conway, *Daily Sketch*, 9 April; Jympson Harman, *Evening News*, 8 April; Derek Granger, *Financial*

Times, 12 April; *London Times*, 12 April; Dilys Powell, *Sunday Times*, 11 April; P. H., *Monthly Film Bulletin*, March–April 1954; William Whitebait, *New Statesman*, 17 April; Fred Majdalany, *Time and Tide*, 9 April.

Mixed or neutral: Reg Whitley, *Daily Mirror*, 9 April; *Daily Telegraph*, 10 April; Beverly Baxter, *Evening Standard*, 8 April; *Manchester Guardian*, 10 April; C. A. Lejeune, *Observer*, 11 April; Virginia Graham, *Spectator*, 9 April.

39. Simsi, *Ciné-Passions*, 25. Positive reviews: *Croix*, 29 July 1954; *Franc-Tireur*, 22 July 1954; Marcel Huret, *Radio Cinéma Télévision*, 18 July 1954.

Negative: Henry Mangan, *Combat*, 13 July 1954; Louis Chauvet, *Figaro*, 19 July 1954.

Mixed: Jean de Baroncelli, *Le Monde*, 22 July 1954.

40. The British reviews (all 1959): Positive: Jympson Harman, *Evening News*, 8 October; John Waterman, *Evening Standard*, 8 October; Peter Burnup, *News of the World*, 11 October; C. A. Lejeune, *Observer*, 11 October; George Sterling, *Sunday Dispatch*, 11 October; Robert Walsh, *Sunday Express*, 11 October; Isabel Quigly, *Spectator*, 16 October; Charles MacLaren, *Time and Tide*, 17 October.

Negative: Campbell Dixon, *Daily Telegraph*, 10 October; Nina Hibbin, *Daily Worker*, 10 October; David Robinson, *Financial Times*, 12 October; *London Times*, 8 October; Dilys Powell, *Sunday Times*, 11 October; P. H., *Monthly Film Bulletin*, no. 310, November 1959; Derek Hill, *Tribune*, 16 October.

Mixed: F. J., *Daily Cinema*, 7 October; David Sylvester, *New Statesman*, 17 October.

41. The U.S. reviews (all 1960): Positive: Marjory Adams, *Boston Globe*, 26 May; *Boston Herald*, 26 May; Philip T. Hartung, *Commonweal*, 3 June; Mandel Herbstman, *Film Daily*, 21 April; *Films in Review*, May 1960; James Powers, *Hollywood Reporter*, 29 April; Lynn Bowers, *Los Angeles Examiner*, 5 May; Philip K. Scheuer, *Los Angeles Times*, 1 May; George Bourke, *Miami Herald*, 5 May; Saul Ostrove, *Motion Picture Herald*, 23 April; *Newsweek*, 9 May; Dorothy Masters, *New York Daily News*, 30 April; Howard Thompson, *New York Times*, 30 April; Myles Standish, *St. Louis Post-Dispatch*, 13 May; *Time*, 16 May; Earn. *Variety*, 14 October 1959; Richard L. Coe, *Washington Post*, 11 June.

Negative: Mae Tinee, *Chicago Tribune*, 18 May; F.H.G., *Christian Science Monitor*, 26 May; Mildred Martin, *Philadelphia Inquirer*, 25 April.

Mixed: Hazel Flynn, *Beverly Hills Citizen*, 5 May.

42. The French reviews (all from 1960): Positive: Claude Garson, *Aurore*, 7 April; *Canard Enchaîné*, 13 April; Jean Rochereau, *Croix*, 27 April; René Quinson, *Dernieres Nouvelles d'Alsace*, 27 December; Samuel Lachize, *Humanité*, 20 April; *Libération*, 11 April; Jean de Baroncelli, *Le Monde*, 13 April; Pierre Laroche, *Noir et Blanc*, 22 April.

Negative: *Arts*, 14 April; Pierre Marcabru, *Combat*, 8 April; *France Observateur*, 14 April.

Mixed or neutral: René Guyonnet, *Express*, 14 April; Louis Chauvet, *Figaro*, 14 April; Marcel Huret, *Radio Cinéma Télévision*, 17 April.

43. Michael Sturma, *South Sea Maidens: Western Fantasy and Sexual Politics in the South Pacific* (Westport, CT: Greenwood, 2002), 26–30.

44. James A. Michener, "Mr. Morgan," in *Return to Paradise* (1951; repr., New York: Fawcett Crest, 1974), 23–45.

45. Oli Holsti, *Public Opinion and American Foreign Policy* (Ann Arbor: University of Michigan Press, 1996), 19.

46. See Syed Hussein Alatas, *The Myth of the Lazy Native: A Study of the Image of the Malays, Filipinos, and Javanese from the 16th Century to the 20th Century and Its Function in*

the Ideology of Colonial Capitalism (London: F. Cass, 1977); Matt K. Matsuda, Empire of Love: Histories of France and the Pacific (Oxford: Oxford University Press, 2005), 117.

47. On this white self-image, see Richard Dyer, White (London: Routledge, 1997), 31.

48. Variety, 5 January 1955.

49. See the ads in the Miami Herald, 15 January 1954; the Detroit News, 3 February 1954; the New York Daily News, 5 February 1954; and Film Daily, 4 January 1954. The memo is in an unnumbered publicity file for His Majesty O'Keefe at the Warner Bros. Archives at USC.

50. Positive: Elinor Hughes, Boston Herald, 9 January 1954; John Rosenfield, Dallas Morning News, 8 January 1954; Alex Murphree, Denver Post, 28 January 1954; Al Weitschat, Detroit News, 4 February 1954; Film Daily, 31 December 1953; M.O.S., Hartford Courant, 15 January 1954; Margaret Harford, Hollywood Citizen News, 29 January 1954; Milton Luban, Hollywood Reporter, 30 December 1953; Sara Hamilton, Los Angeles Examiner, 28 January 1954; David Bongard, Los Angeles Herald & Express, 28 January 1954; Edwin Schallert, Los Angeles Times, 28 January 1954; Jay Remer, Motion Picture Herald, 2 January 1954; Richard C. Seither, New Orleans Times-Picayune, 9 January 1954; Kate Cameron, New York Daily News, 6 February 1954; Archer Winsten, New York Post, 7 February 1954; Edwin Martin, San Diego Union, 4 February 1954; Brog., Variety, 30 December 1953.

Negative: Marjory Adams, Boston Globe, 9 January 1954; Mae Tinee, Chicago Tribune, 16 February 1954; Rod Nordell, Christian Science Monitor, 9 January 1954; Jesse Zunser, Cue, 6 February 1954; W.H.M., Milwaukee Journal, 6 February 1954; Time, 15 February 1954; Richard L. Coe, Washington Post, 9 January 1954.

Mixed: Moira Walsh, America, 13 February 1954; Marion Atchison, Miami Herald, 16 January 1954; Bosley Crowther, New York Times, 6 February 1954; Mildred Martin, Philadelphia Inquirer, 4 February 1954; Luther Nichols, San Francisco Chronicle, 3 February 1954; Myles Standish, St. Louis Post-Dispatch, 29 January 1954.

51. These reviews missed the critique of imperialism: Boston Globe, Boston Herald, Chicago Tribune, Christian Science Monitor, Dallas Morning News, Film Daily, Hartford Courant, Hollywood Citizen News, Los Angeles Examiner, Miami Herald, Milwaukee Journal, Motion Picture Herald, Philadelphia Inquirer, Variety, Washington Post.

52. Positive: Harold Conway, Daily Sketch, 30 April 1954; Kinematograph Weekly, 6 May 1954; Giles Blagrave, New Statesman, 8 May 1954.

Negative: Jympson Harman, Evening News, 29 April 1954; London Times, 6 May 1954; Virginia Graham, Spectator, 30 April 1954; Sunday Chronicle, 2 May 1954.

Mixed or neutral: Reg Whitley, Daily Mirror, 30 April 1954; Campbell Dixon, Daily Telegraph, 1 May 1954; Mark Lewis, Daily Worker, 1 May 1954; Beverly Baxter, Evening Standard, 29 April 1954; C. A. Lejeune, Observer, 2 May 1954; Roy Nash, Star, 30 April 1954.

53. Simsi, Ciné-Passions, 131. Figaro, 17 June 1954; Robert Chazal, Paris-Presse / L'Intransigeant, 24 June 1954.

54. The Daily Herald reported its budget as £225,000; 25 June 1954. The film had a limited release in the United States under the title Land of Fury.

55. D. R., To-Day's Cinema News, 23 June 1954.

56. Peter Limbrick reports that no Maori woman would play the role; see his Making Settler Cinemas: Film and Colonial Encounters in the United States, Australia, and New Zealand (New York: Palgrave Macmillan, 2010), 189.

57. See James Belich, Making Peoples: A History of New Zealanders, from Polynesian

Settlement to the End of the Nineteenth Century (Honolulu: University of Hawaii Press, 1996), 159.

58. John Fitzpatrick, "Food, Warfare and the Impact of Atlantic Capitalism in Aotearo/ New Zealand," *Australasian Political Studies Association Conference: APSA 2004 Conference Papers*, 17–18; online at https://www.adelaide.edu.au/apsa/docs_papers/Others/Fitzpatrick .pdf.

59. See Belich, *Making Peoples*, 148, 187–98.

60. "G.F.D. Presents 'The Seekers,'" *To-Day's Cinema News*, 22 June 1954, 3.

61. Ibid.

62. Josh Billings, *Kinematograph Weekly*, 24 June 1954, 82.

63. D. R., *To-Day's Cinema News*, 23 June 1954.

64. The two positive reviews were Josh Billings, *Kinematograph Weekly*, 24 June 1954; and D. R., *To-Day's Cinema News*, 23 June 1954.

Negative: Paul Holt, *Daily Herald*, 25 June 1954; Mark Lewis, *Daily Worker*, 26 June 1954; Derwent May, *Financial Times*, 28 June 1954; *London Times*, 28 June 1954; D. R. *Monthly Film Bulletin*, no. 247; *Manchester Guardian*, 26 June 1954; Virginia Graham, *Spectator*, 25 June 1954; Cyril Ray, *Sunday Times*, 27 June 1954; Fred Majdalany, *Time and Tide*, 3 July 1954.

Chapter 3 · Westerns

1. See Julian Go, *Patterns of Empire: The British and American Empires, 1688 to the Present* (Cambridge: Cambridge University Press, 2011), 1–4; Jeffrey Ostler, *The Plains Sioux and U. S. Colonialism from Lewis and Clark to Wounded Knee* (Cambridge: Cambridge University Press, 2004), 17. Thomas E. Sheridan says the railroad made Arizona "an extractive colony of the United States"; see his *Arizona: A History* (Tucson: University of Arizona Press, 1995), 122.

2. William Cronon, George Miles, and Jay Gitlin, "Becoming West: Toward a New Meaning for Western History," in *Under an Open Sky: Rethinking America's Western Past*, ed. William Cronon, George Miles, and Jay Gitlin (New York: W. W. Norton, 1992), 275n.2.

3. Edwin R. Sweeney, *Cochise: Chiricahua Apache Chief* (Norman: University of Oklahoma Press, 1991), 128.

4. Elliott West, *The Contested Plains: Indians, Goldseekers, and the Rush to Colorado* (Lawrence: University Press of Kansas, 1998), 92, 312; Robert Wooster, *The Military and United States Indian Policy, 1865–1903* (Lincoln: University of Nebraska Press, 1988), 215; see also Robert M. Utley, *The Indian Frontier of the American West, 1846–1890* (Albuquerque: University of New Mexico Press, 1984), xix.

5. Sheridan, *Arizona*, 66; Odie B. Faulk, *Crimson Desert: Indian Wars of the American Southwest* (New York: Oxford University Press, 1974), 200–201; Utley, *Indian Frontier*, 8.

6. On painter Frederic Remington's admiring view of Indians, see Richard Slotkin, *Gunfighter Nation: The Myth of the Frontier in Twentieth-Century America* (New York: Atheneum, 1992), 96; Brian W. Dippie notes that Indians were less likely to be objects of laughter than were African Americans; see *The Vanishing American: White Attitudes and U.S. Indian Policy* (Lawrence: University Press of Kansas, 1982), 88–89, 91–92.

7. On positive attitudes toward mixing with Indians, see Dippie, *Vanishing American*, 248–50; on Henry Dodge, see Utley, *Indian Frontier*, 49. On whites taking pride in imagined Indian ancestors, see Elizabeth Stone, *Black Sheep and Kissing Cousins: How Our*

Family Stories Shape Us (New York: Penguin, 1988), 188. On playing Indian, see Philip J. DeLoria, *Playing Indian* (New Haven, CT: Yale University Press, 1998); Edward Buscombe, *Injuns! Native Americans in the Movies* (London: Reaktion, 2006), 168; Rayna Green, "The Tribe Called Wannabee: Playing Indian in America and Europe," *Folklore* 99:1 (1988): 30–55; Michelle H. Raheja, *Reservation Reelism: Redfacing, Visual Sovereignty, and Representations of Native Americans in Film* (Lincoln: University of Nebraska Press, 2010).

8. The most vigorous argument that Americans committed genocide is in Ward Churchill, "'Nits Make Lice': The Extermination of the North American Indians, 1607–1996," in *A Little Matter of Genocide: Holocaust and Denial in the Americas, 1492 to the Present* (San Francisco: City Lights Books, 1997), 129–288. Churchill's very broad definition of genocide, which includes harming another people's culture, follows that of Raphael Lemkin, who coined the term in 1944; see "Defining the Unthinkable: Towards a Viable Understanding of Genocide," in *A Little Matter of Genocide*, 431–36. A narrower definition appears in many works, including Frank Chalk and Kurt Jonassohn, *The History and Sociology of Genocide* (New Haven, CT: Yale University Press, 1990). On the problem of definition, see Henry R. Huttenbach, "From the Editor: In Search of Genocide—(Re)focusing on the Existential," *Journal of Genocide Research*, 3:1 (2001): 7–9; Scott Straus, "Contested Meanings and Conflicting Imperatives: A Conceptual Analysis of Genocide," *Journal of Genocide Research* 3:3 (2001): 349–75. On revulsion at massacres, see Utley, *Indian Frontier*, 96; Jeffry D. Wert, *Custer: The Controversial Life of George Armstrong Custer* (New York: Simon & Schuster, 1996), 278.

9. Sweeney, *Cochise*, 318. Ostler, *Plains Sioux*, 168 uses "cultural genocide"; "ethnocidal" is in Ella Shohat and Robert Stam, *Unthinking Eurocentrism: Multiculturalism and the Media* (London: Routledge, 1994), 32.

10. Dippie, *Vanishing American*, 351, 353.

11. Robert F. Berkhofer, Jr., *The White Man's Indian: Images of the American Indian from Columbus to the Present* (New York: Vintage, 1979), 193; Richard J. Perry, *Apache Reservation: Indigenous Peoples and the American State* (Austin: University of Texas Press, 1993), 234. Perry reports that in 1982 "about 75 percent of the population on both of the major Western Apache reservations were able to speak the language"; see Perry, 163. Ostler describes the hardships of the boarding schools but concludes they "did not destroy Indian identity"; see Ostler, *Plains Sioux*, 153, 160.

12. On the termination policy, see Donald L. Fixico, *Termination and Relocation: Federal Indian Policy, 1945–1960* (Albuquerque: University of New Mexico Press, 1986); Roberta Ulrich, *American Indian Nations from Termination to Restoration, 1953–2006* (Lincoln: University of Nebraska Press, 2010); Steve Neale, "Vanishing Americans: Racial and Ethnic Issues in the Interpretation and Context of Post-war 'Pro-Indian' Westerns," in *Back in the Saddle Again: New Essays on the Western*, ed. Edward Buscombe and Roberta E. Pearson (London: British Film Institute, 1998), 18–21.

13. On these images, see Francis Paul Prucha, *The Great Father: The United States Government and the American Indians*, abridged ed. (Lincoln: University of Nebraska Press, 1984), 2; Richard Slotkin, *The Fatal Environment: The Myth of the Frontier in the Age of Industrialization, 1800–1890* (Norman: University of Oklahoma Press, 1985), 53; Utley, *Indian Frontier*, 34; Buscombe, *Injuns!*, 42–43; Gretchen M. Bataille and Charles L. P. Silet, "Introduction," in *The Pretend Indians: Images of Native Americans in the Movies*, ed. Gretchen M. Bataille and Charles L. P. Silet (Ames: Iowa State University Press, 1980), xxi;

Margo Kasdan and Susan Tavernetti, "Native Americans in a Revisionist Western: *Little Big Man*," in *Hollywood's Indian: The Portrayal of the Native American in Film*, ed. Peter C. Rollins and John E. O'Connor (Lexington: University Press of Kentucky, 1998), 122; Berkhofer, *White Man's Indian*, 28.

14. Dippie, *Vanishing American*, 6.

15. John A. Price, "The Stereotyping of North American Indians in Motion Pictures," in Bataille and Silet, *Pretend Indians*, 87; see also Ward Churchill, Mary Anne Hill, and Norbert S. Hill, Jr., "Examination of Stereotyping: An Analytical Survey of Twentieth-Century Indian Entertainers," in *Pretend Indians*, 37.

16. Tom Engelhardt, *The End of Victory Culture: Cold War America and the Disillusioning of a Generation* (New York: Basic Books, 1995), 41.

17. Sweeney, *Cochise*, 160; Wooster, *The Military and United States Indian Policy*, 165; Wert, *Custer*, 257; Utley, *Indian Frontier*, 161.

18. Wooster, *The Military and United States Indian Policy*, 127; Faulk, *Crimson Desert*, 71, 82, 137; Perry, *Apache Reservation*, 101, 106; Utley, *Indian Frontier*, 84, 160, 169; West, *Contested Plains*, 280; Sheridan, *Arizona*, 70; Prucha, *Great Father*, 175.

19. Faulk, *Crimson Desert*, 32.

20. Utley, *Indian Frontier*, 161; West, *Contested Plains*, 153.

21. Berkhofer, *White Man's Indian*, 167; Prucha, *Great Father*, 179; Utley, *Indian Frontier*, 170.

22. J. Hoberman, *The Dream Life: Movies, Media and the Mythology of the Sixties* (New York: New Press, 2003), 127; Michael Coyne, *The Crowded Prairie: American National Identity in the Hollywood Western* (London: I. B. Tauris, 1998), 3, 34; Douglas Pye, "Miscegenation and Point of View in *The Searchers*," in *The Book of Westerns*, ed. Ian Cameron and Douglas Pye (New York: Continuum, 1996), 229.

23. Angela Aleiss, *Making the White Man's Indian: Native Americans and Hollywood Movies* (Westport, CT: Praeger, 2005), 2, 62, 65–71; John H. Lenihan, *Showdown: Confronting Modern America in the Western Film* (Urbana: University of Illinois Press, 1980), 23; Wilcomb Washburn, "Foreword," in Rollins and O'Connor, *Hollywood's Indian*, ix.

24. See Neale, "Vanishing Americans," 15; Thomas Cripps, *Making Movies Black: The Hollywood Message Movie from World War II to the Civil Rights Era* (New York: Oxford University Press, 1993), 175, sees the late 1940s as "a classic case of thermidor" (a return to conservatism); also denying a liberal trend in westerns are M. Elise Marubbio, *Killing the Indian Maiden: Images of Native American Women in Film* (Lexington: University Press of Kentucky, 2006), 65; Churchill, Hill, and Hill, Jr., "Examination of Stereotyping," in Bataille and Silet, *Pretend Indians*, 39; see also Ward Churchill, *Fantasies of the Master Race: Literature, Cinema and the Colonization of the American Indians* (San Francisco: City Lights Books, 1998), 189–90. For a contrary view, see Buscombe, *Injuns!*, 118–19; critic Stephen Handzo argued in 1970 that all westerns since the 1950s *Broken Arrow* were pro-Indian; see *Village Voice*, 10 September 1970.

25. Lary May, *The Big Tomorrow: Hollywood and the Politics of the American Way* (Chicago: University of Chicago Press, 2000), 221; Aleiss, *Making the White Man's Indian*, 89.

26. Positive: Elinor Hughes, *Boston Herald*, 5 December 1947; Mae Tinee, *Chicago Tribune*, 18 October 1947; Fairfax Nisbet, *Dallas Morning News*, 31 October 1947; *Film Daily*, 24 September 1947; *Hollywood Reporter*, 24 September 1947; Edwin Schallert, *Los Angeles Times*, 26 November 1947; James D. Ivers, *Motion Picture Herald*, 27 September 1947; Kate

Cameron, *New York Daily News*, 11 October 1947; Archer Winsten, *New York Post*, 11 October 1947; Gene Peach, *San Diego Union*, 7 January 1948.

Negative: Moira Walsh, *America*, 18 October 1947; Philip T. Hartung, *Commonweal*, 24 October 1947; *Newsweek*, 13 October 1947; John Hobart, *San Francisco Chronicle*, 8 November 1947; Myles Standish, *St. Louis Post-Dispatch*, 18 December 1947; Abel., *Variety*, 24 September 1947; Richard L. Coe, *Washington Post*, 8 January 1948.

Mixed: Marjory Adams, *Boston Globe*, 5 December 1947; Al Weitschat, *Detroit News*, 31 October 1947; Bosley Crowther, *New York Times*, 11 October 1947; Mildred Martin, *Philadelphia Inquirer*, 26 December 1947; *Time*, 27 October 1947.

27. On Custer imagery, see Coyne, *Crowded Prairie*, 59; Steve Neale, "'The Story of Custer in Everything but Name?' Col. Thursday and Fort Apache," *Journal of Film and Video* 47:1–3 (Spring/Fall 1995): 26–32.

28. *Variety*, 5 January 1949.

29. The U.S. reviews, all 1948: Positive: Marjory Adams, *Boston Globe*, 21 May; Elinor Hughes, *Boston Herald*, 21 May; Mae Tinee, *Chicago Tribune*, 1 April; John Rosenfield, *Dallas Morning News*, 29 April; John Finlayson, *Detroit News*, 29 May; Luther Rowsey, *Houston Post*, 29 April; Neil Rau, *Los Angeles Examiner*, 28 May; Edwin Schallert, *Los Angeles Times*, 28 May; R. K., *Motion Picture Herald*, 13 March; Ed Brooks, *New Orleans Times-Picayune*, 13 May; *Newsweek*, 17 May; Kate Cameron, *New York Daily News*, 25 June; Bosley Crowther, *New York Times*, 25 June; John Hobart, *San Francisco Chronicle*, 14 May; Brog., *Variety*, 10 March.

Negative: Philip T. Hartung, *Commonweal*, 11 June; Jesse Zunser, *Cue*, 26 June; Archer Winsten, *New York Post*, 25 June; Myles Standish, *St. Louis Post-Dispatch*, 9 July; *Time*, 10 May; Richard L. Coe, *Washington Post*, 13 May.

Mixed or neutral: *Film Daily*, 10 March; R.E.S., *Hartford Courant*, 15 July; *Hollywood Reporter*, 10 March; *Motion Picture Daily*, 10 March; John McCarten, *New Yorker*, 3 July; Mildred Martin, *Philadelphia Inquirer*, 22 April; Gene Peach, *San Diego Union*, 9 June.

30. The British reviews (all 1948): Positive: *Daily Graphic*, 25 June; *Daily Telegraph*, 28 June; *Star*, 25 June; M. T. McGregor, *Time and Tide*, 3 July.

Negative: *Daily Worker*, 26 June; *Evening News*, 24 June; *People*, 27 June.

Mixed or neutral: *Daily Express*, 25 June; *Daily Herald*, 28 June; Fred Majdalany, *Daily Mail*, no date in British Film Institute clippings file; *Daily Mirror*, 25 June; Milton Shulman, *Evening Standard*, 25 June; *Kinematograph Weekly*, 24 June; *Manchester Guardian*, 26 June; *Monthly Film Bulletin*, no. 175, 31 July; *New Chronicle*, 26 June; William Whitebait, *New Statesman*, 3 July; Virginia Graham, *Spectator*, 2 July.

31. Simon Simsi, *Ciné-Passions: 7e art et industrie de 1945 à 2000* (Paris: Dixit, 2000), 96; the French reviews (all from 1948): Positive: Denis Marion, *Combat*, 28 August; Jean-Jacques Gautier, *Figaro*, 9 July (from Locarno Film Festival); Louis Chauvet, *Figaro*, 20 August; Jean-Pierre Barrot, *Franc-Tireur*, 22 August; Jeander, *Libération*, 26 August; Georges Charensol, *Nouvelles Littéraires*, 26 August; Jacqueline Michel, *Parisien Libéré*, 25 August.

Mixed: *Lettres Françaises*, 30 September; A. F., *Monde*, 26 August.

32. Ford interview with Philip Jenkinson, quoted in Tag Gallagher, *John Ford: The Man and His Films* (Berkeley: University of California Press, 1986), 254.

33. Lenihan, *Showdown*, 27; see also Ken Nolley, "The Representation of Conquest: John Ford and the Hollywood Indian," in Rollins and O'Connor, *Hollywood's Indian*, 84–85; Kathleen A. McDonough, "Wee Willie Winkie Goes West: The Influence of the British

Empire Genre on Ford's Cavalry Trilogy," in *Hollywood's West: The American Frontier in Film, Television, and History*, ed. Peter C. Rollins and John E. O'Connor (Lexington: University Press of Kentucky, 2005), 99–114.

34. Slotkin, *Gunfighter Nation*, 360–61; see Lenihan, *Showdown*, 30–31.

35. See Gallagher, *John Ford*, 531; on the 1947 hearings, see Larry Ceplair and Steven Englund, *The Inquisition in Hollywood: Politics in the Film Community, 1930–1960* (Berkeley: University of California Press, 1979), 257–71.

36. Quoted in Gallagher, *John Ford*, 340.

37. Gallagher says Ford was "basically apolitical"; see Gallagher, *John Ford*, 339; see also Scott Eyman, *Print the Legend: The Life and Times of John Ford* (New York: Simon & Schuster, 1999), 511.

38. *Variety*, 3 January 1951.

39. On Daves, see Cripps, *Making Movies Black*, 281.

40. Philip K. Scheuer, "Indian's Culture Captured in Film," *Los Angeles Times*, 21 May 1950.

41. Sheridan, *Arizona*, 88–89; Frank Manchel, "Cultural Confusion: *Broken Arrow*," in *Hollywood's Indian: The Portrayal of the Native American in Film*, ed. Peter C. Rollins and John E. O'Connor (Lexington: University Press of Kentucky, 1998), 95, 99–100.

42. Stewart is on the list of the ten most profitable stars for 1946–50, 1951–55, and 1956–60; see Paul Kerr, "Stars and Stardom," in *Anatomy of the Movies*, ed. David Pirie (New York: Macmillan, 1981), 109.

43. Rayna Green, "The Pocahontas Perplex: The Image of Indian Women in American Culture," *Massachusetts Review* 16:4 (Autumn 1975): 698–714; see also Marubbio, *Killing the Indian Maiden*, 6–15.

44. Churchill, Hill, and Hill, "Examination of Stereotyping," in Bataille and Silet, *Pretend Indians*, 39. See also Slotkin, *Gunfighter Nation*, 376.

45. Aleiss, *Making the White Man's Indian*, 81; Peter Biskind, *Seeing Is Believing: How Hollywood Taught Us to Stop Worrying and Love the Fifties* (New York: Owl Books, 1983), 236; Buscombe, *Injuns!*, 116; seeing a desire to erase Indian identity is Aleiss, 90–91.

46. Biskind, *Seeing Is Believing*, 238.

47. Buscombe, *Injuns!*, 109, writes that the film favors "the reservation system as a humane solution to the Indian 'problem.'"

48. Biskind, *Seeing Is Believing*, 240, 228; Cripps, *Making Movies Black*, 281; Lenihan, *Showdown*, 25–27; Slotkin, *Gunfighter Nation*, 347–78; Brian Henderson, "*The Searchers*: An American Dilemma," in *Movies and Methods: An Anthology*, vol. 2, ed. Bill Nichols (Berkeley: University of California Press, 1985), 443–49; Joanna Hearne, "The 'Ache for Home': Assimilation and Separatism in Anthony Mann's *Devil's Doorway*," in *Hollywood's West: The American Frontier in Film, Television, and History*, ed. Peter C. Rollins and John E. O'Connor (Lexington: University Press of Kentucky, 2005), 127.

49. Coyne, *Crowded Prairie*, 70.

50. The U. S. reviews (all in 1950): Positive: Moira Walsh, *America*, 29 July; Paul Jones, *Atlanta Constitution*, 25 August; Ben Gardiner, *Boston Herald*, 16 August; Mae Tinee, *Chicago Tribune*, 29 August; Philip T. Hartung, *Commonweal*, 4 August; Jesse Zunser, *Cue*, 22 July; John Rosenfield, *Dallas Morning News*, 24 August; Jose Yglesias, *Daily Worker* (New York), 21 July; Al Weitschat, *Detroit News*, 25 August; *Film Daily*, 14 June; H.V.A., *Hartford Courant*, 17 August; *Hollywood Reporter*, 12 June; George Christian, *Houston Post*, 13 Au-

gust; *Life*, 14 August; Ruth Waterbury, *Los Angeles Examiner*, 19 August; Philip K. Scheuer, *Los Angeles Times*, 19 August; George Bourke, *Miami Herald*, 17 August; B.J.P., *Milwaukee Journal*, 17 August; Buck Herzog, *Milwaukee Sentinel*, 19 August; Fred Hift, *Motion Picture Herald*, 17 June; Robert Hatch, *New Republic*, 31 July; *Newsweek*, 7 August; Kate Cameron, *New York Daily News*, 21 July; Archer Winsten, *New York Post*, 21 July; Mildred Martin, *Philadelphia Inquirer*, 22 July; John Hobart, *San Francisco Chronicle*, 19 August; *Time*, 31 July; Bron. *Variety*, 14 June; Richard L. Coe, *Washington Post*, 31 August.

Negative: B.R.C., *Christian Science Monitor*, 16 August; John McCarten, *New Yorker*, 22 July; Bosley Crowther, *New York Times*, 21 July; Myles Standish, *St. Louis Post-Dispatch*, 18 August.

Mixed or neutral: Marjory Adams, *Boston Globe*, 16 August; Elise Beauchamp, *New Orleans Times-Picayune*, 18 August; Robert Gessner, *Saturday Review*, 5 August; T.A.W., *Wall Street Journal*, 27 July.

51. Simsi, *Ciné-Passions*, 64.

52. Positive: J. Leasor, *Daily Express*, 26 August; P. L. Mannock, *Daily Herald*, 25 August; Fred Majdalany, *Daily Mail*, 25 August; Reg Whitley, *Daily Mirror*, 25 August; *Daily Worker*, 26 August; Jympson Harman, *Evening News*, 24 August; V. G., *Evening Standard*, 24 August; *London Times*, 28 August; *Manchester Guardian*, 26 August; Richard Winnington, *News Chronicle*, 26 August; Ewart Hodgson, *News of the World*, 27 August; C. A. Lejeune, *Observer*, 27 August; *Scotsman*, 10 October; Roy Nash, *Star*, 26 August; Logan Gourlay, *Sunday Express*, 27 August; *Sunday Graphic*, 27 August; *Sunday Pictorial*, 27 August.

Negative: Patrick Gibbs, *Daily Telegraph*, 28 August.

Mixed or neutral: William Whitebait, *New Statesman*, 2 September; *Tribune*, 1 September; Margaret Hinxman, *Time and Tide*, 2 September.

53. Jeanine Basinger, *Anthony Mann* (Middletown, Ct.: Wesleyan University Press, 2007), 72.

54. See Hearne, "The 'Ache for Home,'" 139.

55. *Daily Variety*, 15 May 1950; W.R.W., *Motion Picture Herald*, 6 May 1950; Brog., *Variety*, 17 May 1950.

56. Ad in the *Houston Post*, 29 September 1950.

57. The U. S. reviews (all from 1950): Positive: *Film Daily*, 18 May; M.O.S., *Hartford Courant*, 10 November; Ezra Goodman, *Los Angeles Daily News*, 21 October; Shirle Duggan, *Los Angeles Examiner*, 21 October; George H. Jackson, *Los Angeles Herald & Express*, 21 October; Edwin Schallert, *Los Angeles Times*, 21 October; Wanda Hale, *New York Daily News*, 10 November; Archer Winsten, *New York Post*, 10 November; Bosley Crowther, *New York Times*, 10 November.

Negative: Marjory Adams, *Boston Globe*, 20 October; Mae Tinee, *Chicago Tribune*, 30 September; Jesse Zunser, *Cue*, 11 November; *Hollywood Reporter*, 15 May; *Time*, 9 October; Brog., *Variety*, 17 May.

Mixed or neutral: Moira Walsh, *America*, 25 November; *Boston Herald*, 20 October; H. R., *Christian Science Monitor*, 20 October; Philip T. Hartung, *Commonweal*, 24 November; Richard Harrington, *Houston Post*, 24 September; William R. Weaver, *Motion Picture Herald*, 6 May; *San Francisco Chronicle*, 1 October; Myles Standish, *St. Louis Post-Dispatch*, 16 October.

58. *Christian Science Monitor*, *Film Daily*, *Los Angeles Daily News*, *Los Angeles Examiner*, *New York Daily News*, *New York Post*, *New York Times*, *St. Louis Post-Dispatch*.

59. Also complaining about the casting were the *Boston Herald, Chicago Tribune, Christian Science Monitor, New York Post, St. Louis Post-Dispatch,* and *Variety.*
60. *Variety,* 2 January 1952.
61. The U.S. reviews (all from 1951): Positive: Marjory Adams, *Boston Globe,* 15 February; R.S.T., *Boston Herald,* 15 February; Philip T. Hartung, *Commonweal,* 2 March; *Hollywood Reporter,* 8 January; Ruth Waterbury, *Los Angeles Examiner,* 22 February; John L. Scott, *Los Angeles Times,* 22 February; Robert McDonald, *San Diego Union,* 22 March; Luther Nichols, *San Francisco Chronicle,* 2 February; Brog., *Variety,* 10 January.

Negative: Moira Walsh, *America,* 24 February; Mae Tinee, *Chicago Tribune,* 29 January; Jesse Zunser, *Cue,* 17 February; Archer Winsten, *New York Post,* 19 February; Bosley Crowther, *New York Times,* 19 February.

Mixed: *Box Office,* 13 January 1951; E.F.M. *Christian Science Monitor,* 15 February; John Rosenfield, *Dallas Morning News,* 10 May; *Film Daily,* 8 January; Ann Helming, *Hollywood Citizen News,* 22 February; Floyd Stone, *Motion Picture Herald,* 13 January; Wanda Hale, *New York Daily News,* 18 February; Richard L. Coe, *Washington Post,* 13 February.

62. Kate Buford, *Burt Lancaster: An American Life* (New York: Alfred Knopf, 2000), 137; Lenihan, *Showdown,* 57.
63. Joseph A. Breen letter to Harold Hecht, 26 September 1952, Production Files, Motion Picture Association of America, Production Code Administration Records, *Apache,* 1952–54, Herrick Library, Academy of Motion Picture Arts and Sciences (AMPAS), Beverly Hills, CA.
64. "Robert Aldrich, Interviewed by Joel Greenberg," *Sight and Sound* 38:1 (Winter 1968–69): 9.
65. Buford, *Burt Lancaster,* 137.
66. Joseph A. Breen letter to Harold Hecht, 26 September 1952, Production Files, Motion Picture Association of America, Production Code Administration Records, *Apache,* 1952–54, Herrick Library, AMPAS.
67. Biskind, *Seeing Is Believing,* 245; Aleiss, *Making the White Man's Indian,* 95.
68. Perry, *Apache Reservation,* 61, 80; West, *Contested Plains,* 39.
69. *Variety,* 5 January 1955. U. S. reviews (all 1954): Positive: Elinor Hughes, *Boston Herald,* 5 July; Harold Rogers, *Christian Science Monitor,* 6 July; Jesse Zunser, *Cue,* 10 July; Rual Askew, *Dallas Morning News,* 19 August; Alex Murphree, *Denver Post,* 14 July; Al Weitschat, *Detroit News,* 1 July; *Film Daily,* 7 July; M.O.S., *Hartford Courant,* 5 July; Gene Miller, *Houston Post,* 13 August; Ruth Waterbury, *Los Angeles Examiner,* 22 July; Marion Atchison, *Miami Herald,* 6 August; *Motion Picture Daily,* 30 June; Mandel Herbstman, *Motion Picture Herald,* 3 July; Herman S. Kohlman, *New Orleans Times-Picayune,* 3 July; Dorothy Masters, *New York Daily News,* 10 July; Archer Winsten, *New York Post,* 11 July; John Springer, *San Diego Union,* 19 August; William Hogan, *San Francisco Chronicle,* 2 July; Leo Sullivan, *Washington Post,* 23 July.

Negative: Mae Tinee, *Chicago Tribune,* 7 July; Jack Moffitt, *Hollywood Reporter,* 30 June; Philip K. Scheuer, *Los Angeles Times,* 22 July; Howard H. Thompson, *New York Times,* 10 July; Mildred Martin, *Philadelphia Inquirer,* 26 July; *Time,* 9 August.

Mixed or neutral: Marjory Adams, *Boston Globe,* 5 July; Philip T. Hartung, *Commonweal,* 30 July; Myles Standish, *St. Louis Post-Dispatch,* 30 July; Brog., *Variety,* 30 June.

70. See *Christian Science Monitor, Denver Post, Detroit News, Houston Post, Miami Herald, Motion Picture Herald, New York Post.*

71. All reviews are 1954. Positive: Reg Whitley, *Daily Mirror*, 27 August; *London Times*, 30 August; L.G.A., *Monthly Film Bulletin*, July–August, p. 126; William Whitebait, *New Statesman*, 4 September.

Negative: C. A. Lejeune, *Observer*, 29 August.

Mixed or neutral: Patrick Gibbs, *Daily Telegraph*, 28 August; Janet Wilson, *Daily Worker*, 28 August.

72. Simsi, *Ciné-Passions*, 23. The French reviews (all from 1955): Positive: Jean Rochereau, *Croix*, 25 February; André Bazin, *France Observateur*, 29 February; Jean Néry, *Franc-Tireur*, 23 February; Georges Sadoul, *Humanité*, 26 February; André Bazin, *Parisien Libéré*, 23 February.

Negative: Louis Chauvet, *Figaro*, 22 February; Jean-Paul Faure, *Paris-Presse/L'Intransigeant*, 25 February.

Mixed: *Canard Enchaîné*, 2 March; Paule Sengissen, *Radio Cinéma Télévision*, 27 February.

73. *Variety*, 2 January 1957; "Richard Brooks," *Movie* 12 (Spring 1965): 2–9; the article is a compilation of interviews by Ian Cameron, Mark Shivas, Paul Mayersberg, and V. F. Perkins.

74. The U.S. reviews (all from 1956): Positive: Hazel Flynn, *Beverly Hills Citizen*, 23 February; R.S.T., *Boston Herald*, 21 February; *Box Office*, 18 February; Mae Tinee, *Chicago Tribune*, 8 May; Philip T. Hartung, *Commonweal*, 16 March; Jesse Zunser, *Cue*, 10 March; *Film Bulletin*, 20 February; *Film Daily*, 15 February; Marion Atchison, *Miami Herald*, 1 March; *Motion Picture Exhibitor*, 22 February; Samuel D. Berns, *Motion Picture Herald*, 18 February; Wanda Hale, *New York Daily News*, 1 March; Archer Winsten, *New York Post*, 1 March; Myles Standish, *St. Louis Post-Dispatch*, 1 March; Gene., *Variety*, 15 February.

Negative: Al Weitschat, *Detroit News*, 1 April; Jack Moffitt, *Hollywood Reporter*, 14 February; Sara Hamilton, *Los Angeles Examiner*, 23 February; Philip K. Scheuer, *Los Angeles Times*, 23 February; *Newsweek*, 27 February; *Time*, 5 March.

Mixed or neutral: Moira Walsh, *America*, 10 March; Marjory Adams, *Boston Globe*, 21 February; Frank Gagnard, *Dallas Morning News*, 23 March; Bob Tweedell, *Denver Post*, 15 March; *New Yorker*, 10 March; Bosley Crowther, *New York Times*, 4 March; Paine Knickerbocker, *San Francisco Chronicle*, 20 March; Richard L. Coe, *Washington Post*, 24 February.

75. The British reviews (all from 1956): Positive: *Daily Worker*, 21 April; Jympson Harman, *Evening News*, 19 April; *London Times*, 23 April; *Manchester Guardian*, 21 April; T.J.B., *Monthly Film Bulletin*, no. 269, April–May; Peter Burnup, *News of the World*, 22 April; *Star*, 20 April; Dilys Powell, *Sunday Times*, 22 April.

Negative: Leonard Mosley, *Daily Express*, 20 April; Paul Dehn, *News Chronicle*, 20 April; C. A. Lejeune, *Observer*, 22 April.

Mixed or neutral: *Daily Herald*, 20 April; *Daily Mail*, 20 April; Reg Whitley, *Daily Mirror*, 20 April; Campbell Dixon, *Daily Telegraph*, 21 April; Alan Brien, *Evening Standard*, 19 April; *Times Educational Supplement*, 4 May.

76. Simsi, *Ciné-Passions*, 45. The French reviews: Positive: Claude de Givray, *Cahiers du Cinéma*, no. 74, August–September 1957, 55; Marcel Martin, *Cinéma 57*, September–October 1957, 109–10; Jean Rochereau, *Croix*, 20 July 1957; André Bazin, *France Observateur*, 18 July 1957; W. Giboud, *France Soir*, 21 July 1957; Denis Marion, *Franc-Tireur*, 24 July 1957; *Humanité Dimanche*, 21 July 1957; Christian Rémédy, *Lettres Françaises*, 8 August; André Bazin, *Parisien Libéré*, 12 July; Marcel Ranchal, *Positif*, no. 29, Rentrée [i.e., September] 1958,

35–38; Luc Moullet, *Radio Cinéma Télévision*, 21 July; Roger Fressoz, *Témoignage Chrétien*, 9 August.

Mixed: Eric Rohmer, *Arts*, 17 July.

77. Slotkin, *Gunfighter Nation*, 323–26.

78. David N. Eldridge, "'Dear Owen': The CIA, Luigi Luraschi, and Hollywood, 1953," *Historical Journal of Film, Radio and Television* 20:2 (June 2000): letter 1 (24 January 1953), 159–60, and letter 6 (6 February 1953), 169. See also May, *Big Tomorrow*, 208–9; Frances Stonor Saunders, *The Cultural Cold War: The CIA and the World of Arts and Letters* (New York: New Press, 2000), 290–91.

79. *Variety*, 13 January 1954. Positive: John William Riley, *Boston Globe*, 6 August 1953; Elinor Hughes, *Boston Herald*, 6 August 1953; Steele Hooper, *Dallas Morning News*, 18 February 1954; Alex Murphree, *Denver Post*, 17 August 1953; *Film Daily*, 24 June 1953; M.O.S., *Hartford Courant*, 19 September 1953; Milton Luban, *Hollywood Reporter*, 15 June 1953; Sara Hamilton, *Los Angeles Examiner*, 10 September 1953; Philip K. Scheuer, *Los Angeles Times*, 10 September 1953; Vincent Canby, *Motion Picture Herald*, 20 June 1953; Kermit Tarleton, *New Orleans Times-Picayune*, 17 August 1953; Kate Cameron, *New York Daily News*, 16 September 1953; Archer Winsten, *New York Post*, 16 September 1953; Mildred Martin, *Philadelphia Inquirer*, 17 September 1953; Brog., *Variety*, 17 June 1953.

Negative: Bosley Crowther, *New York Times*, 16 September 1953; William Hogan, *San Francisco Chronicle*, 3 October 1953; Orval Hopkins, *Washington Post*, 21 August 1953.

Mixed or neutral: Moira Walsh, *America*, 19 September 1953; Paul Jones, *Atlanta Constitution*, 11 September 1953; Mae Tinee, *Chicago Tribune*, 25 September 1953; Rod Nordell, *Christian Science Monitor*, 6 August 1953; George H. Jackson, *Los Angeles Herald & Express*, 10 September 1953; *Newsweek*, 14 September 1953; Otis L. Guernsey, Jr., *New York Herald Tribune*, 16 September 1953.

80. *Variety*, 2 January 1952.

81. Ford quoted in Gallagher, *John Ford*, 333.

82. Geoffrey M. Shurlock letter to John Ford, 20 June 1955, in *History of Cinema: Hollywood and the Production Code*, reel 30, Herrick Library, AMPAS.

83. Robert Hatch, *Nation*, 23 June 1956, 536.

84. Arthur M. Eckstein, "Introduction: The Main Critical Issues in *The Searchers*," in *"The Searchers": Essays and Reflections on John Ford's Classic Western*, ed. Arthur Eckstein and Peter Lehman (Detroit: Wayne State University Press, 2004), 3. See also Coyne, *Crowded Prairie*, 52.

85. Slotkin, *Gunfighter Nation*, 463.

86. Gallagher, *John Ford*, 341.

87. Aleiss, *Making the White Man's Indian*, 104, calls the film "undeniably racist" and sees it urging extermination. Biskind, *Seeing Is Believing*, 242, sees it rejecting tolerance and teaching violence, through Martin's eventual killing of Scar.

88. Faulk emphasizes the brutality of the Comanche, for whom "the torturing of prisoners was a prime source of entertainment," and he calls Texan John Robert Baylor an example of "fanatical frontiersmen . . . determined to exterminate the Indians"; see Faulk, *Crimson Desert*, 23, 27, 105.

89. Pye, "Miscegenation and Point of View in *The Searchers*," 233.

90. For examples of those who have objected to the film's treatment of Look, see Green, "Pocahontas Perplex," 711; Marubbio, *Killing the Indian Maiden*, 150–51; Pye, "Miscegena-

tion and Point of View in *The Searchers*," 231–33; Glenn Frankel, *"The Searchers": The Making of an American Legend* (New York: Bloomsbury, 2013), 311–12; Peter Lehman, "Psychoanalysis and Style in John Ford's *The Searchers*," in *The Western Reader*, ed. Jim Kitses and Gregg Rickman (New York: Limelight, 1998), 259–68.

91. Gallagher, *John Ford*, 333; Pye, "Miscegenation and Point of View in *The Searchers*," 229–30; Frankel, *"The Searchers*," 312.

92. Eckstein, "Introduction," 12–13, notes that this was Hollywood's first such imagery of a massacre of Indians.

93. Gallagher, *John Ford*, 333.

94. Noting that it is Martin who kills Scar, Eckstein denies that Ethan is a protector, but this dismisses his vital role in finding Scar; see Eckstein, "Introduction," 26.

95. *Variety*, 2 January 1957.

96. Drew Casper, *Postwar Hollywood, 1946–1962* (Malden, MA: Blackwell, 2007), 345, writes that "the film was dismissed by the industry and critics"; Marubbio, *Killing the Indian Maiden*, 151, says it received "lackluster reviews"; see also Eckstein, "Introduction," 33.

97. The U.S. reviews (all 1956): Positive: Paul Jones, *Atlanta Constitution*, 1 June; Marjory Adams, *Boston Globe*, 31 May; Elinor Hughes, *Boston Herald*, 31 May; Mae Tinee, *Chicago Tribune*, 17 May; Jesse Zunser, *Cue*, 2 June; Bob Tweedell, *Denver Post*, 25 May; Al Weitschat, *Detroit News*, 20 May; *Film Daily*, 13 March; Jack Moffitt, *Hollywood Reporter*, 13 March; Sara Hamilton, *Los Angeles Examiner*, 31 May; Philip K. Scheuer, *Los Angeles Times*, 18 March; George Bourke, *Miami Herald*, 5 June; G. K., *Milwaukee Journal*, 24 May; Richard Gertner, *Motion Picture Daily*, 13 March; William R. Weaver, *Motion Picture Herald*, 17 March; *Newsweek*, 21 May; Kate Cameron, *New York Daily News*, 31 May; Archer Winsten, *New York Post*, 31 May; Bosley Crowther, *New York Times*, 31 May; Edwin Martin, *San Diego Union*, 31 May; Paine Knickerbocker, *San Francisco Chronicle*, 29 May; Myles Standish, *St. Louis Post-Dispatch*, 25 May.

Negative: John Beaufort, *Christian Science Monitor*, 31 May; Philip T. Hartung, *Commonweal*, 15 June; Robert Hatch, *Nation*, 23 June; Mildred Martin, *Philadelphia Inquirer*, 24 May; Holl., *Variety*, 14 March.

Mixed or neutral: Moira Walsh, *America*, 9 June; John Rosenfield, *Dallas Morning News*, 31 May; M.O.S., *Hartford Courant*, 31 May; George Christian, *Houston Post*, 1 June; Albert Goldstein, *New Orleans Times-Picayune*, 8 June; William Zinsser, *New York Herald-Tribune*, 31 May, *Time*, 25 June.

98. *Boston Herald, Los Angeles Times, Philadelphia Inquirer, Variety*.

99. Also puzzled by Ethan were the *Chicago Tribune, Christian Science Monitor, Commonweal, Los Angeles Times, New York Herald-Tribune*, and *Philadelphia Inquirer*.

100. The British reviews (all from 1956): Positive: Leonard Mosley, *Daily Express*, 14 July; Reg Whitley, *Daily Mirror*, 27 July; Thomas Spencer, *Daily Worker*, 28 July; Jympson Harman, *Evening News*, 26 July; Alan Brien, *Evening Standard*, 26 July; *Manchester Guardian*, 28 July; J. W., *Monthly Film Bulletin*, no. 271, June–July; William Whitebait, *New Statesman*, 4 August; C. A. Lejeune, *Observer*, 29 July; Isabel Quigly, *Spectator*, 3 August; Dilys Powell, *Sunday Times*, 29 July; Fred Majdalany, *Time and Tide*, 4 August; R. D. Smith, *Tribune*, 12 October.

Negative: Harold Conway, *Daily Sketch*, 27 July; Lindsay Anderson, *Sight and Sound* 26:2 (Autumn 1956): 94–95.

Mixed: Patrick Gibbs, *Daily Telegraph*, 28 July; Eleanor Wintour, *Tribune*, 3 August.

101. Simsi, *Ciné-Passions*, 121. The French reviews (all from 1956): Positive: Jean Dutourd, *Carrefour*, 22 August; R. M. Arlaud, *Combat*, 14 August; Yves L'Her, *Croix*, 19 August; *Figaro*, 13 August; *Franc-Tireur*, 22 August; Jean de Baroncelli, *Monde*, 15 August; Jacqueline Michel, *Parisien Libéré*, 13 August; Paule Sengissen, *Radio Cinéma Télévision*, 26 August.

Negative: *Arts*, 22 August; *Humanité*, 18 August; H. M., *Lettres Françaises*, 23 August; E. S., *Paris-Presse/L'Intransigeant*, 12 August.

Mixed or neutral: *Canard Enchaîné*, 15 August.

102. Aleiss, *Making the White Man's Indian*, 101, argues that after *The Searchers*, westerns grew more pessimistic about racial coexistence, but only five films about Indians even made *Variety*'s box-office charts for the rest of the decade, and there is no pattern of pessimism in them.

Chapter 4 • The British Empire and Decolonization

1. William Roger Louis, "The Dissolution of the British Empire," in *The Oxford History of the British Empire: The Twentieth Century*, ed. Judith M. Brown and William Roger Louis (Oxford: Oxford University Press, 1999), 343–44. Historical memories of the American war of independence and the conflict in Ireland underlined the costs and drawbacks of colonial wars; see Lawrence James, *The Rise and Fall of the British Empire* (New York: St. Martin's Griffin, 1994), 543.

2. Judith M. Brown, "Epilogue," in Brown and Louis, *Oxford History: Twentieth Century*, 704, 706–7; see also John Darwin, *The End of the British Empire: The Historical Debate* (Cambridge, MA: Basil Blackwell, 1991), 1.

3. Pioneering this revisionism was John M. MacKenzie; see his *Propaganda and Empire: The Manipulation of British Public Opinion, 1880–1960* (Manchester: Manchester University Press, 1984), 2, 253; also his edited volume, *Imperialism and Popular Culture* (Manchester: Manchester University Press, 1986). For a survey of this revisionism, see Andrew Thompson, *The Empire Strikes Back? The Impact of Imperialism on Britain from the Mid-Nineteenth Century* (Harlow, UK: Pearson, 2005). Revisionist works include Catherine Hall and Sonya O. Rose, eds., *At Home with the Empire: Metropolitan Culture and the Imperial World* (Cambridge: Cambridge University Press, 2006); Andrew Thompson, ed., *Britain's Experience of Empire in the Twentieth Century* (Oxford: Oxford University Press, 2012); Stuart Ward, "Introduction," in *British Culture and the End of Empire*, ed. Stuart Ward (Manchester: Manchester University Press, 2001), 1–20. On films, see Wendy Webster, *Englishness and Empire, 1939–1965* (Oxford: Oxford University Press, 2005), 84; Jeffrey Richards, "Imperial Heroes for a Post-Imperial Age: Films and the End of Empire," in Ward, *British Culture*.

4. Bernard Porter, *The Absent-Minded Imperialists: Empire, Society, and Culture in Britain* (Oxford: Oxford University Press, 2004), ix, 5–6, 83, 93, 208, 265, 300. Also downplaying people's interest in empire are Kenneth Morgan and David Cannadine, both quoted in Ward, *British Culture*, 3.

5. MacKenzie, *Propaganda and Empire*, 162; see also Porter, *Absent-Minded Imperialists*, 192–93; Thompson, *Empire Strikes Back?*, 87. On soldiers, see James, *Rise and Fall of the British Empire*, 333; on memories, Porter, *Absent-Minded Imperialists*, 132, 215; see also MacKenzie, *Propaganda and Empire*, 253.

6. Dennis Judd, *Empire: The British Imperial Experience from 1765 to the Present* (London: Fontana, 1996), 13; Porter, *Absent-Minded Imperialists*, 267.

7. "Catching the Public's Ear," *Manchester Guardian*, 23 December 1948. See also John M. MacKenzie, "The Persistence of Empire in Metropolitan Culture," in Ward, *British Culture*, 28; Webster, *Englishness and Empire*, 4.

8. Thompson, *Empire Strikes Back?*, 207–8.

9. Bill Schwarz likens these settlers to other "beleaguered white communities" of the late 1950s, in Arkansas and Algiers; see "'The Only White Man in There': The Re-Racialisation of England, 1956–68," *Race and Class* 38:1 (July–September 1996): 68–71. Bernard Porter, *Empire and Superempire: Britain, America and the World* (New Haven, CT: Yale University Press, 2006), 44, refers to "old fogies" who wrote to the *Daily Telegraph* arguing that "Britain could have held on to her Empire if her people had shown more 'will.'" On the League of Empire Loyalists, see James, *Rise and Fall of the British Empire*, 591.

10. David Carlton, *Britain and the Suez Crisis* (Cambridge, MA: Basil Blackwell, 1989) 6; James, *Rise and Fall of the British Empire*, 577; John Darwin, *Britain and Decolonisation: The Retreat from Empire in the Postwar World* (New York: St. Martin's, 1988), 231; A. J. Stockwell, "Suez 1956 and the Moral Disarmament of the British Empire," in *Reassessing Suez 1956: New Perspectives on the Crisis and Its Aftermath*, ed. Simon C. Smith (Aldershot: Ashgate, 2008), 227; on the Commonwealth idea, see James, *Rise and Fall of the British Empire*, 556; Porter, *Absent-Minded Imperialists*, 319.

11. Nicholas Owen, "Critics of Empire in Britain," in *The Oxford History of the British Empire: The Twentieth Century*, ed. Judith M. Brown and William Roger Louis (Oxford: Oxford University Press, 1999), 208, 205.

12. Those who emphasize indifference include Darwin, *Britain and Decolonisation*, 328; James, *Rise and Fall of the British Empire*, 594; Porter, *Absent-Minded Imperialists*, 318. For a contrary view, see Paul B. Rich, *Race and Empire in British Politics*, 2d. ed. (Cambridge: Cambridge University Press, 1990), 11.

13. Richard Stubbs, *Hearts and Minds in Guerrilla Warfare: The Malayan Emergency, 1948–1960* (Singapore: Oxford University Press, 1989), gives the figure of 1,500 planters and miners (p. 85); T. N. Harper reports that the MPIEA, a planters' association, controlled 1.6 million acres in 1956; see T. N. Harper, *The End of Empire and the Making of Malaya* (Cambridge: Cambridge University Press, 1999), 200.

14. Susan Carruthers notes that the definition had legal implications for collecting on insurance policies; see *Winning Hearts and Minds: British Governments, the Media and Colonial Counter-Insurgency, 1944–1960* (London: Leicester University Press, 1995), 77.

15. The number of planters killed appears in Harper, *End of Empire*, 55. On Templer's policies, see Stubbs, *Hearts and Minds*, 140–91.

16. Webster, *Englishness and Empire*, 129.

17. *Kinematograph Weekly*, 18 December 1952.

18. *London Times*, 18 September 1952.

19. The British reviews (all from 1952): Positive: Elspeth Grant, *Daily Graphic*, 19 September; P. L. Mannock, *Daily Herald*, 19 September; Fred Majdalany, *Daily Mail*, 19 September; Reg Whitley, *Daily Mirror*, 19 September; Campbell Dixon, *Daily Telegraph*, 22 September; *Kinematograph Weekly*, 18 September; C. de la Roche, *Picture Post*, 20 September; J.G.W., *To-Day's Cinema News*, 15 September; R. Rudlater, *Tribune*, 19 September.

Negative: Thomas Spencer, *Daily Worker*, 20 September; Jympson Harman, *Evening News*, 19 September; *Evening Standard*, 18 September; C. B., *Monthly Film Bulletin*, no. 226, p. 155; Richard Winnington, *News Chronicle*, 20 September; Ewart Hodgson, *News of the*

World, 21 September; *New Statesman*, 27 September; C. A. Lejeune, *Observer*, 21 September; Denis Myers, *People*, 21 September; Cyril Ray, *Spectator*, 19 September; *Sunday Chronicle*, 21 September.

Mixed: Leonard Mosely, *Daily Express*, 19 September; *London Times*, 19 September; Philip Hope-Wallace, *Manchester Guardian*, 20 September; Roy Nash, *Star*, 29 September; *Sunday Dispatch*, 21 September; *Sunday Graphic*, 21 September; Dilys Powell, *Sunday Times*, 21 September; *Time and Tide*, 27 September.

20. The others: *Manchester Guardian, Observer, Spectator, Sunday Times, Time and Tide*.
21. *Evening News*, 23 September 1952.
22. *Picture Post*, 24 January 1953.
23. Clippings file, *Planter's Wife*, British Film Institute.
24. See Sue Harper and Vincent Porter, *British Cinema: The Decline of Difference* (Oxford: Oxford University Press, 2003), 45.
25. *Variety*, 7 January 1953. The U.S. reviews: Positive: Marjory Adams, *Boston Globe*, 28 November 1952; R.S.T., *Boston Herald*, 28 November 1952; Jesse Zunser, *Cue*, 29 November 1952; Steele Hooper, *Dallas Morning News*, 4 June 1953; *Film Daily*, 4 December 1952; *Motion Picture Herald*, 15 November 1952.

Negative: John Beaufort, *Christian Science Monitor*, 28 November 1952; Philip T. Hartung, *Commonweal*, 19 December 1952; *Hollywood Reporter*, 8 December 1952; Shirle Duggan, *Los Angeles Examiner*, 8 December 1952; *Newsweek*, 15 December 1952; Myro., *Variety*, 1 October 1952.

Mixed: Philip K. Scheuer, *Los Angeles Times*, 8 December 1952; Dorothy Master, *New York Daily News*, 27 November 1952; Otis Guernsey, *New York Herald-Tribune*, 27 November 1952; Irene Thirer, *New York Post*, 28 November 1952; Bosley Crowther, *New York Times*, 27 November 1952; William Hogan, *San Francisco Chronicle*, 15 November 1952.

26. Susan L. Carruthers writes that the film "ran the risk of antagonizing anti-colonial American audiences"; see her *Winning Hearts and Minds*, 112, and "Two Faces of 1950s Terrorism: The Film Presentation of Mau Mau and the Malayan Emergency," *Small Wars and Insurgencies* 6:1 (Spring 1995): 24.
27. Shirle Duggan's review mentions the documentary, titled *The Hoaxsters*.
28. The *Boston Globe*, *Cue*, *Dallas Morning News*, and *San Francisco Chronicle* mentioned communism.
29. Simon Simsi, *Ciné-Passions: 7e art et industrie de 1945 à 2000* (Paris: Dixit, 2000), 61. The French reviews: Positive: J. F., *Aurore*, 1 January 1953; A. B., *Cahiers du Cinéma*, no. 20, February 1953, p. 61; R.-M. Arlaud, *Combat*, 29 December 1952.

Negative: Pierre Laroche, *Canard Enchaîné*, 7 January 1953; Janine Bouissounouse, *Ce Soir*, 30 December 1952; Armand Monjo, *Humanité*, 2 January 1953; Jean Thevenot, *Lettres Françaises*, 1 January 1953; Georges Charensol, *Nouvelles Littéraires*, 8 January 1953; Claude Brule, *Paris-Presse/L'Intransigeant*, 2 January 1953.

Mixed or neutral: Claude Mauriac, *Figaro Littéraire*, 3 January 1953; Jean Nery, *Franc-Tireur*, 31 December 1952; Jean d'Yvoire, *Radio Cinéma Télévision*, 11 January 1953.

30. The British reviews: Positive: F. J. *Daily Cinema*, 18 December 1957; Anthony Carthew, *Daily Herald*, 20 December 1957; Cecil Wilson, *Daily Mail*, 21 December 1957; Donald Zec, *Daily Mirror*, 20 December 1957; Patrick Gibbs, *Daily Telegraph*, 21 December 1957; Molly Plowright, *Glasgow Herald*, 17 February 1958; *Kinematograph Weekly*, 26 December 1957; Peter Burnup, *News of the World*, 22 December 1957; *New Statesman*, 4 Jan-

uary 1958; Ross Shepherd, *People*, 22 December 1957; Isabel Quigly, *Spectator*, 3 January 1958; Ivon Adams, *Star*, 19 December 1957; *Sunday Dispatch*, 22 December 1957; Milton Shulman, *Sunday Express*, 22 December 1957; *Sunday Graphic*, 22 December 1957; Dilys Powell, *Sunday Times*, 22 December 1957; Derek Hill, *Tribune*, 22 December 1957.

Negative: Harold Conway, *Daily Sketch*, 19 December 1957; Nina Hibbin, *Daily Worker*, 21 December 1957; Jympson Harman, *Evening News*, 20 December 1957; Derek Granger, *Financial Times*, 22 December 1957; *Manchester Guardian*, 21 December 1957; A. T., *Monthly Film Bulletin*, no. 289; C. A. Lejeune, *Observer*, 22 December 1957.

Mixed or neutral: Tom Pocock, *Daily Express*, 21 December 1957; Philip Oakes, *Evening Standard*, 19 December 1957; *London Times*, 23 December 1957; Frank Jackson, *Reynolds News*, 22 December 1957; Charles MacLaren, *Time and Tide*, 28 December 1957.

31. The U.S. reviews: Positive: Jesse Zunser, *Cue*, 4 October 1958; *Film Daily*, 1 October 1958; James Jerauld, *Motion Picture Herald*, 4 October 1958; Kate Cameron, *New York Daily News*, 1 October 1958; Rich., *Variety*, 1 January 1958.

Negative: Ben Crisler, *Christian Science Monitor*, 19 November 1959; Paul V. Beckley, *New York Herald-Tribune*, 1 October 1958; Bosley Crowther, *New York Times*, 1 October 1958; Hollis Alpert, *Saturday Review*, 11 October 1958; *Time*, 10 November 1958.

Mixed: Moira Walsh, *America*, 4 October 1958; Lyon Phelps, *Boston Herald*, 19 November 1959; Archer Winsten, *New York Post*, 1 October 1958.

32. Simsi, *Ciné-Passions*, 5. The French reviews (all from 1959): Positive: *Canard Enchaîné*, 15 July.

Negative: Pierre Marcabru, *Combat*, 13 July; Louis Chauvet, *Figaro*, 14 July; Simone Dubreuilh, *Libération*, 17 July; Maurice Ciantar, *Paris Jour*, 16 July; Michel Aubriant, *Paris-Presse/L'Intransigeant*, 10 July.

Mixed or neutral: Samuel Lachize, *Humanité*, 15 July; C.-M. Tremois, *Radio Cinéma Télévision*, 26 July; R. Regent, *Revue des Deux Mondes*, 1 August.

33. David N. Eldridge, "'Dear Owen': The CIA, Luigi Luraschi, and Hollywood, 1953," *Historical Journal of Film, Radio and Television* 20:2 (June 2000): 188–89n82.

34. *Variety*, 13 January 1954. The reviews, all negative: Marjory Adams, *Boston Globe*, 23 January 1953; Mae Tinee, *Chicago Tribune*, 3 February 1953; Jesse Zunser, *Cue*, 7 February 1953; *Film Daily*, 31 October 1952; *Hollywood Reporter*, 28 October 1952; Philip K. Scheuer, *Los Angeles Times*, 22 January 1953; Vincent Canby, *Motion Picture Herald*, 1 November 1952; A. W., *New York Times*, 4 February 1953; *Time*, 19 January 1953; Brog., *Variety*, 29 October 1952; Richard L. Coe, *Washington Post*, 16 January 1953.

35. G. W., *Monthly Film Bulletin*, no. 217, p. 17.

36. Robert Standish, *Elephant Walk* (London: P. Davies, 1948).

37. Eldridge, "'Dear Owen,'" letters 3 and 6, and nn. 70 and 75.

38. On this film, see James Chapman and Nicholas J. Cull, *Projecting Empire: Imperialism and Popular Cinema* (London: I. B. Tauris, 2009), chap. 5. None of these reviews (all from 1954) saw the film as a metaphor for decolonization: Paul Jones, *Atlanta Constitution*, 7 May; Cyrus Durgin, *Boston Globe*, 30 April; Mae Tinee, *Chicago Tribune*, 17 May; Philip T. Hartung, *Commonweal*, 7 May; John Rosenfield, *Dallas Morning News*, 6 May; *Film Daily*, 29 March; Philip K. Scheuer, *Los Angeles Times*, 27 May; George Bourke, *Miami Herald*, 4 May; Mandel Herbstman, *Motion Picture Herald*, 3 April; Bosley Crowther, *New York Times*, 22 April; William Hogan, *San Francisco Chronicle*, 5 May; *Time*, 19 April; Brog., *Variety*, 31 March; Richard L. Coe, *Washington Post*, 1 May.

39. John Masters, *Bhowani Junction: A Novel* (New York: Viking Press, 1954); on Masters, see John Clay, *John Masters: A Regimented Life* (London: Michael Joseph, 1992).

40. Harper and Porter, *British Cinema*, 120; on Cukor, see Patrick McGilligan, *George Cukor, a Double Life: A Biography of the Gentleman Director* (New York: St. Martin's, 1991).

41. Clay, *John Masters*, 1–2.

42. Lieutenant Colonel E.A.G. Wakefield to George Cukor, 10 March 1955, in George Cukor Papers, file 3-f.25, Herrick Library, Academy of Motion Picture Arts and Sciences (AMPAS), Beverly Hills, CA.

43. Prem Chowdhry, *Colonial India and the Making of Empire Cinema* (Manchester: Manchester University Press, 2000), 265, makes that charge.

44. Freddie Young, *Seventy Light Years* (London: Faber and Faber, 1999), 73.

45. Chowdhry, *Colonial India*, 6, 262–64.

46. *Variety*, 2 January 1957. Harper and Porter, *British Cinema*, 119, present figures showing that the film lost money.

47. See *Milwaukee Journal*, 28 May 1956; *Philadelphia Inquirer*, 3 July 1956.

48. The U.S. reviews (all from 1956): Positive: Moira Walsh, *America*, 9 June; Cyrus Durgin, *Boston Globe*, 14 June; Elinor Hughes, *Boston Herald*, 14 June; Mae Tinee, *Chicago Tribune*, 6 June; Jesse Zunser, *Cue*, 26 May; Bob Tweedell, *Denver Post*, 31 May; Al Weitschat, *Detroit News*, 17 June; *Film Daily*, 7 May; George Christian, *Houston Post*, 27 May; Sara Hamilton, *Los Angeles Examiner*, 7 June; Edwin Schallert, *Los Angeles Times*, 7 June; George Bourke, *Miami Herald*, 25 May; James D. Ivers, *Motion Picture Herald*, 5 May; *Newsweek*, 11 June; Wanda Hale, *New York Daily News*, 25 May; Archer Winsten, *New York Post*, 25 May; Bosley Crowther, *New York Times*, 25 May; Mildred Martin, *Philadelphia Inquirer*, 4 July; Edwin Martin, *San Diego Union*, 8 June; Paine Knickerbocker, *San Francisco Chronicle*, 17 May; Arthur Knight, *Saturday Review*, 2 June; Myles Standish, *St. Louis Post-Dispatch*, 1 June; Hift., *Variety*, 9 May; Richard L. Coe, *Washington Post*, 23 May.

Negative: Marjory Smith, *Atlanta Constitution*, 18 May; John Rosenfield, *Dallas Morning News*, 21 June; Don Gillette, *Hollywood Reporter*, 4 May; E. D., *Milwaukee Journal*, 30 May; John McCarten, *New Yorker*, 2 June.

Mixed or neutral: Philip T. Hartung, John Beaufort, *Christian Science Monitor*, 14 June; *Commonweal*, 8 June; *Time*, 4 June.

49. Also complaining of the film's political timidity were *Commonweal* and the *New Yorker*.

50. The British reviews (all from 1956): Positive: Leonard Mosley, *Daily Express*, 30 August; Emery Pearce, *Daily Herald*, 31 August; Fred Majdalany, *Daily Mail*, 31 August; Reg Whitley, *Daily Mirror*, 31 August; Eric Gillet, *Daily Telegraph*, 1 September; Philip Oakes, *Evening Standard*, 30 August; *Kinematograph Weekly*, 2 August; Dilys Powell, *Sunday Times*, 2 September; R. D. Smith, *Tribune*, 9 November.

Negative: Matt White, *Daily Sketch*, 31 August; Jympson Harman, *Evening News*, 30 August; *London Times*, 3 September; R. B., *Manchester Guardian*, 1 September; *Monthly Film Bulletin*, no. 272, p. 112; William Whitebait, *New Statesman*, 15 September; C. A. Lejeune, *Observer*, 2 September; David Stone, *Spectator*, 8 September.

Mixed or neutral: Thomas Spencer, *Daily Worker*, 1 September; Derek Granger, *Financial Times*, 3 September; Milton Shulman, *Sunday Express*, 2 September; Fred Majdalany, *Time and Tide*, 8 September.

51. Simsi, *Ciné-Passions*, 41. The French reviews (all from 1956): Positive: Eric Rohmer,

Arts, 24 October; Michel Perez, *Cinéma 57*, January 1957, pp. 118–19; R.-M. Arlaud, *Combat*, 18 October; Louis Chauvet, *Figaro*, 19 October; Jean de Baroncelli, *Monde*, 20 October; Robert Chazal, *Paris-Presse/L'Intransigeant*, 14 October; André Bazin, *Radio Cinéma Télévision*, 28 October.

Negative: Michel Mohrt, *Carrefour*, 24 October; *Franc-Tireur*, 20 October; Georges Marescaux, *Humanité*, 17 October; Martine Monod, *Lettres Françaises*, 18 October; Simone Dubreuilh, *Libération*, 22 October.

Mixed or neutral: Claude Garson, *Aurore*, 13 October; *Canard Enchaîné*, 17 October; *Express*, 19 October; Denise de Fontfreyde, *Nouveaux Jours*, 26 October.

52. Bazin's review in *Radio Cinéma Télévision* mentions the translation in the subtitles.

53. Daniel Branch, *Defeating Mau Mau, Creating Kenya: Counterinsurgency, Civil War, and Decolonization* (Cambridge: Cambridge University Press, 2009), xii, 18, 22. For a general history of the conflict, see David Anderson, *Histories of the Hanged: The Dirty War in Kenya and the End of Empire* (New York: W. W. Norton, 2005).

54. See Bethwell Ogot and Tiyambe Zeleza, "Kenya: The Road to Independence and After," in *Decolonization and African Independence: The Transfers of Power, 1960–1980*, ed. Prosser Gifford and William Roger Louis (New Haven, CT: Yale University Press, 1988).

55. See Branch, *Defeating Mau Mau*, 5; Carruthers, *Winning Hearts and Minds*, 165; Caroline Elkins quotes death-toll estimates as high as three hundred thousand; see *Imperial Reckoning: The Untold Story of Britain's Gulag in Kenya* (New York: Henry Holt, 2005), 166.

56. Quoted in Harper and Porter, *British Cinema*, 45. Kenneth M. Cameron, *Africa on Film: Beyond Black and White* (New York: Continuum, 1994), 115, notes that the film's words were more balanced than its images.

57. Webster, *Englishness and Empire*, 121, 129.

58. The British reviews (all from 1955): Positive: Leonard Mosley, *Daily Express*, 20 January; Paul Holt, *Daily Herald*, 21 January; Fred Majdalany, *Daily Mail*, 21 January; Reg Whitley, *Daily Mirror*, 23 January; Harold Conway, *Daily Sketch*, 21 January; Campbell Dixon, *Daily Telegraph*, 22 January; Jympson Harman, *Evening News*, 20 January; W. D. Home, *Evening Standard*, 20 January; *Glasgow Herald*, 14 February; *Kinematograph Weekly*, 20 January; *London Times*, 24 January; *Manchester Guardian*, 22 January; Paul Dehn, *News Chronicle*, 21 January; Peter Burnup, *News of the World*, 23 January; C. A. Lejeune, *Observer*, 23 January; Virginia Graham, *Spectator*, 21 January; Roy Nash, *Star*, 21 January; Harris Deans, *Sunday Dispatch*, 23 January; Derek Monsey, *Sunday Express*, 23 January; *Sunday Graphic*, 23 January; Dilys Powell, *Sunday Times*, 23 January; L.H.C., *To-Day's Cinema News*, 19 January; Peter C. Davalle, *Western Mail*, 5 February.

Negative: *Daily Worker*, 19 January; G. L., *Monthly Film Bulletin*, no. 254 pp. 35–36; William Whitebait, *New Statesman*, 29 January; G. Kaufman, *Tribune*, 28 January.

Mixed: Derek Granger, *Financial Times*, 24 January.

59. *Variety*, 25 January 1956. The U.S. reviews: Positive: Jesse Zunser, *Cue*, 22 October 1955; Bob Tweedell, *Denver Post*, 28 September 1955; *Film Daily*, 29 August 1955; M.O.S., *Hartford Courant*, 17 September 1955; William R. Weaver, *Motion Picture Herald*, 3 September 1955; Kate Cameron, *New York Daily News*, 22 October 1955; Archer Winsten, *New York Post*, 23 October 1955; Howard Thompson, *New York Times*, 22 October 1955; Myles Standish, *St. Louis Post-Dispatch*, 21 October 1955; Myro., *Variety*, 2 February 1955.

Negative: *Atlanta Daily World*, 25 March 1955; George Daniels, *Chicago Defender*, 23 June 1956; Hollis Alpert, *Saturday Review*, 15 October 1955.

Mixed or neutral: Marjory Adams, *Boston Globe*, 15 September 1955; Philip T. Hartung, *Commonweal*, 11 November 1955.

60. *St. Louis Post-Dispatch*, 20 October 1955.

61. Geoffrey M. Shurlock to Dore Schary, MGM, 1 June 1956, Production Files, *Something of Value*, Herrick Library, AMPAS.

62. *Variety*, 8 January 1958.

63. *Detroit News*, 21 June 1957.

64. The U.S. reviews (all from 1957): Positive: Elinor Hughes, *Boston Herald*, 24 June; Mae Tinee, *Chicago Tribune*, 5 July; Melvin Maddocks, *Christian Science Monitor*, 24 June; Larry Tajiri, *Denver Post*, 20 June; Al Weitschat, *Detroit News*, 23 June; *Film Daily*, 30 April; L.E.R., *Hollywood Citizen News*, 8 June; James Powers, *Hollywood Reporter*, 29 April; Kay Proctor, *Los Angeles Examiner*, 8 June; Edwin Schallert, *Los Angeles Times*, 8 June; George Bourke, *Miami Herald*, 27 June; B.J.P., *Milwaukee Journal*, 20 June; Richard Gertner, *Motion Picture Daily*, 29 April; James D. Ivers, *Motion Picture Herald*, 4 May; Kate Cameron, *New York Daily News*, 11 May; Irene Thirer, *New York Post*, 11 May; Mildred Martin, *Philadelphia Inquirer*, 4 July; Charles Hull, *San Diego Union*, 8 July; Paine Knickerbocker, *San Francisco Chronicle*, 21 June; *Time*, 20 May; Hift., *Variety*, 1 May; Richard L. Coe, *Washington Post*, 18 June.

Negative: Paul Jones, *Atlanta Constitution*, 9 August; Philip T. Hartung, *Commonweal*, 31 May; George Christian, *Houston Post*, 16 June; *Newsweek*, 13 May; John McCarten, *New Yorker*, 18 May; Hollis Alpert, *Saturday Review*, 18 May; Myles Standish, *St. Louis Post-Dispatch*, 21 June.

Mixed or neutral: Moira Walsh, *America*, 25 May; Jesse Zunser, *Cue*, 11 May; Rual Askew, *Dallas Morning News*, 20 June; *Life*, 22 July; Robert Hatch, *Nation*, 1 June; Albert Goldstein, *New Orleans Times-Picayune*, 21 June; Stanley Kauffmann, *New Republic*, 21 October; Bosley Crowther, *New York Times*, 11 May.

65. George E. Pitts, *Pittsburgh Courier*, 22 June; the same lines appear in the *Chicago Defender*, 15 June.

66. The British reviews (all from 1957): Positive: Donald Zec, *Daily Mirror*, 28 June; Campbell Dixon, *Daily Telegraph*, 29 June; Robert Kennedy, *Daily Worker*, 29 June; Philip Oakes, *Evening Standard*, 27 June; *Kinematograph Weekly*, 30 May.

Negative: Cecil Wilson, *Daily Mail*, 28 June; Harold Conway, *Daily Sketch*, 28 June; Jympson Harman, *Evening News*, 27 June; *Financial Times*, 15 July; *London Times*, 1 July; P. H., *Monthly Film Bulletin*, no. 283; Elizabeth Frank, *News Chronicle*, 28 June.

Mixed or neutral: Emery Pearce, *Daily Herald*, 28 June; C. A. Lejeune, *Observer*, 30 June.

67. Simsi, *Ciné-Passions*, 26.

68. The French reviews: Positive: Charles Bitsch, *Arts*, 19 March 1958; Steve Passeur, *Aurore*, 28 August 1957; J. D., *Cahiers du Cinéma*, no. 75 (October 1957), 40; M. L., *Canard Enchaîné*, 26 March 1958; J.-G. L., *Cinéma 58*, May 1958, 105–6; Louis Chauvet, *Figaro*, 28 August 1957; Simone Dubreuilh, *Lettres Françaises*, 27 March 1958; *Libération*, 29 August 1957; Simone Dubreuilh, *Libération*, 27 March 1958; Marcel Ranchal, *Positif*, no. 29 (rentrée [September] 1958), 35–38; *Témoignage Chrétien*, 6 September 1957; Jean Carta, *Témoignage Chrétien*, 10 April 1958.

Negative: Eric Rohmer, *Arts*, 5 September 1957; *Combat*, 29 August 1957; *Figaro*, 28 March 1958; Jean de Baroncelli, *Monde*, 29 August 1957.

Mixed or neutral: Louis Marcorelles, *France Observateur*, 3 April 1958; *Humanité Di-*

manche, 23 March 1958; Georges Sadoul, Lettres Françaises, 5 September 1957; Radio Cinéma Télévision, 15 September 1957; Gilbert Salachas, Radio Cinéma Télévision, 23 March 1958; Emmanuel Lecaron, Téléciné, June-July 1958, fiche no. 331.
69. Simone Dubreuilh, Lettres Françaises, 27 March 1958.
70. J.D., Cahiers du Cinéma, no. 75 (October 1957), 40.
71. Louis Marcorelles, France Observateur, 3 April 1958.
72. Radio Cinéma Télévision, 15 September 1957.
73. Combat, 29 August 1957; Simone Dubreuilh, Libération, 27 March 1958.
74. Lettres Françaises, 5 September 1957.
75. Humanité Dimanche, 23 March 1958; others alluding to France's colonial problems were Charles Bitsch, Arts, 19 March 1958, J. D., Cahiers du Cinéma, no. 75 (October 1957), 40; Gilbert Salachas, Radio Cinéma Télévision, 23 March 1958; Témoignage Chrétien, 6 September 1957; Jean Carta, Témoignage Chrétien, 10 April 1958.
76. Variety, 12 February 1958.
77. "Racial Tolerance Film Has Double Dallas Date," Dallas Morning News, 4 April 1959.
78. The U.S. reviews (all from 1958): Positive: Mae Tinee, Chicago Tribune, 8 December; Film Daily, 26 February; Hartford Courant, 4 September; Jack Moffitt, Hollywood Reporter, 11 February; Charles S. Aaronson, Motion Picture Herald, 15 February; Howard Thompson, New York Times, 6 March; Pittsburgh Courier, 14 June; Richard L. Coe, Washington Post, 14 November.

Negative: Jesse Zunser, Cue, 8 March; Bosley Crowther, New York Times, 9 March; Whit., Variety, 12 February.

Mixed or neutral: Moira Walsh, America, 15 March; S. A. Desick, Los Angeles Examiner, 7 August; Geoffrey Warren, Los Angeles Times, 7 August; Archer Winsten, New York Post, 6 March.

79. Philip Dine equates the subject to France's Algeria crisis; see Images of the Algerian War: French Fiction and Film, 1954-1992 (Oxford: Clarendon, 1994), 9.
80. These included Britain's Ourselves Alone (1936), John Ford's The Informer (1935), Ford's film of Sean O'Casey's The Plough and the Stars (1936), and MGM's Parnell (1937).
81. Kevin Rockett, Luke Gibbons, and John Hill, Cinema and Ireland (Syracuse, NY: Syracuse University Press, 1988), 160.
82. Ibid., 162.
83. J. Bowyer Bell, The Secret Army: The IRA, 1916-1970 (New York: John Day, 1971), 145-76; Timothy Pat Coogan, The IRA: A History (Niwot, CO: Roberts Rinehart, 1994), 87-99.
84. On the making of the film, see Jympson Harman, "It's off to a Flying Start," Evening News, 20 April 1959.
85. Variety, 6 January 1960. The U.S. reviews (all from 1959): Positive: Cyrus Durgin, Boston Globe, 3 August; Mae Tinee, Chicago Tribune, 12 June; John Beaufort, Christian Science Monitor, 4 August; Philip T. Hartung, Commonweal, 26 June; Betsy Forsythe, Dallas Morning News, 10 September; Film Daily, 8 May; Jack Moffitt, Hollywood Reporter, 8 May; Ruth Waterbury, Los Angeles Examiner, 4 June; Philip K. Scheuer, Los Angeles Times, 17 May; Vincent Canby, Motion Picture Herald, 9 May; Evelyn Komma, New Orleans Times-Picayune, 15 June; Howard Thompson, New York Times, 25 June; Mildred Martin, Philadelphia Inquirer, 12 June; Paine Knickerbocker, San Francisco Chronicle, 11 June; Leo Sullivan, Washington Post, 10 June.

Negative: Moira Walsh, *America*, 20 June; Archer Winsten, *New York Post*, 11 June; Hollis Alpert, *Saturday Review*, 30 May; *Time*, 20 July.

Mixed or neutral: Elinor Hughes, *Boston Herald*, 3 August; John L. Scott, *Los Angeles Times*, 4 June; Powe., *Variety*, 13 May.

86. The British reviews (all from 1959): Positive: F. J., *Daily Cinema*, 27 May; Margaret Hinxman, *Daily Herald*, 29 May; Campbell Dixon, *Daily Telegraph*, 30 May; Jympson Harman, *Evening News*, 28 May; John Waterman, *Evening Standard*, 28 May; *London Times*, 1 June; P. L. Mannock, *News of the World*, 31 May; Ivon Adams, *Star*, 26 May; George Sterling, *Sunday Dispatch*, 31 May; Derek Prouse, *Sunday Times*, 31 May.

Negative: Leonard Mosley, *Daily Express*, 29 May; Fred Majdalany, *Daily Mail*, 29 May; David Robinson, *Financial Times*, 1 June; *Kinematograph Weekly*, P. H., *Monthly Film Bulletin*, no. 306, 85; Isabel Quigly, *Spectator*, 5 June; Charles MacLaren, *Time and Tide*, 6 June.

Mixed or neutral: Nina Hibbin, *Daily Worker*, 30 May; *Manchester Guardian*, 30 May; William Whitebait, *New Statesman*, 6 June.

Chapter 5 · The French Empire and Decolonization

1. Michael Provence, *The Great Syrian Revolt and the Rise of Arab Nationalism* (Austin: University of Texas Press, 2005), 26.

2. *Variety*, 5 January 1955; Bosley Crowther, *New York Times*, 20 March 1954; *Time*, 12 April 1954.

3. Simon Simsi, *Ciné-Passions: 7e art et industrie de 1945 à 2000* (Paris: Dixit, 2000), 134.

4. On the *grands colons*, see Alistair Horne, *A Savage War of Peace: Algeria, 1954–1962* (New York: Penguin, 1979), 56–58.

5. *Variety*, 13 January 1954.

6. *Variety*, 25 January 1956. The U.S. reviews: Positive: Paul Jones, *Atlanta Constitution*, 28 January 1955; Jesse Zunser, *Cue*, 1 January 1955; John Rosenfield, *Dallas Morning News*, 28 January 1955; Alex Murphree, *Denver Post*, 26 December 1954; Al Weitschat, *Detroit News*, 24 December 1954; *Film Daily*, 24 December 1954; M.O.S., *Hartford Courant*, 15 January 1955; George Bourke, *Miami Herald*, 13 January 1955; Archer Winsten, *New York Post*, 27 December 1954; Edwin Martin, *San Diego Union*, 24 December 1954; William Hogan, *San Francisco Chronicle*, 25 December 1954; Richard L. Coe, *Washington Post*, 22 January 1955.

Negative: Marjory Adams, *Boston Globe*, 15 January 1955; Elinor Hughes, *Boston Herald*, 15 January 1955; Philip T. Hartung, *Commonweal*, 28 January 1955; George Christian, *Houston Post*, 2 January 1955; John L. Scott, *Los Angeles Times*, 14 January 1955; *Newsweek*, 10 January 1955; *New Yorker*, Bosley Crowther, *New York Times*, 27 December 1954; Kenneth Coyle, *Saturday Review*, 15 January 1955; Myles Standish, *St. Louis Post-Dispatch*, 21 January 1955; *Time*, 10 January 1955.

Mixed: Mae Tinee, *Chicago Tribune*, 4 January 1955; Rod Nordell, *Christian Science Monitor*, 15 January 1955; Brog., *Variety*, 22 December 1954.

7. Simsi, *Ciné-Passions*, 162, and the top-films chart for 1955.

8. François Truffaut, *Cahiers du Cinéma*, no. 48 (June 1955), 45. The French reviews (all from 1955): Positive: Truffaut, *Cahiers du Cinéma*, June; André Bazin, *Parisien Libéré*, 16 May; Jean-Paul Faure, *Paris-Presse/L'Intransigeant*, 15 May; J.-G. Pierret, *Radio Cinéma Télévision*, 22 May.

Negative: Claude Garson, *Aurore*, 12 May; R.-M. Arlaud, *Combat*, 30 May.

Mixed or neutral: *Croix*, 21 May; A. L., *France Soir*, 15 May; Jose Zendel, *Lettres Françaises*, 19 May.

9. On the early Indochina films, see Scott Laderman, "Hollywood's Vietnam, 1929–1964," *Pacific Historical Review* 78:4 (November 2009): 578–607.

10. Translation of an April 15, 1955, letter from J. Salberg, Warner Bros. French managing director, to J. S. Hummel of Warner Bros., *Jump into Hell*—Story Memos, #3 of 3, Warner Bros. Archive, University of Southern California, Los Angeles.

11. Making this point about the film are Gina Marchetti, *Romance and the "Yellow Peril": Race, Sex, and Discursive Strategies in Hollywood Fiction* (Berkeley: University of California Press, 1993), 97; Albert Auster and Leonard Quart, *How the War Was Remembered: Hollywood and Vietnam* (New York: Praeger, 1988), 13.

12. Samuel Fuller, *A Third Face: My Tale of Writing, Fighting, and Filmmaking* (New York: Alfred Knopf, 2002), 353–54.

13. It did not appear on *Variety*'s annual charts; see *Variety*, 8 January 1958. The U.S. reviews (all from 1957): Positive: Paul Jones, *Atlanta Constitution*, 21 May; James Powers, *Hollywood Reporter*, 9 May; Ruth Waterbury, *Los Angeles Examiner*, 10 May; John L. Scott, *Los Angeles Times*, 10 May; Samuel D. Berns, *Motion Picture Herald*, 25 May; Jim Walls, *San Francisco Chronicle*, 9 May.

Negative: Marjory Adams, *Boston Globe*, 23 May; Mae Tinee, *Chicago Tribune*, 17 May; Melvin Maddocks, *Christian Science Monitor*, 23 May; Larry Tajiri, *Denver Post*, 13 May; Wanda Hale, *New York Daily News*, 23 May; Archer Winsten, *New York Post*, 23 May; Bosley Crowther, *New York Times*, 23 May; Mildred Martin, *Philadelphia Inquirer*, 24 May; *St. Louis Post-Dispatch*, 23 May; Richard L. Coe, *Washington Post*, 23 May.

Mixed: Elinor Hughes, *Boston Herald*, 23 May; *Film Daily*, 10 May; Whit., *Variety*, 22 May.

14. The ad appears in the *Philadelphia Inquirer*, 22 May 1957.

15. On Hollywood's reluctance to offend foreign audiences, see Ruth Vasey, "Foreign Parts: Hollywood's Global Distribution and the Representation of Ethnicity," in *Movie Censorship and American Culture*, ed. Francis G. Couvares (Washington, DC: Smithsonian Institution Press, 1996), 212–36.

16. Pascal Blanchard, Sandrine Lemaire, and Nicholas Bancel, "La formation d'une culture coloniale en France," in *Culture coloniale en France: De la Révolution française à nos jours*, ed. Pascal Blanchard, Sandrine Lemaire, and Nicholas Bancel (Paris: CNRS/Autrement, 2008), 61–62. Among many others, see also Benjamin Stora, *La gangrène et l'oubli: La mémoire de la guerre d'Algérie* (Paris: La Découverte, 1991); Benjamin Stora, "Guerre d'Algérie: Le Vietnam français?" in *L'Algérie des Français*, ed. Charles-Robert Ageron (Paris: Seuil, 1993); Pascal Blanchard and Isabelle Veyrat-Masson, eds., *Les guerres de mémoires: La France et son histoire; Enjeux politiques, controverses historiques, stratégies médiatiques*, with a preface by Benjamin Stora (Paris: La Découverte, 2008); Herman Lebovics, "La culture métissé," in Blanchard et al., *Culture coloniale*, 489; Claude Liauzu, "Le contingent entre silence et discours ancien combattant," in *La guerre d'Algérie et les français*, ed. Jean-Pierre Rioux (Paris: Fayard, 1990), 509–16.

17. See Dina Sherzer, ed., *Cinema, Colonialism, Postcolonialism: Perspectives from the French and Francophone Worlds* (Austin: University of Texas Press, 1996), 2, 7; Liauzu, "Le contingent," 509.

18. Martine Astier Loutfi, "Imperial Frame: Film Industry and Colonial Representation," in *Cinema, Colonialism, Postcolonialism: Perspectives from the French and Francophone*

Worlds, ed. Dina Sherzer (Austin: University of Texas Press, 1996), 25; Sherzer, *Cinema, Colonialism, Postcolonialism*, 3.

19. On this film, see http://paul.carpita.pagesperso-orange.fr/livrepascal.htm; see also Carpita's obituary in *Humanité*, 26 October 2009, http://www.humanite.fr/node/16321.

20. Carpita discussed the incident on television; see http://www.ina.fr/video/RAC 05006589.

21. Ronald Hyam, *Empire and Sexuality: The British Experience* (Manchester: Manchester University Press, 1990), 214–15.

22. Simsi, *Ciné-Passions*, 102. For purposes of comparison, Jean-Pierre Melville's *Bob le Flambeur* had sold 716,920 tickets in 1956; Robert Bresson's *Pickpocket* sold 435,757 tickets in 1959, and in 1962 François Truffaut's *Jules et Jim* just barely outdid *Mort en fraude*, with 1.5 million tickets; see Simsi, *Ciné-Passions*, 20, 32 (in part 3), 85.

23. The French reviews (all from 1957): Positive: Pierre Laroche, *Canard Enchaîné*, 29 May; Marcel Martin, *Cinéma* 57, June; R. M. Arlaud, *Combat*, 22 May; Jacques Doniol-Valcroze, *France Observateur*, 3 May; Samuel Lachize, *Humanité*, 25 May; François Maurin, *Humanité Dimanche*, 26 May; Henri Magnan, *Lettres Françaises*, 23 May; *Libération*, 27 May; Jean de Baroncelli, *Monde*, 29 May; Jacqueline Michel, *Parisien Libéré*, 22 May; Robert Chazal, *Paris-Presse/L'Intransigeant*, 21 May; Janick Arbois, *Radio Cinéma Télévision*, 2 June.

Negative: Charles Bitsch, *Arts*, 29 May; Claude Garson, *Aurore*, 20 May; Jacques Doniol-Valcroze, *Cahiers du Cinéma*, no. 72 (June), 49; Yves L'Her, *Croix*, 28 May; Denis Marion, *Franc-Tireur*, 28 May; *Positif* (rentrée [September] 1957), September; Gilles Martain, *Rivarol*, 6 June.

Mixed or neutral: *Express*, 24 May; Louis Chauvet, *Figaro*, 24 May; André Lang, *France Soir*, 24 May; Georges Charensol, *Nouvelles Littéraires*, 6 June; Marcel Roy, *Téléciné*, 7 June; Roger Fressoz, *Témoignage Chrétien*, 7 June.

24. Nguyen Khac Vien, *Lettres Françaises*, 18 July 1957.

25. S. D., "Patrouille de choc," *Lettres Françaises*, 18 July 1957.

26. *Aurore*, 17 July 1957, p. 4.

27. On that pattern, see Jacques Dalloz, *La guerre d'Indochine, 1945–1954* (Paris: Seuil, 1987), 145.

28. Simsi, *Ciné-Passions*, 114.

29. André Martin, *Cahiers du Cinéma*, no. 74 (August–September 1957), 50–51; *Combat*, 17 July 1957.

30. The reviews (all from 1957): Positive: *Aurore*, 20 July; André Martin, *Cahiers du Cinéma*, no. 74 (August–September), 50–51; *Combat*, 17 July; Pierre Mazars, *Figaro*, 19 July; Jacques Doniol-Valcroze, *France Observateur*, 11 July; Willy Giboud, *France Soir*, 17 July; S.D., *Lettres Françaises*, 18 July; Simone Dubreuilh, *Libération*, 16 July; Jean de Baroncelli, *Monde*, 21 July; Georges Charensol, *Nouvelles Littéraires*, 25 July; André Lafargue, *Parisien Libéré*, 15 July; *Paris-Presse/L'Intransigeant*, 7 July; Marcel Huret, *Radio Cinéma Télévision*, 28 July; *Téléciné*, October; Roger Fressoz, *Témoignage Chrétien*, 2 August.

Negative: François Maurin, *Humanité*, 17 July; *Humanité-Dimanche*, 28 July.

Mixed or neutral: François Truffaut, *Arts*, 17 July; Jean-Paul Grousset, *Canard Enchaîné*, 17 July; Jean Rochereau, *Croix*, 20 July.

31. The quotes are from Maurin's review in *Humanité*, 17 July.

32. *Libération*, 22 July, printed a Defense Ministry document presenting the changes desired and cited Bernard-Aubert regarding pressure not to show the film.

Chapter 6 · Americans in Postwar Asia

1. Hervé Dumont calls it "an assignment he considered humiliating"; see *William Dieterle: Un humaniste au pays du cinéma* (Paris: CNRS Editions / Cinémathèque Française, 2002), 199.
2. *Variety*, 2 January 1952.
3. On Dmytryk and HUAC, see Larry Ceplair and Stephen Englund, *The Inquisition in Hollywood: Politics in the Film Community, 1930–1960* (Berkeley: University of California Press, 1979), 357–59.
4. Lawrence H. Suid calls this formula "John Waynism"; see *Guts and Glory: The Making of the American Military Image in Film*, rev. ed. (Lexington: University Press of Kentucky, 2002), 247.
5. *Variety*, 25 January 1956. The film's absence from the year-end charts is curious, given that *Variety*'s issue of 5 October reported that it was the number three film in the United States; over the next four weeks it was numbers four, nine, seven, and nine, after which it disappeared from the list.

The U.S. reviews (all from 1955): Positive: John William Riley, *Boston Globe*, 30 September; Elinor Hughes, *Boston Herald*, 30 September; Mae Tinee, *Chicago Tribune*, 5 October; Philip T. Hartung, *Commonweal*, 21 October; Jesse Zunser, *Cue*, 8 October; Frank Gagnard, *Dallas Morning News*, 21 October; Shirley Sealy, *Denver Post*, 4 October; Al Weitschat, *Detroit News*, 21 October; Sara Hamilton, *Los Angeles Examiner*, 29 September; Philip K. Scheuer, *Los Angeles Times*, 29 September; Charles S. Aaronson, *Motion Picture Herald*, 24 September; Edwin Martin, *San Diego Union*, 7 October; Myles Standish, *St. Louis Post-Dispatch*, 28 October; *Time*, 17 October; Brog., *Variety*, 21 September.

Negative: Irene Thirer, *New York Post*, 6 October.

Mixed or neutral: Rod Nordell, *Christian Science Monitor*, 30 September; *Film Daily*, 23 September; *Newsweek*, 10 October; Wanda Hale, *New York Daily News*, 6 October; Paul V. Beckley, *New York Herald-Tribune*, 6 October; A. H. Weiler, *New York Times*, 6 October; Richard L. Coe, *Washington Post*, 13 October.

6. See Turner Classic Movies' *Moguls and Movie Stars: A History of Hollywood*, episode 1.
7. On U.S.-Philippine relations, see Stanley Karnow, *In Our Image: America's Empire in the Philippines* (New York: Foreign Policy Association, 1989); H. W. Brands, *Bound to Empire: The United States and the Philippines* (Oxford: Oxford University Press, 1992).
8. On the Huks, see Benedict J. Kerkvliet, *The Huk Rebellion: A Study of Peasant Revolt in the Philippines* (Berkeley: University of California Press, 1977); and Eduardo Lachica, *The Huks: Philippine Agrarian Society in Revolt* (New York: Praeger, 1971).
9. On Barnwell, see "Eyewitness to Direct 'Huk,' Film on Philippines Fight," *Los Angeles Times*, 26 February 1956.
10. Howard Thompson, *New York Times*, 15 December 1956; Brog., *Variety*, 8 August 1956. Also reviewing the film (all in 1956) were Marjory Adams, *Boston Globe*, 17 September; Elinor Hughes, *Boston Herald*, 17 September; *Film Daily*, 9 August; *Motion Picture Herald*, 4 August; Dorothy Masters, *New York Daily News*, 15 December; Archer Winsten, *New York Post*, 15 December.
11. Simon Simsi, *Ciné-Passions: 7e art et industrie de 1945 à 2000* (Paris: Dixit, 2000), 9.
12. Jean Dutourd, *Carrefour*, 13 March 1957.

13. John Dower notes the occupiers' sense of manifest destiny and their civilizing mission; see *Embracing Defeat: Japan in the Wake of World War II* (New York: W. W. Norton, 1999), 212.

14. Akira Iriye, *The Cold War in Asia: A Historical Introduction* (Englewood Cliffs, NJ: Prentice Hall, 1974), 125.

15. Dower, *Embracing Defeat*, 187, notes that an English-language conversation manual remained "the all-time best selling publication until 1981."

16. On discrimination, see Yukiko Koshiro, *Trans-Pacific Racisms and the U.S. Occupation of Japan* (New York: Columbia University Press, 1999), 58–63, 70–73.

17. Walter LaFeber, *The Clash: A History of U.S.-Japan Relations* (New York: W. W. Norton, 1997), 295, 271; Michael Schaller, *The American Occupation of Japan: The Origins of the Cold War in Asia* (New York: Oxford University Press, 1985), 77–78.

18. See LaFeber, *The Clash*, xxi–xxii, 287.

19. Dower, *Embracing Defeat*, 213; see also John Dower, "Graphic Japanese, Graphic Americans: Coded Images in U.S.-Japanese Relations," in *Partnership: The United States and Japan, 1951–2001*, ed. Akira Iriye and Robert A. Wampler (Tokyo: Kodansha International, 2001), 301–32.

20. *Variety*, 4 January 1950.

21. On Okinawa, see Dower, *Embracing Defeat*, 224, 552.

22. Dower, *Embracing Defeat*, 206, refers to "the conundrum of inducing democracy autocratically."

23. LaFeber, *The Clash*, 317.

24. *Variety*, 8 January 1958; Lawrence J. Quirk, *Motion Picture Herald*, 20 October 1956, 113.

25. The U.S. reviews: Positive: Moira Walsh, *America*, 15 December 1956; Paul Jones, *Atlanta Constitution*, 4 January 1957; Marjory Adams, *Boston Globe*, 24 December 1956; Elinor Hughes, *Boston Herald*, 24 December 1956; Doris Arden, *Chicago Sun-Times*, 20 November 1956; Mae Tinee, *Chicago Tribune*, 20 November 1956; John Beaufort, *Christian Science Monitor*, 24 December 1956; Jesse Zunser, *Cue*, 1 December 1956; Rual Askew, *Dallas Morning News*, 24 January 1957; Larry Tajiri, *Denver Post*, 25 December 1956; Al Weitschat, *Detroit News*, 26 December 1956; *Film Daily*, 17 October 1956; M.O.S., *Hartford Courant*, 21 January 1957; Lowell E. Redelings, *Hollywood Citizen News*, no date in Herrick Library clippings file; James Powers, *Hollywood Reporter*, 17 October 1956; Kay Proctor, *Los Angeles Examiner*, 21 November 1956; Philip K. Scheuer, *Los Angeles Times*, 4 November 1956; John L. Scott, *Los Angeles Times*, 21 November 1956; Lawrence J. Quirk, *Motion Picture Herald*, 20 October 1956; Fritz Haredorf, *New Orleans Times-Picayune*, 1 January 1957; Kate Cameron, *New York Daily News*, 30 November 1956; Irene Thirer, *New York Post*, 30 November 1956; Bosley Crowther, *New York Times*, 2 December 1956; Mildred Martin, *Philadelphia Inquirer*, 26 December 1956; Paine Knickerbocker, *San Francisco Chronicle*, 25 December 1956; Myles Standish, *St. Louis Post-Dispatch*, 26 December 1956; *Time*, 10 December 1956; Kap., *Variety*, 17 October 1956.

Negative: John McCarten, *New Yorker*, 8 December 1956; William K. Zinsser, *New York Herald-Tribune*, 30 November 1956; Hollis Alpert, *Saturday Review*, 22 December 1956; Richard L. Coe, *Washington Post*, 25 December 1956.

Mixed: Philip T. Hartung, *Commonweal*, 14 December 1956; *Newsweek*, 3 December 1956.

26. Objecting were *Commonweal*'s Philip T. Hartung and *Cue*'s Jesse Zunser.

27. The British reviews (all from 1957): Positive: Emery Pearce, *Daily Herald*, 31 May; Harold Conway, *Daily Sketch*, 31 May; Campbell Dixon, *Daily Telegraph*, 1 June; Robert Kennedy, *Daily Worker*, 1 June; Jympson Harman, *Evening News*, 30 May; Philip Oakes, *Evening Standard*, 30 May; Matthew Norgate, *Manchester Guardian*, 1 June; *New Statesman*, 8 June; C. A. Lejeune, *Observer*, 2 June; Isabel Quigly, *Spectator*, 7 June; Derek Prouse, *Sunday Times*, 2 June; Fred Majdalany, *Time and Tide*, 8 June.

Mixed: *London Times*, 29 May; J.A.D.C., *Monthly Film Bulletin*, no. 281 (1957), 67.

28. *La petite maison de thé* opened in September 1957 and sold 619,984 tickets; see Simsi, *Ciné-Passions*, 115.

29. George C. Herring, *America's Longest War: The United States and Vietnam, 1950–1975*, 3rd ed. (New York: McGraw-Hill, 1996), 15–16.

30. George McT. Kahin reports that for fiscal 1954, Washington paid 78 percent of the costs of France's war in Indochina; see Kahin, *Intervention: How America Became Involved in Vietnam* (New York: Anchor, 1987), 42.

31. Herring, *America's Longest War*, 62.

32. Ibid., 74.

33. See Joseph G. Morgan, *The Vietnam Lobby: The American Friends of Vietnam, 1955–1975* (Chapel Hill: University of North Carolina Press, 1997), 4.

34. Anthony Burgess, "Politics in the Novels of Graham Greene," *Journal of Contemporary History* 2:2 (April 1967): 96; Stephen J. Whitfield, "Limited Engagement: The *Quiet American* as History," *Journal of American Studies* 30:1 (1996): 69–70. For the view that Fowler does represent Greene, see William S. Bushnell, "*The Quiet American*: Graham Greene's Vietnam Novel through the Lenses of Two Eras," in *Why We Fought: America's Wars in Film and History*, ed. Peter C. Rollins and John E. O'Connor (Lexington: University Press of Kentucky, 2008), 406.

35. The *London Times* reported on the changes before the film was made; see "'The Quiet American': Film 'Travesty' of the Novel," *London Times*, 9 January 1957. See also Whitfield, "Limited Engagement," 74–75; Jonathan Nashel, *Edward Lansdale's Cold War* (Amherst: University of Massachusetts Press, 2005), 172; Kenneth L. Geist, *Pictures Will Talk: The Life and Films of Joseph L. Mankiewicz* (New York: Scribner, 1978), 269–70. Mankiewicz's Figaro, Inc., sued the Times Publishing Company over its article; see file 35-f.411, Joseph L. Mankiewicz Papers, Herrick Library, Academy of Motion Picture Arts and Sciences (AMPAS), Beverly Hills, CA.

36. See Serguei A. Blagov, *Honest Mistakes: The Life and Death of Trinh Minh Thê (1922–1955), South Vietnam's Alternative Leader* (Huntington, NY: Nova Science Publishers, 2001).

37. Quoted in Geist, *Pictures Will Talk*, 269; and in Brian Dauth, ed., *Joseph L. Mankiewicz: Interviews* (Jackson: University Press of Mississippi, 2008), 141.

38. Quoted in Dauth, *Joseph L. Mankiewicz*, 141.

39. This is Geist's view; see Geist, *Pictures Will Talk*, 271.

40. McDowell to Krim, 16 April 1956, Joseph L. Mankiewicz Papers, *The Quiet American*—Correspondence, 1956–1958, file 34.f-403, Herrick Library, AMPAS.

41. Geoffrey M. Shurlock to Joseph L. Mankiewicz, 5 January 1956; and Mankiewicz to Shurlock, 9 January 1956, Joseph L. Mankiewicz Papers, file 35-f.414, Herrick Library, AMPAS.

42. Edward G. Lansdale letter to Mankiewicz, 17 March 1956, Joseph L. Mankiewicz

Papers, *The Quiet American*—Research (Correspondence) 1956, file 35.f-423, Herrick Library, AMPAS. See also Kevin Lewis, "The Third Force: Graham Greene and Joseph L. Mankiewicz's *The Quiet American*," *Film History* vol. 10 (1998): 482; H. Bruce Franklin, "Our Man in Saigon," *Nation*, 3 February 2003, 43–44.

43. Lewis, "The Third Force," 482; see also Geist, *Pictures Will Talk*, 268.

44. See Nashel, *Edward Lansdale's Cold War*, 152–54.

45. The first part of Fowler's statement follows the novel; see Graham Greene, *The Quiet American* (New York: Penguin, 2002), 113.

46. See Greene, *Quiet American*, 94.

47. Mankiewicz later expressed his disappointment with a film plagued by calamities. Murphy contracted appendicitis during shooting; Redgrave botched his lines, perhaps because of Parkinson's disease; Mankiewicz was dealing with his wife's psychological breakdown shortly before her suicide; some footage was lost and had to be reshot. See Geist, *Pictures Will Talk*, 267; Dauth, *Joseph L. Mankiewicz*, 25; Patrick Brion, *Joseph L. Mankiewicz: Biographie, filmographie illustrée, analyse critique* (Paris: La Martinière, 2005), 568. On Murphy, see William Russo, *A Thinker's Damn: Audie Murphy, Vietnam, and the Making of The Quiet American* (N.p., 2001), 146; on the lost footage and Redgrave's illness, see Russo, 172.

48. See Lewis, "The Third Force," 477; Russo, *A Thinker's Damn*, 223; Nashel, *Edward Lansdale's Cold War*, 168–71.

49. The U.S. reviews (all from 1958): Positive: Hazel Flynn, *Beverly Hills Citizen*, 24 January; Mae Tinee, *Chicago Tribune*, 20 February; Ben Crisler, *Christian Science Monitor*, 4 February; Philip T. Hartung, *Commonweal*, 21 February; Jesse Zunser, *Cue*, 8 February; John Rosenfield, *Dallas Morning News*, 15 March; *Film Daily*, 23 January; M.O.S., *Hartford Courant*, 19 April; *Hollywood Citizen-News*, 28 January; Philip K. Scheuer, *Los Angeles Times*, 24 January; Charles Aaronson, *Motion Picture Herald*, 25 January; Robert Hatch, *Nation*, 8 March; Archer Winsten, *New York Post*, 6 February; Paine Knickerbocker, *San Francisco Chronicle*, 24 January; Arthur Knight, *Saturday Review*, 25 January; Myles Standish, *St. Louis Post-Dispatch*, 14 February; Richard L. Coe, *Washington Post*, 23 January.

Negative: Al Weitschat, *Detroit News*, 2 March; *Hollywood Reporter*, 22 January; Ruth Waterbury, *Los Angeles Examiner*, 27 January; Kate Cameron, *New York Daily News*, 6 February; John McCarten, *New Yorker*, 15 February; Bosley Crowther, *New York Times*, 6 February; Hift., *Variety*, 22 January.

Mixed or neutral: Moira Walsh, *America*, 22 February; Larry Tajiri, *Denver Post*, 10 February; George Christian, *Houston Post*, 2 March; George Bourke, *Miami Herald*, 29 March; Mildred Martin, *Philadelphia Inquirer*, 24 January; Edwin Martin, *San Diego Union*, 13 February; *Time*, 10 February.

50. Nashel, *Edward Lansdale's Cold War*, 168, 171; see also Russo, *A Thinker's Damn*, 223.

51. Charging that Murphy was miscast were Edwin Martin, *San Diego Union*, 13 February; and Hift., *Variety*, 22 January. Praising Murphy were Hazel Flynn, *Beverly Hills Citizen*, 24 January; Ben Crisler, *Christian Science Monitor*, 14 February; John Rosenfield, *Dallas Morning News*, 15 March; and Paine Knickerbocker, *San Francisco Chronicle*, 24 January.

52. Redgrave's reply to the 9 January 1957 article ran on 29 January 1957.

53. The British reviews (all from 1958): Positive: F. J., *Daily Cinema*, 26 March; Jympson Harman, *Evening News*, 27 March; *Kinematograph Weekly*, 3 April; Frank Jackson, *Reynolds News*, 30 March; *Scotsman*, 6 May.

Negative: *Daily Herald*, 28 March; Campbell Dixon, *Daily Telegraph*, 19 January; Nina Hibbin, *Daily Worker*, 29 March; Derek Granger, *Financial Times*, 31 March; Molly Plowright, *Glasgow Herald*, 12 May; *Manchester Guardian*, 29 March; P. H., *Monthly Film Bulletin*, no. 292 (March–April), 59; *News Chronicle*, 28 March; William Whitebait, *New Statesman*, 12 April; David Robinson, *Sight and Sound* 27:4 (Spring 1958), 201; Dilys Powell, *Sunday Times*, 30 March.

Mixed: Leonard Mosley, *Daily Express*, 26 March; *Daily Mail*, 28 March; Philip Oakes, *Evening Standard*, 27 March; Derek Monsey, *Sunday Express*, 30 March; Charles MacLaren, *Time and Tide*, 5 April; Derek Hill, *Tribune*, 18 April.

54. Simsi, *Ciné-Passions*, part 3, p. 42.

55. The French reviews: Positive: *Aurore*, 17 July 1958; Eric Rohmer, *Cahiers du Cinéma*, no. 86 (August 1958), 46–51; C. M., *Carrefour*, 16 July 1958; Claude Gauteur, *Cinéma 58* (September–October 1958), 104–5; Simone Dubreuilh, *Libération*, 16 July 1958; Max Favalelli, *Paris-Presse/L'Intransigeant*, 13 July 1958; Luc Moullet, *Radio Cinéma Télévision*, 20 July 1958.

Negative: Henry Magnan, *Combat*, 19 July 1958; Denis Vincent, *Express*, 17 July 1958; Louis Chauvet, *Figaro*, 12 July 1958; Claude Mauriac, *Figaro Littéraire*, 26 July 1958; Jacques Doniol-Valcroze, *France Observateur*, 24 July 1958; France Roche, *France Soir*, 11 July 1958; Jacques Deltour, *Humanité*, 12 July 1958; P.-L. Thirard, *Lettres Françaises*, 24 July 1958; Jean de Baroncelli, *Monde*, 16 July 1958; Jacqueline Michel, *Parisien Libéré*, 16 July 1958; Elie Fovez, *Téléciné*, no. 80 (January/February 1959).

Mixed or neutral: Jean-Luc Godard, *Arts*, 16 July 1958; Michel Duran, *Canard Enchaîné*, 16 July 1958; Henri Pierre, *Monde*, 30 January 1958.

56. Whitfield, "Limited Engagement," 77.

57. Lewis, "The Third Force," 478; Whitfield, "Limited Engagement," 77; Bushnell, "*The Quiet American*: Graham Greene's Vietnam Novel," 416.

58. Peter Biskind, *Seeing Is Believing: How Hollywood Taught Us to Stop Worrying and Love the Fifties* (New York: Owl Books, 1983), 3, notes that anticommunist films did poorly at the box office in these years.

Part III • Dangerous Liaisons

1. Owen White calls it "an ugly word" implying "somebody has done something wrong"; see his "Miscegenation and the Popular Imagination," in *Promoting the Colonial Idea: Propaganda and Visions of Empire in France*, ed. Tony Chafer and Amanda Sackur (Houndmills, UK: Palgrave, 2002), 133. See also Robert J. C. Young, *Colonial Desire: Hybridity in Theory, Culture, and Race* (London: Routledge, 1995), 9.

2. See Philippa Levine, "Sexuality and Empire," in *At Home with the Empire: Metropolitan Culture and the Imperial World*, ed. Catherine Hall and Sonya O. Rose (Cambridge: Cambridge University Press, 2006), 134; Mary Beltrán and Camilla Fojas, "Introduction: Mixed Race in Hollywood Film and Culture Media," in *Mixed Race Hollywood*, ed. Mary Beltrán and Camilla Fojas (New York: New York University Press, 2008), 10; Gina Marchetti, *Romance and the "Yellow Peril": Race, Sex, and Discursive Strategies in Hollywood Fiction* (Berkeley: University of California Press, 1993), 110.

3. Ann Laura Stoler, *Carnal Knowledge and Imperial Power: Race and the Intimate in Colonial Rule* (Berkeley: University of California Press, 2010), 16; see also Ann Laura Stoler,

Haunted by Empire: Geographies of Intimacy in North American History (Durham: Duke University Press, 2006), 4.

4. Donald L. Kaufmann, "The Indian as Media Hand-me-down," in *The Pretend Indians: Images of Native Americans in the Movies*, ed. Gretchen M. Bataille and Charles L. P. Silet (Ames: Iowa State University Press, 1980), 27; Brian W. Dippie, *The Vanishing American: White Attitudes and U.S. Indian Policy* (Lawrence: University Press of Kansas, 1982), 257. On whites' opposition to mixing with Indians, see Elliott West, *The Contested Plains: Indians, Goldseekers, and the Rush to Colorado* (Lawrence: University Press of Kansas, 1998), 187.

5. Dippie, *Vanishing American*, 248–49. In the early twentieth century, some whites expressed similar attitudes about Asian immigrants; see Henry Yu, "Mixing Bodies and Cultures: The Meaning of America's Fascination with Sex between 'Orientals' and 'Whites,'" in *Sex, Love, Race: Crossing Boundaries in North American History*, ed. Martha Hodes (New York: New York University Press, 1999), 452–56.

6. Renee C. Romano, *Race Mixing: Black-White Marriage in Postwar America* (Gainesville: University Press of Florida, 2003), 2, 8.

7. On visual racism and cinema, see Susan Courtney, *Hollywood Fantasies of Miscegenation: Spectacular Narratives of Gender and Race, 1903–1967* (Princeton, NJ: Princeton University Press, 2005), 112.

8. Dippie, *Vanishing American*, 248.

9. For more detailed figures, see Romano, *Race Mixing*, 186.

10. See Romano, *Race Mixing*, 31–32; see also Courtney, *Hollywood Fantasies of Miscegenation*, 264. On the material foundations of American racism, see George Lipsitz, *The Possessive Investment in Whiteness: How White People Profit from Identity Politics*, rev. ed. (Philadelphia: Temple University Press, 2006).

11. See Romano, *Race Mixing*, 54–55, 66–69, 70, 128, 130.

12. On connections between the Cold War and racial issues, see Mary L. Dudziak, *Cold War Civil Rights: Race and the Image of American Democracy* (Princeton, NJ: Princeton University Press, 2000).

13. Romano, *Race Mixing*, 18.

14. On Robeson in Britain, see Kenneth M. Cameron, *Africa on Film: Beyond Black and White* (New York: Continuum, 1994), 99; Martin B. Duberman, *Paul Robeson: A Biography* (New York: New Press, 1989), 87–91, 118–24.

15. Wendy Webster, *Englishness and Empire, 1939–1965* (Oxford: Oxford University Press, 2005), 150, 173.

16. See Paul B. Rich, *Race and Empire in British Politics*, 2d ed. (Cambridge: Cambridge University Press, 1990), 152–54, 208. On the riots, see Lawrence James, *The Rise and Fall of the British Empire* (New York: St. Martin's Griffin, 1994), 434; Rich, *Race and Empire in British Politics*, 1, 220; Lucy Bland, "White Women and Men of Colour: Miscegenation Fears in Britain after the Great War," *Gender and History* 17 (2004): 29–61. On African American soldiers in Britain, see Romano, *Race Mixing*, 19; and Rich, *Race and Empire in British Politics*,161.

17. Rich, *Race and Empire in British Politics*,127, 132–33; Bill Schwarz, "'The Only White Man in There': The Re-Racialisation of England, 1956–68," *Race and Class* 38:1 (July–September 1996): 74; Webster, *Englishness and Empire*, 157–58.

18. Rich, *Race and Empire in British Politics*, 180. See also Judith M. Brown, "Epilogue," in *The Oxford History of the British Empire: The Twentieth Century*, ed. Judith M. Brown and William Roger Louis (Oxford: Oxford University Press, 1999), 708; Schwarz, "'The Only White Man in There,'" 65; Erik Bleich, *Race Politics in Britain and France: Ideas and Policymaking since the 1960s* (Cambridge: Cambridge University Press, 2003), 39.

19. See Rich, *Race and Empire in British Politics*, 187; Bleich, *Race Politics in Britain and France*, 43; Webster, *Englishness and Empire*, 164; Laura Tabili, "A Homogeneous Society? Britain's Internal 'Others,' 1800–Present," in *At Home with the Empire: Metropolitan Culture and the Imperial World*, ed. Catherine Hall and Sonya O. Rose (Cambridge: Cambridge University Press, 2006), 71.

20. Tyler Stovall, *Paris Noir: African Americans in the City of Light* (Boston: Houghton Mifflin, 1996), 78, 75, 74.

21. Ibid., 75.

22. Owen White, "Miscegenation and the Popular Imagination," in *Promoting the Colonial Idea: Propaganda and Visions of Empire in France*, ed. Tony Chafer and Amanda Sackur (Houndmills, UK: Palgrave, 2002), 136–37.

23. Olivier Barlet and Pascal Blanchard, "Rêver: L'impossible tentation du cinéma colonial (1920–1950)," in *Culture colonial en France: De la révolution à nos jours*, ed. Pascal Blanchard, Sandrine Lemaire, and Nicolas Bancel (Paris: CNRS, 2008), 194; Neil MacMaster, "Imperial Façades: Muslim Institutions and Propaganda in Inter-War Paris," in *Promoting the Colonial Idea*, ed. Chafer and Sackur, 72; White, "Miscegenation and the Popular Imagination," 138.

24. Gilles de Gantès, "Migration to Indochina: Proof of the Popularity of Colonial Empire?" in *Promoting the Colonial Idea*, ed. Chafer and Sackur, 23; Webster, *Englishness and Empire*, 42; Stoler, *Carnal Knowledge*, 49; Ronald Hyam, *Empire and Sexuality: The British Experience* (Manchester: Manchester University Press, 1990), 157–81.

25. On British Puritanism's decline, see S.J.D. Green, "The Strange Death of Puritan England, 1914–1945," in *Yet More Adventures with Britannia*, ed. William Roger Louis (London: I. B. Tauris, 2005), 185–209; see also Hyam, *Empire and Sexuality*, 177.

26. Levine, "Sexuality and Empire," 125–26.

27. "Benjamin Kidd and the Control of the Tropics," in *Imperialism*, ed. Philip D. Curtin (New York: Harper and Row, 1971), 36. See also Stoler, *Carnal Knowledge*, 66.

28. Levine, "Sexuality and Empire," 138; on fears of infertility, see Young, *Colonial Desire*, 8–9; Beltrán and Fojas, "Introduction: Mixed Race in Hollywood Film," 10.

29. Stoler, *Carnal Knowledge*, 110; see also Dina Sherzer, "Race Matters and Matters of Race: Interracial Relationships in Colonial and Postcolonial Films," in *Cinema, Colonialism, Postcolonialism: Perspectives from the French and Francophone Worlds*, ed. Dina Sherzer (Austin: University of Texas Press, 1996), 230; Levine, "Sexuality and Empire," 122; Philip Dine, *Images of the Algerian War: French Fiction and Film, 1954–1992* (Oxford: Clarendon, 1994), 201; Yu, "Mixing Bodies and Cultures," 457.

30. Dennis Judd, *Empire: The British Imperial Experience from 1765 to the Present* (London: Fontana, 1996), 179, calls interracial sex "a perk of the imperial system"; see also Hyam, *Empire and Sexuality*, 210.

31. See Stoler, *Carnal Knowledge*, 2, 48; Hyam, *Empire and Sexuality*, 117, 206; on images of Tahitians as eager sexual partners, see Alan Moorehead, *The Fatal Impact: The Invasion of the South Pacific, 1767–1840* (New York: Harper & Row, 1966), 39; Matt K.

Matsuda, *Empire of Love: Histories of France and the Pacific* (Oxford: Oxford University Press, 2005), 123.

32. The poem appears at http://www.daypoems.net/poems/1800.html.

33. Barot's essay is in John D. Hargreaves, ed. *France and West Africa: Anthology of Historical Documents* (London: Macmillan, 1969), 206–9. On Barot, see Owen White, *Children of the French Empire: Miscegenation and Colonial Society in French West Africa, 1895–1960* (Oxford: Clarendon, 1999), 1–2.

34. Hyam, *Empire and Sexuality*, 115–16.

35. Stoler, *Carnal Knowledge*, 90, 48.

36. Matsuda, *Empire of Love*, 141, 148.

37. See Hyam, *Empire and Sexuality*, 17, 206–7.

38. Hyam, *Empire and Sexuality*, 214–15, calls interracial romance "an act of racial conciliation" that "generates some admiration and affection across" barriers, even mitigating the harshness of rule.

39. Ruth Vasey, "Foreign Parts: Hollywood's Global Distribution and the Representation of Ethnicity," in *Movie Censorship and American Culture*, ed. Francis G. Couvares (Washington, DC: Smithsonian Institution Press, 1996), 221–25.

40. See Courtney, *Hollywood Fantasies of Miscegenation*, 19–22; M. Elise Marubbio, *Killing the Indian Maiden: Images of Native American Women in Film* (Lexington: University Press of Kentucky, 2006), 21; Ella Shohat and Robert Stam, *Unthinking Eurocentrism: Multiculturalism and the Media* (London: Routledge, 1994), 156–59; Marchetti, *Romance and the "Yellow Peril,"* 8–45.

41. On Pocahontas, see Rayna Green, "The Pocahontas Perplex: The Image of Indian Women in American Culture," *Massachusetts Review* 16:4 (Autumn 1975): 698–714; Marubbio, *Killing the Indian Maiden*, 13–14; on Madame Butterfly, see Marchetti, *Romance and the "Yellow Peril,"* 78–89.

42. Beltrán and Fojas, "Introduction: Mixed Race in Hollywood Film," 1; Marubbio, *Killing the Indian Maiden*, 92.

43. Beltrán and Fojas, "Introduction: Mixed Race in Hollywood Film," 10.

44. See Olga J. Martin, *The Literature of Cinema* (New York: H. W. Wilson, 1937), 18.

45. On the operation of the system, see Lea Jacobs, *The Wages of Sin: Censorship and the Fallen-Woman Film, 1928–1942* (Madison: University of Wisconsin Press, 1991), 18–24.

46. Shohat and Stam, *Unthinking Eurocentrism*, 160, argue that the code prohibited "any portrayal of racial and sexual violence toward African-Americans." See also Courtney, *Hollywood Fantasies of Miscegenation*, 103.

47. Beltrán and Fojas, "Introduction: Mixed Race in Hollywood Film," 7–8; Marchetti, *Romance and the "Yellow Peril,"* 128; On the evolution of the code, see http://productioncode.dhwritings.com/multipleframes_productioncode.php; see also Courtney, *Hollywood Fantasies of Miscegenation*, 122, 129–30, 140.

48. On this point see Beltrán and Fojas, "Introduction: Mixed Race in Hollywood Film," 8; and Edward Buscombe, *Injuns! Native Americans in the Movies* (London: Reaktion, 2006), 155.

49. Courtney, *Hollywood Fantasies of Miscegenation*, 103–4.

50. Darryl F. Zanuck to Delmer Daves, Jason Joy, Bob Jacks, and Ray Klune, 15 June 1950, Delmer Daves Papers, box 29, folder 15, Stanford University Libraries, Special Collections, Stanford, CA.

51. See Courtney, *Hollywood Fantasies of Miscegenation*, 133; Mark Harris, *Pictures at a Revolution: Five Movies and the Birth of the New Hollywood* (New York: Penguin, 2008), 182.

52. Emily Belser, "Brutality Gives Movie Censor Most Trouble," *Denver Post*, 17 February 1955. On the studios' questioning whether the ban was enforceable, see Thomas Cripps, *Making Movies Black: The Hollywood Message Movie from World War II to the Civil Rights Era* (New York: Oxford University Press, 1993), 239.

53. Cripps, *Making Movies Black*, 246, 215.

54. Russell Campbell, "The Ideology of the Social Consciousness Movie: Three Films of Darryl F. Zanuck," *Quarterly Review of Film Studies* 3:1 (Winter 1978): 56; on Truman, see Cripps, *Making Movies Black*, 239; on *Pinky*'s effects on Hollywood, see Cripps, 218–19.

55. Beltrán and Fojas, "Introduction: Mixed Race in Hollywood Film," 18; Paul Swann, "The Little State Department: Washington and Hollywood's Rhetoric of the Postwar Audience," in *Hollywood in Europe: Experiences of a Cultural Hegemony*, ed. David W. Ellwood and Rob Kroes (Amsterdam: VU University Press, 1994), 193.

56. Those four were *Unconquered*, *Charge at Feather River*, *The Searchers*, and *The Last Wagon*. Brief allusions in the dialogue appeared in *Drum Beat* and *Pillars in the Sky*.

Chapter 7 · Miscegenation in Westerns

1. On *My Darling Clementine*, see M. Elise Marubbio, *Killing the Indian Maiden: Images of Native American Women in Film* (Lexington: University Press of Kentucky, 2006), 113–17; and Michael Coyne, *The Crowded Prairie: American National Identity in the Hollywood Western* (London: I. B. Tauris, 1998), 34–41.

2. On the directors' credits, see http://www.imdb.com/title/tt0038499/fullcredits?ref_=tt_ov_dr#directors.

3. On Selznick and Vidor, see David Thomson, *Showman: The Life of David O. Selznick* (New York: Alfred A. Knopf, 1992), 451–53; see also King Vidor's comments in his interview with Richard Schickel, "Duel with David," in *The Men Who Made the Movies*, ed. Richard Schickel (New York: Atheneum, 1975), 155.

4. Ronald Haver, *David O. Selznick's Hollywood* (New York: Alfred A. Knopf, 1980), 368; Raymond Durgnat and Scott Simmon, *King Vidor, American* (Berkeley: University of California Press, 1988), 241. Taking it as serious art is Jerome Pryor, "*Duel in the Sun*: A Classical Symphony," *New Orleans Review* 17:4 (Winter 1990): 8–19.

5. Reporting a budget (excluding prints and advertising) of $5,255,000 is Rudy Behlmer, ed. *Memo from David O. Selznick* (New York: Viking Press, 1972), 349. Box Office Mojo says the production budget was $8 million: http://boxofficemojo.com/movies/?id=duelinthesun.htm.

6. On Breen, see Angela Aleiss, *Making the White Man's Indian: Native Americans and Hollywood Movies* (Westport, CT: Praeger, 2005), 85.

7. Coyne, *Crowded Prairie*, calls it "ultraconservative," 43; Aleiss, *Making the White Man's Indian*, considers it progressive for its time, 82.

8. On World War II and cinematic images of Indians, see Aleiss, *Making the White Man's Indian*, chap. 4.

9. See Thomas Cripps, *Making Movies Black: The Hollywood Message Movie from World War II to the Civil Rights Era* (New York: Oxford University Press, 1993), 194.

10. *Variety*, 7 January 1948.

11. Selznick biographer David Thomson calls the releasing strategy "a way of cleaning

up quickly and outflanking bad reviews," and despite the revenues, "still it is uncertain whether it broke even"; see *Showman*, 468, 473; on Selznick's releasing strategy, see Susan Ohmer, *George Gallup in Hollywood* (New York: Columbia University Press, 2006), 223.

12. The U S. reviews: Positive: Marjory Adams, *Boston Globe*, 9 May 1947; *Film Daily*, 31 December 1946; H.V.A., *Hartford Courant*, 8 May 1947; Jack D. Grant, *Hollywood Reporter*, 31 December 1946; Louella O. Parsons, *Los Angeles Examiner*, 1 January 1947; Edwin Schallert, *Los Angeles Times*, 1 January 1947; William R. Weaver, *Motion Picture Herald*, 11 January 1947; Mildred Martin, *Philadelphia Inquirer*, 30 May 1947.

Negative: Paul Jones, *Atlanta Constitution*, 23 May 1947; Elinor Hughes, *Boston Herald*, 9 May 1947; Mae Tinee, *Chicago Tribune*, 17 May 1947; Philip T. Hartung, *Commonweal*, 23 May 1947; Jesse Zunser, *Cue*, 10 May 1947; Fairfax Nisbet, *Dallas Morning News*, 13 May 1947; *Life*, 10 February 1947; Kate Cameron, *New York Daily News*, 8 May 1947; John McCarten, *New Yorker*, 17 May 1947; Archer Winsten, *New York Post*, 8 May 1947; Bosley Crowther, *New York Times*, 8 May 1947; John Hobart, *San Francisco Chronicle*, 9 May 1947.

Mixed or neutral: *Newsweek*, 3 March 1947; *Time*, 17 March 1947; Brog., *Variety*, 1 January 1947; Richard L. Coe, *Washington Post*, 22 May 1947.

13. Thomson, *Showman*, 470.

14. The British reviews (all from 1947): Positive: P. L. Mannock, *Daily Herald*, 22 May; *London Times*, 21 May; Ewart Hodgson, *News of the World*, 25 May; A. E. Wilson, *Star*, no date in British Film Institute clippings file.

Negative: *Daily Mail*, 23 May; Reg Whitley, *Daily Mirror*, 23 May; *Daily Worker*, 24 May; *Evening News*, 22 May; *Manchester Guardian*, 24 May; C. A. Lejeune, *Observer*, 25 May; Geoffrey Bell, *Spectator*, 30 May; *Sunday Chronicle*, 25 May; Stephen Watts, *Sunday Express*, 25 May; Helen Fletcher, *Sunday Graphic*, 25 May; Roger Manvell, *Tribune*, 23 May.

Mixed: *Monthly Film Bulletin*, no. 168 (31 July), 97; Dilys Powell, *Sunday Times*, 25 May.

15. Simon Simsi, *Ciné-Passions: 7e art et industrie de 1945 à 2000* (Paris: Dixit, 2000), 51 and annual chart for 1949. Six French reviews, all negative, were: Yvonne Genova, *Ce Soir*, 9 January 1949; J.-P. Vivet, *Combat*, 5 January 1949; Louis Chauvet, *Figaro*, 27 August 1948; Georges Sadoul, *Lettres Françaises*, 6 January 1949; Henry Magnan, *Monde*, 5 January 1949; *Noir et Blanc*, 19 January 1949.

16. Marubbio, *Killing the Indian Maiden*, 68; Michael Walker, "The Westerns of Delmer Daves," in *The Book of Westerns*, ed. Ian Cameron and Douglas Pye (New York: Continuum, 1996), 128–29; see also John Saunders, *The Western Genre* (London: Wallflower, 2001), 93–94; Joanna Hearne, "The 'Ache for Home': Assimilation and Separatism in Anthony Mann's *Devil's Doorway*," in *Hollywood's West: The American Frontier in Film, Television, and History*, ed. Peter C. Rollins and John E. O'Connor (Lexington: University Press of Kentucky, 2005), 126, 140.

17. Walker, "The Westerns of Delmer Daves," 127.

18. Marubbio, *Killing the Indian Maiden*, 75; *Time*, 19 November 1951.

19. In response to *Time*'s review, MGM's Robert Vogel wrote to the PCA, "Since this publication snipes at the Code frequently, I think they should be answered—not with the idea of seeking a retraction, but to try to wear them down mentally to the point where they, at least, stop making mistakes"; see Robert M. W. Vogel to Joseph Breen, 12 December 1951, PCA Records, Production Files, *Across the Wide Missouri*, Herrick Library, Academy of Motion Picture Arts and Sciences (AMPAS), Beverly Hills, CA.

20. *Variety*, 25 January 1956. The U.S. reviews (all from 1955): Positive: Marjory Adams,

Boston Globe, 7 July; Kay Proctor, Los Angeles Examiner, 30 June; Vincent Canby, Motion Picture Herald, 18 June; Robert Wagner, New Orleans Times-Picayune, 7 July; Dorothy Masters, New York Daily News, 14 July.

Negative: Mae Tinee, Chicago Tribune, 24 August; Rod Nordell, Christian Science Monitor, 7 July; Philip T. Hartung, Commonweal, 15 July; John Rosenfield, Dallas Morning News, 1 July; Al Weitschat, Detroit News, 14 July; Archer Winsten, New York Post, 14 July; A. H. Weiler, New York Times, 14 July; William Hogan, San Francisco Chronicle, 7 July.

Mixed or neutral: Moira Walsh, America, 30 July; R.S.T., Boston Herald, 7 July; Marjorie Barrett, Denver Post, 18 July; Hollywood Reporter, 14 June; Philip K. Scheuer, Los Angeles Times, 30 June; Arthur Knight, Saturday Review, 30 July; Brog., Variety, 15 June.

21. See David N. Eldridge, "'Dear Owen': The CIA, Luigi Luraschi, and Hollywood, 1953," Historical Journal of Film, Radio and Television 20:2 (June 2000): letter 8 (9 February 1953), 170–71, 188.

22. Variety, 8 January 1958.

23. George Stevens Papers, Giant—Previews (first and second): May 22, 1956 (California Theater) and May 23 (El Cajon Theater); file 53.f-661, Herrick Library, AMPAS.

24. Earle L. Kirby letter to Warner Bros. Studio, March 3, 1957, George Stevens Papers, Giant—Correspondence, 1954–1956, file 50.f-604, Herrick Library, AMPAS.

25. The U.S. reviews (all from 1956): Positive: Paul Jones, Atlanta Constitution, 20 November; Marjory Adams, Boston Globe, 2 November; Elinor Hughes, Boston Herald, 2 November; George Daniels, Chicago Defender, 5 November; Will Leonard, Chicago Tribune, 29 October; John Beaufort, Christian Science Monitor, 2 November; Philip T. Hartung, Commonweal, 26 October; John Rosenfield, Dallas Morning News, 11 November; Mandel Herbstman, Film Daily, 10 October; James Powers, Hollywood Reporter, 10 October; Edwin Schallert, Los Angeles Times, 18 October; William R. Weaver, Motion Picture Herald, 20 October; Jack Boyd, Jr., New Orleans Times-Picayune, 1 November; Newsweek, 22 October; Kate Cameron, New York Daily News, 11 October; Bosley Crowther, New York Times, 11 October; Mildred Martin, Philadelphia Inquirer, 10 November; Paine Knickerbocker, San Francisco Chronicle, 2 November; Hollis Alpert, Saturday Review, 13 October; Edward Kosmal, St. Louis Post-Dispatch, 5 November; Time, 22 October; Hift., Variety, 10 October.

Negative: Archer Winsten, New York Post, 11 October.

Mixed or neutral: John McCarten, New Yorker, 20 October; Richard L. Coe, Washington Post, 3 November.

26. John Rosenfield, "Broad Canvas of Film 'Giant,'" Dallas Morning News, 11 November 1956; "Texans Can Take It," Dallas Morning News, 17 November 1956.

27. The British reviews (all from 1957): Positive: Emery Pearce, Daily Herald, 4 January; Jympson Harman, Evening News, 3 January; Manchester Guardian, 5 January; Peter Burnup, News of the World, 6 January; Isabel Quigly, Spectator, 11 January; Roy Nash, Star, 3 January; Dilys Powell, Sunday Times, 6 January.

Negative: Leonard Mosley, Daily Express, 3 January; Harold Conway, Daily Sketch, 3 January; Philip Oakes, Evening Standard, 4 January; London Times, 7 January; Paul Dehn, News Chronicle, 4 January; Milton Shulman, Sunday Express, 6 January; Times Educational Supplement, 8 February.

Mixed or neutral: Robert Kennedy, Daily Worker, 5 January; D. P., Monthly Film Bulletin, no. 277 (February); C. A. Lejeune, Observer, 6 January; Harris Deans, Sunday Dispatch, 6 January.

28. Simsi, *Ciné-Passions*, 69 and the annual chart for 1957.
29. Jean de Baroncelli, *Monde*, 16 March 1957.
30. The French reviews (all from 1957): Positive: Pierre Laroche, *Canard Enchaîné*, 20 March; Jean Dutourd, *Carrefour*, 20 March; Louis Chauvet, *Figaro*, 16 March; Georges Sadoul, *Lettres Françaises*, 21 March; Georges Charensol, *Nouvelles Littéraires*, 28 March; Claude Brule, *Paris-Presse/L'Intransigeant*, 22 March; J.-L. Tallenay, *Radio Cinéma Télévision*, 31 March.

Negative: François Truffaut, *Arts*, 20 March; Claude Garson, *Aurore*, 14 March; R.-M. Arlaud, *Combat*, 22 March; *Express*, 22 March.

Mixed or neutral: Jean Rochereau, *Croix*, 29 March; André Bazin, *Education Nationale*, 28 March; André Bazin, *France Observateur*, 21 March; Armand Monjo, *Humanité*, 20 March; *Libération*, 19 March; D. de F., *Nouveaux Jours*, 23 March.

Chapter 8 · Romance across the Pacific

1. Darryl F. Zanuck letters to Delmer Daves, 14 June and 4 May 1950, Delmer Daves Papers, box 29, folder 15, Stanford University Libraries, Special Collections, Stanford, CA.
2. Gina Marchetti, *Romance and the "Yellow Peril": Race, Sex, and Discursive Strategies in Hollywood Fiction* (Berkeley: University of California Press, 1993), 153, 156.
3. Ibid., 114.
4. Ibid., 111.
5. Ibid., 118. The film conveys what Christina Klein calls "the idea of alliance among independent parties—the model of postwar integration—rather than the idea of an empire unified by blood and force"; see Klein, *Cold War Orientalism: Asia in the Middlebrow Imagination, 1945–1961* (Berkeley: University of California Press, 2003), 146.
6. Ibid., 164.
7. On the McCarran-Walter Act of 1952, see Michael C. Thornton, "The Quiet Immigration: Foreign Spouses of U.S. Citizens, 1945–1985," in *Racially Mixed People in America*, ed. Maria P. P. Root (Newbury Park, CA: Sage, 1992), 67–68; David M. Reimers, *Still the Golden Door: The Third World Comes to America* (New York: Columbia University Press, 1985), 20–22. U.S. Commissioner of Immigration and Naturalization figures appear in Bok-Lim C. Kim, "Asian Wives of U.S. Servicemen: Women in Shadows," *Amerasia* 4:1 (1977): 99. On attention to the issue, see Caroline Chung Simpson, "'Out of an Obscure Place': Japanese War Brides and Cultural Pluralism in the 1950s," *Differences: A Journal of Feminist Cultural Studies* 10:3 (1998): 51–53.
8. The U.S. reviews (all from 1952): Positive: *Boston Globe*, 8 February; Mae Tinee, *Chicago Tribune*, 4 February; Rod Nordell, *Christian Science Monitor*, 8 February; *Dallas Morning News*, 23 February; *Film Daily*, 21 January; M.O.S., *Hartford Courant*, 24 January; John L. Scott, *Los Angeles Times*, 8 February; Fred Hift, *Motion Picture Herald*, 12 January; *Newsweek*, 11 February; Joe Pihodna, *New York Herald Tribune*, 30 January; Brog., *Variety*, 9 January.

Negative: *Time*, 4 February.

Mixed or neutral: R.S.T., *Boston Herald*, 8 February; Irene Thirer, *New York Post*, 30 January.

9. Naoko Shibusawa, *America's Geisha Ally: Reimagining the Japanese Enemy* (Cambridge, MA: Harvard University Press, 2006), 265.
10. Marchetti, *Romance and the "Yellow Peril*," 134–35.

11. Susan Courtney, *Hollywood Fantasies of Miscegenation: Spectacular Narratives of Gender and Race, 1903–1967* (Princeton, NJ: Princeton University Press, 2005), 232; Marchetti, *Romance and the "Yellow Peril,"* 137–38.

12. Producer William Goetz said the accent "was 100 percent Marlon's idea." See Philip K. Scheuer, "'Sayonara' Filming Loaded with High Drama, Intrigue," *Los Angeles Times,* 19 January 1958. See also Truman Capote, *Portraits and Observations* (New York: Modern Library, 2008), 191.

13. Courtney, *Hollywood Fantasies of Miscegenation,* 230; Marchetti, *Romance and the "Yellow Peril,"* 137.

14. On American officials turning a blind eye to interracial sex, see Sarah Kovner, *Occupying Power: Sex Workers and Servicemen in Postwar Japan* (Stanford, CA: Stanford University Press, 2012), 26.

15. William Goetz, memo on telephone conversation with Colonel Miranda, 31 December 1956, Sayonara production files, Warner Bros. Archives, University of Southern California, Los Angeles. The Takarazuka theater troupe also withheld assistance because of its depiction and because of the casting of Ricardo Montalban as a Japanese; see J. E. [Jack] Dagal, letter to Mr. Wolfe Cohen, 15 May 1956, Sayonara production files, WB Archives, USC.

16. Marchetti, *Romance and the "Yellow Peril,"* 140, 139.

17. John Dower, *Embracing Defeat: Japan in the Wake of World War II* (New York: W. W. Norton, 1999), 211.

18. Marchetti, *Romance and the "Yellow Peril,"* 135.

19. *Variety,* 7 January 1959. The U.S. reviews: Positive: Paul Jones, *Atlanta Constitution,* 2 January 1958; Marjory Adams, *Boston Globe,* 26 December 1957; R.S.T., *Boston Herald,* 26 December 1957; Mae Tinee, *Chicago Tribune,* 25 December 1957; *Cue,* 7 December 1957; John Rosenfield, *Dallas Morning News,* 31 December 1957; Larry Tajiri, *Denver Post,* 1 January 1958; Al Weitschat, *Detroit News,* 5 January 1958; Mandel Herbstman, *Film Daily,* 13 November 1957; James Powers, *Hollywood Reporter,* 13 November 1957; Jack Moffitt, *Hollywood Reporter,* 14 January 1958; Ruth Waterbury, *Los Angeles Examiner,* 26 December 1957; Philip K. Scheuer, *Los Angeles Times,* 17 November 1957; Edwin Schallert, *Los Angeles Times,* 26 December 1957; Charles S. Aaronson, *Motion Picture Herald,* 16 November 1957; Virginia Turman, *New Orleans Times-Picayune,* 1 January 1958; Kate Cameron, *New York Daily News,* 6 December 1957; John McCarten, *New Yorker,* 14 December 1957; Archer Winsten, *New York Post,* 6 December 1957; Bosley Crowther, *New York Times,* 6 December 1957; Mildred Martin, *Philadelphia Inquirer,* 26 December 1957; Edwin Martin, *San Diego Union,* 26 December 1957; Paine Knickerbocker, *San Francisco Chronicle,* 26 December 1957; Hollis Alpert, *Saturday Review,* 28 December 1957; Myles Standish, *St. Louis Post-Dispatch,* 7 February 1958; Hift., *Variety,* 13 November 1957; Richard L. Coe, *Washington Post,* 26 December 1957.

Negative: Moira Walsh, *America,* 21 December 1957; *Newsweek,* 9 December 1957.

Mixed or neutral: Ben Crisler, *Christian Science Monitor,* 26 December 1957; Philip T. Hartung, *Commonweal,* 13 December 1957; *Hollywood Citizen News,* 8 January 1958; Robert Hatch, *Nation,* 21 December 1957; *Time,* 16 December 1957.

20. The British reviews (all from 1958): Positive: Frank Entwisle, *Daily Mirror,* 7 February; Campbell Dixon, *Daily Telegraph,* 8 February; *Manchester Guardian,* 8 February; Ivon Adams, *Star,* 6 February.

Negative: Jympson Harman, *Evening News*, 6 February; P.J.D., *Monthly Film Bulletin*, February 1958; William Whitebait, *New Statesman*, 15 February; Frank Jackson, *Reynolds News*, 9 February; Isabel Quigly, *Spectator*, 14 February; Moore Raymond, *Sunday Dispatch*, 9 February.

Mixed or neutral: Leonard Mosley, *Daily Express*, 7 February; Harry Weaver, *Daily Herald*, 7 February; Nina Hibbin, *Daily Worker*, 8 February; Derek Granger, *Financial Times*, 10 February; *London Times*, 6 February; Paul Dehn, *News Chronicle*, 7 February; Peter Burnup, *News of the World*, 9 February; *People*, 9 February; Milton Shulman, *Sunday Express*, 9 February; Dilys Powell, *Sunday Times*, 9 February; Charles MacLaren, *Time and Tide*, 15 February.

21. Simon Simsi, *Ciné-Passions: 7e art et industrie de 1945 à 2000* (Paris: Dixit, 2000), 136. The French reviews (all from 1958): Positive: Jean Rochereau, *Croix*, 12 April; Georges Sadoul, *Lettres Françaises*, 10 April; Pierre Laroche, *Noir et Blanc*, 11 April.

Negative: R.-M. Arlaud, *Combat*, 1 April; André Bazin, *Parisien Libéré*, 31 March; André Bazin, *Radio Cinéma Télévision*, 13 April.

Mixed or neutral: Jean de Baroncelli, *Monde*, 5 April; Luc Moullet, *Radio Cinéma Télévision*, 2 March.

22. Bazin, *Radio Cinéma Télévision*, 13 April.

23. Matt K. Matsuda, *Empire of Love: Histories of France and the Pacific* (Oxford: Oxford University Press, 2005).

Chapter 9 · Black-White Couples and Internal Decolonization

1. See George Lipsitz, *The Possessive Investment in Whiteness: How White People Profit from Identity Politics*, rev. ed. (Philadelphia: Temple University Press, 2006).

2. Charles Palmer, Revised Step Sheet, April 22, 1948, p. 12, in Charles Palmer Papers, Lost Boundaries, file 2.f-20, Herrick Library, Academy of Motion Picture Arts and Sciences (AMPAS), Beverly Hills, CA.

3. Thomas Cripps, *Making Movies Black: The Hollywood Message Movie from World War II to the Civil Rights Era* (New York: Oxford University Press, 1993), 228.

4. Donald Bogle, *Toms, Coons, Mulattoes, Mammies, and Bucks*, 4th ed. (New York: Continuum, 2001), 150.

5. Cripps, *Making Movies Black*, 227–28.

6. Bogle, *Toms*, 150.

7. Cripps, *Making Movies Black*, 227–28.

8. Bogle, *Toms*, 150.

9. *Variety*, annual chart, 4 January 1950; *Variety*, 29 June 1949.

10. See Cripps, *Making Movies Black*, 231.

11. Margaret T. McGehee cites two reviews (the *New York Times* and the *Chicago Defender*) for her claim that the film got mixed reviews; see McGehee, "Disturbing the Peace: *Lost Boundaries*, *Pinky*, and Censorship in Atlanta, Georgia, 1949–1952," *Cinema Journal* 46:1 (Fall 2006): 28.

The U.S. reviews (all from 1949): Positive: *America*, 16 July; Marjory Adams, *Boston Globe*, 16 July; Elinor Hughes, *Boston Herald*, 16 July; Lillian Scott, *Chicago Defender*, 9 July; Mae Tinee, *Chicago Tribune*, 3 September; Philip T. Hartung, *Commonweal*, 15 July; Fairfax Nisbet, *Dallas Morning News*, 21 October; John Finlayson, *Detroit News*, 20 August; *Film Daily*, 28 June; *Hartford Courant*, 15 September; Edwin Schallert, *Los Angeles Times*, 6 August; Charles J. Lazarus, *Motion Picture Herald*, 2 July; Robert Hatch, *New Republic*, 4 July; *Newsweek*, 4 July; Dorothy Masters, *New York Daily News*, 1 July; Archer Winsten, *New York Post*, 30 June; Bosley Crowther, *New York Times*, 1 July; Mildred Martin, *Philadelphia Inquirer*, 24 October; Myles Standish, *St. Louis Post-Dispatch*, 9 December; *Time*, 4 July; Herm., *Variety*, 29 June.

Mixed: Manny Farber, *Nation*, 30 July.

12. S.W.P., *Manchester Guardian*, 6 June 1950; Honor Arundel, *Daily Worker*, 21 June 1950.

13. *London Times*, 23 January 1950.

14. Dilys Powell, *Sunday Times*, 22 January 1950.

15. Ford clashed with Ethel Waters and then claimed illness and quit; see Michael Ciment, ed., *Kazan on Kazan* (New York: Viking, 1974), 59; Leonard Mosley, *Zanuck: The Rise and Fall of Hollywood's Last Tycoon* (Boston: Little Brown & Co., 1984), 238.

16. Russell Campbell, "The Ideology of the Social Consciousness Movie: Three Films of Darryl F. Zanuck," *Quarterly Review of Film Studies* 3:1 (Winter 1978): 66–67; Susan Courtney, *Hollywood Fantasies of Miscegenation: Spectacular Narratives of Gender and Race, 1903–1967* (Princeton, NJ: Princeton University Press, 2005), 190, 343n65; McGehee, "Disturbing the Peace," 33; Miriam J. Petty, "Passing for Horror: Race, Fear, and Elia Kazan's *Pinky*," *Genders OnLine Journal* (http://www.genders.org/g40/g40_petty.html) 40 (2004): paragraphs 15, 35, 38, 43; Michael Rogin, "'Democracy and Burnt Cork': The End of Blackface, the Beginning of Civil Rights," in *Refiguring American Genres*, ed. Nick Browne (Berkeley: University of California Press, 1998), 186, 189; Mark A. Reid, *Redefining Black Film* (Berkeley: University of California Press, 1993), 45; Anna Everett, *Returning the Gaze: A Genealogy of Black Film Criticism, 1909–1949* (Durham, NC: Duke University Press, 2001), 307–8. Rare exceptions to this pattern are Cripps, *Making Movies Black*, 232; and Ginger Clark, "Cinema of Compromise: *Pinky* and the Politics of Post War Film Production," *Western Journal of Black Studies* 21:3 (1997): 186.

17. Bogle, *Toms*, 152; McGehee, "Disturbing the Peace," 41; see also Elspeth kydd [sic], "'The Ineffable Curse of Cain': Racial Marking and Embodiment in *Pinky*," *Camera Obscura* 15:1 43 (2000): 117–18.

18. Zanuck to Michael Abel, quoted in Clark, "Cinema of Compromise," 182.

19. Clark, "Cinema of Compromise," 182.

20. Alan Gevinson, ed., *American Film Institute Catalog: Within Our Gates; Ethnicity in American Feature Films, 1911–1960* (Berkeley: University of California Press, 1997), 777; Cripps, *Making Movies Black*, 235.

21. Darryl F. Zanuck letter to Dudley Nichols, 1 November 1948, in *Memo from Darryl F. Zanuck: The Golden Years at Twentieth Century-Fox*, ed. Rudy Behlmer (New York: Grove Press, 1993), 162. See also Mosley, *Zanuck*, 240.

22. Quoted in Gevinson, *American Film Institute Catalog*, 777; see also Cripps, *Making Movies Black*, 234.

23. Quoted in Gevinson, *American Film Institute Catalog*, 777.

24. Darryl F. Zanuck memo to John Ford, 26 February 1946 in Behlmer, *Memo from Darryl F. Zanuck*, 103.

25. Mosley, *Zanuck*, 239.

26. Fredi Washington, at forty-five, was too old to play a recent graduate; Crain was twenty-three.

27. kydd, "'Ineffable Curse of Cain,'" 101; Petty, "Passing for Horror," paragraph 19; Christopher John Jones, "Image and Ideology in Kazan's *Pinky*," *Literature Film Quarterly* 9:2 (1981):117.

28. Quoted in Gevinson, *American Film Institute Catalog*, 777; see also Cripps, *Making Movies Black*, 234.

29. Quoted in Campbell, "Ideology of the Social Consciousness Movie," 67.

30. Raymond Klune made the suggestion; see Mosley, *Zanuck*, 239.

31. Reid, *Redefining Black Film*, 45.

32. Ibid. Joel Williamson notes that mulattoes provided leadership for southern blacks; see *New People: Miscegenation and Mulattoes in the United States* (New York: New York University Press, 1984), 87.

33. Petty, "Passing for Horror," paragraph 29.

34. Ibid., paragraph 35; see also paragraphs 38, 45.

35. On the origins of the one-drop rule, see Williamson, *New People*, 1–2, 73–75, 97, 108–9; Kerry Ann Rockquemore and David L. Brunsma, *Beyond Black: Biracial Identity in America*, 2d ed. (Lanham, MD: Rowman and Littlefield, 2008), 4–9.

36. Minkah Makalani opposes biracial identity and, for purposes of solidarity, urges people of mixed race to identify as black; see "A Biracial Identity or a New Race? The Historical Limitations and Political Implications of a Biracial Identity," *Souls* (Fall 2001): 83–112.

37. Quoted in George F. Custen, *Twentieth Century's Fox: Darryl F. Zanuck and the Culture of Hollywood* (New York: Basic Books, 1997), 300–301.

38. Mulatto identities declined between 1850 and 1920; see Williamson, *New People*, 113–14, 163. Biracial identities reemerged in the late twentieth century, and in 2000 the U.S. Census let respondents check more than one box for ethnicity. The topic also attracted growing scholarly attention in the 1990s. See Maria P. P. Root, ed., *Racially Mixed People in America* (Newbury Park, CA: Sage, 1992); idem, *The Multiracial Experience: Racial Borders as the New Frontier* (Thousand Oaks, CA: Sage, 1996); Kathleen Odell Korgen, *From Black to Biracial: Transforming Racial Identity among Americans* (Westport, CT: Praeger, 1998); Rockquemore and Brunsma, *Beyond Black*.

39. Malcolm X, *The Autobiography of Malcolm X* (New York: Ballantine Books, 1999), 251.

40. See William L. Van DeBurg, ed., *Modern Black Nationalism: From Marcus Garvey to Louis Farrakhan* (New York: New York University Press, 1997).

41. Cripps, *Making Movies Black*, 237.

42. Ralph Ellison, *Shadow and Act* (New York: Vintage International, 1995), 279–80.

43. Campbell, "Ideology of the Social Consciousness Movie," 66; kydd, "'Ineffable Curse of Cain,'" 111.

44. Jones, "Image and Ideology in Kazan's *Pinky*," 118.

45. *Variety*, 4 January 1950.

46. William Gordon, "Record Crowd Turns Out at First Showing of 'Pinky,'" *Atlanta Daily World*, 18 November 1949; "Racial Picture Packs Theater," *Atlanta Constitution*, 18 November 1949; "'Pinky' Atlanta Bow Calm," *New York Times*, 18 November 1949.

47. The cuts affected the rape scene, the police slapping Rozelia, and Pinky kissing Tom; A. H. Weiler, "By Way of Report," *New York Times*, 6 November 1949.

48. Quoted in Gevinson, *American Film Institute Catalog*, 778.

49. "'Pinky' Atlanta Bow Calm," *New York Times*, 18 November 1949.
50. *Boston Herald*, 7 October 1949; *Atlanta Constitution*, 17 November 1949.
51. Reports on bans appear in *Atlanta Daily World*, 11 July 1950; *Chicago Defender*, 22 July 1950; *Pittsburgh Courier*, 4 February 1950. On the Texas incident, see Gevinson, *American Film Institute Catalog*, 778; McGehee, "Disturbing the Peace," 44; Allen Duckworth, "Censoring of Film to Get Legal Test," *Dallas Morning News*, 3 November 1950.
52. *Chicago Defender*, 27 May 1950.
53. Clark, "Cinema of Compromise," 185, says it received mixed reviews. The U.S. reviews: Positive: Moira Walsh, *America*, 8 October 1949; Paul Jones, *Atlanta Constitution*, 18 November 1949; William Gordon, *Atlanta Daily World*, 18 November 1949; Marjory Adams, *Boston Globe*, 8 October 1949; Elinor Hughes, *Boston Herald*, 8 October 1949; Bob Roy, *Chicago Defender*, 26 November 1949; Mae Tinee, *Chicago Tribune*, 16 November 1949; Philip T. Hartung, *Commonweal*, 14 October 1949; John Rosenfield, *Dallas Morning News*, 16 January 1950; Al Weitschat, *Detroit News*, 3 December 1949; *Film Daily*, 30 September 1949; M.O.S., *Hartford Courant*, 3 December 1949; *Hollywood Reporter*, 30 September 1949; Edwin Schallert, *Los Angeles Times*, 22 October 1949; Elise Beauchamp, *New Orleans Times-Picayune*, 2 December 1949; *Newsweek*, 10 October 1949; Lena Brown, *New York Amsterdam News*, 1 October 1949; Kate Cameron, *New York Daily News*, 30 September 1949; Howard Barnes, *New York Herald Tribune*, 30 September 1949; Archer Winsten, *New York Post*, 30 September 1949; Bosley Crowther, *New York Times*, 30 September 1949 and 9 October 1949; Mildred Martin, *Philadelphia Inquirer*, 1 December 1949; John Hobart, *San Francisco Chronicle*, 28 October 1949; *Time*, 10 October 1949; Herb., *Variety*, 5 October 1949; Richard L. Coe, *Washington Post*, 24 November 1949.

Negative: Robert Hatch, *New Republic*, 3 October 1949.

54. Walter White, "Regrets He Has No Words of Praise for 'Pinky,'" *Chicago Defender*, 29 October 1949.
55. Ellison, *Shadow and Act*, 277, 280.
56. Cab Calloway, "'Cab' Calloway Finds No Problems Solved in 'Pinky,' 'Lost Boundaries,'" *Chicago Defender*, 19 November 1949.
57. The *New York Herald Tribune* used the term "propagandizing"; the *Boston Herald* spoke of "sensationalism"; the *Detroit News* praised the lack of "melodramatics."
58. "Courier's Defense of 'Pinky' Picked Up by Theat Mags," *Pittsburgh Courier*, 29 October 1949; "Record Crowd," *Atlanta Daily World*, 18 November 1949.
59. "Phenomenal Success of 'Pinky' at the Astor," *Boston Globe*, 13 October 1949.
60. The British reviews (all from 1949): Positive: *Daily Express*, 25 November; Paul Holt, *Daily Herald*, 25 November; Fred Majdalany, *Daily Mail*, n.d. in British Film Institute (BFI) clippings file; Reg Whitley, *Daily Mirror*, 26 November; Jympson Harman, *Evening News*, 24 November; V. G., *Evening Standard*, 26 November; *London Times*, 26 November; *Manchester Guardian*, 26 November; P. H., *Monthly Film Bulletin*, no. 192 (31 December 1949), 214; Richard Winnington, *News Chronicle*, n.d. in BFI clippings file; Ewart Hodgson, *News of the World*, 27 November; Joan Lester, *Reynolds News*, 27 November; Virginia Graham, *Spectator*, 2 December; W. A. Wilcox, *Sunday Dispatch*, 27 November; *Sunday Express*, 27 November; Paul Boyle, *Sunday Pictorial*, 27 November; Dilys Powell, *Sunday Times*, 27 November; Margaret Hinxman, *Time and Tide*, 3 December.

Mixed or neutral: Honor Arundel, *Daily Worker*, 26 November; C. A. Lejeune, *Observer*, 27 November; T. R. Fyvel, *Tribune*, 9 December.

61. Simon Simsi, *Ciné-Passions: 7e art et industrie de 1945 à 2000* (Paris: Dixit, 2000), part 3, 19.

62. The French reviews (all from 1950): Positive: Robert Pilati, *Ce Soir*, 8 July; Guy Marester, *Combat*, 3 July; Jean Néry, *Franc-Tireur*, 3 July; J.-G. Pierret, *Radio Cinéma Télévision*, 16 July.

Negative: Claude Garson, *Aurore*, 23 June; Georges Sadoul, *Lettres Françaises*, 20 July; Georges Charensol, *Nouvelles Littéraires*, 6 July.

Mixed: *Libération*, 5 July.

63. Paul Jones, *Atlanta Constitution*, 12 May 1951; Albert Goldstein, *New Orleans Times-Picayune*, 12 July 1951; John Rosenfield, *Dallas Morning News*, 12 July 1951.

64. Larry Ceplair and Stephen Englund, *The Inquisition in Hollywood: Politics in the Film Community, 1930–1960* (Berkeley: University of California Press, 1979), 361, 422.

65. Cripps, *Making Movies Black*, 263.

66. Mosley, *Zanuck*, 289.

67. Ibid., 288–90.

68. Geoffrey M. Shurlock to Harry Cohn, Columbia Pictures, 13 May 1955, Motion Picture Association of America, Production Code Administration Records, Production Files, *Island in the Sun*, Herrick Library, AMPAS.

69. Truman K. Gibson, Jr., to Colonel Frank McCarthy, Twentieth Century-Fox, 19 July 1956, Motion Picture Association of America, Production Code Administration Records, Production Files, *Island in the Sun*, Herrick Library, AMPAS.

70. Unsigned memo on proposed treatment by Alfred Hayes, Production Files, *Island in the Sun*, Warner Bros. (WB) Archives, University of Southern California (USC), Los Angeles.

71. Memo on conference with Mr. Zanuck, 25 October 1955 (on first-draft screenplay of 17 October 1955), Production Files, *Island in the Sun*, WB Archives, USC.

72. Memo of 16 January 1956 on conference with Darryl F. Zanuck and Alfred Hayes on final screenplay of 4 January 1956, Production Files, *Island in the Sun*, WB Archives, USC.

73. Zanuck quoted in Donald Bogle, *Dorothy Dandridge: A Biography* (New York: Amistad, 1997), 387; Sue Harper and Vincent Porter, *British Cinema: The Decline of Difference* (Oxford: Oxford University Press, 2003), 132.

74. On Belafonte's displeasure, see *Variety*, 10 July 1957.

75. Bogle, *Dandridge*, 360, 367.

76. See Bogle, *Dandridge*, 386–87; William A. Payne, "'Island in the Sun' Tops Film Schedule," *Dallas Morning News*, 8 September 1957. That paper ran a letter that read: "Don't let the NAACP hoodwink you into believing that all they want for the Negro race is equal educational opportunities. If you doubt their real motives, just go and see a current movie appearing in Dallas, titled 'Island in the Sun'"; *Dallas Morning News*, 25 September 1957.

77. Bogle, *Dandridge*, 386.

78. C. C. Stockton, letter to State Board of Motion Picture Censors, Virginia, 23 May 1957, Division of Motion Picture Censorship Records, Library of Virginia, box 53, file: Island in the Sun.

79. Landon B. Lane, letter to State Board of Motion Pictures Censors, 24 May 1957,

Division of Motion Picture Censorship Records, Library of Virginia, box 53, file: Island in the Sun.

80. James G. H. Mitchell, Secretary, Defenders of State Sovereignty and Individual Liberties, letter to State Board of Motion Picture Censorship, 1 July 1957, and undated handbill from American Nationalist, Inglewood, Calif., Division of Motion Picture Censorship Records, Library of Virginia, box 53, file: Island in the Sun.

81. Randolph McPherson, letter to Miss Lollie C. Whitehead, Director, Division of Motion Picture Censorship, 15 August 1957, Division of Motion Picture Censorship Records, Library of Virginia, box 53, file: Island in the Sun.

82. J. Lindsay Almond, Jr., Attorney General, letter to (name blacked out), 22 July 1957, Division of Motion Picture Censorship Records, Library of Virginia, box 53, file: Island in the Sun.

83. Lollie C. Whitehead, letter to Mrs. A. W. Goolsby, 26 July 1957, Division of Motion Picture Censorship Records, Library of Virginia, box 53, file: Island in the Sun.

84. Edwin Howard, "Banned 'Island in the Sun'—What It's All About," *Memphis Press-Scimitar*, 3 July 1957.

85. See W. Phillips Davison, "The Third-Person Effect in Communication," *Public Opinion Quarterly* 47 (1983): 1–15.

86. *Variety*, 8 January 1957. *Variety* reported it playing in Louisville, Kentucky; see "South Wavering on 'Island in the Sun'? L'ville Clicks Despite Race Angles," *Variety*, 19 June 1957. *Daily Variety* reported it was "doing boff biz in such segregated southern communities as Owensboro and Henderson, Ky., and Fort Smith, Ark."; see "Memphis Bans 'Sun' as 'Too Frank' a Pic on Miscegenation," *Daily Variety*, 7 August 1957.

87. The U.S. reviews (all from 1957): Positive: G.E.M., *Boston Globe*, 4 July; Rob Roy, *Chicago Defender*, 15 June; Larry Tajiri, *Denver Post*, 14 June; Al Weitschat, *Detroit News*, 16 June; Mandel Herbstman, *Film Daily*, 13 June; Kay Proctor, *Los Angeles Examiner*, 14 June; Edwin Schallert, *Los Angeles Times*, 14 June; George Bourke, *Miami Herald*, 21 June; D.H.D., *Milwaukee Journal*, 15 June; Vincent Canby, *Motion Picture Herald*, 15 June; Wanda Hale, *New York Daily News*, 13 June; Paine Knickerbocker, *San Francisco Chronicle*, 14 June.

Negative: Elinor Hughes, *Boston Herald*, 4 July; Henry Popkin, *Commentary*, vol. 24 (October), 354–57; Philip T. Hartung, *Commonweal*, 5 July; Jesse Zunser, *Cue*, 22 June; *Daily Variety*, 13 June; John Rosenfield, *Dallas Morning News*, 14 September; *Hollywood Citizen News*, 16 July; *Life*, 22 July; Edwin Howard, *Memphis Press-Scimitar*, 3 July; Robert Hatch, *Nation*, 29 June; Philip Roth, *New Republic*, 29 July; *Newsweek*, 1 July; John McCarten, *New Yorker*, 22 June; Bosley Crowther, *New York Times*, 13 and 23 June; Hollis Alpert, *Saturday Review*, 29 June; *Time*, 24 June; Richard L. Coe, *Washington Post*, 15 June.

Mixed or neutral: Mae Tinee, *Chicago Tribune*, 17 June; John Beaufort, *Christian Science Monitor*, 5 July; M.O.S., *Hartford Courant*, 21 June; James Powers, *Hollywood Reporter*, 13 June; Archer Winsten, *New York Post*, 13 June; Mildred Martin, *Philadelphia Inquirer*, 22 June.

88. *Daily Variety*, 13 June.

89. Those were: *Chicago Defender*, *Chicago Tribune*, *Cue*, *Dallas Morning News*, *Detroit News*, *Hollywood Reporter*, *Los Angeles Times*, *New York Daily News*, *Saturday Review*. See also "Island in the Sun: Dandridge, Belafonte Star in Romantic Film," *Ebony*, July 1957, 33.

90. The British reviews (all from 1957): Positive: Reg Whitley, *Daily Mirror*, 26 July; *Kinematograph Weekly*, 4 July.

Negative: Leonard Mosley, *Daily Express*, 24 July; Anthony Carthew, *Daily Herald*, 26 July; Campbell Dixon, *Daily Telegraph*, 22 July; Robert Kennedy, *Daily Worker*, 27 July; Philip Oakes, *Evening Standard*, 25 July; Derek Granger, *Evening Times*, 29 July; London *Times*, 24 July; *Manchester Guardian*, 27 July; J.A.D.C., *Monthly Film Bulletin*, no. 283 (June–July), 97; William Whitebait, *New Statesman*, 3 August; C. A. Lejeune, *Observer*, 28 July; Isabel Quigly, *Spectator*, 2 August; Milton Shulman, *Sunday Express*, 28 July; Dilys Powell, *Sunday Times*, 28 July; Fred Majdalany, *Time and Tide*, 3 August.

Mixed or neutral: Ivon Adams, *Star*, 25 July.

91. Simsi, *Ciné-Passions*, 159. The French reviews (all from 1957): Positive: Marie Perrot, *France Nouvelle*, 12 September; *Franc-Tireur*, 2 September; Samuel Lachize, *Humanité*, 4 September; Simone Dubreuilh, *Libération*, 11 September.

Negative: *Cahiers du Cinéma*, no. 75 (October); *Canard Enchaîné*, 4 September; Pierre Philippe, *Cinéma 57*, 21 (September–October), 102–3; J. P. Vivet, *Express*, 6 September; Jean-Louis Quennessen, *France Soir*, 3 September; Claude Nahon, *Radio Cinéma Télévision*, 15 September; Gilles Martain, *Rivarol*, 5 September.

Mixed or neutral: *Croix*, 7 September; *Figaro*, 14 September; *Humanité Dimanche*, 15 September; Christian Rémedy, *Lettres Françaises*, 12 September; Jacqueline Michel, *Parisien Libéré*, 7 September.

92. Tom Engelhardt, *The End of Victory Culture: Cold War America and the Disillusioning of a Generation* (New York: Basic Books, 1995), 95.

93. Christopher Metress, "Fighting Battles One by One: Robert Penn Warren's *Segregation*." *Southern Review* 32 (Winter 1996): 166–71.

94. E.G.D. [Dougherty], Memo for the files, 14 November 1956, on a meeting with Finlay McDermid, Raoul Walsh, and John Twist of Warner Bros., regarding a script dated 26 September. MPAA, PCA Records, Production Files, *Band of Angels*, Herrick Library, AMPAS.

95. Charles "Chuck" Williams telegram #2954A to Jack Warner, 11 July 1957. Production Files, *Band of Angels*, WB Archives, USC.

96. Martin Harvey, Dean of Students, Southern University, to Jack Warner, 5 June 1957, Production Files, *Band of Angels*, WB Archives, USC. It later opened at a "colored" theater.

97. See Whitney Strub, "Black and White and Banned All Over: Race, Censorship, and Obscenity in Postwar Memphis," *Journal of Social History* 40:3 (Spring 2007): 698.

98. Bruce Dunston, letter to Lollie C. Whitehead, Director, Division of Motion Picture Censorship, date obscured, Division of Motion Picture Censorship Records, Library of Virginia, box 53, file: Band of Angels.

99. *Variety*, 8 January 1958.

100. The U.S. reviews (all from 1957): Positive: Alex Murphree, *Denver Post*, 2 September; Paine Knickerbocker, *San Francisco Chronicle*, 17 August; Whit., *Variety*, 10 July.

Negative: Mae Tinee, *Chicago Tribune*, 5 August; Melvin Maddocks, *Christian Science Monitor*, 15 August; Henry Popkin, *Commentary*, vol. 24 (October), 354–57; Philip T. Hartung, *Commonweal*, 26 July; Jesse Zunser, *Cue*, 13 July; John Rosenfield, *Dallas Morning News*, 15 August; James Powers, *Hollywood Reporter*, 10 July; Ruth Waterbury, *Los Angeles Examiner*, 8 August; Philip K. Scheuer, *Los Angeles Times*, 8 August; *Newsweek*, 29 July; Dorothy Masters, *New York Daily News*, 11 July; John McCarten, *New Yorker*, 20 July; Archer Winsten, *New York Post*, 11 July; Bosley Crowther, *New York Times*, 11 July; Mildred Martin,

Philadelphia Inquirer, 9 August; Myles Standish, *St. Louis Post-Dispatch*, 2 August; *Time*, 5 August; Richard L. Coe, *Washington Post*, 10 August.

Mixed or neutral: Al Weitschat, *Detroit News*, 11 August; *Film Daily*, 10 July; Hazel L. Lamarre, *Los Angeles Sentinel*, 22 August; *Miami Herald*, 25 July; D.H.D., *Milwaukee Journal*, 2 August; Charles S. Aaronson, *Motion Picture Herald*, 13 July; F. McArdie, *New Orleans Times-Picayune*, 8 August; Edwin Martin, *San Diego Union*, 8 August.

101. *Denver Post*, 30 August 1957; *New York Post*, 10 July 1957.

102. This was the case with the *Atlanta Constitution* and *New Orleans Times-Picayune*.

103. Censorship report, August 1957, MPAA, PCA Records, Production Files, *Band of Angels*, Herrick Library, AMPAS.

104. The British reviews (all from 1957): Positive: Campbell Dixon, *Daily Telegraph*, 7 September; Robert Kennedy, *Daily Worker*, 7 September; Paul Dehn, *News Chronicle*, 6 September.

Negative: John Lambert, *Daily Express*, 6 September; Jympson Harman, *Evening News*, 5 September; John Osborne, *Evening Standard*, 5 September; *London Times*, 6 September; *Manchester Guardian*, 7 September; *Monthly Film Bulletin*, no. 285 (August–September), 125; Matthew Norgate, Ross Shepherd, *People*, 8 September; Isabel Quigly, *Spectator*, 13 September; Milton Shulman, *Sunday Express*, 8 September; Dilys Powell, *Sunday Times*, 8 September.

Mixed or neutral: Cecil Wilson, *Daily Mail*, 6 September; Donald Zec, *Daily Mirror*, 6 September; Harold Conway, *Daily Sketch*, 6 September; *Kinematograph Weekly*, 22 August; C. A. Lejeune, *Observer*, 8 September; *Star*, 5 September.

105. Simsi, *Ciné-Passions*, 56. The French reviews (all from 1958): Positive: Eric Rohmer, *Arts*, 15 January; Elsa Casals, *Dauphiné Libéré*, 19 March; Simone Dubreuilh, *Libération*, 14 January; André-S. Labarthe, *Radio Cinéma Télévision*, 19 January.

Negative: Louis Chauvet, *Figaro*, 11 January; Jacques Deltour, *Humanité*, 11 January; Martine Monod, *Lettres Françaises*, 16 January; Jean-Pierre Desportes, *Paris Jour*, 11 January.

Mixed or neutral: R.-M. Arlaud, *Combat*, 17 January; Jean Rochereau, *Croix*, 18 January.

106. It reached the number twenty-seven slot; see *Variety*, 7 January 1959. It sold 933,872 tickets in France; see Simsi, *Ciné-Passions*, 48.

107. On *Night of the Quarter Moon*, see Courtney, *Hollywood Fantasies of Miscegenation*, 218–24.

108. Sirk called the film "a piece of social criticism—of both white and black" but said he "couldn't overcome the material"; see Jon Halliday, *Sirk on Sirk: Conversations with Jon Halliday* (London: Faber and Faber, 1972/1997), 148, 153. On Sirk's reassessment, see Barbara Klinger, *Melodrama and Meaning: History, Culture, and the Films of Douglas Sirk* (Bloomington: Indiana University Press, 1994), 1–35.

109. *Variety*, 6 January 1960. The *New York Daily News* found it "almost as dated as *Uncle Tom's Cabin*," and the *Chicago Defender* called stories about passing "strictly out of style." The U.S. reviews (all from 1959): Positive: Charles S. Aaronson, *Motion Picture Herald*, 14 February; Rex., *Variety*, 4 February.

Negative: Marjory Adams, *Boston Globe*, 30 March; Elinor Hughes, *Boston Herald*, 30 March; Mae Tinee, *Chicago Tribune*, 18 March; John Rosenfield, *Dallas Morning News*, 14 April; Philip K. Scheuer, *Los Angeles Times*, 20 March; *Newsweek*, 13 April; Dorothy Masters, *New York Daily News*, 18 April; John McCarten, *New Yorker*, 25 April; Archer Winsten, *New*

York Post, 19 April; Bosley Crowther, *New York Times*, 18 and 19 April; Richard L. Coe, *Washington Post*, 2 April.

Mixed or neutral: Philip T. Hartung, *Commonweal*, 17 April; Arthur Knight, *Saturday Review*, 11 April; Edward Kosmal, *St. Louis Post-Dispatch*, 13 April.

110. Harry Belafonte, *My Song: A Memoir*, ed. Michael Shnayerson (New York: Alfred Knopf, 2011), 199–200. Courtney, *Hollywood Fantasies of Miscegenation*, 238, claims "the film attempts to preserve . . . the racial and sexual ideologies of dominant culture."

111. John Cassavetes, *Cassavetes on Cassavetes*, ed. Ray Carney (London: Faber, 2001), 59, 55.

112. Prosper Mérimée, "Tamango," in *Nouvelles Completes: Colomba et 10 autres nouvelles*, ed. Pierre Josserand (Paris: Gallimard, 1964), 53–75.

113. See the Berry interview in Patrick McGilligan and Paul Buhle, eds., *Tender Comrades: A Backstory of the Hollywood Blacklist* (New York: St. Martin's, 1997), 55–89.

114. Christopher L. Miller, *The French Atlantic Triangle: Literature and Culture of the Slave Trade* (Durham, NC: Duke University Press, 2008), 238.

115. Ibid., 216.

116. Quoted in Bogle, *Dandridge*, 379.

117. Susan Hayward, *French Costume Dramas of the 1950s: Fashioning Politics in Film* (Bristol: Intellect, 2010), 210. That claim also appears in Robert Harms, "The Transatlantic Slave Trade in Cinema," in *Black and White in Colour: African History on Screen*, ed. Vivian Bickford-Smith and Richard Mendelsohn (Athens: Ohio University Press, 2007), 63.

118. The U.S. reviews: Positive: William Leonard, *Chicago Tribune*, 7 October 1959; Travis Mayo, *Dallas Morning News*, 31 March 1960; Al Weitschat, *Detroit News*, 19 August 1959; *Film Daily*, 26 August 1959; Ruth Waterbury, *Los Angeles Examiner*, 22 October 1959; George H. Jackson, *Los Angeles Herald & Express*, 22 October 1959; Vincent Canby, *Motion Picture Herald*, 5 September 1959; Mosk., *Variety*, 12 February 1958.

Negative: Marjory Adams, *Boston Globe*, 15 October 1959; Elinor Hughes *Boston Herald*, 15 October 1959; Geoffrey Warren, *Los Angeles Times*, 23 October 1959; Wanda Hale, *New York Daily News*, 17 September 1959; Paul V. Beckley, *New York Herald Tribune*, 17 September 1959; Richard Nason, *New York Times*, 17 September 1959; Darcy DeMille, *Pittsburgh Courier*, 10 October 1959; Myles Standish, *St. Louis Post-Dispatch*, 30 October 1959.

Mixed or neutral: Philip T. Hartung, *Commonweal*, 16 October 1959; Jesse Zunser, *Cue*, 19 September 1959; Archer Winsten, *New York Post*, 17 September 1959; Paine Knickerbocker, *San Francisco Chronicle*, 31 October 1959.

119. See Ellen Scott, "Race and the Struggle for Cinematic Meaning: Film Production, Censorship, and African American Reception, 1940–1960" (Ph.D. diss., University of Michigan, 2007), 130.

120. Simsi, *Ciné-Passions*, 145. The French reviews (all from 1958): Positive: Claude Garson, *Aurore*, 27 January; Jacques Deltour, *Humanité*, 29 January; Martine Monod, *Lettres Françaises*, 30 January; Paule Sengissen, *Radio Cinéma Télévision*, 9 February; Jean Carta, *Témoignage Chrétien*, 14 February.

Negative: François Truffaut, *Arts*, 19 January; Etienne Loinod, *Cahiers du Cinéma*, no. 80 (February), 61; Jean Dutourd, *Carrefour*, 29 January; R.-M. Arlaud, *Combat*, 29 January; *Express*, 30 January; Jacques Doniol-Valcroze, *France Observateur*, 30 January; Simone Dubreuilh, *Libération*, 28 January; Jean de Baroncelli, *Monde*, 31 January; Georges Charensol,

Nouvelles Littéraires, 30 January; Jean-Pierre Desportes, *Paris Jour*, 28 January; Gilles Martain, *Rivarol*, 30 January.

Mixed or neutral: Georges Hellio, *Aspects de la France*, 7 February; Jean Rochereau, *Croix*, 4 February; P. Ms., *Figaro*, 1 February; André Lafargue, *Parisien Libéré*, 28 January.

121. See "Rank Cash for Film about Race Riots," *Daily Telegraph*, 10 October 1958.

122. The British reviews (all from 1959): Positive: F. J., *Daily Cinema*, 20 April; Leonard Mosley, *Daily Express*, 8 May; Fred Majdalany, *Daily Mail*, 8 May; Campbell Dixon, *Daily Telegraph*, 9 May; Felix Barker, *Evening News*, 7 May; John Waterman, *Evening Standard*, 7 May; *Kinematograph Weekly*, 23 April; *Manchester Guardian*, 9 May; Paul Dehn, *News Chronicle*, 8 May; Peter Burnup, *News of the World*, 10 May; C. A. Lejeune, *Observer*, 10 May; Ernest Betts, *People*, 10 May; Ivon Adams, *Star*, 7 May; George Sterling, *Sunday Dispatch*, 10 May; Derek Monsey, *Sunday Express*, 10 May; Dilys Powell, *Sunday Times*, 10 May; Charles MacLaren, *Time and Tide*, 16 May.

Negative: P.J.D., *Monthly Film Bulletin*, no. 305 (June); Isabel Quigly, *Spectator*, 15 May.

Mixed or neutral: Nina Hibbin, *Daily Worker*, 9 May; *London Times*, 8 May.

123. Everett, *Returning the Gaze*, 307, writes that "Hollywood now went about business as usual" in racial matters and strove "to reimpose the racial boundaries of America's prewar social order."

124. Six of twenty-six (23 percent) ended well, as opposed to twenty-seven of seventy-three (37 percent) relationships featuring white men.

INDEX

Academy Awards, 35, 38, 43, 50, 53, 57, 67, 109, 128, 200, 210, 230, 267, 285, 301
Achebe, Chinua, 40; *Things Fall Apart*, 40
Acosta, Rodolfo, 251
Across the Pacific (1926), 218
Across the Wide Missouri (1951), 125–26, 259–60, 308
Adams, Marjory, 66, 101, 285, 302, 324
Adams, Robert, 70
Adobe Walls (1953 book), 124
adoption, 47–48, 160, 164–65, 210, 212, 217, 241
Adorno, Theodor, 15
Africa, 44–47, 53–54, 206, 307, 310, 317–18, 323–25, 327, 337, 341; cinematic stereotyping, 12, 251, 289; films on decolonization, 169–70, 179, 216; Mau Mau films, 158–69; postwar situation, 21, 44, 295; trailblazer films, 66–70, 92; white protector films, 70–75
African Americans, 10, 109, 134, 244–45, 255, 267, 289–333, 338–40
African Queen, The (1951), 45
Africa Screams (1949), 45
Agar, John, 99
Ahn, Philip, 210
Alamo, The, 195
Alamo, The (1960), 214
Albert, Eddie, 226
Aldrich, Robert, 118–21, 193–94, 335
Algeria, 188; critics' references to war, 121–22, 150, 157, 169, 194, 198, 206, 222, 325; Sétif violence (1945), 28, 137; war (1954–1962), 11, 53, 182, 190, 199, 203, 339, 346; war and censorship, 200
Algiers (1938), 184

Ali Baba and the Forty Thieves (1944), 191
All About Eve (1950), 232
Alpert, Hollis, 66, 150
Alton, John, 225
America, 36, 61, 78, 87, 110, 115, 170, 177, 285, 294, 314
American Friends of Vietnam, 231, 234, 241
American Indians, 5–6, 10, 58, 61–62, 93–135, 222, 240, 244, 251, 254–64, 270, 338–41, 344; termination policy, 95, 109, 120, 134, 208; vanishing American concept, 95–96, 133
American Indian tribes: Apaches, 94, 99–108, 110–11, 118–24, 126, 143, 253, 258, 261–64, 272; Blackfeet, 125–26, 259–60; Cherokees, 119–20, 127; Cheyennes, 94, 260–61; Comanches, 94, 127–30; Hopis, 106; Navajos, 106; Seminoles, 260–62; Shoshones, 113–15, 258; Sioux, 94, 116–18, 263
American isolationism, 22, 83–84, 337
American Legion, 24, 314
Anderson, Lindsay, 131
Anderson, Michael, 175–76
Ando, Eiko, 63, 65, 332
Anglo-Irish Treaty of 1921, 171–72, 176–78
Ankrum, Morris, 119, 193
Anna and the King (1999), 32
Anna and the King of Siam (1946), 32–37, 51, 55, 227, 277, 343–44
Annakin, Ken, 88, 141
anti-Americanism, 22, 227, 232–33, 235, 238–39, 279–80, 284
anti-communism, 9, 23, 98, 195–97, 209–18, 228–29, 240, 251, 308, 341; Council against Communist Aggression, 232

anti-Semitism, 250, 290, 307, 312
Apache (1954), 118–22, 134, 193, 344–45
Apache Drums (1951), 126
Apache Woman (1955), 261, 331
Arabs, 70, 73–74, 92, 184, 186, 188–89, 271–72, 289
Archers, The (film company), 41
Archuletta, Beulah, 129
Argosy Pictures, 98, 103
Arlaud, R.-M., 194
Armendáriz, Pedro, 99
Arnold, Elliott, 105
Around the World in Eighty Days (1956), 267
Arrowhead (1953), 123–25, 130, 134, 261, 331, 335, 338
Arts (Paris), 66, 82
Askin, Leon, 191
Aslan, Grégoire, 70, 147
Aspects de la France, 51, 325
Atlanta Constitution, 155, 166, 267, 301, 304
Atlanta Daily World, 163, 304
Attlee, Clement, 25
Aubrey, Anne, 69
Aurore, 51, 157, 168, 194, 203, 205, 269, 306
Australia, 6, 151, 175
Aylward, Gladys, 47–54
Aztecs, 57–61

Bacall, Lauren, 79, 214
Back to Bataan (1945), 218
Baer, John, 220
Baines, John V., 158
Baker, Josephine, 289
Balcon, Michael, 173, 307
Balderston, John L., 75
Ball, Suzann, 261
Bancroft, Anne, 263
Bandera, La (1935), 31, 248
Band of Angels (1957), 252, 316–21, 324, 330, 345
Bandung Conference (1955), 315, 325
Bao Dai, Emperor, 28
Barbados, 170
Barbarian and the Geisha, The (1959), 62–66, 276–77
Bardot, Brigitte, 51
Barnwell, John, 220
Baroncelli, Jean de, 52, 157, 269
Barot, Louis, 247

Barri, Mario, 221
Barry, Gene, 196, 212
Barrymore, Ethel, 296, 301
Barrymore, Lionel, 254
Bataan (1943), 218
Batjac Productions, 214
Battle, John Tucker, 57–58
Battle of Manila Bay (1898), 218
Bazin, André, 121, 157, 194, 270, 286
Beatty, Robert, 164, 174
Beau Geste (1939), 82, 184
Belafonte, Harry, 170, 309, 311–12, 322, 332, 336
Belgium, 45, 53–54
Bell, James, 220
Bellah, James Warner, 99, 103
Benavedes, Teddy, 221
Benson, Martin, 74
Bergman, Ingrid, 47–48, 50–51, 55, 273
Bernard-Aubert, Claude, 203–4
Berrell, Lloyd, 85
Berry, John, 323, 335
Best Years of Our Lives, The (1946), 256
Beverly Hills Citizen, 236
Bevin, Ernest, 25
Beyond Mombasa (1956), 163
Bhowani Junction (1956), 153–57, 160, 179–80, 331
Bickford, Charles, 254
Big Sky, The (1952), 126, 259–60, 262, 282, 332
Big Tree, Chief John, 103
Bin Hussan, Sanny, 146
Bird of Paradise (1932), 248–49
Bird of Paradise (1951), 272–73
Birth of a Nation, The (1915), 245, 248, 306, 316, 335
Biskind, Peter, 108
Bitter Tea of General Yen, The (1933), 209, 248
Blachette, Georges, 188
Blackboard Jungle (1955), 122, 164–65, 341
Black Narcissus (1947), 40–44, 48, 54–55, 152, 343
Black Orpheus (1959), 200
Black Tent, The (1956), 289
Blackton, J. Stuart, 218
Blankfort, Michael, 105
Blaustein, Julian, 106
Blood Alley (1955), 214–15, 217, 240–41, 251, 271
Blue, Monte, 119

Blum, Léon, 29
Blum-Byrnes accords, 29
Boetticher, Budd, 260
Bogarde, Dirk, 158, 162, 174
Bogart, Humphrey, 45, 185, 224–25
Bonaparte, Louis-Napoléon, 192, 194–95
Bonaparte, Napoléon, 88
Bond, Anson, 278
Bond, Ward, 98
Borgeaud, Henri, 188
Boston Globe, 48, 66, 82, 101, 116–17, 130, 145, 177, 229, 285, 293–94, 302, 304
Boston Herald, 60, 87, 121, 149, 155, 177, 215, 229, 293, 303, 324
Boyd, Jr., Jack, 267
Boyer, Charles, 151, 184
Brando, Marlon, 175, 225–26, 228, 280, 282, 286
Brandon, Henry, 127
Brazzaville Conference (1944), 27–28
Brazzi, Rossano, 274
Breen, Joseph P., 58, 249–50, 254
Bridge on the River Kwai, The (1957), 235
Brinson, Peter, 51
Britain: Cardiff, 245; Liverpool, 245; London, 42, 47, 170, 173–74, 245, 295, 307, 326–27; Wales, 47, 161
British Academy of Film and Television Arts (BAFTA) Awards, 53, 173
British government, 143, 213, 245; Colonial Office, 70, 72–73, 140; Conservative Party, 25; House of Lords, 310; Labour Party, 25, 144, 147; Ministry of Information, 70
Brodie, John, 90
Broken Arrow (1950), 105–12, 114–16, 120, 123–25, 128, 133–35, 257–60, 270, 272, 282–83, 332, 336–37, 342
Broken Lance (1954), 261
Bronson, Charles, 119
Brooks, Richard, 122–23, 164–65, 335, 341
Brown, Lena, 303
Brown v. Board of Education (1954), 308
Brynner, Yul, 38
Bryon, Kathleen, 41
Buchanan, Edgar, 112
Burgess, Alan, 47
Burma, 25, 35, 137, 150, 276
Burnett, W. R., 124
Burnup, Peter, 268

Burr, Raymond, 188
Burton, Richard, 273
Busch, Niven, 253
Butler, David, 195
Buttons, Red, 281
Bwana Devil (1952), 68–69

Cabot, Susan, 117, 260
Cagney, James, 175, 177
Cahiers du Cinéma, 145, 168, 194, 205, 238
Cairney, John, 146
Calhern, Louis, 113
Call Her Savage (1932), 248
Calloway, Cab, 302, 304
Calvert, Phyllis, 71
Calvet, Corinne, 209–10
Cambodia, 35, 200
Cameron, Earl, 159, 163, 169, 307, 326, 332
Cameron, Kate, 98, 229, 257, 285, 303
Camus, Marcel, 200, 202–3
Canard Enchaîné, 145, 150, 239, 269
Cannes Film Festival, 112, 295
Caplan, Karen, 37
Captain from Castile (1947), 56–62, 75, 77, 92, 216, 344
Captain John Smith and Pocahontas (1953), 261
Cardenas, Elsa, 265, 332
Cardiff, Jack, Jr., 43
Carey, Harry, 127
Carpita, Paul, 199–200
Carradine, John, 184
Carrefour, 131, 157, 222, 238, 325
Cary, Joyce, 70
Casablanca (1942), 183, 185–86
Cassavetes, John, 322
Catholicism, 57–58, 60, 62, 73, 171, 173, 210, 249, 279; Franciscans, 62
Cat People (1942), 189
Cavalry Charge (1951), 126
censorship: in Britain, 42, 165, 248, 338; in France, 169, 182, 199–200, 202, 204, 206, 248, 328, 338, 341; in United States, 238, 249, 293, 297, 312, 320–21, 323, 338
Central Intelligence Agency (CIA), 23–24, 124, 230–31, 266
Centre National de Cinématographie, 17
Ce Soir, 306
Ceylon, 137, 146, 152

Chandler, Jeff, 106–9, 111, 116, 261, 272
Charensol, Georges, 102, 269, 306
Charge at Feather River, The (1953), 123, 251, 261, 341
Charles I (King of England), 88
Charlie Bravo (1980), 203
Charlie Chan in Shanghai (1937), 209
Charly (1968), 220
Chazal, Robert, 88
Chiang Kai-Shek, 49
Chicago Defender, 163, 267, 294, 301–2, 304, 313, 324
Chicago Tribune, 36, 39, 49, 87, 110, 166, 177, 198, 228, 314, 325
Chief Crazy Horse (1955), 118, 344
China: aid to liberation movements, 185; Canton, 212–13; Chinese in Malaya, 140–42; Communist victory (1949), 9, 137, 208, 229, 271, 308, 339; in films, 47–53, 85, 195–96, 209–18, 225, 230, 235–36, 240–41, 271, 275–76, 288, 341; in Korean War, 104, 339; neo-colonialism concept, 8; Peking, 210, 230; Shanghai, 209–12, 216; Shanxi, 47; Tientsin, 47; western imperialism, 34, 64, 209
China Doll (1958), 275–77
China Gate (1957), 196–98, 204, 230, 236, 241, 277, 331
China Girl (1942), 45
Chivington, Colonel John, 260
Christianity: in films, 40–55, 57, 60, 84, 86, 89–91, 103, 106–7, 169–70, 185, 216–17, 263; and imperialism, 22–23, 94;
Christian Science Monitor, 78, 109, 115, 156, 198, 236
Christopher Columbus (1949), 61–62
Churchill, Winston, 25
Cimarron (1930), 248
Cinecittá, 231
Cinéma 57, 123, 203
Cinéma 58, 238
civilizing mission: in films, 33–37, 40, 45–56, 62, 70–71, 81, 91–92, 166, 187, 190, 192, 204–5, 220, 227, 255–56, 272, 283, 344, 345–46; in history, 5, 22, 95–96, 342, 345
Clark, William, 126, 262
Clum, John, 262–63
Cobb, Lee J., 32, 57, 186
Coe, Richard L., 61, 101, 257

Colbert, Claudette, 141, 145
Cold War, 9, 23, 80, 83, 143, 148–51, 189, 196, 204, 209, 211, 216–17, 245, 308, 316, 339; and American anti-colonialism, 22, 198, 208, 341; American culture of, 31, 34, 38, 46, 63, 98, 104, 133, 183, 250, 279, 284–85, 288, 336–37; U.S. policies in, 223, 229, 277
Cole, Nat "King," 196
Collins, Joan, 310
Collins, Michael, 171
Colonial Development and Welfare Bill (1940), 25
colonialism, definition, 4–7; conservative colonialism, 5–6, 46, 73, 95, 148, 161, 179, 342; liberal colonialism, 5–6, 46, 55, 60, 72–73, 90–92, 95, 132–33, 161, 166, 170, 179, 259, 261, 263, 288, 331, 342, 344–45
Columbia Pictures, 163, 185, 191, 279, 309
Columbus, Christopher, 49, 61
Comanche Territory (1956), 135
Combat (France), 37, 79, 102, 145, 150, 168, 194, 203, 205, 306, 321
Command, The (1954), 343
Commentary, 313, 320
Commonweal, 44, 66, 70, 78, 111, 115, 121, 162, 177, 235, 268, 294, 303, 321, 325
Commonwealth, 140, 144
Commonwealth Immigrants Act (1962), 245
communism, 38, 98, 133, 143–49, 154–57, 179, 185, 195–99, 210, 210–18, 222, 225–26, 229–30, 233, 239–40, 250, 308–9, 312, 314, 341
Communist Party: China, 47–48, 137, 141, 196–97, 208, 210–18, 233, 240, 271, 288, 308, 339; France, 28, 29, 52, 195, 199, 315, 340; India, 154–57; Malaya, 141, 147, 179; Philippines, 220; United States, 312, 314; Vietnam, 230–33, 236, 276
Congo, 45, 53
Conner, Rearden, 175
Connors, Chuck, 191
Conrad, Joseph, 85, 88, 271; *Heart of Darkness*, 85; *Lord Jim*, 85
Conway, Harold, 51
Cooper, Gary, 83, 97–98, 193, 218, 260
Cooper, James Fenimore, 96; *Last of the Mohicans*, 96
Corbett, Glenn, 275
Cortés, Hernán, 56–58, 60–61
Cotten, Joseph, 209, 254

Covered Wagon, The (1923), 106
Cowie, Mervyn, 72
Coy, Walter, 127
Craig, Michael, 326
Craigie, Jill, 147–48
Crain, Jeanne, 295, 297, 300–301
Cressan, Alex, 323–25
Crimson Kimono, The (1958), 275
Crisler, Ben, 236
Croix, 52, 123, 131, 194, 202, 205, 269, 315–16, 325
Cromwell, John, 32
Cromwell, Oliver, 172
Crossfire (1947), 250, 269, 290, 297
Crowther, Bosley, 101, 109, 125, 198, 237, 257, 267, 293–94, 302–3
Cue (New York), 36, 87, 115–16, 130, 150, 236–37, 257, 285, 313, 320
Cukor, George, 153–54, 157
Cusack, Cyril, 188
Custer, George Armstrong, 100

Daily Cinema, 237, 327
Daily Express, 112, 131, 143, 161, 314
Daily Herald, 37, 39, 144, 149, 156, 178, 237, 286, 305, 314
Daily Mail, 39, 44, 51, 112, 144, 178, 238, 327
Daily Mirror, 36–37, 50–51, 121, 144, 149, 314
Daily Sketch, 51, 148, 156, 168
Daily Telegraph, 37, 39, 50, 53, 81, 102, 112, 144, 149, 167, 178, 237, 286, 315
Daily Worker (London), 37, 50–53, 81, 88, 131, 144, 148, 156, 162, 168, 178, 229, 268, 286, 295, 305, 314, 327
Daily Worker (New York), 110
Dalio, Marcel, 196, 199
Dallas Morning News, 36, 39, 50, 61, 111, 122, 167, 170, 177, 267, 294, 304, 325
Dances with Wolves (1990), 105, 335
Dandridge, Dorothy, 297, 309, 311–12, 315, 323, 325, 332, 336
Daniels, George, 267–68
Darcel, Denise, 193, 199
Darène, Robert, 68
Darnell, Linda, 33, 36, 253
Da Silva, Howard, 97–98
Daughter of Shanghai (1937), 209
Dauphin, Claude, 231

Dauphiné Libéré, 52
Daves, Delmer, 105–6, 109, 132–33, 272–73, 321
Dean, James, 265
Deans, Harris, 268
Dearden, Basil, 173, 307
De Carlo, Yvonne, 116, 188, 316–17, 320
Deckers, Eugene, 79
decolonization, definition, 7; internal decolonization, 10, 93, 108, 116, 120, 133–34, 339–40
De Gaulle, Charles, 27, 121, 190
Dehner, John, 119, 189
Del Rio, Dolores, 248
DeMille, Cecil B., 50, 97–98, 102, 251, 335
DeMille, Darcy, 324
DeMille, Katherine, 97
Denver Post, 88, 121, 156, 229, 285
De Rochemont, Louis, 290, 293, 295
Detroit News, 111, 155, 166, 235–36, 293–94, 302, 313
Devil's Doorway (1950), 112–17, 120, 134, 258–60, 335–36, 341, 345
Devlin, Father John J., 57–58
Dickinson, Angie, 196
Dickinson, Thorold, 70
Diderot, 82
Diem, Ngo Dinh, 230
Dien Bien Phu, 79, 195, 198, 205, 229
Dien Bien Phu (1992), 195
Dieterle, William, 153, 210
Dietrich, Marlene, 209
Dirty Dozen, The (1967), 194
Disraeli, Benjamin, 40
Dixon, Campbell, 50, 81, 144, 237, 286, 315
Dmytryk, Edward, 212–13, 290
Dolenz, George, 189
Dollar, Clyde, 14
Donat, Robert, 47
Doniol-Valcroze, Jacques, 202
Douglas, Kirk, 252, 259–60
Douglas, Susan, 291
Downs, Cathy, 253
Drach, Michel, 328
Dreyfus, Alfred, 183
Drum Beat (1954), 133
Drums across the River (1954), 135
Drums along the Mohawk (1939), 98
Drums of Tahiti (1954), 191, 198
Du Bois, W. E. B., 1

Dubov, Paul, 196
Duel in the Sun (1946), 251, 253–57, 336, 341
Dulles, John Foster, 22–23, 238
Dunne, Irene, 32, 37
Dunne, Philip, 16, 295
Duras, Marguerite, 286
Dutourd, Jean, 222, 325
Duvivier, Julien, 184
Dwan, Alan, 91
Dyer, Richard, 54

Ealing Studios, 72–73, 173, 307
East India Company (Britain), 40, 247
East India Company (Netherlands), 247
Ebony, 298
Egan, Richard, 262
Egypt, 25, 44, 53, 189, 208, 339
Eisenhower, Dwight, 23, 139
Elephant Walk (1954), 152–53, 179–80, 198
Elise, ou la vraie vie (1970), 328
Ellison, Ralph, 300, 302
Emperor Jones (O'Neill play), 85
Esquire, 36
ethnic miscasting, 13, 36–37, 50, 107–8, 112, 116, 118, 132, 146, 151, 188, 228, 248, 289, 297–98, 318, 321, 329, 342
Evening News, 81, 102, 112, 143–44, 161, 168, 178, 229, 305
Evening Standard, 50–51, 78, 81, 88, 102, 112, 123, 143, 149, 156–57, 167, 237, 305, 314, 327
Express, 52, 54, 82, 239

Facteur s'en va-t-en guerre, Le (1966), 203
Fanon, Frantz, 7
Far Horizons (1955), 126, 262
Farrar, David, 41
Faubus, Orval, 321
Federal Bureau of Investigation (FBI), 217
Federal Council of Churches, 23
Feleo, Juan, 220
Ferber, Edna, 265–67, 307
Ferrer, Mel, 187, 290
Figaro, 37, 51, 88
Figaro, Inc., 230
Figaro Littéraire, 146
Fiji, 85, 191
Film Daily, 87, 101, 110, 115, 122, 294, 324
Financial Times, 51, 79, 81, 161, 168, 178

Finch, Peter, 53, 146, 152
Finlayson, John, 293
First Blood (1982), 120
First Pan-African Congress, 1
Five Gates to Hell (1959), 251, 271, 336
Fleischman, Sid, 214
Fleming, Rhonda, 210
Flemyng, Robert, 147
Fletcher Report (1930), 245
Fonda, Henry, 99
Fong, Benson, 210
Fontaine, Joan, 309, 312
Foot, Michael, 147
Ford, Glenn, 225
Ford, John, 68, 79, 98–99, 101–5, 127–28, 131–32, 183, 253, 295
Ford, Patrick, 79
Ford, Paul, 225
Foreign Legion, 184–85, 188, 195–96
Foreman, Carl, 260
Fort Algiers (1953), 188–89, 198
Fort Apache (1948), 79, 98–105, 110, 129, 135, 336
Fort Laramie Treaty (1868), 117
Foster, Jodie, 32
Fox, William, 16
Foxfire (1955), 263–64, 340
Franc-Tireur, 37, 121, 131, 145, 157, 307, 315
France: Marseille, 199–200; Nice, 323; Paris, 52–53, 91, 245, 253, 309, 315, 323
France Catholique, 52
France Nouvelle, 315
France Observateur, 66, 121, 168, 202, 205–6, 325
France Soir, 315
Franz, Eduard, 260
Free French, 183, 191, 198
Freeman, Mona, 220
French army, 205
French government, 195, 200, 206, 245; Ministry of Colonies, 197; Ministry of Defense, 206; Vichy regime, 51, 183, 191, 198–99, 250
From Here to Eternity (1953), 118
Fuller, Samuel, 196–98, 225, 230, 263, 275–76

Gabin, Jean, 248
Gable, Clark, 68, 125, 212, 259, 317–18
Gam, Rita, 187
Gandhi (1982), 225
Gandhi, Mohandas K., 42, 151, 154–55

Gardner, Ava, 68, 153–55, 252, 307
Garner, James, 281
Garson, Claude, 194, 306
Garvey, Marcus, 299
Gary, Romain, 197
Gast, Michel, 328
Gaynor, Mitzi, 274
Geer, Will, 106
Gélin, Daniel, 200
General Died at Dawn, The (1936), 209
General Film Distributors, 43, 141
Genn, Leo, 163
Gentle Gunman, The (1952), 173–76
Gentleman's Agreement (1947), 75, 250, 290, 295, 297
George VI, 26
Germany, 85–87, 89, 146, 172, 174, 183, 186, 191, 208, 287, 339
Geronimo, 107–8, 118–19, 262
Ghana, 7, 44, 169; Convention People's Party, 44
Ghost and the Darkness, The (1996), 68
Giant (1956), 263, 265–70, 313, 321, 331, 335, 342–43
Gibbs, Patrick, 39
Gibson, Truman K., Jr., 310
Gigi (1958), 52
Gillette, Don, 156
Gish, Lillian, 254
Glasgow Herald, 51, 149, 161, 237
Goddard, Paulette, 98
Godden, Margaret Rumer, 40, 42
Goff, Ivan, 175
Goh, David, 217
Golden Globe awards, 43
Goldwyn, Samuel, 16, 218
Gomez, Thomas, 57
Gone with the Wind (1939), 255, 316, 318–19
Good Earth, The (1937), 209
Graham, Virginia, 306
Granger, Derek, 79
Granger, Stewart, 66, 122, 153
Grant, Ulysses S., 107
Grayson, Charles, 63
Great Depression, 21–22, 25, 183
Green, F. L., 173
Green Berets, The (1968), 214
Greene, Graham, 73, 230–39
Guardian. See *Manchester Guardian*

Gunga Din (1939), 75, 335
Gunman's Walk (1958), 261

Haggard, H. Rider, 66–67
Hale, Barbara, 260
Hale, Wanda, 325
Hall, Jon, 184
Hallatt, May, 41
Hal Roach Distribution Corporation, 324
Hammerstein, Oscar, 32, 274, 307
Han Suyin (Rosalie Chow), 215–16, 273–74, 276
Harman, Jympson, 81, 178, 305
Harmand, Jules, 31
Harris, Townsend, 62–66, 92
Harrison, Rex, 32, 36–37
Hartford Courant, 110–11, 235–36, 293, 302, 313
Hartung, Philip, 111, 121, 235, 268, 303, 325
Haskin, Byron, 85
Hatch, Robert, 128, 235, 301, 313
Hathaway, Henry, 45
Hawkins, Jack, 88, 141, 272
Hawks, Howard, 126, 259
Hayakawa, Sessue, 224–25
Hayes, Alfred, 309
Hayes, Bully, 85
Haynes, Roberta, 84
Hayward, Susan, 45, 55, 212
Heart of the Matter, The (1953), 72
Hecht, Harold, 84, 118, 120
Hecht-Lancaster Productions, 193
Heflin, Van, 116, 260
Heisler, Stuart, 224
Henty, G. A., 82
Hepburn, Audrey, 53, 55
Hepburn, Katherine, 45
Hernandez, Juano, 165, 169
Herrmann, Bernard, 32
Heston, Charlton, 123, 261–62
Heusken, Henry, 63, 65
Heyes, Herbert, 216
Hibbin, Nina, 50–51, 53, 81, 148, 178, 286, 327
High Noon (1952), 129, 260
High Sierra (1941), 124
Hill, Derek, 81, 148
Hinduism/Hindus, 79–80, 82, 154
Hinxman, Margaret, 178
Hiroshima, mon amour (1959), 286–88
His Majesty O'Keefe (1954), 84–88, 92, 274–75, 337

Hiss, Alger, 308
Hitler, Adolf, 174
Hobart, William, 257, 302
Ho Chi Minh, 28, 196–97, 229
Hogan, William, 125
Holden, William, 215
Hollywood Citizen News, 117, 285, 314
Hollywood Reporter, 39, 49, 66, 82, 110, 121, 130, 145, 156, 167, 177, 235–36, 268, 285, 302–3, 320
Hollywood Ten / blacklist, 11, 23, 212, 240, 290
Home of the Brave (1949), 297
Homestead Act (1862), 114
Hong Kong, 25, 85, 210, 212–17, 240, 273, 277
Hong Kong (1952), 210
Hope, Bob, 69
Hopper, Dennis, 265
Hordern, Michael, 146
Horkheimer, Max, 15
Hougron, Jean, 200
House Committee on Un-American Activities (HUAC), 23, 98, 101, 104, 116, 210, 228, 240, 308–9, 323, 336
House of Bamboo (1955), 225, 276
Houston Post, 36, 155, 236
Howard, Trevor, 73, 172, 271
Hudson, Rock, 164, 166–68
Hughes, Elinor, 87, 229
Huk! (1956), 218–22, 240–41, 337
Humanité, 52, 66, 121, 131, 145, 150, 157, 202, 205, 239, 269, 321, 325
Humanité Dimanche, 169, 315–16
Hunchback of Notre Dame, The (1939), 182
Hunter, Jeffrey, 127
Hurricane, The (1937), 83, 183
Hurst, Brian Desmond, 158–59
Huston, John, 45, 62–63, 65
Huston, Walter, 254
Hylton, Richard, 290

Illing, Peter, 153
Imitation of Life (1934), 248–49
Imitation of Life (1959), 322
imperialism, definition, 7
Inclán, Miguel, 99
India, 8, 21, 25–26, 40–44, 75–82, 137, 139–41, 150–57, 175, 251, 337; Darjeeling, 41–42; Mutiny (1857), 40, 76

Indian Fighter, The (1955), 259–60
Indian National Congress, 42, 153, 155–56
Indochina, 11, 22, 28, 35, 53, 68, 103, 137, 145–46, 182, 185, 195–208, 229–39, 287, 339
Indonesia, 89, 137, 150
Inn of the Sixth Happiness, The (1958), 47–55, 83, 227, 273, 277, 335, 343
International Rescue Committee, 233
In the Heat of the Night (1967), 220
Iran, 189, 208; Tehran, 39
Iraq, 25
Ireland, 5, 25, 41, 84, 88, 99, 102, 171–81, 338, 345; Dublin, 84, 172, 175, 177–78; Irish Republican Army (IRA), 171–78, 182
Isabella (Queen), 61
I See a Dark Stranger (1946), 171–73, 336
Islam/Muslims, 76–77, 79–82, 151, 154, 188, 190, 246, 337
Island in the Sun (1957), 170–71, 179–80, 309–16, 324, 330, 342, 345
Israel, 137, 139
I Walked with a Zombie (1943), 189

Jackson, Frank, 51
Jackson, Freda, 153
Jaeckel, Richard, 211
Jaffe, Sam, 63
Jamaica, 307
Japan, 25, 28, 47–48, 62–66, 84, 92, 140–42, 191, 208–9, 218–19, 222–29, 239, 241, 276–88, 337–38; Edo, 63; geishas, 62–66, 278; Hiroshima, 66, 287; Shimoda, 63–64, 92; Tokyo, 224–25
Japanese Americans, 275; internment, 23, 275, 278
Japanese War Bride (1952), 277–79, 283, 308
Jeander, 103
Jeans, Ursula, 79
Jeffries, Lionel, 252
Jim Thorpe—All American (1951), 118, 120
J'irai cracher sur vos tombes (1959), 328, 330, 345
Johar, I. S., 79
Johns, Glynnis, 89
Johnston, Eric, 266
Jolson Sings Again (1949), 301
Jones, Barry, 83–84
Jones, Jennifer, 215, 251, 253
Jones, Paul, 267, 304

Jordan, 137
Jordan, Dorothy, 127
Jourdan, Louis, 272
Juarez (1939), 193
Jump into Hell (1955), 195, 205, 240
Jurado, Katy, 124, 260–61, 332
Jurgens, Curt, 47–48, 50–51, 273, 323
Justin, John, 77, 309, 312

Kam Tong, 216
Karloff, Boris, 97
Kauffmann, Stanley, 166–67
Kazan, Elia, 252, 290, 295, 297–98, 300
Kelly, Grace, 68, 260
Kennedy, John F., 148
Kennedy, Robert (British critic), 168
Kenya, 69, 72–74, 139, 142, 158–69, 180, 339; Mombasa, 73–74
Kenyatta, Jomo, 158
Kerima, 272
Kern, Jerome, 307
Kerr, Deborah, 38, 41, 55, 66, 151, 171
Kerr, John, 274
Kidd, Benjamin, 246
Killers of Kilimanjaro (1959), 69, 92, 336–37
Kimathi, Dedan, 158
Kimura, Mitsuko, 280
Kinematograph Weekly, 37, 44, 78, 90, 143, 148, 161, 178
King, Henry, 56, 75, 216
King, Martin Luther, Jr., 170
King and I, The (1956), 32, 38–40, 55, 267, 277, 288, 343–44
King of the Khyber Rifles (1953), 75–79, 216, 273, 308
Kings Go Forth (1958), 321
King Solomon's Mines (1937), 66
King Solomon's Mines (1950), 66–69
Kipling, Rudyard, 78, 81–82, 85, 156, 220, 227, 247, 285; Gunga Din, 81; Mandalay, 247; Man Who Would Be King, 85; White Man's Burden, 220
Kitt, Eartha, 169
Knight, Arthur, 235
Knight, Esmond, 41
Korean War, 53, 65, 83, 104, 109, 141, 145, 196, 208–10, 224, 229, 273, 278, 280, 287, 308, 339
Krasker, Robert, 173, 232

Krim, Arthur, 232
Ku Klux Klan, 297, 315, 321
Kyô, Machiko, 226, 332

La Bigorne, Caporal de France (1958), 68–69
Lachize, Samuel, 150, 315
Ladd, Alan, 151
Lady of the Tropics (1939), 248
Lamarr, Hedy, 184, 248
Lancaster, Burt, 84–85, 87, 118, 120–21, 191, 193
Landon, Margaret, 32
Lang, Walter, 38
Lansdale, Edward, 230, 232
Laroche, Pierre, 37
Las Casas, Bartolomé, 58, 60
Lasky, Jr., Jesse, 91
Last Hunt, The (1956), 122–23, 134, 164–65, 251, 261, 335, 341
Last Train from Gun Hill (1959), 251, 261
Launder, Frank, 171
League of Empire Loyalists, 140
League of Nations, 28, 186
Lee, Canada, 290
Lee, Spike, 299
Legion of Decency, 24–25, 43, 58, 84, 249
Lejeune, C. A., 305, 327
LeMay, Alan, 127
Leonowens, Anna, 32, 35, 38, 41, 46, 48, 54, 63
Leopold, King of Belgium, 45
Letter to Three Wives, A (1949), 232
Lettres Francaises, 54, 66, 102, 123, 131, 146, 157, 168–69, 194, 202–3, 257, 269, 306, 315, 321
Levien, Sonya, 153
Lewin, Albert, 187
Lewis, Meriwether, 126, 262
Libération, 52, 103, 150, 169, 205–6, 238, 269, 306, 325
Liberation of L. B. Jones, The (1970), 220
Life, 110, 167, 257
Life of Emile Zola (1937), 183
Li Hua Li, 275, 332
Lincoln, Abraham, 34–35, 58
Little Caesar (1931), 124
Lives of a Bengal Lancer (1935), 45, 75
Lloyd, Frank, 210
Lodge, Jr., Henry Cabot, 22
Logan, Joshua, 274, 280

Lom, Herbert, 79
London, Julie, 321
Loo, Richard, 213
Los Angeles Examiner, 36, 78, 111, 130, 166–67, 177, 215, 237, 314, 321, 325
Los Angeles Sentinel, 320
Los Angeles Times, 61–62, 78, 82, 87, 110, 152, 167, 229, 235–36, 285, 302, 324
Losch, Tilly, 254
Lost Boundaries (1949), 290–99, 301–2, 305, 329, 331, 340, 344
Lost Command (1966), 83
Loti, Pierre, 247
Love Is a Many-Splendored Thing (1955), 215–16, 240, 273, 276
Lubin, Arthur, 191
Luce, Henry, 257
Lundigan, William, 295
Luraschi, Luigi, 152, 266

Macao, 212–13
MacArthur, Douglas, 104, 221, 223, 283
MacDonald, Moira, 84
MacDougal, Roger, 173
MacDougall, Ranald, 322
Macmillan, Harold, 2
Macomber Affair, The (1947), 45
Macon, Georgia, 301
Macready, George, 193
Madagascar, 28, 68–69, 137, 187; Île Sainte-Marie, 68–69
Madame Butterfly (1903 opera), 248, 285
Madame Du Barry (1934), 183
Magsaysay, Ramon, 221
Maitland, Marne, 147, 165, 169
Majdalany, Fred, 39, 44, 51, 131, 178, 327
Malaya, 25, 31, 35, 137, 139–50, 179–80, 271, 339; Kuala Lumpur, 144
Malcolm X (1992), 335
Maltz, Albert, 105, 258, 335
Man Called Horse, A (1970), 14
Manchester Guardian, 44, 91, 140, 143, 148, 161, 295, 327
Manifest Destiny, 22, 94–95
Manila Calling (1942), 218
Mankiewicz, Joseph L., 58, 59, 230–35, 237–38
Mann, Anthony, 112, 183, 341
Mann, Daniel, 225

Mao Zedong, 104, 137, 173, 196, 209, 229–30
March, Frederic, 61
March of Time (1935–1951), 290
Marester, Guy, 306
Marie Antoinette (1938), 183
Marion, Denis, 102
Mark of the Hawk, The (1958), 169–70, 179–80, 216–17, 240, 343–44
Marly, Florence, 224
Marquand, Christian, 328
Marqués, María Elena, 125, 332
Marshall, Herbert, 253
Marshall, Texas, 301
Marshall, William, 165
Martain, Gilles, 325
Martin, Dewey, 259
Martin, Edward (Senator), 23
Martin, Marcel, 203
Martin, Mildred, 267, 303, 320
Martinelli, Elsa, 260
Martins, Orlando, 70–71, 74, 159, 326
Marx, Karl, 210
Mason, James, 170, 173, 310
Massey, Raymond, 183
Massie, Paul, 326
Masters, John, 153, 156
Matatumua, Chief Mamea, 83
Matthews, Francis, 153
Mature, Victor, 118, 163, 189, 191, 253, 275
Maufray, André, 200
Mau Mau, 158–69, 179
Mau Mau (1955), 163
Mauriac, Claude, 146
Maurin, François, 205–6
Maximilian I, Emperor of Mexico, 193
Mayo, Virginia, 91, 191, 273
McCarten, John, 36, 102
McCarthy, Joseph, 308, 315
McDowell, Arthur G., 232
McIntire, John, 118, 169
McKenna, Virginia, 158, 162
McKinney, Nina Mae, 295, 297
McQueen, Butterfly, 255, 257
Méchard, Anne, 201
Memmi, Albert, 6
Men of Two Worlds (1946), 70–72, 75
mental colonization, 6, 40, 256, 300
Mérimée, Prosper, 323, 325

Metro-Goldwyn-Mayer (MGM), 52, 66, 68, 112, 115, 122, 125, 153–55, 164, 187, 225, 239, 259, 293, 322
Mexican Americans, 10, 124, 265–70
Mexico, 124–26, 253, 260–62; border with United States, 104; French conquest, 192–95; Spanish conquest, 56–60, 90; U.S. conquest, 265
Miami Herald, 82, 110, 121, 236, 313, 320
Michael Collins (1996), 177
Michener, James A., 83, 274, 280
Micronesia, 85
Miles, Vera, 261
Miller, Arthur C., 32
Miller, Marvin, 210
Mills, John, 174
Milwaukee Journal, 111, 320
Mineo, Sal, 266
Miracle decision (1952), 24
Misérables, Les (book), 119
missionaries, 40–54, 83–84, 91, 163, 169–70, 197, 210–11, 213, 216–17, 225, 251, 343
Mitchum, Robert, 45
Moctezuma (Aztec Emperor), 57, 59–60
Moffitt, Ivan, 153
Moffitt, Jack, 36, 49, 66, 121, 177
Mogambo (1953), 68
Mohammed V (Morocco), 187
Mohawk (1956), 261
Mohrt, Michel, 157
Moll, Giorgia, 231
Monde, Le, 3, 52, 79, 102, 157, 206, 238, 269
Monjo, Armand, 269
Monroe Doctrine, 193
Monsey, Derek, 237–38
Montalban, Ricardo, 125, 282
Montgomery, George, 220
Monthly Film Bulletin, 39, 70, 81, 148–49, 152, 161, 178, 268, 305, 314
Moore, Terry, 77, 273
Moorehead, Alan, 151
More, Kenneth, 79
Moreno, Rita, 38, 262, 332
Moretti, Jeanine, 200
Morley, Robert, 272
Morocco, 183, 186–88, 190; Istiqlal Party, 185
Mort en fraude (1957), 200–203, 205–7, 276, 282, 335, 337, 344

Mosley, Leonard, 131, 143, 314
Mossadegh, Mohammed, 189
Motion Picture Alliance for the Preservation of American Ideals, 23, 98
Motion Picture Daily, 101, 111, 130
Motion Picture Herald, 44, 49, 66, 82, 111, 115, 215, 222, 228–29, 236
Motion Picture Producers and Distributors Association of America, 249, 266
Movement for Colonial Freedom, 140
Mudie, Leonard, 190
Muhammad, Elijah, 299
Mullen, Barbara, 175
Mundy, Talbot, 75
Murphy, Audie, 231, 234–36, 262
Murphy, Richard, 279
Murray, Don, 175
Music Corporation of America (MCA), 24
Mussolini, Benito, 83, 88
Mutiny on the Bounty (1935), 210
My Darling Clementine (1946), 98–99, 253, 257, 260

Nash, Roy, 78
Nasser, Gamal Abdel, 39, 189
Nation, 128, 235, 313
National Association for the Advancement of Colored People (NAACP), 257, 297, 301, 312
National Film Finance Company (Britain), 27
Nationalist Party, China, 47, 210–13, 215–16
Nazis, 23, 26–27, 61, 117, 123, 186, 194, 217, 306
Neame, Ronald, 146
Nehru, Jawaharlal, 78, 151
Nelson, Admiral Horatio, 58
neo-colonialism, defined, 7–8
Néry, Jean, 307
Newman, Alfred, 57
New Orleans Times-Picayune, 49, 121, 130, 166, 267, 304, 314
New Republic, 166–67, 301
News Chronicle, 168
News of the World, 268
New Statesman (London), 112, 156, 237
Newsweek, 44, 50, 66, 145, 268, 313
New York Amsterdam News, 303
New York Daily News, 98, 116, 162, 198, 229, 236, 257, 285, 294, 303, 325

New Yorker, 36, 50, 102, 313
New York Herald-Tribune, 130, 150, 302
New York Post, 43, 111, 115–16, 121–22, 150, 155–56, 162, 166–67, 235–36, 257, 268, 285, 293–94, 302, 313
New York Times, 3, 50, 70, 99, 101, 109, 116, 125, 170, 177, 198, 222, 235, 237, 257, 267, 293, 302
New Zealand, 88–91, 272; Maoris, 88–91, 272
Nichols, Dudley, 295
Nicol, Alex, 116
Nigeria, 169
Night of the Quarter Moon (1959), 321, 330, 340, 345
1984 (book), 211
1984 (1956 film), 211
Nkrumah, Kwame, 7–8, 44
noble savage concept, 12, 83, 95–96, 105, 126, 183, 227–28, 255, 272
Nord, Pierre, 68
North Africa, 157, 184, 188, 198, 269, 328, 332
Northern Ireland, 139, 171, 173–78; Belfast, 173–74
North West Frontier (1959), 79–82, 336
Nouveaux Jours, 51
Nouvelles Littéraires, 52, 102, 146, 205–6, 269, 306
Nugent, Frank S., 79, 99, 101, 103, 127
Nun's Story, The (1959), 53–55, 343
Nuyen, France, 274, 332

Oakes, Philip, 156, 167
O'Brien, Edmond, 210
Observer, 122, 143, 305, 314, 327
Odd Man Out (1947), 173
O'Hara, Maureen, 261
Okada, Eiji, 287
O'Keefe, Dennis, 192
O'Neal, Frederick, 295
O'Neill, Eugene, 85
opinion polls, 2, 16, 22, 140, 244–45; Mass Observation (Britain), 140
Opium Wars, 64
Orphans of the Storm (1921), 183
Orwell, George, 211
Osborn, Paul, 280
Outcast of the Islands (1952), 271–72

Outpost in Morocco (1949), 185, 188, 198
Owens, Patricia, 281

Pagan Love Song (1950), 277
Paget, Debra, 106, 111, 122, 251, 257, 272
Painted Veil, The (134), 209
Pakistan, 25, 80, 137, 139, 153, 208; Peshawar, 78
Palance, Jack, 124–25
Palestine, 25, 139
Palmer, Charles, 291
Palmer, Ernest, 109
Pan-Pacific Productions, 219
Paramount case (*United States v. Paramount Pictures, Inc.*), 24
Paramount Pictures, 75, 123–24, 150, 152, 184, 210, 266
Parisien Libéré, 123, 194, 205, 315
Paris-Presse/L'Intransigeant, 88, 205
Parks, Rosa, 308
Passage to Marseille (1944), 183
Pate, Michael, 164
Patrick, John, 216, 225
Patrick, Nigel, 326
Patrouille de choc (1957), 203–7, 337, 343
Pearl of the South Pacific (1955), 91–92, 273
Pearson, Beatrice, 290
Peck, Gregory, 251, 254, 276
Peckinpah, Sam, 122
Peking Express (1951), 209–11, 271
Pennebaker Productions, 175
Pepé le Moko (1937), 31, 184, 253
Périer, François, 68
Perrot, Marie, 315
Perry, Commodore Matthew C., 62, 64, 222
Pétain, Philippe, 27, 51, 186
Pétainisme, 51, 103
Peters, Jean, 57, 60, 118, 121
Philadelphia Inquirer, 36, 50, 61, 101, 198, 229, 236–37, 267, 303, 320
Philippines, The, 9, 22, 65, 137, 208, 218–23, 225, 240, 278
piastres scandal, 200–201, 204
Pickup on South Street (1953), 196
Picture Post, 144
Pierre, Henri, 238
Pierret, J. G., 306
Pillars of the Sky (1956), 343
Pinewood Studios, 41, 141, 146

Pink Panther films, 224
Pinky (1949), 75, 252, 295–310, 316, 329–31, 336, 340, 342, 344–45
Pittsburgh Courier, 167, 170, 304, 324
Planter's Wife, The (1952), 141–46, 153, 159–60, 179, 196, 335
Plowright, Molly, 51, 149, 237
Pocahontas, 248
Podesta, Rossana, 68
Poitier, Sidney, 164, 166–67, 169, 317, 319–20
Polynesians, 192, 272–75, 277
Pool of London (1951), 307, 329
Popkin, Henry, 313, 320
Portes, Jacques, 29
Portman, Eric, 71
Portugal, 40, 139
Positif, 202
Potemkin, Prince Grigory, 58
Powell, Dilys, 39, 81, 131, 143, 237, 295, 305
Powell, Michael, 40
Power, Tyrone, 56, 60, 75–76, 273
Powers, James, 268, 285, 320
Pressburger, Emeric, 40
Price, Will, 79
Princesse Tam-Tam (1932), 31, 246
Proctor, Kay, 314
Production Code Administration, 24, 58, 84, 119–20, 128, 164, 230, 232, 243, 249–51, 254, 256, 258–59, 276, 289–90, 296–97, 305, 308–10, 318, 321, 323, 336, 338
protectionism, 26, 28–29
Protestantism/Protestants, 22, 52, 171, 173
public opinion, 2–4, 9, 18, 180–81, 331, 340–41, 344; definition, 3
Puerto Rico, 9, 208, 314
Purcell, Noel, 88
Purple Plain, The (1954), 276

Quality (1946 book), 295
Quiet American, The (1955 book), 230
Quiet American, The (1958 film), 230–41, 275–77
Quigley, Martin, 49
Quigly, Isabel, 327
Quinn, Anthony, 260

Radio Cinéma Télévision, 131, 150, 168, 194, 205–6, 238, 306
Raft, George, 185

Rage of Vultures, The (1948 book), 151
Rains, Claude, 183
Rains Came, The (1939), 273
Rains of Ranchipur, The (1955), 273
Raki, Laya, 89, 272
Rank Organisation, 43, 79, 81, 141, 146, 158, 162, 179, 326
Ray, Aldo, 279
Raymond, Paula, 113
Reader's Digest, 290
Reagan, Ronald, 126, 210
Real Glory, The (1939), 45, 218
Red Cloud, 116–17, 260, 344
Red Dust (1932), 68
Redgrave, Michael, 176–77, 231, 235–37
Reed, Carol, 173, 271
Reed, Donna, 163, 262
Reign of Terror (1949), 183
Rendez-vous des quais, Le (1955), 199–200, 341
Rennie, Michael, 62, 76, 212, 262
Republic Pictures, 210, 212
Resnais, Alain, 286–87
Return to Paradise (1953), 83–84, 91–92, 275, 277, 308, 337, 343
Reynolds News, 51, 286
Rice, Joan, 85, 87
Richardson, Ralph, 271
Rio Grande (1950), 104
Riva, Emmanuele, 287
Rivarol, 316, 325
River, The (1946 novel), 40, 42
River, The (1951 film), 40
RKO Pictures, 75, 103, 290
Roberts, Ben, 175
Robeson, Paul, 245
Robespierre, Maximilien, 183
Robinson, David, 81, 178
Robson, Flora, 41
Robson, Mark, 47, 52, 83
Rochereau, Jean, 325
Rodgers, Richard, 32, 274
Rogue's Regiment (1948), 195
Rohmer, Eric, 157, 238
Rolfe, Guy, 76, 79
Roman, Ruth, 211
Romero, Cesar, 56, 59–60, 193
Roosevelt, Franklin D., 310
Rosenberg, Ethel, 308

Rosenberg, Frank P., 75
Rosenberg, Julius, 308
Rosenfield, John, 304
Rossen, Robert, 309, 314
Rotha, Wanda, 187
Rousseau, Jean-Jacques, 88
Roxas, Manuel, 219–20
Royal College of Music, 326
Ruark, Robert, 164
runaway films, 11, 27, 29, 53, 69, 163, 175, 199, 309, 337
Run of the Arrow (1957), 263
Russell, Jane, 263
Russia, 65, 185, 211, 224, 234–35; Moscow, 230
Ruysdael, Basil, 91, 106, 296

Saadia (1953), 187–88, 190, 198, 289, 343
Sabu, 43
Sacajawea, 262
Sadoul, Georges, 269, 306
Safari (1956), 163, 179
Said, Edward, 7
saltwater fallacy, 9
Sand Creek Massacre (1864), 116–17, 260
San Francisco Chronicle, 36–37, 50, 61, 87, 117, 125, 130, 155, 235, 257, 302
Santana Pictures, 224
Sapphire (1959), 326–28, 339
Sarraut, Albert, 32
Saturday Review, 50, 55, 150, 156, 162, 235
Savage, Archie, 85
Sayonara (book), 280
Sayonara (1957), 280–86, 314, 332, 342
Scaramouche (1923), 183
Scarface, (1932), 124
Schallert, Edwin, 78, 87, 285
Scheuer, Philip K., 82, 110, 235, 285
Schiaffino, Laurent, 188
Schoendoerffer, Pierre, 195
Scott, Lillian, 294
Scott, Martha, 281
Searchers, The (1956), 79, 127–32, 251, 262
Seekers, The (1954), 88–91, 272
Selander, Lesley, 188
Selznick, David O., 251, 253–57
Seminole (1953), 260–61
Serra, Father Junípero, 62, 262
Seven Cities of Gold (1955), 62, 262

Seyler, Athene, 47
Shadows (1959), 322
Shake Hands with the Devil (1959), 175–80, 198, 240, 335, 345
Shane (1953), 124, 129
Shanghai Express (1932), 209
Shanghai Gesture, The (1941), 209
Shanghai Story, The (1954), 195, 210–13, 215, 217, 240, 251, 271
Shaw, Susan, 307
Shaw, Victoria, 275
Shellabarger, Samuel, 56
Sheridan, Dinah, 72
Sheridan, General Philip, 122
She Wore a Yellow Ribbon (1949), 79, 103
Shigeta, James, 275, 332
Shimada, Teru, 224
Show Boat (1951), 307–8, 316, 318
Shulman, Milton, 39, 149, 314
Shurlock, Geoffrey, 250, 310
Siam (Thailand), 32–39, 54; Mongkut, King of Siam, 32–39, 48, 63, 344; Prince Chulalongkorn, 33, 35
Sierra Leone, 73
Sight and Sound, 131
Silliphant, Stirling, 220–21
Silverheels, Jay, 56, 107–8
Silverstein, Elliot, 14
Silvestre, Armando, 332
Sim, Sheila, 74
Simba (1955), 158–65, 179
Simmons, Jean, 43
Simon, Michel, 187
Simsi, Simon, 17, 37
Sinatra, Frank, 321
Sinden, Donald, 159
Singapore, 25, 338
Sirk, Douglas, 322
Sirocco (1951), 185–87, 189, 198, 240, 337, 341
Sitting Bull (1954), 118, 344
slavery, 38, 59, 70, 73, 92, 97, 190, 247, 251, 275, 289–90, 306–7, 309, 311, 316–21, 323–25
Slave Ship (1937), 316
Slotkin, Richard, 43
Smith, Adam, 5
Smith, C. Aubrey, 184
Smith, Christine, 301
Smith, Kent, 281

Smith, R. D., 131
Sneider, Vern J., 225
Snows of Kilimanjaro, The (1952), 45
Sofaer, Abraham, 85, 154
Soldier Blue (1970), 116, 135
Soldier of Fortune (1955), 212–14, 240–41
Something of Value (1956), 164–69, 179, 198, 240, 344–45
Song of Bernadette (1943), 253
Song of Freedom (1936), 245
South, the. *See* United States South
South Africa, 102, 245; Johannesburg, 328
Southeast Asia, 33, 35, 38–39, 149, 229
Southern University, 319
South Pacific (1958), 274–75, 342
South Seas films, 12, 82–92, 183, 191–92, 198, 218, 251, 255, 272, 274–75, 343
South Sea Woman (1953), 191, 198
Soviet Union, 9, 22, 47, 104, 185, 189, 195–97, 211, 214, 220, 230, 270, 308, 339
Spain, 56–62, 90, 124, 262; conquistadors, 57–59, 61–62; Inquisition, 57, 59, 61; Santa Hermandad, 57, 59
Spanish-American War, 218
Spartacus (1960), 324
Spectator, 81, 102, 148–49, 161, 306, 327
Spencer, Thomas, 156
Stack, Robert, 68, 276
Stafford, John, 144
Stagecoach (1939), 79, 98
Stalin, Josef, 196, 230
Standish, Myles, 121, 166, 293, 294
Standish, Robert, 152–53
Stanley and Livingstone (1939), 66
Stanwyck, Barbara, 251
Star (London), 78, 144, 315
Steel, Anthony, 72–73, 142
Steel Helmet, The (1951), 196
Steiger, Rod, 263
Stevens, George, 265, 268
Stewart, James, 105, 107, 257
St. Louis Post-Dispatch, 37, 49–50, 87, 109, 115, 121, 162, 166, 229, 235, 268, 293–94, 324
Stowe, Harriet Beecher, 38
Suez Crisis of 1956, 39, 53, 80–81, 139–40, 146, 338
Sullivan, Francis L., 192
Sumner, Cyd Ricketts, 295

Sunday Dispatch (London), 268, 286
Sunday Express (London), 39, 149, 156, 237, 268, 286, 314
Sunday Graphic (London), 112
Sunday Pictorial (London), 112
Sunday Times (London), 39, 44, 81, 123, 131, 143, 161, 237, 295, 305, 327
Supplement to the Voyage of Bougainville (1772), 82
Sutton, John, 57
Sweden, 51
Swerling, Jo, 150
Sydney, Basil, 310
Syria, 28, 185–87, 198, 337; Damascus, 186–87

Tahiti, 184, 191–92
Taiwan, 49, 215
Tajiri, Larry, 285
Taka, Miiko, 281, 332
Tale of Two Cities, A (1935), 183
Tamango (1958), 252, 323–25, 329–30, 335, 341, 345
Tamblyn, Russ, 122
Tanganyika, 71
Taylor, Don, 278
Taylor, Elizabeth, 152
Taylor, Robert, 69, 112, 116, 122, 341
Taza, Son of Cochise (1954), 118
Teahouse of the August Moon (1956), 225–29, 239, 241, 276, 280, 313, 342, 344
Teal, Ray, 317
Téléciné, 205
Témoignage Chrétien, 202, 205, 325
Temple, Shirley, 75, 79, 99
Templer, Sir Gerald, 31
Thê, Trình Minh, 232–33
Thompson, Carlos, 188
Thompson, Howard, 170
Thompson, J. Lee, 79
Thorndike, Sybil, 175
Threatt, Elizabeth, 259
Three Musketeers, The (1948), 182
Three Stripes in the Sun (1955), 279–80, 282–84, 332, 337, 343
Thunder in the East (1952), 150–52, 179–80, 198, 337
Thurmond, Strom, 297, 301
Timbuktu (1959), 189–90, 198, 337

Time, 48, 50, 61, 82, 87–88, 110–11, 116, 149, 155, 166, 215, 235–36, 257, 268, 294, 303, 313
Time and Tide (London), 112, 131, 148, 305
Times (London), 3, 44, 79, 112, 121, 143, 148, 168, 178, 229, 237, 268, 295, 305
Times Educational Supplement (London), 51
To-Day's Cinema News, 91
Tokyo Joe (1949), 224–25, 241
Tomahawk (1951), 116–17, 260, 344
Tourneur, Jacques, 189–90, 199
Trader Horn (1931), 66
Travers, Bill, 153
Tribune (London), 81, 131, 148, 157, 161, 237, 305
Trooper Hook (1957), 251, 331
Trosper, Guy, 112
Trotti, Lamar, 58
Truffaut, François, 194, 269, 325
Truman, Harry S., 9, 23, 29, 209, 240, 250, 297
Tuaregs, 189, 337
Tunisia, 6, 190
Turner, Lana, 273
Turney, Catherine, 278
Twentieth Century-Fox, 32, 35, 38, 45, 47, 49, 56–58, 62, 75–76, 105, 196, 212, 215, 250, 272, 277, 290, 295, 309–10
Two Cities Films, 70

Ukraine, 150, 212
Ullman, James Ramsey, 146
Ulzana's Raid (1972), 194
Umeki, Miyoshi, 281, 332
Uncle Tom's Cabin (1852 book), 38
Uncle Tom's Cabin (1927), 316
Unconquered (1947), 97–98, 106, 251, 257, 335–36, 341
Union Française, 28
United Artists, 68, 83, 118, 120, 184–85, 188–89, 193, 222, 230, 232
United Malays National Organisation, 141
United Negro Improvement Association, 299
United States: Alabama, 312; Alaska, 10; Arizona, 126, 159, 263–64; Atlanta, 285, 293, 301; Boston, 50, 177, 290, 292, 295, 299; California, 62, 76, 91, 154, 216, 278; Chicago, 290, 308, 310; Colorado, 116; Dallas, 285, 294; Denver, 299; Florida, 121; Georgia, 290, 294; Hawaii, 9, 10; Kentucky, 317; Little Rock, 23, 274, 315, 321, 328; Los Angeles, 57, 110, 145, 197, 256, 275, 277; Louisiana, 193, 317; Maryland, 265, 268; Memphis, 293, 312, 320; Minneapolis, 312; Mississippi, 295; Montgomery, 308; New Hampshire, 290; New Jersey, 274, 290; New Orleans, 285, 314, 317; New York, 50, 228, 231, 256–57, 263, 285, 293, 297, 303, 322–23, 328; North Carolina, 312–23; Oklahoma, 119; Salinas, 278; San Diego, 62, 267; San Francisco, 322; Savannah, 87; South Carolina, 267, 297, 311; St. Louis, 119; Texas, 127–28, 262, 265–69; Tucson, 106–8; Utah, 189; Virginia, 312, 320–21; Washington, D.C., 219, 234, 262; Wyoming, 112–13
United States Civil War, 192–93, 317–21
United States government, 101, 104, 106–7, 110, 114–15, 117, 185, 195, 208–9, 215, 219, 222–23, 225–27, 229–30, 232–33, 277, 280, 284, 339; Department of Defense, 280; Department of Justice, 24; Department of State, 26, 29, 152, 220, 250, 280; Republican Party, 9, 209; Supreme Court, 24, 308, 311, 313, 338
United States military: Air Force, 281–83; Army, 96, 112, 135, 225–29, 258, 285; cavalry, 101, 103, 115, 127, 129, 132, 159; Marines, 234; Navy, 212, 290, 292, 294; Supreme Commander for the Allied Powers (SCAP), 223–25
United States South, 23, 167, 267, 285, 291, 293–302, 304, 306, 308–9, 311–13, 315–21, 324, 329
Universal-International Pictures, 264
University of Dakar, 325
Ure, Mary, 146

Van Cleef, Lee, 230
Varden, Evelyn, 296
Variety, box-office charts, 17, 35, 38, 43, 53, 67, 82, 97, 100, 105, 124, 130, 132, 145, 152, 166, 188, 210, 215, 234, 251, 256, 301; reviews, 49, 61, 115–16, 155–56, 162, 167, 170, 222, 235–36, 293–94, 313, 324
Venice Film Festival, 168
Vera Cruz (1954), 193–95, 198, 240, 337
Vian, Boris, 328
Victoria, Queen, 40
Vidor, Charles, 150
Vidor, King, 253, 272, 277–78

Vietminh, 22, 28, 195–96, 200–202, 204, 229–30, 239
Vietnam, 31, 104, 195–207, 229–40, 251, 339, 346; Hanoi, 28; Saigon, 200, 231–32
Voltaire (1933), 183

Wakefield, Alan, 154
Walk the Proud Land (1956), 262, 340
Wall Street Journal, 110–11
Walsh, Moira, 87, 285, 314
Walsh, Raoul, 316
War Arrow (1953), 261
War Eagle, John, 108, 116
Warfield, William, 308
Warner, Jack, 283, 319
Warner Bros., 53, 118, 191, 195, 250, 265–66, 280, 316, 318
Warren, Charles Marquis, 123
Warren, Robert Penn, 316–17
Warrender, Harold, 72
Warwick, Robert, 189
Warwick Films, 69, 163
Washington, George, 58
Washington Post, 61, 78, 101, 110, 155, 257, 303
Wasserman, Lew, 24
Waterbury, Ruth, 177, 237, 321, 325
Waterman, John, 327
Waters, Ethel, 295, 301
Watson, Douglas, 281
Waugh, Alec, 170, 309
Way Down South (1939), 316
Wayne, John, 62–65, 99, 103, 127–28, 131, 214–15, 335
Weaver, Harry, 286
Webb, Robert, 62
Webster, Wendy, 26
Wee Willie Winkie (1937), 75
Welles, Orson, 16
Wellman, William, 125, 184, 214
Werker, Alfred L., 290
Western Mail (Cardiff), 161
Western Samoa, 83
West of Shanghai (1937), 209
West of Zanzibar (1954), 73–75, 160, 337
Where No Vultures Fly (1951), 72–75, 337–38
White, Walter, 297–98, 301, 304
White, William L., 290
Whitebait, William, 237

White Feather (1955), 261
White Shadows in the South Seas (1928), 83
White Witch Doctor (1953), 45, 54–55, 69, 343
Whitley, Reg, 314
Wiata, Inia Te, 89
Wild Bunch, The (1969), 122
Wilde, Cornel, 163, 187
Wilkerson, Billy, 106, 108
Williams, Charles, 319
Willow Bird, Chris, 108
Windom's Way (1959), 146–50, 179–80, 343–44
Windsor, Marie, 185, 278
Win Min Than, 276
Winsten, Archer, 121, 150, 235–36, 257, 268, 285, 293–94, 302–3, 313
Wood, Natalie, 127, 321
Worden, Hank, 129
World, the Flesh, and the Devil, The (1959), 322, 329
World War I, 21, 25, 27, 175, 245
World War II, 84, 153, 196, 223; Dunkirk, 195; effects on decolonization, 1, 21, 274; effects on empire films, 75, 97; effects on West, 24–28, 31, 185, 208; effects on Western attitudes, 58, 245, 250, 287, 337, 339; in films, 218, 266, 275–76, 279, 190–91, 321; memory of, 121–22, 142; Pearl Harbor, 65–66, 209, 339
Wynter, Dana, 175

X, Malcolm, 299

Yah Ming, 142
Yamaguchi, Shirley, 276, 278, 332
Yamamura, Sô, 63
Yank in Indo-China, A (1952), 195
Yap, 85–86, 88, 337
Yellowstone Kelly (1959), 126, 261
Young, Freddie, 311
Young, Terence, 163

Zanuck, Darryl F., 32, 38, 56–59, 75–77, 170, 249, 252, 272–73, 290, 295, 297–98, 301–4, 309–12, 314, 329, 336, 340
Zec, Donald, 50
Zinnemann, Fred, 53, 260
Zukor, Adolph, 16
Zulu (1964), 102